History of the American Nation

JOHN PATRICK • CAROL BERKIN

TEACHER'S MANUAL
Richard Wilson • Margaret Altoff

MACMILLAN PUBLISHING COMPANY, NEW YORK
COLLIER MACMILLAN PUBLISHERS, LONDON

Margaret Altoff is co-author of this Teacher's Manual and author of the Tests included in it. She teaches American history and heads the social studies department at Northeast Middle School in Baltimore, Maryland.

Richard Wilson, co-author of this Teacher's Manual and author of the Worksheets, is Coordinator of Secondary Social Studies in Montgomery County, Maryland. He has taught American history and served as curriculum writer for the Baltimore school system.

Macmillan Publishing Company
866 Third Avenue, New York, New York 10022
Collier Macmillan Canada, Inc.
Printed in the United States of America
ISBN 0-02-151010-5
10 9 8 7 6 5 4 3 2

History of the American Nation

Contents

PROGRAM FEATURES

Highly Readable, Narrative Style

America's history is presented in a strong, compelling storyline that brings enjoyment and drama to the classroom.

Balanced Political and Social History

The scope includes all the landmark events in American political history plus the history of the American people, the majority and minorities, women, and family life, during the nation's development.

Clear Chronological Approach

The text's careful chronological format highlights the sequence and relationships of events in American history. The consistency of this approach provides a solid and dependable base for teaching and learning American history.

Efficient Organization

Every Chapter Opener includes clearly stated content goals to be developed within the chapter. These same goals are then specifically reviewed in the Chapter Summary.

Each chapter has three to five sections designed as daily lessons, each with its own section review.

Special Emphasis on Citizenship Awareness

Throughout the text, and in the special features, emphasis is given to the origin and development of America's ideals and heritage.

History of the American Nation

Systematic Reading and Vocabulary Development

The entire text is carefully written and easy to read. It is accompanied by frequent headings that serve as a helpful outline of main ideas. All new history words are consistently identified, defined, and repeatedly reinforced.

Strong Integration of Geography Content and Skills

The geographic setting underlying historical events is effectively developed as a theme throughout the text and reinforced by a richly abundant in-text map program. This focus successfully builds essential geography skills.

Comprehensive Study Aid Program

Consistent end-of-section checkup questions and a full range of exercises and activities in the chapter and unit reviews provide ample basis to chart mastery of vocabulary, factual knowledge, and history study skills.

Complete Teacher's Manual with Free Tests and Activity Sheets on Blackline Masters

This separate manual provides a specific lesson plan for each daily lesson. Also included are a complete set of chapter, semester, and end-of-year Tests and a substantial package of Worksheets—both on Blackline Masters.

EFFICIENT ORGANIZATION
with chronology and content goals clearly designated and developed in comfortable daily lessons.

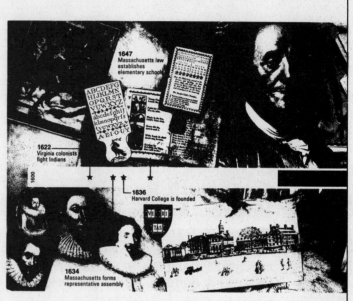

CHAPTER 6

Colonists Develop New Ways of Life (1600's-1700's)

106

Europeans Start Colonies

47

THE CHAPTER OPENER

● Easy-to-read Timeline in which the decades to be studied are clearly indicated, and the events and personalities are visually depicted

● Introductory narrative that peaks interest in the material to be studied

● Outline of content goals

THE UNIT OPENER

● Stunning full-color original art that evokes the events and personalities to be studied

● Outline of chapters in which the chronological span is always specified

1 Different Ways to Make a Living Develop in the Colonies

When we ask how the colonists lived, we think first about the ways in which they earned their living. What did they grow? What items did they make? What different kinds of work did they do? Were they rich or poor or just ordinary people?

Some New Englanders are farmers. [Th]e geographical location and physical [fea]tures of a colony helped to form its [eco]nomy—the way it produced, used, and [ma]naged its crops or goods. It took a while [for] the colonists to learn what crops they [cou]ld grow in their regions. By about the [ear]ly 1700's, it was clear that the New [Eng]land Colonies, Middle Colonies, and [Sou]thern Colonies had developed different [kin]ds of economies.

The early colonists found farming in [Ne]w England to be very difficult. Why? [Firs]t, much of New England is too hilly [and] rocky for farming. In the fairly level [area]s, settlers had to spend many weeks [and] months clearing fields of the rocks, [ston]es, and even boulders that filled the [soil]. Second, the soil was not very fertile. [Fin]ally, the growing season there was [shor]t. A family was able to plant and har[vest] only one crop before the ground froze [and] the winter snows began.

Nonetheless, New Englanders soon pro[duc]ed enough on their farms to live com[fort]ably. They grew vegetables and picked [berr]ies, plums, and apples in their orchards. [Mos]t families owned livestock. Therefore, [the]y had cheese, butter, milk, and eggs, [as w]ell as chicken, hams, and bacon. They [use]d wood from nearby forests to build [thei]r homes and furniture.

Sometimes New England farm families [had] extra food that they sold to neighbors. [The]y also exchanged it for some food they [nee]ded. However, these families did not pro-

duce a *cash crop*, a crop grown specifically to sell after the harvest. This was because New England farms were small and also because they did not grow things needed by the other colonies or by Great Britain. New England farming was a *subsistence economy*—families grew just what they needed for themselves.

Other New Englanders work at sea. Because of the difficulty of farming in their region, some New Englanders chose to fish for a living rather than to farm. The Atlantic waters of New England were filled with many different kinds of fish. Fleets from seacoast towns such as Marblehead, Massachusetts, brought in catches of halibut, herring, mackerel, and cod.

Many men from Nantucket Island took up whaling. Whale blubber, or fat, was valuable. It was made into oil for use in oil lamps. Whalers also sold spermaceti (spur′mə set′ē), a liquid from the whales which was used for candlemaking.

New England businesses and trade develop. New Englanders needed ships to go to sea. Soon colonists opened shipyards to build fishing sloops and ocean-going vessels. Carpenters, blacksmiths, and coopers found jobs in the shipyards. In the forests, lumberjacks cut trees for the shipyards. Small factories produced ships' supplies, such as tar and turpentine, from the hardwood white pines of New Hampshire.

Soon New Englanders found other new ways of earning their living. Merchants in the seaport towns and cities salted the fish they bought to preserve it. Then some shipped it with lumber and other products to the sugar plantations of the West Indies. The West Indian plantation owners who bought these goods exchanged them for sugar, molasses, or money. Back in New England, the merchants either sold the molasses to Great Britain or had it made into rum. They shipped the rum to Africa, where it was exchanged for slaves. The shippers and merchants who sold these slaves in the

---

In a small New England town in the 1700's, 15-year-old Elizabeth Fuller closes her diary and places it beside the bed. Tired, she carefully blows out the candle, settles in beside her sisters, and goes to sleep.

Suppose you could read Elizabeth Fuller's diary. What would you find there— accounts of school, dating and parties, of arguments with her parents?

Elizabeth Fuller's diary has none of these things. Instead, it is filled with long lists of work completed and chores to be done. Looking at the latest pages, you can see that in the last three months Elizabeth has been very busy. She has baked pies, made candles, scrubbed floors, chopped meat for sausages, made cheese, and spun and woven many yards of cloth.

Elizabeth's diary entry for tonight tells us that her household chores are over for one precious, short moment. She writes: "Welcome sweet Liberty, once more to me. How I have longed to meet again with thee."

Elizabeth Fuller's life of household work seems harsh and unfair to us. She was not a servant or a slave. Her family was not particularly poor. She was, we might argue, only a teenage girl. Elizabeth's parents would not understand this argument. Neither would Elizabeth Fuller herself.

How did the colonists live, work, and entertain themselves? What was the quality of life for Indians and blacks in the colonies? How were the colonies governed? In this chapter you will read about life in colonial society. You will see how American ways of living developed.

- Different Ways to Make a Living Develop in the Colonies
- [Fam]ilies Contribute to Colonial Life
- [Colon]ists Establish a Rich Community

[India]ns and Blacks Live in the Colonies
[Settle]rs Develop Colonial Governments

107

1750
Philadelphia is largest colonial city

1732
Franklin begins publishing *Poor Richard's Almanac*

1739
Cato leads slave rebellion

1769
Dartmouth College is founded

CHAPTER SUMMARY

1. Different Ways to Make a Living Develop in the Colonies. New Englanders had a varied economy that included farming, fishing, and trade. The Middle Colonies were mainly agricultural and were known as the "bread basket" of the colonial world. They also had important trade centers. The Southern Colonies were agricultural, with such cash crops as tobacco, rice, and indigo.

2. Families Contribute to Colonial Life. Colonial families were large. Husbands worked to support their families, while wives ran the home. Only men could vote and sue in court. They controlled the family's property and wealth. Women had few legal rights. Children often started to work in the home and in the fields at age seven.

3. Colonists Establish a Rich Community Life. Most of the colonists were Protestant, mainly Puritan or Anglican. Maryland, Pennsylvania, and Rhode Island had colonists of many religions because they were the first colonies to guarantee religious free-

INTEGRATION OF GEOGRAPHY CONTENT AND SKILLS

consistently developed throughout the text.

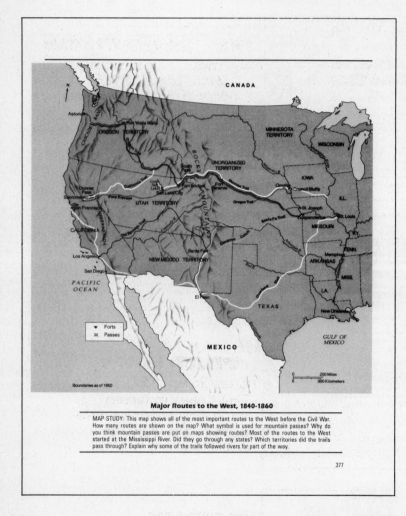

Major Routes to the West, 1840-1860

MAP STUDY: This map shows all of the most important routes to the West before the Civil War. How many routes are shown on the map? What symbol is used for mountain passes? Why do you think mountain passes are put on maps showing routes? Most of the routes to the West started at the Mississippi River. Did they go through any states? Which territories did the trails pass through? Explain why some of the trails followed rivers for part of the way.

377

IN-TEXT DEVELOPMENT

The geographic setting underlying the development of the American nation is detailed throughout the text and reinforced by a strong in-text map program. These maps are accompanied by caption questions that result in a significant addition to the geography skills development found in this text.

CHAPTER REVIEW

Every Chapter Review section includes a "Linking Geography and History" section in which history-related geography skills are effectively reinforced.

5. Congress established the Utah Territory.   e. 1836

LINKING GEOGRAPHY AND HISTORY

Throughout history, different methods have been used by nations to annex new territory. Chapter 16 discusses the annexation of Texas, Oregon, the Mexican Cession, and the Gadsden Purchase. What methods were used by the United States to annex each?

THINKING ABOUT AMERICAN HISTORY

PLUS—AN EXTENSIVE FULL-COLOR ATLAS FOR EASY REFERENCE

SYSTEMATIC VOCABULARY DEVELOPMENT with the clear introduction, development, and reinforcement of each new word.

Elizabeth ake such n was not e. She, as il Adams, had been eclaration rights of

Should women have the right to vote? However, one of Stanton's proposals stunned even the most concerned women at the convention. In it she called for women's *suffrage,* or the right of women to vote. Women's suffrage! Even Lucretia Mott rose to speak out against such a daring and unexpected idea.

TEXT IDENTIFICATION

New history vocabulary words are identified and clearly defined where they first appear in the text.

Elizabeth Stanton (left), Carrie Catt (center), and Lucretia Mott (right) are honored on this American stamp. They led the fight for women's *suffrage.*

CAPTIONS

Many of these same words are illustrated, and are italicized in captions.

REVIEWING KEY WORDS

Write the letter of the answer that correctly defines each of the

1. reform
2. temperance
3. abolitionists
4. emancipation
5. suffrage

a. the freeing of slaves
b. less drinking of alcoholic beverages
c. the right to vote
d. people who worked to end slavery
e. to correct or improve society's social

APPLIED USAGE

Every Section, Chapter, and Unit Review includes a vocabulary review exercise in which new words are reinforced.

ies: colonies own leaders ny political

upper house es Congress, ators elected

have no crops left over to trade or to sell for cash.
suburbs (sub'urbs) smaller communities near large cities.
suffrage (suf'rij): the right to vote.
summit meeting (sum'it): a meeting of the leaders of the most powerful countries.

vaquero (vä the Southv
veto (vē'tō): ecutive to by a legisla

GLOSSARY

All vocabulary words are listed and defined in the glossary at the end of the book.

Name _____ Class_____ Date_____

Chapter 15 Test
REVIEWING KEY WORDS

Write the letter of the correct word that is defined in each of the following descriptions.

1. _____ the right to vote — A suffrage — B temperance
2. _____ places where teachers were trained — A normal schools — B religious revivals
3. _____ the freeing of slaves — A abolition — B emancipation
4. _____ to improve or correct society's social problems — A reform — B utopian

CHECKING UP ON THE FACTS

CHAPTER TEST

A "Reviewing Key Words" section is included in each Chapter Test.

SPECIAL FEATURES with effective emphasis on citizenship development.

IDEALS IN THE LIVES OF AMERICANS

Dramatic biographical descriptions that personalize major American ideals by demonstrating their importance in the lives of individual Americans.

Questions are provided that highlight these ideals for the student.

Ideals In The Lives of AMERICANS

Clara Barton

On July 21, 1861, the people of Washington, D.C., were shocked and frightened. Federal troops had just been defeated by the Confederates at nearby Bull Run in Virginia. Hundreds of wounded and dead soldiers were being carried back to the nation's capital. Washington itself might be attacked at any moment.

One resident of Washington, Clara Barton, was too busy to be afraid. Barton was a clerk in the Patent Office, a department in the federal government that handles inventions. She was 40 years old when the fighting started. She immediately organized a group of women to nurse the wounded soldiers, and their care saved many lives.

Although women were not allowed at the front lines, in 1862 Barton went to Cedar Mountain, Virginia. She brought a wagon train of food, clothing, and medical supplies to the battlefield. And she remained there taking care of the sick and wounded for five days.

Barton risked her life helping soldiers on other battlefields. She became known as the "Angel of the Battlefield," and by the end of the War she was famous. President Lincoln called her a hero.

After the war Barton learned of the valuable services performed by the International Red Cross. She worked hard to establish an American Red Cross and finally succeeded in 1881. Barton served as President of the American Red Cross until 1904.

Although the Red Cross was originally set up to help wounded soldiers in wartime, Barton knew it would be needed in peacetime, too. Today the Red Cross aids Americans who are victims of disasters like floods or blizzards.

1. What was Clara Barton's goal in setting up the Red Cross?
2. What are some of the ideals that Clara Barton stands for today?

434

Landmarks OF LIBERTY

Monument to Jackson, "The People's President"

Andrew Jackson was called "the people's President." He believed that all citizens, rich and poor alike, and not just property owners, should be able to vote. Jackson also felt that the nation's leaders should be ordinary people who used common sense to guide them in public office. His motto was "Let the people rule."

Jackson favored greater political power for ordinary Americans. And he also took a strong interest in their well-being. His ideas became known as Jacksonian Democracy. For the first time, the common people, ordinary Americans, were the center of a President's political program. The people, in turn, responded warmly to Jackson and made him one of the most popular Presidents in American history.

After Jackson's death Congress decided that a m[...] should be built to honor t[...] Sculptor Clark Mills was [...] create a bronze statue of [...] placed in Lafayette Park, [...] the White House.

Mills had never met [...] However, he had long ad[...] Hickory's" courage and de[...] Thus, he decided to portr[...] dent on horseback in a bo[...] rous pose. The heroic bro[...] created by Mills, seems to [...] the White House, where Jackson lived from 1829 to 1837.

The statue was hailed as a great work when it was completed in 1853. It is a lasting symbol of the opportunities in a free nation, where a common person may achieve uncommon goals.

1. What were some of the main features of Jacksonian democracy?
2. For what achievements and ideals is Jackson honored today?

307

LANDMARKS OF LIBERTY

Focused descriptions of places and objects that symbolize the American nation and its heritage. Accompanied by questions that develop the student's awareness of this heritage.

What Life Was Like

The families who left their homelands to settle the 13 colonies brought with them many rich cultural traditions. These settlers combined European crafts and African farming skills with the Indians' knowledge of the land to create a new American culture.

In the settlements along the Atlantic Coast, colonists developed special skills such as making silverware, brass objects, clothing, and pottery. These colonists also enjoyed reading newspapers and almanacs.

In the countryside, colonists worked hard to start their farms and plantations. Families living in simple log cabins often had beautiful quilts and other items handmade by their owners. A few wealthy colonial families were able to build large, elegant homes.

Some of the items made during colonial times and the years soon after are shown in the photographs on these two pages. Starting at the top left of page 116, they are:

1. A Pennsylvania Dutch dish
2. Handmade quilt
3. Painting of a Southern plantation
4. An almanac printed in Pennsylvania
5. Brass tea kettle
6. Flag of the Society of Pewterers
7. A painting of colonial children
8. Painted wooden toys

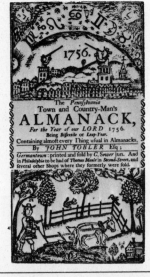

116

117

WHAT LIFE WAS LIKE

Two-page photo essays that illuminate the customs and traditions from various periods of America's past. Care has been taken to include aspects of the lives of young people from each period.

Sources of Freedom ★ Patrick Henry's "Give Me Liberty" Speech

Gentlemen may cry peace, peace. But there is no peace. The war is actually begun! The next gale that sweeps from the north will bring to our ears the clash of resounding arms! Our brethren are already in the field! Why stand we here idle? What is it that gentlemen wish?

What would they have? Is life so dear, or peace so sweet, as to be purchased at the price of chains and slavery? Forbid it, Almighty God! I know not what course others may take; but as for me, give me liberty or give me death!

Virginia, 1775

153

SOURCES OF AMERICAN FREEDOM

Students are acquainted with the great documents of American history and, at the same time, develop an understanding of primary source materials.

COMPREHENSIVE STUDY AID
PROGRAM that is unrivaled in quality and scope.

★ ★ ★ ★ ★ ★ HISTORY ★ ★ ★ ★ ★ ★ ★
STUDY SKILLS

Using a Line Graph

The percentage of voters who voted in America's presidential elections changed from 1824 to 1840. Studying the graph on this page can help you understand that change. Changes in numbers over the years are often shown on line graphs. Why? These graphs show clearly whether numbers stay the same, increase, or decrease.

Read All the Labels on the Graph. Before you start studying the graph, look at its title. The title will tell you what information the graph shows. The left side of the graph is called the vertical axis. Here, this label reads "Percentage of Voters." This percentage means the percentage of all eligible voters (not including slaves, Indians, and women) who took part in each presidential election listed.

The bottom of the graph is called the horizontal axis. This axis is labeled "Presidential Election Years." Since presidential elections are held every four years, the bottom line shows each of the elections from 1824 to 1840.

Find Where the Horizontal and Vertical Axes Meet. Suppose you want to find the percentage of Americans who voted in 1824. Find 1824 on the horizontal axis at the bottom of the graph. Next follow the axis upward from 1824 until you reach the point where it meets the line running across the graph. At that point the vertical axis shows about 26 percent. Now look at the year 1828. What percentage of the population voted in that election? (58 percent)

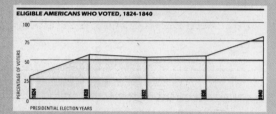

Now practice reading information on this line graph.

1. What percentage of the population voted in 1832? in 1840?
2. Compare the percentage of voters in 1828 and 1840. In which year was the percentage largest?
3. Did the percentage of Americans who voted in the years from 1828 to 1840 increase, decrease, or remain the same? How did the percentage of Americans who voted during Jackson's years change?

HISTORY STUDY SKILLS
These special lessons at the end of each chapter teach, review, and apply the skills basic to a sound understanding of American history. Among the skills developed are reading maps, tables, graphs; interpreting paintings, photos, and cartoons; outlining, reviewing, and text study.

German invaders out of their country.

SECTION REVIEW

1. **IDENTIFY:** Pearl Harbor, General Douglas MacArthur, Battle of the Coral Sea, Erwin Rommel, General Dwight D. Eisenhower, General Bernard Montgomery
2. **DEFINE:** convoys
3. How did the United States become fully involved in World War II?
4. Why was the Battle of Midway considered a "turning point" in the Pacific war?
5. **SKILL PRACTICE:** Study the photograph of General MacArthur on page 677. What kind of person did MacArthur seem to be?

SECTION REVIEWS
Consistently review and reinforce vocabulary, content, and skills

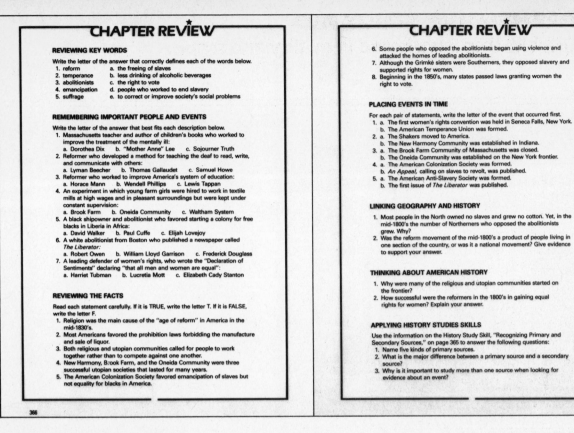

CHAPTER REVIEW

REVIEWING KEY WORDS

Write the letter of the answer that correctly defines each of the words below.
1. reform   a. the freeing of slaves
2. temperance   b. less drinking of alcoholic beverages
3. abolitionists   c. the right to vote
4. emancipation   d. people who worked to end slavery
5. suffrage   e. to correct or improve society's social problems

REMEMBERING IMPORTANT PEOPLE AND EVENTS

Write the letter of the answer that best fits each description below.
1. Massachusetts teacher and author of children's books who worked to improve the treatment of the mentally ill:
   a. Dorothea Dix   b. "Mother Anne" Lee   c. Sojourner Truth
2. Reformer who developed a method for teaching the deaf to read, write, and communicate with others:
   a. Lyman Beecher   b. Thomas Gallaudet   c. Samuel Howe
3. Reformer who worked to improve America's system of education:
   a. Horace Mann   b. Wendell Phillips   c. Lewis Tappan
4. An experiment in which young farm girls were hired to work in textile mills at high wages and in pleasant surroundings but were kept under constant supervision:
   a. Brook Farm   b. Oneida Community   c. Waltham System
5. A black shipowner and abolitionist who favored starting a colony for free blacks in Liberia in Africa:
   a. David Walker   b. Paul Cuffe   c. Elijah Lovejoy
6. A white abolitionist from Boston who published a newspaper called The Liberator:
   a. Robert Owen   b. William Lloyd Garrison   c. Frederick Douglass
7. A leading defender of women's rights, who wrote the "Declaration of Sentiments" declaring "that all men and women are equal":
   a. Harriet Tubman   b. Lucretia Mott   c. Elizabeth Cady Stanton

REVIEWING THE FACTS

Read each statement carefully. If it is TRUE, write the letter T. If it is FALSE, write the letter F.
1. Religion was the main cause of the "age of reform" in America in the mid-1830's.
2. Most Americans favored the prohibition laws forbidding the manufacture and sale of liquor.
3. Both religious and utopian communities called for people to work together rather than to compete against one another.
4. New Harmony, Brook Farm, and the Oneida Community were three successful utopian societies that lasted for many years.
5. The American Colonization Society favored emancipation of slaves but not equality for blacks in America.

366

CHAPTER REVIEW

6. Some people who opposed the abolitionists began using violence and attacked the homes of leading abolitionists.
7. Although the Grimké sisters were Southerners, they opposed slavery and supported rights for women.
8. Beginning in the 1850's, many states passed laws granting women the right to vote.

PLACING EVENTS IN TIME

For each pair of statements, write the letter of the event that occurred first.
1. a. The first women's rights convention was held in Seneca Falls, New York.
   b. The American Temperance Union was formed.
2. a. The Shakers moved to America.
   b. The New Harmony Community was established in Indiana.
3. a. The Brook Farm Community of Massachusetts was closed.
   b. The Oneida Community was established on the New York frontier.
4. a. The American Colonization Society was formed.
   b. An Appeal, calling on slaves to revolt, was published.
5. a. The American Anti-Slavery Society was formed.
   b. The first issue of The Liberator was published.

LINKING GEOGRAPHY AND HISTORY

1. Most people in the North owned no slaves and grew no cotton. Yet, in the mid-1800's the number of Northerners who opposed the abolitionists grew. Why?
2. Was the reform movement of the mid-1800's a product of people living in one section of the country, or was it a national movement? Give evidence to support your answer.

THINKING ABOUT AMERICAN HISTORY

1. Why were many of the religious and utopian communities started on the frontier?
2. How successful were the reformers in the 1800's in gaining equal rights for women? Explain your answer.

APPLYING HISTORY STUDIES SKILLS

Use the information on the History Study Skill, "Recognizing Primary and Secondary Sources," on page 365 to answer the following questions:
1. Name five kinds of primary sources.
2. What is the major difference between a primary source and a secondary source?
3. Why is it important to study more than one source when looking for evidence about an event?

367

CHAPTER REVIEW A complete range of exercises and activities for effective reinforcement of content and skills for each chapter.

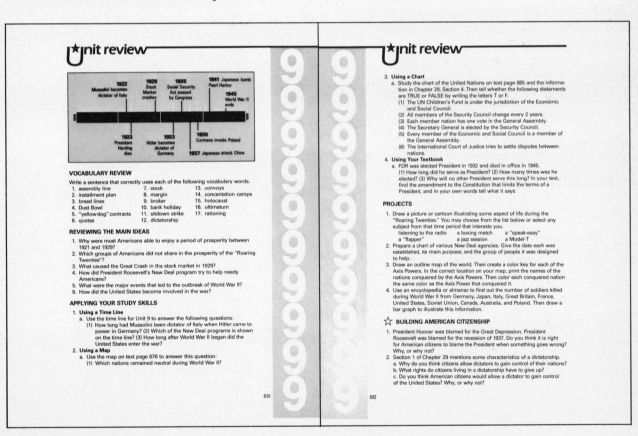

Unit review

VOCABULARY REVIEW

Write a sentence that correctly uses each of the following vocabulary words.
1. assembly line   7. stock   13. convoys
2. installment plan   8. margin   14. concentration camps
3. bread lines   9. broker   15. holocaust
4. Dust Bowl   10. bank holiday   16. ultimatum
5. "yellow dog" contracts   11. sitdown strike   17. rationing
6. quotas   12. dictatorship

REVIEWING THE MAIN IDEAS

1. Why were most Americans able to enjoy a period of prosperity between 1921 and 1929?
2. Which groups of Americans did not share in the prosperity of the "Roaring Twenties"?
3. What caused the Great Crash in the stock market in 1929?
4. How did President Roosevelt's New Deal program try to help needy Americans?
5. What were the major events that led to the outbreak of World War II?
6. How did the United States become involved in the war?

APPLYING YOUR STUDY SKILLS

1. Using a Time Line
   a. Use the time line for Unit 9 to answer the following questions:
   (1) How long had Mussolini been dictator of Italy when Hitler came to power in Germany? (2) Which of the New Deal programs is shown on the time line? (3) How long after World War II began did the United States enter the war?
2. Using a Map
   a. Use the map on text page 676 to answer this question:
   (1) Which nations remained neutral during World War II?

691

Unit review

3. Using a Chart
   a. Study the chart of the United Nations on text page 685 and the information in Chapter 29, Section 4. Then tell whether the following statements are TRUE or FALSE by writing the letters T or F.
   (1) The UN Children's Fund is under the jurisdiction of the Economic and Social Council.
   (2) All members of the Security Council change every 2 years.
   (3) Each member nation has one vote in the General Assembly.
   (4) The Secretary General is elected by the Security Council.
   (5) Every member of the Economic and Social Council is a member of the General Assembly.
   (6) The International Court of Justice tries to settle disputes between nations.
4. Using Your Textbook
   a. FDR was elected President in 1932 and died in office in 1945.
   (1) How long did he serve as President? (2) How many times was he elected? (3) Why will no other President serve this long? In your text, find the amendment to the Constitution that limits the terms of a President, and in your own words tell what it says.

PROJECTS

1. Draw a picture or cartoon illustrating some aspect of life during the "Roaring Twenties." You may choose from the list below or select any subject from that time period that interests you.
   listening to the radio   a boxing match   a "speak-easy"
   a "flapper"   a jazz session   a Model-T
2. Prepare a chart of various New Deal agencies. Give the date each was established, its main purpose, and the group of people it was designed to help.
3. Draw an outline map of the world. Then create a color key for each of the Axis Powers. In the correct location on your map, print the names of the nations conquered by the Axis Powers. Then color each conquered nation the same color as the Axis Power that conquered it.
4. Use an encyclopedia or almanac to find out the number of soldiers killed during World War II from Germany, Japan, Italy, Great Britain, France, United States, Soviet Union, Canada, Australia, and Poland. Then draw a bar graph to illustrate this information.

☆ BUILDING AMERICAN CITIZENSHIP

1. President Hoover was blamed for the Great Depression. President Roosevelt was blamed for the recession of 1937. Do you think it is right for American citizens to blame the President when something goes wrong? Why, or why not?
2. Section 1 of Chapter 29 mentions some characteristics of a dictatorship.
   a. Why do you think citizens allow dictators to gain control of their nations?
   b. What rights do citizens living in a dictatorship have to give up?
   c. Do you think American citizens would allow a dictator to gain control of the United States? Why, or why not?

692

UNIT REVIEW Thorough reinforcement of chronology, vocabulary, content, and skills for each unit. With a special "Projects" section for more extensive activities.

COMPLETE TEACHER'S MANUAL
with Free Tests and Activity Sheets.

Name _____ Class_____ Date_____

Chapter 14 Test
REVIEWING KEY WORDS
Write the letter of the answer that correctly completes each sentence below.

A metropolis   B prejudice   C Lyceum
    D clipper ship   E packet line

1. _____ People who traveled by sea preferred to take their trips on a ___?___ because these ships ran on a regular schedule.

2. _____ During the 1800's Americans showed their ___?___ against foreigners by voting against immigrants who ran for public office.

3. _____ During the 1800's Americans who wished to hear the latest information on science, politics, or religion, often attended lectures at the ___?___.

_____ The ___?___ was a beautiful ocean-going vessel that used many sails to increase its speed.

_____ A big city like New York or Philadelphia is called a ___?___ because it serves as a center of business, education, culture, and politics.

...KING UP ON THE FACTS
...he letter of the answer that correctly completes each statement below.

_____ All of the following are examples of literature in the 1800's except
A *Rip Van Winkle.*
B *The Pathfinder.*
C "Raftsmen Playing Cards."
D *The Yemmassee.*

---

3. The stagecoach.
4. Improved method of making paper; new ways of setting type; invention of a rotary printing press.

SECTION 3: Cities and Their Populations Change

OBJECTIVES
After completing this section, students will be able to:
- Identify the reasons for the growth of towns and cities.
- List some of the problems that developed in urban areas.
- Identify the national origins of American immigrants and the reasons they came to America.
- Discuss the reaction of Americans to the arrival of the immigrants.

MOTIVATION
Ask students if they know the meaning of the word metropolis (large city that is a center of business, education, culture, and politics). Have volunteers name American cities today that they feel fit that description. Then have them guess which of those cities were already regarded as metropolises in the 1860's.

SUGGESTED ACTIVITIES
1. **Directed Reading.** Have the students read this section, and use the following as guide questions:
   A. Why did the population of cities increase between the 1820's and the 1850's? (offered job opportunities, waves of immigrants)
   B. What problems developed in urban areas as a result of this growth in population? (poor sanitation, poor housing, crime)
   C. Why were some Americans upset by the increase in immigration? (jobs threatened, afraid their way of life would change)
2. **Map Study.** Utilizing a wall map of the United States, ask students to locate the nine cities classified *metropolises* in 1860. Have students define "metropolis." Ask them about the population figure and other attributes that qualified each of these cities for that designation.
3. **Using an Almanac to Make a Table.** Using a current almanac, have students find the population of each of the nine cities above both for the year 1860 and for the current year. Ask them to create a table Nine Largest Cities in America in 1860 and _____ (the current year). You may wish to provide slower students with the necessary information but out of order. Then ask them to reorganize it in the form of a table, matching the correct cities and population figures in 1860 with those for the current year.
4. **Making a Table.** Have students draw a table to organize the information concerning the immigrant groups that came to America. Use the following headings:

IMMIGRATION TO AMERICA
COUNTRY OF ORIGIN	REASONS THEY CAME	WHERE THEY SETTLED

5. **Reviewing Graphs.** Duplicate Worksheet 38, *Immigration.* It will offer an excellent review of the History Study Skill for Chapter 9 and also give students more information about the nations from which immigrants came to America between 1800 and 1860.

BUILDING AMERICAN CITIZENSHIP
Duplicate Worksheet 37, *A Nation of Immigrants.* This activity reviews the History Study Skills for Chapters 5 and 10, and also provides insights about the contributions of three immigrant groups to American society.

SECTION 3 REVIEW ANSWERS
1. **IDENTIFY: potato blight:** a disease tha... potato crop in Ireland in the 1840's; Kn... group of American Protestants who for... the Star Spangled Banner, whose memb... vote against Catholics and foreigners... fice.
2. **DEFINE: metropolis:** a large city that... business, education, culture, and poli... dislike of a group of people because of... other reasons.
3. Many new settlers came to cities, inc... ambitious people looking for new b... tunities, and immigrants. Some cities g... a special industry in the area, others be... located near a transportation route, a... because they were port cities where... landed.
4. Irish: to escape starvation after the p... 1845; Germans: mainly for political r... escape punishment for criticizing the... Dutch and Scandinavians: mainly to... freedom.

SECTION 4: Technology Chan... Life and Work

OBJECTIVES
After completing this section, students...
- List several inventions that changed lif... the farms and in the factories.
- Describe working conditions in a typi... 1800's.
- Explain the differences between worki... and working at home .

MOTIVATION
Refer students to the time line in the... beginning of Chapter 14. Have them sel... tions on the time line that they have not... (reaper, revolver, sewing machine, and s... them to look at the pictures in Section 4 ... these inventions are shown. Remind stud... of this section and ask how they think th... tions might have changed everyday life a...

Name _____ Class_____ Date_____

★ **Building American Citizenship**

The Star-Spangled Banner

The "Star-Spangled Banner" is the national anthem of the United States. You read in Chapter 11 how it was written by Francis Scott Key in 1814 during the British invasion of the United States. Key wrote the words as a poem. Within a few days of the battle, however, the words had been set to music. The song was an immediate success and was soon recognized by the Army and Navy as our country's anthem. In 1931, Congress officially adopted the "Star-Spangled Banner" as our national anthem.

Below is the first verse of "The Star Spangled Banner." Read it carefully and answer the questions that follow.

THE STAR-SPANGLED BANNER

Oh! say! can you see, by the dawn's early light,
What so proudly we hailed at the twilight's last gleaming?
Whose broad stripes and bright stars through the perilous fight,
O'er the ramparts we watched were so gallantly streaming?
And the rockets' red glare, the bombs bursting in air,
Gave proof through the night that our flag was still there.
Oh, say, does that Star-Spangled Banner yet wave
O'er the land of the free and the home of the brave?

1. Look up in a dictionary and write down the meaning of the following words:

   twilight _____

   perilous _____

   ramparts_____

   star-spangled (Look up "Spangled" first.) _____

2. What is the star-spangled banner? _____

3. What questions does Francis Scott Key ask? (Restate the question in your own words.)
   _____
   _____

4. Write down the words of "The Star Spangled Banner" that described the United States.
   _____
   _____

5. About what time of day do you think Francis Scott Key wrote his verse? Explain your answer. _____
   _____
   _____

©Macmillan Publishing Co.

Worksheet 29, Chapter 11   207

DAILY LESSON PLANS
The heart of the Teacher's Manual is the full lesson plan for each chapter section. These sections are designed for completion in a single class period. Thus, in this Manual, the teacher is provided with a complete lesson plan for each day of teaching. The lesson plan includes objectives, motivational techniques, suggested activities, strategies for building citizenship, and Section Review answers.

FREE BLACKLINE MASTERS
The Teacher's Manual also includes a complete set of chapter and semester Tests and a substantial Activity Sheet package on Blackline Masters. Both of these items are also available in workbook form as separate ancillaries.

CONTENTS—Student Text

UNIT **1** (Prehistory to 1500's)

The First Settlers Arrive

Introducing the Unit

Unit One surveys the settlement of the Americas from the arrival of the first peoples in the Western Hemisphere, in prehistoric times, through the establishment of the earliest Spanish colonies in the Caribbean in the early 16th century. The first peoples to migrate to the Americas came from Asia across a land bridge that linked Siberia to Alaska during the last Ice Age, some 28,000 to 10,000 years ago. These Asian peoples, who later became known as Indians, gradually dispersed throughout North and South America, and over the millenia developed many different lifestyles and cultures to suit their varying environments and needs.

By contrast, the first European contact with North America occurred less than than 1,000 years ago. It started as European explorers began to search first for new lands and later for all-water trade routes to Asia.

Chapter 1 describes how the first Americans—nomads—fanned out from their northern entry point. They moved slowly, following animal herds and trails until some reached the southern part of South America some 10,000 years ago. Gradually, some evolved from hunters to farmers and established settlements. All of these peoples, throughout North and South America, developed many different cultures, which were greatly influenced by the natural regions in which they lived. By the time of Columbus, many of these early settlements in Mexico and South America, for example, had become the great empires of such peoples as the Maya, the Aztecs, and the Incas, each comprising unique and complex societies. The entire Western Hemisphere, by this time, was widely populated by many different groups of Indians.

Chapter 2 surveys five centuries of European quests for new lands and all-water trade routes to Asia. The Vikings were first, arriving at Newfoundland around 1000 A.D. However, it was not until some 500 years later, with the voyage of Christopher Columbus, that a permanent contact was established between Europe and the Americas. Columbus was but one of many seafarers who sailed south and west looking for a new trade route to Asia. However, his "discovery" of the "New World" modified the objectives of future explorers. Soon, the acquisition of colonies and of gold, silver, and other treasures became the goals of many European nations, seeking to emulate the wealth and power of Spain. By the early 16th century, many European nations were caught up in a rivalry for power that hinged on control of the New World.

The Unit Opener in the textbook depicts many of the outstanding persons and events of this period. You may want to use these illustrations to help introduce the Unit. The statue in the lower central part of the page is of the ancient Mexican god Quetzalcoatl. Beginning in the lower left-hand corner and moving in a clockwise direction are a mastodon and hunter; a Pacific Northwest Indian ceremonial mask; a Viking ship; a stone age spear; the explorer Christopher Columbus; and a pueblo in New Mexico.

Another major feature in this and several other units in the textbook is a photo essay, *What Life Was Like.* It is designed to evoke the quality and flavor of daily life in different types of American communities at various times in the nation's history. In Unit one, the photo essay shows several early Indian tribes, mostly hunters and gatherers.

Unit Themes and Ideas

There are three major themes in Unit One. The first is the migration, throughout North and South America, of the groups of Asians who arrived in the Western Hemisphere between 28,000 and 10,000 years ago. The land bridge theory is discussed in detail because it is basic to our understanding of how the first peoples came to North America. The second important theme is the development of cultures by these immigrant groups. Geography is presented as a major influence of cultural variations among different Indian groups. Indians adapted their cultures to make the best use of their physical environments. Some Indians developed large, highly organized empires. Others remained in small, nomadic clans.

The European drive for exploration, and discovery is the third major theme of Unit One. Undaunted by early lack of success in finding those sought-after trade routes to Asia, the Europeans kept trying. In the process, America was "discovered" by the Europeans and life on the Western Hemisphere was forever changed.

The themes and ideas of Unit One are organized into the two chapters below:

Chapter 1 - *Indians Settle in the Americas (Prehistory to 1500's)*
Chapter 2 - *Europeans Come to the Americas (1000-1500's)*

CHAPTER 1

Indians Settle in the Americas (Prehistory to 1500's)

Chapter Objectives

After completing this chapter, students will be able to:
1. Explain the land bridge theory regarding the migrations of nomad hunters from Asia to the Americas.

1

2. Describe the eight natural regions of North America.
3. Identify major Indian groups in the Americas.
4. Describe the cultures of major Indian groups in the Americas.

Chapter Chronology

Chapter 1 covers the development of Indian cultures throughout North and South America from prehistoric times to just before the arrival of European explorers. Many of the most important events of this long period are highlighted on the time line in the textbook Chapter Opener. In 28,000 B.C., hunters started to come to North America from Asia. They dispersed very slowly over the continents, some reaching the tip of South America by 10,000 B.C. By 5000 B.C. the Indians of Mexico were beginning to farm. In 2500 B.C., the farmers of the Southwest were digging irrigation canals. The Aztecs in Mexico built their empire in 1428 A.D. In 1438 A.D., the Incas built their empire in Peru. The Iroquois League was founded in 1570.

Motivation

Show students an outline map of the Western Hemisphere. Tell them that scientists believe that about 50,000 years ago, there were probably no people living in North and South America. Next, suggest four theories about how people came to the Americas:
1. They came from Asia to the west coast of South America in seaworthy boats.
2. They walked across a "land bridge" between Siberia and Alaska. The land bridge later sank beneath the Bering Strait.
3. They came from Africa to the east coast of South America in strong reed boats.
4. They came from other continents, long ago, when all continents were very close together.

Ask students to discuss the merits of each theory. Keep student responses on the board and review them after they have read the chapter.

Geographical Setting

Chapter 1 introduces the physical environment of North America and the lifestyles of its inhabitants prior to the European colonization of the continent. The first map, *Hunters' Routes into the Americas*, illustrates the migration routes from Asia into the Americas. The map *Indian Groups of North America in 1492* shows the major Indian groups that existed on the continent at that time. The physical features of the continent are illustrated in the map *Physical Features of North America*. The great Indian empires in the Americas are shown in the map of that title. This is a good point at which to teach basic locational geography as all of the physical features illustrated are mentioned in the text.

History Study Skills

The History Study Skill in Chapter 1 is *Locating Information in a Book*. This activity focuses on the Table of Contents, Index, Glossary, and other parts of a book that help students locate information. Use this activity as soon as possible so that students will improve their use of the textbook as a resource.

Bibliography

Teacher References
Driver, Harold E., *Indians of North America*. University of Chicago Press, Chicago, Ill., 1969.
Josephy, Jr., Alvin, *The Indian Heritage of America*. Knopf, New York City, 1968.
Student References
Billard, Jules B., ed.,*The World of the American Indian*. National Geographic Society, Washington, D.C., 1974. This beautiful book on American Indians includes origin and migration stories, cultural descriptions, historical events and verse and art.
Witt, Shirley Hill, *The Tuscaroras*. Macmillan, New York City, 1972. This book traces the history of the Tuscaroras, a tribe of the Iroquois Confederacy, from earliest times to the present day.

Audio-Visual Materials

Indians of North America, National Geographic Society. Five sound filmstrips, color. This program surveys American Indians from ancient to modern times.
American Indians Before European Settlements, BFA films, 10½ minutes. This film portrays Indian life, before the arrival of the Europeans, in five regions of the United States: the Eastern Woodlands, Great Plains, Southwest, Far West, and Northwest Coast.

SECTION 1: People Move Into North America

OBJECTIVES

After completing this section, students will be able to:
- Explain how the first peoples came to North America.
- Describe the nomadic life style of the first Americans.
- List the types of artifacts used by archeologists to learn about the first Americans.

MOTIVATION

Use the strategy suggested in the chapter introduction in this manual. Write the four theories on the chalkboard. Then discuss the merits of each theory, as well as the possible difficulties people would have faced in each instance. Point out to students that Section 1 identifies one of the theories and explains it in detail. Challenge them to name and explain this theory when they have finished the reading.

SUGGESTED ACTIVITIES

1. **Directed Reading.** As students read the information in Section 1, have them answer the following guide questions:
   A. How did the formation of glaciers affect the movement of people to North America? (The formation of glaciers led to the creation of a land bridge when the sea level was lowered. People were able to walk over this bridge from Asia to North America.)
   B. What type of life did these early peoples lead? (Nomadic; they could use fire, make weapons, tools, and clothing, and often lived in caves.

Hunters and gatherers of food, they did not know how to farm.)

   C. What have archeologists learned about the early North Americans from studying artifacts? (Where they lived, how they lived, when they crossed the continent)

    Review the answers to the questions with students. As a summary, refer to the four theories discussed during the motivation. Ask students to identify the one they have just read about and to explain it.

2. **History Study Skills.** As suggested in the chapter introduction in this manual, this activity should be introduced as soon as possible. Refer students to the History Study Skill, *Locating Information in a Book,* on textbook page 23. Read through the information with students. Then have them answer the questions in the activity. You may wish to provide additional examples. These can be excerpted from the Table of Contents and Index.

3. **Using the Glossary.** Ask students to find another part of their textbook that would help them to locate information. (The glossary) Have them state the purpose of the glossary. (To find the meaning of words.) Ask them to identify the words in Section 1 for which they could find meanings in the glossary. (Printed in heavy blue type.) Have them locate each word in the glossary and read the definitions orally. Ask them to complete the "Define" part of the Section Review in writing. This would make an excellent home assignment which could be enhanced by having students use each word in a sentence.

4. **Creative Writing Assignment.** Have students pretend that they were born on another planet and trained as archeologists. They are assigned to take a voyage to the earth and discover how people there lived in the late 20th century. Ask students to make a list of "artifacts" they might find and to describe what each would tell about the way people lived during this time.

BUILDING AMERICAN CITIZENSHIP

    Explain to students that the first Americans were citizens of the nomadic society in which they lived. Ask them what qualities of good citizenship these people would have had to possess in order to contribute to the survival of their group. (Cooperation; a willingness to share what they had)

SECTION 1 REVIEW ANSWERS

1. **IDENTIFY: Peter Lord:** Loucheaux Indian who discovered an animal bone about 27,000 years old in an Indian village in Alaska; **last Ice Age:** about 50,000 years ago when glaciers spread slowly across the earth from the north; **George McJunkin:** black cowboy who discovered evidence of ancient people near Folsom, New Mexico, in the 1920's; **Mound Builders:** early Indians who lived in the North Central region of the United States, who honored their dead by burying them along with their possessions in huge graves.

2. **DEFINE: glaciers:** huge masses of ice and snow; **land bridge:** a land connection between North America and

Asia, formed when glaciers lowered the sea level; **nomads:** people who move from place to place in search of food; **archeologists:** scientists who study the remains of ancient cultures; **artifacts:** objects made by early humans and other physical remains of an ancient culture.

3. They followed the herds of animals that moved across the land bridge to North America.

4. Objects such as weapons and tools made by early people, bones, markings on the land, and other physical remains.

SECTION 2: North America Has Many Regions

OBJECTIVES

    After completing this section, students will be able to:
- Identify the eight natural regions of the United States.
- Chart distinguishing features of each of the eight regions.

MOTIVATION

    Refer students to the map, *Physical Features of North America* on textbook page 9. Ask them to study it carefully and then to name the bodies of water North, East, West, and South of North America. Next, using the information on the map, have them name the regions into which North America seems to be divided. Ask them to state how one region seems to differ from another. Explain that Section 1 identifies all of these regions and the ways in which they differ.

SUGGESTED ACTIVITIES

1. **Directed Reading.** As students read, have them complete the following table, *Regions of North America.* Provide one example for them, and work through the second example with them. Then, circulate among the students as they complete the table to assist with questions or problems.

NAME OF REGION	LOCATION	PHYSICAL FEATURES	CLIMATE
Pacific Coast	From Alaska in North to California Peninsula in the South	High mountain ranges; green valleys; rivers	Mild and humid with much rain

    Place the table on the chalkboard. Check student entries by having students go to the chalkboard and write the information in the appropriate column. As a summary, cover the table and have students close their notebooks. Then name an entry from one of the columns and have students identify the region to which it is related.

2. **Research.** Have students use Section 2 as their *only* resource. Ask them to identify the region in which each of the following would be located:
   A. Mount McKinley (Pacific Coast)
   B. Great Plains (Central Lowlands)
   C. Hudson Bay (Canadian Shield)
   D. Cloud-covered volcanoes (Mexican Highlands)
   E. Dismal Swamp (Atlantic Coast)
   F. Piedmont Plateau (Appalachian Region)

G. Mississippi River (Central Lowlands)
H. Continental Divide (Rocky Mountains)
I. Death Valley (Intermountain Plateau)

3. **Map Study.** Review the meaning of the term "tributaries." (Have students use their dictionaries, if necessary.) Use the information in Section 2 to name the river in the middle of the continent (Mississippi) and the two river systems that flow into it (Ohio and Missouri). Then, have students refer to an atlas or other library source to list the main tributaries of both the Ohio River System and the Missouri River System.

4. **History Study Skills.** Duplicate Worksheet 1, *Locating Information in a Book.* This activity requires students to apply the skill introduced in the previous section. Have them answer the questions in Part I only. (Part II should be utilized with Section 3.) You may wish to assign this for homework, allowing students to practice the skill independently.

BUILDING AMERICAN CITIZENSHIP

How would the location, climate, and physical features of North America's natural regions help determine how citizens in each one might make a living? Give examples to support your answer.

SECTION 2 REVIEW ANSWERS

1. **IDENTIFY: Continental Divide:** crest of the Rocky Mountains from which the rivers on the east flow into the waterways to the east, and the rivers on the west flow to the Pacific Ocean: **Canadian Shield:** worn-down land that remained after the glaciers melted, stretching from the Great Lakes to the Arctic Ocean.
2. **DEFINE: natural region:** all the conditions and geographical features of an area; **plateau:** a dry highland plain where few plants can grow; **intermountain plateau:** plateau between the mountains on the coast and the Rocky Mountains; **canyons:** deep valleys with steep sides, cut by rivers; **prairie:** grassland; **fall line:** the geographical line marking the beginning of a plateau, usually marked by waterfalls.
3. The younger mountains are more rugged because wind and water have not yet rounded their peaks.
4. The Ohio River and its tributaries flow into the Mississippi from the East, and the Missouri River and its tributaries flow into the Mississippi from the West, thus linking both to one another and to the South. Water from the Great Lakes flows into the St. Lawrence River to the Atlantic Ocean, forming a link between the Middle West and the East Coast.

SECTION 3: Indians Develop Many Different Cultures

OBJECTIVES

After completing this section, students will be able to:
• Identify the major Indian groups that lived in North America.
• Give examples of the lasting heritage of American Indians.

MOTIVATION

Ask the class to read the Landmarks of Liberty selection, *Mesa Verde National Park,* on textbook page 12. Then have students answer the two questions at the end and discuss them. Make sure students can identify the Anasazi and the area in which they lived. Explain that the Anasazi are one of the many groups of Indians that lived in the United States. Tell students that they will be learning about some of the differences among these groups today.

SUGGESTED ACTIVITIES

1. **Directed Reading.** As students read, have them complete a list of the Indian groups identified in Section 3 and the areas in which they lived. Students may title this classwork *Indians in North America.*

INDIAN GROUP	AREA IN WHICH THEY LIVED
Anasazi	Southwestern United States

When students have completed the activity, check their work by having them write their answers on the chalkboard. As they do, discuss distinguishing features of the culture of each group. Summarize by discussing some of the effects of our Indian heritage on the lives of students.
2. **History Study Skills.** Refer students to Worksheet 1. Direct them to complete Part II of the Worksheet, which is related to material in Section 3.
3. **Making a Table.** Duplicate Worksheet 2, *Culture and Environment.* This activity will enable students to organize the information they have read about in Section 3. Suggest that students refer to the information in Section 2. This will help them complete the last column of the table.
4. **Round Robin.** This technique enables many students to participate orally in reviewing factual information. Call on a student volunteer to state one important fact from the reading. Then, call on a second student to repeat that fact, and to state a different one. A third student volunteer then repeats the second fact given and states still another one. You may continue the activity as time and resources allow. If this type of exercise is new to students, you may wish to let them use their textbooks as an aid.

BUILDING AMERICAN CITIZENSHIP

Review the information on the Iroquois League. What are the similarities between this League and the way our government operates today? (Our government performs some of the same functions. The League settled disputes, dealt with outsiders or foreign nations, and decided whether or not to make war. States today elect representatives to Congress just as the Iroquois selected chiefs to represent them. Individual states rule their people just as the individual tribes of the Iroquois League ruled theirs.)

SECTION 3 REVIEW ANSWERS

1. **IDENTIFY: Maya:** Indians of southern Mexico whose culture lasted from about 1000 B.C. to about 800 A.D., who were skilled farmers and mathematicians and who

built splendid palaces and temples decorated with jewels, gold, and fine sculptures; **Aztecs:** Indians who built a great empire in the highlands of central Mexico about 1428 A.D.; **Hohokam and Anasazi:** early Indian peoples who lived in the American Southwest; **Yukis:** California Indians who made beautiful baskets, blankets, and pottery; **Iroquois:** the most powerful of the Eastern Woodlands Indians; **Chippewa:** a nomadic Indian group around Lake Superior and Lake Michigan who lived by hunting and gathering and who built wigwams for shelter; **Eskimos:** a group of hunters (who called themselves *Inuit*) in the treeless, frozen land of the Arctic who depended entirely on hunting and fishing and special skills to survive; **Haida:** a group of Indians who lived on islands near the Pacific coast of Canada, who used the wood from forests to build canoes and houses of cedar and who carved totem poles as family symbols.

2. **DEFINE: cultures:** ways of life; **confederation:** union; **potlatches:** feasts held by the Indians of the Northwest Pacific Coast; **descendants:** one's children, their children and their children's children; **heritage:** traditions handed down from the past.

3. Mexican Indians, Southwestern Indians, California Indians, Eastern Woodlands Indians, Southeastern Indians, Eskimos, Northwest Pacific Coast Indians, and Plains Indians.

4. By having parties, called potlatches, where all guests were given gifts; the number and value of the gifts indicated the importance of the host, who was usually a chief.

CHAPTER 1 REVIEW ANSWERS

IDENTIFYING KEY WORDS

1. b.   2. a.   3. b.   4. b.   5. a.

REMEMBERING IMPORTANT PEOPLE

1. e.   2. c.   3. d.   4. b.   5. a.

REVIEWING THE FACTS

1. F   2. T   3. T   4. T   5. F

PLACING EVENTS IN TIME

1. D   2. E   3. B   4. C   5. A

LINKING GEOGRAPHY AND HISTORY

The ways the Indians made their living—hunting, farming, or gathering—were influenced by the land on which they lived. The ways they built their homes were determined by the materials available and the climate of the region.

THINKING ABOUT AMERICAN HISTORY

1. Answers will vary.
2. Answers will vary.

APPLYING HISTORY STUDIES SKILLS

1. Table of Contents or Index.
2. Glossary.
3. Index.

CHAPTER 2

Europeans Come to the Americas (1000-1500's)

Chapter Objectives

After completing this chapter, students will be able to:
1. Explain why Europeans were seeking new trade routes.
2. Identify European explorers, the countries they represented, and their accomplishments.
3. Describe the importance of Columbus' voyages to the "New World."

Chapter Chronology

Chapter 2 covers the years 1000 to the 1500's, the earliest period of European exploration, motivated by the search for new trade routes and new lands. Many of the most important persons and events of this time are highlighted on the time line in the textbook Chapter Opener. In 1001, Leif Ericsson voyaged to North America. Marco Polo visited China in 1271. In Portugal in 1418, Prince Henry started a school for navigators. In 1487, the Portuguese explorer, Bartholomeu Dias rounded Africa's Cape of Good Hope. Just five years later, in 1492, Christopher Columbus reached the Americas. In 1497, Vasco da Gama, a Portuguese explorer, sailed to the East Indies. In the same year, John Cabot, an Italian sailing for England, reached North America. In 1513, Vasco Núñez de Balboa became the first European to see the Pacific Ocean. Six years later in 1519, Ferdinand Magellan, a Portuguese navigator sailing for Spain, began a voyage around the world.

Motivation

To prepare students for the main ideas in Chapter 2, have them look closely at each of the maps in it. Use the following questions to guide their studies:
1. *Trade Routes Between Europe and Asia Before and After 1498*—What seems to be the goal of these European trade routes?
2. *The Voyages of Columbus*—Did Columbus have the same goal? Did he go about achieving it differently? Was he successful?
3. *Early Voyages to the Americas*—What other countries are also interested in the same goal?
4. *Magellan's Voyage, 1519-1522*—What was Magellan's major discovery?

Do not try to answer student questions at this time. They will be able to answer many themselves at the end of the chapter.

Geographical Setting

The voyages taken by the major European explorers are the geographical focus of Chapter 2. The map *Early Voyages to the Americas* on textbook page 38 shows the early efforts of the European explorers to find new trade routes and new lands. Though they did not always discover the better new routes that they sought, the voyages of many, especially to the Americas, were not without some measure of success. Each resulted in a land claim that signaled an era of colonization and colonial rivalry among European nations.

History Study Skills

The History Study Skill introduced in Chapter 2 is *Using Time Lines.* The focus is on explorers who sailed to the New World between 1000 and 1600. The emphasis is on how events are related and on cause and effect. This activity may be used to introduce Sections 1 and 2 or as a summary of the events in the chapter.

Bibliography

Teacher References

Morison, Samuel Eliot, *The European Discovery of America: The Northern Voyages, A.D. 1500-1600.* Oxford University Press, New York City, 1971.

Quinn, David, *North America from Earliest Discovery to First Settlements.* Harper, New York City, 1977.

Student References

Irwin, Constance, *Strange Footprints on the Land: Vikings in America.* Harper, New York City, 1980. This book presents interesting facts, hypotheses, and unresolved controversies about the Vikings who ventured to North America some 500 years before Columbus.

Heinmann, Susan, *Christopher Columbus.* Franklin Watts, New York City, 1973. This excellent biography of Columbus, illustrated with authentic prints, documents, and maps, includes many interesting facts about the man and his voyages.

Audio-Visual Materials

Europe and the Age of Discovery. Guidance Associates, 2 filmstrips, 2 cassettes, Library Kit, Teacher's Guide. This program, which illustrates many facets of European exploration and discovery, includes the Norse expeditions as well as those of Columbus, Vasco da Gama, and Magellan.

Discovery and Exploration, Educational Enrichment Materials. Five sound filmstrips and a teacher's guide. Paintings and authentic period maps are used to illustrate the seafaring expeditions of such explorers as Cartier and Hudson in the American wilderness. There is also an excellent description of the Spanish conquest of the Incas and Aztecs.

SECTION 1: Europeans Seek New Trade Routes

OBJECTIVES

After completing this section, students will be able to:
• Identify the Viking explorers and their achievements.
• Explain the changes brought about in Europe by the Crusades.
• Describe the explorations of Portuguese seafarers.

MOTIVATION

Have the class read the textbook Chapter Introduction. Ask students why Ericsson and his crew were ex-cited about their discovery. Ask why people today consider this journey to be important. Direct students to read the three questions in the last paragraph of the Chapter Introduction. Tell them to concentrate on the first two questions as they read and that each will be discussed when they have finished.

SUGGESTED ACTIVITIES

1. **Directed Reading.** Section 1 deals primarily with three topics: the Viking explorers, the changes brought about in Europe by the Crusades, and the explorations of Portuguese seafarers. Write the statements below on the chalkboard. Have students copy them and fill in the correct information about each topic.

   A. The Vikings, or ___(NORSEMEN)___, named North America ___(VINLAND)___. They established settlements there but were driven out by ___(SKRAELINGS)___. Others learned of these settlements from Viking ___(SAGAS)___.

   B. European nations started wars "for the Cross" called ___(CRUSADES)___ to fight the ___(MUSLIMS)___ and win back the ___(HOLY LAND)___. As a result of these wars, ___(TRADE)___ with the nations of ___(ASIA)___ increased.

   C. Portugal built better ___(SHIPS)___ and trained better ___(SAILORS)___. ___(PRINCE HENRY)___ started a school for sailors where they learned to use instruments such as the ___(ASTROLABE)___ and ___(COMPASS)___. Eventually, their ships reached ___(INDIA)___ by sailing around the southern end of ___(AFRICA)___.

   Review the answers with students. Summarize by discussing the first two questions in the last paragraph of the textbook Chapter Introduction.

2. **Mix and Match.** Have students match the individuals described in Section 1 by finding the correct description in the right-hand column.

1. Thorfinn Karlsevni	A. leader of the Vikings who settled in Vinland around 1009
2. Leif Ericsson	B. first to sail around the Cape of Good Hope
3. Bartholomeu Dias	C. established a school for sailors in Portugal
4. Marco Polo	D. spent 24 years in Asia; then returned to Europe to inform Europeans about that land
5. Prince Henry	E. he and his crew were the first Europeans to see North America
6. Vasco da Gama	F. found Vinland and explored it before returning to Greenland
7. Bjarni Herjolfsson	G. sailed from Europe to India around the southern tip of Africa

   Answers:
   1-A; 2-F; 3-B; 4-D; 5-C; 6-G; 7-E

3. **History Study Skills.** Refer students to the History Study Skill, *Using Time Lines,* on textbook page 42.

The focus of this activity is on explorers who sailed to the New World between 1000 and 1600. Emphasize those events described in Section 1. Ask students if there are any other events that could have been incorporated on the time line. Also, ask them which individuals they might expect to read about in Section 2.

4. **Comprehension Check.** Determine students' understanding of Section 1 by having them complete the following TRUE-FALSE exercise. If the statement is FALSE, require students to explain why.

   A. Evidence of Viking settlements has been discovered in Canada and the northeastern United States. (T)

   B. The Crusades increased European interest in trade with Asia. (T)

   C. Most of the trade with Asia was controlled by Portuguese merchants. (F—Italian merchants)

   D. The Portuguese invented the compass and astrolabe. (F—they learned how to use them from the Arabs)

   E. The Portuguese searched for a route to Asia by sailing westward across the Atlantic. (F—sailing around the southern tip of Africa)

BUILDING AMERICAN CITIZENSHIP

Citizens can make contributions to their nations in many ways. What contributions did Prince Henry make to Portugal? (He established a school that built up the Portuguese fleet and prepared seafarers to make successful expeditions into unknown waters.) What contributions were made by Marco Polo to Italy? (The stories of his travels aroused his nation's interest in trade with the countries of Asia and eventually resulted in great wealth for Italian merchants.)

SECTION 1 REVIEW ANSWERS

1. **IDENTIFY: Leif Ericsson:** Viking who explored several places in North America before returning to Greenland in 1001; **Bjarni Herjolfsson:** Norwegian whose ship blew off course and accidentally landed on the coast of North America in 986 A.D.; **Thorfinn Karlsevni:** leader of a group of Norse settlers who set up a settlement, called Vinland, in North America in about 1009; **Muhammed:** founder of the Islam religion; **Holy Land:** Palestine; region on the eastern shore of the Mediterranean Sea; **Marco Polo:** Italian who spent 24 years in Asia, then returned to Venice with stories of life there; **Prince Henry:** brother of the king of Portugal who started a school for sailors.

2. **DEFINE: manors:** large estates in Europe owned by noble lords; **Crusades:** wars fought by the Roman Catholic Church to regain the Holy Land from the Muslims; **monopoly:** complete control of something; **compass:** an instrument that indicates directions accurately; **astrolabe:** a navigation instrument used by explorers that measured the location of the stars; **caravel:** a small, sturdy ship that used lateen sails.

3. The overland trade routes were difficult; caravans had to travel vast distances across mountains and deserts. Also, the trade routes were controlled by Muslims, on which Italian merchants had a monopoly.

4. They opened up a new trade route to India by sailing around the southern end of Africa. Portugal was able to make huge profits from this new trade route to Asia.

SECTION 2: Columbus Sails Across the Atlantic

OBJECTIVES

After completing this section, students will be able to:

- Describe Columbus' first voyage to America.
- Identify the lands found by Columbus.
- Explain how the "New World" came to be called America.
- Explain the importance of Columbus' voyages of discovery.

MOTIVATION

Ask "Who discovered America?" Likely responses would include the Indians, Leif Ericsson, and Christopher Columbus. Ask students why Columbus is given credit for the discovery if the Indians and Ericsson arrived first. Ask why the land was called America if Columbus, or Ericsson, or the Indians discovered it. Tell students they should be able to answer these questions after reading Section 2.

SUGGESTED ACTIVITIES

1. **Directed Reading.** As students read Section 2, have them answer the following guide questions:

   A. What factors enabled Columbus to voyage westward across the Atlantic? (He was an expert navigator; had made detailed calculations regarding the distance of his planned route; and won the financial support of the King and Queen of Spain.)

   B. Why did Columbus call the people in the new land "Indians"? (He thought he had reached the Indies in Asia.)

   C. Why did Columbus make three more voyages to the "Indies"? (He wanted to find China.)

   D. How did America get its name? (A German mapmaker named it after the Italian explorer Amerigo Vespucci.)

   Discuss the answers to these questions with students. As a summary, refer to the questions posed during the Motivation. Have students support their answers with information from Section 2. Also, discuss the importance of Columbus' voyages.

2. **Map Study.** Refer students to the map *The Voyages of Columbus* on textbook page 34. Have them answer the following questions:

   A. From which European nation did each voyage begin? (Spain)

   B. Which islands did Columbus visit on his first voyage? (San Salvador, Cuba, and Hispaniola)

   C. How many voyages to the "Americas" did Columbus make? (Four voyages)

   D. During which voyage did Columbus explore the coast of Central America? (The fourth voyage)

3. **Ideals in the Lives of Americans.** Have students read the selection on Bartolomé de las Casas on textbook page 36 and then discuss the answers to the two

questions that follow. Ask students if they think Columbus treated the Indians as most Spanish did, or as Las Casas did. You may wish to refer students to Columbus' letter describing the Arawaks in the textbook for evidence to support their opinions.

4. **Sequence.** Have students place the following events from Section 2 in chronological order.
   A. Columbus founded Santo Domingo.
   B. Columbus founded San Salvador.
   C. Columbus gained the support of the King and Queen of Spain.
   D. Columbus left Spain in August 1492.
   E. Columbus led an expedition to West Africa.
   ANSWERS: E - C - D - B - A

BUILDING AMERICAN CITIZENSHIP

Each year the citizens of the United States celebrate holidays commemorating important events in American history. One of these events is described in this section. Can you identify it? (Columbus Day) What event is commemorated on this day? (Columbus' landing on San Salvador) On what date is it celebrated? (Oct. 12) Can you name another holiday that celebrates an important event in American history? (Independence Day, July 4, celebrates the signing of the Declaration of Independence.)

SECTION 2 REVIEW ANSWERS

1. **IDENTIFY: King Ferdinand and Queen Isabella:** rulers of Spain who financed the voyages of Columbus; **Amerigo Vespucci:** Italian for whom America was named; **"the Indies":** name given to the islands in the Caribbean discovered by Columbus, which he thought to be the Indies in Asia; the **"New World":** the continents of North and South America, first known to Europe after the voyages of Columbus.
2. Columbus thought this route would be shorter and easier.
3. On his first voyage Columbus reached San Salvador, Cuba, and other islands in the Caribbean, which he named Hispaniola; on a later voyage he landed on the coast of Venezuela and sailed along the coast of Central America.

SECTION 3: Europeans Explore and Settle the Americas

OBJECTIVES

After completing this section, students will be able to:
- Explain why explorers searched for a Northwest Passage.
- Identify the explorers, their accomplishments, and the nations for which they sailed.
- Describe the Spanish colonization of the Caribbean Islands.

MOTIVATION

Review the voyages of Columbus. Did he accomplish what he set out to do? (No—he never reached the Indies or China.) Why is he so well remembered? (He was the

first to make Europe aware of the new lands to the West.) Once people realized what Columbus had found, what do you think they were going to do next? (Explore the new land; look for a way to get around it to Asia). If students do not have any answers, have them read the first paragraph of Section 3. Explain that it describes European exploration of the New World.

SUGGESTED ACTIVITIES

1. **Directed Reading.** As students read Section 3, have them write one or two sentences about each explorer, including his full name, the country for which he sailed, and his achievements. For example: "John Cabot was an Italian who sailed for England. He claimed Newfoundland for England." When students have completed the assignment, you may check it with them by having them read the sentences out loud or write them on the chalkboard. Use the following activity to summarize.
2. **Using Time Lines.** Duplicate Worksheet 3, *Explorers, 1499-1609.* This activity has a dual purpose. It will allow students to apply the History Study Skill introduced in Section 1 and also provide a review of the explorers they read about in Section 3. When students have completed the activity, ask them to identify those explorers on the time line about whom they wrote sentences. Then, have them add to the time line those explorers that were not included. (Cabot, Balboa, and Magellan) Finally, have students identify those explorers that they have not yet read about.
3. **Discussion on Colonization.** Begin by asking students to define the word "colony." Then, ask: Why does a nation start colonies? Which European nation was the first to start colonies? Where were they started? How did this nation control the colonies? How did they treat the people who lived in the colonies? How did these people respond? What sources of wealth were found in the colonies?
4. **Crossword Puzzle.** Duplicate Worksheet 4, *European Exploration.* This activity will give students an opportunity to review the contents of the chapter in preparation for completion of the Chapter 2 Review and the Chapter 2 Test in the manual. Some students may want to use it as a model to create their own puzzle, using other facts in the chapter.

BUILDING AMERICAN CITIZENSHIP

Were the citizens of the colonies founded by Spain treated fairly? What methods could the Spanish have used to rule these citizens with less brutality? (Answers will vary.)

SECTION 3 REVIEW ANSWERS

1. **IDENTIFY: Northwest Passage:** a water passage that Europeans thought would lead to Asia from the New World; **John Cabot:** Italian sailor hired by England who, while searching for the Northwest Passage, discovered Newfoundland; **Giovanni Verrazano:** Italian sailor hired by France to find the Northwest Passage, who explored the eastern coast of North America; **Jacques Cartier:** French explorer who claimed part of northeastern North

American for France; **Pedro Cabral:** Portuguese explorer whose ship was blown off course and reached the northeast coast of South America, which later led to Portugal's establishment of a colony in Brazil; **Ferdinand Magellan:** Portuguese navigator who led the Spanish expedition that made the first voyage around the world; **Ponce de León:** Spanish explorer who claimed Florida for Spain.

2. **DEFINE: colony:** territory that is controlled and often settled by people of another country.
3. They wanted to find a water route from the Americas to Asia.
4. The expedition proved that the best and shortest sea route to Asia was around Africa.

CHAPTER 2 REVIEW ANSWERS

REVIEWING KEY WORDS

1. b.   2. e.   3. a.   4. c.   5. d.

REMEMBERING IMPORTANT PEOPLE

1. c.   2. e.   3. d.   4. a.   5. b.
6. b.   7. a.   8. c.   9. e.   10. d.

REVIEWING THE FACTS

1. T   2. F   3. F   4. T   5. T

PLACING EVENTS IN TIME

1. a.   2. b.   3. a.   4. a.   5. b.

LINKING GEOGRAPHY AND HISTORY

In their search for a Northwest Passage to Asia, they explored the Americas and gained new knowledge about previously unknown areas of the earth.

THINKING ABOUT AMERICAN HISTORY

1. Columbus made Europeans aware of a "New World."
2. He failed to find a shorter route to Asia.

APPLYING HISTORY STUDIES SKILLS

491 years.

UNIT 1 REVIEW ANSWERS

VOCABULARY REVIEW

Answers will vary.

REVIEWING THE MAIN IDEAS

1. People came because the Ice Age changed the earth's climate. The glaciers that spread from the north lowered the sea level, and land appeared, forming a land bridge between Asia and North America.
2. Through the artifacts that remain.
3. The eight regions are: the Pacific Coast, the Intermountain Plateau, the Rocky Mountains, the Central Lowlands, the Canadian Shield, the Appalachian Mountains, the Atlantic Lowlands, and the Highlands of Central Mexico.
4. The cultures of the different Indian groups differed in language, beliefs, ways of providing food, shelter, clothing, organization, laws, and so on. For example, the Eskimos lived in igloos, while the Plains tribes lived in tepees. The Plains tribes hunted buffalo, while those in the northern part of the Intermountain Plateau were gatherers and hunters of small game.
5. Columbus discovered the Americas for Europeans, making them aware of these lands. What he saw led others to explore the Western Hemisphere and other parts of the world.
6. They were looking for a shorter route to Asia.

APPLYING YOUR STUDY SKILLS

1. **Using a Time Line**
   a. (1) Dias and Da Gama
      (2) 1570 Iroquois League formed

2. **Using a Map**
   a. Europe, Africa, and Asia

3. **Using Your Textbook**
   a. 70 days
   b. (1) Table of Contents or Index
      (2) Index
      (3) Glossary
      (4) Table of Contents or Index
      (5) Table of Contents or Index

PROJECTS

Answers will vary.

BUILDING AMERICAN CITIZENSHIP

Courage, intelligence, a spirit of adventure, a good organizer, a leader who could earn respect from his crew, as well as sailing and navigational skills.

A good crew member would also have to have courage, be adventurous, able to take orders, get along well with other crew members, be willing to face hardships, and so on.

UNIT 2 (1500's-1700's)
Europeans Start Colonies

Introducing the Unit

Unit Two surveys the exploration and colonization of large areas of North and South America that occurred in the sixteenth, seventeenth, and eighteenth centuries. During most of this period, Spain, France, and England competed with each other for domination of the Americas. Occasionally their interests conflicted, particularly in North America. This unit begins with the conquests of the Spanish explorer Cortés and ends around 1750 with the arrival of English colonists in Georgia.

Discussed first are some two-and-a-half centuries of Spanish expansion, from Cortés' conquest of the Aztecs in 1521 to the settlement of California in the 1770's. Spanish expansion may be divided into two phases. The first, spanning the years from the 1520's to the 1530's, concentrated on Central America and the Aztec and Incan empires. The second period covers the well over 200 years that Spain took to extend its power into South America and the southern and western parts of the present-day United States.

Although the French began to explore North America in 1534, they were very slow to build a colonial empire there. The great explorer Champlain did establish a trading post at Quebec in 1608, but by 1660 there were fewer than 3,000 settlers in New France. It was French explorers, among them Joliet, Marquette, and La Salle, and fur traders who established and maintained France's hold on the continent.

Early English efforts at colonization failed in the late 1500's. However, a fledgling colony at Jamestown in 1607 became a success by 1620, and the English quickly began to colonize the east coast of North America. Plymouth in 1620 was followed by many more colonies, the last being Delaware founded in 1776.

The unit's last chapter is an in-depth study of the economic, political, social, and cultural development of the English colonies through the 1750's. The emphasis is on the evolution of colonial American civilization.

The Unit Opener in the textbook depicts many of the significant persons and events of this period. You may wish to use these illustrations to help introduce the unit to the class. The central picture is of the Mayflower. Beginning in the lower left-hand corner, in a clockwise direction, are a Spanish explorer, an unknown Indian, Peter Stuyvesant, a Pilgrim woman, and a Spanish church and mission.

Another feature in this and several other units in the textbook is a photo essay, *What Life Was Like.* It is designed to evoke the quality and flavor of daily life in different types of American communities at various times in the nation's history. In Unit Two, the photo essay shows life in American towns and villages mostly during colonial times.

Unit Themes and Ideas

Exploration and colonization are the two major themes in Chapters 3, 4, and 5. Students should learn that there were economic, political, and religious reasons for exploration and colonization. The promise of wealth, and the political power it might bring, provided the economic incentives for monarchs and established businesspeople as well as ordinary persons. Religion also played a major role. However, while Spain and France sought to spread Catholicism among the non-Christian inhabitants of the New World, the English were primarily interested in acquiring religious freedom for themselves. All three countries were rivals for hegemony in Europe.

The major theme of the Unit's final chapter is life in the English colonies in the 1600's and 1700's. Students should be made aware of the diversity of experience and life styles that comprised this newly evolving and uniquely American society. The unit is organized into the four chapters below:

Chapter 3 - *Spaniards Colonize the Americas (1500's - 1700's)*
Chapter 4 - *The French Settle in North America (1600's - 1700's)*
Chapter 5 - *The English Colonize North America (1500's - 1700's)*
Chapter 6 - *Colonists Develop New Ways of Life (1600's - 1700's)*

CHAPTER 3

Spaniards Colonize the Americas (1500's-1700's)

Chapter Objectives

After completing this chapter, students will be able to:
1. Identify Spanish explorers and conquerors who gained an empire for Spain in the Western Hemisphere.
2. Name major Spanish settlements in the Americas.
3. Describe how Spain governed its colonies in the Americas.
4. Identify the influence of Spanish culture in the Americas.

Chapter Chronology

Chapter 3 covers the exploration and conquest of large areas of the Americas by the Spaniards in the period of the 1500's to the 1700's. Major events of the Spanish conquest are highlighted in the Chapter Opener time line, beginning in 1521 when the Aztecs surrendered to Cortés. A decade later, Pizarro conquered the Incas, and soon thereafter Narváez and de Vaca reached Mexico. During the next two centuries, the Spaniards extended their claims into the borderlands. Coronado explored the Southwest, de Soto reached the Mississippi River, Cabrillo explored the coast of California, and Onate reached New Mexico. Florida, Texas, and California all became part of Spain's empire in the Americas, leaving an imprint that is still apparent today.

Motivation

Use a wall map of the world or the map *The Spanish Empire in the Americas in 1650* on textbook page 52 to introduce the geographical areas that are the focus of Chapter 3. Have students look at the time line on the Chapter Opener page. Ask students to locate each place on the map that is named on the time line. Most students will be familiar with some of the names. As students locate each place on the time line, ask them to explain what they think was happening at that point. (Exploring, settling, building) This strategy will give students a sense of the vast geographical area to be studied and the major concepts in the chapter.

Geographical Setting

The geographical focus of Chapter 3 is the Spanish Empire in the Americas. The three maps in the chapter illustrate the expansion of Spain in the area, beginning with Spanish exploration and settlement of the Caribbean Basin, including the islands of Hispaniola and Cuba. The Aztec Empire conquered by Cortés is shown as is the Inca Empire won by Pizarro. The Spanish holdings in both North and South America during this period, including Mexico and the borderlands in the southern part of present-day United States are also shown. Emphasis is given to settlements that the Spanish established as they extended their empire northward. Students should note the locations of Sante Fe, San Diego, and San Antonio. This is a good point to review basic place geography of the Americas, especially bodies of water and landforms.

History Study Skills

The History Study Skill introduced in Chapter 3 is *Studying the Parts of a Map.* The map used for this activity is *Spanish Exploration in North America.* Students will study different parts of the map including the title, the legend, scale, political features, routes of explorers, and physical features. It is best to use this activity as early as possible so that the skills may be reinforced with the other two maps in Chapter 3. Further reinforcement is provided by Worksheet 6 in this guide.

Bibliography

Teacher References
Gibson, Charles, *Spain in America.* Harper, New York City, 1966.
Haring, C.H., *The Spanish Empire in America.* Harcourt, New York City, 1963.
Student References
Steele, William, *The Wilderness Tattoo.* AMS Press, New York City, 1972. This is a fictional account of the exploits of Juan Ortiz, who accompanied the De Soto expedition to the Mississippi River.

Audio-Visual Materials

El Dorado, Educational Enrichment Materials, American Heritage filmstrip collection, sound filmstrip, color. This is a visually striking introduction to Spanish exploration and colonization.
Legacy of the Incas, New York Times, six sound filmstrips, color. These filmstrips contain a complete study of the Incas, the achievements of their civilization, and Pizarro's conquest of them.

SECTION 1: Spain Claims an Empire in the Americas

OBJECTIVES

After completing this section, students will be able to:
- Use a map to locate the lands conquered by Cortés and Pizarro.
- Complete a chart comparing the conquest of the Aztecs to the conquest of the Incas.
- Explain how the Spaniards were able to conquer the empires of the Aztecs and Incas.

MOTIVATION

Have students look at the textbook Chapter Introduction. Using the map *The Spanish Exploration in North America 1513-1545,* ask them to trace the travels of Cortés after he left Spain. Include Hispaniola, Cuba, the Gulf of Mexico, and Mexico. Then ask students to name some reasons why Cortés made these journeys (wealth, power and fame). Ask students to think about the answers to the questions at the end of the Introduction. If available, use appropriate frames from the sound filmstrip *El Dorado* to provide additional information on Cortés.

SUGGESTED ACTIVITIES

1. **Directed Reading.** Before beginning to read, have students practice pronunciation of the different Spanish names. Focus on the first question at the end of the Chapter Introduction: What happened in Mexico as a result of Hernando Cortés's quest for gold? When students have completed the reading discuss the answer to the question at the end. Rephrase the question for a discussion of Pizarro's conquests.
2. **Table.** Have students utilize the information in Section 1 to complete the following table:

	Aztec Empire	Inca Empire
Location	(Mexico)	(West Coast of South America)
Emperor	(Moctezuma)	(Atahualpa)
Spanish Conqueror	(Cortés)	(Pizarro)
Indian Treatment of Spanish	(friendly)	(friendly)
Spanish Treatment of Indians	(cruel)	(cruel)
New Spanish Cities	(Mexico City)	(Lima)

3. **Research-Comparison.** The information in this chapter indicates that the city of Tenochtitlán was larger and grander than any in Spain at that time. Have students use library references to research some early sixteenth century Spanish cities. (Toledo, Cordoba, Ávila) Have them compare their findings to the textbook description of Tenochtitlán, noting as many similarities and differences as possible. Ask above-average students to make an oral report to the class.
4. **Writing Assignment.** Allow students to choose to imagine themselves as a part of either Cortés' or Pizarro's expedition, or as a member of the Inca or Aztec civilization. Ask the students to write a paragraph describing their reactions and feelings (as Spaniard or Indian) on the day the Spanish and Indians first encountered each other.

BUILDING AMERICAN CITIZENSHIP

What rights of the Aztec and Inca Indians were violated by their Spanish conquerors? (To live, own property, to be free) What steps were taken by the Indians to defend their rights? (They fought back.) Could the Indians have used peaceful means to defend their rights? Explain your answer. (Answers will vary.)

SECTION 1 REVIEW ANSWERS

1. **IDENTIFY: Hernando Cortés:** Spanish explorer who conquered the Aztecs; **Doña Mariña:** Indian woman who traveled with and helped Cortés and the Spaniards; **Moctezuma:** emperor of the Aztecs; **Tenochtitlán:** capital city of the Aztec Empire; **Francisco Pizarro:** Spanish explorer who conquered the Incas; **Atahualpa:** emperor of the Incas; **Peru:** name given to the southern part of the Spanish empire in the Americas; **New Spain:** name given to the northern part of the Spanish empire in the Americas.
2. Moctezuma thought that Cortés was a god who had promised revenge on the Aztecs.
3. The Spaniards had superior weapons, and many Aztecs were also killed by such diseases as smallpox, measles, and influenza.
4. Central America and South America came under the control of Spain.

SECTION 2: Spaniards Start to Settle the Borderlands

OBJECTIVES

After completing this section, students will be able to:
• List the settlements started in the borderlands of Spain's American empire.
• Identify the individuals responsible for starting the settlements.
• Explain the reasons why these settlements were established.

MOTIVATION

Use the map *Mexico and the Borderlands by 1776* on textbook page 60. Have students study the legend to identify the kinds of communities started by the Spaniards in these areas. Ask the students what basic structures, other than homes and property were most important to them and why. For example, a fort would have been built to protect people or property. If students have difficulty with the word "mission," have them use the glossary to determine its meaning. Ask: How many forts are shown on the map? Settlements? Missions? Is it possible to determine if any one type of community was more important to the Spanish than the others? Have students explain their reasoning.

SUGGESTED ACTIVITIES

1. **Directed Reading.** As students read the chapter, have them list the names of the communities, the type (fort, mission, settlement), and the reason each was established. This information may be organized in chart form. As the answers are reviewed, have students add the names of the individuals involved in starting the communities. Discuss again the last question under Motivation.
2. **Map Exercise.** Using the list of communities they compiled above, have students name the state in which each is now located.
   Have students consult a map of the United States today. As a further challenge, have them use the cardinal and intermediate directions to identify the part of the state in which each is located. (San Diego — Southern Calif.; Sante Fe — Northern New Mexico, and so on.)
3. **Putting Events In The Right Order.** Duplicate Worksheet 5, *The Spanish in America.* It will provide a good review of both Sections 1 and 2 of this chapter. You may wish to assist below-average students by working with them to complete the first two or three entries.
4. **Flash Card Review.** Prepare two sets of flash cards. On the first set, write the names of the Spanish communities. On the second set, write the names of the individuals associated with the establishment of the communities. Try to use marking pens of different colors to help students differentiate among the difficult Spanish names. Distribute the two sets of cards among the students. Have one student bring a card to the front of the room. The student with the correct match should do the same. This activity should provide an excellent review, and may be repeated as often as needed.

BUILDING AMERICAN CITIZENSHIP

The people from New Spain who established communities in the borderlands demonstrated their bravery by setting out to face unknown challenges. What types of risks did they have to take? (Unfriendly Indians, lack of regular food supply, lack of sturdy shelter, unfamiliarity with the terrain) In today's society, citizens must still face unknown challenges and take risks. Think of some situations in which you or your family would have to prove your bravery by risking the unknown. (Changing schools, changing jobs, moving to a new neighborhood) What types of challenges would you have to face? (Answers will vary.)

SECTION 2 REVIEW ANSWERS

1. **IDENTIFY: Huguenots:** people who had broken away from the Catholic Church of France; **St. Augustine:** oldest city in the United States, lived in from about 1565 to the present. **Estéban:** a slave who searched for gold in the territory north of Mexico after being freed; **Francisco Coronado:** Spanish explorer who searched for gold in what later became the southwestern part of the United States, allowing Spain to claim vast territories in that area; **Hernando de Soto:** Spanish explorer who discovered the Mississippi River; **Juan Bautista de Anza:** Spanish explorer who marked an overland trail to California from Mexico.
2. **DEFINE: borderlands:** unsettled lands along the edges of a nation's territory; **convert:** to persuade someone to change from one religion to another; **missions:** religious communities that taught Indians about the Roman Catholic religion.
3. Florida.
4. It allowed Spain to claim new lands in the area of the Mississippi River.

SECTION 3: Spanish Culture Is Spread to New Spain

OBJECTIVES

After completing this section, students will be able to:
- Describe the concept of mercantilism.
- Explain the established structure of social groups in New Spain.
- List the ways in which aspects of Spanish and Indian customs combined to form a new culture in New Spain.

MOTIVATION

Display the following items in front of the classroom: box of sugar, lemon, orange, banana, can or ear of corn, can of beans or fresh beans, a pepper, cocoa, a potato, and a tomato. Number each item. Have students give their opinion as to which items were brought to America and which were already growing here and used by the Indians.

SUGGESTED ACTIVITIES

1. **Directed Reading.** Use the following guide questions to help students understand the information in Section 3:
   A. How did the rulers of Spain expect the colonies of New Spain to help them become wealthy?
   B. What were the major classes of society in New Spain?
   C. What parts of the new culture of New Spain were taught by the Spanish to the Indians? What parts were taught by the Indians to the Spanish?
   Discuss the answers to each of these questions. As a summary activity, return to the display items used for the motivation. Have students use information from Section 3, to give the correct origin of each item.
2. **Vocabulary Development-Acrostic.** The vocabulary list for this section is extensive. Use the following puzzle to provide additional practice for students in learning the meaning of the words.

haCienda	C - a large estate in New Spain
mestizOs	O - person who was part Spanish and part Indian
puebLos	L - towns of New Spain
criOllos	O - colonists born in New Spain by Spanish parents
mercaNtilism	N - theory that a colony existed to make the parent country wealthy
viceroY	Y - title given to the governor of New Spain

There are two words which are not included in the puzzle. Ask students to identify and define them. (Presidio—fort in New Spain; and peninsulares—people born in Spain)
3. **Research.** The information in this section states that there are more than 2,000 cities and towns, and many rivers, mountains and valleys in the United States with Spanish names. Have above-average students use the library to compile a list of 10 to 25 places with Spanish names in the United States and ask them to identify the state in which each is located. Supply average students with a list of Spanish place names and ask them to identify the state in which each is located.
4. **Map Exercise.** To summarize what the students have learned about the colonies of New Spain, duplicate Worksheet 6, *Spanish Conquests.* Ask students to add to this map some of the cities, towns, rivers, mountains, and valleys that were listed in activity 3. Have them create symbols for each type of place, and add these to the map legend.
5. **Landmarks of Liberty.** Have students read *New Mexico's Inscription Rock* and answer the two questions at the end. Relate the reading to the concepts developed in Section 3 by asking students the following question: In what way might Inscription Rock be seen as a symbol of the culture of New Spain? (It too combined the Indian and Spanish cultures-messages were written on it by both over hundreds of years).

BUILDING AMERICAN CITIZENSHIP

A viceroy was appointed to govern the colony of New Spain. Review the information in Section 3 concerning his duties, loyalties, and appointment. Then discuss the role of state governors today. What are their duties? How are they selected? To whom do they owe loyalty?

SECTION 3 REVIEW ANSWERS

1. **IDENTIFY: Don Antonio de Mendoza:** first viceroy of New Spain; **Sister Juana Inés de la Cruz:** a Catholic nun who became the greatest poet of New Spain.
2. **DEFINE: viceroy:** a governor who ruled in the name of a king or queen; **mercantilism:** the theory that a colony existed to make its parent country richer and stronger; **hacienda:** a huge estate in New Spain; **pueblos:** towns; **presidio:** a fort; **criollos:** people born in New Spain of Spanish parents; **mestizos:** people who are part

Spanish and part Indian; **peninsulares:** colonists born in Spain.
3. Mexico City.
4. They divided the land into haciendas; they established pueblos, missions, and presidios.

CHAPTER 3 REVIEW ANSWERS

REVIEWING KEY WORDS

1. c.   2. e.   3. d.   4. a.   5. b.

REMEMBERING IMPORTANT PEOPLE

1. e.   2. a.   3. b.   4. d.   5. c.
6. d.   7. c.   8. a.   9. b.   10. e.

REVIEWING THE FACTS

1. b.   2. b.   3. a.   4. c.   5. b.

PLACING EVENTS IN TIME

1. d.   2. e.   3. a.   4. c.   5. b.

LINKING GEOGRAPHY AND HISTORY

1. They no longer had to worry about Indian opposition to their colonization.
2. North.

THINKING ABOUT AMERICAN HISTORY

1. Indians often lost their land and their gold and silver; Indians were sometimes used as slave labor; some Indians were forced to convert to Christianity.
2. Spanish design in buildings; Spanish words and names of geographic locations, towns, and cities; Spanish foods such as tacos and paella.

APPLYING HISTORY STUDIES SKILLS

1. T   2. F   3. T   4. T

CHAPTER 4

The French Settle in North America (1600's-1700's)

Chapter Objectives

After completing this chapter, students will be able to:
1. Name the explorers who built an empire in North America for France.
2. Identify major French settlements in New France.
3. Describe the importance of New France to the parent country.

Chapter Chronology

Chapter 4 covers the period of French expansion in North America, much of it concurrent with Spanish activity to the south. The Chapter Introduction in the textbook, describes the success of Jacques Cartier in establishing French claims to what is now Canada. The rest of the chapter is a chronological narrative of French explorations in the region. Among the economic activities, and settlements, important elements highlighted on the time line on the Chapter Opener page are the founding of Quebec by Champlain in 1608, followed more than a half century later by the expedition of Joliet and Marquette in 1673. In 1682, La Salle claimed Louisiana for the King of France. In 1707, the Kingdom of Great Britain was formed and the English also began to be known as the British. Six years later, following a major war between France and Britain, the victorious British received vast French territories in North America through the Treaty of Utrecht. The chapter ends with the founding of New Orleans at the mouth of the Mississippi River in 1718.

Motivation

Use a wall map of the physical features of North America or the map *Physical Features of North America* on textbook page 9 to prepare students for the extraordinary exploration and utilization of rivers in North America by the French. Have the students make a list of the rivers they see. Then refer students to the Chapter Introduction in the textbook, and suggest they pretend to be part of Cartier's expedition in 1534, anchored just south of Newfoundland. Have students hypothesize how far inland Cartier could have sailed. Then ask how far inland he could have gone if he and his crew had used canoes. List the rivers mentioned by students. As students read Chapter 4, have them compare their list of rivers to the rivers mentioned in the text.

Geographical Setting

Chapter 4 covers a large part of the North American continent from the icy northern reaches of what is today Canada to the vast stretches of Louisiana, down to the warm coast of the Gulf of Mexico. Since the French expertly utilized the rivers of New France, this is an excellent place to teach students the river systems of eastern and central North America. The French exploration of the St. Lawrence and Mississippi river systems are illustrated in the maps on textbook pages 69 and 73. Students should see the relationship between the French fur trade and the use of interior waterways throughout New France for commercial transportation. The fur trade was their business. Nothing else compared to it in importance. And the rivers were the life blood of the fur trade.

History Study Skills

The History Study Skill in Chapter 4 is Reading History Maps. The map used to develop these skills is *French Exploration of the Mississippi 1673-1682* on textbook page 73. The focus is on distinguishing the characteristics of a map that shows more than one site, or place geography. Students should learn to recognize all of the information on maps that is situational, that is, events, travel or trade routes, population, or land claims. Use this skill activity at the beginning of Section 2, as an introduction to the reading on Joliet and Marquette and La Salle.

Bibliography

Teacher References
Eccles, W.C., *France in America.* Harper, New York City, 1972.

Parkman, Francis, *Pioneers of France in the New World.*
Corner House Publishers, Williamstown, Mass.,
1970.

Student References

Ferguson, Linda, *Canada.* Scribner, New York City,
1979. This is a lively well-balanced history of
Canada.

Moody, Barry, *The Acadians.* Franklin Watts, New York
City, 1982. This is an illustrated account of the Acadians, one of Canada's earliest groups of settlers.

Audio-Visual Materials

French Explorations in the New World, Coronet Films,
10½ minutes. This covers the explorations of Verrazano, Cartier, Champlain, Marquette, Joliet and
La Salle.

Marquette and Jolliet: Voyage of Discovery, Coronet
Films, 14 minutes. This is a documentary recreation
of the journey as recorded in Marquette's journal.

SECTION 1: France Begins to Build an American Empire

OBJECTIVES

After completing this section, students will be able to:
• Name the different groups of French people who settled in New France.
• Describe the role of the Indians in helping the French
to become established in New France.
• Name and locate the rivers, lakes, and cities associated
with the French exploration of North America.

MOTIVATION

Have students read the Chapter Introduction in the
textbook. Check student comprehension of the reading
by asking the following questions:
1. How many voyages did Cartier make to North
America?
2. What was he trying to find?
3. What were his accomplishments?
  Then ask the following questions about Champlain:
1. Why did Champlain come to North America?
2. What were his accomplishments?
3. Why is he known as the father of New France?

SUGGESTED ACTIVITIES

1. **Directed Reading.** As students read this section,
have them a) name the explorers, b) list bodies of
water on which they traveled, c) describe the farthest
extent of their travels. This may be done in sentence
form. For example:
    Cartier sailed on the St. Lawrence River to
villages near present-day Quebec and Montreal.
    Champlain sailed along the east coast of North
America, on the Atlantic Ocean, as far south as
Massachusetts. He also explored the St. Lawrence
River and established the town of Quebec.
    As a summary activity, have students read the
answers orally. Those with the best-phrased answers
might write them on the board.
2. **History Study Skills.** Have students complete the

activities found on textbook page 79. One of the objectives for this section is that students familiarize
themselves with the geographic features of the northern part of North America. To help them achieve
this goal, have them draw their own map of the area,
labeling the St. Lawrence River, the Great Lakes, Montreal, and Quebec. Then ask them to visualize and
trace the probable routes of Étienne Brulé and Jean
Nicolet. Either have them consult an atlas to find the
location of Chesapeake Bay and Green Bay or provide
this information for them.

3. **Comparison.** Have students compare the hierarchy
suggested in the social structure of New France to that
of New Spain. For example, the *peninsulares* of New
Spain were similar to the *seigneurs* of New France.
Have students make two lists, one of the Spanish and
one of the French hierarchies in the Americas and
compare them. What were some of the similarities in
the two social structures? What were some of the differences?

4. **Round Robin.** Use this activity, introduced earlier in
this manual. Ask a student volunteer to state a fact re-
tained from the reading of this section. A second
volunteer repeats the first fact and adds a new one. A
third volunteer repeats the second fact and adds a new
one, and so on. Slower students may use their textbook of class notes to participate in the activity.

BUILDING AMERICAN CITIZENSHIP

What basic right was denied to the early citizens of
New France? (Freedom of religion) How did this affect the
growth of New France? (It deterred large numbers of immigrants.) Do you think that freedom of religion is any
more or less important today than it was in New France
in the 1600's? Why? (Answers will vary.)

SECTION 1 REVIEW ANSWERS

1. **IDENTIFY: Samuel de Champlain:** French explorer who
became known as the "father of New France"; **Quebec:**
first permanent French settlement in North America;
Wendat: Indian tribe whose French name was "Huron";
Étienne Brulé: explorer who expanded the French
trading area into the Great Lakes region; **Jean de
Brébeuf:** French priest killed by the Iroquois for helping
the Hurons; **Huguenots:** French Protestants.
2. **DEFINE: coureurs de bois:** French woods runners who
were both explorers and suppliers in the fur trade;
seigneurs: French nobles who received grants of land in
New France; **habitants:** farmers who worked the land
for seigneurs and paid them yearly rent.
3. Champlain established several communities, including
Quebec, and mapped the Ottawa River region, Lakes
Ontario and Huron, and discovered Lake Champlain.
4. For trading furs with the Indians.

SECTION 2: The French Explore North America's Interior

OBJECTIVES

After completing this section, students will be able to:
• Describe the boundaries of the land claimed by La
Salle for France.

15

- Explain why the Indians and the French remained friendly.
- Discuss the operation of the French trade and trapping network.

MOTIVATION

As suggested in the chapter introduction in this manual, use the History Study Skill on textbook page 79 to introduce Section 2. After students have completed this activity, ask them to close their textbooks and visualize the map. Ask for volunteers to first describe the route taken by Joliet and Marquette and then the route taken by La Salle. Jot down the major points from their descriptions on the chalkboard. This activity will make students aware of the difference between the written description of a journey and its depiction on a map.

SUGGESTED ACTIVITIES

1. **Directed Reading.** As students read about the explorations of Joliet and Marquette and of La Salle, have them refer to the points listed on the chalkboard during the Motivation. Have them write in their notebooks any aspects of the journey that were omitted. As a summary activity, fill in the missing information on the chalkboard. Compare the final written descriptions to their depictions on the map, *New France in 1750*, on textbook page 72.
2. **Sequencing Events.** Continue to emphasize the theme of describing a journey. Cover the descriptions on the chalkboard and ask students to close their notebooks. Display the following list of events of Joliet and Marquette's journey on the overhead projector, or write it on another part of the chalkboard. Have students place the events in the correct sequence.

   The Journey of Marquette and Joliet

   Canoed from the Wisconsin River to the Mississippi River (4)
   Portaged canoes from the Fox River to the Wisconsin River (3)
   Paddled down the Mississippi River to the point where the Arkansas flows into it (5)
   Canoed along Lake Michigan to Green Bay (1)
   Canoed south on the Fox River as far as they could go (2)
3. **History Study Skills.** Duplicate Worksheet 7 *French Explorers*. This activity is designed to reinforce the study skill *Reading History Maps*, introduced in the previous section. Although students are familiar with Cartier and Champlain, you may wish them to do additional research on Verrazano's role in the development of New France. Students should be encouraged to use library sources to learn more about him.

BUILDING AMERICAN CITIZENSHIP

The early French explorers got along very well with the Indians. Why was this so? (They did not try to take their land; they provided them with goods from France in exchange for furs; they sought the cooperation of the Indians) In a sense, the French treated the Indians as good neighbors. What can you do, as a citizen, to remain on good terms with the people in your neighborhood? (Avoid being noisy, avoid littering, volunteer in community activities)

SECTION 2 REVIEW ANSWERS

1. **IDENTIFY: Father Jacques Marquette:** French explorer of the Mississippi River as far south as the Arkansas River; **Louis Joliet:** French explorer who accompanied Marquette on his exploration of the Mississippi River; **La Salle:** first European to explore the Mississippi River all the way to the Gulf of Mexico.
2. **DEFINE: portage:** carrying canoes overland between bodies of water.
3. Louisiana.
4. The French were interested only in the fur trade, not in taking Indian lands for new settlements and farms.

SECTION 3: Settlers and Traders Come to Louisana

OBJECTIVES

After completing this section, students will be able to:
- Explain the importance of the French settlements established in Louisiana and Illinois.
- Discuss the causes of conflict between French and English fur traders and trappers.
- List examples of French culture still found in North America.

MOTIVATION

Ask and discuss the question: What did the French in New France have that aroused envy in others? (Control of a vast area in the interior of the continent; a thriving fur trade; friendship with many Indian tribes.) Continue the discussion by asking who might wish to have some or all of these valuable things. (Spanish, English, Indians) Finally, ask by what means they could have been gotten? (Treaty, war, stealing)

SUGGESTED ACTIVITIES

1. **Directed Reading.** Direct students to read Section 3 to determine the accuracy of the answers given during the motivational discussion.
   A. What things did the French have that were also of value to others?
   B. Who wanted to have what the French possessed?
   C. How did they go about trying to take them?
   Compare the actual answers to those given in the motivational discussion. As a summary, ask the students what the French could have done to avoid conflict with the English? (Claimed the Hudson Bay earlier; given more to the Indians for their furs; been forceful sooner with English intruders.)
2. **History Study Skills.** Duplicate Worksheet 8, *Spain and France.* This will provide an excellent review of Chapters 3 and 4. You may want to assist slower students by providing the page numbers in Chapter 3 or 4 on which the information can be found. You may ask above-average students to suggest other areas of comparison that were not included in this chart.
3. **Research.** The information in this section suggests

that there are many cities, towns, rivers, mountains, and valleys with French names. Send students to the library to compile a list of 10 to 25 places with French names. Then have them identify the state in which each is located today. Another activity would have students use cookbooks to find out popular American food dishes and beverages of French origin. Ask the students to list each item and accompany it with a brief description of the dish or beverage.

4. **Ideals in the Lives of Americans.** Have students read the selection on Pierre de la Vérendrye, found on textbook page 77. Although Section 3 emphasizes the exploration and settlement of Louisiana, this reading should help students realize that exploration and claiming of land in the Western territories also occurred during this period.

BUILDING AMERICAN CITIZENSHIP

In Chapter 3, the class read about the contributions of early Spanish citizens to American culture. In Chapter 4, it has read about the influence of the French heritage on American culture. What other groups have influenced American culture? (Indians, blacks) What were some of their contributions to the heritage and culture of the United States? (Answers will vary).

SECTION 3 REVIEW ANSWERS

1. **IDENTIFY: Sieur de Bienville:** founder of New Orleans; called the "father of Louisiana"; **Pierre de Charlevoix:** Jesuit priest who toured Illinois and urged the French king to encourage more settlements there; **Hudson Bay Company:** company established by the English to control the fur trade on the Hudson Bay.
2. To establish permanent French colonies in both areas.
3. They competed over the fur trade and control of Hudson Bay; the English established trading posts on lands claimed by France.

CHAPTER 4 REVIEW ANSWERS

REVIEWING KEY WORDS

1. d.   2. a.   3. c.   4. e.   5. b.

REMEMBERING IMPORTANT PEOPLE AND PLACES

1. T   2. F   3. T   4. F   5. T

PLACING EVENTS IN TIME

1. A   2. D   3. B   4. C   5. E

LINKING GEOGRAPHY AND HISTORY

1. Those explorers who went looking for the Northwest Passage never found it. However, as a result of their search, new areas were explored and new discoveries were made.
2. There were waterways leading from present-day Illinois in every direction. From there, travelers and traders could go in nearly any direction they wished.

THINKING ABOUT AMERICAN HISTORY

1. The French traders and trappers depended on the Indians to provide furs and to transport them to market.

APPLYING HISTORY STUDIES SKILLS

1. mission   2. outline of a canoe   3. Arkansas River

CHAPTER 5

The English Colonize North America (1500's-1700's)

Chapter Objectives

After completing this section, students will be able to:
1. Name explorers and important colonists who established North American colonies for England.
2. Identify major English colonies in North America.
3. List the different purposes for which the various English colonies were founded.
4. Describe how England gained control over New Netherland and New Sweden.

Chapter Chronology

Chapter 5 covers the English colonization of North America from the mid-1500's to the mid-1700's. England's expansion began under the reign of Queen Elizabeth (1558-1603), discussed in the textbook Chapter Introduction. With the defeat of the Spanish Armada, England looked to increase its territories. The time line in the Chapter Opener highlights the major colonies established by the English, beginning with Jamestown in Virginia in 1607. Over the next century and a half, colony after colony was founded. The landing of the Pilgrims at Plymouth in 1620 was followed by the formation of the Massachusetts Bay Colony in 1630, of Maryland in 1634, and Rhode Island in 1644. Before the seventeenth century had passed, four more colonies were established, including Connecticut, New York, New Hampshire, and Pennsylvania. The first colony to be formed in the eighteenth century was New Jersey in 1702. Of the original 13 colonies, the last four to be established were Georgia in 1733, North and South Carolina in 1744, and Delaware in 1776.

Motivation

Write the statements below on the chalkboard:

CAPTAIN JOHN SMITH:
1. ran away from home in England at 16 to fight the Spaniards in the Netherlands.
2. set out for Hungary at 20 to fight the Turks.
3. captured at sea by pirates whom he joined and became a wealthy man.
4. killed three Turkish soldiers in hand-to-hand combat.
5. was later captured by the Turks and placed on a slave ship from which he escaped.
6. walked back to England from Central Europe.
7. came to Jamestown in 1607 aboard the first ship with settlers for the new colony.

Ask students what qualities Smith had that may have helped make him an ideal leader of the first successful English colony in North America. Ask them also to think about what were some of the problems that he might have had to solve in Jamestown.

Geographical Setting

Chapter 5 focuses on the east coast of what is today the United States. In this region occur the major developments of early American history. The original 13 colonies are illustrated in several maps in Chapter 5. You may want to point out that these are the colonies that became the United States of America after the Revolution.

Alert students to be aware of the role, if any, environment played in the formation and development of the New England Colonies, Middle Colonies, and Southern Colonies. This theme will be explored in Chapter 6.

History Study Skills

The History Study Skill in Chapter 5 is *Reading for the Main Idea* on textbook page 103. Use it at the beginning of the chapter. Encourage students to practice the skill for each section of the chapter.

Bibliography

Teacher References

Bremer, Francis J., *The Puritan Experiment.* St. Martin's Press, New York City, 1976.

Vaughn, Alden, *American Genesis: Captain John Smith and the Founding of Virginia.* Little Brown, Boston, Mass., 1975.

Student References

Tunis, Edwin, *Colonial Living.* Harper, New York City, 1976. This is an excellent and well-illustrated reference book for the colonial period in American history.

Siegel, Beatrice, *Fur Trappers and Traders: The Indians, the Pilgrims, and the Beaver.* Walker, New York City, 1981. An illustrated account of the fur trade and the conflicts among the people involved.

Audio-Visual Materials

Colonial America, Educational Enrichment Materials, five sound filmstrips, color. These beautifully illustrated materials, from the American Heritage Filmstrip collection, cover the colonial period from 1607 to 1763.

The Pilgrim Adventure, McGraw, 54 minutes, color, 16mm. This narrative of the Pilgrims' journey to America includes the reasons for their coming and the hazards they faced on the way and once they settled.

SECTION 1: England Challenges the Power of Spain

OBJECTIVES

After completing this section, students will be able to:
- Describe how Queen Elizabeth worked to increase England's wealth and power.
- List the names of English explorers and adventurers and their accomplishments.

- Discuss the importance of England's defeat of the Spanish Armada.

MOTIVATION

Use the time line on textbook page 82 and ask students the following questions:
1. How many events are registered on the time line? (14)
2. How many years are there between the date of the first event and the date of the last? (188)
3. How many of the events took place in the 1500's? (1) the 1600's? (9) the 1700's? (4)
4. Thirteen of the fourteen events involve the names of colonies. Which one does not? (1588 — Defeat of the Spanish Armada)
5. Why would this event be included if it does not involve a colony? (Answers will vary and will be speculative.)

SUGGESTED ACTIVITIES

1. **Directed Reading.** Have students answer the following guide questions as they read Section 1:
   A. What steps were taken by Queen Elizabeth to increase the wealth and power of England?
   B. Why were England's first attemps to establish colonies in America unsuccessful?
   C. How was the small English navy able to defeat the powerful Spanish Armada?
   After you have finished discussing the answers to these questions, summarize by repeating the last question in the Motivation. Students should be able to explain that the defeat of the Armada was on the time line because this meant that Spain could no longer interfere with England's plans to colonize America.
2. **Preparing Reports.** Eight important individuals appear in this section. Have average and above-average students use the library to prepare reports on important events in the lives of these people that are NOT included in this section. For example, what did Sir Francis Drake do after the defeat of the Spanish Armada? Slower students should list the eight individuals and identify each one, using information from Section 1.
3. **Reading for the Main Idea.** Use the History Study Skill activity on textbook page 103. If students can apply the skill in conjunction with Section 1, you will be able to reinforce it in each of the remaining sections.

BUILDING AMERICAN CITIZENSHIP

Were the English right to support the adventurers who brought wealth and power to their nation? Should citizens of any nation be willing to support *any* action that gives it wealth and power and a sense of pride and confidence? Why, or why not? If Sir Francis Drake were alive today and taking similar actions how do you think the British would react? Explain your answer.

SECTION 1 REVIEW ANSWERS

1. **IDENTIFY: "sea dogs":** English pirates; **Sir Francis Drake:** favorite "sea dog" of Queen Elizabeth who captured many Spanish treasure ships; commander of the English navy against the Spanish Armada. **Sir Humphrey Gilbert:** former sea dog who tried but failed to

establish an English colony in what is now New-foundland; **Sir Walter Raleigh:** founder of an English colony at Roanoke Island; **Virginia Dare:** first English child born in America; **Roanoke:** English colony whose colonists mysteriously disappeared.
2. DEFINE: **charter:** a document granting one or more persons title to land and governing rights over colonists who settled there; **armada:** a fleet of warships.
3. Drake sailed westward, around the world, to England.
4. It marked the end of Spain's control of the seas.

SECTION 2: The English Start a Colony In Virginia

OBJECTIVES

After completing this section, students will be able to:
- Discuss the hardships suffered by the first English colonists in America.
- Explain why indentured black servants began to be treated differently than indentured white servants.
- Describe the role of Captain John Smith in helping to save the colony of Jamestown.

MOTIVATION

If you did not use the Motivation suggestion from the chapter introduction in the manual, you might wish to use it now. If you have already worked with it, have students recall the leadership qualities of John Smith. Remind them also to recall their ideas on the types of problems he might have had to solve. Ask the students to pretend that they are colonists. Conduct a general class discussion about the difficulties involved in planning a trip to America, making the voyage, and establishing a colony after their arrival.

SUGGESTED ACTIVITIES

1. **Directed Reading.** Use the following guide questions:
   A. How did English merchants raise the money needed to finance a colony in America?
   B. What difficulties did the colonists face when they arrived in America?
   C. How did John Smith save the colony?
   D. Why did life in Jamestown improve after the first few difficult years?
   After discussing the answers to these questions, talk about the role of others, including James I, Pocahontas, and John Rolfe in the founding of Jamestown. Ask students to hypothesize what might have happened to the colony without the help of these three individuals.
2. **Role Playing.** Divide the class into groups. Have each group select one of the following topics and prepare a skit to indicate what they think actually happened. Above-average students may be required to research their topic in order to make the presentations more accurate.
   A. John Smith's rescue by Pocahontas
   B. A black servant seeking release on the last day of indenture
   C. The first meeting of the House of Burgesses

D. The arrival of the first ship carrying women to Jamestown
E. John Smith taking control of the colony
F. Landing of the first ships at Jamestown
3. **Locating Information In Your History Book.** After students read the section, ask them to close the book. Display the following questions on the overhead projector or write them on the board. Ask the students how they would use their book to answer these questions.
   1. On which page did the section begin?
   2. On which page did you read about John Rolfe?
   3. What is the House of Burgesses?
   4. What is the title of this chapter?
   5. On which page did you read about John Smith?
   6. What is an indentured servant?
   Go through the questions with students, and have them try to answer each question. Go through them a second time, asking them to identify the part of their textbook that would help them find the information without having to scan the section again. Answers: 1—Table of Contents; 2—Index; 3—Glossary; 4—Table of Contents; 5—Index; 6—Glossary.
4. **History Study Skills.** Duplicate Worksheet 9, *Jamestown and Plymouth,* and distribute to students. Two of the paragraphs deal with information in Section 2. Choose additional paragraphs in the section from which students should be able to select the main idea. You can also provide students with the main idea, and a page number, and have them identify the paragraph with which it is associated.
5. **Landmarks of Liberty.** Have students read the selection on Colonial Williamsburg on textbook page 96. Explain to students that the capitol had been moved from Jamestown to Williamsburg because of the swampy area in which Jamestown was located and because of a fire that destroyed much of that area. Have students answer the questions at the end of the reading. Then ask them how long Williamsburg served as the capitol of Virginia? (81 years) Using the information in Section 2, have them determine which city served as the capitol longer—Jamestown or Williamsburg. (Williamsburg—81 years; Jamestown—80 years.)

BUILDING AMERICAN CITIZENSHIP

What citizens were allowed to take part in Virginia's government? (Land-owning, free males) What citizens were not allowed to take part in government? (Women, indentured servants, slaves) Today, are there any citizens who are not allowed to take part in the government of your state? (Those under 18; those with felony records; those that do not meet residency requirements) How have the requirements for taking part in a state's government changed since 1619? (Answers will vary.)

SECTION 2 REVIEW ANSWERS

1. **IDENTIFY: Virginia Company:** a company formed by a group of London and Plymouth merchants, who shared the costs of starting a colony; **Jamestown:** English settlement founded in 1607; **Captain John Smith:** leader of the Jamestown colony; **Powhatans:** Indian tribe near

Jamestown who gave supplies to the colony; **Pocohontas:** 12-year-old daughter of the chief of the Powhatans who supposedly saved John Smith's life; **"starving time":** winter of 1609 to 1610 when food in the Jamestown colony ran low, causing many to starve; **John Rolfe:** colonist who began cultivation of tobacco in Virginia; **House of Burgesses:** the first representative assembly of Virginia.

2. **DEFINE: joint stock company:** a company in which many people buy stock and share profits or losses; **indentured servants:** people who agreed to work for 3 to 7 years to repay the cost of their passage to America; **royal colony:** a colony completely controlled by the king.

3. Many died of disease, cold, or starvation; they knew nothing about living in the wilderness or how to perform everyday tasks.

4. Tobacco.

SECTION 3: Pilgrims and Puritans Colonize New England

OBJECTIVES

After completing this section, students will be able to:
- Name and locate the New England Colonies.
- Explain why the Puritans came to America.
- Identify the reasons why colonists left Massachusetts to start other colonies.

MOTIVATION

Refer students to the Chapter Opener time line on textbook page 82. Ask them to name the colonies started between the years 1620 and 1679. (Plymouth, Massachusetts, Maryland, Rhode Island, Connecticut, New York, and New Hampshire) Next, have them look at the map of the New England Colonies on textbook page 91. Ask them to name the colonies started between 1620 and 1679 that are NOT New England colonies. (Maryland and New York) As a summary activity, have them list the names of the New England Colonies in their notebook with their founding dates.

SUGGESTED ACTIVITIES

1. **Directed Reading.** As students read this section, have them take notes on each colony, including the date it was founded, the person or group who established it, and the reason(s) for its establishment. EXAMPLE: Plymouth - 1620 - Pilgrims - Religious freedom

If you prefer, this information may be organized in chart form.

2. **Writing Assignment.** Have students write a paragraph comparing the establishment of Plymouth Colony with the founding of Jamestown. You may wish students to include the following: date of establishment; length of voyage; types of people who first settled there; problems during the first year; dealings with the Indians; and cooperation among themselves. Slower students should be required to compare only a few of these items. Above-average students should be required to incorporate all of them.

3. **Puzzles.** Ask students to create a puzzle using the names of the colonies, the names of individuals, and history vocabulary words. You may want all students to do one type of puzzle, such as a word search puzzle, an acrostic or a crossword puzzle, or you may give them a choice. Each puzzle should contain a minimum of 10 items and provide clues so that other students can solve them. Have students exchange and solve puzzles.

4. **Identification.** Have students select one historical figure from Section 3. Ask them to write one or two sentences, in the first person, identifying the role of the individual in establishing a New England colony. Call on students to read their sentences. Have other students identify the individual.
EXAMPLE: I am the King of England who granted Roger Williams a charter for the colony of Rhode Island. ANSWER: King Charles

BUILDING AMERICAN CITIZENSHIP

Duplicate Worksheet 10, *The Mayflower Compact.* Have students complete the activity. To encourage critical thinking, ask the following questions:
Would you be willing to sign a document such as this in order to remain a citizen in the town or city in which you now live? Why, or why not?

SECTION 3 REVIEW ANSWERS

1. **IDENTIFY: Anglican Church:** official Protestant Church of England; **Mayflower:** the ship on which the Pilgrims traveled to America in 1620; **Mayflower Compact:** a plan of government written by the Pilgrims; **Squanto:** an Indian leader who helped the Pilgrims; **Roger Williams:** a minister who started the colony of Rhode Island after being ordered to leave Massachusetts for his religious beliefs; **Thomas Hooker:** a minister who started a settlement in what is now Hartford, Connecticut.

2. **DEFINE: Puritans:** English people who wanted to purify the Anglican Church by making it less Catholic and more Protestant; **Separatists:** a group of Puritans who left the Anglican Church and formed a church of their own; **Fundamental Orders:** a plan of government for the people of Connecticut; first written Constitution in America.

3. They taught the colonists how to plant corn, how to hunt in the forests, and how to clear fields by setting fires.

4. Roger Williams.

5. It was founded by colonists from Massachusetts, who felt that Massachusetts was become too crowded. They later received a charter from the king.

SECTION 4: Settlers Establish the Southern Colonies

OBJECTIVES

After completing this section, students will be able to:
- Name and locate the Southern colonies.
- Discuss the reasons why each colony was established.
- Identify the specific problems that arose in each colony during the early years of its existence.

MOTIVATION

Pass around samples of rice and tobacco and have students identify each substance. Ask students if they know how these crops are grown (rice is grown underwater), and what is needed to help them grow (much land and many workers). Ask if they can identify the area of the United States in which these crops are still widely grown. (South)

SUGGESTED ACTIVITIES

1. **Directed Reading.** Have students continue taking notes on each colony, listing the year it was established, the person or group responsible, and the reason(s) for its establishment.
   EXAMPLE: Maryland - 1634 - Lord Baltimore and his family - A place where Catholics could worship as they wished

   After concluding this activity and discussing student answers, repeat the questions asked during the Motivation. Have students answer them again, using the information from this section.
2. **Identification of the Colonies.** Write a list of "clues" about the Southern Colonies on the chalkboard. Have students identify the colony described in the clue.
   Savannah was its only town for several years (G)
   Toleration Act granted freedom of religion (M)
   Settlers were given free land (M)
   Eight proprietors or owners named it after their king (C)
   Virginians searching for new farmlands settled there (NC)
   It was created as a haven for debtors (G)
   Charter granted to Lord Baltimore (M)
   Colonized by people from England, Germany, France and the West Indies (SC)
   All able-bodied men had to be prepared to fight the Spaniards (G)
   The "Dismal Swamp" divided the colony into 2 parts (C)
3. **Class Discussion.** Review the problems encountered by the founders of Jamestown and Plymouth. Discuss the problems encountered by colonists in each of the Southern Colonies. (Maryland—religion; Carolinas—creation of an unequal society; Georgia—Oglethorp's many rules and regulations). Ask students about the differences and similarities between the problems of the New England Colonies and those of the Southern Colonies.
4. **Map Activity.** On a chalk map, or a blank outline map projected on the overhead, number each of the Southern Colonies. Have students identify each of the Southern Colonies by writing the number and corresponding colony on notebook paper. As a review, repeat the process for the New England Colonies.

BUILDING AMERICAN CITIZENSHIP

In England, what happened to people who could not pay their debts? In your opinion, was this a good or bad practice? Why? In the United States today, what happens to citizens who find themselves in debt? (They can borrow; refinance loans; declare bankruptcy) How are these citizens protected from being thrown into prison? (Americans are protected by laws and cannot be thrown into prison except by a court of law.)

SECTION 4 REVIEW ANSWERS

1. **IDENTIFY: Lord Baltimore:** English noble who established the colony called Maryland; **Toleration Act:** a law in Maryland guaranteeing all Christians the right to worship as they wished; **Dismal Swamp:** a large swampy area separating the Albermarle area from the rest of Carolina; **James Oglethorpe:** Englishman who started the colony of Georgia especially for debtors in English prisons.
2. **DEFINE: proprietors:** people who were given charters by the king to start colonies in America.
3. Maryland.
4. The climate was bad; the proprietors created an unequal society by offering huge amounts of land to a few people, expecting most colonists to work for the large landowners instead of for themselves.
5. That every able-bodied man in the colony must be willing and prepared to fight the Spaniards, if necessary.

SECTION 5: Settlers Move to the Middle Colonies

OBJECTIVES

After completing this section, students will be able to:
- Name and locate the Middle Colonies.
- Describe how the English gained control of New Netherland.
- Explain the reasons for the growth and prosperity of Pennsylvania.

MOTIVATION

Using a chalkmap or transparency of an outline map, show the class Delaware, New York, Pennsylvania, and New Jersey, all located between the New England and Southern Colonies. Ask students to suggest an appropriate name for this group. If they do not suggest "Middle," have them open their book to the first page of Section 5 to find the name in the title.

SUGGESTED ACTIVITIES

1. **Directed Reading.** Have students continue to practice their note-taking skills on the colonies using the pattern established in the first activity in the two previous sections.
   EXAMPLE: Pennsylvania - 1681 - William Penn - Provide a place where Quakers could worship as they wished

   After concluding this activity have students close their textbooks and notebooks. Again, using the chalkmap or transparency of an outline map, point to each of the Middle Colonies. Ask students to name them and to recall one important fact concerning the establishment of each one. As a review of the chapter, you may wish to repeat this process for all 13 colonies.
2. **Chronology.** Six important dates are mentioned in section 5: 1626, 1638, 1664, 1682, 1702, and 1776.

Ask students to draw a time line (1 inch = 30 years). Have them make sure to position the six dates correctly and write the events that occurred in each year on the time line. You may wish to assist slower students by using a blank transparency and showing them how to construct the line step-by-step. Demonstrate the placement of the first few dates and show them how to write in the events.

3. **Outline.** This assignment can easily be differentiated for groups of varying abilities. The title for all groups is: *The 13 English Colonies.* Slower students would restrict their outline to main topics (New England, Middle, and Southern Colonies) and limited subtopics (names of the colonies). Average and above-average students should use their notes from the Directed Reading activity to provide information for other subtopics (date, founder, reason for establishment)

4. **Organizing Facts.** Duplicate Worksheet 11, *English Colonies.* Have students scan the 17 statements on it and select those related to the establishment of the Middle Colonies (3, 4, 5, 7, 10, 12, 14, 17). Then, ask them to read the nine other statements to determine with which each of the remaining two groups of colonies would be associated.

BUILDING AMERICAN CITIZENSHIP

Four colonies in Chapter 5 took steps to grant self-government to their colonists. What were the names of the colonies and the steps that were taken?

Plymouth—Mayflower Compact
Virginia—House of Burgesses
Connecticut—Fundamental Orders of Connecticut
Pennsylvania—Frame of Government

Each of these colonies believed in the importance of laws made with the consent of the people, who also agree to obey them. Ask: Do you think it is possible to live in a nation where there are no laws? Explain your answer. Which laws do you think are *most* important to citizens today? Which laws do you think are the *least* important to citizens today? (Answers will vary).

SECTION 5 REVIEW ANSWERS

1. **IDENTIFY: Henry Hudson:** English sea captain who sailed to America for the Dutch and whose voyage enabled the Dutch to claim land along the Hudson River; **New Amsterdam:** Dutch settlement begun in 1621 on the island of Manhattan, for which the Dutch paid the Indians $24 in jewelry, tools, and other small items; **New Netherland:** the entire Dutch colony in New York; **Peter Stuyvesant:** unpopular Dutch governor who surrendered New Amsterdam to the British without firing a shot; **James, Duke of York:** brother of King Charles I who became proprietor of the former Dutch colony of New Netherland; **Lord John Berkeley;** one of the two original owners of New Jersey; **Sir George Carteret:** one of the two original owners of New Jersey; **William Penn:** founder of the colony of Pennsylvania; where Quakers could worship without fear of punishment.

2. **DEFINE: patroons:** Dutch landowners of huge estates in New Netherland; **Quakers:** a religous group also known as the Society of Friends; **Frame of Government:** Pennsylvania's plan of government, which gave the colonists a representative assembly and religous freedom.

3. About $24 in tools, jewelry, and other small items.
4. England sent warships to Manhattan Island, and the Dutch governor surrendered.
5. Penn founded the colony as a place where Quakers could worship freely and where people could live according to the Quaker ideals of honesty, charity, and peacefulness.

CHAPTER 5 REVIEW ANSWERS

REVIEWING KEY WORDS

1. d.   2. a.   3. e.   4. c.   5. b.

REMEMBERING IMPORTANT PEOPLE

1. d.	2. c.	3. a.	4. e.	5. b.
6. c.	7. e.	8. b.	9. a.	10. d.

REVIEWING THE FACTS

1. T   2. F   3. T   4. T   5. F

PLACING EVENTS IN TIME

1. D   2. A   3. C   4. E   5. B

LINKING GEOGRAPHY AND HISTORY

1. The English colonies no longer had to worry about Spanish ships interfering with their shipping and trade.
2. Text describes the abundant land for farming, forests for lumber, and ample hunting for game and animals. Map shows many rivers for transportation and fishing; good harbors for trade and commerce.

THINKING ABOUT AMERICAN HISTORY

1. Answers will vary.
2. Ship could get lost or be destroyed by storms; spoiled food or shortage of food supply; disease; attack by pirates and so on.

APPLYING HISTORY STUDIES SKILLS

1. To gain control of the seas, thus giving England freedom to settle in the New World.
2. A joint stock company was formed to raise funds and equip settlers for the colony.

CHAPTER 6

Colonists Develop New Ways of Life (1600's-1700's)

Chapter Objectives

After completing this chapter, students will be able to:
1. Identify the different ways that colonists made their living in the various colonies.
2. Describe family structure and traditions during colonial times.

3. Explain the importance of religion and education to colonial communities.
4. Identify the status of Indians and blacks in colonial America.
5. Describe how colonists gained increasing political control through their local governments.

Chapter Chronology

Chapter 6 surveys various aspects of colonial life in America from the mid-1600's to the mid-1700's. Representative events of the period are highlighted in the time line on the textbook Chapter Opener page. In 1634, Massachusetts became the second colony to establish a representative assembly (Virginia was first in 1619 with the House of Burgesses). By 1750, not only did all the colonies have assemblies, but they had all gained more power. Higher education was assuming increased importance in the colonies. Two major institutions, Harvard (1634) and Dartmouth (1769) were among several major universities and colleges founded during this time. Meanwhile, unrest among slaves in the colonies began to surface. One of the earliest slave rebellions was led by a slave named Cato in South Carolina in 1739.

Motivation

Ask students the following questions and list their responses on the chalkboard.
1. How do members of your family make a living?
2. What do you do to help out in your family?
3. How do different people in your community make a living?

Then ask students to imagine themselves as Colonists and answer the questions again. List their responses on the chalkboard and refer to them at the end of Section 2.

Geographical Setting

Chapter 6 is an economic, social, and political survey of the original 13 colonies. Geographical setting plays a major role mostly in Section 1, where students learn how the location and physical features of a colony helped shape its economy. New Englanders, plagued with poor soil and harsh winters, turned to fishing, whaling, and trade. The Middle Colonies became the breadbasket region because farmers there produced far more than they needed to feed themselves. This farm surplus needed to be shipped to consumers in other regions and both Philadelphia and New York City, with excellent natural harbors, became major seaports. In the Southern Colonies the climate and soil conditions resulted in a commitment to one crop agriculture, notably tobacco. In each of these three regions, the environment influenced the types of economic activities that developed.

History Study Skills

The History Study Skill introduced in Chapter 6 is Studying Trade Routes on Maps and the focus is on colonial trade routes. This activity should be used in conjunction with Section 1 and the text information on colonial trade routes. This activity is the place to review map skills developed in Chapters 3 and 4.

Bibliography

Teacher References
Henretta, James, *The Evolution of American Society, 1700-1818*. Heath, Boston, Mass., 1973.
Wright, Louis B., *The Cultural Life of the American Colonies, 1607-1763*. Harper, New York City, 1957.
Student References
Morris, Richard B., *Life History of the United States, Volume I, Before 1775*. Silver Burdette, Morristown, N.J., 1974. This beautifully illustrated volume covers the people and events of early American history.
Speare, Elizabeth, *The Witch of Blackbird Pond*. Houghton-Mifflin, Boston, Mass., 1958. This historical novel takes place in Connecticut in 1687. Kit Tyler, a young woman had lived in Barbados for 16 years before emigrating to the Northern Colonies. Her high spirits and unconventional upbringing eventually led to her involvement in witch trials.

Audio-Visual Materials

The Beginnings of American Industry, SVE, sound filmstrip, color. This excellent overview of colonial home industries, offers good use of paintings and documents.

Life in Colonial America, National Geographic, two sound filmstrips, color. These filmstrips survey daily life in the colonies, including fishing, farming, education, and religion.

SECTION 1: Different Ways to Make a Living Develop in the Colonies

OBJECTIVES

After completing this section, students will be able to:
• Identify the various occupations of people living in the New England, Middle, and Southern Colonies.
• Discuss the influence of environment and geography on the development of occupations in each area.
• Define specific words related to the occupations of people in each group of colonies.

MOTIVATION

Use the Motivation suggested in the chapter introduction in the manual. In addition, discuss with students the differences in life that might exist on a New England farm, Middle Colony farm, and Southern plantation.

SUGGESTED ACTIVITIES

1. **Directed Reading.** Provide a simple outline framework on the chalkboard or the overhead. Ask students to copy the outline, and complete it as they read the chapter.

Occupations In The Colonies

I. New England	II. Middle	III. Southern
A.	A.	A.
B.	B.	B.
C.		

When students have completed the assignment, review the correct format for an outline and make sure their facts are correct. As a summary activity, return to the motivational discussion. Discuss the differences and similarities in New England, Middle, and Southern farms. Students should include geographic and climatic factors, size of farms, and types of crops grown.

2. **Vocabulary Development.** Many new terms, including economy, cash crop, subsistence economy, triangular trade, apprentice, staple, and artisan are introduced in Section 1. Prepare a set of flashcards, placing a term on each card. Write the definition on sentence strips and distribute them to the students. Have one student come to the front of the room with a sentence strip and hold it up for the class to see. The student with the matching flashcard should also bring it to the front of the room. The two students should read the term and its definition in unison. Collect the materials and repeat the exercise as often as time allows.

3. **Class Discussion.** The topic to be discussed is: Why did the New England, Middle, and Southern colonies develop different types of economies? This question should be written on the chalkboard. In a class with above-average students, you may wish to divide the students into discussion groups. One student from each group should then report to the class, with others making corrections and additions. You may wish to lead the discussion for average and below-average students. You may also wish to encourage participation by asking such questions as: Why were there no plantations in New England? Why were there more seaports in the North than in the South? The goal of this discussion is to help students recognize the influence of climate and geography on the development of occupations.

BUILDING AMERICAN CITIZENSHIP

The colonists utilized their abilities to develop occupations suited to the climate and geographic features of the region in which they lived. Which, if any, jobs in your area are determined by climate and geography? What occupations would be totally unsuitable for the area in which you live?

SECTION 1 REVIEW ANSWERS

1. **IDENTIFY: economy:** the way an area produces, uses, and manages its crops or goods; **cash crop:** a crop grown to sell after the harvest; **subsistence economy:** an economy in which farmers produce just what they need for themselves; **triangular trade:** a trading route in the shape of a triangle between New England, the West Indies, and Africa; **artisans:** skilled craftworkers; **commercial farming economy:** an economy in which farmers grow cash crops for sale or trade; **apprentices:** trainees who worked without wages while they learned a craft or skill; **staples:** principal crops or products; **frontier:** a thinly settled area beyond which the wilderness lay.

2. Farming, fishing, whaling, as merchants, as shipyard workers.
3. Commercial farming, loading ships, selling goods, as craftworkers.
4. Tobacco, rice, and indigo.

SECTION 2: Families Contribute to Colonial Life

OBJECTIVES

After completing this section, students will be able to:
• List the responsibilities of men, women, and children in colonial society.
• Compare family life in colonial society with family life today.
• Compare the legal rights of unmarried women and widows to the rights of married housewives.

MOTIVATION

On the board, provide a list of responsibilities that are generally shared by families:

Earning a living	Buying household goods
Cooking	Caring for infants
Voting	Washing and ironing
Cleaning	Keeping order

Discuss how these duties are divided up among members of a family today—Mom, Dad, children. In some cases, more than one answer would be acceptable. Then, tell students that in colonial society things were very different. When students finish reading Section 2, they should know the responsibilities of each colonial family member.

SUGGESTED ACTIVITIES

1. **Directed Reading.** As students read Section 2, have them compile a list of the major differences between family life in colonial America and family life now. In colonial time, for example:
   A. Women married at a younger age.
   B. Families were larger.
   C. There were more deaths from disease.
   D. The responsibilities and rights of husbands and wives differed greatly.
   E. Only men could vote.
   F. Married women had fewer rights than unmarried women.

   Using the students' lists, compile one master list on the chalkboard. Return to the motivational activity. Now that they have read Section 2, ask students to tell which member of a colonial family held each responsibility.
2. **Research.** Have students use a current almanac to answer the following questions:
   A. What is the current infant mortality rate today?
   B. What is the average age at which men marry? Women?
   C. What is the average number of children per family today?
   D. What disease is responsible for the greatest number of deaths?

E. What is the average age of death for men? Women?

Compare the answers to these questions to the information in Section 2 concerning life in colonial America. Although precise figures are not always available for this period, students should become aware of the vast differences between then and now.

3. **Writing Assignment.** Each student should pretend to be a man, woman, or ten-year-old child living in colonial America. Ask students to write a paragraph or two describing a typical day in their lives, from dawn to dusk.

4. **Drawing.** Ask students to select one of the responsibilities of a man, woman, or child in a colonial society. Have them draw a picture of the person performing a task associated with that responsibility. You may want to provide a list of possibilities for slower students. Use the best samples of student work by displaying them and having the rest of the class identify the tasks.

BUILDING AMERICAN CITIZENSHIP

As suggested in Section 2, colonial families had to rely upon themselves to provide food, clothing, shelter, and other necessities of life. Today, many of these necessities can be purchased rather than made by the family. However, family members still rely upon each other to fulfill many needs. What are some of these needs? (Love, support, discipline)

SECTION 2 REVIEW ANSWERS

1. **IDENTIFY: "notable housewives":** women who ran orderly, pleasant, and thrifty households; **spinster:** an unmarried woman who, in colonial times, spent much of her life spinning.
2. There were fewer women in the colonies, and men wanted wives to help run their farms.
3. Colonists had little medical knowledge and skills; there were few infection-fighting drugs; and people were not immunized against infectious diseases.
4. Men controlled the family's property; they could vote, sue in a court, and sign a will. Women could do none of these things.

SECTION 3: Colonists Establish a Rich Community Life

OBJECTIVES

After completing this section, students will be able to:
• Compare religious, educational, and leisure time activities in the New England, Middle, and Southern colonies and in frontier communities.
• Categorize activities as being educational, religious, or social.
• Explain the differences between ways of life in established colonies and on the frontier.

MOTIVATION

Introduce the three terms—educational, religious, and leisure. Be sure that students understand the meaning of each. Discuss all three in terms of today's society.

Education—What is the purpose of education? What are the goals of most students today?
Religion —What are some of the major religions? Do people spend much time in houses of worship today?
Leisure —How do you spend your free time? How do your friends, parents, and neighbors spend theirs?

Introduce the purpose of today's lesson—to determine the importance of each in the lives of colonial Americans.

SUGGESTED ACTIVITIES

1. **Directed Reading.** Have students write in their notebooks, three column headings for the three topics utilized in the motivational discussion. As they read, have them jot down specific information related to each. After the item, they should note whether it refers to New England, Middle, or Southern Colonies. As a summary, have students close notebooks and textbooks. Orally, give them examples of religious, educational, or social activities, and have them categorize each. Example include:
   A. First public schools (NE)
   B. Long visits to homes of neighbors (S)
   C. Attending Theaters (M)
   D. Church forming the center of social life (NE)
2. **Life in the English Colonies.** Duplicate Worksheet 12 with this title. Have students use the information in this section to complete the last three boxes of the chart. Have them complete the first four boxes of the chart, using the information from Sections 1 and 2. This will provide an excellent review of the material students have covered so far in Chapter 6.
3. **Reading for the Main Idea.** Review the Chapter 5 History Study Skill. Provide students with a list of main ideas from this section and have them select the paragraphs with which they are associated.
   A. The colonists lived in an oral society.
   B. People looked to churches to provide an education for their children.
   C. What people did for enjoyment depended upon their sex and their age, where they lived, and how wealthy they were.
   D. On the frontier, colonists turned many of their chores into social events.

BUILDING AMERICAN CITIZENSHIP

The American colonists learned to develop "tolerance" of religious beliefs other than their own. What does the word "tolerance" mean? Why is "tolerance" an important characteristic for all citizens to develop? In what ways can you demonstrate your "tolerance" of others? (Answers will vary.)

SECTION 3 REVIEW ANSWERS

1. **IDENTIFY: denominations:** different Protestant religious groups; **tolerance:** acceptance of religious beliefs other than one's own.
2. In the North people lived within walking distance and went to church every Sunday. In the South people lived

too far apart and depended on a monthly visit from a traveling minister.

3. People in New England passed laws requiring that children be taught to read, and most towns had schools. In the Middle Colonies, there were church schools for wealthy children. In the South, wealthy planters hired tutors. Only boys were educated in all areas.

4. Southern planters entertained at home, visited each other, or went to stay in the city. New Englanders used the church as a center for social life. On the frontier, people turned chores, such as "house-raising," sheep-shearing, quilting, weaving, and spinning, into social events.

SECTION 4: Indians And Blacks Live In the Colonies

OBJECTIVES

After completing this section, students will be able to:
- Describe the difference between the Indian and British ways of life.
- Discuss the development of slavery in the colonies.
- Describe the similarities and differences between slaves and free black Americans.

MOTIVATION

Have students look at the map of *Ocean Trade Routes of the Colonies* on textbook page 109 to answer these questions:
1. What products were shipped from the American colonies to Africa? (rum, iron bars)
2. What products were shipped from Africa to the colonies? (slaves, gold)
3. Where did the ships stop on their voyage from Africa to the colonies? (West Indies)
4. Why do you think they stopped there?
Explain that the last question will be answered in today's reading.

SUGGESTED ACTIVITIES

1. **Directed Reading.** As students read Section 4, have them look for the answers to the following questions:
   A. Why did the British colonists and the Indians become enemies?
   B. What was the difference between a newly captured African and a "seasoned slave?"
   C. What were the differences and similarities between slaves and free black Americans?
   Discuss the answers to these questions with students. As a summary, have students study the pictures in this section and state one fact from their reading that is related to each picture.
2. **Research.** As the information in Section 4 suggests, Indian tribes inhabited every colony before the arrival of white colonists. Ask students to use the library to list some of the tribes that lived in the colonies. This information can be organized in chart form.
   Colony in Which/What Happened
   Indian Tribe/They Lived   /to Them
3. **Writing.** Have students pretend that they are slaves from Africa. They are to place themselves in any one of

the following situations and describe what happened to them:
   A. Being captured from an African village
   B. Traveling aboard ship from Africa to the West Indies
   C. Working in the sugarcane fields of the West Indies
   D. Taking part in a slave rebellion and surviving
   E. Buying their freedom and moving to a free black community
   You may ask above-average students to do additional research so that their assignments reflect a greater knowledge of actual events, rather than hypothesis.
4. **History Study Skills.** Have students complete the Chapter 6 History Study Skill, *Studying Trade Routes on Maps,* on textbook page 130. This activity relates directly to the ideas developed in the Motivation and to the material in Section 4 about the transportation of slaves from Africa.

BUILDING AMERICAN CITIZENSHIP

Freed black Americans in the colonial period were denied rights that other colonists took for granted, and that all American citizens today take for granted. List the rights denied to freed black Americans. (To vote, appear in court, travel freely, live where they wished)

SECTION 4 REVIEW ANSWERS

1. **IDENTIFY: Cato:** a black slave who led a rebellion in South Carolina in 1739; **Phillis Wheatley:** an ex-slave who became a well-known colonial poet; **Benjamin Banneker:** an ex-slave who became a self-educated scientist, mathematician, and surveyor, and one of the planners of Washington, D.C.
2. **DEFINE: pagans:** people who worship many gods rather than one; **Middle Passage:** the voyage of slaves in small, overcrowded ships from Africa across the Atlantic Ocean; **slave codes:** laws passed in the colonies to control the lives of slaves.
3. Differences in attitudes toward land, the earth, and animals and in religious beliefs.
4. They continued traditions such as working together and community ownership of food grown in their gardens, giving their children "day" names and teaching them traditional skills in music, dancing, fishing, and cooking.

SECTION 5: Settlers Help Develop Colonial Governments

OBJECTIVES

After completing this section, students will be able to:
- Describe the organization of the British government.
- Describe the organization of colonial governments.
- Compare and contrast colonial governments with modern state governments.

MOTIVATION

If possible, secure a picture of your state's governor and its legislative bodies. Label and display these so that all students can clearly see and identify them. Discuss what the governor and the members of the legislative bodies do and how they get and keep their jobs. Also, discuss why the governments of each of the 50 states are similarly organized. Finally, ask students how they think this type of government organization got its start.

SUGGESTED ACTIVITIES

1. **Directed Reading.** Using the information in the motivational activity, have students copy the table below:

STATE GOVERNMENTS	COLONIAL GOVERNMENTS	BRITISH GOVERNMENT
Governor		
(Name of) Upper House		
(Name of) Lower House		

Have them add the next two columns, to be completed as they read. When students have finished, check to be sure that their information is correct. Refer again to the last question in the Motivation, which students should now be able to answer with ease.

2. **Ideals in the Lives of Americans.** Have students read the selection on John Peter Zenger, on textbook page 128. Have them answer the questions at the end. Ask them how his story is related to the information in Section 5. (British rights included trial by jury) (The colonists continued the tradition of the British, who had fought for their rights over many years).

3. **Building Citizenship Skills.** Duplicate Worksheet 14, *Colonial Governments.* When completed, students will have an adequate summary of the information in Section 5. Allow slower students to use their textbooks to complete the table and answer the questions.

4. **Research.** Among the most interesting types of laws, passed by colonial assemblies were those dealing with personal behavior. Punishments inflicted on colonists who broke those laws were often harsh. Find and show pictures of stocks, pillories, and dunking stools to create student interest in the topic. Have above-average students investigate the laws governing personal behavior and the punishments inflicted upon those who broke the laws. If possible, have them name the colony in which the law was passed. Then, let students present their findings to the class.

5. **History Study Skills.** Duplicate Worksheet 13 *Spanish Trade.* The purpose of this activity is to review the History Study Skills developed in the previous section. It should also remind students that Spain's colonial empire coexisted with that of Britain on the North American continent. Have students recall the type of colonial government that was established in New Spain. Ask them to compare this structure with the type of government in the British colonies.

BUILDING AMERICAN CITIZENSHIP

In colonial America, the assemblies became very important to the colonists. Ask students to recall some of the reasons why this was so. In modern society, state legislatures have replaced colonial assemblies. Do you think they are *as* important to a state's citizens as the assemblies were in colonial America? Why or why not?

SECTION 5 REVIEW ANSWERS

1. **IDENTIFY: monarch:** a king or queen; **Parliament:** England's two-house lawmaking body; **royal colonies:** colonies under the direct control of the monarch; **proprietary colonies:** colonies owned or controlled by individuals; **self-governing colonies:** colonies which elected their own political leaders; **legislature:** lawmaking body.
2. To rule for, not over, the people.
3. Colonists knew what was needed and how to get the job done; they became more cooperative and law-abiding; such a government attracted more colonists.
4. Councils were usually appointed by the governor to advise him. Council members were expected to consider the wishes of the king or proprietor before those of the local colonists.

CHAPTER 6 REVIEW ANSWERS

REVIEWING KEY WORDS

1. e.	2. b.	3. d.	4. a.	5. B.
6. c.	7. e.	8. d.	9. a.	10. b.

REMEMBERING IMPORTANT PEOPLE

1. c.   2. a.   3. b.

REVIEWING THE FACTS

1. c.	2. c.	3. b.	4. a.	5. a.	6. b.
7. T	8. F	9. F	10. T	11. T	12. T

LINKING GEOGRAPHY AND HISTORY

1. They lived near the sea. The land was too rocky and hilly and the growing season too short for farming.
2. Rich soil, mild climate, long, deep rivers.
3. A lot of land was needed to grow their crops of tobacco, rice, and indigo.

THINKING ABOUT AMERICAN HISTORY

1. Colonial families were larger; women married younger; only boys went to school; many children died of disease; colonial women had fewer rights; colonial children began working at a younger age.
2. Two-house legislatures; governments existed to rule FOR the people; the second house, representing the common people, was more powerful; the colonial council was modeled on the House of Lords.

APPLYING HISTORY STUDIES SKILLS

1. West Indies   2. Africa
3. Southern Colonies   4. Northeast coast
5. Africa   6. West Indies

UNIT 2 REVIEW ANSWERS

VOCABULARY REVIEW

Answers will vary.

REVIEWING THE MAIN IDEAS

1. a. Spain: South America; southwestern and southeastern part of North America
   b. France: Canada (as it is called today); the Great Lakes Region; Mississippi River Valley
   c. England: East coast of present-day United States

2. Cortés searched in Mexico and found gold; Estéban searched north of Mexico and was killed; Coronado searched in the area that became the southwestern part of the United States but found no gold; De Soto searched in the area of the Mississippi River, found no gold, and died of a fever.
3. The French and the Indians were friendly; the French and the English competed for land claims and trading rights and became enemies.
4. To get rich; to find freedom of religion; to find adventure; to get out of prison; to get cheap land.
5. A royal colony was controlled directly by the king; a proprietary colony was controlled by a person or persons to whom the king granted a charter.
6. New England Colonies: fishing, sea-related trades, whaling, some farming. Middle Colonies: commercial farming, crafts, ship loading, shopkeeping. Southern Colonies: large-scale farming.
7. Puritans and Pilgrims—Massachusetts. Dutch Reform—New York. Catholics—Maryland. Quakers—Pennsylvania. (See Chapter 6, Section 3.)
8. They did not have the same ideas concerning land ownership or religious beliefs. Their cultures were too different for them to remain friendly.
9. They had no rights. Laws were passed to control their actions.

APPLYING YOUR STUDY SKILLS

1. **Using a Time Line**
   a. Cortés; Mexico; 1519
2. **Using Maps**
   a. Mississippi River
   b. Answers will vary.
   c. New England Colonies: iron, ships, fish, whaling
   Middle Colonies: grain, flour, cattle, iron
   Southern Colonies: tobacco, rice, indigo

PROJECTS

Answers will vary.

BUILDING AMERICAN CITIZENSHIP

1. **Spain:** loyalty to government and spirit of adventure and enterprise were good; greed and cruel treatment of Indians were bad.
   France: fair treatment of Indians was good; lack of religious toleration was bad.
   England: allowing colonists to help govern themselves was good; settlers fighting among themselves in Jamestown and the practice of slavery was bad.
2. The right to vote, own property, hold public office, travel freely, testify in court, and so on.

UNIT 3 (1754-1789)
Americans Win Independence

Introducing the Unit

Unit Three surveys the years before, during and immediately after the American Revolution, 1754 to 1789. It described the development of the 13 colonies, only loosely bound by traditions and proximity, into a unified new nation, the United States of America. After 1775 with the British attack on the citizens of Concord and Lexington, the colonies became committed to fight for their independence from their increasingly harsh and unyielding parent country. Those shots were among the first in the long and difficult war that followed. America's victory resulted in freedom and the creation of a new government. Three chapters, 7-9, make up this Unit.

Discussed first are the events between 1754 and 1776 that led to war. British-American tensions increased after the defeat of the French in the French and Indian War in 1763. Beginning with the Proclamation of 1763, which closed the Ohio Valley to colonial settlers, the British issued other harsh measures, including a series of taxes and other rulings that the colonies regarded as unjust. Neither peaceful colonial protests nor acts of defiance seemed to have any effect on Britain's policy, and talk of revolution became widespread.

Independence was officially declared on July 4, 1776. Americans now began a fierce and organized fight for that independence. Through triumphs and setbacks the war raged on, spreading across the land. Patriot defeats in Quebec and New York City were followed by America's successes in New Jersey and also Saratoga, in 1777, after which the French began to aid America openly. In the next few years, the war shifted to the seas and the Southern Colonies, where it ended abruptly with the surrender of Cornwallis at Yorktown in 1781.

After the war the new nation faced the problems of creating a strong and lasting government. After a transition period under the Articles of Confederation, the Constitutional Convention met in 1787. For the next few years, delegates from all the states concentrated on hammering out and then ratifying the Constitution of the United States.

The Unit Opener in the textbook depicts many of the significant persons and events of this period. You may wish to use these illustrations to help introduce the unit to the class. The central figure is George Washington. Beginning in the lower left-hand corner in a clockwise direction are the American eagle, John Adams, the first American flag, Paul Revere, a woman sewing an American flag, American soldiers in the War of Independence.

Unit Themes and Ideas

The major theme of Unit Three is the revolutionary spirit that urged acceptance of a break with Great Britain, helped sustain the fledgling nation during years of war, and endured to help shape the new form of government established in 1787 at Philadelphia. This spirit is supported by the concepts of self-determination, independence, perseverance, and respect for democratic ideals. Continuity between 1764 and 1787 is maintained since many of the important leaders prior to the Revolution became national figures afterwards. This unit is organized into the three chapters below:

Chapter 7 - *Americans Rebel Against Great Britain (1754 - 1776)*

Chapter 8 - *Americans Fight for Independence (1776 - 1783)*

Chapter 9 - *Americans Create a New Form of Government (1783 - 1789)*

CHAPTER 7

Americans Rebel Against Great Britain (1754-1776)

Chapter Objectives

After completing this chapter, students will be able to:
1. Explain how the British defeated the French in the French and Indian War
2. Identify changes in Britain's colonial policy towards the colonies after the French and Indian War
3. Describe American reactions to changes in British colonial policy
4. Identify important Americans whose ideas helped lead the colonies towards independence
5. Describe the ideas that inspired the colonists to seek independence

Chapter Chronology

Major events of the 20-year period covered here are highlighted in the chapter opener time line, starting in 1754 when fighting broke out between the French and the British. The war, fought from 1756 to 1763 ended with the Treaty of Paris. After 1763, Britain developed a new colonial policy, designed to tighten up on the American colonies. Such measures as the Sugar Act of 1764 showed the colonists that Britain was ending her "neglect" of the colonies. The Stamp Act of 1765 caused American protests and a boycott of British goods. Although the Stamp Act was finally repealed, it was followed by other harsh measures, including the Townshend Acts of 1767. At every turn, the Americans protested, and sometimes violence erupted, notably at the Boston Massacre in 1770. After the Boston Tea Party, in 1773, Parliament passed the Coercive, or Intolerable, Acts. In the same year, the colonists began to act collectively through a Continental Congress. The shots fired at Lexington and Concord in 1775 marked the start of a war of independence that had been a decade in the making.

Motivation

Have students read the Chapter Introduction on textbook page 137. When they get to the first question at the end of the reading, ask them to look at the titles of sections 2 through 5 for clues that might help them answer the question. For example, students might guess that the words "New Policy" in the title of Section 2 might be bad for the colonists. The "Liberty in Danger" part of the Section 3 title certainly should catch students' attention. Be sure to ask students for examples that might fit each of these clues. After the titles have been analyzed, ask students to examine the time line on textbook page 136. Ask if there are any more clues there that might help them answer the original question. Students may already know something about the Boston Tea Party. Keep a list of students' thoughts and responses and refer back to them as students go through the chapter.

Geographical Setting

The territories that the British won in New France as a result of the French and Indian War can be seen on the map, *North America in 1763*, on textbook page 145. The geographical setting of the remainder of Chapter 7 is the American colonies. Boston, Philadelphia, and New York are the three principal colonial cities mentioned in the text. Have students discuss why Philadelphia was chosen as the site for the Continental Congress. The pivotal confrontations at Lexington and Concord are shown in the map on textbook page 152. It should be used in conjunction with the Chapter Introduction in the textbook.

History Study Skills

The History Study Skill introduced in Chapter 7 is *Comparing Historical Maps*. The focus is on the elimination of France as a power to be reckoned with in North America. This skill activity may be used to introduce Section 1 if students are told the results of the war first and *then* asked to find out what happened. Or, it may be used at the end of Section 1 to illustrate the results of the war that students have just studied.

Bibliography

Teacher References

Gross, Richard, *The Minutemen and Their World.* Hill and Wang, New York City, 1976.

Maier, Pauline, *From Resistence to Revolution.* Random House, New York City, 1972.

Student References

O'Dell, Scott, *Sarah Bishop.* Houghton-Mifflin, Boston, Mass., 1980. This is a story of a Tory family on Long Island before, during, and after the American Revolution.

Audio-Visual Materials

Colonial America: The Roots of Revolution 1607-1775, Benchmark. This excellent two-part sound filmstrip

program analyzes the varying life-styles among the colonists and also surveys the period from 1754 to 1776. A teacher's guide is included.

Decades of Decisions, National Geographic. This program consists of six color films that deal with the Revolutionary period. An excellent teacher's guide accompanies each film.

SECTION 1 : The French and Indian War Is Fought

OBJECTIVES

After completing this section, students will be able to:
- Explain the causes of the French and Indian War.
- List the advantages and disadvantages faced by each of the nations involved in the war.
- Identify the important leaders and battles of the war.

MOTIVATION

Use the map of the French and Indian War on textbook page 139 to familiarize students with places they will be reading about in Section 1. These include the Ohio and Mississippi Rivers, the Ohio Valley, the Great Lakes, the Appalachian Mountains, Forts Duquesne and Necessity, Albany, Quebec, and Montreal. Have students close their textbooks temporarily. Show students a transparency of an outline map or a chalkmap on which the features are marked but nameless, and then have them identify each place again. Tell students that you will refer to the outline map again later. At that time, they will have to identify and name each place and also explain its significance in Section 1.

SUGGESTED ACTIVITIES

1. **Directed Reading**. Use the following questions to focus student attention on important concepts:
   A. Why was the French and Indian War fought?
   B. What were the main battles of the war?
   C. How were the British able to defeat the French?
   In discussing the answers to these questions, refer frequently to the map of the French and Indian War. As a summary, point to a specific location on the outline map, such as Albany, and have students identify it and explain its significance in Section 1.

2. **Who's Who?** Chapter 7 contains the names of many individuals, some of whom, such as George Washington, students will be familiar with. However, students may have difficulty remembering what role these figures played before the American Revolution. Therefore, ask students to begin a "Who's Who?" page in their notebooks. Have them record the names of the individuals and identify their role in a sentence or two.

   EXAMPLE: William Pitt: He was appointed by England's King George II to lead the English nation and to direct its efforts in the French and Indian War.

3. **Chronology.** With this activity, students practice the skill of placing events in the order in which they happened. Write a list of events, such as the one below, on the chalkboard. Have them locate and provide the date of each event and finally, recopy the list in chronological order.
   A. The capture of Quebec (1759)
   B. The meeting of the Albany Congress (1754)
   C. France and Great Britain formally declare war (1756)
   D. The fighting ended with the capture of Montreal (1764)
   E. Washington surrendered at Fort Necessity (1753)
   F. General Braddock's army was defeated in the Ohio Valley (1755)

Correct sequence: E - B - F - C - A - D

4. **History Study Skills.** Duplicate Worksheet 15, *Colonies in 1650 and 1700.* This activity reviews information learned by students in Chapter 5. Use the map activity as a basis for a critical thinking exercise. Have students recall how England gained control of New Netherland and compare this with how they gained control of the French Empire in North America. Again, ask students to state differences and similarities.

BUILDING AMERICAN CITIZENSHIP

Can the advice or actions of one person make a difference in the outcome of historical events? Have students consider General Braddock's refusal to take Washington's advice. Have them consider Wolfe's decision to make the treacherous climb to the Plains of Abraham in the dead of the night. Focus the discussion at the personal level. How can you, as a student, influence the outcome of an event at school, such as an election? How can you, as a citizen, affect the outcome of events in your neighborhood, such as a clean-up campaign?

SECTION 1 REVIEW ANSWERS

1. **IDENTIFY: George Washington:** leader of troops from Virginia into the Ohio Valley to fight the French; **Fort Duquesne:** French fort built where the Monongahela and the Allegheny rivers meet; **Albany Plan of Union:** a plan for colonial military cooperation against the French, which called for a Grand Council made up of representatives from each colony; **Benjamin Franklin:** author of the Albany Plan of Union; **William Pitt:** appointed by George II to direct Britain's war against France; **James Wolfe:** leader of British troops at the Battle of Quebec; **Louis Montcalm:** leader of French troops at the Battle of Quebec.
2. **DEFINE: veto:** to turn down.
3. Both Britain and France claimed the Ohio Valley. However, the French had been fur trapping in the valley since the early 1700's. When British fur trappers and farmers began moving into the area in the 1740's, trouble developed.
4. In the dead of night, the British used an unguarded path up the cliffs to reach the Plains of Abraham outside of Quebec, surprising the French troops.

SECTION 2: Great Britian Begins a New Colonial Policy

OBJECTIVES

After completing this section, students will be able to:
• Describe the shifts in French and British land ownership in North America from 1763.
• Identify the problems Great Britain faced after the French and Indian War.
• List the methods used by Great Britain to try to solve its problems.
• Explain the causes and results of Pontiac's Rebellion.

MOTIVATION

Have students recall how the French and Indian War ended (capture of Quebec and Montreal). Ask them what usually happens to the losing country (made to pay for damages, give up land). Ask what happens to nations who win (take land, prisoners, and other spoils of war). Ask what type of agreement is signed between winning and losing nations (treaty). Finally, ask students if they can think of any problems that might arise after a war has ended (debts, what to do with new territories and their inhabitants). Discuss these questions with students. Tell them that these issues will be discussed again after this section is read. Write the questions below on the chalkboard.
1. What did the French lose as a result of the war?
2. What did the British gain as a result of the war?
3. What problems did Great Britain have after the war ended?
4. How did the British try to solve these problems?

SUGGESTED ACTIVITIES

1. **Directed Reading.** Have students read this section to answer the four questions above. Refer to the map of North America in 1763 on textbook page 145 when discussing the answers to questions 1 and 2. As a summary activity, have students add George III and Lord Grenville to their Who's Who?
2. **Time Line.** Ask the students to begin a time line of events leading to the American Revolution. Using a 6-inch line, have them mark each inch on the line and, beginning with the year 1763, number the line every two years until 1775. Ask students to place the events of this section on the time line. You may wish to include the following:

   Pontiac's Rebellion (1763)   Sugar Act (1764)
   Proclamation of 1763   Quartering Act (1765)

   Remind students to keep the time line in their notebook and to bring it to class daily.
3. **Writing Exercise.** Based on what they have read in Section 2, have students write a paragraph to answer the following question:
   Do you think Great Britain had a right to expect the colonists to pay for the cost of the war and for the defense of the new North American empire?

BUILDING AMERICAN CITIZENSHIP

Initiate a discussion about taxes. What are they? Why does a government tax its people? Why do certain people complain about taxes? Who decides what things are taxable? What differences are there between the policy of taxing the British colonists after 1763 and the way Americans are taxed today?

Elicit from the class that the colonies were not being taxed by their own government, but rather by a king and Parliament 3,000 miles (4,800 kilometers) away. Today taxes are levied by a government elected by the people. Also, although no one likes paying taxes, they are necessary to pay for such services as police and fire protection, armed forces, unemployment insurance, and social security.

SECTION 2 REVIEW ANSWERS

1. **IDENTIFY: Pontiac's Rebellion:** an unsuccessful rebellion in May 1763 of several Indian tribes led by Pontiac, the Ottawa chief, against the British; **Proclamation of 1763:** a proclamation issued by the British forbidding further settlement of the Ohio Valley to give Britain time to make peace with the Indians; **Lord George Grenville:** prime minister of Great Britain responsible for tightening British control of the colonies; **Navigation Acts:** British trade laws that regulated American trade with Britain and with foreign countries; **Sugar Act:** British act passed in 1764 that placed a 3¢-a-gallon import tax on all foreign molasses and sugar brought into the colonies; **Quartering Act:** British act passed in 1765 requiring colonists to pay the cost of housing and feeding British soldiers stationed in their area.
2. **DEFINE: customs duties:** taxes on goods imported into America from foreign countries.
3. Britain had huge war debts; it needed funds for a bigger defense budget; it also needed money to establish new governments in Canada and the Ohio Valley.
4. The colonists were upset because they had not been consulted before passage of the new tax laws; they felt that having to pay the cost of housing and feeding British soldiers was a way to make them pay part of Britain's defense budget.

SECTION 3: America's Liberty Is in Danger

OBJECTIVES

After completing this section, students will be able to:
- List the ways the colonists protested British colonial practices.
- Describe the effects of colonial protest on British policy.
- Arrange the events described in sections two and three in chronological order.

MOTIVATION

The concept of "protest" is important in understanding Section 3. Select a current event that has been the subject of widespread protest. Discuss the event (nuclear disarmament, pollution, unemployment). Then discuss the methods used by people to show their dissatisfaction

with current policies (letters to Congress, demonstrations, meetings). Redirect the discussion to the colonial period from 1763-1775. What British actions would the colonists wish to protest (Proclamation of 1763, Sugar Act, Quartering Act). How could they show their dissatisfaction? Have students look at the pictures in this section to get ideas. Tell students that, in this section, they will be learning about more actions taken by Parliament and the means of protest used by colonists to object to these actions.

SUGGESTED ACTIVITIES

1. **Directed Reading.** Go over the vocabulary in this section: boycott, repeal, delegates, subjects, writs of assistance. Have students draw a line down the center of a sheet of paper, making two columns. Label one column BRITISH ACTIONS and the second column COLONIAL ACTIONS PROTESTING BRITISH POLICY. As students read the textbook, have them write down some of the British actions and the colonial methods of protest. As a summary activity, ask students to evaluate the success or failure of the various colonial protests.
2. **Time Line.** Add the following to the time line.
   Stamp Act - 1765
   Repeal of Stamp Act - 1766
   Declaratory Act - 1766
   Townshend Acts - 1767
   Boston Massacre - 1770
   Repeal of Townshend Acts - 1770
3. **Chronology.** List the following on the board and ask students to copy them in chronological order. As the correct order is checked, have students identify each event by telling what it involved.

Stamp Act (3)	Townshend Acts (5)
Boston Massacre (6)	Declaratory Act (4)
Proclamation of 1763 (1)	Sugar Act (2)

4. **Drawing a Cartoon.** Have students draw a cartoon illustrating one of the means of protest (a town meeting, Patrick Henry giving his speech in the Virginia House of Burgesses, the burning of a copy of the Stamp Act, the Boston Massacre).
5. **Who's Who?** Have students add the following to their list: Patrick Henry, Samuel Adams, Thomas Preston, Crispus Attucks, Frederick Lord North.
6. **Sources of Freedom.** Patrick Henry's speech before the House of Burgesses in Virginia is mentioned in Section 3. Provide students with the opportunity to read his historic comments, which can be found on textbook page 153. Since the 18th-century writing style differs markedly from that of the 20th century, you may wish to help students interpret Henry's speech.

BUILDING AMERICAN CITIZENSHIP

One of the most important duties of a citizen is to obey the law.
1. Do you think that most people today obey the laws passed by our government?
2. Did the colonists have good reasons to question and then disobey the laws passed by Parliament?
3. Can you think of any situation in which a law should be questioned?
4. Is it *ever* right to disobey a law?

SECTION 3 REVIEW ANSWERS

1. **IDENTIFY: Stamp Act:** British law that taxed such items as playing cards, newspapers, and all legal documents; **Sons of Liberty:** colonists who organized to protest the Stamp Act: **Patrick Henry:** Virginia lawyer who organized political protests against the Stamp Act and urged leaders to stand up for their liberties; **Stamp Act Congress:** a New York meeting of delegates from 9 colonies to protest the Stamp Act; **Townshend Acts:** British laws that put customs duties on paint, lead, tea, paper, and wine coming to America; **Samuel Adams:** colonial leader who warned of dangers to American liberties as long as Parliament governed the colonies: **Crispus Attucks:** a black Bostonian killed at the Boston Massacre; **Lord North:** new prime minister of Great Britain who believed in disciplining the colonists.

2. **DEFINE: boycott:** to refuse to buy or sell goods; **repeal:** to withdraw or do away with a law; **delegates:** representatives; **British subjects:** members of the British empire; **writs of assistance:** documents, like search warrants, allowing British officers to enter buildings to look for smuggled goods.

3. No American voted in Parliament's elections or served in the British Parliament; therefore, Parliament had no right to tax Americans.

4. British troops stationed in Boston were frequently taunted and jeered by crowds. When an angry mob surrounded a small group of British soldiers on March 5, 1770, shots were fired into the crowd, killing five people.

SECTION 4: The Colonists Resist British Policies

OBJECTIVES

After completing this section, students will be able to:
- Explain the purpose of the Committees of Correspondence.
- State the causes of the Boston Tea Party.
- Describe the results of the Boston Tea Party.

MOTIVATION

Have students study a picture of the Boston Tea Party. Ask these questions:
1. Where is the action taking place? (Boston Harbor)
2. What is being thrown into the water? (Tea)
3. Who is doing the damage? (Colonists disguised as Indians)
4. What is the reaction of the people on the docks? (Cheering)
5. Why was the tea dumped in the harbor? (Answers may vary.)
6. What do you think happened in Boston after this event? (Answers may vary.)

SUGGESTED ACTIVITIES

1. **Directed Reading.** Have students read Section 4 to answer the last two questions in the motivation. Afterwards discuss the answers to both questions. Important points to mention include:
   A. (Question 5 above):
   The financial difficulties of the East India Company

The low price that colonists would be paying for tea
The tax that remained on the tea
Governor Hutchinson's determination to see the tea unloaded
   B. (Question 6 above):
   Passage of the Coercive, or Intolerable, Acts closing of the port of Boston
   The taking away of the right of self-government
   The fact that colonists had to provide food and housing for more British soldiers

2. **Cause and Effect.** Duplicate Worksheet 16, *The American Revolution.* Then, immediately after students have read the introductory paragraph, ask them to give an example from Section 4 of one cause of the Boston Tea Party, and one effect. Then have them answer the questions. Afterwards, test their mastery of the skill by randomly selecting salient points from activity 1. Ask students to identify each statement as a cause or effect.

3. **Writing Assignment.** Have students pretend they are members of a Committee of Correspondence from a colony other than Massachusetts. Have them write a letter to Boston's Committee describing the reactions of people in their colony to the Boston Tea Party and the Coercive Acts.

4. **Making Additions to Other Activities.** Have students add Thomas Hutchinson to their Who's Who? list. Also, have them add the Boston Tea Party (1773) and the Coercive Acts (1774) to their time lines.

BUILDING AMERICAN CITIZENSHIP

To protest the tea tax, the colonists broke the law by destroying private property. For this they were punished. Could the colonists have used legal means of protest? What could they have done? If citizens today are unhappy with a law, what legal means can they use to get it changed? (Writing letters to politicians, giving speeches, going to court, staging a peaceful demonstration)

SECTION 4 REVIEW ANSWERS

1. **IDENTIFY: Committees of Correspondence:** committees that were set up in all colonies to communicate with each other about important political happenings; **Tea Act:** law allowing the British East India Company to sell its tea directly to America without paying British import taxes; **Thomas Hutchinson:** governor of Massachusetts who was determined to see the cargoes of tea unloaded in Boston; **Boston Tea Party:** the dumping of the East India tea into Boston harbor by people disguised as Indians; **Intolerable Acts:** laws designed to punish the people of Massachusetts by closing the port of Boston until the tea dumped into Boston harbor was paid for and by taking away their right of self-government; **Quebec Act:** law that gave French Canadians religious freedom and their own legal system but no representative assembly.

2. **DEFINE: monopoly:** sole control over the buying and selling of a product.

3. They feared that once the British East India Company

gained a monoply of the American tea market, it might raise its prices. Also, Britain might plan other monopolies in the future.

4. It passed what colonists called the Intolerable Acts, which closed the port of Boston, weakened the power of the Massachusetts colonial assembly, and brought more British troops to the colony.

SECTION 5: Americans Choose Independence

OBJECTIVES

After completing this section, students will be able to:
- Describe the actions taken by the First and Second Continental Congress.
- Tell how the war between the colonists and Great Britain began.

MOTIVATION

Find a copy of Henry Wadsworth Longfellow's poem, commonly known as "Paul Revere's Ride." It begins with the lines "Listen my children and you shall hear of the midnight ride of Paul Revere." Read the first two verses to the class. Jot down these questions on the chalkboard.
1. When did Paul Revere make his ride?
2. What was its purpose?
3. How did he know which route the British were taking?
4. Where were the British troops going? Why?

Explain that Longfellow wrote a beautiful poem. However, he left out a few important historical details. For example, he did not tell where the British troops were going, or why. Also, he omitted the role played by two other patriotic riders that evening.

SUGGESTED ACTIVITIES

1. **Directed Reading.** Have students read Section 5 to determine the information omitted by Longfellow:
   A. Where were the British going? Why?
   B. Who else helped warn the colonists about the British?
   C. What happened to the British troops on April 19, 1775?
   To help students visualize the events as they occurred, refer them to the map of the Battle of Lexington and Concord on textbook page 152. Several other events that transpired that fateful evening are not included in the poem. For example, Revere and Dawes both reached Lexington. But Revere was captured west of Lexington, and it was Dr. Samuel Prescott who rode on to warn the people of Concord.
2. **Research Activity.** The textbook provides only part of the story of Revere's ride. You may wish to assign a few students the task of learning what happened to Revere, Dawes, and Prescott. If possible, make this assignment before teaching the lesson, so that students will be prepared to present their findings when the topic is discussed.
3. **Making Additions to Other Activities.** Have students add Paul Revere, William Dawes, Samuel

Prescott, and Thomas Paine to their Who's Who lists. Have students add the following to their time lines:
The First Continental Congress (1774)
Battles of Lexington and Concord (1775)
Second Continental Congress (1775)

4. **Landmarks of Liberty.** The statue of the "Minuteman of Concord" commemorates the events described in this section. Ask students to read the Landmark of Liberty selection on textbook page 143. Then have them answer the questions that follow it.

BUILDING AMERICAN CITIZENSHIP

Duplicate Worksheet 17, *Methods of Protest.* The concept of "protest" was introduced in the motivation for Section 3. This citizenship activity should reinforce the concept, which can be applied to sections 4 and 5 of this chapter as well.

SECTION 5 REVIEW ANSWERS

1. **IDENTIFY: First Continental Congress:** 1774 meeting in Philadelphia of delegates from 12 states to protest British tyranny; **Declaration of Rights:** a statement drawn up by the delegates of the First Continental Congress of terms they considered acceptable as a compromise with Britain; **Paul Revere:** Massachusetts silversmith who warned the colonists that British troops were marching to Lexington and Concord; **Thomas Paine:** author of *Common Sense.*
2. **DEFINE: militia:** a group of citizens trained to fight in emergencies; **Redcoats:** name given to British troops because their coats were red.
3. It approved Massachusetts' call for a militia; approved a boycott of trade with Great Britain; drew up a Declaration of Rights.
4. On the Lexington Green in Lexington, Massachusetts.

CHAPTER 7 REVIEW ANSWERS

REVIEWING KEY WORDS

1. c.	2. a.	3. e.	4. b.	5. d.

REMEMBERING IMPORTANT PEOPLE AND EVENTS

1. b.	2. b.	3. c.	4. a.	5. c.

REVIEWING THE FACTS

1. F	2. T	3. T	4. T	5. F
6. T	7. T	8. T	9. F	10. F

PLACING EVENTS IN TIME

1. b.	2. a.	3. c.	4. e.	5. d.

LINKING GEOGRAPHY AND HISTORY

1. It took a long time for news of the passage of the Stamp Act to travel from Britain to America; it also took time for the news to reach all the colonies and then for the delegates to travel to New York.

THINKING ABOUT AMERICAN HISTORY

1. The war had been costly to Britain; therefore it looked to the colonies to help pay its war debt. It began to enforce trade laws and collect customs duties it had "neglected" to enforce. It also passed the Proclama-

tion of 1763 in an effort to end problems with the Indians in the Ohio Valley who had rebelled against British rule. The proclamation banned further settlement in the Ohio Valley. Britain also passed the Sugar Act and the Quartering Act to collect more money from the colonies. All of these measures reflected Britain's new policy of greater control of the American colonies.

2. They wrote newspaper articles offering suggestions for keeping the peace; they sent a direct appeal to the king to ask him to serve as peacemaker; they sent an "Olive Branch" petition to the king.

APPLYING HISTORY STUDIES SKILLS

1. Great Britain   2. Russia   3. Spain

CHAPTER 8

Americans Fight for Independence (1776-1783)

Chapter Objectives

After completing this section, students will be able to:
1. List reasons why Americans decided to fight for independence.
2. Identify important military battles during the Revolution.
3. Trace the movement of the war from New England, through the Middle colonies and into the South.
4. Describe how the Revolution changed the lives of Americans.

Chapter Chronology

Chapter 8 covers the American Revolution and the War of Independence. The time line in the chapter opener on textbook page 158 highlights the most important events of this period. The Battle of Bunker Hill, the first major battle of the war, occurred in June 1775, just under one year before the signing of the Declaration of Independence. American defeat at Bunker Hill was followed by American victories elsewhere, notably at Saratoga in 1777. After Saratoga, the French began to aid America openly. After some setbacks, the tide finally turned in 1780 with an American victory at Kings Mountain in North Carolina. This victory set the stage for the final battle at Yorktown, Virginia, in 1781. The British were defeated and their General Cornwallis surrendered to George Washington. With the signing of the Treaty of Paris in September 1783, the War for Independence was officially at an end.

Motivation

By Chapter 8, students have already studied the battles at Lexington and Concord and know that the war had started. Begin by having students "size up" the two sides. Ask them to think of the resources necessary to wage war. Responses should include human resources (to fight, grow crops, make weapons), material resources (guns, ships), and moral resources (courage, conviction, unity). Ask students to compare Great Britain and the 13

colonies in each of these resource categories. Have students predict what problems each side will have during the Revolutionary War.

Geographical Setting

Chapter 8 describes the American Revolution in all parts of the colonies. This is an excellent point to reinforce map skills because the four maps in the chapter illustrate all of the colonies, including many important physical features and locations where key events occurred. The maps trace the war's movement from New England into the other colonies and the western territories. The role of geographical factors in war may be illustrated in this chapter. For example, both the British and Americans try to make use of waterways and the ocean for troop movements. Cornwallis at Yorktown is bottled up on a peninsula, and vulnerable to navel and land artillery. Finally, refer students to the map showing the boundaries of the United States in 1783 on textbook page 187 in Chapter 9.

History Study Skills

The History Study Skill introduced in Chapter 8 is *Reading Historical Documents*. Students will read the Declaration of Independence and analyze it. They will also examine some of the characteristics of historical documents. This skill activity should be used during Section 1 where students read about the Declaration and the thoughts of its author, Thomas Jefferson.

Bibliography

Teacher References

Norton, Mary Beth, *Liberty's Daughters: The Revolutionary Experience of American Women 1750-1800*. Little, Brown, Boston, Mass., 1980.

Wills, Gary, *Inventing America: Jefferson's Declaration of Independence*. Random House, New York City, 1978.

Student References

Collier, James Lincoln and Collier, Christopher, *Jump Ship to Freedom: A Novel*. Set in Connecticut in the Revolutionary period, this story is about a 14-year-old slave boy's efforts to buy freedom for his mother and himself.

Fritz, Jean, *Traitor: The Case of Benedict Arnold*. Putnam, New York City, 1981. This is an illustrated biography. It includes many of Arnold's good qualities as well as his questionable ones.

Milgrim, Shirley, *Haym Salomon: Liberty's Son*. The Jewish Publication Society of America, Philadelphia, Pa., 1975. This is the biography of a Jewish immigrant from Poland, who arrived in New York in 1772 and became an ardent revolutionary, and financier, raising needed funds for the War of Independence.

Audio-Visual Materials

The Declaration of Independence, National Geographic. This filmstrip highlights the writing of the Declaration of Independence. Main points of the Declaration are illustrated and the grievances that led to the revolution.

The American Revolution, Guidance Associates. Two filmstrips, cassettes, Library Kit, Teacher's Guide. Historical documents and contemporary works of art are used to survey the events and issues that led to the American Revolution.

SECTION 1: The Colonists Declare Their Independence

OBJECTIVES

After completing this section, students will be able to:
- State the reasons why Americans decided to fight for their independence.
- Explain the advantages and disadvantages the Americans had in preparing to fight Great Britain.
- Identify the ways in which foreign governments helped Americans fight the Revolution.

MOTIVATION

Use the Motivation suggested in the chapter introduction. Have students discuss and compare Great Britain with the 13 colonies in each of the resource categories, using the terms ''advantage'' and ''disadvantage.'' Note their responses on the chalkboard. Example: Which side held the advantage in the number and types of weapons available? In addition, ask students to recall why this war began.

SUGGESTED ACTIVITIES

1. **Directed Reading.** Have students read Section 1 to answer the following questions:
   A. How did the colonists let the British know why they were fighting?
   B. Who wrote this statement? When? Where?
   C. What were the advantages and disadvantages of the American Army in preparing to fight Great Britain? List them.
   Discuss the answers to the three questions. As a summary, compare students' lists in response to question C. with the one formulated during the motivation. Ask students to add any resources they may have missed. Have them close books and notebooks, and orally drill them by asking them questions.
   EXAMPLES: Which side had better trained troops? Knew their home ground?
2. **History Study Skills.** As suggested in the introduction to this chapter, the History Study Skill, *Reading Historical Documents* on textbook page 181, could best be used with Section 1. It will provide students with an opportunity for an in-depth look at the reasons for Americans going to war with Britain.
3. **Sources of Freedom**. Refer students to the Declaration of Independence on textbook page 162. This will reinforce the History Study Skill and lead into the next activity.
4. **Building American Citizenship**. Duplicate Worksheet 18, *Declaration of Independence*. This will provide an excellent extension of the History Study Skill activity. It will also help clarify some of the complex language used in the Declaration of Independence.

5. **Research Activity**. The last paragraph of Section 1 lists the names of individual foreigners who helped the Americans. Have your students use encyclopedias and other reference sources to determine how each individual helped. You may wish to encourage above-average students to try to discover the names of other, less well-known foreigners who gave assistance.

BUILDING AMERICAN CITIZENSHIP

Thomas Jefferson blamed the king for all the wrongs listed in the Declaration of Independence. Why? (He was better known than the members of Parliament; he stood for the government of the nation). Whom do citizens usually blame today when something goes wrong in the nation? (The President) Do you think this is fair? (Answers will vary.) Who passes the laws for American citizens? (Congress) Shouldn't American citizens also criticize Congress as well as the President? Why or why not? (Answers will vary.)

SECTION 1 REVIEW ANSWERS

1. **IDENTIFY: Thomas Jefferson:** author of the Declaration of Independence; **Declaration of Independence:** the written statement or document explaining why Americans felt they must rebel against Great Britain.
2. **DEFINE: preamble:** an introduction stating the purpose of a document; **mercenaries:** hired soldiers; **Hessians:** German soldiers hired by the British to fight the American colonists.
3. Abuse of personal rights.
4. **Advantages:** American soldiers believed in their cause; they fought on their home ground; British troops had poor military leaders; Americans had help from foreigners.
   Disadvantages: The American army was small, undisciplined, poorly equipped, and inexperienced; its officers were untrained in military affairs; the Americans had no navy to carry troops or supplies; they lacked money to build factories or ships or to pay soldiers.

SECTION 2: The War Spreads Across the Nation

OBJECTIVES

After completing this section, students will be able to:
- Describe the Battle of Bunker Hill.
- Identify other battles fought in 1775 and 1776.
- Locate the sites of battles fought in 1775 and 1776.

MOTIVATION

Have students look at the picture of the Battle of Bunker Hill in Section 2. Have students carefully describe what is happening in the picture. Ask them if it is possible to predict the outcome of this battle based on what they have seen.

SUGGESTED ACTIVITIES

1. **Directed Reading.** As students read Section 2, have them list the name of each battle described and its

location. When they have finished, ask a student to write the name of the first battle and its location on the board. (Bunker Hill) Discuss the details with students and have them use the map *Revolutionary War in the North* on textbook page 166 to pinpoint the exact location. Repeat this procedure for each of the battles in the section.

2. **Making a Chart**. Using the information from the above activity as a starting point, have students begin a battle chart. Use the sample below as a guide:

BATTLE	DATE	LOCATION	OUTCOME
Lexington	April 19, 1775	Massachusetts	Colonists killed; British move on to Concord
Concord	April 19, 1975	Massachusetts	British retreated to Boston

3. **Research Activity.** You may wish to add two more columns to the battle chart started in activity 2. These would be labeled British Commander and American Commander. Have students use the textbook as their first source. For example, the textbook names only the British commander at Bunker Hill, General Howe, but not the American commander. Students will have to use other references to find this information.

   You may wish to have below-average students limit their research to the textbook. If a commander is not named, they could leave that section of the chart blank, or the teacher could provide the information for them.

4. **Time Line**. Use the time line on the textbook Chapter Opener page. Ask students which of the battles from Section 2 is depicted on the time line. (Bunker Hill) Be sure to point out that this battle was fought *before* the Declaration of Independence was signed. Have students name the other battles that could be put on the line for 1775 and for 1776 *without* consulting their battle charts.

BUILDING AMERICAN CITIZENSHIP

Citizens fighting in a war often make many sacrifices. The soldiers who fought with General Benedict Arnold in Canada are a good example. Reread the story of the Canadian campaign. What sacrifices were made by these citizen-soldiers? (Some killed or captured; others forced to camp through the bitter winter, fighting bravely to slow down British troops on Lake Champlain in the face of sure defeat.)

Today, our army's soldiers are professionals. Do you think they would be willing to make the same types of sacrifices as the citizen-soldiers of Arnold's army? Why or why not? (Answers will vary.)

SECTION 2 REVIEW ANSWERS

1. **IDENTIFY: Thomas Gage:** commander of British troops in Boston; **Benedict Arnold:** American leader in the battles at Fort Ticonderoga, Quebec, and Lake Champlain; **Ethan Allen:** leader of the "Green Mountain Boys" who took part in the capture of Fort Ticonderoga; **Henry Clinton:** commander of British troops defeated at Charleston, S.C.
2. **DEFINE: Loyalists:** American colonists who remained loyal to Britain; **siege:** a strong military attack.

3. After capturing Fort Ticonderoga, the Americans moved the cannon from there overland to Boston.
4. Arnold and his troops built a makeshift navy and fought the British on Lake Champlain. Although they lost, the battle forced the British to turn back at the onset of winter.

SECTION 3: The War Moves to the Middle States

OBJECTIVES

After completing this section, students will be able to:
• Name and locate the battles fought in the Middle States.
• Discuss the errors made by the British and Hessians in these battles.
• Describe the hardships endured by American soldiers at Valley Forge.

MOTIVATION

Read the Ideals in the Lives of Americans selection on Haym Salomon on textbook page 176. Have students discuss the answers to the two questions at the end. Ask them why Washington's soldiers at Valley Forge would need the money and supplies donated by Salomon and Morris? Tell students that they will be able to answer this question after reading Section 3.

SUGGESTED ACTIVITIES

1. **Directed Reading**. Have students continue work on the battle chart, begun in Section 2. Direct them to add the battles described in Section 3 and to supply the necessary information in each column.

   As a summary, have students review the information to determine if it is correct. A teacher-prepared transparency of the chart, projected on the overhead, would make this task easier. Also, discuss the answer to the question posed in the motivation.
2. **Discussion.** Present the class with this statement: British mistakes helped American soldiers to win the Revolution. Ask students if they think it is true or false, and have them give examples from the reading to defend their answers. They should include information on the failure of the British to follow Washington as he retreated into New Jersey; the failure of Hessian soldiers to prepare fortifications at Trenton; and the communication failure among the British commanders about plans to cut off New England from the rest of the country.
3. **Map Interpretation**. Have students use the map, *The Revolutionary War in the Middle Colonies*, on textbook page 170 to answer TRUE or FALSE to the following questions:
   A. Washington had to cross a river to attack Trenton. (T)
   B. Washington retreated from New York in a southeasterly direction. (F)
   C. General Burgoyne's troops were traveling south from Canada when defeated by the Americans. (T)
   D. General St. Leger's army was stopped near the town of Oriskany. (T)
   E. Valley Forge is located west of Philadelphia. (T)

4. **Writing Assignment**. Ask students to imagine that they are soldiers in the American army. Have them write a diary entry describing participation in one of the following:
   A. The retreat from New York to New Jersey
   B. The Battle of Saratoga
   C. The attack on Trenton
   D. A spying mission against the British in Philadelphia
   E. The hardships of spending a winter at Valley Forge

BUILDING AMERICAN CITIZENSHIP

Nathan Hale volunteered for a spying mission, stating, "I wish to be useful." He died as a result of that mission. Other than serving as a soldier or a spy, how else might citizens prove themselves "useful" when their country is at war? (Donating money, nursing wounded soldiers, volunteer work with the Red Cross, donating blood.)

SECTION 3 REVIEW ANSWERS

1. **IDENTIFY: Nathan Hale:** captain in the Continental Army, hanged as a spy by the British; **Johann Rall:** commander of the Hessian troops at Trenton, N.J.; **General John Burgoyne:** commander of British troops defeated at the battle at Saratoga; **Valley Forge:** the army quarters near Philadelphia where General Washington and his troops spent the winter of 1777 to 1778; **General Von Steuben:** German military expert who trained American troops at Valley Forge; **John Paul Jones:** American naval hero who commanded the *Bonhomme Richard* and defeated the British ship *Serapis.*
2. **DEFINE: privateers:** privately owned American ships that were encouraged to attack British warships.
3. From there, Howe could march south on Philadelphia or north into New England.
4. European nations no longer saw the American cause as hopeless. After the American victory, the French king signed a treaty of friendship with the Second Continental Congress. The French were now willing to openly help the Americans.

SECTION 4: The War Ends in the South

OBJECTIVES

After completing this section, students will be able to:
• Name and locate the battles fought in the West.
• Name and locate the battles fought in the South.
• Identify the important terms of the Treaty of Paris of 1783.

MOTIVATION

Have the class study the maps of the war in the Southern Colonies on textbook page 175 *and* the map of the war in the West on textbook page 173. Ask students to list the battles fought in the West, and have them practice the pronunciation of each one (Vincennes, Cahokia, and Kaskaskia). Ask students to name the battles in the South that they have already studied (Charleston,

Moore's Creek Bridge). Then have them list the ones they have not yet read about (Savannah, Cowpens, Kings Mountain, Guilford Court House, Yorktown). Have them tell which side won each battle. Ask whether it is possible to tell from the map where the last battle was fought, or the outcome.

SUGGESTED ACTIVITIES

1. **Directed Reading.** As students read, have them complete the battle chart started in Section 2. Again, review the information carefully with students to make sure it is correct. Have them utilize the chart to answer such questions as:
   A. In which part of America were most of the battles fought?
   B. In which year were the most battles fought?
   C. How many of the battles were won by the British? The Americans?
   D. Which British commander took part in the greatest number of battles?
   E. How many years passed between the first battle of Charleston and the second battle of Charleston?
2. **Review—Making a Time Line**. Duplicate Worksheet 19, *The American Revolution.* This activity will provide an excellent review of major events in the first four sections. You may wish to allow average and below-average students to use their charts as an aid. Ask above-average students to complete the activity without references to assist them.
3. **Review—Reading for the Main Idea.** Duplicate Worksheet 20, *The Swamp Fox.* This activity expands on the role played by this prominent individual. You may wish to encourage above-average students to research the three other patriots mentioned in Section 4—George Rogers Clark, Nathanael Greene, and Daniel Morgan. Using the worksheet as a sample, have them prepare a similiar written activity to trade with other students for further practice in this skill. They may also be collected and distributed to average and below-average students who need additional practice.
4. **Treaty of Paris of 1783.** Use the overhead projector or chalkboard. Have students copy the following paragraph and fill in the blanks:

   In the year *1783*, the Treaty of *Paris* was signed. In it, Great Britain recognized the *independence* of the United States and agreed to remove its *troops* from American territory. The *Mississippi* River was established as the new western *boundary* of the United States. The United States, in turn, agreed to pay its *debt* to British merchants and to repay *Loyalists* for lost homes and property.

BUILDING AMERICAN CITIZENSHIP

With the surrender of General Cornwallis at Yorktown, the war ended. One of the postwar problems faced by Americans was how to treat the defeated Redcoats. How should citizens of a victorious nation treat citizens of a defeated nation? How should citizens of a victorious nation treat fellow citizens who were loyal to the enemy? Give reasons for your answers. (The answers may vary considerably.)

SECTION 4 REVIEW ANSWERS

1. **IDENTIFY: George Rogers Clark:** commander of American troops in the West; **General Cornwallis:** commander of British troops in the South; **"No Quarter" Tarleton:** British captain responsible for the massacre of American forces at Waxhaws, S.C.; **Daniel Morgan:** American raider whose troops trapped and defeated Tarleton's troops at Cowpens, S.C.; **Nathanael Greene:** commander of American troops in the South.
2. Kaskaskia, Cahokia, and Vincennes.
3. The Americans won both battles.
4. French navy blocked Cornwallis' escape by sea while Washington's troops laid siege to Yorktown.

SECTION 5: The Revolution Changes American Life

OBJECTIVES

After completing this section, students will be able to:
* Describe the duties and responsibilities assumed by women during the Revolution.
* Explain the role of black Americans during the Revolution.
* Identify the problems of Loyalists during and after the Revolution.

MOTIVATION

Discuss the idea that war often brings about changes in the life of a nation. Indicate that two groups which had been in the background heretofore played important roles during the Revolution and contributed greatly to the American victory. Ask students who the members of these two groups were (women and American blacks). Ask students how women might have helped to win the Revolution. Jot down their ideas on the chalkboard. Then ask students what they think the role of black Americans might have been in the Revolution. Explain to students that this section will reveal the many ways in which both groups helped America to win.

SUGGESTED ACTIVITIES

1. **Directed Reading.** Have students continue to add to the list of ways women helped to win the Revolution. In addition, have them describe the part taken by blacks in the Revolution. As a summary, compare the roles of the two groups. Then compare what happened to the two groups after the war with what happened to the Loyalists.
2. **Outlining.** Have students use their lists of contributions made by women during the Revolution to construct an outline. Above-average students should be able to determine a title and several topics without assistance. You may wish to provide average and below-average students with several suggested topics. Those suggested in this section are appropriate:
   I. American women support the Revolution
   II. Women take on new roles
   III. Women's activities after the war
3. **Writing Reports.** The textbook provides an excellent overview of the roles of black Americans and women. In order to give students an appreciation of

specific contributions, have them prepare a brief report on one of the following. Students should restrict their report to information related to activities involving the Revolution.

Peter Salem	Martha Washington
Prince Hall	Mary Hays
Cuff Hayes	Deborah Sampson
James Armistead	Caesar Dickerson
Mercey Otis Warren	Catherine Schuyler
Margaret Corbin	Abigail Adams
Saul Matthews	

4. **Discussion.** The population of the colonies on the eve of the Revolution approached 2,500,000. Estimates concerning the number of Loyalists vary between 160,000 and 384,000. Reveal these numbers to students. Ask them to give reasons why the estimates vary so greatly. For example, many Loyalists left the colonies early in the war; many never admitted they were Loyalists. You may wish to have above-average students try to find additional information concerning the role of Loyalists and their subsequent problems.

BUILDING AMERICAN CITIZENSHIP

Most of the 2,500,000 Americans supported the War of Independence from Great Britain. Those who did not lose their property were sometimes imprisoned and were despised by their neighbors. Many of these people simply preferred to stay out of the conflict. Were these citizens treated fairly? Give a reason for your answer.

SECTION 5 REVIEW ANSWERS

1. **IDENTIFY: "Molly Pitchers":** American women who served at the front, reloading muskets and carrying pitchers of water to the soldiers; they sometimes engaged in actual combat. **Mary McCauley:** the original "Molly Pitcher" who fought in the Revolution at the Battle of Monmouth, New Jersey, in 1778. **Mercy Otis Warren:** the historian of the Revolution.
2. **DEFINE: "Republican Motherhood":** the theory that women strengthened the nation by teaching children the principles of democracy and American history, which led to the establishment of schools for women and a recognition of the importance of women in public affairs; **emancipate:** to set free; **confiscate:** to take away or take possession of another person's property.
3. Women organized boycotts of British-made goods, wrote poems and plays in support of the Revolution, collected money for the army and metal household items to be melted down into ammunition, made clothing and blankets for the soldiers, took charge of family businesses while the men were away fighting, became "Molly Pitchers," served as nurses in army hospitals and as spies.
4. They were promised their freedom in return for fighting for the British.

CHAPTER 8 REVIEW ANSWERS
REVIEWING KEY WORDS

1. e.   2. c.   3. a.   4. b.   5. d.

REMEMBERING IMPORTANT PEOPLE

1. d.   2. b.   3. e.   4. a.   5. c.
6. c.   7. e.   8. a.   9. d.   10. b.

REVIEWING THE FACTS

1. c.   2. b.   3. b.   4. a.   5. a.

PLACING EVENTS IN TIME

1. C   2. E   3. A   4. D   5. B

LINKING GEOGRAPHY AND HISTORY

1. Americans could plan their war strategy based on their knowledge of the land. They knew the best places for an ambush, for sudden retreats, for shortcuts between places, for good areas for setting up camps, for running a spy network safely, and so on.
2. Yorktown was on a peninsula. From there Cornwallis could get supplies and replacements by water and yet have only one "front" to defend against American attack.

THINKING ABOUT AMERICAN HISTORY

1. Americans showed that they could defeat a large British army, making an American victory in the war seem more likely. European nations, particularly France, no longer believed that the American cause was hopeless and began to support the Americans openly.
2. By refusing to obey Clinton's orders, Cornwallis created confusion in British strategy. While the British generals argued, the French and Americans cooperated to trap Cornwallis at Yorktown.

APPLYING HISTORY STUDIES SKILLS

1. The Constitution, Patrick Henry's Speech, Washington's Farewell Address, Monroe Doctrine, Seneca Falls "Declaration of Sentiments," the Gettysburg Address, Martin Luther King's Speech.
2. Both begin with preambles, or introductions.
3. Martin Luther King's speech because it is written in modern language. Answers will vary.

CHAPTER 9

Americans Create a New Form of Government (1783-1789)

Chapter Objectives

After completing this chapter, students will be able to:
1. Identify the strengths and weaknesses of the Articles of Confederation.
2. Name important leaders who helped create the Constitution.
3. Explain how compromise was used in developing the Constitution.
4. List the arguments of those who were for and those who were against ratification of the Constitution.
5. Describe the plan of government formulated under the Constitution.

Chapter Chronology

Chapter 9 covers the decade of the 1780's. It traces the development of government in the United States from the Articles of Confederation through the ratification of the Constitution. Many of the major persons and events of the period are highlighted in the textbook Chapter Opener. The first important event of the decade was the ratification of the Articles of Confederation in 1781. Troubled times for the new nation ensued, reflected in such serious outbreaks of violence as Shays' Rebellion in 1786. In the following year, American representatives met in Philadelphia for the Constitutional Convention. 1787 was also the year in which the Northwest Ordinance, insuring fair and peaceful settlement of the West, was passed. In 1788, the Constitution was ratified and George Washington was elected first President. The Bill of Rights was added to the Constitution three years later.

Motivation

Ask students to imagine that they are in charge of the government of the United States in 1783. Have them make a list of all of the steps that must be taken for the United States to maintain its independence. After these have been listed, ask students to think about what the new nation's most immediate problems, domestic and foreign, would be and how the new government should go about solving them. Domestic issues should be divided into economic, political, and social issues. Have students make a list and keep it for reference as they read the chapter.

Geographical Setting

The geographical focus in Chapter 9 is concentrated largely in Section 1, in which the plan for settling the Northwest Territory is described. The plan for settlement of the land west of the Appalachians became a model by which other territories later became states. The importance of New Orleans and the Mississippi River to Americans who settled in the Northwest Territory is also explained in Section 1. The rest of the chapter deals with the Constitutional Convention and the development of the United States government.

History Study Skills

The History Study Skill introduced in Chapter 9 is *Studying Illustrations*. The example used is an illustration of many of the most prominent delegates at the Constitutional Convention. This skill may be used in either Section 1 or 2, although the specific leaders in the picture are discussed in Section 2.

Bibliography

Teacher References

Wood, Gordon S., *The Creation of the American Republic, 1776-1787*. Norton, New York City, 1969.
Jensen, Merrill, *The New Nation: A History of the United States During the Confederation*. New University Press, Chicago, Ill., 1950.

Student References

Cabral, Olga, *So Proudly She Sailed: Tales of Old Iron-*

sides. Houghton, Boston, Mass., 1981. This book contains narratives about the *Constitution*, or "Old Ironsides" as the ship was affectionately known, from her launching in 1797 through her many voyages.

Hilton, Suzanne, *We The People: The Way We Were 1783-1793*. Westminister Press, Philadelphia, Pa., 1981. This is a well-illustrated description of what life was like for young people in the nation's first decade.

Audio-Visual Materials

The Federal System—Checks and Balances, Associated Press/Prentice Hall Media, Inc. Color; two sound filmstrips, including Learning Activity Packet. The three branches of national government are explained. References to state and local governments are included in Part I. Part II contains a contemporary view of checks and balances.

Our Federal Government, United Learning. Five sound filmstrips, student materials, including 38 spirit masters. The five parts are the U.S. Constitution, the Presidency, the Legislative Branch, the Judicial Branch, and a System of Checks and Balances.

SECTION 1: The Government of the Confederation Is Weak

OBJECTIVES

After completing this section, students will be able to:
* State the weaknesses of the national government under the Articles of Confederation.
* Describe the foreign and domestic problems experienced by Americans living under the new government.
* Identify the successes of the national government under the Articles of Confederation.

MOTIVATION

Begin with the following statement: The War of Independence is over, the treaty is signed, and American soldiers have gone home. Therefore, in 1783, our nation had no problems. Then ask: Is this true? Students will obviously give a negative reply. Ask the class to think about a major problem faced by the people of a new nation. (How to rule themselves) Now proceed with the motivation suggested in the chapter introduction in the Teacher's Manual. You may wish to write the list of suggested problems on the chalkboard for easy reference during the subsequent discussion.

SUGGESTED ACTIVITIES

1. **Directed Reading.** Write the following questions on the chalkboard to guide students' reading of the material:
   A. Why were the years 1783 to 1787 a troubled time for the nation? List as many specific reasons as you can.
   B. Why was the government under the Articles of Confederation unable to solve the problems that arose?
   C. What was the purpose of the Northwest Ordinance?

As a summary, discuss the answers to these questions. In addition, return to the list compiled during the Motivation. Delete inaccuracies and add problems that had been omitted. Be sure to add the five "tasks" listed in Worksheet 21 to be used as the next activity.

2. **The Articles of Confederation**. Duplicate Worksheet 21 of this title. This activity builds on what students learned during the Directed Reading activity, and should be used as an immediate follow-up.

3. **Vocabulary.** In Section 1 several terms are introduced that will appear often in this chapter. Check student understanding of their meanings by having them complete this short puzzle:

confederaTion **T** - a loose union of friendship
curRency   **R** - money
natiOnal   **O** - government with authority over all the states
repUblican   **U** - government in which citizens elect officials to represent them
Barter   **B** - trade
seLf-governing **L** - each state has power to make and carry out its own laws
ratifiEd   **E** - officially accepted

BUILDING AMERICAN CITIZENSHIP

What is a major difference between the taxation policy under the Articles of Confederation and taxation policy today? (Then, only states could raise taxes. Today, taxes are collected by both the state and national governments.) What would happen if there was a return to taxation by states only? (Citizens might feel better off at first because there would be fewer taxes. However, they would soon see that the national government could do nothing without their tax money.) What changes would there be in our government today if we still had the same taxing policy? (Many—no government money for defense, education, welfare)

SECTION 1 REVIEW ANSWERS

1. **IDENTIFY: Articles of Confederation:** the plan of government approved by the 13 states in 1781, under which each state was self-governing and the power of the national government was limited; **Daniel Shays:** leader of a rebellion in Massachusetts to get citizens more power in the state government; **Land Ordinance of 1785:** a law that worked out a system for dividing up the land in the Northwest Territory; **Northwest Ordinance:** a law that stated how territories could become states.

2. **DEFINE: constitution:** a plan of government; **confederation:** a loose union of states.

3. People believed that a strong national government would destroy the rights of the 13 state governments and take away citizens' liberties.

4. The national government could not force the states to obey laws; it had no president to make decisions and coordinate activities; it could not tax people in the states and therefore could not raise money to pay the nation's debts; members of Congress were paid by and more loyal to their states than to the national government; there was little national feeling among citizens; it could not regulate trade or commerce in or between

states; it could not create a national currency because it had no money to buy gold and silver; its weakness led to confusion and riots and rebellions; foreign countries refused to make agreements with it because it had not paid its debts and was seen as being in a state of disorder.

SECTION 2: The Constitutional Convention Meets

OBJECTIVES

After completing this section, students will be able to:
• Identify important individuals who participated in the Constitutional Convention in Philadelphia in 1787.
• Explain why the delegates changed the purpose of the convention.

MOTIVATION

Review the weaknesses of the Articles of Confederation. Ask students what the states could do to eliminate these weaknesses. Elicit from them the importance of a "meeting" of the states to talk their problems out. Introduce the word "convention" and name several groups today that periodically hold conventions, such as political parties, teachers, or dentists, among others. Discuss the reasons why these groups hold conventions. Ask what some of the items for discussion would be at a convention of states in the 1780's. Also, ask what term is used to describe individuals attending such conventions (delegates).

SUGGESTED ACTIVITIES

1. **Directed Reading.** As students read, have them identify the delegates to the convention and the states they represented. When they have completed this activity, ask specific questions covering those listed: Who was the oldest delegate? The youngest? Who presided over the meetings? Who took notes at every meeting? Which state sent no delegates? What was the first thing the delegates did at the convention? Also, discuss why the delegates decided to keep their meetings closed to the public.
2. **Research Activity**. Divide your class into 12 groups. Assign each group the name of a state (omitting Rhode Island). Ask each group to research the names, age, and occupations of the delegates from their assigned state. In addition, have them determine the experience each delegate brought to the convention by completing a checklist:

Name: _____ Age at the time of convention:_____
Occupation:_____
(1) Took part in the Revolution	YES NO
(2) Served in the Continental Congress	YES NO
(3) Had been a state government official	YES NO
(4) Considered wealthy	YES NO
(5) Well educated	YES NO

From this research, you may wish to compile a profile of the 55 delegates. For example, how many merchants, lawyers, plantation owners were there? How many were in each of the "YES" categories

above? This would provide a specific description of the types of individuals who participated in the convention.

3. **History Study Skills**. Have students complete the History Study Skill activity, Studying Illustrations, on textbook page 222. You may wish to ask some additional questions about the picture:
   A. Can you identify any other delegates in the picture?
   B. Why didn't the artist paint all 55 delegates?
   C. Why would the artist paint so many of the delegates in a standing position?
4. **Studying Illustrations.** Duplicate Worksheet 22, *Shays Rebellion*. This activity will provide reinforcement and additional practice in applying the study skill. It will also allow students to review one of the major events of Section 1. Have students recall why the rebellion shocked so many Americans. Ask what the delegates to the Convention might include in a Constitution to avoid such a problem in the future.

BUILDING AMERICAN CITIZENSHIP

Although the states were experiencing problems, they showed a spirit of cooperation by sending delegates to Philadelphia to consider government reforms under the Articles. How do the 50 states today show their willingness to cooperate with one another? (Common water rights, freedom of movement between borders, turning over requested captured criminals)

SECTION 2 REVIEW ANSWERS

1. **IDENTIFY: James Madison:** an outstanding young leader in the Virginia state government who played a significant role at the Constitutional Convention in Philadelphia; **Alexander Hamilton:** a New York lawyer who, along with Madison, urged Congress to call a convention to revise the Articles of Confederation; **Constitutional Convention:** the meeting of delegates from the states held in Philadelphia in May 1787 for the purpose of reforming the national government and where the Constitution was written; **Independence Hall:** the name given to the State House in Philadelphia where the Constitutional Convention met to honor it as the birthplace of the nation.
2. **DEFINE: convention:** a meeting; **quorum:** the number that must be present at a meeting in order to conduct business.
3. Rhode Island.
4. The delegates decided that they had to do more than revise the Articles of Confederation and decided instead to write a new plan of government.

SECTION 3: The Convention Writes a New Constitution

OBJECTIVES

After completing this section, students will be able to:
• Explain the Virginia, New Jersey, and Connecticut plans for a national legislature.
• Discuss the compromises necessary to settle the differences between North and South.

- Describe Franklin's role in gaining the delegates' approval of the Constitution.

MOTIVATION

Present the following situation to students: "It is Friday evening and you are planning to visit a friend. You ask your parents if you may stay to watch a movie that ends at midnight. Your parents say you must be home at 10:00 P.M., but may watch the movie at home. How can this 'disagreement' be settled peacefully?" Students may suggest such solutions as watching half the movie with the friend and returning home at 11:00 P.M. Discuss the idea of having both sides adjust their demands, with each giving something up and each getting something in return. Introduce the term "compromise." Tell students that the delegates to the convention often found it necessary to compromise.

SUGGESTED ACTIVITIES

1. **Directed Reading**. Have students read Section 3 to determine the disagreements among the delegates that had to be settled by compromise. Tell them that they should list four of the disagreements:
   A. The question of representation of big and small states in Congress
   B. Counting slaves as part of the population
   C. The slave trade
   D. Control of foreign trade
   Then summarize by having students describe the compromises that were reached in order to settle each disagreement.
2. **Comparison**. Have students compare the Virginia Plan with the New Jersey Plan by answering the following questions:
   A. Which plan seemed to favor the small states? (N.J.)
   B. Which plan called for selection of the judiciary by Congress? (VA)
   C. Which plan stated that national authority would rank higher than state law? (N.J.)
   D. Which plan provided more representatives in Congress for the larger states? (VA)
   E. Which plan called for a one-house legislature? (N.J.)
   After reviewing the answers, have students go back over each question and tell what the *other* plan stated concerning the issue.
3. **Comprehension Check**. Determine students' grasp of the information presented in Section 3 by having them answer the following TRUE-FALSE questions:
   A. The Great Compromise settled the argument over slavery between the North and the South. (F)
   B. The delegates agreed that the slave trade would end in 1808. (T)
   C. The Virginia Plan called for a one-house legislature. (F)
   D. A compromise between large and small states resulted in slaves being counted for representation and tax purposes. (F)
   E. The delegates agreed to tax imports but not exports. (T)
4. **Landmarks of Liberty.** Have students read the selection *The Charters of Freedom*, on textbook page 192. In addition to answering the two questions at the end of the reading, ask students to describe the special care given to these documents. You might also ask students which document they think is the most important, and why.
5. **Sources of Freedom**. Students should be given their first opportunity to look at the Constitution as one of the activities for this section. Refer them to the document on textbook page 204. Depending upon the ability level of the students, you may wish to have them locate the parts of the document that describe the compromises they listed in Activity 1.

BUILDING AMERICAN CITIZENSHIP

The delegates to the Constitutional Convention settled their disputes by compromising. What do the two sides in any dispute have to be willing to do in order to reach a compromise? (Give something up) In trying to settle a dispute, how can you, as a citizen, demonstrate your respect for the rights of others? (Listen to what they have to say.)

SECTION 3 REVIEW ANSWERS

1. **IDENTIFY: William Randolph:** the delegate at the Constitutional Convention who proposed the Virginia Plan of government, giving the larger states greater representation than small states in the legislature; **William Paterson:** the delegate at the Constitutional Convention who proposed the New Jersey Plan, giving equal representation to all states in the legislature.
2. **DEFINE: legislative branch:** the branch of the federal government that makes the laws; **executive branch:** the branch of the federal government that carries out the laws; **judicial branch:** the branch of the federal government that judges the meaning of laws and the ways in which they are applied; **compromise:** an agreement in which each side in a dispute gives up part of what they want and in return gets part of what they want; **House of Representatives:** the lower house of the two-house legislature, with membership based on population; **Senate:** the upper house of the two-house legislature, with each state having equal representation; **federal republic:** a government in which the power is divided between the states and the national government.
3. The Virginia Plan based the number of representatives each state would have on population, thus giving greater power to large states; the New Jersey Plan gave equal representation to all states, thus increasing the power of the small states.
4. The Great Compromise proposed a two-house legislature, with representation in the lower house based on population, as in the Virginia Plan, and with equal representation in the upper house, as in the New Jersey Plan.

SECTION 4: The States Ratify the Constitution

OBJECTIVES

After completing this section, students will be able to:
- Identify the Federalists and the Anti-Federalists.

- Discuss arguments used by those for and by those opposed to ratification of the Constitution.

MOTIVATION

Review the following information with students:
1. Why was the Constitution written?
2. Where was it written?
3. When was it written?
4. What were the major compromises involved?

Finally, ask the question: Who had to approve the Constitution before it could go into effect? Would it be easy or difficult to gain approval? Why?

SUGGESTED ACTIVITIES

1. **Directed Reading**. Draw two columns on the chalkboard and label them as follows:

   Leaders Who Favored the Constitution/
   Leaders Who Opposed the Constitution

   As students read Section 4, have them enter, under the appropriate heading, the names of individuals whom they have encountered in earlier sections. When this assignment has been completed and checked, have students further label each column as "Federalist" or "Anti-Federalist." Discuss the reasons given by individuals for favoring or opposing ratification. Summarize by having students review their answers to the last question under Motivation.
2. **Sequencing**. Present students with a list of the 13 states in random order, along with the date of ratification. Then have them arrange the states in the order in which ratification occurred:

   Maryland—April 26, 1788
   North Carolina—November 21, 1789
   Virginia—June 25, 1788
   Delaware—December 7, 1787
   Massachusetts—February 6, 1788
   New Hampshire—June 21, 1788
   New York—July 26, 1788
   Connecticut—January 9, 1785
   Georgia—January 2, 1788
   New Jersey—December 18, 1787
   Pennsylvania—December 12, 1787
   Rhode Island—May 29, 1790
   South Carolina—May 23, 1788
3. **Round Robin**. Use this method, as introduced in Chapter 1: Have a student volunteer state a fact from Section 2. Have a second volunteer repeat the fact, and state another. Have a third student volunteer repeat the fact stated by the second, and state another. Continue this activity, as time and resources allow.

BUILDING AMERICAN CITIZENSHIP

During the 1780's there were few means available to citizens who were trying to persuade others that their point of view was the correct one. How did citizens convey their ideas to others at that time? (Newspaper articles, handbills, speeches, meetings) How do citizens today try to persuade others to support their point of view? (television, radio, speeches, newspapers, bumper stickers, buttons, posters)

SECTION 4 REVIEW ANSWERS

1. **IDENTIFY: *The Federalist Papers:*** a series of articles written by Madison, Jay, and Hamilton supporting ratification of the Constitution; **Amos Singletary:** Massachusetts delegate who spoke for farmers opposed to ratification of the Constitution; **Jonathan Smith:** Massachusetts delegate who spoke for farmers in favor of ratification of the Constitution.
2. **DEFINE: Federalists:** those who backed the Constitution because they wanted a strong federal government; **Anti-Federalists:** those who were against the Constitution.
3. Nine.
4. They were opposed to the loss of rights of state governments and feared that citizens would lose civil rights and liberties.

SECTION 5: The Constitution Is Our Plan of Government

OBJECTIVES

After completing this section, students will be able to:
- Explain the responsibility of government as stated in the Constitution's Preamble.
- Identify the three branches of government and the function of each.
- Give examples of the system of checks and balances.
- Explain the process for amending the Constitution.

MOTIVATION

Have students look at the copy of the Constitution on textbook pages 204-221. Ask the following questions:
1. What are the parts into which the Constitution is divided? (Articles, sections, paragraphs)
2. How many articles are there? (7)
3. Skim the beginning of Article I. With which branch does it deal? (Legislative) Article II? (Executive) Article III? (Judicial)
4. Which of the remaining articles deals with ratification? (VII)
5. What are "amendments"? (Use Glossary to define)

Explain to students that they have just received a brief overview of the document's organization. Also, tell them that today's lesson will explain some of the important parts of the Constitution, and that they will be referring to it again after they have read Section 5.

SUGGESTED ACTIVITIES

1. **Directed Reading.** As students read Section 5, have them answer these questions:
   A. How does the Constitution divide power between the national government and the state governments?
   B. What is the function of each of the three branches of government?
   C. What guarantees of civil liberties does the Constitution contain?

   As you discuss the answers to these questions, have students use the terms included in the Chapter Review on textbook page 223. For example, the answer to the first question alone should incorporate the use of the term "concurrent powers."

2. **Using Documents**. Duplicate Worksheet 23, *The Constitution*. This activity will increase student familiarity with the document itself. In addition, it will aid student understanding of the three branches of government. For average and above-average students, you may wish to add questions on sections 4 through 7 of Article I.

3. **Which Branch Does This?** Duplicate Worksheet 24, of this title. When students have completed this activity, have them prepare an outline. The title would be *Branches of Government*. The main topics are the names of the three branches and the subtopics the items on the worksheet. This outline will provide a better study guide for students to keep in their notebooks.

BUILDING AMERICAN CITIZENSHIP

Study the Bill of Rights carefully. Which of these rights is most important to you as an adolescent citizen? (Answers will vary.) How would you be treated differently if the Bill of Rights did not exist? (Answers will vary.) Which of these rights will not apply to you until you are an adult citizen? (Right to bear arms)

SECTION 5 REVIEW ANSWERS

1. **IDENTIFY: Bill of Rights:** the first Ten Amendments to the Constitution.
2. **DEFINE: federalism:** the theory of government in which power is divided between the national government and state governments and in which the states have powers not specifically denied to them or given to the national government; **concurrent powers:** powers that are shared by both the national and state governments, such as raising taxes and chartering banks; **checks and balances:** the system provided by the Constitution to prevent any branch of government from getting too much power; **judicial review:** in cases brought before it, the Supreme Court's power to overrule a law passed by Congress and signed by the President that goes against the Constitution; **civil liberties:** the rights that people have as citizens of the nation; **amend:** to change; **elastic clause:** a special clause in the Constitution allowing Congress to pass laws and use powers not mentioned in the Constitution.
3. Freedom of speech and press, of assembly, and of petition; equal treatment under the law for all citizens; right to a fair trial; protection from cruel punishments; protection of life and property.
4. By a two-thirds vote of Congress or by a national convention when two-thirds of the states request a convention for that purpose. To ratify an amendment, three-fourths of the state governments, or at a special convention three-fourths of the states, must approve it.

CHAPTER 9 REVIEW ANSWERS
REVIEWING KEY WORDS

1. c.   2. b.   3. b.   4. a.   5. c.

REMEMBERING IMPORTANT PEOPLE AND EVENTS

1. b.	2. e.	3. c.	4. a.	5. d.
6. c.	7. e.	8. b.	9. d.	10. a.

REVIEWING THE FACTS

1. T   2. T   3. F   4. F   5. T

PLACING EVENTS IN TIME

1. b.   2. a.   3. b.   4. a.   5. b.

LINKING GEOGRAPHY AND HISTORY

1. **Size:** The large states wanted representation according to population; the small states wanted equal representation for all states. **Location:** The Southern states wanted slaves counted as part of the population, a continuation of the slave trade, and no taxes placed on the agricultural goods they exported.

THINKING ABOUT AMERICAN HISTORY

1. The Constitution tied the nation more closely together by increasing the power of the national government. It eliminated the confusion that existed under the Articles of Confederation when each state could make its own laws.
2. The Constitution can be changed or amended to meet changing conditions and problems. The elastic clause gives it additional flexibility.

APPLYING HISTORY STUDIES SKILLS

1. The caption tells what the picture is about — continental currency.
2. The section in which it is found is on the weaknesses of the national government under the Articles of Confederation. A major weakness of the government was its lack of power to create a national currency. The chapter is on the national government under the Articles of Confederation.

UNIT 3 REVIEW ANSWERS
VOCABULARY REVIEW

Answers will vary.

REVIEWING THE MAIN IDEAS

1. Both the French and the British claimed land in the Ohio Valley. They fought over this land and ownership of an empire in the Ohio Valley.
2. The colonists felt that the laws of Parliament and the tyranny of the king were no longer acceptable.
3. George Washington, Benjamin Franklin, Thomas Jefferson, Benedict Arnold, Nathanael Greene, Ethan Allan, Nathan Hale, John Paul Jones.
4. A. Women took part in the protests against unfair British laws, made clothing for the army, served as "Molly Pitchers" and nurses, ran family businesses, served as spies.
   B. Some black slaves fought for the British in exchange for their freedom; over 5,000 blacks fought in the Patriot army; after the war some states and slave owners freed black verterans.

C. Many Loyalists lost their homes and property; some were imprisoned; many moved to Canada, Great Britain, or the West Indies.

5. After five days of discussion, the delegates decided that they had to do more than revise the Articles of Confederation because it was no longer an adequate plan of government.

6. The language of the Constitution is not so specific that change is prevented. It is given even greater flexibility by the "elastic clause," which allows Congress to pass laws and use powers not specifically written into the Constitution.

APPLYING YOUR STUDY SKILLS

1. **Using a Time Line**
   a. 25 years
2. **Using Your Textbook**
   a. Delaware, New Jersey, Georgia, Pennsylvania, Connecticut, Massachusetts, Maryland, South Carolina, New Hampshire, Virginia, New York, North Carolina, Rhode Island
   (1) Delaware (2) Rhode Island (3) New Hampshire

3. **Using a Map**

   (1) False   (2) True   (3) False   (4) False   (5) True

4. **Completing an Outline**
   Major Battles of the American Revolution

   I. Battles in the Northern States
      A. Lexington
      B. Concord
      C. Boston
      D. Saratoga

   II. Battles in the Southern States
      A. Charleston
      B. Cowpens
      C. Yorktown

   III. Battles in the Middle States
      A. Fort Ticonderoga
      B. New York City
      C. Trenton
      D. Princeton
      E. Brandywine

   IV. Battles in the West
      A. Kaskaskia
      B. Cahokia
      C. Vincennes

PROJECTS

Answers will vary.

BUILDING AMERICAN CITIZENSHIP

1. Answers will vary.
2. a. By speaking or writing letters to delegates; by writing newspaper or magazine articles.
   b. By telephone, telegraph, or letters to local and national leaders and to newspapers; joining citizen-action or political groups.

UNIT **4** (1789-1828)

Americans Build a Nation

Introducing the Unit

Unit Four surveys the dramatic first four decades of the new American nation, the period from 1789 to 1828. It begins with the inauguration, in April 1789, of George Washington as first President of the United States. For the next 40 years, the United States would embark on a course of increasing strength and purposefulness. The American nation would be forged from a weak, loose confederacy of 13 states to a united country ready to challenge European activities in the Western Hemisphere.

The Unit's first chapter describes key events of the Washington and Adams administrations. Under their leadership, the new government began to work. The Bill of Rights was passed in 1789, a few months after the inauguration of Washington who, as the first President, helped better define and shape the executive branch of government. Both Washington and Adams were confronted with many problems—domestic, including the Whiskey Rebellion in 1794 and foreign, including the French bribery scandal of 1798, known as the XYZ Affair.

Chapter 11 describes the peaceful change of government from Federalist to Republican control, that is, from President Adams to President Jefferson, in 1801, and the remarkable progress in the period that followed. This included success with quelling the troublesome Barbary pirates; the purchase in 1803 of the Louisiana Territory, a vast area that doubled the size of the United States; victory over Great Britain in the War of 1812; and notice, in 1823, to European nations that the Western Hemisphere was closed to further colonization. The most striking political development of the time was the elevation, under Chief Justice John Marshall, of the Judiciary to a footing almost equal to that of the Executive and Legislative branches.

In Chapter 12, the evolution of a distinctly American way of life is examined. The frontier experience had been and continued to be a key influence in the development of American traditions. Settlers poured into the trans-Appalachian West, and, by 1820, the number of states had risen from 13 to 24. Nine of these states were in this frontier region. In the South cotton became "king," while in the North, manufacturing took hold. Already the seeds were sown for that sectional split which finally occurred in 1860. The unit closes in 1828 with the United States a strong and firmly established nation.

The Unit Opener in the textbook depicts many of the significant persons and events of the period. You may wish to use these illustrations to help introduce the unit to the class. The two central figures are Thomas Jefferson on the left and Zebulon Pike on the right. Beginning in the lower left-hand corner and moving in a clockwise direction are the Barbary pirates; the Liberty Bell; Slater's Mill; Dolley Madison; and the American flag.

Another major feature in this and several other units in the textbook is a photo essay, *What Life Was Like*. It is designed to evoke the quality and flavor of daily life in different types of American communities at various times in the nation's history. In Unit Four, the photo essay illustrates what life was like for pioneer families on the frontier from the late 1700's to the early 1800's.

Unit Themes and Ideas

Unit Four deals with two major themes. The first traces the evolution of our national government from an untested set of ideas in 1789 to a well organized, smoothly functioning structure capable of solving important problems. At first this process was carried on largely in the executive and legislative branches of government. By 1801, however, under John Marshall, the judicial branch began to play an increasingly powerful and important role in government. The American government wrestled with financial problems and with crises in foreign relations. Washington's Farewell Address in 1796 is reflected in the Monroe Doctrine of 1823. The United States walked a tightrope in trying to maintain a strong and independent position and simultaneously avoid war.

The second major theme of this unit is that of territorial expansion and westward movement. With the Louisiana Purchase in 1803, Jefferson doubled the size of the United States. Pioneers continued to stream across the Appalachians in large numbers to settle in the West. Expansion and migration led to clashes with Indians and the demand for internal improvements. The Northeast turned to manufacturing to fill the needs of frontier settlers in both the Old Northwest and the burgeoning cotton lands of the South. The nation was beginning to see the development of distinct sections within its borders.

The themes and ideas of Unit Four are organized into the three chapters below:

Chapter 10 - *The Federalists Build a Strong Government (1789-1801)*
Chapter 11 - *The Nation Moves Ahead (1801-1824)*
Chapter 12 - *Different Sections Develop in America (1789-1828)*

CHAPTER 10

The Federalists Build a Strong Government (1789-1801)

Chapter Objectives

After completing this chapter, students will be able to:
1. Describe how the legislative and executive branches of the national government began to function.

2. Identify important national problems that were dealt with and solved during Washington's administration.
3. Explain how the United States developed a foreign policy.
4. Describe the differing viewpoints of the Federalists and Republicans in 1800.

Chapter Chronology

Chapter 10 covers the first dozen or so years of American history following the ratification of the Constitution and the inauguration of the nation's first President, George Washington. Many of the important persons and events of the period are highlighted on the time line on the textbook Chapter Opener page. The decade of the 1790's began with the passage of Hamilton's Funding Bill in 1790. The following year, the Bank of the United States opened its doors. In 1791, also, the Bill of Rights was ratified. In foreign affairs, Jay's Treaty with the British was ratified in 1795. In 1796, John Adams became the second American President. In his administration the Department of the Navy was formed in 1798. Two years later, in 1800, Thomas Jefferson was elected President.

Motivation

To help students gain an understanding of the people and events of this time period, lead them through a quick preview of the portraits of political leaders in Chapter 10. They will be familiar with some of these men, including Jefferson, Hamilton, and Adams. As students look at their pictures, ask them to summarize what they already know about these men and to theorize about what their roles might be in the new government. Suggest that some might have held several government positions in their lifetimes. Ask if students know anything about Jay or Burr? Do not try to answer student questions at this time. Instead write them down for consideration and discussion as they work through the chapter.

Geographical Setting

The political questions addressed in Chapter 10 overshadowed the geographical setting. Most of the "action" in this period took place in our nation's capitals—first New York City, then Philadelphia, and finally Washington, D.C. Conflicts with the British over their forts in the Ohio Valley and Great Lakes regions as well as Spanish control over the Mississippi River served as constant reminders of foreign threats to American independence. Be sure to stress the importance of the Ohio and Mississippi Rivers to American economic development. Abroad, a prolonged war between Britain and France threatened to entangle the new American nation. Three new states joined the union at this time—Vermont, Kentucky, and Tennessee.

History Study Skills

The History Study Skill introduced in Chapter 10 is *Improving Your History Writing.* Students are taught how to plan and write a brief report. This skill may be taught at any time during the chapter.

Bibliography

Teacher References
Miller, John C., *The Federalist Era, 1789-1801.* Harper, New York City, 1960.
Shepherd, Jack, *The Adams Chronicles: Four Generations of Greatness.* Little, Brown, Boston, Mass., 1975.
Student References
Freidel, Frank, *Our Country's Presidents.* National Geographic, Washington, D.C., 1969. This is a well-illustrated collection of biographies of American Presidents.
Fencher, E. B., *The American Legal System.* Franklin Watts, New York City, 1980. The book describes the legal processes through the experiences of two teenagers—one on trial as a juvenile, the other as an adult.

Audio-Visual Materials

Benjamin Banneker: Man of Science, Encyclopedia Britannica, color, 9 minutes. Shows some of Banneker's achievements in math, science, and planning Washington, D.C.
A New Nation: The Struggle to Survive 1789-1850. Benchmark Films, color, 26 minutes. This film provides an excellent overview of the period, delineating the social, economic, and political uncertainties that faced our new nation.

SECTION 1: Federalists Organize the National Government

OBJECTIVES

After completing this section, students will be able to:
- Name and explain laws passed by Congress in its first session.
- Name the executive departments created by Congress and describe the function of each.
- List the precedents established during Washington's Presidency.
- Explain the results of the first census.

MOTIVATION

Have students read the Chapter Introduction on textbook page 229. Discuss the differences and similarities between Washington's inauguration and that of more recent Presidents. For example, they took the same oath of office and gave inaugural addresses. However, Washington's inaugural was viewed by a small group, whereas recent ones were telecast around the world and seen by countless millions.

Pay careful attention to the questions in the last paragraph. Have students use context clues to match the questions with the sections in which they will be answered. Emphasize the question for Section 1: How did the Federalists shape and organize the national government?

SUGGESTED ACTIVITIES

1. **Directed Reading.** Ask students to write two col-

umns on their paper, as in A. and B. below. Instruct them to jot down specific accomplishments of the first Congress and the first President under the appropriate column.

A. Actions Taken to Organize the Government
1) passage of Bill of Rights
2) passage of Judiciary Act of 1789 to set up a federal court system
3) the taking of a census

B. Actions Taken to Shape the Government
1) establishment of a Cabinet
2) President's right of dismissal of appointed officials without Senate approval
3) establishment of right of "executive privilege"

After the work has been completed and checked, have students close notebooks. Ask them to identify the word used in the book for actions taken to shape the government. (Precedents) Read several of the statements on the lists at random and have students identify them as organizational acts or precedents.

2. **Building Citizenship Skills.** Duplicate Worksheet 25, *The Bill of Rights.* Review the directions carefully before having students complete the activity. As an extension, review with students the process by which the Bill of Rights became part of the Constitution.

3. **Create A Puzzle.** Ask students to create an acrostic or crossword puzzle using the chapter vocabulary, the names of executive departments, and the laws passed by Congress. Have them include clues. Students may be paired off for an exchange of puzzles, or the work of one class may be collected and distributed to another. This activity will provide a review of the factual content of the chapter.

4. **Comprehension Check: The First Census.** Have students answer TRUE or FALSE to each of the following statements.
A. The 1790 Census revealed that nearly 4 million people lived in the United States. (T)
B. According to the 1790 Census, the United States was a rural nation. (T)
C. In 1789, the largest city in the United States was New York. (F)
D. In 1790, the slave population made up 40 percent of the population. (F)
E. In 1790, most families were large. (T)

BUILDING AMERICAN CITIZENSHIP

The Judiciary Act of 1789 set up a federal court system. Why is this system important to American citizens? (Courts make certain that laws are applied equally in each state.) How would life for American citizens be different if we had no such court system? (Answers will vary)

SECTION 1 REVIEW ANSWERS

1. **IDENTIFY: Alexander Hamilton:** the first Secretary of the Treasury; **John Jay:** the first Chief Justice of the Supreme Court.

2. **DEFINE: jurisdiction:** authority to interpret and apply the law; **appeal:** request that a case be heard again in the hopes that the lower court's decision will be overturned; **judicial review:** power of the Supreme Court to set aside laws that go against the Constitution; **precedents:** unwritten laws or customs developed over the years and used as examples for actions in the future; **President's Cabinet:** heads of the executive departments that meet with and advise the President on important matters; **"executive privilege":** a precedent established by President Washington, giving the Chief Executive the right to keep certain documents secret in the best interests of the nation; **census:** population count.

3. The Department of the Treasury: for managing financial affairs of the government; State Department: for handling the nation's relations with foreign governments; War Department: for directing the nation's military affairs.

4. President's Cabinet; presidential power to dismiss appointed officials; "executive privilege."

SECTION 2: The Federalists Solve National Problems

OBJECTIVES

After completing this section, students will be able to:
- Explain why the national government was in debt.
- List the methods used to raise money to pay the national debt.
- Describe the functions of the Bank of the United States.
- State the causes and effects of the Whiskey Rebellion.

MOTIVATION

Discuss these questions with students:
1. How do people get out of debt?
2. What means can people use to get out of debt?
3. How do governments get into debt?
4. What means can a government use to get out of debt?

SUGGESTED ACTIVITIES

1. **Directed Reading.** Use the following to guide students' reading of Section 1:
A. Why was the national government in debt?
B. How did the national government get out of debt?
C. Why did the farmers of Pennsylvania complain about the methods used to get out of debt?
Discuss the answers to these questions with the class.

In addition, have students consider the role of Alexander Hamilton in the events discussed in this chapter. Why did the President and Congress have so much confidence in him? What were his major accomplishments as Secretary of the Treasury?

2. **Biographical Study.** The life of Alexander Hamilton both before and after he served as Secretary of the Treasury should be of interest to students. You may wish to assign several students or the entire class to prepare reports about his life, using library sources. You may wish to offer the guide questions below:
A. Where was Hamilton born, and when?
B. What is known about his early life?

C. What was his role during the American Revolution?
D. What contributions did he make to the new government?
E. When and how did he die?

3. **Ideals In the Lives of Americans.** The story of Benjamin Banneker's life is directly related to the information in Section 2. Have students read this selection on textbook page 233, and discuss the answers to the two questions at the end. Ask students to describe the relationship between this story and what they learned about the conflict of the location of the nation's capital in Section 2. (Jefferson and Hamilton compromised over the location of the capital. Jefferson's plan to have it located between Maryland and Virginia was approved.)

4. **Time line.** Have students look at the time line on the textbook Chapter Opener page. Ask them which of the events described in Chapter 10, Section 2, are found on the line. (Bank of the United States opens) Ask them to name at least two other events that could have been placed on the line. (Paying of the foreign debt—1796; Funding Bill—1790; Whiskey Rebellion — 1794)

BUILDING AMERICAN CITIZENSHIP

Do you agree with President Washington's decision to send American troops against American citizens during the Whiskey Rebellion? (Answers will vary.) Can you think of any situation today in which American troops might be asked to stand against American citizens? (To assist police in controlling riots that threaten the safety of other Americans; to help enforce, if necessary, Court decisions, such as desegregation of schools)

SECTION 2 REVIEW ANSWERS

1. **IDENTIFY: Assumption Act:** law passed by Congress that gave the federal government responsibility for the debts of state governments, mostly incurred during the American Revolution; **national bank:** the Bank of the United States established by Hamilton, with a central or a main office and branch banks in large cities; **Whiskey Rebellion:** rebellion by a group of Pennsylvania farmers who refused to pay the federal tax on whiskey.

2. **DEFINE: national debt:** money the government owes to American citizens and to foreign governments; **tariff:** a tax on imports; **excise taxes:** fees on the manufacture, sale, or consumption of certain products, such as whiskey or sugar.

3. By taxes, sale of federal lands, and loans from private citizens.

4. Because Hamilton agreed to support Jefferson's plan to locate the nation's capital in the South.

SECTION 3: Other Nations Challenge America

OBJECTIVES

After completing this section, students will be able to:
• Describe the problems the United States had in dealing with other nations.

• Explain the methods used by the United States to try to solve its problems with other nations.
• State the main ideas of Washington's Farewell Address.

MOTIVATION

Use a chalkmap or outline map of the world to locate Spain, France, and England. Have students recall the last time the U.S. dealt with each nation. EXAMPLE: France helped the United States during the American Revolution. Ask students how they think each of these nations might regard and treat the new United States. They should be able to recall some pertinent information from what they read in Chapter 9, Section 1. Have them look at the title of Section 3, and define the term "challenge." Explain that the goal of today's lesson is to describe how America was challenged and to explain how it dealt with this.

SUGGESTED ACTIVITIES

1. **Directed Reading.** Before the reading begins, place the following chart on the chalkboard, and have students copy it. Ask them to supply the information as they read.

AMERICA IS CHALLENGED BY OTHER NATIONS		
NATION	PROBLEM(S)	PROPOSED SOLUTION

Students should complete the chart for England, France, Spain, and the Barbary Coast nations.

2. **History Study Skills.** Have students complete the History Study Skill activity on textbook page 247. Use it at this point, because the paragraph that is examined here is taken from Section 3. You may wish to give students a choice of topics for their paragraph. For example, they may write about Problems at Home or Problems with Other Nations.

3. **Reading for the Main Idea.** Have students read the information under the heading "Washington Says Farewell to the Nation." Have them select the main ideas of Washington's speech. These would include:
A. Americans should be proud of their nation.
B. Opposing political groups could threaten the structure of the Union.
C. The United States should remain neutral in foreign affairs.
   You may wish to have above-average students research the original text of the speech to identify main ideas that were not included in the textbook. You may also ask students to discuss what they think about these points for the United States today.

4. **Improving Your History Writing.** Duplicate Worksheet 26, *The Barbary Pirates.* If students completed activity 2 in class, this activity should be utilized as a homework assignment in which they are required to practice this skill independently.

5. **Sources of Freedom.** The last few paragraphs of Section 3 give a general idea of the contents of Washington's Farewell Address. Allow students to examine Washington's actual words by reading the document on textbook page 239.

BUILDING AMERICAN CITIZENSHIP

In his Farewell Address, Washington told citizens that their main duty was "guarding and preserving the Union of the whole." What do you think he meant by this? (Keeping the nation together.) How can citizens of the United States work to preserve the "Union of the whole" today? (Work to solve problems between citizens of different states; welcome those from other regions or states that move into your area; think and act as Americans rather than as a citizen from a particular state)

SECTION 3 REVIEW ANSWERS

1. **IDENTIFY: Jay's Treaty:** agreement with Great Britain ending British restrictions on American trade; **Thomas Pinckney:** American envoy who negotiated a treaty with Spain.
2. **DEFINE: tribute:** money paid to the Barbary states to protect American trading ships and sailors from Barbary pirates in the Mediterranean; **revenue:** income; **neutral:** not taking sides in a conflict; **impressed:** kidnapped.
3. The United States was not prepared for and might be seriously damaged by a war; the French-American treaty was made with the French monarchy, not the new republic; a war with Britain would cut off trade, which was a valuable source of money for the American government.
4. Jay's Treaty didn't end problems of British interference with American shipping or impressment of sailors.

SECTION 4: Federalists Clash with Republicans

OBJECTIVES

After completing this section, students will be able to:
- Name the first two political parties and the leaders of each.
- Describe the differences that developed between the two parties.
- Explain the difficulties that John Adams faced as President.

MOTIVATION

Have students name two major American political parties today. Ask them why people choose to join one party or the other. (To support the principles and ideas for which the party stands) Ask students what the purposes of a political party are. (To influence government decisions, to get its leaders elected) If students are unable to answer the questions, write them on the board, for discussion after students have read Section 4. Tell them that today's lesson explains the origin of political parties. It also describes the differences between the nation's first two parties.

SUGGESTED ACTIVITIES

1. **Directed Reading.** Have students skim the first page of Section 4 to find the names of the first two political parties and their leaders. Write them on the board and have students write them in their notebooks. As students read, have them note down the differences between the parties. You may wish to help them with the first example to be sure they are following directions correctly.

FEDERALISTS—HAMILTON
1. Loose construction
2. Supported Great Britain
3. Favored interests of factories and cities

REPUBLICANS—JEFFERSON
1. Strict construction
2. Supported France
3. Favored interests of farmers and workers

To encourage students to think critically about what they have read, ask them to compare today's political parties with those formed in the 1790's. Which party of today is similar to the Federalists? Which is similar to the Republicans? Have students give reasons for their answers.

2. **Tables.** Place the following table on the chalkboard or on an overhead projector. It is merely a different method of organizing the notes taken by students in the previous activity and should provide an opportunity to test their understanding of that information.

	FEDERALISTS	REPUBLICANS
Leaders		
Sections of the U.S. in which the party was strong		
View of powers of the central government		
View of interpretation of the Constitution		
Beliefs about the future of the U.S.		
Major points of foreign policy		

3. **Flash Cards.** The Section Review contains six names to be identified and seven terms to be defined. Since this may be an excessive number for students to comprehend easily, prepare two separate sets of flash cards. The first set should contain cards with the names and cards with sentences identifying each name. The second set should contain cards with the terms and cards with the definition of those terms. Divide the class into two groups. Distribute the first set to the first group and the second to the second group. Have them match the cards in each set. Then collect and redistribute, with the first set going to the second group and vice versa. Get as many students as possible involved.

BUILDING AMERICAN CITIZENSHIP

Do you think that political parties help to keep the nation together or divide it? Why? What can citizens do if they disagree with the beliefs of both political parties? (Answers will vary. However, the idea of registering as an "Independent" or joining a third party should be brought out.)

SECTION 4 REVIEW ANSWERS

1. **IDENTIFY: Federalists:** political party that supported a strong national government and loose construction of the Constitution; **Republicans:** political party that supported states' rights and strict construction of the Constitution; **John Adams:** second President of the United States; **Alien Acts:** laws designed to "protect" American citizens from foreigners; **Sedition Act:** law making it a crime to criticize the President, members of Congress, or the federal government; **Virginia and Kentucky Resolutions:** statements saying that the Alien and Sedition Acts had no legal force in those states and setting forth the theory of states' rights.

2. **DEFINE: political party:** a group of people with similar ideas and beliefs about the government and how it should be run; **loose construction:** interpretation of the Constitution based on meaning, leaving open the possibility of powers not specifically stated; **strict construction:** interpretation of the Constitution limiting the powers of government to those specifically stated in the Constitution and no more; **caucuses:** secret political meetings; **deport:** to force to leave or send out of the country; **sedition:** to act or speak against the government in order to cause unrest or rebellion; **state's rights theory:** the theory that each state has the right to determine whether the federal government has gone beyond its constitutional powers and can decide whether or not to obey federal laws.

3. Hamilton was leader of the Federalists; Jefferson and Madison were leaders of the Republicans.

4. Federalists generally represented wealthy bankers, manufacturers, and business owners in cities in the Northeast; they supported a strong national government, loose construction of the Constitution, and the growth of business and industry. Republicans favored the interests of small farmers, craftworkers, and shopkeepers, and drew most of their support from the South; they believed in the ability of ordinary people to govern themselves and supported states' rights, strict construction of the Constitution, and called for a system of public education to help people defend their rights.

SECTION 5: Republicans Replace the Federalists in Power

OBJECTIVES

After completing this section, students will be able to:
- Describe the events involved in the unusual election of 1800.
- Explain why the Federalist Party declined.

MOTIVATION

Discuss procedures used in the presidential elections. Who elects a President? The most obvious response is "the people." That is wrong! Refer students to Article II, Section 1, of the Constitution, and the Twelfth Amendment. Be sure they understand the electoral system before proceeding. Finally, ask them why they think the Twelfth Amendment was added to the Constitution. If they do not know, jot the question on the board to be discussed after they have read Section 5.

SUGGESTED ACTIVITIES

1. **Directed Reading.** As students read Section 5, have them answer the following guide questions:
   A. Why did John Adams lose the election of 1800? (Lost Hamilton's support; Federalists were anti-French, but most Americans and Republicans now favored France)
   B. What made the election of 1800 so unusual? (Tie electoral vote for President; failure of the House to elect a President after 30 ballots; Hamilton's support of Jefferson)
   C. What had the Federalists contributed to the development of the American nation before losing power? (Helped organize a government; paid the nation's debt; started a national bank; won the respect of other nations)
   Be sure to return to the final question posed during the motivation. Students should be able to state clearly why the Twelfth Amendment had been passed.

2. **Biographical Study.** Aaron Burr was and has remained a controversial historical figure. As stated in Section 5, both Hamilton and Jefferson mistrusted him. What were the reasons for this mistrust? You may wish to assign several students, or the entire class, to use library sources to prepare reports about his life. (The pattern would be similar to that used for Hamilton in Section 2.) Provide students with the following guide questions:
   A. Where and when was Burr born?
   B. What is known about his early life?
   C. How did he contribute to the American cause during the Revolutionary War?
   D. Why was he mistrusted by Hamilton and Jefferson?
   E. What happened after his defeat in the presidential contest of 1800?
   F. When and how did he die?
   You may wish to assign one question to each student, so that at least 6 reports would have to be heard before the entire story is known.

3. **The Election of 1800.** Duplicate Worksheet 27 of this title. Before having the students complete the Worksheet, familiarize them with the map by asking a few simple questions:
   A. How can you tell the difference between the states that voted for Adams and those that voted for Jefferson?
   B. Name two states that voted for Adams.
   C. Name two states that voted for Jefferson.
   D. What was the southernmost state that voted for Hamilton?
   E. What was the nothernmost state that voted for Jefferson?

BUILDING AMERICAN CITIZENSHIP

Do you understand the role of the average citizen in presidential elections? If so, answer this question: If electors actually elect the President and Vice-President, why should citizens vote in presidential elections? (The votes of citizens determine which party's electors will be voting.)

SECTION 5 REVIEW ANSWERS

1. **IDENTIFY: Aaron Burr:** Republican candidate for Vice-President in the election of 1800; **John Marshall:** appointed Chief Justice of the Supreme Court by President Adams.
2. Because of a flaw in the election rules and the resulting confusion in the election of 1800. The amendment calls for electors to vote separately for the President and the Vice-President.
3. It lost touch with the people and their needs.

CHAPTER 10 REVIEW ANSWERS

REVIEWING KEY WORDS

1. i.	2. d.	3. h.	4. e.	5. f.
6. a.	7. c.	8. b.	9. g.	10. j.

REMEMBERING IMPORTANT PEOPLE AND EVENTS

1. c.	2. a.	3. c.	4. b.	5. b.

REVIEWING THE FACTS

1. c.	2. e.	3. b.	4. d.	5. a.

PLACING EVENTS IN TIME

A. 3	B. 2	C. 1	D. 5	E. 4

LINKING GEOGRAPHY AND HISTORY

1. The Republicans favored the interests of farmers and workers. Many farmers and landowners lived in the South. The Federalists represented the interest of bankers, manufacturers, and business owners. Many of these people lived in the Northeast.
2. Americans needed the river to ship their goods to market, and they needed the port of New Orleans as a center for trade.

THINKING ABOUT AMERICAN HISTORY

1. Under Hamilton's management, the United States was able to pay its foreign debts, thus establishing a good credit rating and respect of the world's nations as well as increased confidence of American citizens in their government. Hamilton also created a national banking system, giving the nation a uniform, dependable money supply and encouraging trade among the states.
2. There was a tie vote between Jefferson and Burr, leaving the outcome unclear as to which one had won the Presidency. In accordance with the Constitution, the contest had to be decided by the House of Representatives.

APPLYING HISTORY STUDIES SKILLS

1. Detail or facts support the main idea.
2. The topic sentence introduces the main idea.
3. The concluding sentence sums up what the paragraph is saying.
4. The Twelfth Amendment was passed to avoid tie votes in the electorial college for the candidates for President and Vice-President. The Twelfth Amendment requires electors to vote separately for each.

CHAPTER 11

The Nation Moves Ahead (1801-1824)

Chapter Objectives

After completing this chapter, students will be able to:
1. Explain how the decisions of Chief Justice John Marshall increased the importance of the judicial branch of government.
2. Identify territory added to the United States during this period.
3. Describe the events that led the United States to war with Great Britain.
4. Define and give examples of the American spirit of nationalism that emerged after the War of 1812.
5. Compare the Monroe Doctrine with Washington's Farewell Address.

Chapter Chronology

Chapter 11 surveys the period from the early 1800's to the 1820's. It begins with Jefferson's first administration and ends with his death in 1825. Many of the major persons and events of the period are highlighted on the time line on the textbook Chapter Opener page. The purchase, by Jefferson, of the Louisiana Territory in 1803 doubled the size of the United States. He then sent Meriwether Lewis and William Clark to explore it in 1804. A new President, James Madison, was elected in 1808. He was reelected in 1812, the year Congress declared war on Great Britain. That conflict, the War of 1812, ended two years later with the signing of the Treaty of Ghent. At the next presidential election in 1816, James Monroe was elected. Under his administration, the United States purchased Florida in 1819. In 1823, he issued the Monroe Doctrine, which warned European nations to stay out of the political affairs of the Western Hemisphere.

Motivation

To prepare students for the main ideas in Chapter 11, have them look carefully at each of the maps in it. As they look at each map, ask: (1) What is its subject? (2) What is happening in it? (3) How might the President of the United States have been involved with these events? Do not try to answer student questions at this time. Instead write them down for consideration as students work through the chapter.

Geographical Setting

Chapter 11 is an excellent point at which to emphasize place geography and map skills. The map *The Barbary War, 1803-1815*, illustrates the steps by which America finally ended the tyranny of the Barbary pirates over its ships. the territorial expansion of the United States during this period is shown in the maps, *The Louisiana Purchase and Western Exploration 1803-1806*, and *The United States Gains Florida, 1810-1819*. Newly independent Latin American countries are depicted in the map *Independence in Latin America, 1825*. These maps are excellent resources to review map-reading skills.

The *War of 1812* map is a good introduction to the History Study Skill emphasized in Chapter 18, *Using Military Maps.*

History Study Skills

The History Study Skill introduced in Chapter 11 is *Using Circle Graphs.* Emphasis is on the Elections of 1800 and 1804. This skill should be used at the end of Section 1 in order to reinforce the information in the text on the Election of 1804. Students might be encouraged to look through newspapers and magazines for examples of circle graphs. An extension of the circle graph skill is found in Worksheet 28 that accompanies this chapter. The students learn to make their own circle graphs using data on the elections of 1812 and 1816.

Bibliography

Teacher References
Smelser, Marshall, *The Democratic Republic, 1801-1815.* Harper, New York City, 1968.
Malone, Dumas, *Jefferson and His Time,* (5 volumes). Little, Brown, Boston, Mass., 1948-1981.

Student References
Jassem, Kate, *Sacajawea: Wilderness Guide.* Troll Associates, Mahwah, N.J., 1979. This is a readable, well-illustrated biography of the Indian woman who served as a guide for Lewis and Clark.
Phelen, Mary Kay, *The Story of the Louisiana Purchase.* Harper, New York City, 1979. The book vividly describes the Louisiana Purchase.

Audio-Visual Materials

The Mountain Men, BFA, 15 minutes, color. The Lewis and Clark expedition is shown here and the Mountain Men who followed to pave the way for settlers.
Thomas Jefferson: Architect of Liberty, Guidance Associates. Two filmstrips and cassettes, Library Kit, Teacher's Guide. This is a detailed account of Jefferson's life, including his work as a diplomat, political philosopher, and President of the United States.

SECTION 1: President Jefferson Leads the Nation

OBJECTIVES

After completing this section, students will be able to:
- Explain the concept of judicial review as set forth in the case of *Marbury v. Madison.*
- Locate the Louisiana Territory and state the facts concerning its purchase.
- Trace the route of Lewis and Clark through the western lands to the Pacific Ocean.

MOTIVATION

Have students read the textbook Chapter Introduction, describing Jefferson's inauguration. Ask them to compare it to Washington's inauguration as described in the opening paragraph of Chapter 10. In what ways was it similar? (Both took the same oath of office and gave an inaugural address.) How was it different? (Different city;

Jefferson's was private, while Washington's was in front of a crowd.) Ask which three Presidents they will read about in this chapter? (Jefferson, Madison, and Monroe) Refer to the Chapter Opener time line. How many terms did each one serve? (two) What does this tell you about them? (They were popular.) Which events can you expect to read about during Jefferson's administration? (Louisiana Purchase; Lewis and Clark Expedition) Tell students that when they finish reading Section 1, they should think of at least three other events during Jefferson's administration that could have been placed on the time line.

SUGGESTED ACTIVITIES

1. **Directed Reading.** As students read, have them note down what they consider to be *the* most important fact about each event on the time line. Also, remind them to add three other events that could be placed on the time line for Jefferson's administration. These could include the 1801 repeal of the Judiciary Act; the case of *Marbury v. Madison* in 1803; France forcing Spain to return Louisiana in 1802; and the reelection of Thomas Jefferson in 1804. As a summary, have students state one important fact about each of those three added events.

2. **History Study Skills.** As suggested in the chapter introduction in this manual, the History Study Skill *Using Circle Graphs* on textbook page 271 should be used with Section 1. To further stimulate critical thinking skills ask: Why did the percentage of Federalist votes drop so drastically between 1800 and 1804? Some students may recall the reasons for the decline in Federalist popularity stated in Chapter 10. Others might infer that people were pleased with the actions taken by Jefferson during his first term.

3. **Comparing History Maps.** This is a good place to review the Chapter 7 History Study Skill on textbook page 155. Have students compare the map of the *Louisiana Purchase and Western Exploration 1803-1806* on textbook page 253 with the map of *North America in 1783* on textbook page 187. First have students state the differences between the two maps. (One shows the entire United States, the other only the western half; the Louisiana Purchase is outlined on one and not on the other; the dates are different) Next, have students state similarities in the two maps (Spanish claimed the West and Southwest; both show the Mississippi River)

4. **Audio-Visual.** If possible, use the BFA film entitled *The Mountain Men,* listed under Chapter 11 Audio-Visual Materials in this manual. As they view the film, have students list the names of the mountain men who followed Lewis and Clark into the Louisiana Territory, and also the major contribution of each.

5. **Writing Activity.** Continue to provide practice for students in improving their history writing skills, as presented in the Chapter 10 History Study Skill. Have students write a paragraph to answer this question: Why was Thomas Jefferson a popular President?

BUILDING AMERICAN CITIZENSHIP

Section 1 describes the government's first application of the power of impeachment. Review the process with the students, including the ways in which the House of Representatives and Senate become involved. Ask students how the average citizen might be able to influence a congressional decision concerning the impeachment of a government official. (Writing, calling, or telegraphing their representative or Senator to express their opinion)

SECTION 1 REVIEW ANSWERS

1. **IDENTIFY:** *Marbury v. Madison:* the Supreme Court case that established the Court's power of judicial review, or the power to declare a law unconstitutional; **Toussaint L'Ouverture:** the leader of a successful slave revolt against French plantation owners in Haiti; **Meriwether Lewis:** former soldier and scout sent by President Jefferson to explore the Louisiana Territory; **William Clark:** former soldier and scout sent by President Jefferson to explore the Louisiana Territory; **Sacajawea:** Shoshone Indian woman who served as an interpreter and guide to Lewis and Clark; **Zebulon Pike:** explorer of the Louisiana Territory as far west as the Rocky Mountains (for whom Pike's Peak is named) and south into Spanish territory in what is now the American Southwest.
2. **DEFINE: impeach:** the power given the House of Representatives by the Constitution to bring charges of wrongdoing against government officials; **judicial review:** the power of the Supreme Court, in cases brought before it, to declare a law passed by Congress unconstitutional; **versus:** against.
3. The Constitution does not specifically grant the federal government power to buy land, and as a strict constructionist, Jefferson was particularly concerned about his decision to purchase the Louisiana Territory.
4. Lewis, Clark, and Pike.

SECTION 2: America Defends Its Rights Against Enemies

OBJECTIVES

After completing this section, students will be able to:
- State the cause, events, and results of the War with the Barbary States.
- Describe Tecumseh's struggle to resist pioneer settlement of the frontier.
- List the events that caused the War Hawks to demand military action against Great Britain.

MOTIVATION

Use the map *The Barbary War, 1803-1815* on textbook page 257. Have students name the Barbary States and the continent on which they are located. Use a chalkmap of the world to have them pinpoint the location of these nations and where they were in reference to the United States. Ask students why the United States might go to war with these nations?

SUGGESTED ACTIVITIES

1. **Directed Reading.** As students read Section 2, have

them answer the following guide questions, in sentences:
A. Why did the United States go to war with the Barbary States?
B. Why did the United States stop trading with the nations of Europe in 1807?
C. Why was the battle of Tippecanoe fought?

As the answers to these questions are reviewed, go over the people and events involved with each. For example, with Question A, discuss William Eaton and Stephen Decatur; with Question B, discuss the *Chesapeake-Leopard* Affair; with Question C, discuss Tecumseh, the Prophet, and William Henry Harrison.

2. **Cause and Effect.** Review the meaning of each term. A *cause* is something that brings about an event. It is what makes something happen. An *effect* is a result. Use the example of Tecumseh. What was the cause of his war against people on the frontier? (Settlers moving into Indian Territory) What was the result? (Battle of Tippecanoe; death of many white settlers) For each of the following events have students list one cause and one effect.
A. War with the Barbary States
B. Embargo Act of 1807
C. Battle of Tippecanoe
D. War Hawks', cries for action against England

3. **Acrostic.** Puzzles often provide an interesting way to review facts with students. Place the following on the chalkboard to help students review the events described in Section 2.

DecaTur	T - ____ led the American fleet that won a naval battle against Algeria.
WaR Hawks	R - Congressmen who wanted military action against England were called ____.
embargO	O - An ____ is a government order to stop trade.
TecUmseh	U - A Shawnee warrior, ____, organized Indian tribes to fight settlers on the frontier.
BarBary	B - Morocco, Tripoli, and Algeria were the ____ States.
Henry CLay	L - ____ was a leader of the Congress members who wanted war with Britain.
ChesapEake	E - The ____ was attacked by the *Leopard* in 1807.

4. **Chronology.** Have students place the following events, described in Section 2, in chronological order:
A. Chesapeake-Leopard Affair
B. Peace Treaty signed with ruler of Tripoli
C. Election of James Madison
D. Battle of Tippecanoe
E. Embargo Act
Answers: B -A -E -C - D

BUILDING AMERICAN CITIZENSHIP

Review Tecumseh's attempts to organize an Indian Confederacy. Ask students why Tecumseh was trying to form a confederacy. (To unite all tribes to fight pioneer settlers) Do you see any advantages in trying to unite people who have the same problem? Explain your answer. (Yes. There is a sense of caring and sharing. Also, a group is often able to succeed where an individual cannot.)

SECTION 2 REVIEW ANSWERS

1. **IDENTIFY: Stephen Decatur:** commander of an American fleet that won a naval battle against Algeria in 1815, thus ending the piracy of the Barbary states; *Chesapeake-Leopard* **affair:** an event in which British sailors on the *Leopard* attacked and boarded the American ship *Chesapeake* and forced sailors from the ship; **James Madison:** elected President of the United States in 1808, succeeding Jefferson; **Tecumseh:** Shawnee Indian leader who waged war against frontier settlers; **William Henry Harrison:** governor of the Indiana Territory who led a successful attack against the Indians at the Battle of Tippecanoe; **"War Hawks":** members of Congress who wanted war with Great Britain; **Henry Clay:** a Kentucky Congressman who led the War Hawks.
2. **DEFINE: embargo:** a government order to stop trade.
3. The Barbary pirates seized the crews and cargoes from American ships; the British navy seized over 1,000 American ships and kidnapped more than 6,000 sailors.
4. He tried to unite all Indian tribes and give them a feeling of pride in order to strengthen their fight against settlers on Indian lands.

SECTION 3: Troubles with Britian Lead To The War of 1812

OBJECTIVES

After completing this section, students will be able to:
• List the reasons why the United States went to war against Great Britain in 1812.
• Name and locate the major battles of the War of 1812.
• Explain the results of the War of 1812.

MOTIVATION

Use the map of the *War of 1812* on textbook page 261. Have students name the major battles fought during the War of 1812. Ask them why navies were needed to fight the war by both the Americans and the British. (Most of the battles were fought along the coast or on the Great Lakes.) Ask students which battles were won by the British and which by the Americans. Ask if, by looking at the map, it is possible to tell why the war started or what the results were.

SUGGESTED ACTIVITIES

1. **Directed Reading.** As students read Section 3, assign the Chapter Review skill exercise at the end of the chapter. Have them do an outline of the war, listing its major causes, events, and results. As you check the outline with students, refer frequently to the map so that students can locate the battle sites and relate the outcome of each battle.
2. **Map Interpretation.** Once again, use the map of the

War of 1812. Check students' ability to read the map by asking the following questions:
A. Which Chesapeake Bay cities were attacked by the British? (Washington and Baltimore)
B. In which direction did Jackson travel to reach New Orleans from Horseshoe Bend? (South)
C. What body of water was crossed by the British to reach New Orleans (Gulf of Mexico)
D. Where was the westernmost battle of the war fought? (New Orleans)
E. The British traveled south from Canada. The Americans traveled north and east from Lake Ontario. Where did they clash in battle? (Plattsburg)
F. Which was the only battle fought on the Great Lakes? (Battle of Lake Erie)
3. **Building American Citizenship.** Duplicate Worksheet 29, *The Star-Spangled Banner.* Before completing the activity, review the circumstances under which Francis Scott Key came to write the poem. Also, read through both verses with students, helping them to pronounce any words with which they might have difficulty.
4. **History Study Skills.** Duplicate Worksheet 28, *The Elections of 1812 and 1816.* Have students do the activity. For further practice, you may also wish to have students research casualty figures for the War of 1812. This would give them an opportunity to draw another circle graph:

CASUALTIES FOR THE WAR OF 1812
Number of British who died
Number of Americans who died
Number of Indians who died
You may have to help students convert figures to percentages in order to complete this activity.

BUILDING AMERICAN CITIZENSHIP

As stated in Section 3, the war became an important issue in the election of 1812. Those who favored war were responsible for the reelection of James Madison. What other "big" issues might help determine the outcome of a presidential election? (A depression, an unpopular law that the President approved)

SECTION 3 REVIEW ANSWERS

1. **IDENTIFY: Oliver Hazard Perry:** captain of an American fleet that defeated a British fleet at a battle on Lake Erie; **Dolley Madison:** wife of President James Madison who risked capture by the British to save important papers kept in Washington; **Francis Scott Key:** author of the "Star-Spangled Banner" written during a battle at Fort McHenry; **Andrew Jackson:** leader of the American troops that defeated the British at the Battle of New Orleans; **Treaty of Ghent:** the peace treaty signed at Ghent, Belgium, ending the War of 1812.
2. **DEFINE: anthem:** a song of praise.
3. Lake Erie; Thames; Fort McHenry; New Orleans.
4. American ships enjoyed freedom of the seas; the fighting power of the Indians in the Ohio Valley was destroyed, encouraging new settlers to the frontier; it gave Americans great national pride and brought respect from other nations.

SECTION 4: An Era of National Pride Follows the War

OBJECTIVES

After completing this section, students will be able to:
- List the accomplishments of Madison and the Republican Congress during the final years of his Presidency.
- Explain why the "Era of Good Feelings" was given that name.
- Identify cases in which the Supreme Court made nationalist decisions.

MOTIVATION

Introduce the phrase "Era of Good Feelings." Define the word "era" if students are unfamiliar with the term. Ask students what they would expect to find during a period of time that is given this name. (Peace, prosperity)

SUGGESTED ACTIVITIES

1. **Directed Reading.** Have students read Section 4 to determine if their expectations were correct. If they stated that prosperity helped create such a period, have them write a sentence or two proving they were right. Expectations for which there is no proof should not be included. Other elements, such as a strong feeling of nationalism, should be added. As a summary, ask students to give an informal opinion about this question: Could the final years of Madison's Presidency have been included in the "Era of Good Feelings?" (Although answers may vary, the response generally should be "yes." This is because of the cooperation between the Republican Congress the the President concerning the bank, the tariff, and money for roads and canals.)

2. **Class Discussion.** Direct a discussion of the following topic: How did the Supreme Court support the cause of nationalism? In answering, students should explain the decisions in the cases of *McCulloch v. Maryland* and *Gibbons v. Ogden*. They should also conclude that these decisions gave more power to the federal government than to state government.

3. **Research Assignment.** Section 4 describes two Supreme Court decisions made while John Marshall was Chief Justice. Have students use library resources to prepare reports on other cases of the period that increased the power of the federal government. These could include:
   - 1816—*Martin v. Hunter's Lessee* which reaffirmed the Court's power to overrule a state court.
   - 1819—*Dartmouth College v. Woodward* in which a New Hampshire law altering the college's charter was declared to be unconstitutional.
   - 1821—*Cohen v. Virginia* in which citizens convicted in state courts were given the right to appeal to the federal judiciary.

4. **Ideals In The Lives Of Americans.** Have students read the selection on Noah Webster on textbook page 265. Discuss the answers to the two questions at the end of the selection. Section 4 stresses the strong mood of nationalism in the United States at that time.

You may wish to ask how Webster contributed to the feeling. The last paragraph of the selection provides the answer.

BUILDING AMERICAN CITIZENSHIP

The first paragraph of Section 4 describes ways in which citizens expressed their patriotic feelings towards the nation in 1815. How do citizens express their feelings of patriotism today? (Saluting the flag, standing for the national anthem, singing patriotic songs, flying the flag on designated days)

SECTION 4 REVIEW ANSWERS

1. **IDENTIFY: James Monroe:** elected President in 1816 and in 1820; *McCulloch v. Maryland:* Supreme Court case in which the supremacy of federal law over state law was upheld; *Gibbons v. Ogden:* Supreme Court case in which the Court ruled that commerce among the states is ruled by the federal government, not the states.

2. **DEFINE: inflation:** an increase in the amount of money in circulation, resulting in a decrease in its value and a rise in prices; **protective tariff:** a tax on imports, which raises the prices of goods from other countries; **interstate commerce:** trade between states; **monopoly:** a business that has no competition.

3. It was a time when national unity was stronger than sectional feelings or party loyalties.

4. The Supreme Court struck down state laws that violated federal law or the Constitution. Its decisions upheld the supremacy of federal law over state law.

SECTION 5: America's Influence in Foreign Affairs Grows

OBJECTIVES

After completing this section, students will be able to:
- State the terms of the Rush-Bagot Agreement.
- Tell how the United States acquired Florida.
- Summarize the main points of the Monroe Doctrine.

MOTIVATION

Ask the question: How could the "Era of Good Feelings" be extended to our dealings with other nations? Students might answer that other nations would treat us fairly, and that the United States would reciprocate. Explain that the purpose of today's lesson is to examine the foreign policy of the period—to see what specific nations we dealt with during this time and the outcome of our efforts.

SUGGESTED ACTIVITIES

1. **Directed Reading.** As students read Section 5, have them list the nations that the United States dealt with during this period and the various decisions that were reached. For example:
   A. England: Rush-Bagot Agreement fixed the boundary between Canada and the United States.

B. Spain: Florida was sold to the United States after pressure was placed on it to govern the area properly or cede it to the United States

C. All European Nations: The Monroe Doctrine warned them to stay out of the political affairs of the Western Hemisphere.

In summarizing the lesson, be sure to discuss the individuals involved with each of the decisions. These include (A) Secretary of State Richard Rush; (B) Andrew Jackson, John Quincy Adams; and (C) James Monroe.

2. **Map Study.** Have students use the *Independence in Latin America* map on textbook page 268 to answer the following questions:

A. According to the map, how many independent nations were there in Latin America in 1825? (10—Mexico, United Provinces of Central America, Great Colombia, Haiti, Peru, Brazil, Paraguay, Argentina, Chile, Bolivia)

B. Which British colonies are shown? (British Honduras, Trinidad, British Guiana, Jamaica, and Bahamas)

C. Which nation possessed the islands south of Florida? (Spain)

D. Why does Chapter 11 include a map of Latin America? (The United States recognized the nations of Latin America in 1823 and warned European nations to stay out of the political affairs of the Western Hemisphere.)

3. **Research Activity.** Section 5 gives the date of death for Thomas Jefferson and John Adams. This may prompt questions from students regarding the deaths of Madison and Monroe. Have students list the names of the first six Presidents. (Section 5 mentions John Quincy Adams) Have them use library sources to make a chart of the dates of birth and death of each to determine who was the oldest at the time of death and who was the youngest. If student interest broadens to include all Presidents, have them continue their research to determine who was the oldest and youngest of all Presidents at the time of death.

4. **Organizing History Facts.** Duplicate Worksheet 30 for an excellent review of all of the major facts in the chapter. You may wish to have students organize the facts dealing with domestic events (question 2) in chronological order. Then have students discuss the major developments associated with each of the 18 facts mentioned.

5. **Sources of Freedom.** One of the most important documents dealing with foreign policy in American history is the Monroe Doctrine. Refer students to it on textbook page 269. Ask them to describe, in their own words, what the various parts of the statement mean.

BUILDING AMERICAN CITIZENSHIP

The Monroe Doctrine warned the nations of Europe to stay out of the political affairs of the Western Hemisphere. This included both North and South America. In your opinion, did the United States government have the right to speak for the citizens of independent Latin American countries? Explain your answer. (Answers will vary.)

SECTION 5 REVIEW ANSWERS

1. **IDENTIFY: Rush-Bagot Agreement:** agreements worked out with Great Britain fixing the boundary between Canada and the United States along the 49° parallel of latitude, postponing the settlement of both nations' claims to the Oregon Territory until 1828, and granting Americans fishing rights off the coast of Labrador and Newfoundland in eastern Canada; **John Quincy Adams:** the Secretary of State under President James Monroe who arranged the purchase of Florida from Spain and whose advice led to the Monroe Doctrine; **Monroe Doctrine:** foreign policy statement by President Monroe in 1823 warning European powers to stay out of the political affairs of the Western Hemisphere.

2. Rush-Bagot Agreement with Great Britain; the purchase of Florida from Spain and Spain's agreement to give up all claims to the Oregon Territory; the Monroe Doctrine.

3. The United States warned Russia that it would stop any European nation from gaining new colonies in the Western Hemisphere, which led to a treaty with Russia establishing the boundary between Russia and Oregon at 54° 40′ parallel of latitude.

CHAPTER 11 REVIEW ANSWERS

REVIEWING KEY WORDS

1. c. 2. b. 3. e. 4. a. 5. d.

REMEMBERING IMPORTANT PEOPLE AND EVENTS

1. c. 2. a. 3. d. 4. e. 5. b.
6. c. 7. b. 8. d. 9. a. 10. e.

REVIEWING THE FACTS

1. F 2. T 3. T 4. T 5. F

PLACING EVENTS IN TIME

1. a. 2. a. 3. b. 4. b. 5. a.

LINKING GEOGRAPHY AND HISTORY

1. People in the West wanted to conquer Canada to cut off the base of British support of the Indians who attacked frontier settlers, and they also wanted to gain rich farm land for new settlements. People in the Northeast depended on foreign trade for a living; they feared that war with Britain would cut off their trade completely.

THINKING ABOUT AMERICAN HISTORY

1. A protective tariff places a tax on imports, which raises the price of foreign goods. Americans are therefore encouraged to buy American goods because they are cheaper.

2. When Congress declared war on Great Britain on June 18, 1812, it was not aware of the fact that two days earlier the British government had decided to stop attacking American ships.

APPLYING HISTORY STUDIES SKILLS

A graph should be drawn, showing the appropriate percentages.

CHAPTER 12

Different Sections Develop in America (1789-1828)

Chapter Objectives

After completing this chapter, students will be able to:
1. Explain why and how pioneers settled west of the Appalachians.
2. Identify important transportation improvements that helped pioneers move west.
3. Describe how industry began to develop in the Northeast.
4. Explain why slavery developed in the South.
5. Describe important characteristics of the various sections of the United States.

Chapter Chronology

Chapter 12 surveys the period of sweeping change that was occurring in the United States between 1789 and 1828. Major persons and events of this period are highlighted on the time line on the textbook Chapter Opener page. Westward movement begins here with Daniel Boone who led settlers to Kentucky in 1775. Meanwhile, industry was beginning to develop in the Northeast and less than two decades later, Samuel Slater opened his cotton mill, the first American factory. Two years later, Eli Whitney invented the cotton gin. Shortly after the turn of the century, in 1807, the steamship *Clermont,* built by the American inventor, Robert Fulton, sailed on the Hudson River. Another kind of landmark in transportation history in America was the opening of the National Road in 1818. The Missouri Compromise in 1820 was a clear signal that sectionalism was a growing problem for the new nation. In 1824, John Quincy Adams became president. In his administration, there was another great transportation landmark, the opening of the Erie Canal in 1825. The chapter ends with the election of Andrew Jackson, the first "western" president in 1828.

Motivation

Have students look at the time line on the textbook chapter opener page. They will see that the first event listed on it is the opening of Samuel Slater's Cotton Mill in Pawtucket, Rhode Island. Discuss the other persons and events mentioned on the time line, using the material under Chapter Chronology for additional background information. Ask students to think about how each entry on the time line might fit in with the chapter title, Different Sections Develop in America. Remember, not all events on the time line may have an obvious relationship to the title. Then begin Section 1 in the chapter.

Geographical Setting

Geography is a major factor in Chapter 12. The westward movement described in Section 1, provides a good opportunity for students to review the major migra-

tion routes used by pioneers going to the frontier settlements. The Cumberland Gap—National Road—Ohio River route was the most important. Those who preferred to go by way of water could travel the Erie Canal—Great Lakes route all the way to the Mississippi River. The map, *Canals in the United States in 1840,* can be found on page 282. Industrial development in the northeast depended upon the availability of water power. Thus, the majority of mills and factories were located near rivers and waterfalls. Most of the cities noted in Chapter 12 were situated near waterfalls or located along major transportation routes.

The rise of cotton and the growth of slavery are interrelated. The environment of the South, including its soil and climate resulted in the development of an economy and culture that was very different from other sections of the country. Finally, the Missouri Compromise created a geographical boundary that promised to limit the spread of slavery and cool the fires of sectionalism.

History Study Skills

The History Study Skill introduced in Chapter 12 is *Separating Facts from Opinions.* It focuses on two descriptions of Lincoln. This skill activity could be used in Section 1 after students read about Lincoln or at the end of the chapter, after the Missouri Compromise. Lincoln is a good example of an American who lived in a slave state, Kentucky, and later in several free states, north of the Ohio River.

Bibliography

Teacher References

Genovese, Eugene, *Roll Jordon, Roll: The World the Slaves Made.* Random House, New York City, 1974.

Wade, Richard E., *The Urban Frontier: The Rise of Western Cities, 1790-1830.* Harvard University Press, Cambridge, Mass., 1959.

Student References

Coit, Margaret K., *Life History of the United States, Volume 3, 1789-1829.* Silver Burdette, Morristown, N.J., 1974. This is a beautifully illustrated survey of the social, political, and military events of the period.

Tebbel, John, *The Battle of Fallen Timbers.* Franklin Watts, New York City, 1972. This book describes the third and victorious final campaign against British and Indian forces in the Ohio Valley, following the American Revolution.

Audio-Visual Materials

Slavery and Slave Resistance, Coronet Films, 23 minutes. This vivid account of slavery and slave resistance talks about such figures as Phyllis Wheatley, William Wells Brown, and Frederick Douglass.

Presidents of the United States, Part I—Washington, Adams and Jefferson, National Geographic Educational Services. Three filmstrips and cassettes. This thorough coverage of the first three Presidents of the United States emphasizes their personalities, early lives, families, and careers.

SECTION 1: Pioneers Settle West of the Appalachians

OBJECTIVES

After completing this section, students will be able to:
- Explain why and how pioneers settled west of the Appalachian Mountains.
- Identify important transportation improvements of the early 1800's.
- Name and locate the three sections of the country.

MOTIVATION

Have students read the textbook Chapter Introduction. Ask them to name the various methods of transportation used by Mr. Flower to reach his destination. (Ship, Conestoga wagon, flat boat) Ask students where he was going (Edwards County, Illinois) and in what part of the country this was located (Northwest). Remind students that in Chapter 11 the nationalistic feelings of the nation were described. According to the Chapter Introduction, what other feelings were developing at the same time? (Sectional) Ask students to name the three sections of the country. (Northeast, South, and West) Ask them to describe where the "WEST" is located. (West of the Appalachians) The Northeast and South? (East of the Appalachians) Which section is dealt with in Section 1 of this chapter? (West)

SUGGESTED ACTIVITIES

1. **Directed Reading.** Use the five "W's and "H" below to guide students' comprehension of the material in Section 1:
   - A. Who went West? (People looking for a better life.)
   - B. What means of transportation did people use to get there? (Wagons, flatboat, horses)
   - C. Where was "the West" in the early 1800's? (West of the Appalachians and east of the Mississippi)
   - D. When did the western territories become states? (By 1821)
   - E. Why did people go there? (To get land, for adventure, to escape to the East)
   - F. How was the West linked to the East? (Wilderness Road)

   In summarizing the material, be sure to have students describe the role of Daniel Boone, and families like the Lincolns, in settling the West.

1. **Using Numbers.** Apply mathematical facts and concepts to history by having students use the information in Section 1 to answer the following:
   - A. What was the total population of Kentucky in 1800? (220,000)
   - B. What percentage of the population was slaves? (18 percent)
   - C. What was the approximate population of Kentucky in 1810? (440,000)
   - D. According to federal law, what was the maximum total amount a family would pay for 160 acres? ($320)
   - E. How much younger was Abraham Lincoln than his sister Sarah? (2 years)
   - F. How old was Abraham Lincoln when his mother died? (9 years)

   - G. How long did it take to build and open the National Road after it received Congressional approval? (12 years)
   - H. How many miles did the Clermont travel in its trip from New York City to Albany and back. (310 miles)

3. **History Study Skills.** Have students turn to textbook page 294 and complete the activity that teaches them to separate facts from opinions. Have students try to select at least one other example each of a "fact" and of an "opinion" from Chapter 11, and perhaps even from Chapter 10.

4. **Separating Facts from Opinions.** Duplicate Worksheet 31, *Pioneers Move Westward.* The activity is designed to allow students an additional opportunity to apply the study skill. Assuming that students completed the previous activity in class, this may be used as a homework assignment so that they can practice the skill independently.

5. **Landmarks of Liberty.** Ask students to read the selection on the Wilderness Road found on textbook page 283. Have them answer the questions at the end of the reading. Then ask students how the road then would have been different from the modern highway that follows its path today.

BUILDING AMERICAN CITIZENSHIP

Have students define the term "self-reliance." Ask them how pioneer families such as the Lincolns demonstrated self-reliance. (Worked hard, paid their debts, and raised and educated children, usually without the help of hospitals and often without formal schools) How do families demonstrate self-reliance today? (Answers will vary.)

SECTION 1 REVIEW ANSWERS

1. **IDENTIFY: Daniel Boone:** leader of pioneers who settled in Kentucky; **National Road:** road that connected Cumberland, Maryland, to the town of Wheeling on the Ohio River; **Robert Fulton:** inventor of the steamboat *Clermont*, which Fulton sailed from New York City to Albany and back in 1807; *Seneca Chief:* a freight barge pulled from Buffalo to Albany on the new Erie Canal in 1825; **Erie Canal:** a continuous water route connecting the Great Lakes to the Atlantic Ocean.

2. **DEFINE: turnpikes:** private roads named after the spiked poles used at the toll gates; **toll:** fee charged for using a road; **Wilderness Road:** Indian trail used by pioneers to cross the Appalachian Mountains.

3. New opportunities; chance to own more and less costly land; chance for a better life; adventure; escape cities; the soil on farms and plantations was worn out.

4. The National Road was built; steamboats used on rivers and canals.

SECTION 2: Industry Develops in the Northeast

OBJECTIVES

After completing this section, students will be able to:
- List the changes that took place in America as a result of the Industrial Revolution.

- Describe the system of mass production, including the use of interchangeable parts and division of labor.
- Explain why Philadelphia became an important cultural center in the early 1800's.

MOTIVATION

Purchase four identical ball point pens and take them apart. Place the parts in four boxes: 1) pen tops; 2) pen bottoms; 3) springs; 4) fillers. Without explaining the contents of the boxes, have student volunteers walk by them, examine the contents, and assemble the pens. Then ask the following questions:

1. Why were students able to assemble the pens so easily? (Parts are all alike.)
2. Suppose, this were your job but instead of assembling the whole pen, all that was required was to add one piece or part to it the whole day? What difference would this make? (Task would be simpler, but more boring.)
3. What products could be made using this system? (Cars, shoes, radios, candy bars)

Explain that in today's lesson, students will learn what the system is called, who developed it, and what effects it had.

SUGGESTED ACTIVITIES

1. **Directed Reading.** Place the following information on lined tagboard or overhead transparency:
   A. Making parts of a product that are exactly alike (Interchangeable Parts)
   B. Giving each worker one or two simple tasks (Division of labor)
   C. Making many goods in large numbers and in a short time (Mass Production)
   D. Inventor of the system (Eli Whitney)
   E. Effects: (Used in many factories; rise of factory system; growth of cities)
   Have students use these terms as they read Section 2. To check their understanding, discuss application of the system to the production of a bicycle or other item of interest to students.
2. **Preparing Reports.** Assign students to prepare written reports on the lives of the early American industrialists named in Section 2: Moses Brown, Samuel Slater, Francis Lowell, and Eli Whitney. Require them to include a bibliography with their report, and stress that they must use at least one source other than an encyclopedia.
3. **Separating Facts from Opinions.** Apply the History Study Skill introduced on textbook page 294 by having students determine whether these statements from Section 2 are facts or opinions. Have students give reasons to support their answers.
   A. Many people thought Philadelphia the most beautiful city in North America. (O)
   B. Philadelphia had many black residents, all of whom were free. (F)
   C. Cities were exciting places to live in or visit. (O)
   D. In 1810, Philadelphia was the second largest American city, with a population of over 87,000. (F)
   E. Philadelphia city was well laid out. (F)
4. **Comparison.** Have students use the information in Chapter 10, Section 1, from the 1790 Census and compare it to the information in this section to answer the following:
   A. Did the number of people living on farms increase or decrease between 1790 and 1810? (Decrease)
   B. By how much did it decrease? (About 5%)
   C. Which was America's largest city in 1790? (Philadelphia) In 1810? (New York)
   D. Of Philadelphia, New York, and Boston, which city's population increased the most? (New York) By how much? (Over 77,000)
   E. What city's population increased the least? (Boston)

BUILDING AMERICAN CITIZENSHIP

Samuel Slater had to memorize the blueprints of machinery made in Britain in order to copy it and set up the first factory in America. Do you think it was right for Slater to acquire the plans for British machines in this way? Explain your answer. (Answers will vary.) Can you think of any circumstances today when it would be right for a citizen to acquire something in a similar way from a neighbor, community, or country? (Answers will vary.)

SECTION 2 REVIEW ANSWERS

1. **IDENTIFY: Industrial Revolution:** the change brought about by the invention of new machines and the consequent ways of producing goods; **Moses Brown:** a wealthy merchant in Rhode Island who offered money to anyone who could make machines as good as those in Great Britain; **Samuel Slater:** ex-factory worker in British cotton mills who set up the first factory in America, a cotton mill in Rhode Island in 1791; **Francis Lowell:** inventor of a power loom, a machine to make cloth; **Eli Whitney:** inventor of a system of making all parts of a product exactly alike, which made parts interchangeable.
2. **DEFINE: factories:** buildings built to hold large machines for producing goods; **factory system:** using machinery and workers to make large amounts of goods; **mill:** a factory in which only one or two simple operations are performed; **interchangeable parts:** parts of a product that are made exactly alike; **division of labor:** dividing up work so that each worker has one or two simple jobs; **mass production:** making goods in very large numbers in a short time and at a lower cost.
3. New England had many swift-running rivers to supply power to run factory machines; people there had money to invest in building factories; many people there needed jobs.
4. Philadelphia was the nation's leading center of trade; it was an important political center, having been the nation's capital for ten years; it was well laid out; it had a rich cultural life; it had many products for sale made by skilled craftworkers.

SECTION 3: Cotton Becomes "King" In The South

OBJECTIVES

After completing this section, students will be able to:
- Explain how cotton became the main cash crop of the South.

- Describe the living conditions of the slaves in the South.
- Identify methods of resistance used by slaves.

MOTIVATION

Discuss the concept of *resistance* with students. Relate it to their daily lives in school and at home. For example, if they are dissatisfied with their school assignments, how can they resist? (Do nothing, walk out of class, complain to the teacher) What result could they expect from such actions? (Responses ranging from disapproval to punishment) Select a similar example from students' home life. Suppose they were assigned to clean their rooms, and didn't want to do it. How could they resist? Explain to students that, in this section, they will be reading about the life of slaves in the South. They will learn the ways that the slaves found to resist unfair treatment.

SUGGESTED ACTIVITIES

1. **Directed Reading.** Use the following as guide questions for students as they read Section 3:
   A. How did the invention of the cotton gin affect the growth of slavery in the South?
   B. Why was the life of a slave such a hard one?
   C. What methods were used by slaves to resist unfair treatment?
   Discuss the answers to these questions. As a summary, ask students to identify individuals associated with the answers to each question. For example, Eli Whitney would be associated with question 1.
2. **Separating Facts from Opinions.** Apply the skill by having students determine which of the following statements are facts and which are opinions. Be sure to have students give reasons for their answers.
   A. Subsistence farmers dreamed of owning more land one day. (O)
   B. From 1791 to 1807, the value of America's exports increased by almost $30 million. (F)
   C. The planters believed that slave labor was the cheapest and best way to produce cotton. (O)
   D. Congress passed a law ending the slave trade after January 1, 1808. (F)
   E. Pierce Butler argued that slaves were better off and happier than the free, white factory workers in the North. (O)
3. **Slavery and Slave Resistance.** If available, show the 23 minute film, *Slavery and Slave Resistance* by Coronet Films. As students view it, have them note down examples of slave resistance as discussed in the Motivation and Directed Reading.
4. **Interpreting Data.** Have students use the graph, *Cotton Production, 1790-1825* on textbook page 288 to answer the following questions:
   A. How many bales of cotton were produced in 1790? 3,000
   B. How many *more* bales were produced 20 years later? 332,000
   C. During which interval of time did the smallest increase in production take place? What was the increase? 1790-1795; only 14,000 bales

D. During which interval of time did the largest increase in production take place? What was the increase? 1820-1825; 126,000 bales

BUILDING AMERICAN CITIZENSHIP

Review the methods of resistance used by slaves. (Doing little work, escaping, rebelling) Ask students if they feel the slaves were right to use these methods. Were there other methods they could have used? What methods are used by citizens today to resist laws they feel are unfair? (Disobey the law, go to court to change the law, write congresspersons, plan demonstrations)

SECTION 3 REVIEW ANSWERS

1. **IDENTIFY: Pierce Butler:** Georgia plantation owner who defended slavery; **Gabriel Prosser:** a slave who led an unsuccessful slave rebellion in Virginia in 1800; **Nat Turner:** a slave who led the bloodiest slave rebellion in Virginia in 1831.
2. **DEFINE: subsistence farmers:** farmers who produce enough crops to feed themselves, with little left for trade or sale.
3. Eli Whitney's cotton gin.
4. They claimed that slaves were better off than white factory workers in the North; slaves were cared for when they were sick or old; they always had food, clothes, and shelter and were never out of a job.

SECTION 4: Sectional Clashes Divide the Nation

OBJECTIVES

After completing this section, students will be able to:
- Summarize the main points of the Missouri Compromise.
- Explain the influence of sectionalism on the election of 1824.
- Describe the differences between the National Republican Party and the Democratic Party.

MOTIVATION

Have students look at the time line on the textbook Chapter Opener page. Ask them to name the events they have already read about, and to state one fact related to each event. Then, have students name those events they have not yet read about: Missouri Compromise, election of John Quincy Adams, and the election of Andrew Jackson. How many terms did John Quincy Adams serve? (1) Who was the only other President before him to serve only one term? (His father) Tell students that by the end of this section they should be able to tell something about each of the remaining events on the time line. They should be able to explain why John Quincy Adams served only one term.

SUGGESTED ACTIVITIES

1. **Directed Reading.** Have students read the first paragraph and name the three sections of the country. Set up the following chart on the chalkboard. Tell the class that there are three basic issues on which the

sections disagreed. The students are to name these issues in the lefthand column and then tell how each section felt or acted in the appropriate column to the right.

ISSUE	NORTH	SOUTH	WEST
1. Slavery	(Against)	(For)	(Undecided)
2. Political parties	(National Republicans)	(Democrats)	(Democrats)
3. Tariff	(For)	(Against)	(Undecided)

Discuss the answer for each block and have students give reasons for their entries. As a summary, relate each of the events on the time line to one of the issues discussed.

2. **Using Circle Graphs.** Have students review the steps required for drawing a circle graph as outlined in Chapter 11 on textbook page 271. Then, have them draw a circle graph using the figures for the electoral vote in the election of 1824. Do not provide the figures. Part of the activity should include students' ability to locate these in the chapter.

3. **Americans Compromise.** Duplicate Worksheet 32, of this title. You may wish to allow below-average students to use the information in the textbook to complete the activity. It not only reviews the Missouri Compromise and the Tariff of Abominations, but requires students to create compromises for specific situations.

4. **Causes of Sectionalism.** Duplicate Worksheet 33 of this title. This activity will provide a good check on students' grasp of sectional conflict. It also offers an opportunity to apply the Chapter 10 History Study Skill *Improving Your History Writing.*

BUILDING AMERICAN CITIZENSHIP

Check a map of the United States today. How many sections are there? (5) Name them. (Northeast, South, Midwest, West, and Southwest) Can you name any sectional issues that citizens argue about today? (Answers may vary, but generally, no) Do citizens living in the United States today consider themselves as sectionalists —Northerners, Southerners, and so on—or as Americans? (Again, answers may vary, but, in general, Americans) Why do you think this is so? (Answers will vary.)

SECTION 4 REVIEW ANSWERS

1. **IDENTIFY: Missouri Compromise:** compromise proposed by Henry Clay and passed by Congress in 1820 to ease the sectional conflict over admitting Missouri as a slave state; it maintained the balance of power in the Senate by admitting Maine as a free state and Missouri as a slave state; it also closed the area north of the 36°36' line to slavery. **John Quincy Adams:** Secretary of State under Monroe; elected President in 1824 by the House of Representatives; **Democratic Party:** political party formed by Andrew Jackson after he lost the election of 1824; **Tariff of Abominations:** Tariff of 1828, a protective tariff which placed a high tax on imported goods and displeased many people.

2. **DEFINE: revenue tariffs:** taxes placed on imported goods to raise money.

3. It admitted Missouri as a slave state and Maine as a free state, thus keeping the number of Senators from the North and South balanced.

4. It led to the creation of a rival political party when, after his defeat, Andrew Jackson started the Democratic Party.

CHAPTER 12 REVIEW ANSWERS

REVIEWING KEY WORDS

1. c.   2. e.   3. b.   4. a.   5. d.

REMEMBERING IMPORTANT PEOPLE AND EVENTS

1. b.   2. c.   3. a.   4. c.   5. b.

REVIEWING THE FACTS

1. T	2. T	3. F	4. T	5. F.
6. T	7. T	8. T	9. F	10. F

PLACING EVENTS IN TIME

1. c.   2. d.   3. e.   4. a.   5. b.

LINKING GEOGRAPHY AND HISTORY

Slavery: North opposed; South favored; West had mixed opinions. **States' rights:** North opposed; South favored; West had mixed opinions. **Tariffs:** North opposed tariffs on raw materials but favored tariffs on textiles and manufactured goods; farmers in the South and West opposed tariffs on manufactured goods but favored tariffs on farm products.

THINKING ABOUT AMERICAN HISTORY

1. The new means of transportation increased trade, helping both farmers and merchants grow richer, and gave jobs to more people and brought Americans closer together.

2. Philadelphia was a center of trade, an important political city, and well laid out. Money made in trade was spent to build a playhouse, a library, and a museum.

APPLYING HISTORY STUDY SKILLS

1. Something we know for certain.
2. A view, a judgment, a belief about something.
3. The major difference is evidence. Facts are supported by evidence; opinions are not.
4. Answers will vary.

UNIT 4 REVIEW ANSWERS

VOCABULARY REVIEW

Answers will vary.

REVIEWING THE MAIN IDEAS

1. People had different attitudes and beliefs about governments. They formed groups with those who shared their beliefs in order to gain power and control the government.

2. Judicial review; political parties; purchasing territory from other nations; President's Cabinet; executive privilege

3. To gain control of the port of New Orleans and the Mississippi River for Western farmers to trade and ship their goods; to prevent Westerners from being at the mercy of a foreign power; Napoleon offered to sell it at a bargain price.

4. To stop British attacks on American ships and the kidnapping of American sailors; to end British support of Indians who attacked pioneers on the Western frontier.

5. After the cotton gin was invented, the production of cotton increased enormously, making cotton the South's chief crop.

6. The people of the North were mainly business people, factory owners, and workers, who depended on trade to make a living. They opposed slavery and states' rights and supported a tariff to keep out cheaper foreign manufactured goods. The people of the South were mainly farmers and plantation owners who supported slavery and states' rights. They opposed a tariff on manufactured goods because it raised prices on goods they needed, but they supported a tariff on farm products. Many people in the West were pioneers and farmers. Generally, they opposed tariffs but had mixed feelings on slavery and states' rights.

APPLYING YOUR STUDY SKILLS

1. **Using a Time Line**
   a. (1) Louisiana; Florida (2) 1803; 1819

2. **Using Maps**
   a. (1) Tripoli, Algiers, Morocco (2) On the coast of North Africa (3) Mediterranean Sea
   b. Montana, Wyoming, Colorado, North Dakota, South Dakota, Nebraska, Kansas, Oklahoma, Minnesota, Iowa, Missouri, Arkansas, Louisiana

3. **Using Your Textbook**
   a. (1) George Washington (2) John Adams (3) Thomas Jefferson (4) James Madison (5) James Monroe (6) John Quincy Adams

PROJECTS

Answers will vary.

BUILDING AMERICAN CITIZENSHIP

1. Answers will vary.
2. Answers will vary.

UNIT 5 (1820's-1850's)
The Nation Grows Stronger

Introducing the Unit

Unit Five covers the landmark years of the 1820's to the 1850's in America's national development. This period is often referred to as the Age of Jackson. Many historians believe that Andrew Jackson's election in 1828 was a catalyst that spurred Americans to redouble their efforts to improve their lives and literally broaden their horizons. Unit Five depicts many of the events that shaped this time.

The period was characterized by great energy and vitality. The pioneers headed out west to the Mexican territory of Texas in the 1820's and 1830's and, beginning in the 1840's, to California, another Mexican territory. By 1848, under President Polk, the United States had won both Texas and California from Mexico, as well as vast new additional territories, including Utah and Colorado. Pioneer families also streamed into the Oregon Country, claimed by both Britain and the United States. By 1846, the Oregon question was settled peacefully, adding still more land to our country.

Several important movements designed to improve the quality of American life developed during this period. The abolitionist movement achieved national status in the 1830's after William Lloyd Garrison founded his anti-slavery newspaper, *The Liberator.* In 1833, the American Anti-Slavery Society was established. It attracted thousands of Americans, whose combined efforts resulted in some progress. However there were also increasing acts of violence by those opposed to the abolitionist movement.

Many women were active abolitionists and worked in other reform movements as well, including those designed to help alcoholics, the mentally ill, and the handicapped. Women also participated in such experiments in communal living as Oneida and Brook Farm. Soon women began to call for full citizenship rights for themselves. Their efforts culminated in the Seneca Falls Convention in 1848.

The Unit Opener in the textbook depicts many of the significant persons and events of this period. You may wish to use these illustrations to help introduce the unit. The central figure is Jackson himself. Beginning in the lower left-hand corner in a clockwise direction are the abolitionist, Harriet Beecher Stowe, the suffragist, Lucretia Mott, the flag of the Republic of California and the Lone Star flag of Texas, a gold miner, the U.S. Cavalry, a steamship, and a Plains Indian warrior.

Unit Themes And Ideas

Unit Five deals with five major themes, all of them developing concurrently during this period. The rise of the common man, a theme closely associated with Jackson and Jacksonian democracy, is developed in Chapter 13. Unprecedented economic prosperity and technological advancement are interwoven themes in Chapter 14. Social reform is the key theme in Chapter 15 in the work of reformers committed to the abolition of slavery, increased opportunities for women, and help for the downtrodden in American society. Expansion is the theme of Chapter 16 and Manifest Destiny is the unifying idea. These themes, show this period of American history to be one of growth and improvement—economically, socially, and politically. The unit is organized into the four chapters below:

Chapter 13- *A Democratic Era Begins Under Jackson (1820's - 1840's)*

Chapter 14- *Prosperity Leads to a Changing America (1820's - 1850's)*

Chapter 15- *Reformers Improve American Life (1820's - 1850's)*

Chapter 16- *The Nation Gains Western Territories (1820's - 1850's)*

CHAPTER 13

A Democratic Era Begins Under Jackson (1820's-1840's)

Chapter Objectives

After completing this chapter, students will be able to:
1. Give reasons why Jackson was known as the "champion of the common people."
2. Explain the nullification crises and how it was resolved.
3. Discuss Jackson's Indian Removal plan and what it meant to the Indians.
4. Describe how Jackson defeated the Second Bank of the United States.
5. Explain why the Whig Candidate, William Henry Harrison, won the election of 1840.

Chapter Chronology

Chapter 13 covers the period from the 1820's to the early 1840's. Many of the important persons and events of the period are highlighted on the time line on the textbook Chapter Opener page. Andrew Jackson was elected President in 1828. In 1830, the Indian Removal Act was passed. Two years later, in 1832, Jackson was reelected and in the same year, the Whig Party was formed. The second Seminole War began in 1835. One year later, in 1836, Martin Van Buren was elected President. The Trail of Tears spanned the years 1838 to 1839. In the following year, 1840, William Henry Harrison was elected President.

Motivation

From time to time, an extraordinary leader emerges, influential and powerful, who affects the course of a nation's history. Andrew Jackson was such a leader. Ask the students to make a list of some of the qualities that they think such a leader must have, including grace under pressure, imagination, perseverance, courage, and forcefulness. Ask them to keep the list while they study the chapter, making additions and deletions as they read. At the end of the chapter they should have a "portrait of Jackson."

Geographical Setting

The Age of Jackson shifted the nation's focus from the East Coast to the frontier, west of the Appalachians. Jackson was a product of the frontier and drew his strongest support from the western settlers. This is a good place to review the major frontier areas of the period—the Old Northwest and the Old Southwest. Use the map in Chapter 12 on page 278 for this purpose.

To help students discover the results of Jackson's Indian Removal Policy use the map *Relocation of American Indians, 1830-1840*, on textbook page 310. Have the students identify the Indian tribes that were removed. Then ask them to locate the traditional Indian homelands, their new homes, and the routes they used to get there.

History Study Skills

The Chapter 13 History Study Skill is *Using a Line Graph*. The information graphed illustrates the increase in the number of voters between 1824 and 1840. You might want to use this skill in Section 5.

Bibliography

Teacher References
Ward, John William, *Andrew Jackson, Symbol for an Age.* Oxford University Press, N.Y., 1955.
Latner, Richard B., *The Presidency of Andrew Jackson: White House Politics, 1829-1837,* University of Georgia Press, Athens, Ga., 1979.
Student References
Remini, Robert V., *The Revolutionary Age of Andrew Jackson.* Harper & Row, New York City, 1976. This is a book whose human interest emphasis will interest most young readers.
Oppenheim, Joanne, *Sequoyah, Cherokee Hero.* Troll Associates, Mahwah, N.J., 1979. This is an excellent illustrated biography that concentrates on Sequoyah's invention of his Cherokee alphabet.

Audio-Visual Materials

The Jackson Years. The New Americans, Learning Corp. of America. Color, 27 minutes. This film illustrates the development of new American attitudes and the rise of popular democracy in the Jackson years.

The American Indian Speaks, Encyclopedia Britannica, color, 23 minutes. This is a documentary about the heritage of the American Indians with a look into what may lie ahead for them.

SECTION 1: The People Choose Jackson as President

OBJECTIVES

After completing this section, students will be able to:
- Explain Andrew Jackson's appeal to the common people of America.
- Describe the voting requirements for American citizens in the 1820's.
- Explain the "spoils system."
- Explain rotation in office in the federal government.

MOTIVATION

Ask the students to imagine themselves as American settlers and farmers in the 1820's. Have them describe their way of life—building and protecting their houses, working in the fields, making all the necessities of daily life in their homes. Then ask them to list the kind of leader they would feel most comfortable with and trust—someone born on the frontier, a hard worker, self-made person, brave soldier—leader willing to share hardships with troops.

SUGGESTED ACTIVITIES

1. **Directed Reading**. Now, write Andrew Jackson's name on the board. Inform students that they will be reading about his life and his accomplishments as President. As they read this section, ask them to note down the ways in which he showed his concern for "the common people." (He demonstrated a great willingness to fight for the causes of farmers, settlers, and working people, and gave Americans a feeling of greater participation in their government by giving them opportunities to hold government jobs.) Write the student responses on the chalkboard.

2. **Landmarks of Liberty.** Have the class read *Monument to Jackson, "The People's President"* on textbook page 307. Ask the students why they think this monument was built. As a follow-up and extension of the reading, have them answer the following questions:
   A. Why do you think Jackson is shown in uniform on horseback? (As a reminder of his exploits as a military leader)
   B. How else might he have been shown? (As president)
   C. In what other ways could Jackson have been honored? (Portrait on coins, places named after him)

3. **Writing Assignment**. Send above-average students to the library to investigate the voting laws in their state. Ask them first to list the requirements for voting, including age, residence, and registration. Then ask the students to write a paragraph comparing voting requirements today with those in the 1820's.

   Ask average and slower students to read the material in the textbook under the heading *The common people gain power* to answer the following questions:
   A. Who determined the voting qualifications of American citizens? (State governments)

B. Which citizens were allowed to vote in the 1820's? (All free adult white males)
C. Which groups of citizens were still denied the right to vote at that time? (Women, free blacks—in most states—and slaves)

4. **History Study Skills**. As suggested in the chapter introduction in this manual, have students complete the line graph activity at the end of Section 1. It will serve as a reinforcement for the information on the elections of 1824 and 1828 and preview voter trends for the remaining years covered by this chapter.

BUILDING AMERICAN CITIZENSHIP

When President Jackson took office, he tried to make the government more democratic by introducing the practice of "rotation in office." After reading this section, the students will realize that this practice is now obsolete. Ask students to think of ways in which the President and the Congress try to bring the democratic spirit to the nation's government. (The President, members of the Cabinet, and members of Congress appear frequently on television to share information with the people. In addition, the President and Congress members travel around the country, talking and listening to people. Citizens are encouraged to write letters to the President or their Representatives in Congress. Many Americans come to Washington, D.C., where they visit the Capitol to watch Congress at work, or tour government buildings to see the government in action. Citizens may also apply to get government jobs.

SECTION 1 REVIEW ANSWERS

1. **IDENTIFY: Kitchen Cabinet:** group of President Jackson's friends, mostly from the West, who met with Jackson at home to advise him on government matters.
2. **DEFINE: suffrage:** the right to vote; **nominating conventions:** special meetings called by people in cities, towns, or counties to choose candidates to run for public office; **spoils system:** the practice by winners to political office of hiring friends for jobs and firing enemies.
3. Instead of being chosen by Senators and members of Congress, party candidates were chosen by the people at nominating conventions held in cities, towns, and counties. When national elections were held, state nominating conventions were called to select presidential candidates.
4. Jackson fought laws harmful to farmers, frontier settlers, or working people. Serving ordinary Americans was his first concern.

SECTION 2: President Jackson Preserves the Union

OBJECTIVES

After completing this section, students will be able to:
- Explain the meaning of a protective tariff, its purposes, and how it works.
- Describe the national crises that resulted from the Tariff Act of 1828.
- Explain how the nullification crisis was solved.
- Organize a selected list of events in correct sequential order.

MOTIVATION

Use simple drawings on the chalkboard to help students understand what happens when imported goods are taxed. Automobiles, radios, or television sets would make good examples. Have students volunteer brand names of both American and foreign products. Ask which usually costs more—an American or imported product. Use made-up prices and show the effects of made-up taxes.

EXAMPLE:	Manufactuer's Price	Government Tax	Total Price
American radio	$50.00	0	$50.00
Imported radio	$50.00	20%	$60.00

Ask students which radio they would rather buy and why? Ask them why they think the government places taxes on imported goods? (To raise money, to encourage Americans to buy American products) Introduce the term "tariff" to the students. Explain to them that they are going to read about the most serious tariff problem in the nation's history.

SUGGESTED ACTIVITIES

1. **Directed Reading**. After they have read Section 2, ask the students to answer each of the questions below.
    (a) Why were the planters of South Carolina particularly unhappy about the Tariff of 1828? (b) What was the national crisis that came about as a result of the Tariff? (c) How was the crisis resolved? Direct the students to write the answer to each question in complete sentences in their notebooks. As a summary activity, discuss the answers to the questions. To develop critical thinking skills, discuss what might have occurred if it had been necessary to send federal troops into North Carolina.
2. **Sequencing.** This section provides an excellent opportunity for students to practice the skill of ordering events sequentially. You may use the list below.
    A. South Carolina passes a Nullification Act.
    B. President Jackson declares that the Union must be preserved.
    C. Henry Clay designs a compromise tariff.
    D. Senators Webster and Hayne debate states' rights.
    E. John C. Calhoun resigns as Vice-President.
    F. Congress passes the Tariff Act of 1828.
    The correct sequence would be F-D-B-E-A-C. In reviewing the correct answers to this exercise, you may want to ask students to state the cause of each event. For example: "F" was caused by the desire of Congress to protect American-made goods against competition from foreign nations' goods.
3. **Reading Documents**. This skill was introduced in Chapter 8 and can be practiced here. Ask students to go to the library to find the text of the following documents mentioned in this section.
    A. The Tariff Law of 1828
    B. Senator Hayne's speech to Congress
    C. Senator Webster's speech to Congress
    D. The South Carolina Nullification Act
    E. Jackson's Proclamation to the People of South Carolina

An alternative approach would be to read selected sections from these documents to the students. Then have them identify the document or the person with whom it would be associated.

BUILDING AMERICAN CITIZENSHIP

Throughout the nullification crisis, Jackson's main aim was the preservation of the Union, and all his decisions and subsequent actions were directed toward that end. The tone and content of his public statements ranged from conciliatory to provocative. For example, his behind-the-scenes efforts with Congress to lower the tariff rate had little or no effect on the crisis. His famous toast to the Union simply restated his view on the preservation of the Union. However, his "Proclamation to the People of South Carolina" was a serious warning and heated up the situation considerably.

Ask the students if they agree with Jackson's handling of the crisis. Have them discuss alternative actions that he might have taken. For example, could the crisis have been averted if Jackson had been more persistent in working to lower the tariff? Relate this activity to the students' experiences by having them discuss specific situations in their own lives and decisions that they have had to make. Have them consider alternative actions and their consequences.

SECTION 2 REVIEW ANSWERS

1. **IDENTIFY: John C. Calhoun:** Vice-President under Andrew Jackson who formed the doctrine of states' rights; **Robert Y. Hayne:** Senator from South Carolina who defended the doctrine of states' rights; **Daniel Webster:** Massachusetts Senator who defended the Union and upheld the power of the federal government to make laws for all the states; **Nullification Act:** law passed in South Carolina in 1832 declaring that the Tariff of 1828 was not to be enforced in that state.
2. **DEFINE: tariff:** tax placed on foreign goods sold in the United States; **protective tariff:** a tax on certain foreign goods, designed to protect American industries; **nullify:** to refuse to recognize or obey; **doctrine of states' rights:** the belief that state governments have certain rights and duties that are even more important than their ties to the federal government and that a state may nullify a federal law if it is harmful to the state's citizens.
3. South Carolina. People there felt that the law unfairly helped manufacturers of the Northeast while requiring Southerners to pay high prices for needed goods. They also felt the tariff hurt their sales of cotton to Britain because the tariff cut down on the sale of British goods in America.
4. In Clay's compromise, Congress agreed to pass a law lowering the tariff, and South Carolina accepted it.

SECTION 3: Jackson Moves the Indians West

OBJECTIVES

After completing this section, students will be able to:
• Name the tribes removed from their homelands in the Southeastern United States and the Old Northwest.

• Describe the feelings of the Indian groups removed from their homelands.
• State how the removal of Indians from their homelands was protested by them and by a few others.
• Use a map to gain specific information.

MOTIVATION

Use the map, *Relocation of American Indians, 1830-1840* on textbook page 310 to introduce the lesson. Have students answer the following questions orally.
1. What is the title of the map? (*Relocation of American Indians, 1830-1840*)
2. What is the meaning of the word "relocation"? (To transfer from one location to another)
3. Which tribes were relocated from the Southern part of the U.S.? (Cherokee, Creek, Chickasaw, Choctaw, Seminole)
4. Which tribes were relocated from the northern part of the United States? (Sauk and Fox)
5. Does this map tell you why the Indians were relocated from their lands? (No)
6. Does the map tell you how they were relocated? (No)
7. Does the map tell you when the Indians were relocated? (Yes, between 1830 and 1840)
8. Does the map tell you if anyone besides the Indians was involved in this predicament? (No)
9. Does the map tell you how the Indians felt about moving? (No)

This is a good time to review the functions of maps. Remind students that maps can show location, distance, and directions. However, they cannot tell why an event occurred, how it happened, or how people felt about it.

SUGGESTED ACTIVITIES

1. **Directed Reading.** On the board, rewrite questions 5, 6, 8, and 9 from Motivation. Use them as guide questions for the students to answer as they read this section. Ask the students to write the questions and answers in their notebooks. The answers are.
   5) White settlers and farmers demanded the lands owned by the Indians. Jackson agreed and proposed a plan for the removal of the Indians.
   6) Some were removed peacefully, after signing treaties. Others, including the Sauk, Fox, Cherokee, and Seminole tribes fought with federal troops, who forced them to leave.
   8) People involved other than the Indians including Andrew Jackson, Senator Frelinghuysen, General Wiley Thompson, and Justice John Marshall. Federal troops and settlers were also involved.
   9) The Indians did not want to give up their lands. Some protested peacefully, while others fought to keep them.
2. **Reviewing Map Skills.** Duplicate Worksheet 34, *Indian Relocation.* The questions on the Worksheet extend the information in the text while reviewing the map skills developed in previous chapters. You may wish to compare the map of Indian Relocation on textbook page 310 with the Worksheet map. Ask students to list the differences between the maps. (The Worksheet map shows only the five Southeastern tribes, whereas the textbook map shows the reloca-

tion of Northern tribes. The Worksheet map shows the specific locations of each tribe within the states; the textbook map indicates the states from which the tribes were relocated.

3. **Research Assignment**. Several Indians who fought against removal are mentioned by tribe. These include the Cherokee leader, John Ross; the Sauk chief, Black Hawk; and the Seminole chief, Osceola. Have students identify each of these leaders and the roles they played in trying to prevent removal of their tribes. Ask the students to identify the chiefs of other tribes involved and how they reacted to Jackson's removal policy.

4. **Statistical Study**. In this section the students learn the estimated combined population (60,000) of the five Southern tribes discussed, prior to their removal. Have your above-average students research the population figures for each tribe before removal. Then have them find the number in each tribe that were actually resettled in Indian Territory. This information may be recorded in table form or converted to a bar graph. For average and below-average students, you may wish to provide the figures and demonstrate how to convert them to a graph or table.

BUILDING AMERICAN CITIZENSHIP

Ask students to define "discrimination" (showing prejudice). Then have them read the statements of Governor John Gayle of Alabama and Senator Theodore Frelinghuysen in this chapter. Ask students which of the two statements is discriminatory and why? (Gayle points to differences in language and customs to "prove" Indians' inequality with white people)

Ask the students why Gayle's conclusions about the Indians are invalid? (He was looking for reasons to deprive the Indians of their property; he wrongly assumed that the language, customs, and laws of white people are more important than those of Indians)

SECTION 3 REVIEW ANSWERS

1. **IDENTIFY: "Sharp Knife":** Creek and Seminole Indian name for Andrew Jackson; **Indian Removal Act:** law passed in 1830 that granted Jackson $500,000 to buy Indian land; **John Ross:** Cherokee leader who asked the Supreme Court to rule on the right of the Cherokees to keep their land in Georgia; *Worcester v. Georgia:* Supreme Court case in which Chief Justice John Marshall ruled that Georgia had no right to pass laws requiring the removal of the Cherokees; **Chief Black Hawk:** leader of the Sauk and Fox Indian tribes in their battles to keep their lands in Illinois and Wisconsin; **Osceola:** leader of the Seminole Indians in their fight to keep their land in Florida and resist moving to Indian Territory.

2. Jackson's policy was to pay Indians for their land and to resettle them in Indian Territory—land set aside for them west of the Mississippi River.

3. The Cherokees challenged the constitutionality of Georgia laws threatening their rights and appealed to the Supreme Court to rule on their right to keep their lands.

4. The Sauk, Fox, and Seminole tribes.

SECTION 4: Jackson Fights the National Bank

OBJECTIVES

After completing this section, students will be able to:
- Identify Jackson's reason for destroying the Bank of the United States.
- Explain Jackson's new banking plan.
- State the results of Jackson's banking policies.

MOTIVATION

Set up a role-playing situation around the Bank of the United States. You will need: chalkboard, a sign saying "banker," and play money. Arrange to meet with five students the day before the lesson for a rehearsal as described below.

To begin, write BANK OF THE UNITED STATES as well as its current assests ($10,000) on the chalkboard, and set up a banker's station (a desk) in front of it. Provide the teller with a supply of "money" of which a running total must be kept on the board as the skit proceeds.

STUDENT #1: (Mr. Blacksmith) "I wish to deposit my year's savings of $100."
BANKER: "Thank you very much."
STUDENT #2: (Mrs. Storekeeper) "I wish to deposit last week's profits of $1,000."
BANKER: "Thank you very much."
STUDENT #3: (Mr. Rich Property Owner) "I wish to borrow $11,000 to build a new factory."
BANKER: "Glad to be of service, sir."
STUDENT #4: (Mr. Farmer) "I wish to borrow $50 to fix my fences."
BANKER: "Sorry, that is impossible right now."
STUDENT #3: (Mr. Rich Property Owner) pays back $100 of his loan.
STUDENT #2: (Mrs. Storekeeper) returns to withdraw $500 to buy more supplies.
BANKER: "Sorry, all I have is $200. Here you are, Madam."
STUDENT #1: (Mr. Blacksmith) returns to withdraw $50 to buy new tools.
BANKER: "Sorry, we are out of money and must close now. Please come back another time when we are open."

Start a discussion with students concerning the Bank's practices. Whom does the Bank seem to favor? (Mr. Rich Property Owner—those who have money.) Whom does the Bank ignore? (Mr. Farmer—the common man.) What happened to the rest of the money owed by Mr. Property Owner? (Special easy payment arrangements are made for the wealthy.)

Ask the students how they would solve this financial crisis, if like President Jackson, they were leaders who swore to protect the common people. List their suggested solutions on the board.

SUGGESTED ACTIVITIES

1. **Directed Reading**. Have students read this section and then answer the following guide questions:
   A. Why did Jackson destroy the Bank of the United States?

B. What was Jackson's plan for making the distribution of the government's money more equal across the nation?

C. What were the results of Jackson's money policies?

As a summary activity, compare Jackson's actions with the list of solutions suggested by students.

2. **Puzzle.** Use an acrostic to review the meaning of the vocabulary developed in the section.

reDeem	D -	to cash in
chartEred	E -	given a contract to operate
Pet banks	P -	23 state banks into which the government's money was deposited in 1833
bank nOtes	O -	paper money
Speculators	S -	persons who invest money hoping to make quick profits
specIe	I -	gold or silver
VeTo	T -	the president's power to disapprove of a law

3. **Reading for the Main Idea**. Review the important points of the Chapter 5 History Study Skill. Select specific paragraphs from the various headings in this section and have students identify the main idea in each.

Examples:

A. Paragraph One under *The banks and paper money*. Main idea: During the 1820's and 1830's, some bankers misused their depositors' money.

B. Paragraph One under *The Bank of the United States*. Main idea: First sentence.

C. Last paragraph under *Jackson makes war on the Bank*. Main idea: Difficult banking problems had to be solved now that the "monster" was dead.

D. Paragraph One under *Jackson's bank plan causes trouble*. Main idea: Jackson's plan to deposit the government's money throughout the states did not work very well.

For below-average students, you may want to list the main ideas on the chalkboard. Then have the students find the sentences in the paragraphs from which they were selected. Students should be able to state details from the paragraphs to support their choices.

4. **Cartoon Analysis.** Have students study the cartoon of Jackson's fight with the Bank of the United States on textbook page 315 to answer the following questions.

A. What is Jackson holding in his hand? (An order to remove the government's money.)

B. How is the destruction of the Bank of the United States represented in the cartoon? (Falling pillars)

C. Why is the man next to Jackson smiling? (He agrees with Jackson's orders.)

D. Whom might this figure represent? (The common people)

BUILDING AMERICAN CITIZENSHIP

Sometimes people allow their personal feelings and opinions to affect their judgments and decisions. Have students give instances from their own lives. Example: joining a school club that does not really interest you because a good friend is joining. Draw a parallel with Jackson's decisions during the national bank crisis. What personal opinions and feelings affected his judgment? (Unwillingness to forgive a political enemy, dislike for wealthy Americans, impatience, unwillingness to listen to financial advisers) What were the unfortunate results of his decisions? (Decrease in the value of paper money, bank closings, a serious business depression)

SECTION 4 REVIEW ANSWERS

1. **IDENTIFY: Nicholas Biddle:** President of the Second Bank of the United States in Philadelphia; **Specie Circular:** order issued by President Jackson in 1836 requiring people to pay for government land in gold or silver only.

2. **DEFINE: bank notes:** paper money; **redeem:** to cash in paper money for gold or silver; **specie:** gold or silver; **chartered:** given a contract to operate; **"pet banks":** nickname given by newspaper writers to the 23 state banks in which Jackson deposited the federal government's money; **speculators:** persons who invest money hoping to make quick profits.

3. Jackson felt that the government's money gave special advantages to wealthy Americans, expecially in the East; he also felt that it had too much political power in its lending money to Congress members running for reelection.

4. The state banks were hard to control; they printed too much paper money, and as a result, the value of paper money fell and prices began rising. People began to borrow recklessly, especially to buy government land.

SECTION 5: The Whig Party Challenges the Democrats

OBJECTIVES

After completing this section, students will be able to:
• Compare various selected characteristics of Presidents Jackson, Van Buren, and Harrison.
• State the reasons for Van Buren's growing unpopularity among the voters.
• List the campaign tactics used by the Whigs in the election of 1840.

MOTIVATION

Create a display of campaign memorabilia for your classroom. This may include bumper stickers, posters, buttons, pamphlets, pictures, newspaper articles, and advertisements, banners, hats, etc. Ask students to identify familiar names (nicknames) of the candidates, the offices they seek, the promises they make, and their slogans as indicated by these items. Ask students why these items are used (to help get candidates elected). Ask students to name other methods used by candidates (speeches, radio and television commercials, traveling to all parts of the country, visiting neighborhoods, schools, businesses) Explain that this section includes the story of the first campaign to use such items.

SUGGESTED ACTIVITIES

1. **Directed Reading**. As students read this section, have them write down the methods used by the Whigs to get their candidate elected in 1840. These include handing out banners, campaign buttons, hats, and flags; holding rallies and organizing parades; singing political songs and giving away free cider. Review this list with students after they have read the section. As a summary activity, compare the methods used in the campaign of 1840 with those used today. Which of today's popular methods were not in use in 1840? (e.g., bumper stickers because there were no cars; radio and television advertising)

2. **Comparison and Contrast.** Have the class read about Van Buren and Harrison. Then ask students to compare them with Andrew Jackson in terms of backgrounds, political views, and ability to deal with people. This can best be accomplished by directing students to construct a simple table as shown below:

	JACKSON	VAN BUREN	HARRISON
BACKGROUND	(Military hero, self-made man)	(Self-made man)	(Military hero, claimed to be self-made man)
POLITICAL VIEWS	(Opposed nullification; supported Indian removal, opposed the Second Bank)	(Supported Jackson's views completely)	(Favored states' rights, willing to spend federal money to build roads and canals.)
ABILITY TO DEAL WITH PEOPLE	(A champion of the common people)	(Had skill in dealing with political leaders and voters)	(Could talk with ordinary Americans and attract their support)

From the information on the table, have students answer these questions:

A. In which ways were all three presidents very much alike? (Ability to deal with people)
B. How was William Henry Harrison most unlike the other two? (Political views)
C. Which president, do you think, was the least popular? Why? (Probably Van Buren because of his failure to deal effectively with the 1837 Depression)

3. **Oral Reports**. Many important events occurred during the administrations of Jackson and Van Buren. A partial list follows. Ask each student to choose an event and, using the library, to investigate and prepare an oral report to present to the class.

A. The election of the first President born after the achievement of American independence. (Van Buren)
B. The murder of Elijah P. Lovejoy
C. The Battle of San Jacinto
D. The birth of "Uncle Sam"
E. Samuel Colt's invention of the six-shooter

F. The publication of the first McGuffey Reader
G. The invention of the daguerreotype
H. The results of the 1840 census
I. The "Restook" War
J. The invention of the screw propeller

As students present their reports, the rest of the class should note the event and the date on which it occurred. Draw a time line on the chalkboard, indicating which events occurred during the administration of each President.

4. **Planning a Political Campaign, 1840.** Duplicate Worksheet 36. The type of campaign tactics used in the election of 1840, were emphasized in Section 5. This activity points out *where* they should be utilized. It may also be used to practice map skills. Have students trace or draw an outline map of the United States. Ask them to label each state and its total electoral votes, and to create a map key to distinguish slave and free states. Finally, have them underline the names of the 14 states they have selected as crucial in planning their campaign.

5. **History Study Skills.** Duplicate Worksheet 35, *Farm Size and Land Prices.* Relate the activity to the content of Section 5 by asking students to speculate about the cost of land in the years 1836 and 1840. Using their knowledge of the business depression, the shortage of currency, and the failure of the subtreasury system, students should be able to give an opinion regarding the direction of the lines on the graph.

BUILDING AMERICAN CITIZENSHIP

Citizens join political parties for a variety of reasons. In this section, students have read about the types of people who joined the new Whig Party and why they did. Review this information found in the text under the heading *The Whigs challenge the Democratic Party.* Ask the students to decide which of the two political parties they would have joined and why.

You may wish to ask students also to think about which of today's political parties they would join and why. An informal poll of the results can serve as a follow-up to this lesson, with emphasis on the reason or reasons for joining a party.

SECTION 5 REVIEW ANSWERS

1. **IDENTIFY: Independent Treasury System:** the system proposed by President Van Buren in which the federal government removed money from state banks and placed it in "subtreasuries" in cities across the nation; **William Henry Harrison:** Whig candidate elected President in 1840; **John Tyler:** Whig candidate elected Vice-President in 1840.
2. The Whig Party.
3. In the 1830's Americans did not believe that the federal government should be directly involved in the lives of its citizens.
4. The Whigs borrowed the campaign tactics of Jackson and Van Buren. They handed out banners, campaign buttons, hats, and flags. They held parades and rallies and tried to create the image that Harrison was a man of the people.

CHAPTER 13 REVIEW ANSWERS

REVIEWING KEY WORDS

1. d.   2. b.   3. a.   4. e.   5. c.

REMEMBERING IMPORTANT PEOPLE AND EVENTS

1. c.   2. a.   3. c.   4. b.   5. b.

REVIEWING THE FACTS

1. T   2. T   3. F   4. T   5. F

PLACING EVENTS IN TIME

1. E.   2. B.   3. C.   4. A.   5. D.

LINKING GEOGRAPHY AND HISTORY

The swamps—known as the Everglades—made an excellent place to hide. The federal troops did not know their way around the swamps.

THINKING ABOUT AMERICAN HISTORY

1. Cotton farmers wanted to start plantations on the rich soil held by the Indians. Pioneer farm families wanted to clear the forests held by the Indians to gain new land for farming. Also, some people thought that the Indians were inferior people who were not "civilized" and that Indians and whites could not live together peacefully.
2. Van Buren was President when it happened. Also, he took very little action to try to stop it.

APPLYING HISTORY STUDIES SKILLS

1. To compare numbers to see how they change.
2. Title, vertical axis, horizontal axis.
3. 16.   4. 1828 and 1836
5. 30.7 percent.   6. 1832.
7. 1824: John Quincy Adams
   1832: Andrew Jackson
   1836: Martin Van Buren
   1840: William Henry Harrison

CHAPTER 14

Prosperity Leads to a Changing America (1820's-1850's)

Chapter Objectives

After completing this chapter, students will be able to:
1. Explain why the shipping industry was so important to the prosperity of the American economy.
2. Identify the various technological improvements in transportation and communication that occurred during this period.
3. Describe some of the changes and shifts in American population between the 1820's and the 1850's.
4. Name several important inventions and how they changed the life in America during this period.
5. Identify some American writers and their works that were representative of a newly emerging national culture.

Chapter Chronology

Chapter 14 covers the period from the 1820's to the 1850's. Numerous major technological developments and inventions occurred during this time. Many of the important persons and events of the period are highlighted on the time line on the textbook Chapter Opener page. In 1830, *Tom Thumb* made its run in Maryland. One year later, Cyrus McCormick invented the reaper. Samuel Colt invented the revolver that bears his name in 1835. In the city of Boston, the nation's first paid police force was organized in 1837. In that year Sarah Josepha Hale became editor of *Godey's Lady's Book*. In 1845, the first American clipper ship set sail and the Know-Nothings were organized. Two major inventions of the 1840's were Elias Howe's sewing machine, invented in 1846 and the improved steel plow, invented in 1847.

Motivation

Ask students to read the introductory anecdote about Samuel Colt in the text. Then have them read the titles of the five chapter sections. Ask students to define the key words in each title (trade and commerce, transportation and communications, cities and population, technology and culture.) Finally, have students look at the time line for Chapter 14. Ask them to guess in which section each of the events listed on it will be discussed.

Geographical Setting

In the first section student attention is focused on China, Japan, the Mediterranean region, and Cape Horn, as well as the coast of present-day Oregon—areas that attracted American traders. Use a map of the world to show students those areas. The rest of Chapter 14 is domestic in focus, concentrating on expansion of trade and population in the United States. Refer students to the map, *Railroads in the United States in 1860* on textbook page 330. Ask students where most railroads start? Where do they go? How does geography influence the location of railroads?

History Study Skills

The History Study Skill in Chapter 14 teaches how to interpret data on a map. One of the maps in this chapter is *Major Roads in the United States in 1840*. Teach it just before beginning Section 2, when the focus shifts to domestic transportation. The skill page is an excellent way to introduce students to domestic transportation routes while teaching them map interpretation skills.

Bibliography

Teacher References

Nye, Russel B., *Society and Culture in America, 1830-1860.* Harper and Row, New York City, 1974.

Weisberger, Bernard A., *They Gathered at the River: The Story of Great Revivals and Their Impact Upon Religion in America.* Octagon Books, New York City, 1958.

Student References

Blumenthal, Shirley, and Ozer, Jerome S., *Coming to America: Immigrants from the British Isles.* Delacorte Press, New York City, 1980. This book contains excellent photographs, prints, and stories.

Fisher, Leonard E., *The Railroads*. Holiday House, Inc., New York City, 1979. This is a thorough survey of the development of railroads throughout the 19th century.

Audio-Visual Materials

Stephen Foster and His Songs, Coronet, color, 16 minutes. This is a life of Foster which provides the historical background to his songs.

The Transportation Revolution, Learning Corp of America, color, 21 minutes. Students will see how changing modes of transportation shaped life in the United States.

SECTION 1: American Trade and Commerce Grows

OBJECTIVES

After completing this section, students will be able to:
- Identify the types of ocean-going vessels used during the first half of the 1800's.
- Explain how shipping helped America prosper.
- Describe the appearance and capabilities of clipper-ships.

MOTIVATION

Use the first activity under Geographical Settings in the manual chapter introduction. After students have located Asia, China, the Mediterranean region, Cape Horn, and the coast of present-day Oregon, discuss the types of transportation that they might use today to reach these locations. Help them determine the amount of time each might take. Then discuss the different means of transportation available during the 1800's to reach the various locations, and the time involved in each. Students should realize that the only way to reach Asia, Cape Horn, and the Mediterrean region during the 1800's was by ship.

SUGGESTED ACTIVITIES

1. **Directed Reading.** Using the discussion under Motivation as a springboard, ask students to read this section and answer the questions below:
   A. Why did people want to travel to Asia? (To trade)
   B. What was the fastest means of transportation available during the first half of the 1800's? (Clipper ship)
   C. Why was travel temporarily interrupted between the years 1807 and 1815? (The 1807 embargo followed by the War of 1812)
   Summarize the activity by having students list both the various items that Americans shipped to other nations and the items that we wished to purchase from other countries.
2. **Writing a Report**. Direct average and below-average students to write a brief report on the development of the clipper ship. Have them use the information in the chapter. The report should focus on the following questions:
   A. Who designed the ship?
   B. In what ways did this ship differ from other ocean-going vessels?

C. What was the name of the first ship of this type?
D. When was it built?
E. Who was responsible for improving the design?
F. How did the ship help to increase trade with other nations?
Above-average students may be sent to the library to prepare a similar report on the development of steamships. They may use the same questions as an outline for their research.
3. **Outlining**. The Motivation activity in the manual chapter introduction suggests the main topics for an outline of Chapter 14: transportation, trade, population, technology, and culture. Begin this outline with Section 1. Using "transportation" as the first topic, develop the first part of the outline as follows:
   I. Transportation
      A. Improvements in water transportation
         1. Packet lines
         2. Clipper ships
         3. Steamships
The outline should be kept in students' notebooks for ready reference so that additions can be made as they study the next four sections of the chapter.

BUILDING AMERICAN CITIZENSHIP

One of the basic freedoms of all American citizens is the selection of the occupation of their choice. This section details many of the occupations associated with the shipbuilding industry. Ask students to list these occupations. Then have them add whatever new ones have resulted from modern improvements in the shipping industry. A partial list of both old and new shipping related occupations would include dockworkers, sailors, shipbuilders, merchants, bookkeepers, lumberjacks, computer operators, and managers. Discuss the benefits and drawbacks of these different types of occupations. You may also want to ask those students who seem especially interested to investigate educational requirements, physical requirements, and salary scales for these occupations.

SECTION 1 REVIEW ANSWERS

1. **IDENTIFY: Robert Shaw:** American sea captain who began American's China trade in 1874 when he sailed the *Empress of China* from New York harbor to Canton, China; **Robert Gray:** sea captain who traded with Indians in Oregon for furs, which he took to China to trade; **John Griffith:** naval architect who in 1845 designed the first American clipper ship; **David McKay:** designer of faster clipper ships, often called Yankee Clippers.
2. **DEFINE: packet lines:** shipping companies that operated on fixed arrival and departure schedules; **clipper ship:** a beautiful ocean-going sailing ship that used many sails to increase its speed.
3. Clipper ships were faster than other ships, thus enabling the United States to take over most of the China and East Asian trade. They also created many jobs, not only for the large crews needed to handle the sails but also for lumberjacks, shipbuilders, manufacturers, storeowners, and the government, which collected taxes on the sales of foreign goods.

4. Money made from trade was often invested in new businesses, which resulted in new ways of producing wealth, goods, and jobs for Americans.

SECTION 2: Transportation and Communication Improve

OBJECTIVES

After completing this section, students will be able to:
- Describe improvements in stagecoach and railroad transportation.
- Name two ways in which communication improved during the early 1800's.
- Continue the outline they began in Section 1.

MOTIVATION

Have students complete the History Study Skill on textbook page 345. When they have done the map interpretation exercise, ask them to name the types of transportation that people would use to travel from one place to another on these roads (carts, wagons, carriages, horses, walking). Then ask which of those modes of transportation are still used today.

SUGGESTED ACTIVITIES

1. **Directed Reading**. Students should read this section before adding to the outline started in Section 1. Encourage above-average students to accomplish this independently. You may wish to offer suggestions to average and below-average students.

   B. Improvements in Land Transportation
      1. Stagecoaches
         a. Roof flattened
         b. Spring suspension introduced
      2. Locomotive
         a. T-rail   b. Spike
   II. Communication
      A. Telegraph invented by Samuel Morse
      B. More newspapers printed
         1. Rotary press invented
         2. Penny press became popular

   As a summary activity, ask students how each of the improvements made a difference in the lives of the American people.

2. **Coding and Decoding**. Secure a copy of the Morse Code. Duplicate it so that each students can have a copy. Ask students to translate a short sentence of their own into Morse Code and write it down. Then have them exchange papers and decode the message written by a classmate. If possible, borrow several telegraph keys from the science department. Ask for volunteers to "send" messages using the keys. Have the class try to decode them. Ask students to explain why this invention was so important in the early 1800's (made it possible to send messages from one part of the country to another) and why it is less important today (faster means of communications are avaliable).

3. **Categorization**. This section deals with improvements and inventions in four areas: the stagecoach, the locomotive, the telegraph, and newspapers. Write them as form heads on one side of the board. On the other side, copy the items in the list below. Direct students to list these items under the correct head. This activity will reinforce the outlining skills that are being practiced throughout the chapter.
   A. Making paper (N)   F. Rotary press (N)
   B. Spike (L)   G. Flat roof (S)
   C. Dots and dashes (T) H. Spring suspension (S)
   D. Setting type (N)   I. Electric signals (T)
   E. Copper wire (T)

4. **Writing Reports.** Four inventors, Richard Hoe, Samuel Morse, Robert Stevens, and Peter Cooper, are mentioned in this section. Ask students to go to the library and prepare short reports on the inventions of each person. You may wish to suggest that students emphasize the problems encountered in designing the invention and then have it accepted by the American people. After the reports are presented to the class, introduce for discussion the question, "Which inventor was the most important? Why?"

5. **History Study Skills**. As suggested in the chapter introduction in this manual, use the map interpretation exercise with this section. The map shows transportation routes, the theme of Section 2. Ask students specific questions regarding these routes. For example:
   A. Which rivers were most likely used for transportation?
   B. Which roads were used by settlers moving to the West?

6. **Using Multi-Purpose Maps**. Duplicate Worksheet 39, *Roads in 1840.* This activity will help reinforce students' awareness of American transportation before railroads were built.

BUILDING AMERICAN CITIZENSHIP

The four inventors described in this section had to use their abilities and get them accepted. Students should realize the difficulties the inventors had to overcome after preparing and presenting the reports in activity 4. Although not everyone has the talent to become an inventor, all people have the capacity to use their abilities to the fullest. Encourage students to apply this concept to their own lives. Ask them to list their own special talents and abilities. Then have them think of various ways in which they can use those abilities both now and in the future.

SECTION 2 REVIEW ANSWERS

1. **IDENTIFY: Peter Cooper:** an American who ran the steam locomotive *Tom Thumb* on tracks between Ellicot City and Baltimore in a challenge with a horse-drawn carriage; *Tom Thumb:* a steam engine; **Robert Stevens:** designer of the "T" rail and the spike and other railroad improvements; **Samuel F. B. Morse:** American painter and artists who invented the telegraph and the Morse code; **Richard M. Hoe:** designer of a rotary printing printing press that could print 8,000 newspapers an hour.

2. **DEFINE: spike:** a long, square-headed metal nail that attached iron rails to wooden ties; **Morse Code:** a code using short and long pulses of sound, called dots and dashes, by which messages could be sent over a telegraph wire.

3. The stagecoach.
4. Improved method of making paper; new ways of setting type; invention of a rotary printing press.

SECTION 3: Cities and Their Populations Change

OBJECTIVES

After completing this section, students will be able to:
- Identify the reasons for the growth of towns and cities.
- List some of the problems that developed in urban areas.
- Identify the national origins of American immigrants and the reasons they came to America.
- Discuss the reaction of Americans to the arrival of the immigrants.

MOTIVATION

Ask students if they know the meaning of the word metropolis (large city that is a center of business, education, culture, and politics). Have volunteers name American cities today that they feel fit that description. Then have them guess which of those cities were already regarded as metropolises in the 1860's.

SUGGESTED ACTIVITIES

1. **Directed Reading**. Have the students read this section, and use the following as guide questions:
   A. Why did the population of cities increase between the 1820's and the 1850's? (offered job opportunities, waves of immigrants)
   B. What problems developed in urban areas as a result of this growth in population? (poor sanitation, poor housing, crime)
   C. Why were some Americans upset by the increase in immigration? (jobs threatened, afraid their way of life would change)
2. **Map Study**. Utilizing a wall map of the United States, ask students to locate the nine cities classified *metropolises* in 1860. Have students define "metropolis." Ask them to state the population figure and other attributes that qualified each of these cities for that designation.
3. **Using an Almanac to Make a Table**. Using a current almanac, have students find the population of each of the nine cities above both for the year 1860 and for the current year. Ask them to create a table Nine Largest Cities in America in 1860 and _____ (the current year). You may wish to provide slower students with the necessary information but out of order. Then ask them to reorganize it in the form of a table, matching the correct cities and population figures in 1860 with those for the current year.
4. **Making a Table.** Have students draw a table to organize the information concerning the immigrant groups that came to America. Use the following headings:

IMMIGRATION TO AMERICA		
COUNTRY OF ORIGIN	REASONS THEY CAME	WHERE THEY SETTLED

5. **Reviewing Graphs**. Duplicate Worksheet 38, *Immigration*. It will offer an excellent review of the History Study Skill for Chapter 9 and also give students more information about the nations from which immigrants came to America between 1800 and 1860.

BUILDING AMERICAN CITIZENSHIP

Duplicate Worksheet 37, *A Nation of Immigrants*. This activity reviews the History Study Skills for Chapters 5 and 10, and also provides insights about the contributions of three immigrant groups to American society.

SECTION 3 REVIEW ANSWERS

1. **IDENTIFY: potato blight:** a disease that destroyed the potato crop in Ireland in the 1840's; **Know-Nothings:** a group of American Protestants who formed the Order of the Star Spangled Banner, whose members promised to vote against Catholics and foreigners running for office.
2. **DEFINE: metropolis:** a large city that is the center of business, education, culture, and politics; **prejudice:** dislike of a group of people because of race, religion, or other reasons.
3. Many new settlers came to cities, including farmers, ambitious people looking for new business opportunities, and immigrants. Some cities grew because of a special industry in the area, others because they were located near a transportation route, and still others because they were port cities where new immigrants landed.
4. Irish: to escape starvation after the potato blight in 1845; Germans: mainly for political reasons and to escape punishment for criticizing their government. Dutch and Scandinavians: mainly to find religious freedom.

SECTION 4: Technology Changes Everyday Life and Work

OBJECTIVES

After completing this section, students will be able to:
- List several inventions that changed life in America on the farms and in the factories.
- Describe working conditions in a typical factory of the 1800's.
- Explain the differences between working in a factory and working at home .

MOTIVATION

Refer students to the time line in the textbook at the beginning of Chapter 14. Have them select those inventions on the time line that they have not yet read about (reaper, revolver, sewing machine, and steel plow). Ask them to look at the pictures in Section 4 to see which of these inventions are shown. Remind students of the title of this section and ask how they think these four inventions might have changed everyday life at that time.

SUGGESTED ACTIVITIES

1. **Directed Reading.** As students read this section, have them list the inventions mentioned and have them state one way in which each helped to change everyday life.
   Example: the steel plow made plowing easier in the upper West.
   As a summary activity, have students review their notes orally, and name the person responsible for each invention.

2. **Outlining.** Continue the outline developed in Sections 1 and 2. Ask students to make suggestions for the third topic, or provide them with the information that follows:
   III. Improved Technology
      A. Inventions change farm life
         1. Steel plow   2. Reaper   3. Thresher
      B. Invention change factory work
         1. Interchangeable or standard parts
         2. Sewing macine

3. **Writing Assignment**. Ask students to write a short composition on one of the following topics:
   A. The differences between working in a factory and working at home during the 1800's.
   B. The differences between working in a factory in the 1800's and working in a factory today.

4. **Preparing a Report**. This assignment is similar to the one suggested in Section 2. Have students go to the library to prepare short reports on one of the inventors mentioned in this section. Again, have students emphasize the problem each person encountered in designing the invention and having it accepted by the American people. After the reports have been presented in class, have students discuss the question, "Which invention was the most important? Why?"

5. **Landmarks of Liberty**. Have students read *The Smithsonian Institution* on textbook page 338. After they have answered the questions at the end of the reading, ask them to name some of the people in Section 4 whose contributions and inventions they think might be found in the Smithsonian. Ask them to recall other people from previous sections whose work might also be represented there.

BUILDING AMERICAN CITIZENSHIP

A major aspect of any career that a person might choose is having a sense of pride in one's job. This is also true of one's career as a student. Ask students to describe what aspects of their lives as students give them the most satisfaction. Discuss ways of developing a sense of pride in their school, home, town, and country.

SECTION 4 REVIEW ANSWERS

1. **IDENTIFY: John Deere:** a blacksmith who invented a steel plow in 1847; **Cyrus McCormick:** inventor of a horse-drawn reaper; **Samuel Colt:** inventor of a revolver with interchangeable parts; **Elias Howe:** New England farmer who invented a sewing machine; **Isaac Singer:** inventor of an improved sewing machine.

2. A steel plow, a reaper, and a thresher.
3. Factories were dark, poorly lit, poorly ventilated buildings. Workers had no places to eat, rest, or wash up. Many factory machines were made without proper safety features. Workers worked 12 to 13 hours with little time for meals. There was very little satisfaction for workers who did only one job.

SECTION 5: The Nation Develops an American Culture

OBJECTIVES

After completing this section, students will be able to:
- Identify the elements that made up the newly emerged American culture of the 1800's.
- Associate the names of individuals with their particular cultural contribution.

MOTIVATION

Write the title of this section on the chalkboard. Discuss the meaning of the word "culture," with emphasis on what aspects of life could be identified as culture. Ask the students to skim the section, reading only the headings emphasized in bold type. From the headings, they should be able to discover that culture comprises literature, including prose and poetry, history, painting, and music.

SUGGESTED ACTIVITIES

1. **Directed Reading.** As students read this section, have them complete the outline of the chapter. The fourth main topic should be "culture." The subtopics should be these elements identified in the Motivation. Example:
   IV. Culture
      A. Literature
         1. Washington Irving
         2. James Fenimore Cooper
      B. Poetry
         1. Henry Wadsworth Longfellow
         2. William Cullen Bryant
   Summarize the lesson by having students name one contribution by each of the figures named.

2. **Preparing a Report**. Many of the books and poems mentioned in this section are appropriate for readers in this age group. They should be available in the school or community library. Ask above-average students to select one of these literary works and complete a report on it. Direct them to use the following question as a guide:
   A. What is the main ideas of the work?
   B. What does it tell you about life in the 1800's?
   C. Did you enjoy reading this work? Why or why not?
   Assign selected excerpts to average and below-average students. Then ask them to write a brief report in answer to question B above.

3. **Round Robin**. Use this method, as introduced in Chapter 1: Have a student volunteer state a fact from Section 5. Have a second volunteer repeat the fact, and state another. Have a third student volunteer repeat the fact stated by the second, and state another. Continue this activity, as time and resources allow.

BUILDING AMERICAN CITIZENSHIP

With the class, review Emerson's ideas as they are stated under the heading, *The Concord Group writes about self-reliance.* Have students explain what is meant by "self-reliance." Ask them how they can put Emerson's ideas into practice in their own lives, with emphasis on the following:
A. Daring to be individuals
B. Looking toward the future
C. Being self-reliant
D. Taking pride in their own nation

SECTION 5 REVIEW ANSWERS

1. **IDENTIFY: Washington Irving:** first American writer to become famous from writing about his own country; **James Fenimore Cooper:** author of stories about the New York frontier; **Herman Melville:** author of stories about the sea, notably *Moby-Dick;* **Henry Wadsworth Longfellow:** best-loved poet of New England, author of *The Song of Hiawatha* and "Paul Revere's Ride"; **Nathaniel Hawthorne:** author of novels about the conflicts caused by Puritan beliefs; **Ralph Waldo Emerson:** New England philosopher, known as "the Sage of Concord"; **Henry David Thoreau:** New England writer who left his home to live simply at Walden Pond, where he wrote *Walden;* **Edgar Allan Poe:** Southern author of poems and short stories; creator of detective stories; **George Bancroft:** popular historian who wrote a 10-volume history of the United States; **Thomas Cole:** American artist and founder of the Hudson River School, where he taught younger artists; **Stephen Foster:** the most popular songwriter of the 1800's, who wrote about ordinary people in the South in such songs as "My Old Kentucky Home" and "Oh, Susanna."
2. **DEFINE: lyceum:** a lecture hall where people heard speakers on science, politics, religion, and other subjects.
3. Americans were developing a sense of pride in their nation's history and in their own opinions and ways of doing things. They stopped imitating European culture. Many Americans read books by American writers. Artists and writers used American themes and settings for their works.
4. Many artists and writers celebrated nature in their works.

CHAPTER 14 REVIEW ANSWERS
REVIEWING KEY WORDS

1. e.	2. d.	3. a.	4. c.	5. b.

REMEMBERING IMPORTANT PEOPLE AND EVENTS

1. e.	2. d.	3. a.	4. c.	5. b.
6. b.	7. a.	8. c.	9. e.	10. d.

REVIEWING THE FACTS

1. c.	2. b.	3. c.	4. a.	5. c.

PLACING EVENTS IN TIME

1. C.	2. A.	3. B.

LINKING GEOGRAPHY AND HISTORY

They wrote about places they knew. For example, Irving wrote about New York, Cooper wrote about the frontier, Melville wrote about the sea, Longfellow wrote about the New England Indians, and Thoreau wrote about living simply in the woods around Walden Pond.

THINKING ABOUT AMERICAN HISTORY

1. Answers will vary.
2. New farm technology made work easier and faster for farmers. New farm machines and tools made it possible to turn formerly useless land or land used for grazing into productive farmland. New technology for mass production in factories led to a greater selection of goods for consumers and at cheaper prices. However, factory workers suffered from a poor working environment, long hours, and little personal satisfaction in their work.

APPLYING HISTORY STUDIES SKILLS

1. The North.
2. Along the Atlantic Coast and between the Appalachian Mountains and the Mississippi River.
3. Chicago, St. Louis, New York, Boston.
4. The North.

CHAPTER 15

Reformers Improve American Life (1820's-1850's)

Chapter Objectives

After completing this chapter, students will be able to:
1. Name some of the reformers who worked to correct serious social problems in American society.
2. Understand the reasons why some Americans established special communities in the United States.
3. Trace the development of the antislavery movement in the United States.
4. Describe the beginnings of efforts to gain full citizenship rights for women.

Chapter Chronology

Chapter 15 covers the major reform movements that occurred in America between the 1820's and the 1850's. Many of the major persons and events of the period are highlighted on the timeline on the textbook Chapter Opener page. In 1829, David Walker published *An Appeal.* Two years later, in 1831, William Lloyd Garrison's *The Liberator* was first published. The American Anti-Slavery Society was founded in 1833. Another reform organization, the American Temperance Union was formed in 1836. Two famous communities were founded at this time, the religious Oneida Community in 1840 and the utopian Brook Farm in 1841.

Motivation

Put the following statements on the board:
1. In the 1850's over 3 million people in America were living in slavery.

2. In the 1880's mentally ill people in the United States were often thrown into prisons.
3. In the 1850's American women were not allowed to vote in elections.

Discuss each statement with the students. Ask them to explain why these statements represent situations that needed to be changed. Also ask students how they think such changes would have been accomplished.

Geographical Setting

Many of the reform movements originated in the eastern part of the nation and gradually spread westward. Both the abolitionist movement and the women's movements were based in the North, with little or no activity in the southern states.

The utopian communities were usually located in isolated rural areas, both in the East and later west of the Appalachian Mountains. After they have read the appropriate section, you might want to have students discuss reasons why utopians would want to be located away from other settlements.

History Study Skills

The History Study Skill in Chapter 15 is *Recognizing Primary and Secondary Sources*. This activity may be used effectively at any time during the chapter. However, the earlier it is used the better, as it will provide students with an opportunity to practice the skill during the rest of the chapter. There are many source references throughout Chapter 15.

Bibliography

Teacher References
Berkin, Carol Ruth and Norton, Mary Beth, *Women of America: A History*. Houghton, Boston, Mass., 1979.
Perry, Lewis, and Fellman, Michael, eds., *Anti-slavery Reconsidered: New Perspectives on the Abolitionists*. Louisiana State University Press, Baton Rouge, La., 1979.
Welter, Barbara, *Dimity Convictions: The American Woman in the Nineteenth Century*. Ohio University Press, Athens, Ohio, 1976.
Student References
Faber, Doris, *The Perfect Life: Shakers in America*. Farrar, Straus, New York City, 1974. This is an objective account of Shakers and their communities.
Meltzer, Milton, *All Times, All People: A World History of Slavery*. Harper, New York City, 1980. This is an excellent, well illustrated introduction to the history of slavery throughout the world.

Audio-Visual Materials

The Angry Prophet: Frederick Douglass, Films, Inc., color, 24 minutes. This offers the words, speeches, and writings of the famous black abolitionist.
American Civilization 1783-1840, Guidance Associates. 3-part sound-slide program. This is a survey of the social ideas of Americans during the nation's first 50 years.

SECTION 1: Reformers Help Many Groups in America

OBJECTIVES

After completing this section, students will be able to:
• List some of the problems that American reformers tried to solve.
• Name some of the individuals who worked to solve those problems.
• Chart specific information on various reform movements.

MOTIVATION

Use the material suggested under Motivation in the manual chapter introduction. Then have students read the section headings, indicated in bold face type, to list other problems that Americans tried to solve during this period. As students read and discuss the chapter contents, make a complete list on the chalkboard for easy reference.

SUGGESTED ACTIVITIES

1. **Directed Reading**. Use the above list as the basis for beginning a table. As students read, they should find the information necessary to complete the following format:

Problem /	Actions Taken To Solve The Problem/	Groups or Individuals Who Worked To Solve The Problem/
Example: Alcoholism /	Speeches, poems, songs, meetings/	American Temperance Union, Washingtonians

After students have completed the table, you will want to review the answers to be sure their information is correct. In the process, discuss the degree of success of each reform effect.

2. **Comparison Writing Assignment**. Have students select one of the problem areas described in this section. For example, direct students who chose the problem area of the mentally ill to write a paragraph comparing the treatment of them in the 1800's with that of today.

Above-average students may be encouraged to use the library to investigate the problem they have selected in greater detail. Average and below-average students should rely on the information in the chapter to complete the assignment.

3. **Flash Cards**. Use large index cards to prepare three sets of flash cards. On one set, write the names of individual reformers or reform groups. On the second set, write the names of the problems they attempted to solve. On the third set, write vocabulary words or terms used in the sections, such as temperance, utopian societies, peculiar institution. It would be helpful to use a different colored marker in preparing each set. Pass all the cards out. Call on one student to bring his or her card to the front. Continue until all cards have been correctly shown by students. Slower students may be allowed to consult their charts to help complete this activity.

4. **History Study Skills**. Use this chapter's History Study Skill here. Used at this point in the chapter this activity will provide students with opportunities to practice the skill as they read the subsequent sections. After they have completed the activity, ask students to identify the sources related to this section. (The first two)

BUILDING AMERICAN CITIZENSHIP

Reformers have many characteristics in common. For example, most have a desire to help others. What other qualities would a person need in order to help reform specific problems, either in the 1800's or today? (A belief that people want to improve their lives; a willingness to work tirelessly; a belief that what one is doing is important; the ability to overcome discouragement)

SECTION 1 REVIEW ANSWERS

1. **IDENTIFY: Dorothea Dix:** Massachusetts teacher and author who devoted herself to getting better treatment for the mentally ill; **Thomas Hopkins Gallaudet:** reformer who developed a method of teaching the deaf to read, write, and communicate with others; **Samuel Gridley Howe:** reformer who developed special books using raised letters so that the blind could "read" with their hands; **Horace Mann:** leader of educational reforms who set up an elementary public school system in Massachusetts.
2. **DEFINE: reform:** to correct or improve; **religious revival:** a renewed interest in religion; **temperance:** reduction in the drinking of alchoholic beverages; **normal schools:** teacher-training schools.
3. Slavery, the educational system, treatment of the handicapped and mentally ill, and alcoholism.
4. Massachusetts and other states built special hospitals where the mentally ill received treatment and good care.

SECTION 2: Americans Try New Ways of Living Together

OBJECTIVES

After completing this section, students will be able to:
* Name some of the religious and utopian societies founded in the late 1700's and early 1800's.
* Explain why people joined religious and utopian societies.
* Locate the states in which the religious and utopian societies established themselves.

MOTIVATION

Have students read the title of this section. Ask those that have been to summer camp to describe the experience of group living and sharing. Explain that in the early 1800's some people set up special social and religious communities in which they lived and worked together. Discuss the reasons why people might have decided to try such an experience and how it might be different from life in an average town or city.

SUGGESTED ACTIVITIES

1. **Directed Reading**. Use the motivational discussion above to establish a purpose for reading. Have students read to answer these guide questions:
   A. Why did people join religious and utopian societies? (They expected to improve society by showing that their ideas worked. They wanted to worship as they pleased, or to make specific changes such as ending poverty, racial prejudice, or bad working conditions.)
   B. How did life in these societies differ from life in other towns or communities of that time? (People were willing to cooperate and share both the work and the profits. They did not compete with one another.)
2. **Extending History Study Skills.** Information in Section 2 lends itself to additional practice of the history study skill. Direct students to tell whether the following are primary or secondary sources:
   A. A copy of the Shaker hymn "Simple Gifts" (P)
   B. Excerpts from a diary of one of the Waltham girls (P)
   C. An original edition of *The Blithedale Romance* (P)
   D. Robert Owen's written plans for the town of New Harmony (P)
   E. A visitor's description of Brook Farm (S)
   Ask above-average students to create their own examples of primary and secondary sources, using the information in this section.
3. **Map Study**. Display a map of the United States. Have students locate the states in which the religious and utopian societies discussed in this section were started. Ask the following questions based on these determinations:
   A. In which direction did the Amana Society members travel in their journey from New York to Iowa? (SW)
   B. If a Shaker family wished to move from the Shaker community in Indiana to one in Ohio, in which direction would it travel? (East)
   C. One religious community and one utopian community started settlements in Indiana. Name them. (Shakers and New Harmony)
   D. The Waltham System and Brook Farm were both established in what state? (Massachusetts)
4. **Reformers Work to Improve American Life**. Duplicate Worksheet 40, of this title. It may be begun and partially completed when students have finished Section 2. This Worksheet will provide both a good review and a preview of the next two sections.

BUILDING AMERICAN CITIZENSHIP

"Cooperation" is a major theme developed in Section 2. American citizens who joined religious and utopian societies worked together to accomplish their tasks and goals. Ask students to discuss the following questions:
1. Why is it necessary for citizens of a community to cooperate with one another?
2. Can you give examples of how people in your neighborhood or community have worked together to accomplish difficult tasks or to achieve a common goal?

SECTION 2 REVIEW ANSWERS

1. **IDENTIFY: "Mother Ann" Lee:** founder of the Shaker community; **Robert Owen:** Scottish immigrant who established a utopian society, called New Harmony, in Indiana; **Waltham System:** a system whereby female factory workers were paid high wages, given pleasant surroundings and living quarters but were held under constant supervision; **Brook Farm:** a Massachusetts community whose members wanted a place to enjoy a cultural life away from competition from the outside world; **Oneida Community:** a community whose goal was to work together and share equally and to create a perfect world; famous for their silverware.
2. An increasing flow of immigrants provided cheap labor, thus ending the mill owners' need for help.
3. To try to end poverty, racial prejudice, bad working conditions, and inequality between men and women.

SECTION 3: Reformers Work to Abolish Slavery

OBJECTIVES

After completing this section, students will be able to:
- List the arguments used by Southerners to defend slavery.
- Identify abolitionists who worked to end slavery.
- Describe the actions taken by abolitionists to end slavery.

MOTIVATION

Find and display pictures of famous abolitionists, including William Lloyd Garrison, Frederick Douglass, Harriet Tubman, Angelina Grimké, David Walker, and Elijah Lovejoy. Introduce the term "abolitionist" and ask students to define it. Discuss the methods that abolitionists might have used to help free the slaves.

SUGGESTED ACTIVITIES

1. **Directed Reading.** As students read this section, have them list the methods proposed and used by anti slavery reformers to try to free the slaves. Introduce and define the terms "extreme" and "moderate." Then have the students classify each of the proposals and methods listed as extreme or moderate. As a summary activity, ask students to name the methods used by each of the abolitionists whose pictures were used to motivate the lesson.
2. **Reformers Work to Improve American Life.** Have students continue adding to Worksheet 40. Four of the people on it are taken from this section.
3. **Extending History Study Skills.** There is ample opportunity in this section for students to practice identification of primary and secondary sources. Depending on the ability level of the students, you may wish to provide examples, or have them create their own. Examples that you might use include:
   A. 1945 biography of William Lloyd Garrison (S)
   B. Speech given by Frederick Douglass on August 19, 1841, in Nantucket, Massachusetts (P)
   C. A copy of David Walker's *Appeal* (P)

D. Your textbook's account of the murder of Elijah Lovejoy (S)

4. **Chronology.** This section describes the abolitionist movement from its beginnings to the mid-1800's. Check students' understanding of the sequence of major developments by having them place the facts below in chronological order:
   A. First issue of *The Liberator* (1831)
   B. Murder of Elijah Lovejoy (1838)
   C. Establishment of the American Anti-Slavery Society (1833)
   D. Formation of the American Colonization Society (1817)
   E. The abolitionists split into extreme and moderate groups (1840)

5. **Ideals in the Lives of Americans.** Have students read about Prudence Crandall on textbook page 355. In addition to the two questions at the end of the reading, have students answer the following:
   A. Why is this activity incorporated as part of Section 3? (Prudence Crandall was an abolitionist, and fought for the rights of black people.)
   B. If this activity had been completed as part of Section 1, under which topic would Prudence Crandall have been included? (Reformers in education)
   C. Could she have been included in Section 2? Explain. (Yes. She and her husband began a school in Illinois, and might have been labeled "Utopians" at that time.)

BUILDING AMERICAN CITIZENSHIP

This section points to the fact that although many citizens disagreed with the abolitionists, they defended the abolitionists' right of free speech. Which other "rights" were exercised by the abolitionists in their efforts to end slavery? (Freedom of the press and assembly) How were these rights violated by citizens who opposed the abolitionists? (Crowds broke up meetings, stoned speakers, killed Elijah Lovejoy, destroyed printing presses, damaged meeting halls, and attacked the homes of abolitionists.) How can citizens be stopped from violating the rights of other citizens? (Answers will vary)

SECTION 3 REVIEW ANSWERS

1. **IDENTIFY: American Colonization Society:** one of the earliest white anti-slavery societies in America, whose members wanted freed blacks sent "home" to Africa; **Paul Cuffe:** a free black shipowner who took blacks on his ships to Liberia in Africa for resettlement; **David Walker:** a free black abolitionist who published *An Appeal,* calling for blacks to rise up and fight for their freedom; **William Lloyd Garrison:** a white abolitionist, editor of a newspaper called *The Liberator,* which called for the immediate emancipation of slaves; **Frederick Douglass:** a black abolitionist and former slave, a famous speaker and an editor of an anti-slavery newspaper; **Harriet Tubman:** former slave who helped hundreds of slaves escape to the North.
2. **DEFINE: abolitionists:** those who worked to bring an end to slavery; **emancipation:** the freeing of slaves.

3. They urged Congress to free the slaves; they organized anti-slavery societies and held anti-slavery conventions; they wrote books and published newspapers calling for an end to slavery; they helped slaves escape.
4. Some were afraid of losing their jobs to freed blacks; others feared the cotton trade would be destroyed; Northerners who were friends of Southern slaveowners felt they should support them.

SECTION 4: Reformers Call for Full Rights for Women

OBJECTIVES

After completing this section, students will be able to:
• Identify leading women reformers of the period.
• Explain the specific rights that women were seeking to acquire.
• Form an opinion on how successful the women's reform movement was.

MOTIVATION

Discuss the Equal Rights Amendment (ERA), as proposed by Congress in March 1972. It reads, in part:

"Equality of rights under the law shall not be denied or abridged by the United States or by any State on account of sex."

Ask students what this statement means? Ask them to list the rights women are fighting for today? (Equal pay, equal job opportunities) Explain to students that the struggle for women's rights began in the 19th century. This section will tell the story of that early struggle.

SUGGESTED ACTIVITIES

1. **Directed Reading**. As students read Section 4, have them list the rights that women were seeking in the 1800's and the methods they used in their efforts to gain these rights. As a summary activity, compare this list with the one made under Motivation above. Discuss the differences and similarities in the types of rights women sought then and now. Also, discuss the role of men in helping women in their struggle, both in the 1800's and today.
2. **Extending History Study Skills**. At this point, students should need no assistance in selecting examples of primary and secondary sources from the text. Have them give specific examples from Section 4. These might include:
   A. A newspaper article attacking the actions of the Grimké sisters. (P)
   B. Catherine Beecher's book, *The American Woman's Home*. (P)
   C. The textbook description of the Anti-Slavery Convention in London. (S)
   D. The newspaper notice announcing the Seneca Falls Convention. (P)
   E. A Copy of the "Declaration of Sentiments." (P)

      As a further extension of this chapter's History Study Skill, duplicate Worksheet 41, *Slaves Tell Their Story*. Ask students to read the excerpt. Then have them respond to the questions and discuss the answers.

3. **Reformers Work to Improve American Life.** Have students complete Worksheet 40. The last three names on the chart are provided in this section. This Worksheet is an excellent study guide for students as they prepare for their chapter test.
4. **Crossword Puzzle**. Duplicate Worksheet 42, *Reform in America*. Clues 4, 7, 12, 16, and 17 deal specifically with information in Section 4. However, the puzzle should serve as an excellent review of the entire chapter.
5. **Sources of Freedom**. Section 4 describes several of the proposals or resolutions on women's rights that were part of the "Declaration of Sentiments" from the Seneca Falls convention. Have students read the primary source material on textbook page 363. Have them try to pick out the actual statements in which the resolutions were made.

BUILDING AMERICAN CITIZENSHIP

In the 1800's, women contributed to the success of a number of reform movements, including the abolitionist movement and the campaign for better care of the mentally ill. Women also are leaders in many reform movements today. What, if any, specific contributions do women make to such modern reform efforts as environmentalism, the anti-nuclear movement, campaigns against drugs, child abuse, and drunk driving? Do men and women have equal public influence today?

SECTION 4 REVIEW ANSWERS

1. IDENTIFY: **Sarah and Angelina Grimké:** sisters from South Carolina who were among the earliest abolitionists and defenders of women's rights; **Lucretia Mott:** a leading defender of women's rights and an organizer of the 1848 Women's Rights Convention in Seneca Falls, N.Y.; **Elizabeth Cady Stanton:** a leading defender and speaker on women's rights and, along with Lucretia Mott, an organizer of the Women's Rights Convention in Seneca Falls; famous for her speech the "Declaration of Sentiments."
2. DEFINE: **suffrage:** the right to vote.
3. Some felt the struggle against slavery should be won first. Others felt that women should not speak publicly or take leadership roles.
4. The right to vote, hold property of their own if married, keep the wages that they earned, speak out in public, the right to custody of their children, better educational and job opportunities.

CHAPTER 15 REVIEW ANSWERS
REVIEWING KEY WORDS

| 1. e. | 2. b. | 3. d. | 4. a. | 5. c. |

REMEMBERING IMPORTANT PEOPLE AND EVENTS

| 1. a. | 2. b. | 3. a. | 4. c |
| 5. b. | 6. b. | 7. c | |

REVIEWING THE FACTS

| 1. T | 2. F | 3. T | 4. F |
| 5. T | 6. T | 7. T | 8. F |

PLACING EVENTS IN TIME

1. b.   2. a.   3. a.   4. a.   5. b.

LINKING GEOGRAPHY AND HISTORY

1. Some Northerners feared losing their jobs to freed blacks. Some who depended on the cotton trade feared that ending slavery would ruin their businesses. Also, some had friends who were Southern slaveowners, whom they wanted to support.
2. It was national, involving all parts of the country. The religious and utopian societies flourished in the West. Reforms in education and care of the mentally ill began in the Northeast. Abolitionists and supporters of equal rights for women came from both the North and South.

THINKING ABOUT AMERICAN HISTORY

1. Since there were fewer people living on the frontier, the communities could experiment with new ideas without annoying others. They had more freedom to make mistakes and enjoy success.
2. Some states began to pass laws allowing women to control their property, to sue or to be sued in court, and to have custody of their children. But success was limited. Women did not gain the right to vote until the twentieth century.

APPLYING HISTORY STUDIES SKILLS

1. Statements, letters, diaries, objects, and pictures that remain from the time of the event.
2. A primary source comes from the time the event actually occurred; a secondary source does not.
3. Some source materials may not record information correctly. Also, some sources may contain the writer's opinions instead of facts.

CHAPTER 16

The Nation Gains Western Territories (1820's-1850's)

Chapter Objectives

After completing this chapter, students will be able to:
1. Trace the development of Texas from a Spanish possession in 1815 to statehood in 1845.
2. Explain why Oregon was so attractive to many American pioneers.
3. Describe how America resolved its boundary disputes with Mexico and Great Britain.
4. Identify America's territorial acquisitions between 1845 and 1853.
5. Contrast the reasons for the rush of settlers to California and Utah.

Chapter Chronology

Chapter 16 covers the expansion of the United States during the period from the late 1820's to the 1850's.

Many important persons and events of the period are highlighted on the time line on the textbook Chapter Opener page. In 1835 the Texas War began. Five years later, in 1840, William Henry Harrison was elected President. After Harrison's death, in 1841, John Tyler became President. Three years later, in 1844, James Polk was elected President. Also in 1844, Texas was admitted to the Union. The Mexican War began in 1846, the same year that the Oregon boundary dispute was settled. The Mormons settled in Utah in 1847, one year before the discovery of gold in California.

Motivation

Chapter 16 has five maps, all of which deal with American territorial expansion. Before having students look at each map, have them write Westward Expansion at the top of a page in their notebooks. On the chalkboard, write the following four questions:
1. Where is the expansion taking place? (Texas, California, etc.)
2. What settlements are involved? (San Antonio, Omaha, etc.)
3. Where is the activity occurring?
4. What activity or changes are shown on the map? (War, travel, etc.)

Ask students to keep the question in mind as they look at the maps. Discuss each map separately with the class. Have the students make a heading for each map and write the answers to the questions underneath it. This information will give students a background for the chapter's themes.

Geographical Setting

In Chapter 16, students are introduced to the geography of the American Southwest in their study of Texas and its road to statehood. Another new geographical setting—the American Northwest—is introduced in the Oregon question. Have students compare and contrast these two environments as well as the reasons why pioneers decided to settle in each area. In Utah, the Mormons showed how people can change their environment to make it more livable. The study of California, in the far West provides an opportunity to develop students' map skills including tracing routes and identifying natural resources.

History Study Skills

The History Study Skill in Chapter 16 is *Studying Your History Vocabulary*. It may be used near the beginning of the chapter because it relies on the text to provide the vocabulary "clues." It can also be used at the end of the chapter, at which point most of the students should be familiar with the new history words. A similar activity may be used with any chapter in the text with the clues applied to the new vocabulary in each chapter.

Bibliography

Teacher References

Lander, Ernest M., Jr., *Reluctant Imperialists: Calhoun, the South Carolinians, and the Mexican War.* Louisiana State University Press, Baton Rouge, La., 1980.

Merk, Frederick, *Manifest Destiny and Mission in American History: A Reinterpretation.* Random House, New York City, 1963.

Student References

Levitin, Sonia, *The No-Return Trail.* Harcourt, New York City, 1978. This is the story of a 17-year-old pioneer wife and mother on the first wagon train from Missouri to California.

McCall, Edith, *Heroes of the Western Outposts.* Children's Press, Chicago, Ill., 1980. This is an interesting account of the exploits of some well-known and some lesser-known heroes who opened up the West.

Audio-Visual Materials

Gone West, Time Life, 52 minutes, 16 mm. This is a documentary on the Westward movement from the Louisiana Purchase to the Gold Rush.

Westward Expansion, Guidance Associates. Two filmstrips and cassettes, Library Kit and Teacher's Guide. This is a chronological over-view of America's westward movement.

SECTION 1: American Pioneer Families Move to Texas

OBJECTIVES

After completing this section, students will be able to:
- Identify leaders in the Texas struggle for independence.
- Explain the steps by which Texas became a state.
- Arrange selected events of the history of Texas in chronological order.

MOTIVATION

Have students read the **Landmarks of Liberty** story of the Alamo on textbook page 374 and answer the questions orally. Ask them to locate the Alamo on the map of the *War for the Independence of Texas, 1835-1836* on textbook page 371.

Remind the students that the battle of the Alamo, though very important for morale, was only one in a series of events in Texas history between 1815 and 1845. Explain that one of the goals of today's lesson is to determine some other events that also were of major importance.

SUGGESTED ACTIVITIES

1. **Directed Reading**. As students read about the Texas War, have them keep a list of major "landmarks" during the war. Use the map decribed above in the Motivation to locate these sites. As a summary, have students describe—orally, or in their notebooks—why each of these places was important. To develop critical thinking skills, ask students if any of these places might be considered as or *more* important than the Alamo and, if so, why.
2. **Writing Reports.** Many of the historical figures in this section gained fame through their involvement in historical events surrounding the war for Texas' independence. Have students prepare reports to present

to the class about other important happenings in the lives of: Stephen F. Austin, Santa Anna, William Travis, Jim Bowie, Davy Crockett, Sam Houston, John C. Calhoun, James K. Polk, and Henry Clay. Average and below-average students may use the information in this section to identify the roles of these persons in Texas' history.
3. **Chronology**. The steps by which Texas became a state are described in this section. Texas was first a colony, then an independent republic, and finally a state. To help clarify the correct sequence of events have students place the following statements in correct chronological order:
   A. Texas became the Lone Star Republic.
   B. The Battle of the Alamo was fought.
   C. Santa Anna gained control of the Mexican government.
   D. Stephen Austin established a colony in Texas.
   E. Texas became the twenty-eighth state.
   F. Texas declared its independence from Mexico.
   CORRECT SEQUENCE: D - C - F - B - A - E
4. **History Study Skills.** Use the *Studying Your History Vocabulary* activity early in the chapter as suggested in the manual chapter introduction. An initial reading of Section 1 will familiarize students with several of the vocabulary words. Completion of the activity at this point could enhance their feelings of success.

BUILDING AMERICAN CITIZENSHIP

Duplicate Worksheet 43, *Setting Up a Government.* This activity requires students to think critically about the choices open to Texans in their development of a government. It also requires them to redefine the concepts of "dictatorship" and "democracy."

SECTION 1 REVIEW ANSWERS

1. **IDENTIFY: Stephen F. Austin:** continued his father's project of establishing an American colony in Mexican-owned Texas; **Santa Anna:** leader of Mexico during the Texas-Americans' war for independence; **the Alamo:** an empty mission where the Texans set up their defense; **Sam Houston:** commander of the Texas army and first president of the Lone Star Republic; **Lone Star Republic:** the name given to Texas when Texas-Americans declared their independence from Mexico.
2. **DEFINE: annex:** to add onto.
3. The Mexican government wanted Americans to give up slavery, to speak Spanish, and become Catholics. The Texas-Americans refused.
4. Santa Anna refused to listen to their requests for reforms and led his army to drive them out of his empire.

SECTION 2: "Oregon Fever" Draws Settlers to the West

OBJECTIVES

After completing this section, students will be able to:
- List the groups that claimed the Oregon Country.
- Explain how disputes in the Oregon Country were settled.

- Describe the journey made by pioneer families over the Oregon Trail.

MOTIVATION

Use the map *Major Routes to the West, 1840-1860* on textbook page 377. Ask students to describe a journey to Oregon, using the geographical features on the map. They should be able to tell you about the rivers and mountains that had to be crossed, as well as the Indian Territory. This should lead the class into a discussion of the dangers these pioneers faced along the trail. List them on the chalkboard.

SUGGESTED ACTIVITIES

1. **Directed Reading.** Use the section review questions as guide questions. The answers will summarize the important material in this section. As students read the information under the heading "The Oregon Trail Marks a Route to the West," have them note the textbook description of the river and mountain crossings. As they read further in the section, have them compare the textbook description of the journey's hardships and dangers with those listed on the chalkboard.
2. **Writing Exercise.** Based on the information in this section, have the average and below-average students prepare a diary entry of a typical day's journey over the Oregon Trail. You may ask above-average students to prepare a more detailed story by researching information from existing diaries of pioneers journeying westward.
3. **Skill Practice.** Review the Chapter 15 History Study Skill, *Recognizing Primary and Secondary Sources*. Have students select examples of each from this section or use the following list to practice the skill:
   A. A map drawn by Jim Bridger of a path through the montains (P)
   B. The textbook's description of Dr. Whitman's efforts to help the Indians (S)
   C. An excerpt from Lavinia Porter's diary (P)
   D. A copy of the Oregon Constitution of 1843 (P)
   E. A newspaper article describing the Oregon Territory of 1846 (S)
4. **Map Interpretation.** Use a modern highway map of the United States. Have students prepare a description of an automobile trip from either Independence or St. Joseph, Missouri, to Portland, Oregon. They should include major highways to be traveled. Students should also prepare a timetable estimating the number of miles (kilometers) to be covered each day and the total travel time. Based on their reading of this section, you may also want students to compare how long it took pioneers to make the journey with the amount of time it takes today.

BUILDING AMERICAN CITIZENSHIP

The United States and Great Britain solved the boundary dispute in Oregon peacefully, by reaching a compromise. Review the meaning of the term "compromise" with students. Ask them how they could apply this principle in their own lives. Have them think of issues or problems today among individual citizens, groups of citizens, or nations that might best be solved by com-

promises. (Placement of new prisons or sanitary land-fills; OPEC's attempts to set prices for oil; salary dispute between an employer and an employee)

SECTION 2 REVIEW ANSWERS

1. IDENTIFY: **Mountain Men:** fur trappers who braved the cold and heights of the Rocky Mountains and survived in the wilderness and who were the first Americans to blaze a trail to the Oregon Country; **Continental Divide:** line that divides the rivers flowing to the Atlantic and the Pacific oceans; **Reverend Jason Lee:** a Methodist minister, the first missionary to reach Oregon; **"Fifty-four forty or fight!":** President Polk's campaign slogan, indicating that the United States should own the entire Oregon country.
2. Spain, Russia, France, Great Britain, the Indians, and the United States.
3. Leaving their homes, friends, and cherished belongings; loneliness; long days of walking; heat of deserts and mountain cold; prairie fires; Indian attacks.

SECTION 3: America Wins Vast Territories from Mexico

OBJECTIVES

After completing this section, students will be able to:
- State the reasons for America's declaration of war against Mexico.
- Describe the American strategy for winning the war.
- Explain the results of the Mexican War.

MOTIVATION

Use a large rubber band to demonstrate the concept of expansion. Stretch the band to its fullest extent, and ask students to describe this action. Above-average students may use the word to explain what happened. Others may give synonyms. Have students state some of the ways in which the United States had already expanded (the Louisiana Purchase; the annexation of Texas; the acquisition of the Oregon Territory by treaty with England.) Ask students to look at the map, *Territorial Growth of the United States by 1853*, on text page 385. Have them name the areas that remained to be acquired, and establish the purpose of this lesson—to learn how and why these territories were obtained.

SUGGESTED ACTIVITIES

1. **Directed Reading.** The information in this section can be understood in terms of slogans, nicknames, and treaties. As they read this section, ask above-average students to list and identify each. For average and slower students, you may want to provide a list, including the following: Manifest Destiny, "Mexico or Death," "Mr. Polk's War," "Old Rough and Ready," "Old Fuss and Feathers," the Bear Flag Republic, the Mexican Cession, and the Gadsden Purchase. As a summary, have the class identify each item from the descriptions written and read aloud by selected students.
2. **Reading for the Main Idea.** Have students review the History Study Skill for Chapter 5 on textbook page

103. Have them apply the skill by writing a sentence or two stating the main ideas of this section in their own words.

3. **Improving Map Skills**. Duplicate Worksheet 44, *Westward Expansion*. Above-average students should be able to complete the activity without reference to the above-mentioned map on textbook page 385. Average and below-average students can use the text map as a study guide.

BUILDING AMERICAN CITIZENSHIP

Abraham Lincoln criticized the war against Mexico, as did many citizens from New England. Should citizens be allowed to criticize the policies of the government when it is at war with other nations? Under what, if *any* circumstances, should citizens not be allowed to criticize their government?

SECTION 3 REVIEW ANSWERS

1. **IDENTIFY: Manifest Destiny:** belief that it was the fate of the United States to own all lands from Texas to the Pacific Ocean; **Zachary Taylor:** American general chosen to lead an invasion of northern Mexico, nicknamed "Old Rough and Ready"; **Winfield Scott:** American general chosen to lead an attack on Mexico City, nicknamed "Old Fuss and Feathers"; **Bear Flag Republic:** name given to the independent government of California; **Treaty of Guadalupe Hidalgo:** the peace treaty ending the war between Mexico and the United States; **Mexican Cession:** the area given up by Mexico after the Mexican-American War; **Gadsden Purchase:** the strip of land south of the Gila River purchased from Mexico for $10 million.
2. **DEFINE: expansionists:** Americans who supported the westward expansion of the United States.
3. Trouble between the two countries began over the Texas revolution in the 1830's. Mexico felt that the United States was trying to take its lands; the United States felt that Mexico was trying to block the westward progress of democracy and that Mexico had invaded its territory by crossing the Rio Grande River.
4. New Englanders feared any new lands won in a war would become slave states; some people felt that the United States could not claim that Mexico had invaded American soil since the land was disputed territory.

SECTION 4: More Settlers Journey to the West

OBJECTIVES

After completing this section, students will be able to:
- State the effects of the California Gold Rush.
- Describe life in a typical mining camp.
- Explain why the Mormons chose to settle in Utah.

MOTIVATION

An excellent film, *Western Movement*, Part V: *The Gold Rush*, (Encyclopedia Brittanica, 1966), should be shown to the students, if available. It is about the life of the 49er gold seekers and should create enthusiasm for the topic. If the film is unavailable, use the pictures in this section to begin a discussion.

SUGGESTED ACTIVITIES

1. **Directed Reading.** Since this section has two topics, split the class into two groups, and make one responsible for the gold seekers and one for the Mormons. As guide questions, have each group use the five W's and H. (Who, what, when, where, why, and how?)
   Gold Seekers:
   A. Who discovered gold?
   B. When?
   C. Where?
   D. What was life like in a mining camp?
   E. Why did some miners give up?
   F. How did the miners get to California?
   Mormons:
   A. Who led them?
   B. Where did they finally settle?
   C. When?
   D. Why did they move there?
   E. What were they searching for?
   F. How were their beliefs different form those of other religions?
   Have each group "teach" the essential information to the others by sharing the answers to these questions. This may be done by pairing students from each group or by having selected students report orally to all students.

2. **Group Reports.** The lives of four individuals in this section could be researched outside the scope of this narrative. With above-average students, modify suggested Activity 1 by creating six class groups. Two of the groups should do Activity 1. The other four should use the library to investigate: John Sutter, James Marshall, Joseph Smith, or Brigham Young. Their investigation should emphasize happenings in the lives of these men that occurred before or after the events described in this section. All six groups would take turns presenting their findings to the class. You may wish to exempt some average and below-average students from completing Activity 1 and have them complete Activity 2 instead.

3. **Relating History and Mathematics.** Use the following activity with students: You have just completed three weeks working on your claim, finding an average of $40 of gold a day. The following are your needs for the next month. Assume that coffee costs $25 per pound, bacon $50 per pound, and beans $30 a sack. Other prices are in your textbook. Answer the following:
   A. What were your total earnings for a 3-week period? ($840)
   B. Here is your grocery list. Compute the cost of each item and the total bill.

½ barrel of flour	($200)
5 pounds of sugar	($40)
4 pounds of bacon	($200)
4 pounds of coffee	($100)
7 sacks of beans	($210)
TOTAL	($750)

   C. How much profit would you have made? ($90)
   D. How could you have spent your profits? (Answers will vary)

4. **Role-Playing**. Select two groups of three to six students. One group is to imagine that they are Mor-

mons living in Nauvoo. The other group, living in the same town, is to imagine that they are their neighbors. Have these two groups discuss those aspects in the Mormon religion described in the text that caused controversy among the citizens of Nauvoo. You can also have students reenact the death of Joseph Smith and the decision of the Mormons to move West.

5. **Studying Your History Vocabulary.** Duplicate Worksheet 45, *Using Vocabulary Clues.* Do *not* allow students to use the glossary until they have skimmed the entire chapter using "vocabulary clues" to determine the meaning of all words. Conduct an oral review of students' answers for column 1. Then have students use the glossary to complete the second column. If the meanings are the same, write the word "same." Discuss the advisability of having a glossary if most words are defined by clues. (It serves as a quick reference—one does not have to search through the chapter for definitions).

BUILDING AMERICAN CITIZENSHIP

The treatment of the Mormons provides a striking example of a group being persecuted by other groups because of its beliefs or ideas. Ask students to think how they would have acted as citizens living at that time. Have students name other groups in American history who were discriminated against. (Indians, blacks, immigrants) Ask them what they, as citizens, can do to act against this type of unfair treatment in today's society?

SECTION 4 REVIEW ANSWERS

1. **IDENTIFY: John Sutter:** owner of the land on which gold was discovered in California; **James Marshall:** one of Sutter's carpenters who discovered gold at Sutter's mill; **Gold Rush:** the rush of thousands of people to California to search for gold; **"Forty-niners":** the name given to the people who went to California in 1849 to find gold; **Joseph Smith:** founder of the Mormon Church; **Brigham Young:** Mormon leader who succeeded Joseph Smith and who established the Mormon settlement near Salt Lake in Utah.
2. **DEFINE: vigilantes:** citizens in the gold-mining camps who formed groups to keep order and take the law into their own hands.
3. Poor living conditions in the mining camps, extremely high prices for supplies, and lack of law and order.
4. They were disliked by many people who did not approve of their practice of polygamy or their belief that they were chosen people. After having been forced to move several times and then the death of Joseph Smith and his brother at the hands of any angry mob, Brigham Young decided that the Mormons could not live in peace with other Christians and decided to move them to the wilderness near the Great Salt Lake.

CHAPTER 16 REVIEW ANSWERS
REVIEWING KEY WORDS

1. b.   2. c.   3. a.

REMEMBERING IMPORTANT PEOPLE AND EVENTS

1. b.   2. a.   3. c.   4. a.
5. b.   6. a.   7. b.

REVIEWING THE FACTS

1. c.   2. e.   3. b.   4. d.   5. a.
6. F   7. T   8. F   9. T   10. T

PLACING EVENTS IN TIME

1. d.   2. b.   3. e.   4. c.   5. a.

LINKING GEOGRAPHY AND HISTORY

Texas: After the Texans had fought and won their independence from Mexico, the United States annexed Texas by a joint resolution of Congress. **Oregon:** by a treaty with Great Britain. **Mexican Cession:** by winning a war with Mexico, then by treaty. **Gadsden Purchase:** by a treaty.

THINKING ABOUT AMERICAN HISTORY

1. Many became farmers and ranchers and started orchards or raised wheat and cattle. Some became shopkeepers and merchants. Others sought gold in other areas.
2. The United States might have found itself fighting against both Great Britain and Mexico.

APPLYING HISTORY STUDIES SKILLS

1. **proposals:** resolutions—text.
2. **custody:** care and keeping of children—text.
3. **suffrage:** the right to vote—text and Glossary.
4. **assert:** defend—text.
5. **redressed:** corrected—text.

UNIT 5 ANSWERS

VOCABULARY REVIEW

Answers will vary.

REVIEWING THE MAIN IDEAS

1. Problems with South Carolina over the Tariff Act of 1828; the nullification controversy; resettlement of the Indians; the Bank War.
2. Clipper ships; steamships; steam locomotives; the telegraph; the rotary printing press.
3. Work on the farms was made easier and faster by new machines for plowing, planting, and harvesting crops. New machines also reduced the amount of human labor needed to run farms. Work in factories was made simpler, with each worker doing one or two simple operations. However, factory workers could no longer take pride in the finished product and therefore found little personal satisfaction in their work. They also suffered from long hours, an unhealthy environment, and dangerous factory machines.
4. Alcoholism; poor prision conditions; cruel treatment of the mentally ill; neglect of the handicapped; inadequate educational system; slavery; unequal treatment of women.
5. Many people thought they could improve their lives by living in special communities where they could take

part in religious practices or earn a living by cooperating instead of competing with others. Many hoped to improve society by showing that their ideas worked.

6. Through the annexation of Texas, settlement of the Oregon boundary dispute, victory in the war with Mexico resulting in the Mexican Cession, and arrangement of the Gadsden Purchase.

APPLYING YOUR STUDY SKILLS

1. (1) Jackson
   (2) 1828
   (3) Indian Removal Act
2. a. California, Nevada, and Utah; parts of Wyoming, Colorado, Kansas, Oklahoma, and New Mexico
   b. (1) the Southeast (2) the Northeast
      (3) the Southwest (4) the Northwest
      (5) the South (6) the West
3. "Inventions of the Mid-1800's"
   I. Inventions in Transportation and Communication
      A. Clipper ships
      B. Steam locomotive
      C. T-rail and spike
      D. Telegraph
      E. Rotary printing press
   II. Inventions That Changed Farm Life
      A. Iron plow
      B. Horse-drawn reaper
   III. Inventions That Changed Factory Life
      A. Sewing machine
      B. Improved sewing machine

PROJECTS

Answers will vary.

BUILDING AMERICAN CITIZENSHIP

1. Germany, Scandinavia, and Ireland. Today: Cuba, Haiti, Mexico, and Southeast Asia. Freedom of speech, religion, press, the freedom to choose their own way of making a living, and the freedom to choose where they want to live.
2. Drug abuse, child abuse, racial prejudice, overcrowding of prisons, abuse of the environment, unemployment, women's rights, political corruption, and so on.

UNIT 6 (1850-1877)
Conflict Splits The Nation

Introducing the Unit

Unit Six surveys 25 of the most difficult and troubled years in American history—1850-1877. It traces the events leading up to the Civil War, covers the war itself, and finally deals with the political, social, and economic aftermath. Unit Six relates the issues, events, and personalities that dominated this remarkable period.

The unit's first chapter covers the decade before the outbreak of hostilities. Tensions between North and South were increasing over the issue of the spread of slavery to the new territories in the West. Attempts at compromise, including the Compromise of 1850 and the Kansas-Nebraska Act of 1854 only widened the split. Meanwhile abolitionists were becoming more outspoken. Harriet Beecher Stowe's *Uncle Tom's Cabin* created a sensation at its publication in 1852. Violence erupted in Kansas, leading to bloodshed between pro-slavery and anti-slavery forces. Lincoln's election in 1860 resulted in the ultimate manifestation of sectionalism—secession.

Chapter 18 focuses on the Civil War years from the birth of the Confederacy in 1861 to the war's end in 1865. Fighting began at Fort Sumter in April 1861. Victorious in the West for the next two years, the Union was unable to defeat Lee's Army of Virginia. The war's turning point came in July 1863 when the Confederates at Vicksburg surrendered to Grant, and Lee was defeated by Meade at Gettysburg. Sherman's invasion of Georgia in 1864 and Grant's unrelenting pressure on Lee brought the war to a sudden conclusion in 1865.

Reconstruction is covered in Chapter 19. After Lincoln's assassination in 1865, Andrew Johnson tried, ineffectively, to implement the fallen leader's plan of restoring the Southern states to the Union. By 1866, Congress had taken over Reconstruction. The Freedmen's Bureau was created in 1865 to help freed slaves find work and to provide them with legal protection and education. Between 1865 and 1870 three amendments to the *Constitution*, relating to civil rights, were passed. In 1867, Congress passed the Military Reconstruction Act that provided the structure for government in the South for almost a decade. One by one, the Southern states were "reconstructed" and readmitted to the Union. Reconstruction ended in 1877 as the country lost interest in the problems that it had confronted.

The Unit Opener in the textbook depicts many of the significant persons and events of this period. You may wish to use these illustrations to help introduce the unit. The central figure is Abraham Lincoln. Beginning in the lower left-hand corner, in a clockwise direction, are Ulysses S. Grant, the Confederate flag, Sojurner Truth, Clara Barton, a group of slaves, Jefferson Davis, and the Confederate army.

Unit Themes and Ideas

Throughout Unit Six, in all three chapters, there is a continuous theme—the importance of leadership to the well-being of a nation. Without a strong leader the United States was unable to resolve the strong sectional differences that ultimately resulted in war—a war that might otherwise have been avoided. Chapter 18 illustrates how Lincoln, a great leader, was able to keep the Union together throughout the four difficult years of the Civil War. In Chapter 20, post-war leadership is assumed by certain members of Congress, who resolve the issues of Reconstruction and how to deal with the freed men. Throughout this period, good leadership or its absence is the critical factor in determining the course of events in the United States.

The themes and ideas of Unit Six are organized into the three chapters below:

Chapter 17 - *Sectional Conflict Divides the Nation (1850-1861)*

Chapter 18 - *Sectional Conflict Leads to War (1861-1865)*

Chapter 19 - *The Union is Restored (1865-1877)*

CHAPTER 17

Sectional Conflict Divides the Nation (1850-1861)

Chapter Objectives

After completing this chapter, students will be able to:
1. Explain how sharply differing ways of life helped divide Northerners and Southerners.
2. Identify attempts to deal with sectional differences through compromise.
3. Evaluate the effects of the major compromises of the 1850's.
4. List the steps in the movement of the South towards secession.

Chapter Chronology

Chapter 17 focuses on events in the 1850's that led the United States to the brink of secession. Many of the important persons and events of the period are highlighted in the textbook Chapter Opener. The first major event of the decade was the acceptance by Congress of the Compromise of 1850. Two years later Harriet Beecher Stowe's powerful abolitionist novel *Uncle Tom's Cabin* was published. In 1853, Franklin Pierce became President and another compromise, the Kansas-Nebraska Act of 1854, was passed during his administration. In 1857

James Buchanan became President. In the same year, the Supreme Court made the Dred Scott decision. The Presidential election of 1860 resulted in the victory of Lincoln. In the next year, the Southern states formed the Confederate States of America.

Motivation

Have students look at the textbook Chapter Introduction. Ask them to read about Brooks' attack on Sumner. Remind them that it took place on the Senate floor and inform them that Brooks was much younger than Sumner. Tell students that Brooks used a cane in his attack, hitting Sumner with such force that it shattered. A number of Southerners approved of Brooks' actions and sent him new canes to replace the one he broke. Ask students to look at the first question at the end of the introduction and recall all the events that had caused the bitter feelings to erupt between North and South.

Geographical Setting

The dominant political issue of the period is the extension of slavery into the Western territories and they provide the geographical focus for much of Chapter 17. The map *Free and Slave Areas of the United States 1850-1854*, includes Kansas and Nebraska, which became battlegrounds between slavery and antislavery forces. Students should study the map, *The Expansion of Cotton Growing Areas, 1839-1859*, to understand that the expansion of cotton growing from the East to the Western territories resulted in the debates over the extension of slavery into those new areas.

History Study Skills

The History Study Skill introduced in Chapter 17 is *Using Bar Graphs*. The information graphed is the growth of slavery from 1800 to 1860. Have students do this activity along with Section 1 because it helps them understand why the South was so committed to the institution of slavery. This skill is reinforced in Worksheet 47, *The Election of 1860*.

Bibliography

Teacher References
Oates, Stephen B., *To Purge this Land With Blood: John Brown*. Harper, New York City, 1970.
Potter, David M., and Fehrenbacher, Don E., *The Impending Crisis: 1848-1861*. Harper, New York City, 1976.
Student References
Jacob, Helen Pierce, *The Diary of the Strawbridge Place*. Atheneum, New York City, 1978. This novel focuses on the many families that aided runaway slaves.
Scott, John Anthony, *Woman Against Slavery, The Story of Harriet Beecher Stowe*. Harper, New York City, 1978. This is an excellent biography of Harriet Beecher Stowe.

Audio-Visual Materials

Follow the North Star, Time-Life, 47 minutes, color. 16 mm. This adventure drama deals with the sectional dispute over slavery.

John Brown: Violence in America, Multi-Media Production, color. This single sound filmstrip describes the life of John Brown.

SECTION 1: Different Ways Divide North and South

OBJECTIVES

After completing this section, students will be able to:
- Complete a table detailing the major differences between North and South.
- Identify spokesmen for the Northern and Southern positions.
- Discuss the bonds of unity holding the North and South together.

MOTIVATION

Use the Motivation suggested in the chapter introduction in this manual. Tell students that, after reading this section, they should be able to name four differences in ways of living that divided North and South.

SUGGESTED ACTIVITIES

1. **Directed Reading.** Place the following three-column table on a transparency or chalkboard (without answers). Have students look at and use the various headings in Section 1 to help them complete column one. (You may need to help them with the last one, states' rights.) As they read the chapter, they should fill in the other two columns.

DIFFERENCES IN WAYS OF LIVING	NORTH	SOUTH
(POPULATION)	(Fast growing cities Large population)	(Only 2 large cities Smaller population)
(ECONOMIC ACTIVITIES)	(Jobs in businesses and factories)	(Agriculture)
(SLAVERY)	(Opposed the spread of slavery in the West)	(Defended slavery)
(STATES' RIGHTS)	(States had right to decide to permit laws)	(Against allowing states to nullify laws)

As a summary, have students discuss the bonds of unity between North and South. Ask if they can think of others besides those mentioned in the book.

2. **Map Interpretation.** Ask students to study the map *The Expansion of Cotton Growing Areas, 1839-1859*. Then have them answer the following questions:
A. How many states were involved in growing cotton in 1839?
B. How many more states were involved in growing cotton in 1859?
C. In which direction did the expansion of cotton-growing areas occur?
D. Does this map tell you why expansion of cotton growing areas occurred? Explain your answer.
E. What was the northernmost state that grew cotton in 1839? In 1859?
F. What was the westernmost state that grew cotton in 1839? In 1859?

3. **Using Bar Graphs.** The History Study Skill for Chapter 17 is directly related to the contents of Section 1. Therefore, as suggested in this manual's chapter introduction, students would derive the greatest benefit from completing the activity, at this point. You may wish to add some questions, particularly for above-average students. These might include:
A. During which 10-year period did the smallest growth in the slave population occur? (1800-1810)
B. During which 10-year period did the greatest growth in the slave population occur? (1850-1860)
C. Does the graph tell you why the slave population increased? Explain.

4. **Ideals In the Lives of Americans.** Have students read the selection on Harriet Tubman on textbook page 400. It describes her life before and after her involvement with the Underground Railroad. Then have students answer the two questions at the end. Encourage them to do additional research on the various activities of Harriet Tubman during the Civil War. Students may also wish to investigate her family life. If Harriet Tubman was 30 in 1849, have students calculate her age at death. (94)

BUILDING AMERICAN CITIZENSHIP

One of the major issues dividing North and South was that of state sovereignty. Have students reread the last two paragraphs of Section 1 if it is necessary to review the meaning of the concept. Ask students if they can think of any issue today that might cause states to claim the right to decide for themselves whether or not to obey a federal law? (Answers will vary.)

SECTION 1 REVIEW ANSWERS

1. **IDENTIFY: George Fitzhugh:** Virginia plantation owner and leading defender of slavery; **Solomon Northup:** a free black who was kidnapped and sold into slavery and later wrote about his experiences in *Twelve Years a Slave;* **Harriet Tubman:** well-known black conductor of the underground railroad.
2. **DEFINE: underground railroad:** name given the escape routes from the South to the free states of the North and Canada.
3. (a) Population of the North was twice as large as that of the South. (b) Economic activities in the South were mainly agricultural; in the North there were more factories and businesses. (c) States' rights were defended by Southerners, some of whom believed in their right to nullify federal laws; Northerners were against states' rights and defended national unity.
4. People of the North and South spoke the same language and shared many customs and beliefs.

SECTION 2: North and South Try to Compromise

OBJECTIVES

After completing this section, students will be able to:
• Explain the differing positions of Northern and Southern members of Congress on the status of new states admitted to the Union.

• Describe the political issues that influenced the elections of 1848 and 1852.
• State the main features of the Compromise of 1850.

MOTIVATION

Review the meaning of the word "compromise." Have students consult the glossary if they cannot recall the meaning. Encourage them to give examples of compromises they have made in their own lives. Recall historical compromises discussed in earlier chapters (Great Compromise of the Constitutional Convention, Missouri Compromise). Recall the main points of the Missouri Compromise. Tell students that they will be reading about another important compromise in today's section and that they will be comparing it to the Missouri Compromise.

SUGGESTED ACTIVITIES

1. **Directed Reading.** As students read, have them write down the name of the compromise approved by Congress, the Compromise of 1850 and answer the following questions:
A. Who wrote it?
B. What was its purpose?
C. What did it say?
D. What did the North give up? What did it get?
E. What did the South give up? What did it get?
F. What were the results of the compromise?

In discussing the answers to these questions, place special emphasis on D and E. The answers to these two will reveal if students grasp the concept of "compromise." As a summary, have them compare the Compromise of 1850 with the Missouri Compromise by answering the above set of questions about the Missouri Compromise. In conclusion, ask in what ways the two were similar (author, purpose). In what ways were they different? (Content, year)

2. **Class Discussion.** The topic for the discussion should be: How did the issue of slavery affect the elections of 1848 and 1852? Students should bring out the following points: the names of the candidates; their positions on slavery; the creation of a third party in 1848; and the results of the elections.

3. **Identification.** Section 2 describes the positions of a number of people on the issue of slavery. Place the following list on the chalkboard. Have students identify the positions of each person as FOR slavery, AGAINST slavery, or VIEWS UNKNOWN.
A. Stephen Douglass - Against
B. Winfield Scott - VU
C. John C. Calhoun - For
D. Robert Toombs - For
E. John P. Hale - Against
F. Martin Van Buren - Against
You may wish to have below-average students read the sentence in the section from which they were able to identify each person's position.

4. **Studying Your History Vocabulary.** Have students apply this skill, learned in Chapter 16, to this section. Ask them to use clues in the reading to define these terms: abolish, proviso, popular sovereignty, vernal, unobserved, and disruption. Ask students which of these words they think would also be defined

in the glossary (proviso, popular sovereignty), and how they know this. (Words are printed in blue) Have them compare the chapter definitions with those found in the glossary.

BUILDING AMERICAN CITIZENSHIP

Duplicate Worksheet 46, *Compromise Fails in the 1850's.* Ask students to complete the first few questions. Have them apply the information they have learned about compromise by asking them to think of some issues before Congress recently that might require compromise. (Answers will vary.)

SECTION 2 REVIEW ANSWERS 14

1. **IDENTIFY: Wilmot Proviso:** a law proposed by David Wilmot, a Democratic Congressman from Pennsylvania, banning slavery in new territories won from Mexico; **"Platform of the South":** Calhoun's argument that Congress had no constitutional right to ban slavery in any part of the United States; **Stephen A. Douglas:** Illinois Senator who proposed the idea of popular sovereignty; **Zachary Taylor:** elected President in 1848; **Free Soil Party:** political party formed in 1848 to support banning slavery in new territories; **Henry Clay:** Senator from Kentucky and author of the Missouri Compromise, who proposed the Compromise of 1850; **Compromise of 1850:** Henry Clay's proposal for organizing the territories won in the Mexican War to cool the sectional conflict over slavery.

2. **DEFINE: proviso:** a special condition added to a bill or treaty; **popular sovereignty:** the idea that the people of each territory should decide by a majority vote whether or not to ban slavery.

3. To make the South's power in Congress equal to that of the North.

4. The South agreed to accept it if (1) the Fugitive Slave Law was enforced; (2) slavery continued to be allowed in the District of Columbia; (3) territories asking to be admitted as slave states not be denied admission to the Union.

5. 1½ million

SECTION 3: Compromises Fail to Settle Conflicts

OBJECTIVES

After completing this section, students will be able to:
- Explain the influence of *Uncle Tom's Cabin.*
- Describe the effects of the Kansas-Nebraska Act.
- Explain the importance of the Dred Scott case.

MOTIVATION

Use the illustration in Section 3. Have students read the captions carefully. Ask students how they think each illustration might be related to the main issue of this section. Tell students that these illustrations will be discussed again when they have completed the reading.

SUGGESTED ACTIVITIES

1. **Directed Reading.** Review the meaning of the terms "cause" (what makes something happen) and "effect" (the result). As students read, have them draw three

columns on a sheet of paper. Ask them to list the four sectional conflicts discussed in Section 3 in the middle column labelled Event. In the left column, labelled Cause, they should write what caused the conflict, and in the right column, labelled Effect, one result.
EXAMPLE:

CAUSE	EVENT	EFFECT
Senator Douglas' desire for a trans-continental rail-road	Kansas-Nebraska Act	"Bleeding Kansas"

2. **Chronology.** To check students' awareness of the sequence of events described in Section 3, have them arrange the following chronologically.
   A. Birth of the Republican Party
   B. Publication of *Uncle Tom's Cabin*
   C. Dred Scott case
   D. Kansas-Nebraska Act
   E. Compromise of 1850
   Answers: E - B - D - A - C

3. **Using Circle Graphs.** Review this History Study Skill from Chapter 11 by having students construct a circle graph using the results of the *electoral* voting in the election of 1856. Ask them to reread the skill page on textbook page 271. You may wish to assist them in converting the actual figures into percentages.

CANDIDATE	VOTES	PERCENTAGES
Buchanan	174	59%
Fremont	114	38%
Fillmore	8	3%

4. **Round Robin.** Call for a volunteer to state one important fact from Section 3. Ask a second volunteer to repeat that fact and add a new one. Ask a third student to repeat the second fact and add a new one and so on. Continue until all students have had the opportunity to participate. You may wish to allow below-average students to use their textbook or class notes while doing this activity.

BUILDING AMERICAN CITIZENSHIP

Instruct students to answer the remaining questions from Worksheet 46, *Compromise Fails in the 1850's.* Ask students the following questions when they have completed the activity:
   A. Do you think Senator Douglas would have proposed the Kansas-Nebraska Act if he had known it would result in violence?
   B. Can violence ever be used as a means of compromise? Why?

SECTION 3 REVIEW ANSWERS

1. **IDENTIFY: Harriet Beecher Stowe:** author of *Uncle Tom's Cabin;* **Uncle Tom's Cabin:** Stowe's novel published in 1852 describing the tragedies of slavery; **Kansas-Nebraska Act:** a bill proposed by Senator Douglas of Illinois for organizing the territories of Kansas and Nebraska and granting each the right of popular sovereignty; **Dred Scott:** a slave who sued for his freedom, resulting in the Supreme Court case in

which the Court ruled that slavery was protected by the Constitution.
2. Pro-slavery and anti-slavery forces tried to gain control of the state, which led to violence between the two groups.
3. It intensified the sectional conflict between the North and South. Southerners supported the Court's decision; Northerners opposed it.

SECTION 4: The South Moves Toward Secession

OBJECTIVES

After completing this section, students will be able to:
• Compare the positions of Lincoln and Douglas in the 1858 Senatorial debates.
• Describe people's reactions to John Brown's raid on Harpers Ferry, Virginia.
• Explain why the Southern states seceded from the Union.

MOTIVATION

Review the differences in ways of living in the North and South (Section 1). Review the attempts to settle sectional differences. (Missouri Compromise, Compromise of 1850, Kansas-Nebraska Act) Review the events that increased sectional conflict. ("Bleeding Kansas," *Uncle Tom's Cabin,* Dred Scott case) Ask students where all of this is leading? Have them look at the title of Section 4 for a possible answer. Check the glossary to be sure students can define the term "secession." Tell them that at the conclusion of this section, they should be able to identify the specific reasons for the secession of the Southern states.

SUGGESTED ACTIVITIES

1. **Directed Reading.** As students read the section, have them answer the following questions either orally or in their notebooks:
   A. How did Lincoln become famous all across the country?
   B. What were the reactions of Northerners and Southerners to John Brown's raid on Harpers Ferry?
   C. How was Lincoln able to win the election of 1860? Discuss the answers to each question. As a summary, ask students to identify the specific reasons for the secession of the Southern states.
2. **Using Bar Graphs.** Duplicate Worksheet 47, *The Election of 1860.* This activity gives students an opportunity to practice the History Study Skill introduced in Section 1, and to review information on Lincoln's election. Before beginning, familiarize students with the information on both graphs by asking the following questions:
   A. What is the title of the graph?
   B. What information is on the vertical axis?
   C. What information is on the horizontal axis?
   D. What is the biggest difference between the two graphs? (One is electoral, the other popular)

3. **Acrostic:** Review the major events leading to secession by having students complete the following acrostic:

Uncle Tom'S Cabin	S - book about slavery by Harriet B. Stowe
rEpublican	E - political party founded in 1850's to oppose the spread of slavery
Dred SCott case	C - Supreme Court's decision involving slave rights and protection of slavery under the Constitution
Harpers FErry	E - location of John Brown's raid on a federal arsenal
Lincoln-Douglas Debates	D - public discussions between candidates running for the Illinois Senate seat in 1858
Kansas-NEbraska Act	E - law allowing people settling in the territories of the Great Plains to decide about slavery for themselves

4. **Cause and Effect.** Duplicate Worksheet 48, *The 1850's.* It will provide an excellent application of the skill, while simultaneously allowing students to review the major events of the chapter. You may wish to work with students on the first example. Allow them to do the next two, and then check their progress before completing the remainder of this activity. This will permit you to work with students who are having problems

BUILDING AMERICAN CITIZENSHIP

What was Lincoln's stand on slavery? Knowing that his position could lead to war, should he have changed it? Why or why not? Should presidents act on what they think is right, no matter what the consequences for the nation may be? (Answers will vary.) Can you think of any presidential decisions since the mid-1900's that caused a great national outcry? (Panama Canal Treaty, Pardon of President Nixon)

SECTION 4 REVIEW ANSWERS

1. **IDENTIFY: Lincoln-Douglas debates:** public debates on slavery between Lincoln and Douglas during their election campaigns in the Illinois senatorial election of 1858; **John Brown:** leader of an anti-slavery group in an unsuccessful raid on a federal arsenal at Harper's Ferry, Virginia; **Crittenden Compromise:** proposal by John Crittenden of Kentucky, rejected by Congress, for a constitutional amendment guaranteeing slavery where it already existed and reestablishing the Missouri Compromise line for slavery; **Confederate States of America:** name given to the new nation formed by the Southern states that seceded from the Union.
2. **DEFINE: secession:** leaving or withdrawing from the Union.
3. Slavery, popular sovereignty, rights of citizenship for black Americans.

4. They argued that Southern states had lost their rights (to own slaves) in the territories and therefore they had cause to cut their ties with the Union.
5. **SKILL PRACTICE:**

34

CHAPTER 17 REVIEW ANSWERS

REVIEWING KEY WORDS

1. e.	2. b.	3. a.	4. d.	5. c.

REMEMBERING IMPORTANT PEOPLE AND EVENTS

1. c.	2. e.	3. a.	4. b.	5. d.
6. e.	7. a.	8. d.	9. c.	10. b.

REVIEWING THE FACTS

1. T	2. T	3. F	4. T	5. T F

PLACING EVENTS IN TIME

1. B.	2. E.	3. D.	4. A.	5. C.

LINKING GEOGRAPHY AND HISTORY

Congress had to decide whether the states formed from the new territory would be open to slavery. This led to arguments between Northerners and Southerners.

THINKING ABOUT AMERICAN HISTORY

1. In the conflict following passage of the Kansas-Nebraska Act in 1854, the Whig Party split apart. Pro-slavery Whigs in the South joined the Democratic Party. Anti-slavery Whigs in the North joined Free-Soilers to form the Republican Party. Thus, the Republican Party was formed to fight the spread of slavery.
2. There were four candidates running for President. The Democratic Party split between the North and supporters of popular sovereignty (who nominated Stephen A. Douglas) and the South and supporters of the Dred Scott case (who nominated John C. Breckinridge). The Republicans nominated Lincoln, who believed slavery should be allowed where it already existed, but in their platform the Republicans continued to oppose slavery in the territories. A fourth candidate, John Bell of Tennessee, was nominated by the Constitutional Party, which supported the Union and the Constitution.

APPLYING HISTORY STUDIES SKILLS

1. compare.	2. title.
3. vertical axis.	4. horizontal axis.
5. 1850.	6. ½ million.
7. 5.	8. increase.

CHAPTER 18

Sectional Conflict Leads to War (1861-1865)

Chapter Objectives

After completing this chapter, students will be able to:
1. Explain why secession led to civil war.

2. List the war aims of the North and South.
3. Name major military battles and campaigns.
4. Describe how Northern strength wore down and ultimately defeated the South.
5. Explain how the war changed the nation.

Chapter Chronology

Chapter 18 covers the events immediately preceding the Civil War and during the war itself. Many of the most important persons and events of the period are highlighted in the textbook Chapter Opener. Confederate firing on Fort Sumter in April 1861, marked the beginning of the war. Three months later, at the Battle of Bull Run, the Confederates won the war's first major battle. In 1862, Union forces, under U.S. Grant captured Fort Donelson in Tennessee. Lincoln issued the Emancipation Proclamation in 1863. In the same year there were two major Union victories, one at Vicksburg, the Confederacy's last stronghold on the Mississippi River, and one at Gettysburg. Union occupation of Atlanta under Sherman in 1864 dealt a crushing blow to the Confederacy. In April 1865, Lee surrendered at Appomattox Court House. Just weeks earlier, Lincoln had been inaugurated to his second term as President.

Motivation

The complex network of events that brought on the Civil War has always fascinated historians and students of history. In the previous chapter, students read about the movement toward secession, and they should know that they will now study the Civil War. Below are some causes of the Civil War from the points of view of two major figures of the time and from the later perspective of two 20th century historians. Have students discuss each cause and comment on it. Be sure that students understand that causes may be short-range or long-range. Have students reconsider their comments at the end of the chapter, by which time some may have changed their opinions.

Jefferson Davis, speaking to the Confederate Congress, Spring 1861.
  • Lincoln's Declaration of War on April 15, 1861
  • Northern movement against slavery
  • Tariff
Abraham Lincoln, speaking to Congress, July 1861
  • Attack on Fort Sumter
  • Southern prevention of federal mail delivery and other federal functions
  • Failure of Southern states to give troops to the Union army
James Ford Rhodes, historian, 1913
  • Slavery
Avery Craven, historian, 1950
  • Failure of leadership in the 1850's

Geographical Setting

Chapter 18 covers the major campaigns of the Civil War, which except for Antietam and Gettysburg, took place in the South. Geography played a very important part in determining Northern strategy. The Union used a naval blockade to stop Southern shipping. Union forces concentrated on gaining control of the Mississippi River to separate the West from the Confederacy. Much of the fighting took place along railway lines and rivers. Although the war intruded into all parts of the Confederacy, Chapter 19 focuses on the area between Richmond and Washington, D.C.; Grant's victories at Vicksburg and Chattanooga in the West; and Sherman's March through Georgia. The first map in this chapter shows the *Union and the Confederate States 1861*. It is followed by maps showing *The Civil War, 1861-1865, The Civil War in the East, 1861-1863,* and *The Last Major Battles of the Civil War, 1864-1865.*

Bibliography

Teacher References

Catton, Bruce, *The Centennial History of the Civil War*, 3 Volumes. Doubleday, New York City, 1963.

Massey, Mary, *Bonnet Brigades: American Women and the Civil War.* 1966.

Student References

Colt, Margaret, *The Fight for Union.* Houghton-Mifflin, Boston, Mass., 1961. This book describes the events leading up to the Civil War and emphasizes the influence of contemporary Americans, including Henry Clay, John C. Calhoun, Daniel Webster, and John Brown.

Katz, William, *An Album of the Civil War.* Franklin Watts, New York City, 1974. This clearly written, well-illustrated history of the Civil War, includes a short summary of its aftermath and also offers good coverage of the role of black Americans.

Audio-Visual Materials

The Civil War: A Unit of Study, United Learning. This eight-part sound filmstrip package includes an extensive program guide with activities and ditto masters.

The Civil War, National Geographic. This three-part sound filmstrip program covers the events before, during, and after the Civil War.

SECTION 1: The South Leaves the Union and War Begins

OBJECTIVES

After completing this section, students will be able to:
• Explain the differences between the Confederate Constitution and the United States Constitution.
• Describe the battle of Fort Sumter in South Carolina.
• Discuss the difficult decisions made by Northerners and Southerners at the beginning of the War.

MOTIVATION

Use the Motivation suggested in the chapter introduction of this manual. When the discussion is complete, make a statement similar to the following: We now have some ideas as to why the war was fought. But who started it? Where did it begin and why? These are some of the questions that will be answered in Section 1.

SUGGESTED ACTIVITIES

1. **Directed Reading.** As students read Section 1, have

them answer the following questions—who, what, when, where, why, and how.
A. When did the Civil War begin? (April, 1861)
B. Where did it begin? (Fort Sumter, S.C.)
C. How did it begin? (Bombardment of the fort)
D. Who were the important people involved? (Union Commander—Robert Anderson; Confederate Commander—Pierre Beauregard)
E. What were the results of this event? (Patriotism in the North, support for Lincoln)
F. Why would Lincoln not be displeased with what happened here? (The Confederacy fired the first shots and this started the war.)

After reviewing the answers to these questions, ask students if they think there might have been any way to avoid the battle that occurred at Fort Sumter.

2. **Discussion and Writing.** The topic for class discussion is taken directly from the reading: "Why was it so difficult for people to choose sides at the beginning of the war?" Students should point out that numerous people disagreed with their state and local leaders. Some even disagreed with their families. For many, the decision to be made was whether to follow their personal beliefs or to adopt the loyalties of their state, local area, or family.

At the conclusion of the discussion, have students write a paragraph summarizing their ideas. You may wish to have them review the Chapter 10 History Study Skill on textbook page 247 before completing the assignment.

4. **Preparing Reports.** Have students use library sources to prepare reports on each of the following individuals: Jefferson Davis, Pierre Beauregard, Robert Anderson, Robert E. Lee, and Mary Todd Lincoln. Have students emphasize important aspects of their lives before and after the war, as well as during the conflict.

BUILDING AMERICAN CITIZENSHIP

What qualities made Robert E. Lee a leading citizen and military leader of the Confederacy? (Loyalty, a sense of duty and honor, ability to inspire others, willingness to take the initiative) Which of these qualities would you consider important in the people who are leading America today? (Answers will vary.)

SECTION 1 REVIEW ANSWERS

1. **IDENTIFY: Jefferson Davis:** elected President of the Confederate States of America; **Abraham Lincoln:** Republican candidate who became President of the United States in 1861; **Fort Sumter:** fort held by Union troops in the harbor of Charleston, South Carolina, that was fired on by Confederate troops on April 12, 1861, marking the beginning of the Civil War; **Major Robert Anderson:** commander of Union troops at Fort Sumter; **General Pierre Beauregard:** commander of Confederate forces in Charleston, whose troops fired on Fort Sumter; **Robert E. Lee:** officer who resigned from the Union Army to become general of the Confederate Army.

2. **DEFINE: recognize:** to agree to the existence of a government; **abolitionists:** people who were opposed to slavery.

3. The Confederate States of America.
4. Lincoln believed that no state had the right to secede from the Union.

SECTION 2: The North and South Have Different War Aims

OBJECTIVES

After completing this section, students will be able to:
- State the plans of the North and South for winning the war.
- Compare the resources held by the North and South at the start of the war.
- Describe the Baltimore Riot and the First Battle of Bull Run.

MOTIVATION

Review the names of the wars studied by students so far this year. (French and Indian, War of Independence, Barbary Pirates, War of 1812, Texas War for Independence, and the Mexican War) Since students have studied some six wars to this point, challenge them to use their "expertise" to list all of the things it takes to win a war. Write their responses on the chalkboard and have students explain why each is essential. Take a poll among students to determine whether the North or South has the advantage in each area, and label with "N," "S," or "?" if students are unsure. State the goals of this lesson:
1. To add to the list anything that may have been forgotten
2. To determine, finally, which side had the advantage in each case
3. To see what difference, if any, these resources made in the war's first major battle.

SUGGESTED ACTIVITIES

1. **Directed Reading.** Be sure students are aware of the goals established during the Motivation. As they read, ask them to list the resources of the North and South, mentioned in this section, and also to determine, which side held the advantage. Examples include:

   Good strategy (Opinion)
   Strong military tradition (S)
   Expertise in handling firearms (S)
   Large population (N)
   Industrial power (N)
   Weapons (N)
   Railway system (N)
   Food (N)

   It should become apparent to students that the North held the advantage. As a summary, discuss what, if any, difference this advantage made in the war's first major battle—Bull Run.
2. **Comprehension Check.** In order to determine students' understanding of the material in Section 2, have them answer TRUE or FALSE to each of the following. If the answer is FALSE, the students should be able to explain why.
   A. Part of the Confederate Plan to win the war was to invade the North as often as possible. (F)
   B. Part of the North's Plan to win the war was to stop Confederate trade with other countries. (T)
   C. The Union's advantages in resources made victory a certainty. (F)
   D. Neither the North nor South were prepared to fight a war. (T)
   E. The Baltimore Riot was started by Confederate troops stationed in the city. (F)
   F. The first Union invasion of Confederate territory failed. (T)
3. **Time Line.** Have students begin a time line of the major events of the four years of the Civil War. They may use a scale of 1½" = 1 year or 2" = 1 year. You may wish to have them indicate the months of the year. Included on the line should be such events in Section 1, as the birth of the Confederacy and the Battle of Fort Sumter. For Section 2, include the Baltimore Riot (have students look up the exact month) and the First Battle of Bull Run.
4. **Recognizing Primary and Secondary Sources.** Review the Chapter 15 History Study Skill on textbook page 365. Then have the students identify each of the following as a primary or secondary source.
   A. Eyewitness account of the Battle of Manassas (P)
   B. Copy of Lincoln's orders to Union forces to restore control of the city of Baltimore. (P)
   C. An 1861 recruitment poster for the Confederate Army (P)
   D. A filmstrip about the Battle of Bull Run. (S)

BUILDING AMERICAN CITIZENSHIP

Whose responsibility is it to make plans for fighting a war? (President, Generals) Do you think military men should be allowed to make all of the decisions or should they seek the advice of other citizens in making their plans? (Answers will vary.) Explain your answer.

SECTION 2 REVIEW ANSWERS

1. **IDENTIFY: General Winfield Scott:** commander of the United States Army who helped President Lincoln work out a plan to defeat the Confederacy; **Battle of Bull Run (Battle of Manassas):** the first major battle in the Civil War; **"Stonewall" Jackson:** hero of the Confederate Army who blocked the Union advance at Bull Run.
2. **DEFINE: emancipation:** the freeing of slaves.
3. By capturing Richmond, the capital of the Confederacy; by gaining control of the Mississippi River to separate the eastern and western parts of the Confederacy; and by stopping Confederate trade with other nations.
4. By defending the South against invasion and by holding out until the North grew tired of war and recognized the Confederacy.

SECTION 3: The War Is Hard Fought for Two Years.

OBJECTIVES

After completing this section, students will be able to:
- List and locate Confederate and Union victories from 1861 to 1863.
- Explain the importance of the Emancipation Proclamation.

- Describe the role of black soldiers during the war.
- Identify the difficulties associated with the draft law and disloyal citizens.

MOTIVATION

Use the military map, *The Civil War in the East, 1861-1863,* on textbook page 425. Have students identify the battles fought in the East from 1861 to 1863 and the year in which they were fought. Also, ask them to speculate about how free blacks and slaves might have been able to help the Union win the war. Tell them that this section will provide information on both these topics. 4

SUGGESTED ACTIVITIES

1. **Directed Reading.** As students read, have them answer the following questions:
   A. What battles were fought from 1861 to 1863? Which side won each battle?
   B. What were the effects of the Emancipation Proclamation?
   C. What problems did Lincoln and the government have to solve during the early years of the war?
      After reviewing the answers with students, be sure to discuss the ways in which blacks contributed to the war effort.
2. **History Study Skills.** Several of the battles depicted on the military map have already been discussed. This is therefore a good time to introduce the Chapter 18 History Study Skill, *Using Military Maps,* on textbook page 437. It will serve both as a review of the battles already discussed and as an introduction to those gone into in the remaining two sections.
3. **Using Military Maps.** Duplicate Worksheet 49, *The Battle of Antietam.* This exercise will reinforce the History Study Skill introduced in the previous activity. You may wish to assign it for homework. This would give students an opportunity to apply the skill independently. You may also wish to review the details of the battle as described in the text and have students compare this information with what they have learned from the military map.
4. **Building American Citizenship.** Duplicate Worksheet 50, *The Emancipation Proclamation.* This will allow students to examine part of the actual statement, and should encourage them to think about what it says.

BUILDING AMERICAN CITIZENSHIP

Opposition to the war and the government increased as the war progressed. How did citizens show their discontent during the war? (Riots, formation of secret societies) How did Lincoln react? (Sent soldiers to stop the rioting, suspended the right of *habeas corpus*) Should a President be allowed to suspend citizens' rights during a war? At any other time? Explain your answer. (Answers may vary, but should include the need of a president to do what is necessary for the nation during a time of crisis.)

SECTION 3 REVIEW ANSWERS

1. **IDENTIFY: Ulysses S. Grant:** commander of the Union troops in the West; **Emancipation Proclamation:** pro-

clamation issued by President Lincoln freeing the slaves in Confederate states; **Copperheads:** members of secret societies in the North who opposed the Civil War.
2. **DEFINE: unconditional surrender:** having to give up everything after a military defeat; **conscription:** a national draft; **bounty system:** a system in which federal, state, and local governments offered money to those who volunteered to serve in the army; ***habeas corpus:*** a citizen's right to appear before a court before being jailed.
3. The Northern army took control of Missouri and Kentucky and won battles at Fort Donelson and Antietam. The Confederate army won a battle near Richmond, the second Battle of Bull Run, a battle at Chancellorsville, and several others.
4. Lincoln suspended several civil liberties for the length of the war, including the right of *habeas corpus.*

SECTION 4: Northern Power Wears Down the South

OBJECTIVES

After completing this section, students will be able to:
- List and locate the battles fought from 1863 to 1865.
- Describe the effects of the Union blockade of Southern ports.
- Explain how the war ended.

MOTIVATION

Use the time line in the textbook Chapter Opener. Ask students to identify events they have already discussed. Have them identify those that remain to be covered. Tell them that Section 4 will provide information on all of these events except one. Challenge students by stating that after they have read this section, you will ask them to identify other events that could have been depicted on the time line as well as the one event on it that was not discussed in the reading of this section.

SUGGESTED ACTIVITIES

1. **Directed Reading.** As students read, have them answer the following question by providing as many possible reasons as they can give.
   Why was the South beaten during the last two years of the war?
   Possible answers include:
   A. South was unable to successfully invade the North.
   B. South had too few soldiers or supplies to defend its territory.
   C. North was able to gain control of the Mississippi River
   D. North began destroying almost everything that could be of use to the South
   E. the President found a general who seemed to be more determined than the others
   F. South was effectively blockaded
   Be sure also to discuss other events that could be added to the time line, including the *Monitor* vs. the *Merrimac,* the Battle of Cold Harbor, and the capture of Richmond. Remind students about the one event

which was not discussed in Section 4. (Lincoln's reelection)

2. **Time Line.** Continue with the emphasis on time study. Have students add events from Sections 3 and 4 to the time line they began constructing in Section 2.

3. **Research.** Chapter 18 describes the major battles of the Civil War. However, there were hundreds of other battles that students could investigate. Ask students to select one of those listed below, or another in which they have expressed an interest. Have them prepare a report on the battle, including its exact location, the leaders involved, the date, unusual occurrences or incidents, the results, and any other information of interest.

> Cedar Mountain, Virginia
> Spotsylvania, Virginia
> Stones River, Tennessee
> Kennesaw Mountain, Georgia
> Olustee, Florida
> Nashville, Tennessee
> Mobile Bay, Alabama
> Pea Ridge, Arkansas
> Wilson's Creek, Missouri
> Lookout Mountain, Missouri
> Bentonville, North Carolina
> Shiloh, Tennessee

5. **Sources of Freedom—The Gettysburg Address.** Have students read and interpret the excerpts from the *Gettysburg Address* on textbook page 429. Relate the primary source material to the information in Section 4 by having students recall specific details about the occasion on which it was given. These would include when, where, and why the speech was made and the major ideas it contains.

BUILDING AMERICAN CITIZENSHIP

During his march from Atlanta to Savannah, Georgia, Sherman's army destroyed everything in its path that could have been of use to the Confederate Army. Do you think an army should destroy military targets only or everything of use to private citizens as well? (Answers will vary.)

SECTION 4 REVIEW ANSWERS

1. IDENTIFY: **General George Meade:** commander of Union forces in the battle at Gettysburg in 1863; **Gettysburg Address:** speech given by President Lincoln at Gettysburg in which he honored the soldiers who had died there and described the meaning of the war; the *Virginia (Merrimac):* a ship captured by the Confederates and refitted with iron armor; the *Monitor:* a new ironclad warship of the North that battled with the *Virginia,* marking the beginning of modern naval warfare; **Appomattox Court House:** site of Lee's surrender to Grant on April 9, 1865.

2. DEFINE: **blockade runners:** fast ships of the Confederates that outran federal ships; **siege warfare:** continuous attack, used by General Grant to force Lee's army to stay in trenches until they ran out of supplies and soldiers.

3. Gettysburg and Vicksburg.

4. In their marches through Georgia and South Carolina, Sherman's army of 60,000 soldiers destroyed most of the South's resources. They also freed slaves along the way.

SECTION 5: The Civil War Changes the Nation

OBJECTIVES

After completing this section, students will be able to:
- List the costs of the Civil War.
- Describe the opportunities gained by women and blacks as a result of the war.
- Describe the political changes brought about by the war.

MOTIVATION

Have students read the title of Section 5. Ask them to speculate about the changes brought on by the war. They will undoubtedly mention the end of slavery. Have them look at the picture and read the caption. Then have them name other changes, in addition to the widespread destruction in the South indicated here. Challenge students to identify other changes as they read.

SUGGESTED ACTIVITIES

1. **Directed Reading.** Have students skim the headings in Section 5 to identify areas of change. As they read, have them develop an outline of the changes that occurred. The topics could include: Ways of Doing Battle, New Opportunities for Women, New Opportunities for Blacks, and Political Changes. Provide below-average students with the topics. Other students should be able to develop their own. As a summary activity, discuss each change and identify those that were not included in the motivational discussion.

2. **Identication Puzzle.** There are some names in this chapter which students may be encountering for the first time. Have them create a crossword puzzle or an acrostic, with clues, for all of the people mentioned. For additional reinforcement, you may wish to have students exchange papers to solve the puzzles. If students become curious about the exact roles of the individuals, encourage them to use library resources to do additional research.

3. **Ideals In The Lives Of Americans.** Have students read the selection on Clara Barton, on textbook page 434. Ask additional questions to have students think critically about what they have read. For example:
   A. When was Clara Barton born?
   B. What dangers would she have faced in performing her work?
   C. Why were women not allowed on the front lines of battlefields?
   D. Where did she get the supplies that were needed?

4. **Recognizing Primary and Secondary Sources.** Duplicate Worksheet 51, *Letters From A Soldier.* Relate this activity to the previous one by asking students what types of work Clara Barton might have been doing if she had been present in Sam's various camps.

BUILDING AMERICAN CITIZENSHIP

For four years, Southern Congressmen from the seceded states did not participate in the governing of the nation. What difference did this make? (Republicans gained control of Congress and passed laws that the Southern Congress members would have opposed.) In today's Congress, all states are represented. Some members of Congress, however, do not attend all sessions of Congress. Should they be required to attend? Explain your answer. (Answers will vary.)

SECTION 5 REVIEW ANSWERS

1. **IDENTIFY: Elizabeth Blackwell:** a doctor who worked for improved medical care for soldiers; **Clara Barton:** a nurse who helped wounded soldiers on the battlefield; **Mary Chesnut:** Southern writer who kept a diary recounting Civil War experiences; **Homestead Act:** law passed in 1862 to open land to frontier farmers; **Morrill Act:** law passed in 1862 that gave public land in the West to the states, enabling them to sell the land to raise money for colleges.
2. **DEFINE: total war:** a war in which all of a country's resources are used; **land-grant colleges:** educational institutions opened with funds as a result of the Morrill Act.
3. Repeating rifles, machine guns, ironclad warships, long-range artillery, telescopic sights, naval mines and land mines.
4. Women took over men's jobs in managing farms, businesses, and plantations, and worked in factories. They led organizations that helped soldiers and their families and began working in civil service jobs. Black Americans won their freedom, fought courageously as soldiers, and some took over plantations and ran them successfully.

32 pp 438-439

CHAPTER 18 REVIEW ANSWERS

REVIEWING KEY WORDS

1. b.   2. e.   3. d.   4. c.   5. a.

REMEMBERING IMPORTANT PEOPLE

1. d.   2. c.   3. b.   4. a.   5. e.

REVIEWING THE FACTS

1. S   2. N   3. N   4. N   5. S.
6. c.   7. c.   8. b.   9. b.   10. a.

PLACING EVENTS IN TIME

1. B.   2. E D   3. D A   4. A E   5. C.

LINKING GEOGRAPHY AND HISTORY

1. Control of the Mississippi River would split the Confederacy into two parts, cutting the states west of the Mississippi off from the rest of the South. The Union could ship supplies freely to Union armies, and it would open the heart of the South of Union attack.
2. It reduced the South's chances of winning because the blockade cut off the source of needed supplies. The blockade also cut off their income from trade with other nations.

THINKING ABOUT AMERICAN HISTORY

1. Lincoln hesitated to declare emancipation without first winning a military victory; otherwise, critics would say he was trying to gather support in the face of defeat. Also, he hoped the Southern states would rejoin the Union if they were allowed to keep their slaves.
2. Neither army was really prepared at the onset of the war. They had to train troops and gather supplies. Also, both sides were confident in their ability to win quickly.

APPLYING HISTORY STUDIES SKILLS

1. F   2. T   3. T   4. F   5. F

CHAPTER 19

The Union is Restored (1865-1877)

Chapter Objectives

After completing this chapter, students will be able to:
1. Describe the Reconstruction programs of Lincoln and Johnson.
2. Explain the role of Congress in Reconstruction and how it helped the freedmen.
3. Identify the provisions of the Thirteenth, Fourteenth, and Fifteenth Amendments.
4. Describe the ways in which many Southerners resisted Reconstruction.
5. Explain the reasons for the end of Reconstruction.

Chapter Chronology

Chapter 19 is a survey of the period in American history, from 1865 to 1877, that is known as Reconstruction. Many of the important persons and events of the time are highlighted in the textbook Chapter Opener. The assassination of Lincoln in 1865 was an immeasurable national tragedy. He was succeeded by Andrew Johnson. Two years later, the Southern states were placed under military control. In 1868, Johnson was impeached by the House of Representatives but not convicted by the Senate. The Fourteenth Amendment was ratified in the same year, and Ulysses S. Grant was elected President. In 1870, the Fifteenth Amendment was ratified. Grant was reelected in 1872. Five years later, with the Compromise of 1877, Reconstruction ended.

Motivation

Among the many issues of Reconstruction, two stand out:
1. Helping the former slaves in their transition from slavery to freedom.
2. Creating state governments in the Confederate states that would be loyal to the Union.

Write these two issues on the chalkboard and ask students to suggest possible solutions. This may be done as a group activity or by the whole class. Keep student responses for reference as they work through the chapter.

Geographical Setting

In chapter 19 the geographical focus is on the Southern states that seceded from the Union in 1860-1861. Social and political issues predominate with little or no geographical emphasis. Worksheet 52 is a map skill activity. It illustrates the dates when Southern states regained admission to the Union and control of their own state governments.

History Study Skills

The History Study Skill introduced in Chapter 19 is *Putting Events in Chronological Order* and the focus is on the sequence of events in Chapter 19. This activity is best used at the end of the chapter as a review of Reconstruction. The activity allows students to review each event as well as the order in which each event occurred.

Bibliography

Teacher References

Franklin, John Hope, *Reconstruction After the Civil War.* University of Chicago Press, Chicago, Ill., 1961.

Gillette, William, *Retreat From Reconstruction: 1869-1879.* Louisiana State University Press, Baton Rouge, La., 1980.

Student References

Buckmaster, Henrietta, *Freedom Bound.* Macmillan, New York City, 1965. This dramatic account of the Reconstruction period deals with the aspirations and disappointments of both whites and blacks in this period.

Longsworth, Polly, *I, Charlotte Forten, Black and Free.* Crowell, New York City, 1970. This is the gripping biography of a free black woman, who helped establish the famous school for freed slaves in Port Royal, South Carolina.

Audio-Visual Materials

The Civil War: Postwar Period, Coronet, 16 minutes. This film, on the years of crisis and bitterness after the Civil War, includes mention of the conflicts between Johnson and Congress, of the carpetbaggers, and of the birth of the Ku Klux Klan.

Presidents of the United States, Part IV, National Geographic. This two-part filmstrip set describes the lives of Lincoln, Johnson, and Grant, the presidents during Reconstruction and also provides information on the problems and process of Reconstruction.

SECTION 1: Leaders Argue About Reconstruction

OBJECTIVES

After completing this section, students will be able to:
- Distinguish between President Lincoln's plan for Reconstruction and that of President Johnson.
- Describe the treatment of blacks by the newly "restored" Southern state governments.
- Explain why Congress took charge of Reconstruction.

MOTIVATION

Use the textbook Chapter Introduction, which describes Lincoln's assassination. Discuss this selection by asking the following questions:
A. How did Lincoln plan to deal with the conquered South?
B. Why was Lincoln assassinated, and by whom?
C. What did Stanton mean when he said "Now he belongs to the ages."?
D. Why was Lincoln missed in the years following the war?
E. What problems for the restoration process of the defeated Southern states might have arisen as a result of Lincoln's death?

Questions "A" to "D" are based on the reading. "E" is designed to have students think about the possibility of the new president's plans differing from those of Lincoln.

SUGGESTED ACTIVITIES

1. **Directed Reading.** As students read Section 1, have them list the major points of each plan for Reconstruction: Lincoln's, Johnson's, and that of Congress. When students have done this, compare the programs. What were the similarities? the differences? Also, have students select an adjective to describe each plan. For example: Lincoln's—moderate; Johnson's—mild; Congress—harsh.

2. **Research Report.** Students are generally fascinated by the events surrounding the assassination of President Lincoln. Divide the class into groups and assign each the following questions to be researched:
A. What happened to John Wilkes Booth after the assassination?
B. Who were the other people who worked with Booth? What happened to them?
C. Who was Dr. Samuel Mudd? What happened to him?
D. Why wasn't Lincoln more carefully guarded at Ford's Theatre?

3. **Comprehension Check.** To determine students' understanding of the various plans for Reconstruction, have them answer the following TRUE-FALSE questions. If a statement is false, students should be able to explain why.
A. President Lincoln's plan for Reconstruction stated that all Southerners who swore loyalty to the Union would be pardoned. (F) *Johnson's Plan*
B. Congressional plans for Reconstruction required new state constitutions to recognize the freedom of blacks. (T)
C. Most moderate and radical Republicans felt that Johnson's plan for Reconstruction was weak. (T)
D. Johnson's plans for Reconstruction allowed each state to establish its own voting laws. (T)
E. Congressional plans for Reconstruction included acceptance of newly elected representatives and senators to Congress. (F)

BUILDING AMERICAN CITIZENSHIP

The President often disagrees with Congress about how to solve problems that involve American citizens. In what sense was this true during Reconstruction? Is such frequent disagreement a good way to solve the nation's problems? Explain your answers.

SECTION 1 REVIEW ANSWERS

1. **IDENTIFY: Andrew Johnson:** Vice-President elected in 1864 who became President after Lincoln's death in 1865; **Freedmen's Bureau:** agency created by the federal government in 1865 to supply freed blacks with food, clothing, medical care, and help in finding jobs, legal protection, and in the opening of schools for black children; **Thaddeus Stevens:** Pennsylvania Congressman who was a leader of Radical Republicans in Congress.
2. **DEFINE: Reconstruction:** period of rebuilding the nation after the Civil War, 1865-1877; **Radical Republicans:** members of Congress who supported harsh measures for Reconstruction; **Black Codes:** laws passed by Southern state governments limiting the rights and opportunities of former slaves.
3. President Johnson required the former Confederate states to admit they were wrong, repeal secession laws, abolish slavery, and pledge loyalty to the United States government.
4. Congress felt that President Johnson's terms were too mild, that lasting freedom for blacks had not been achieved, and that many former Confederates were back in power controlling the state governments in the South.

SECTION 2: Congress Takes Charge of Reconstruction

OBJECTIVES

After completing this section, students will be able to:
- Identify the laws passed by Congress to carry out its Reconstruction plans.
- List the actions required of Southern states before they could be readmitted to the Union.
- Explain the reasons for the impeachment of President Johnson.

MOTIVATION

Review the meaning of the term "impeachment." Have students recall the reasons why a President may be impeached, and which Congressional body is responsible for trying the President. Refer students to the Constitution on textbook pages 204-221. Use Article I, Section 3, Article II, and Article III, Section 4. Ask students why Congress wanted to impeach President Johnson.

SUGGESTED ACTIVITIES

1. **Directed Reading.** The disagreements between President Johnson and Congress resulted from the series of laws passed by Congress in 1866 and 1867. As students read, have them complete the following table:

LAW/DATE PASSED/CONTENTS/PRESIDENTIAL REACTION

As a summary, ask students to identify the law which led directly to the impeachment of President Johnson by the House of Representatives. Return to

the questions asked in the Motivation and have students state the reason why Congress was eager to impeach the President.

2. **Improving Your History Writing.** Have students review the Chapter 10 History Study Skill. Then have them answer the following question: Why did Congress fail to remove President Johnson from office?
3. **Separating Facts from Opinions.** Review the Chapter 12 History Study Skill. Have students apply the skill to Section 2 by determining whether each of the statements below is a "fact" or an "opinion." Have students give reasons for their answers orally.
   A. President Johnson believed the federal government had no constitutional right to support the Freedmen's Bureau. (O)
   B. In June, 1866 Congress proposed the Fourteenth Amendment. (F)
   C. Few Southern states rejected the Fourteenth Amendment. (F)
   D. Radical Republicans claimed that Johnson's Reconstruction policies betrayed the fallen Union soldiers. (O)
   E. Former Confederate states were outraged at the idea of military rule. (O)

BUILDING AMERICAN CITIZENSHIP

President Andrew Johnson is the only American president ever to have been impeached. Why do you think this is so? If a President breaks a law, should he be treated differently from other American citizens? (Answers will vary.)

SECTION 2 REVIEW ANSWERS

1. **IDENTIFY: Civil Rights Act:** act passed by Congress in 1866 to overturn the Black Codes; **Fourteenth Amendment:** amendment proposed by Congress in 1866 that guarantees the right of citizenship to native-born and naturalized Americans and due process of law to all citizens; **Military Reconstruction Act:** law that placed ten Southern states under military authority; **Command of the Army Act:** a law limiting Johnson's constitutional power as Commander-in-Chief by requiring the President to give orders to the army through its commanding general, whom he could not remove from office; **Tenure of Office Act:** a law requiring that the President have the consent of the Senate before firing federal officials.
2. **DEFINE: disenfranchised:** denied the right to vote; **impeach:** the constitutional right given the House of Representatives to bring charges of misconduct against a federal official.
3. Most voters supported Reconstruction and chose Radicals over Johnson, thus electing a majority of Republicans to office.
4. For breaking Tenure of Office Act, making speeches against Congress, and failing to uphold Reconstruction Act.

SECTION 3: Reconstruction Changes the South

OBJECTIVES

After completing this section, students will be able to:
1. Distinguish among scalawags, carpetbaggers, and copperheads.

2. Explain the gains made by black Americans during Reconstruction.
3. List the changes made by state governments during Reconstruction.

MOTIVATION

Introduce the terms scalawags, carpetbaggers, and copperheads. Assign these names to various groups of students—"Those of you in the second row are all scalawags; those in the fourth row are carpetbaggers" and so on. Ask students if they like these nicknames and to explain the reasons for their answers. (All sound somewhat disparaging though students probably will not know why.) As students read Section 3, have them identify what the role of their group would have been during Reconstruction.

SUGGESTED ACTIVITIES

1. **Directed Reading.** Use the following guide questions to help students gain a better understanding of what they have read:
   A. What requirements had to be met by Southern states wishing to be readmitted to the Union?
   B. How did the carpetbaggers and scalawags become involved in Reconstruction politics in the South?
   C. Why was the Fifteenth Amendment introduced in Congress?
   D. In what ways did the Southern states try to help both poor blacks and poor whites?
   Discuss the answers to each of these questions. In addition, discuss the outcome of the election of 1868 and how black voters helped elect President Grant. Summarize by asking students to identify their roles as scalawags, carpetbaggers, or copperheads.

2. **Landmarks of Liberty.** Have students read the selection on Tuskegee Institute on textbook page 452. Discuss the answers to the questions at the end of the reading. Then ask students the following:
   A. Was Tuskegee Institute started during the Reconstruction Era? (No)
   B. Why was it incorporated in a chapter on Reconstruction? (The goals of the Institute—to educate blacks and to teach them not to rely too much on others for help, were also goals of Reconstruction.)

3. **History Study Skills.** Duplicate Worksheet 52, *Reconstruction.* This activity provides a review of map skills and a preview of the chapter's History Study Skill, *Putting Events in Chronological Order.* At this point, have students complete part 1 only of the activity. It is directly related to the content of Section 3. In reviewing the answers, you may wish to have students recall the requirements which had to be met by each state before it could be readmitted. Students will do the History Study Skill on textbook page 460 in Section 4 and complete the second part of this activity in Section 5 to reinforce what they have learned.

BUILDING AMERICAN CITIZENSHIP

Duplicate Worksheet 53, *Equality Under the Law.* In order to answer the questions, have students refer to the

amendments as they actually appear in the Constitution on textbook pages 204-221.

SECTION 3 REVIEW ANSWERS

1. **IDENTIFY: Fifteenth Amendment:** amendment passed by Congress in 1869 designed to protect black voting rights; **copperheads:** Northerners who had sympathized with the South during the Civil War.
2. **DEFINE: scalawags:** white Southerners who joined the Republican Party and were willing to carry out the Radical Republican program; **carpetbaggers:** Northern Republicans who traveled South to live and work;
3. They felt both groups were in the South to make money for themselves rather than to help the people.
4. They established free public education, state-supported hospitals and mental health institutions, better transportation systems, and supported the opening of factories and businesses.

SECTION 4: Many Southerners Resist Reconstruction

OBJECTIVES

After completing this section, students will be able to:
• List and explain the methods used by Southern whites to limit the opportunities and rights of black Americans.
• Describe the pressures placed on whites who tried to help black Americans.
• Identify and describe examples of corruption in government.

MOTIVATION

Ask students how they would react if a new school board president were to issue the rules below, that all must follow:
A. Girls must wear skirts or dresses every day.
B. Boys must wear shirts and ties every day.
C. The cafeteria will be closed. All students must bring their lunches.
D. Lockers may be used before school and after school only.
E. Students will only be allowed to use the lavatories at certain times of the day.
   These are sample statements only. You may wish to revise them as the situation in your school warrants. Read the entire list. Then discuss student reactions which will include disbelief, outrage, anger, resentment, and resistance. Ask students what they might be able to do to change the new rules.
   Explain to students that the purpose of this activity was to give them some idea of how the Southerners felt about the requirements being placed on them by Congress. They, too, were angry and looked for ways to resist the changes.

SUGGESTED ACTIVITIES

1. **Directed Reading.** As students read the section, have them list the methods used by Southern whites to

resist laws designed to protect the former slaves. These would include the sharecropping system, segregation, terror, and pressure against sympathetic whites. As a summary, ask students why the federal government did so little to stop the resistance efforts of Southerners. (Their attitude and attention was focused on other problems, chiefly, corruption.)

2. **Research.** This section offers several topics that would allow students to expand their interest and knowledge about Reconstruction. Suggestions are offered below. You may wish to have below-average students confine their study to information in the textbook. Other students should be required to use library sources.
   A. Sharecropping
   B. James Rapier
   C. Ku Klux Klan
   D. Scandals in Grant's administration (the Whiskey Ring)
   E. William "Boss" Tweed
   F. Horace Greeley

3. **History Study Skills.** Have students complete *Putting Events in Chronological Order*, the History Study Skill on textbook page 460. All of the events for which they are required to find dates have been mentioned in the first four sections of Chapter 19. The search for events that occurred in 1875 and 1876 will provide a preview of the last section. Students usually experience great success in working with this skill. Allow them to share that success by writing their answers on the chalkboard or on lined tagboard.

BUILDING AMERICAN CITIZENSHIP

The Ku Klux Klan continues its activities in many states today. Why do you think this hate group is still in existence today? (Answers will vary.) Should citizens be arrested for joining groups such as the Ku Klux Klan? (Answers will vary.)

SECTION 4 REVIEW ANSWERS

1. **IDENTIFY: Ku Klux Klan:** a secret society formed in Tennessee in 1865 to oppose equal rights and opportunities for black Americans; **Force Acts:** laws passed by Congress in 1870 and 1871 giving the President the authority to use the army to stop violence against Southern blacks and to protect their rights under the Fifteenth Amendment; **Amnesty Act:** law passed in 1872 restoring full citizenship to all white Southerners except some 500 former Confederate leaders.

2. **DEFINE: sharecropping:** a farming system in which farmers give part of their crops to the land owner in return for use of the land; **segregation:** separation of races.

3. They promoted the sharecropping system, enforced segregation, used threats and force, and scorned Republicans publicly.

4. Between 1873 and 1877 President Grant and other government leaders gave less and less attention to the needs of black citizens and the cause of Reconstruction.

SECTION 5: Reconstruction Is Ended

OBJECTIVES

After completing this section, students will be able to:
• Explain how Democrats were able to regain control of Southern state governments.
• Describe the "Compromise of 1877."
• Tell how Southern states avoided enforcement of the Fifteenth Amendment.

MOTIVATION

Turn to the History Study Skill on textbook page 460. Have students restate the event they listed for the year 1876. (Disputed election—Tilden v. Hayes) Ask them why there might have been a problem in this election. Have them recall who resolves disputed elections. (Congress) Tell students that they should be able to describe the details of this dispute and how it led to the end of Reconstruction when they have finished reading Section 5.

SUGGESTED ACTIVITIES

1. **Directed Reading.** Have students complete an outline, using the following topics:
   I. Democrats "redeem" Southern states
   II. Disputed Election of 1876
   III. "Compromise of 1877"
   IV. Southern blacks lose their rights
   Review the important details students have incorporated under each topic. As a summary, return to the questions posed during the motivation:
   A. Why were there problems in the election of 1876?
   B. How did the solution to these problems lead to the end of Reconstruction?

2. **History Study Skills.** Have students complete Worksheet 52, *Reconstruction*, that they began in Section 3. This would include questions 2, 3, and 4. Ask students to recall why the federal government released control of state governments, and what occurred after they were released.

3. **Interpreting Line Graphs.** Duplicate Worksheet 54, *Voter Participation*. After reading about the election of 1876, students should have no difficulty answering the interpretive questions. Set the stage for the answering of these questions by asking students others that will familiarize them with the graph. For example:
   A. How many people voted in 1860? (Nearly 5 million)
   B. How many people voted in 1868? (Nearly 6 million)
   C. How many different elections are depicted? (5)
   D. In which year did nearly 6½ million people vote? (1872)
   E. Can you recall who won each election? (1860, 1864 — Lincoln; 1868, 1872 — Grant; 1876 — Hayes)

4. **Studying Your History Vocabulary.** Review the Chapter 16 History Study Skill. Have students apply this skill to Section 5 by defining each of the following terms: A) redeem; B) unredeemed; C) stalwarts; (d) status quo; E) patronage.

BUILDING AMERICAN CITIZENSHIP

Throughout the Reconstruction period, blacks won important civil and political rights. At the end of Reconstruction, they lost many of these. What rights could not be taken away? (Citizenship, freedom from slavery) What right did many southern state governments make almost impossible for them to exercise? (Right to vote) Could a group of citizens be denied their basic rights in today's society? Explain your answer. (Answers will vary.)

SECTION 5 REVIEW ANSWERS

1. **IDENTIFY: Senator Blanche K. Bruce:** Republican Senator from Mississippi who unsuccessfully appealed to the Senate for help against violation of black civil rights; **Samuel J. Tilden:** Democratic candidate in the contested election of 1876; **Rutherford B. Hayes:** Republican candidate elected President as a result of the Compromise of 1877; **Compromise of 1877:** an agreement ending the election deadlock in which Republicans agreed to end Reconstruction and Southern Democrats agreed to accept Hayes as President.
2. **DEFINE: patronage:** power of appointment to federal jobs.
3. The Amnesty Act of 1872 gave many more whites the opportunity to vote; blacks were discouraged from voting by threats of violence; the withdrawal of federal troops weakened Republican power.
4. It ended in a deadlock, resulting in a compromise agreement in which the Republicans agreed to end Reconstruction.

CHAPTER 19 REVIEW ANSWERS

REVIEWING KEY WORDS

1. c.   2. a.   3. b.   4. e.   5. d.

REMEMBERING IMPORTANT PEOPLE AND EVENTS

1. c.   2. a.   3. c.   4. b.   5. b.

REVIEWING THE FACTS

1. c.   2. d.   3. b.   4. d.   5. a.
6. T   7. F   8. T   9. T.   10. F

PLACING EVENTS IN TIME

1. a.   2. d.   3. c.   4. e.   5. b.

LINKING GEOGRAPHY AND HISTORY

In 1868, the Southern black votes were a source of Republican strength. Without their support, Grant might have lost the election and fewer Republicans would have gained seats in Congress.

In 1877, three "unredeemed" Southern states—Florida, South Carolina, and Louisiana—were contested, resulting in an election deadlock. A compromise agreement was finally worked out, resulting in the election of Rutherford B. Hayes.

THINKING ABOUT AMERICAN HISTORY

1. Black sharecroppers were usually in debt to property owners, who thus controlled their lives; sharecroppers usually voted according to property owners' "orders." Sharecroppers were free, and therefore they could leave or move elsewhere.
2. The Amnesty Act gave more whites the right to vote; federal troops were being withdrawn from the Southern states; blacks were terrorized into not voting; the mood of the nation had turned away from the problems of Reconstruction.

APPLYING HISTORY STUDIES SKILLS

4., 2., 1., 3., 5.

UNIT 6 REVIEW ANSWERS

VOCABULARY REVIEW

Answers will vary.

REVIEWING THE MAIN IDEAS

1. Publishing of *Uncle Tom's Cabin;* John Brown's raid; Kansas-Nebraska Act; Lincoln's running for President; Dred Scott case.
2. Failure to find another compromise to save the Union; increased disagreements over states' rights; fear that Lincoln would free the slaves and Lincoln's vow to preserve the Union; the belief of Southerners that they had lost their rights (to own slaves) in the territories.
3. Southerners felt secure in their vast lands, knowing it would take a huge army to conquer all their territory; they felt that the Union's will to fight was much weaker and if they held out long enough, the North would grow tired and end the war.
4. Grant was determined to win and refused to quit. He believed in action rather than in careful planning and was flexible in his battle plans.
5. The South's economy was destroyed; there was a lot of bitterness between the North and South; slaves gained their freedom; the North became a major industrial power; women gained new opportunities; the argument over secession ended once and for all.
6. How to readmit the defeated Southern states to the Union; how to help former slaves gain their rights as citizens; how to overcome the bitterness between North and South.
7. Southern states found ways to get around the Fifteenth Amendment; the Ku Klux Klan and other groups terrorized blacks who tried to exercise their rights; there were no federal troops in the South after 1877 to protect black citizens; Southern Democrats failed to live up to their promises to give fair treatment to blacks; Northerners and political leaders lost interest in black civil rights.

USING YOUR STUDY SKILLS

Answers will vary.

PROJECTS

Answers will vary.

BUILDING AMERICAN CITIZENSHIP

1. Educational and travel opportunities; learning job skills; monetary bonuses; slogans for different branches of the service and appeals to patriotism.
2. Through such programs as welfare, food stamps, medical and other assistance through the Social Security program.

UNIT 7 (1865-1900)
Industry Changes America

Introducing the Unit

Unit Seven covers a period of great change in America, the period from 1865 to the turn of the 20th century during which a rural, agrarian, and nativist America was transformed into an urban, industrial, and heterogeneous society. One of the most striking visual changes was on the face of the land itself. In the 1850's, the American West, that great roughly defined territory west of the Mississippi River, was still sparsely populated. Post-Civil War travelers through the region, however, saw an increasing number of barns and windmills, barbed-wire fences, and new farm machinery. They also saw more and more railroad junctions, cowtowns, and mining settlements.

By 1887, all of the Plains ranches were fenced in. The Indians had fought the pioneers for control of the last frontier from 1850 to 1890 and finally lost. Chapter 20 chronicles the disappearance of the frontier and the accompanying decline in the fortunes of the Indians.

Remarkable industrial growth was another outstanding characteristic of this period. The beginnings of industrialization in America had begun long before 1865. However, in the postwar years, the nation's industrial performance multiplied at an incredible rate, made possible by and spurred on through a series of technological triumphs, many of which are highlighted in Chapter 21. These inventions include the Bessemer/Kelly converter, the telegraph, the telephone, the turbine, the dynamo, and the light bulb. Along with these technological developments came a revolution in business practices. Mail-order businesses and department stores became popular and profitable. Successful tycoons ran mammoth corporations that controlled such businesses as the steel, oil, and meatpacking industries.

The Industrial Revolution in America also brought about much social change, described in Chapter 22. Many people left the countryside to find work in American cities. Soon, over one-third of all Americans were living in communities of more than 8,000 persons. Immigrants streamed into America in record-breaking numbers. Urban crowding, in both living and factory space, led to the development of apartment hotels and skyscrapers. Rural areas also changed. Farmers fluctuated between prosperity and depression. Many farm families gave up and headed for the cities. Rapid urbanization created problems, which urban reformers attempted to solve. American society in 1900 was increasingly heterogeneous, undergoing a shift in values. The country was becoming, in every sense of the term, a "modern nation."

Many of the changes in this period had undesirable effects. By the end of the century, Americans had begun to protest some of the evils of industrial change. Chapter 23 examines the efforts of reformers to regulate business, improve on the quality of government, and provide a measure of self-realization for working people. Some progress was made, but in 1900 the United States was still in need of many reforms.

The Unit Opener in the textbook depicts many of the significant persons and events of this period. You may wish to use these illustrations to help introduce the unit. The central figure is Thomas Edison. Beginning in the lower left-hand corner, in a clockwise direction are General George Custer, some steel factories, Boss Tweed, Susan B. Anthony, a cluster of oil wells, and Chief Sitting Bull.

Another major feature in this and several other units in the textbook is a photo essay, *What Life Was Like*. It is designed to evoke the quality and flavor of daily life in different types of American communities at various times in the nation's history. In Unit Seven, the photo essay shows how people lived in America's cities from 1865 to 1900.

Unit Themes and Ideas

The main theme for Unit Seven is the rapid growth and development of the United States between 1865 and 1900. This theme is supported by the important subordinate themes of industrialization and urbanization, which while they benefited countless Americans, at the same time they created serious new problems. Both the benefits and the problems are well documented throughout the unit. One of the most positive developments during this period was technological advancement. Few Americans were untouched by improvements in such areas as transportation and communication. All these factors brought on great social change, another constant during this period. There was movement in and to America, and both immigration and migration created an American society marked by complexity and challenge. These themes and ideas are organized into the four chapters below:

Chapter 20- *The Last Frontier is Settled (1865 -1900)*
Chapter 21- *America Becomes an Industrial Nation (1865 - 1900)*
Chapter 22- *Industrial Progress Changes The Nation (1865 - 1900)*
Chapter 23- *An Age of Protest Begins (1865 - 1900)*

CHAPTER 20

The Last Frontier Is Settled (1865-1900)

Chapter Objectives

After completing this chapter, students will be able to:
1. Describe how railroads opened the last frontier.

2. Explain how miners and ranchers helped settle the last frontier.
3. Identify problems facing farmers who settled the last frontier.
4. Describe what happened to Indians living on the last frontier.

Chapter Chronology *Read to class*

Chapter 20 covers the settlement of America's last frontier from the post-Civil War era to the turn of the 20th century. Many of the important persons and events of this period are highlighted on the time line in the textbook Chapter Opener. Just two years after the end of the Civil War, Joseph McCoy started the Chisholm Trail. In 1869, the transcontinental railroad was completed. A new kind of fence was used on Western farms and ranches after Joseph Glidden invented barbed wire in 1873. In the ongoing battle over the last frontier, Indians continued to lose, and in 1877, Chief Joseph of the Nez Percés surrendered. The Dawes Act was passed 10 years later in 1887. Two years later, Oklahoma was opened to homesteaders. With the Battle of Wounded Knee, in 1890, the last Indian resistance ended.

Motivation

Have students turn to their textbooks and read the first paragraph under the Section 4 heading. Then ask them to read about Chief Joseph under the sidehead "Custer's Last Stand Is an Indian Victory." Next have them read the section titles for Chapter 20 on textbook page 467. Ask students how the encroaching railroads, miners, ranchers, and farmers might have forced Chief Joseph to respond as he did. Ask students to think back to the Indian Removal section of Chapter 13. Were the forces then similar to the ones that threatened Indians in the West a generation later? Save student responses for reference as they work through the chapter.

Geographical Setting

The term "last frontier" refers to the sparsely settled areas in the trans-Mississippi west. The four maps in Chapter 20 illustrate the major activities carried out in the West during the second half of the 19th century. These include the establishment of major cattle trails that ran from Texas to Kansas. The map *Cattle Trails and Railroads in the West, About 1870,* on textbook page 473, when used in conjunction with a physical features map, illustrates the relative flatness of the Great Plains. The map *Mining in the West, About 1890,* on textbook page 472, shows mining in the West. When used in conjunction with a physical features map, this map shows students that mining was usually located in highland regions. As they study the map *Transcontinental Railroads in the West, 1890,* on textbook page 469, students should note that the railroad routes were carefully planned to make use of mountain passes and narrow places in the rivers. The map *Indian Reservations in the West, 1890* illustrates the continual encroachment of pioneers on Indian lands.

History Study Skills

The Chapter 20 History Study Skill is *Using Relief Maps.* The information illustrated is the location of min-

ing sites in the West. The best place to use this skill is in Section 2 as a supplement to the text on mining. At this point, you may wish students to use an atlas, so they can examine current mining sites in the West.

Bibliography

Teacher References
Coel, Margaret, *Chief Left Hand: Southern Arapaho.* University of Oklahoma Press, Norman, Okla., 1981.
Merk, Frederick, *History of the Westward Movement.* Knopf, New York City, 1978.

Student References
Alderman, Clifford, *Annie Oakley and the World of Her Time.* Macmillan, New York City, 1979. This story about one of America's most famous 19th-century women covers her childhood, marriage, and stage career.
Johnson, Dorothy, *All the Buffalo Returning.* Dodd, Mead, New York City, 1979. This powerful story of a Sioux Indian leader includes the Battle of Little Big Horn in 1876 and the Wounded Knee Massacre in 1890.

Audio-Visual Materials

Railroads and Westward Expansion: 1865-1900, BFA, 16 min., color. This film shows how the railroad transformed the West.

The Sodbusters; Bedbugs, Fleas and Grasshopper Traps, Listening Library, Inc. 2 sound filmstrips. This is the story of the pioneers who turned the buffalo grasses of the Plains into rich, productive farmland.

SECTION 1: Railroads Open the Last Frontier

OBJECTIVES

After completing this section, students will be able to:
- Tell how James J. Hill became a railroad tycoon.
- List the problems encountered in building the transcontinental railroads.
- Explain the effects of the railroads on the towns and settlers of the West.

MOTIVATION

where?

Have students read the Chapter Introduction on textbook page 467 and answer these questions. When did the event occur? What companies were involved? Why was this such a celebrated event? Have students look at the picture in Section 1. Ask them what problems were probably encountered in the building of the railroad. List their responses on the chalkboard. Ask how the railroad affected the lives of the people of the time. List possible answers on the chalkboard. Tell students their lists will be checked after they have completed the reading.

SUGGESTED ACTIVITIES

1. **Directed Reading**. As students read, have them answer the following questions:
   A. Why did the government subsidize the building of railroads?

B. How did James J. Hill become a railroad tycoon?

C. What methods were used to build the transcontinental railroads?

D. Why did Westerners complain about railroad practices?

Review the answers to these questions when students have completed their reading. In addition, discuss the questions posed as part of the motivation. Have students add to their answers based on the information they have read.

2. **Map Interpretation**. Have students use the map entitled *Transcontinental Railroads in the West, 1890,* on textbook page 469 to answer the following:

A. Which railroad line connected the cities of Portland and St. Paul? (Northern Pacific)

B. Which cities are connected by the Southern Pacific railroad line? (Los Angeles and El Paso)

C. Which states are crossed by the Northern Pacific railroad line? (Minnesota, North Dakota, Montana, Idaho, and Washington)

D. Approximately how far would you travel by rail between St. Louis and Kansas City? (About 225 miles or 360 kilometers)

E. Which two railroad lines would you take to travel from San Francisco to Omaha? (Central Pacific and Union Pacific)

3. **Making a Line Graph**. Duplicate Worksheet 55, *Railroad Mileage*. Once students have constructed the graph, ask the following questions to interpret the information.

A. How many miles of track were there in 1900? (259,000)

B. How much more was this than the number of miles in 1850? (24,000) 250,000

C. During which 10-year period did the number of miles increase the most? (1890-1900)

D. During which 10-year period did the number of miles increase the least? (1860-1870: 13,000) Can you think of any reason for this? (Civil War Period and Reconstruction) 1850-60

E. During which 10-year period did the amount of travel increase by 40,000 miles? (1870-1880)

4. **Research Activity.** Section 1 describes the manner in which James J. Hill became a tycoon. Six other tycoons are mentioned: Charles Crocker, Mark Hopkins, Collis P. Huntington, Leland Stanford, Cornelius Vanderbuilt, and Jay Gould. Have students select one of these men and investigate the manner in which they earned their fortunes from railroads. Their reports may be submitted orally or in writing.

BUILDING AMERICAN CITIZENSHIP

How were the railroads treating Western citizens unfairly? (Charging higher rates for short hauls) To whom would these citizens complain? (The railroad companies, the government) If citizens were treated unfairly today by a company or business, to whom could they complain? (Better Business Bureau, their Congressperson, Consumer Protection Agency) Do you think it was easier then or would it be easier now for citizens to get someone to take action against unfair business practices? (Answers will vary.)

106

SECTION 1 REVIEW ANSWERS

1. **IDENTIFY: James J. Hill:** builder of the Great Northern Railway.

2. **Define: subsidies:** special government aid, such as grants of land and loans; **tycoons:** people of great wealth and power.

3. The government considered fast, long-distance transportation important, and Americans were eager to reach the Far West.

4. They had to tunnel through mountains; they had to deal with supply problems such as getting iron rails, wooden ties, food, water, and tools to the building sites.

SECTION 2: Miners and Ranchers Come to the Frontier

OBJECTIVES

After completing this section, students will be able to:
• Describe the life and work of a miner.
• Describe the life and work of a cowhand.
• List the problems that brought an end to the era of the cattle kingdom.

MOTIVATION

Ask students to describe the life of miners and cowboys based on television shows or films they have seen. You might lead the discussion by asking: What types of work does a cowboy do? What dangers might he face? The same questions might be asked about the miners. Tell students that at the end of this section, they will compare the textbook description to the fictional portrayals on television and in films.

SUGGESTED ACTIVITIES

1. **Directed Reading.** Have students complete the following table as they read.

	Miners	Ranchers
Why did they go to the Great Plains?	(Search for gold and silver)	(Raise herds of cattle to be shipped east on railroad)
What types of work did they do?	(Created passageways; put in drainage and air intake systems; dug out rock)	(Delivered calves; chased strays; branded; rode all day to keep watch on herd.)
What dangers did they face?	(Heat in the tunnels; accidents)	(Stampedes; storms)
Why did their jobs disappear?	(Ore veins gave out)	(The open range was fenced in; prices fell; blizzards wiped out the herds)

This table should provide an excellent basis for a summary comparison between television and movie fictionalization of the lives of miners and ranchers, and what their existence was really like.

2. **History Study Skills**. Have students complete the activity *Using Relief Maps* on textbook page 483. This map shows the location of the "boom towns" described in Section 2. After using the map to determine the land's height, you might also have students compare it to the railroads map in Section 1 to find out which mining towns were located on or near major railroad lines. You might also wish to check students' ability to use the map scale by having them calculate distances between several of the mining towns.

3. **Acrostic.** Section 2 contains many terms associated with mining and ranching. To check students' knowledge of their meanings, put the following puzzle on the chalkboard or on a transparency for them to complete.

oPen range	P -	unclaimed land where cattle grazed
vigiLante committee	L -	volunteers who took law and order into their own hands in mining towns
vAqueros	A -	Spanish word for cowhands
ChIsholm Trail	I -	McCoy's route for driving cattle to Abilene, Kansas
cowtowNs	N -	communities in which cattle were loaded into railroad cars
ghoSt towns	S -	abandoned communities

4. **Map Interpretation.** Have students study the map *Cattle Trails and Railroads in the West, About 1870,* on textbook page 473 and answer the following questions:
   A. Which trail was the longest? (Western Trail)
   B. Which trail ended in Abilene, Kansas? (Chisholm)
   C. Which trail was the westernmost? (Goodnight Loving)
   D. Use the map scale to determine how far cattle were driven on the Chisholm Trail from San Antonio to Abilene. (About 650 miles)
   E. Compare this map to the map *Transcontinental Railroads in the West, 1890* on textbook page 469. Which railroad line transported cattle that had traveled the Western Trail? (Union Pacific)

BUILDING AMERICAN CITIZENSHIP

Duplicate Worksheet 56, *Law and Order.* When students have given their "decisions" and the cases have been fully discussed, ask how each of these arguments might be settled in today's system of maintaining law and order. (By the courts) Ask what they think a modern judge would do in each case and what alternatives are available today that were not available to the pioneer courts. (Answers will vary.)

SECTION 2 REVIEW ANSWERS

1. **IDENTIFY: Comstock Lode:** the richest silver vein in the nation discovered in Nevada in 1859; **Alfred Nobel:** Swedish scientist who invented dynamite; **Joseph McCoy:** originator of the Chisholm Trail, the trail used to drive cattle herds from Texas to Kansas.

2. **DEFINE: lode:** rich vein of silver; **vigilante committee:** a group of volunteers organized to bring law and order to Western towns; **boom towns:** fast-growing towns near gold and silver mines; **ghost towns:** empty towns where no one lived; **vaqueros:** Mexicans and California Indians who worked as cowhands; **open range:** unclaimed land on the Plains. *missing cowtowns*
3. The search for gold and silver.
4. Herds had grown too large for the available grass; beef prices fell; two harsh winters and a dry summer destroyed many of the herds.

5. Texas

SECTION 3: Farm Families Settle the Plains

OBJECTIVES

After completing this section, students will be able to:
• List the problems of homesteaders on the Great Plains.
• State the importance of barbed wire to the homesteaders on the Plains.
• Explain how Oklahoma was opened to homesteaders.

MOTIVATION

Have students look at the time line on the textbook Chapter Opener page. Tell them that Section 3 contains information on three events listed there. Have students use the following clues to determine which they are.
A. The first occurred seven years earlier than the completion of the transcontinental railroad. (Homestead Act)
B. The second occurred 11 years later. (Glidden invents barbed wire)
C. The third event occurred 27 years after the first one. (Oklahoma is opened to settlers)
Inform students that their task will be to tell what difference each of the three events made to farmers settling in the West.

SUGGESTED ACTIVITIES

1. **Directed Reading.** On the board list the three events from the Motivation. As students read, have them write a sentence or two next to each, answering the question posed during the Motivation: What difference did it make to farmers settling on the Plains?

   As a summary, discuss the problems of homesteaders, and the methods they used to solve the problems. For example, lack of a good water supply led to dry farming.
2. **Hazards of the Plains.** Have students discuss the problems faced by farmers. Then, compare these with the difficulties faced by the miners and ranchers. To summarize, have them identify which group had to deal with each of the following hazards:
   A. cave-ins (M)   E. heat in the tunnels (M)
   B. thunderstorms (R) F. sick calves (R)
   C. insects (F)   G. building materials (F)
   D. fuel (F)   H. water supply (F)
3. **Creating a Puzzle.** Have students use the important people, laws, and terms mentioned in Section 3 and the previous sections to create a puzzle. This could be a word puzzle, an acrostic, or a crossword puzzle. A word bank should be provided for the word puzzle, and clues should be given for the other two. You may

wish to have students exchange papers to solve the puzzles. Set a limit on the number of items depending on the ability level of the class. For example, below average, 5-7, above average, 10-15.

4. **Recognizing Primary and Secondary Sources.** Review the Chapter 15 History Study Skill. Then have students identify each of the following as a primary (P) or secondary (S) source. This activity can be written on the chalkboard.
   A. A Kansas sod house (P)
   B. President Harrison's order opening the Oklahoma Territory (P)
   C. Fred Wenner's description of Oklahoma's land rush (S)
   D. A two-foot section of Glidden's barbed wire (P)
   E. A deed to a homesteader's land (P)

BUILDING AMERICAN CITIZENSHIP

According to the Census Bureau, the "frontier" did not exist after 1890. Many citizens felt that opportunities for adventure did not exist after this date. Do you think this was true? What "frontiers" are there for citizens to conquer today? (Space, finding cures for diseases, solving problems)

SECTION 3 REVIEW ANSWERS

1. **IDENTIFY: Homestead Act:** 1862 law granting 160 acres of land to any citizen or to any person who intended to become a citizen; **Joseph Glidden:** a cattle rancher who invented barbed wire; **Oliver Dalrymple:** famous bonanza farmer who lived in the Dakota Territory and homesteaded 25,000 acres of wheat.
2. **DEFINE: homesteader:** person granted land under the Homestead Act; **dry farming:** planting crops in a way that keeps the soil moist longer; **bonanza farms:** large-scale farms in North Dakota and Minnesota that used the newest farming methods and machinery.
3. Blizzards, floods, and droughts; insects; few trees for wood; lack of water.
4. In order to open up Oklahoma land to homesteaders.

SECTION 4: Indians Lose the Last Frontier

OBJECTIVES

• List the ways in which the Indians depended upon and used the buffalo.
• Describe the struggles of the Indians to resist white settlers' attempts to control the Plains.
• Explain why Indians were dissatisfied with reservation life.

MOTIVATION

Have students study the map *Indian Reservations in the West, 1890* on textbook page 481. Ask them to define the term "reservation." If necessary, check the Glossary. Then, discuss the following questions:
A. Which tribes settled on the lands?
B. Why did Indians settle on reservation lands?
C. How well did they adjust to reservation life?

You may also wish to discuss the different ways that Indians are usually portrayed on television and in movies.

SUGGESTED ACTIVITIES

1. **Directed Reading.** As students read Section 4, have them list each of the tribes mentioned. Then have them add what happened to them as a result of clashes with white settlers. These include:
   A. Navaho—surrendered
   B. Apache—resisted until 1886, then surrendered
   C. Cheyenne—grew weary of fighting; some massacred at Sand Creek; others surrendered
   D. Sioux—some tried reservation life; others resisted and were forced to surrender
   As a summary, discuss again the questions posed during the Motivation.

2. **Ideals in the Lives of Americans.** Have students read the selection on Chief Joseph of the Nez Percés. After they have answered the two questions at the end of the reading, ask students why Chief Joseph may have chosen to resist resettlement. (His people were being moved from their homeland in Idaho to a reservation in Oregon.) Ask what problems the Nez Percés may have had adjusting to reservation life in Oklahoma. (Different land and climate, not used to staying in one place)

3. **Research.** Several Indian leaders are mentioned in Section 4, and students may be interested in the stories of their resistance to white settlers. Capitalize on students' curiosity by having them prepare written reports on encounters with these leaders and the settlers. The following is a partial list of leaders from which students may choose:

Geronimo	Quonah Parker	Gall
Red Cloud	Roman Nose	Wovoka
Sitting Bull	Crazy Horse	Looking Glass
Black Kettle	Captain Jack	Cochise

4. **Showing Relief.** Duplicate Worksheet 57, *Western Land Forms.* This activity will allow students to practice the History Study Skill introduced in Section 2. When students have completed the activity, have them recall details of events that occurred within each area.

BUILDING AMERICAN CITIZENSHIP

The citizens who moved to the Plains had difficulty dealing with Indians for a number of reasons. Can you name them? (Disputes over land, differences in language and customs, differences in ways of living) What should our government have done to protect these native Americans and their property? (Answers will vary.) How could the government have made it easier for the Indians to live on reservation lands? (Locate them on or near the Indians homelands, allow them to keep their customs, continue hunting)

SECTION 4 REVIEW ANSWERS

1. **IDENTIFY: Geronimo:** Apache Indian chief who continued to resist white settlers until 1886; **Chivington's Massacre:** 1864 massacre of the Cheyenne Indians at

Sand Creek, Colorado; **Indian Bureau:** federal government agency created to provide food, clothing, and supplies to Indians; **General George Custer:** army officer who led an unsuccessful attack on the Sioux Indians and their allies in June 1876, during which all of his troops died; **Dawes Act:** 1887 law offering Indians 160 acres of land to become farmers, the purpose of which was to force Indians to give up their customs and become Americanized; **Ghost Dance:** Indian dance symbolizing Indians' faith in a new religion promising a return to their old ways of life; **Wounded Knee:** battle in the Black Hills in which 200 Indians died, marking the end of Indian resistance.

2. **DEFINE: nomad:** wanderers who move about in search of food; **reservations:** lands set aside especially for Indians.
3. They did not want to leave their homes; the soil on reservations was often poor; Indian agents on the reservations often cheated the Indians and showed no respect for their customs.
4. They depended on the buffalo for food, clothing, tools, weapons, and even for part of their shelter.

CHAPTER 20 REVIEW ANSWERS

REVIEWING KEY WORDS

1. c.   2. e.   3. a.   4. d.   5. b.

REMEMBERING IMPORTANT PEOPLE

1. b.   2. d.   3. e.   4. a.   5. c.

REVIEWING THE FACTS

1. d.   2. b.   3. a.   4. c.   5. c.

PLACING EVENTS IN TIME

1. A.   2. D.   3. B.   4. C.   5. E.

LINKING GEOGRAPHY AND HISTORY

(1) Cattle trails led to the development of towns. (2) Mining led to a population increase and the development of towns. (3) Railroads provided transportation for people and products and led to the development of new lands and the growth of towns. (4) Removal of Indians to reservations opened up new lands for settlement.

THINKING ABOUT AMERICAN HISTORY

Answers will vary.

APPLYING HISTORY STUDIES SKILLS

1. under 5,000.   2. Denver.   3. above 10,000
4. yellow.   5. 2,000 - 5,000 feet.

CHAPTER 21

America Becomes an Industrial Nation (1865-1900)

Chapter Objectives

After completing this chapter, students will be able to:
1. Identify the different resources that helped make America an industrial nation.

2. Explain how new inventions spurred on industrial growth.
3. Describe new methods of buying and selling that came about during the Industrial Revolution.
4. Relate the problems of labor to the growth of big business.

Chapter Chronology

Chapter 21 surveys America's developments as an industrial nation between 1865 and 1900. The time line in the textbook Chapter Opener highlights many of the important persons and major events of the period. Numerous important inventions emerged during this time. One of the first, in 1866, was the laying of telegraph cable across the Atlantic by Cyrus Field. Meanwhile, on the burgeoning areas of business and labor, other events were taking place. The Knights of Labor was formed in 1869. Three years later, a mail-order business was established by Montgomery and Ward. In 1876, Alexander Graham Bell invented the telephone. And in the same decade, in 1879, Thomas Alva Edison invented the electric light. In 1879, also, the Standard Oil Trust was formed. Another important labor organization, the American Federation of Labor, was founded in 1886. Urban transportation received a great boost in 1887 when the first trolley system was designed and 10 years later in 1897, with the opening of the nation's first subway in Boston.

Motivation

Have students read the textbook Chapter Introduction on Thomas Edison. Then, ask them why they think the invention of the electric light was so important to Americans of Edison's day. Ask students to think about some of Edison's other inventions (phonograph, storage battery). Have them name some important inventions of the 20th century. How have these inventions improved the lives of Americans?

Geographical Setting

Chapter 21 has no explicit geographical focus, and there are no maps in the text. However, several important places are mentioned—the Great Lakes and its region of mineral deposits; the stretch of the transatlantic cable from Canada to Ireland; Niagara Falls, New York, and its power plant; Boston and its subway; Chicago and its beef industry; and Pittsburgh and its steel industry. As students read the text, have them locate these places on a map. Students should understand that the surge of industrial activity took place throughout the United States.

History Study Skills

The History Study Skill used in Chapter 21 is *Using Tables.* The activity could be used at several places in the chapter since it involves industrial growth, one of the chapter's main concepts. You might also find it useful to summarize the chapter.

Bibliography

Teacher References

Degler, Carl N., *The Age of the Economic Revolution.* Scott, Foresman, Glenview, Ill., 1977.

Livesay, Robert H., *Samuel Gompers and Organized Labor in America.* Little Brown, Boston, Mass., 1978.

Wiebe, Robert H., *The Search for Order, 1877-1920.* Hill and Wang, New York City, 1968.

Student References

Hilton, Suzanne, *The Way It Was—1876.* Westminster, Philadelphia, Pa., 1975. This is a highly readable, well-illustrated story about everyday life in the United States during our centennial year.

Weisberger, Bernard, *Captains of Industry.* Harper, New York City, 1966. This well-illustrated group of ten vignettes about American industrial giants after the Civil War discusses Rockefeller, Morgan, Carnegie, Vanderbuilt, and Ford among others.

Audio-Visual Materials

The Industrial Revolution in America, Guidance Associates, 2 filmstrips, 2 cassettes, library kit and teacher's guide. These filmstrips illustrate the economic, social, and technological changes that resulted in the American Industrial Revolution.

The Rise of Industrial Giants, McGraw, 25 minutes, color. This film shows the rapid industrialization that took place in the United States at the turn of the century.

SECTION 1: America's Resources Help Industries Develop

OBJECTIVES

After completing this section, students will be able to:
- List the advantages that allowed America to become an industrial power.
- Explain the contributions of Cornelius Vanderbilt to improve the nation's railway system.
- Explain the government's policy towards big business and industry.
- Identify the sources of human resources needed for American factories.

MOTIVATION

Have students divide themselves into groups of four or five and use the following scenario: "I am now going to wave my magic wand and make you all millionaires—at least for the next few minutes. In order to make more money, you and a group of fellow millionaires have decided to go into business and to build a factory together. A meeting has been called to discuss exactly what you will need to start this factory. Select someone in your group to take notes. (Wait a minute or two.) Once again, let me state the purpose of your meeting. You are going to build a factory and start a business. Discuss and note down everything you will need." After about 10 minutes, call on the note takers in each group to read their lists. Discuss possible additions and deletions with the entire class.

SUGGESTED ACTIVITIES

1. **Directed Reading.** Have students remain in their groups as they read Section 1. Now ask them to add a second column on their list of things needed to start a factory. Under this column, they should write all of the things they find in this section that were not on their lists before. Again, have the note takers read their second list. Collect these from each group. As a summary, use the chalkboard to make a master list. It should include investors, a source of heat for the factory, minerals needed to produce the goods, a method of transporting the products, and workers.

2. **Applying Map and Research Skills.** Have students list the natural resources and minerals mentioned in Section 1. Next, refer them to an almanac to determine the states in which these are found. Then, have them use an outline map (they may draw it or you may provide it) of the United States and label the states. Finally, ask students to create a map legend that includes symbols for each resource, and have them place the symbols in the correct states.

3. **Improving Your History Writing.** Have students apply the Chapter 10 History Study Skill by writing a paragraph to answer this question: Why was it necessary to improve the nation's transportation system? (In order to bring people and natural resources to industrial centers [cities] and also to ship out the finished products to consumers.)

4. **Comprehension Exercise.** To determine whether or not students understand the information presented in Section 1, have them answer TRUE or FALSE to the following:
   A. Many of America's natural resources are located underground. (T)
   B. Without the help of foreign investors, America may not have had the capital needed for starting and running businesses. (T)
   C. Cornelius Vanderbilt began the system of setting railroad tracks at standard widths and sizes. (F)
   D. Government followed a total "hands-off" policy towards big business. (F)
   E. Immigrants and former farm workers provided the human resources needed for factories. (T)

5. **History Study Skills.** Have students complete the activity *Using Tables* on textbook page 505. This activity is directly related to Activity 3 above, and should be helpful to students by allowing them to visualize the value of resources they have already researched and mapped out.

BUILDING AMERICAN CITIZENSHIP

In the late 1800's, most American citizens supported the government's decision not to regulate big business. What is the attitude of American citizens today regarding the regulation of big business? (They want to have it regulated.) Why do you think the attitude of citizens changed? (Answers may vary.) Tell students they should be able to give more reasons for this change by the time they finish reading Chapter 21.

SECTION 1 REVIEW ANSWERS

1. **IDENTIFY: Cornelius Vanderbilt:** railroad tycoon who offered the first continuous railroad service between New York and Chicago.

2. **DEFINE: heavy industry:** an industry that produces materials, such as coal or steel, to make other goods; **laissez-faire:** government "hands-off" policy concerning the activities of business and industry.
3. Rich natural resources, wealthy people willing to invest in American industries, inventors, government and public support for the growth of businesses, and an inexpensive labor supply.
4. A good railway system was needed to move raw materials to factories and products from factories to markets and harbors for shipping. It was also needed to transport workers.

SECTION 2: New Inventions Help Industry Grow

OBJECTIVES

After completing this section, students will be able to:
- Explain why industrialists supported inventions.
- Identify American inventors of the time and their inventions.
- State the reasons for locating factories in urban areas.
- List improvements made in urban transportation.

MOTIVATION

Have students recall what they read about Thomas Edison in the Chapter Introduction. Ask them what name is applied to a person who, like Edison, thinks up and creates new things or dramatically improves on old ones to make life more comfortable or efficient. The answer, of course, is "inventor." Check the library picture file for pictures of some of the inventions mentioned in this chapter. Have the class identify these. Then tell students that they will learn when, by whom, and for what reason these things were invented.

SUGGESTED ACTIVITIES

1. **Directed Reading.** Place the following table with column 1 filled in on the chalkboard, and have students copy it in their notebooks. Ask students to read Section 2, and then have them complete the table by filling in the remaining three columns.

INVENTION	DECADE	INVENTOR	IMPROVEMENTS
Making steel	(1850's)	(H. Bessemer)	(Stronger, safer rails for railroad tracks)
Transatlantic cable	(1860's) 50's	(C. Field)	(Cut communication time between Europe and America from weeks to minutes)
Telephone	(1870's)	(A. Bell)	(People could talk using wires)
Oil well	(1850's)	(E. Drake)	(New method for drawing oil up from underground)
Turbine	(1870's)	—	(More efficient use of water and steam power)
Dynamo	(1870's)	—	(Changed steam/water into electricity
Trolley	(1880's)	(F. J. Sprague)	(Moved city people quickly, cheaply and safely)
Subway	(1890's)	—	(Moved city people quickly, cheaply and safely)

As a summary, have students orally review all of the information for the table. Then apply the study skill for Chapter 19 by having students arrange the inventions in chronological order.

2. **Research Activity.** Section 2 stresses some of the well-known inventions of the late 1800's that improved people's lives and their businesses. However, there are hundreds of smaller, less famous inventions that affect students' lives daily. Below is a partial list.

ballpoint pen	camera
shoelaces	x-rays
zipper	vacuum cleaner
elevator	frozen food processing
radio	wristwatch
television set	adding machine

Encourage students to use the *People's Almanac* or another reference book to help them answer the following questions about one of the inventions above.
A. When was it invented?
B. Who invented it?
C. How has it improved or changed people's lives or businesses?

You may want to chart this information in a manner similar to the one completed in Directed Reading. This could provide the basis for a bulletin board display.

3. **Ideals in the Lives of Americans.** Have students read the selection on George Washington Carver, on textbook page 490. Ask them to tell why Carver should be included with the other inventors presented in Section 2. Have students add his name, and the other required information, to their charts.

4. **Flash Cards.** In order to help students learn the names of the inventors and their inventions, make three sets of flash cards, using tagboard of three different colors. On one set, write the names of the inventors, on the second set the inventions, and on the third set the decade in which they were created. Distribute the cards to students at random. Have individuals come to the front of the class to match the cards. Repeat the exercise at least once.

BUILDING AMERICAN CITIZENSHIP

Section 2 describes how the various inventions improved the lives of people and helped industry. Consider the opposite point of view. Look at the list of inventions again. What possible problems did each invention create for ordinary citizens and for businesses? Which of these problems still exist today? (Answers will vary.)

14

SECTION 2 REVIEW ANSWERS

1. **IDENTIFY: Alexander Graham Bell:** inventor of the telephone; **George Westinghouse:** inventor of air brakes for railroad cars; **Henry Bessemer:** inventor of a process for turning iron ore into steel; **Cyrus Field:** inventor who was responsible for laying the first transatlantic cable between Europe and North America; **Edwin Drake:** American who drilled the first oil well in Pennsylvania.

2. **DEFINE: patent:** a grant by the federal government giving an inventor the sole right to make, sell, or use an invention; **turbine:** a steel motor that used water or steam power more efficiently; **dynamo:** a machine that changed power from steam or water into electricity; **electric motors:** machines powered by electricity.

3. Machines, means of communication and transportation, sources of power.

4. Kerosene, natural gas, and gasoline.

5. *Els, trolleys, railways*

SECTION **3:** New Ways of Buying and Selling Appear

OBJECTIVES

After completing this section, students will be able to:
• Distinguish between specialty stores, department stores, chain stores, and mail-order houses.
• Identify individuals who introduced new ways of buying and selling.
• Explain how advertising and brand names were used to increase product sales.

MOTIVATION

If possible, display items labeled with the names of the following or similar stores: Sears, Woolworth's, Wards, the A&P, and a local specialty shop. You might also use shopping bags, circulars, catalogues, or newspaper advertisements by one or more of these businesses. Ask students to name some of the goods available at these stores. Ask them where they might do their shopping if such stores were not available. Ask them to name other stores in your area which offer similar goods and services. Tell them that today they will be learning how each of these companies began and what made their ideas of buying and selling so different in the late 19th century.

SUGGESTED ACTIVITIES

1. **Directed Reading.** As students read, have them write down the various ways in which people began to do their shopping during the late 1800's. They should explain what each involved, and give an example. Example:
   A. Specialty shop—sold only one kind of item (shoe store or hat store)
   B. Department store—filled with many things to buy (Macy's, Wanamaker's)
   As a summary, discuss the differences and similarities between the various means available for buying and selling goods.

2. **Categorization.** Have students read each statement carefully, and decide which of the following is described: A) Specialty Shops, B) Department Stores, C) Chain Stores, or D) Mail-Order Houses.
   1. People shopped without ever leaving their homes (D)
   2. People were provided with entertainment as well as a variety of goods (B)
   3. Clerks gave personal treatment to their regular customers (A)
   4. People could shop in stores with the same name and products wherever they went (C)
   5. These were most popular with people in rural areas (D)
   Repeat the above directions—this time, however, using the names of stores or individuals.
   1. George Huntington Hartford (C)
   2. Frank W. Woolworth (C)
   3. Richard Sears (D)
   4. Aaron Montgomery Ward (D)
   5. Wanamaker's (B)
   6. Macy's (B)
   Add to the list, using names of other stores in your area, including specialty shops such as bakeries, shoe stores, or florists.

3. **Using Tables.** Duplicate Worksheet 58, *The Shift from Farm to Factory.* Have students complete the activity. Then, relate it to the material in Section 3 by asking the following questions:
   A. How would farm workers learn about new products to buy?
   B. What advantages would non-farm workers have when they decided to do some shopping?
   C. Which method of purchasing new products would most likely appeal to farm workers? To non-farm workers?

4. **Round Robin.** Use the oral-review technique first described in Chapter 1. Ask for a student volunteer to state one important fact from Section 3. Call on a second student to repeat that fact and add another. Call on a third student to repeat the second fact and add a new one. Repeat the process until all important information has been reviewed or until each student has had an opportunity to participate.

BUILDING AMERICAN CITIZENSHIP

New methods of advertising were created so that one store could gain an advantage over others in the competition for customers. Is advertising fair to the citizens who purchase a store's products? Explain your answer. (Some may say "yes" because it provides notice of available products, sales, and prices at various stores. Others may say "no" because the advertisements are not always truthful, and prices of the goods are sometimes driven up to pay for the cost of the advertising.)

14

SECTION 3 REVIEW ANSWERS

1. **IDENTIFY: Wanamaker's:** a large department store and amusement attraction in Philadelphia; **A & P:** the first chain store; **Frank W. Woolworth:** a salesclerk who started the first five-and-ten-cent chain stores in the United States and Canada; **Aaron Montgomery Ward:**

founder of a mail-order business in 1872; **Richard Sears:** founder of the mail-order firm Sears Roebuck and Company in 1886; **National Biscuit Company:** a pioneer in the use of brand names.

2. **DEFINE: department stores:** large stores offering many different kinds of goods, including clothing, furniture, and food; **chain stores:** stores with branches in many places, each with the same name and the same products; **mail-order houses:** businesses that sell goods by mail, using catalogues to advertise their goods for sale; **brand name:** the name that tells the maker or manufacturer of a product.

3. Convenience of buying everything in one store; free delivery; lower prices.

4. The opening of mail-order houses meant that people in rural areas no longer had to go to a store to shop. They could buy a wide range of goods at low prices.

5. 4 pv.

SECTION 4: Tycoons Create Vast Business Empires

OBJECTIVES

After completing this section, students will be able to:
- Explain the advantages of corporations over individually owned businesses or partnerships.
- Compare the methods used by Swift, Carnegie, and Rockefeller to become "captains of industry."

MOTIVATION

Place the following headings on the board: STEEL PRODUCTION / MEAT-PACKING INDUSTRY / PETROLEUM INDUSTRY. Ask students if they can name any companies associated with these industries. Ask if they can name any individuals who were pioneers in these industries. Have them look at the pictures in Section 4 and identify the individuals associated with the start of each industry. Tell students that each created a business empire and at the end of the lesson they will be comparing the men and the methods they used.

SUGGESTED ACTIVITIES

1. **Directed Reading.** As students read Section 4, have them complete the following chart. This can be placed on the chalkboard or a transparency for the overhead projector. Students should copy the headings in their notebooks and provide the information for each column.

ENTREPRENEUR	INDUSTRY	LOCATION	METHODS FOR SUCCESS
Swift	(Meat packing)	(Chicago, Ill.)	(Lower prices, selling to chains, advertising)
Carnegie	(Steel)	(Pittsburgh, Pa.)	(Lower prices, gained control of everything needed, kept costs low)
Rockefeller	(Oil)	(Cleveland, Ohio)	(Cut production costs, eliminated middlemen, created a monopoly)

As a summary, compare the early lives of these entrepreneurs and the methods they used to achieve success. Have students rank the three according to their concern for the customers. Ask students to give reasons for their answers.

2. **Reading for the Main Idea.** Duplicate Worksheet 59, *Andrew Carnegie.* This activity will let students apply the History Study Skill learned in Chapter 5. You may want to review the contents of page 103 before having students complete the worksheet. You may also wish to select one or more paragraphs from Section 3 that describe the other two entrepreneurs. Then have students identify the main idea of the paragraphs.

3. **Vocabulary Review.** Some students may find the vocabulary in Section 4 difficult. To provide additional practice with the words, use the skill exercise in the Section Review. You may also use the following matching exercise as a drill, review, or summary activity. It can be written on the chalkboard or on a transparency for the overhead projector.

1. Entrepreneurs (F)   A. Large companies that raise capital by selling shares or stock

2. Corporation (A)   B. Those who distribute, sell, or transport a product before it is sold

3. Stockholders (G)   C. Combination of two or more corporations

4. Middlemen (B)   D. A giant organization that centralizes management and standarizes practices in an industry

5. Monopoly (E)   E. Total control over a product or business

6. Merge (C)   F. Tycoons who developed new businesses, or new ways of doing business

7. Trust (D)   G. People who buy stock in a corporation, thereby becoming joint owners of it

4. **Improving Your History Writing.** Have students review the Chapter 10 History Study Skill and then write a paragraph on one of the topics below:
   A. How does a corporation work?
   B. For which of the entrepreneurs would you like to work? Why?
   C. What are the advantages of establishing a business corporation?

BUILDING AMERICAN CITIZENSHIP

How did Carnegie use his wealth to help society? (See text) Contributing money is only one way that citizens can help society. In what ways can people without money serve the common good? (Volunteer work; fulfilling the responsibilities of a citizen, such as obeying the laws; voting; donations of food and clothing to those in need)

SECTION 4 REVIEW ANSWERS

1. **IDENTIFY: Gustavus Swift:** a butcher who changed the meat industry by butchering cattle in Chicago and shipping the meat East in refrigerated cars; **Andrew**

Carnegie: creator of a nationwide steel industry who made a fortune by producing large quantities of steel and selling it at lower prices than his competitors; **John D. Rockerfeller:** entrepreneur who made a fortune by gaining a monopoly of the oil business in the United States.

2. **DEFINE: entrepreneurs:** people who develop new businesses using original methods; **corporations:** business organizations that raise capital by selling shares of stock; **monoply:** nearly total control over an industry; **merger:** the combining of corporations; **trust:** a business organization in which stockholders in the corporations that form a trust give their stock to a group of trustees and in exchange receive shares in the trust and dividends on its profits.

3. A corporation can raise money by selling stock; it can continue to operate even if one of its owners dies; if the corporation fails, the stockholders lose only the money they paid for their investment. In a private business, the owner is responsible for all of the debts of the company, and the business closes down when the owner dies.

4. To gain greater control of the oil business.

SECTION **5**: American Workers Struggle to Get Ahead

OBJECTIVES

After completing this section, students will be able to:
- State the reasons for the formation of unions in the 19th century.
- Identify the unions, their leaders, and their goals.
- List the methods used by employers to prevent workers from organizing and joining unions.
- Explain the importance of the Haymarket Affair and the creation of the A. F. of L.

MOTIVATION

Have students study the time line at the beginning of this chapter. Ask them to identify the events they have already studied, and to review important information about each one. Have them name the two events which they have yet to read about: 1869—Knights of Labor formed, and 1866—American Federation of Labor founded. Ask students if they know what these types of organizations are called. Refer them to the section title and repeat the question. If they still cannot guess the word "unions," tell it to them. Have them name some of the unions with which they are familar. Ask them to describe the purposes of unions and why people joined them.

SUGGESTED ACTIVITIES

1. **Directed Reading.** As students read, have them answer the following questions:
   A. What were the names of the unions started during the 1800's?
   B. Why were these unions founded?
   C. How did union members try to get what they wanted?
   D. Why were these early unions unsuccessful?

Discuss the answers to the questions when students finish reading this section.

2. **Vocabulary Review.** Students may find a vocabulary review helpful at this point. Write this paragraph and the vocabulary words below on the chalkboard. Have the students fill in the blank spaces with the correct words:

Skilled craftspeople, or (A), were the first to form labor organizations to improve working conditions. These labor organizations were called (B), and the method they most often used to win their demands was (C). Employers used the (D) to stop strikes, simply closing down their factories. Workers left without jobs were sometimes forced to live in "cardboard communities" called (E). In the meantime, employers often hired non-union workers, or (F), to replace those who left their jobs.

ANSWERS: (A) artisans, (B) unions, (C) strike, (D) lockout, (E) shantytowns, (F) scabs

3. **Factual Review.** Have students copy the following sentences and fill in the correct answer in each.
   1. The leader of the Knights of Labor was (Terence Powderly).
   2. The A. F. of L. was a union created by (Samuel Gompers) in 1886.
   3. The Knights of Labor were blamed for a bombing in Chicago, which became known as the (Haymarket Affair).
   4. The (NLU) was a national union formed in Baltimore, Maryland, in 1866.
   Have students arrange the events in the order in which they occurred.

BUILDING AMERICAN CITIZENSHIP

Duplicate Worksheet 60, *To Strike or Not to Strike?* Spend some time discussing the question posed: What are our rights and responsibilities as good citizens where strikers are concerned? In reviewing students' answers for the two activities, be sure to have them defend their choice of how other citizens would be affected by such a strike or the use of scabs.

SECTION 5 REVIEW ANSWERS

1. **IDENTIFY: NLU:** the National Labor Union, formed by a group of factory workers' unions in Baltimore in 1866; **Knights of Labor:** a union formed in Philadelphia in 1869 that later represented all types of workers; **Terence Powderly:** leader of the Knights of Labor; **Rose Schneiderman:** an immigrant labor organizer; **Haymarket Affair:** a peaceful rally in Chicago that ended in violence when a bomb was thrown into a group of police officers, for which the Knights of Labor was blamed; **Samuel Gompers:** creator of the A.F. of L. in 1886; **A.F. of L.:** the American Federation of Labor, a group of craft unions, each representing skilled workers in a certain trade.

2. **DEFINE: unions:** labor organizations formed to raise wages, protect rights of workers, and improve working conditions; **artisans:** skilled craftworkers such as blacksmiths, printers, bakers, weavers, and so on; **strike:** the

114

refusal of workers to do their jobs until employers agree to certain demands; **lockout:** closing down factories, leaving striking workers with no jobs; **scabs:** nonunion workers who replace union workers on strike.

3. Higher wages, shorter workdays, better working conditions, protection of workers' rights.
4. The A.F. of L. organized only skilled workers, refusing to admit unskilled workers, blacks, or women.

CHAPTER 21 REVIEW ANSWERS

REVIEWING KEY WORDS

1. b.   2. c.   3. c.   4. b.   5. b.

REMEMBERING IMPORTANT PEOPLE AND EVENTS

1. b.   2. b.   3. a.   4. a.   5. b.
6. b.   7. b.   8. a.

REVIEWING THE FACTS

1. T   2. F   3. F   4. T
5. F   6. T   7. T

PLACING EVENTS IN TIME

1. E.   2. C.   3. D.   4. A.   5. B.

LINKING GEOGRAPHY AND HISTORY

1. It was more convenient for people who lived in rural areas where it was difficult to get to stores or where there were few department stores.
2. The population of the West would have grown more rapidly, and instead of the East Coast, large cities would have grown up along the West Coast.

THINKING ABOUT AMERICAN HISTORY

1. Methods of advertising have changed since the invention of radio and television, which advertise products nationally. Other answers may vary.
2. Automobiles, airplanes, helicopters, space ships.

APPLYING HISTORY STUDIES SKILLS

1. iron and steel.   2. iron and steel.
3. $427,000,000.   4. $749,000,000.
5. lumber and forest products; food processing.

CHAPTER 22

Industrial Progress Changes the Nation (1865-1900)

Chapter Objectives

After completing this chapter, students will be able to:
1. Describe life in American cities at the turn of the century.
2. Identify problems facing rural Americans in this period.
3. Explain how reformers worked to improve life for city dwellers.
4. Describe how writers and artists captured the American scene.

Chapter Chronology

Chapter 22 , like Chapter 21, surveys several concurrent movements in American history between 1865 and 1900, with emphasis on social issues. The time line in the textbook Chapter Opener highlights several of the major events and occurrences of the period. In 1867, the Grange, a secret organization to help farmers solve their economic problems, was founded. A tragedy in a major city occurred in 1871 when the Chicago fire broke out. Although many immigrants came to America during this time, they were not welcomed by all Americans. In 1882, Chinese immigration was limited. To accommodate business expansion, skyscrapers began to be built, the first one rising in Chicago in 1885. Jacob Riis' *How the Other Half Lives*, about the terrible hardships endured by the poor in New York City, was published in 1890. Immigration to America continued at a steady rate as when in 1896, many people from Eastern and Southern Europe began to arrive in large numbers.

Motivation

Ask students to name some things that attract people to cities today. Ask them to name some things that cause people to move from cities today. Repeat the same questions for farms or small towns. Record all student answers. Ask students which of their answers may also have been true in the 1870's-1890's. Were there "push-pull" factors then that are not present today? As students read the chapter, refer back to their answers.

Geographical Setting

Chapter 22, like the previous chapter in this unit, has no explicit geographical focus. However, there are several geographic references in the chapter. Have students look at the map of Europe and find the countries generally labeled as being in Northern, Western, Eastern and Southern Europe to help them identify the changes in immigration patterns that occurred in the 1890's. Students should study a map of the United States to find the agrarian states of the Midwest and Great Plains that suffered from agricultural depression and the subsequent migration to urban areas of many farm families. Refer students to the *Major American Cities in 1900* map on textbook page 512 to pinpoint and review the locations of such major cities mentioned in this chapter as New York, Chicago, Boston, and Washington, D.C.

History Study Skills

The History Skill introduced in Chapter 22 is *Studying Statistics*. The information highlighted is the population shift from rural to urban areas from 1860 to 1900. This activity is best used in conjunction with Section 2, which examines the forces that created rural migration.

Bibliography

Teacher References

Handlin, Oscar, *The Uprooted*, 2d ed. Little, Brown, Boston, Mass., 1973.
Chudacoff, Howard, *The Evolution of American Urban Society*, rev. ed. Prentice Hall, Englewood Cliffs, N.J., 1981.

Student References

Giblin, James, *The Skyscraper Book.* Harper, New York City, 1981. This well-illustrated book presents a historical view of modern tall buildings, as well as the political, economic, and social issues that are involved in their construction.

Lehmann, Linda, *Better than a Princess.* Lodestar Books, New York City, 1978. This autobiography of an immigrant girl, who came to America with her family at age 7, describes how they worked their way westward during the early 1900's, finally settling in Missouri.

Audio-Visual Materials

Boss Tweed: City Growth and Municipal Corruption, Listening Library, Inc., 2 sound color filmstrips. This program shows how William Tweed built the most famous political machine in post war America.

The American Experience: Becoming an American, BFA, 1975. This film shows Italian-Americans, Mexican-American, and Chinese-Americans working to solve problems faced by immigrant groups.

SECTION 1: The Modern City Takes Shape

OBJECTIVES

After completing this section, students will be able to:
* Distinguish between "old" immigrants and "new" immigrants.
* Explain the opposition of some Americans to immigration.
* Describe the methods used by immigrants to make themselves at home in their new land.
* Identify new types of city buildings, some designed to house people and others planned for businesses.

MOTIVATION

Check in the school library for 19th-century pictures of immigrants, individual buildings, including skyscrapers and apartment houses, and cities. Display them prominently in the front of the classroom for students to study. Remind students of the title of Section 1 and ask them how each picture might be related to the "shaping" of cities. Tell them you will discuss this question again when they have finished the reading.

SUGGESTED ACTIVITIES

1. **Directed Reading.** The questions guiding student reading are related to the pictures used in the motivation. If you have displayed these on the chalkboard, you may wish to write the questions above or below the appropriate picture.
   A. From which nations did most immigrants come until 1895?
   B. From which nations did most of them come after 1895?
   C. What affects did immigrants have on the "shaping" of American cities?
   D. Name the new types of buildings designed during the late 1800's and the purpose of each.

As a summary, use the pictures again and repeat the question posed during the Motivation. Also, if a chalkmap of Europe or of the world is available, have students locate and label the nations from which the immigrants came. This may be done with two different colors of chalk to distinguish between "old" and "new" immigration.

2. **Landmarks of Liberty.** Refer students to the selection on the Statue of Liberty, on textbook page 514. Before they read it, ask them to recall what they already know about it from what they have studied in Section 1. For example, when did we get it? From whom did we get it? Why was it important to immigrants? After they have read this selection, pose the following questions:
   A. How would you describe the statue?
   B. Who created it?
   C. What materials were used to construct the statue?
   D. Why was a museum established at its base?
      Also, discuss the two questions at the end of the reading.

3. **Studying Your History Vocabulary.** Section 1 provides an excellent opportunity to apply the Chapter 16 History Study Skill. After having students review the key features, ask them to define the following words from Section 1: steerage, docked, ethnic, slums, tenement, apartment hotels, and dumb-waiters.

4. **Reading a Bar Graph.** Duplicate Worksheet 61, *Immigration.* Allow students to become familiar with the graph by asking the following questions before having them complete the accompanying activity:
   A. What information is found on the vertical axis? (Countries or sections of Europe)
   B. What information is found on the horizontal axis? (Number of people)
   C. What is the smallest number shown on the chart? (206,000)
   D. What does this number represent? (Number of people from Southern Europe living in the United States in 1890)
   E. What is the largest number on the chart? (3,702,000)
   F. What does this number represent? (Number of people from Eastern Europe living in the United States in 1910)

BUILDING AMERICAN CITIZENSHIP

The bar graph on immigration that you studied showed that millions of American citizens were born in other countries. Why do you think these people wanted to come to America? How accurate were the claims, by people who opposed immigration, that immigrants took jobs from Americans? Do immigrants coming to America today face similar responses from citizens born here?

SECTION 1 REVIEW ANSWERS

1. **IDENTIFY: Ellis Island:** official immigration center established by the federal government in 1891 in New York harbor; **Statue of Liberty:** giant statue presented as a gift to the United States from France in 1886; **Workingman's Party:** a group of people in California who op-

posed Chinese immigration; **Immigration Restriction League:** a group of people in Boston who tried to get a law passed requiring immigrants to pass a literacy test; **William Le Baron Jenney:** architect who designed the first skyscraper, built in Chicago in 1885.

2. **DEFINE: immigrants:** newcomers from foreign lands; **slums:** rundown sections in cities; **tenements:** apartment buildings or rooming houses in cities that are usually in poor condition and overcrowded; **skyscrapers:** a building many stories high.

3. "Old" immigrants came from the northern and western nations of Europe; "new" immigrants came from the eastern and southern nations of Europe.

4. To provide housing for middle-class families to keep them from moving out of the cities into the suburbs.

SECTION 2: Life in the Countryside Changes

OBJECTIVES

After completing this section, students will be able to:
- List the reasons for the change from prosperity to depression for American farmers.
- Describe the changes in the lives of farmers resulting from the worldwide depression in farm prices.
- Explain the goals of the National Grange of the Patrons of Husbandry.

MOTIVATION

Ask this question: If you were a farmer, what would be your most important concerns? Possible answers include: the weather, the price of crops, and the care and condition of equipment. Then ask: As a farmer, what problems might eventually influence you to give up this way of life for something else? Possible answers include: a few years of bad crops, continued low prices for crops, a disaster such as a fire or tornado wiping out the farm. Then, focus on the last half of the 1800's. Tell students to think about these questions as they read Section 2.

SUGGESTED ACTIVITIES

1. **Directed Reading.** Use the two questions posed in the Motivation to guide students' reading of this section, and add a third:
   A. What were the major concerns of farmers in the late 1800's?
   B. Why did so many farmers give up their way of life?
   C. How did those who remained farmers try to solve their problems?
   Have students write the answers to these questions in their notebooks. As a summary, have students complete the next activity.
2. **Cause and Effect.** Review the meaning of the terms "cause" and "effect." A cause is what makes something happen. An effect is a result. Have students identify each of the following as a "cause" or an "effect" of changes in farm life:
   A. Drop in farm prices (C)
   B. Founding of the Grange (E)
   C. Rising costs (C)
   D. Bad Weather (C)

E. Farmers organizing nationally (E)
F. Families becoming confused and bitter (E)
G. Young people leaving the farm (E)
H. Specializing in one crop (C)
I. People pitying farm families (E)
J. Competition with farmers in other nations (C)

3. **History Study Skills.** Have students complete the History Study Skill, *Studying Statistics*, on textbook page 527. The table included as part of this exercise may be used to extend students' skills in other areas:
   A. Have students compare the table to the bar-graph activity in Worksheet 61 duplicated for Section 1. Ask them to state the similarities (both are methods of presenting data, both include dates and numbers). Ask them to state the differences (the type of data presented, the organization of the data).
   B. Have students convert the data in the table to a double bar graph using the years and the numbers of people living in cities and on farms.
   C. To determine if the trends suggested by the table continue, have students utilize an almanac to extend the table to include each decade for the 1900's. This would include applying suggested methods to convert numbers to percentages.
4. **Separating Facts from Opinions.** Review the Chapter 12 History Study Skill. Then have students identify each of the following as "fact" or "opinion":
   A. In the 1890's, prices for many farm products dropped by almost 80%. (F)
   B. Many farm families became confused and bitter about the changes they faced. (O)
   C. Living on a farm made people honest, hardworking, and dependable. (O)
   D. In 1867, the National Grange of the Patrons of Husbandry was founded. (F)
   E. The farmers created a new political party, called the Populist Party. (F)

BUILDING AMERICAN CITIZENSHIP

If a group of citizens share a common problem, what might be a good way for them to solve it? (Work together as a group) How did the farmers try to solve their problems in the late 1800's? (Joined the Grange, formed the Populist Party) What other groups have citizens formed to solve problems? (Sons of Liberty, vigilantes, environmentalists protesting nuclear war)

SECTION 2 REVIEW ANSWERS

1. **IDENTIFY: Oliver Kelley:** founder of the Grange in 1867, a social and family organization for farmers; *Munn v. Illinois:* Supreme Court case in which the Court ruled that states have the right to regulate businesses that widely affect the public interest; overturned in 1886; **Populist Party:** political party formed by farmers in 1892.
2. **DEFINE: cooperatives:** groups formed by farmers in which members shared costs and profits of their business activities.
3. Prices for crops fell; competition from farmers in other countries; rising costs; change in Americans' opinion of farmers from admiration to ridicule and pity.

4. It was an organization for farmers designed to bring farm families together and create a sense of community. It became a political-action group to solve farmers' problems, particularly the high rates charged by railroads.

SECTION 3: Reformers Try to Improve City Life

OBJECTIVES

After completing this section, students will be able to:
* List the changes made in cities to improve services to their inhabitants.
* Describe the methods used by reformers and ministers to improve living conditions in the cities.
* Explain how political machines gained the support of the people.

MOTIVATION

Ask students to name the major problems in their city or community today. These might include crime, poverty, drugs, vandalism. Next, ask them who works to solve these problems. They may say police, politicians, or local citizens groups. Finally, ask them to name some problems people in cities may have had 100 years ago that we do not have today.

SUGGESTED ACTIVITIES

1. **Directed Reading.** As students read, have them compile two lists. Sample entries are provided:

Problems of Cities in the 1800's	Actions Taken to Correct the Problems
Dirty streets	Street cleaners
Disease and death	Requirements in new buildings for fresh air circulation and clean water
Poverty	Establishment of settlement houses and social services by some churches
Dishonest politicians	Reformers running for office

Write the headings of Columns A and B on the chalkboard. As a review have one student go to the chalkboard to make an entry in Column A and another to match it with the correct entry for Column B.

2. **Discussion.** One of the major topics emphasized in Section 3 is political corruption. Conduct a class discussion on this topic, beginning with the following question. Why were people willing to allow corrupt politicians to control the cities in the 1800's? Then ask students if they think corrupt political leaders still pose a problem in our large cities today? Ask what safeguards there are to prevent city leaders from taking millions of dollars?

3. **Picture Study.** Have students examine the picture of the tenements in Section 3. Ask specific questions based on the picture to help students recall the important information from the reading. In studying the picture of the tenements, what indicates to you that living conditions there were probably bad? How did

reformers like Jane Addams try to help those in need? Questions should encourage students to infer as much information as possible from what they see.

4. **Comprehension Check.** To determine whether or not students understood what they have read, have them complete the following. You may wish to provide an answer bank for low-ability students.

Reformers tried to end (A) and (B) in cities by campaigning for (C) and (D). At the same time, ministers turned their attention to (E). Other reformers established (F) to provide services to the poor. These people faced problems dealing with the (G) and their (H), who sometimes helped the poor but usually helped themselves by (I) from the city.
ANSWERS:
  A and B - disease, overcrowding, death, poverty
  C and D - clean water, better sewage, fresh air, better plumbing
  E - social problems
  F - settlement houses
  G - political bosses
  H - machines
  I - stealing

BUILDING AMERICAN CITIZENSHIP

Duplicate Worksheet 62, *The Tweed Ring.* This activity will provide students with practice in determining the main idea while working with details concerning Tweed's life. It will make them more aware of the positive qualifications they might demand in a political leader when they begin to vote.

SECTION 3 REVIEW ANSWERS

1. **IDENTIFY: "social gospel":** actions proposed by ministers and churches primarily to improve conditions in slums; **White City:** a small model city built on the shores of Lake Michigan; **Tweed Ring:** a group of corrupt politicians who ran New York City from 1868 to 1872; **Samuel "Golden Rule" Jones:** famous reformer elected mayor of Toledo, Ohio, in 1896.
2. **DEFINE: architects:** people who design buildings; **environment:** surroundings; **settlement houses:** houses set up in slum neighborhoods to provide services to the poor; **city bosses:** dishonest politicians who controlled city governments; **commission:** a group of city leaders who shared powers, replacing a mayor; **city manager:** a person trained in managing city affairs, replacing a mayor.
3. Reformers campaigned for clean water, more fresh air, improved sewage disposal, and better plumbing in city buildings. They also started settlement houses. Ministers founded schools for slum children, ran health clinics, and created loan associations for the poor.
4. They got the support of city officeholders and neighborhood political party leaders. They won the trust of the people by helping them in many ways, such as giving those in need food and money, helping them get jobs, and so on.

SECTION 4: Writers and Artists Describe Modern America

OBJECTIVES

After completing this section, students will be able to:
- Distinguish between the "realist" and "naturalist" movements of the 19th century.
- Identify realist and naturalist writers and artists.

MOTIVATION

Select two paragraphs to read to students, one by a realist author, such as Mark Twain, and one by a naturalist author, such as Frank Norris or Stephen Crane. Try to select passages that illustrate differences in style. Ask students to note the differences and similarities between the two. Tell students that they will be reading about American writers and painters of the 1800's. Remind them that you will be asking them again at the end of class to identify the styles and perhaps the authors.

SUGGESTED ACTIVITIES

1. **Directed Reading.** As students read, have them complete the following outline.

   American Writers and Artists of the 1800's
   I. *(Realists)* write about ordinary people and events in the real world
      A. (Joel Chandler Harris)
      B. (Mark Twain)
      C. (William Dean Howells)
   II. *(Naturalists)* write about how their environment and our human nature shape and control people's lives as they struggle to survive
      A. (Frank Norris)
      B. (Stephen Crane)
      C. (Theodore Dreiser)
   III. *(Realist artists)* paint what they see
      A. (John Singer Sargent)
      B. (Winslow Homer)
      C. (James Abbott McNeill Whistler)

   As a summary, reread the earlier passages to see if students can identify the style and/or the authors.

2. **Using Chronology.** The birthdates of several of the authors and painters are available in Section 4. Have students find the year of birth of each of the following and determine the age of each in 1890. Then arrange them chronologically according to their age in that year.

William Dean Howells	1837
Theodore Dreiser	1871
Henry James	1843
Winslow Homer	1836

   You may wish to have students research the years of birth of the other authors and artists mentioned to increase the learning value of this activity.

3. **Improving Your Writing.** Have students select one of the topics they read about in the first three sections of Chapter 22. Direct them to write a paragraph about one of these topics in either the "realist" or "naturalist" style. You may wish to review the History Study Skill for Chapter 10 on textbook page 247 before beginning. Students should not identify the style of their paragraph in any way. Select several students to read their paragraphs and have the rest of the class identify the style.

4. **Identification.** Provide clues for students and have them identify the individual associated with the clue. This may be done verbally, by using the chalkboard, or by placing the clues on a transparency. Examples include:
   A. Used the Southern dialect for his "Uncle Remus" stories (Harris)
   B. Wrote about life along the Mississippi River (Twain)
   C. "Dean of American letters" (Howell)
   D. Often wrote about the worst side of life, especially for the poor (Dreiser)
   E. Painter of realist portraits (Sargent)
   F. Artist who painted *Arrangement in Gray and Black No. 1* (Whistler)

BUILDING AMERICAN CITIZENSHIP

As an American citizen in the late 1900's what subjects would you suggest to realist authors to write about today? What struggles of average citizens could naturalist authors describe in their works? (Answers will vary.)

SECTION 4 REVIEW ANSWERS

1. **IDENTIFY: Bret Harte:** writer of stories about life in the California mining camps; **Joel Chandler Harris:** a Southerner who wrote the famous "Uncle Remus" stories; **Samuel Clemens:** known as Mark Twain; best-known local colorist who wrote about life along the Mississippi River; **William Dean Howells:** leader of the realist writers in America in the late 1800's; **Theodore Dreiser:** most famous naturalist writer whose greatest work was *An American Tragedy;* **Henry James:** novelist known for his character studies, particularly of innocent Americans living in Europe; **Winslow Homer:** painter famous for his watercolors depicting the struggles of people against the forces of nature; **Thomas Eakins:** finest American painter of the 1800's, who was a master at painting the human body; **James McNeill Whistler:** painter who was part realist and part romantic, best known for his portrait "Whistler's Mother."

2. **DEFINE: dialect:** local language of a region; **naturalism:** a style of realism in writing in which all aspects of reality, including the most unpleasant, are reported.

3. Realists wrote about life as they saw it; naturalists often wrote about the unpleasant aspects of reality, emphasizing the struggle of human beings against society's injustice and their own human weaknesses.

CHAPTER 22 REVIEW ANSWERS

REVIEWING KEY WORDS

1. b.	2. c.	3. a.	4. a.	5. b.

REMEMBERING IMPORTANT PEOPLE AND EVENTS

1. e.	2. a.	3. c.	4. b.	5. d.
6. b.	7. d.	8. e.	9. c.	10. a.

REVIEWING THE FACTS

1. F   2. T   3. T   4. F   5. T

PLACING EVENTS IN TIME

1. C   2. B   3. A   4. E   5. D

LINKING GEOGRAPHY AND HISTORY

Bret Harte wrote about life in the California mining camps in which he had lived. Joel Chandler Harris, a Southerner, based his Uncle Remus stories on folk tales he had heard from slaves and had his characters speak in a Southern dialect. Mark Twain's stories were based on his experiences along the Mississippi River and in the West. William Dean Howells, Frank Norris, and Stephen Crane wrote about the problems in society they saw around them. Henry James lived in Europe and wrote novels about Americans living in Europe.

THINKING ABOUT AMERICAN HISTORY

1. Many city bosses were immigrants themselves and knew the problems immigrants faced. They attended neighborhood weddings, funerals, and other important events. They found jobs for the newly arrived immigrants, helped those in trouble with the law, and provided food and loans for those in need, thus gaining immigrants' trust—and their votes.
2. Politicians still visit neighborhoods to learn the views and problems of their constituents. They attend important events, help people in various ways, and try to get to know as many of the voters in their districts as possible.
3. Today, both laws and citizen-action groups place greater limits on what the politicians can do. Today's voters are more sophisticated, requiring different political tactics. Answers will vary.

APPLYING HISTORY STUDIES SKILLS

1. a.   2. b.   3. b.   4. a

5. b.   6. b.   7. a.

CHAPTER 23

An Age of Protest Begins (1865-1900)

Chapter Objectives

After completing this chapter, students will be able to:

1. Define the term "Gilded Age" as it applies to American history.
2. Explain why many political leaders were strong supporters of big business.
3. Describe how reformers worked to regulate big business.
4. Identify reforms associated with the Populists.
5. Describe the role of William Jennings Bryan in the political and economic scene of the period.

Chapter Chronology

Chapter 23 covers the same period as the other chapters in this unit. Corruption existed in certain areas of business and politics and was a continuing need for economic reform as well. Many of the major figures and events of this period are highlighted on the time line in the textbook Chapter Opener. In 1876, Rutherford B. Hayes was elected President. In 1880, James Garfield was elected President. However, he was assassinated in 1881 and was succeeded immediately by Chester A. Arthur. In his administration the Pendleton Act, establishing the Civil Service, became law in 1883. In the next year, Grover Cleveland was elected President, followed four years later, in 1888, by Benjamin Harrison. In 1890, the Sherman Antitrust Act was passed by Congress. In the following year, farmers got together and established the Populist Party. The year 1892 saw the reelection as President to a second term of Cleveland. He was followed by William McKinley, elected in 1896.

Motivation

Have students read the textbook Chapter Introduction. After they have read about the party at Delmonico's in 1890, make sure they note the concerns expressed by Americans about corrupt practices in business and government. Record student comments for reference as they read the chapter.

Geographical Setting

Chapter 23, like the two preceding chapters in this unit, has no explicit geographical focus. Rural America is significant here in terms of its being the base for the Populist movement.

History Study Skills

The History Study Skill introduced in Chapter 23 is *Getting Information from Newspapers*. This activity is probably best used with Sections 1 and 2.

Bibliography

Teacher References

Goodwyn, Lawrence, *Democratic Promise: The Populist Movement in America.* Oxford, New York City, 1976.

Weisberger, Bernard A., *The New Industrial Society.* John Wiley, New York City, 1969.

Student References

Weisberger, Bernard A., *Life History of the United States, 1890-91.* Silver Burdette, Morristown, N.J., 1974. This is Volume 8 in this excellent series and includes outstanding photo-essays on the period as well as biographical sketches about major figures.

Hoopes, Ray, *Political Campaigning.* Franklin Watts, New York City, 1979. This clear, concise overview of the presidential campaigning process is ideal as an extension of the text information on the presidential campaigns in the Gilded Age.

Audio-Visual Materials

Money on the Land, Time-Life Films, 52 minutes, color. This film, for above-average students, discusses factors responsible for the change in the American economy between 1865 and 1900.

Progressives, Populists and Reform in America, Guidance Associates. 2 filmstrips, 2 cassettes, library kit, teacher's guide. This program examines specific objectives sought by reform groups, such as the Populists.

SECTION 1: Politicians Grow Rich in the Gilded Age

OBJECTIVES

After completing this section, students will be able to:
• Give the origin and meaning of the term "Gilded Age."
• Explain the problems associated with the spoils system.
• Describe the achievements of the Presidents who served during the Gilded Age.

MOTIVATION

Use the Motivation suggested in the Chapter Introduction on page 531 of the manual. After reviewing the list of problems in America during that period, ask students for examples of corruption uncovered in recent years. Ask who is responsible for correcting corrupt practices and solving problems in the nation. (People, Congress, President) Tell students that in Section 1 they will learn how some people tried to reform corrupt practices in the late 1800's.

SUGGESTED ACTIVITIES

1. **Directed Reading.** Tell students to skim the section and read the headings. Ask them to write down the names of the Presidents mentioned, in their notebooks, under a column marked Presidents. Then, have them add three other columns to make a chart like the one below and fill them in.
   PRESIDENT / TERM OF OFFICE / POLITICAL PARTY / ACCOMPLISHMENTS
   Have students discuss the information placed in each column. Also, talk about why each of these Presidents, except for Cleveland, served only one term in office. Then, use the following activity to summarize.
2. **Identification.** Have students identify the President associated with each of the following statements. These may be placed on the chalkboard or on a transparency for the overhead projector.
   A. "An ideal self-made man" (Garfield)
   B. Signed the Pendleton Civil Service Act into law (Arthur)
   C. Supported a plan to lower tariffs (Cleveland)
   D. Started an investigation into political corruption in New York State (Hayes)
   E. Defeated James G. Blaine in the 1884 election (Cleveland)
   F. "The human iceberg" (Harrison)
   G. Assassinated by Charles Guiteau (Garfield)
   H. Signed the McKinley Tariff into law (Harrison)
   I. The only President elected to two non-consecutive terms (Cleveland)

3. **Research Activity.** In Section 1 there are several topics suggested that you may wish students to investigate, using library sources. (Roscoe Conkling, Charles Guiteau, the Mugwumps, James G. Blaine, and any of the Presidents they have studied) Allow students to make their choices. You may wish those who choose a President to emphasize his private life as well as his career following his term in office.

BUILDING AMERICAN CITIZENSHIP

What is "mudslinging"? (Name calling and attacking the character of a political opponent) Why has mudslinging long been part of political campaigns? (It often seems easier to attack someone personally than to study and critically evaluate the issues.) Should there be a law passed to outlaw mudslinging in political campaigns? Explain your answer. (Answers will vary.)

SECTION 1 REVIEW ANSWERS

1. **IDENTIFY: Rutherford B. Hayes:** Republican candidate elected President in 1876; **"Stalwarts":** a powerful group within the Republican Party; **James A. Garfield:** Republican candidate elected President in 1880 and assassinated less than a year later; **Charles Guiteau:** disappointed office seeker who shot President Garfield; **Chester A. Arthur:** Vice-President who became President on the death of President Garfield; **Pendleton Act:** law passed in 1883 creating a merit system for government jobs and requiring all who applied for certain government jobs to take an examination; **James G. Blaine:** corrupt Republican Senator from Maine who was defeated in the presidential election of 1884; **Mugwumps:** those who left the Republican Party in 1884 to support the Democratic presidential candidate; **Grover Cleveland:** Democratic candidate elected President in 1884; **Benjamin Harrison:** Democratic candidate elected President in 1888; **McKinley Tariff:** law passed in 1888 setting high duties on imports.
2. **DEFINE: civil service jobs:** certain government jobs for which applicants must pass an examination.
3. "Gilding" is applying a thin layer of gold over a cheaper metal. Twain thought that the shiny surface of America's government covered up corruption and greed.
4. Garfield was assassinated; Presidents Hayes and Arthur were not renominated; Cleveland was not renominated until eight years later.
5. Hayes, Garfield, Cleveland

SECTION 2: Political Leaders Support Big Business

OBJECTIVES

After completing this section, students will be able to:
• Explain why political leaders opposed the regulation of business.
• List and describe the methods used by business leaders to control competition and prices.
• Identify the role of bankers in helping business leaders to create trusts.

MOTIVATION

Write the words "pool," "trust," and "panic" on the board. Have students use the words in sentences. This should be an oral exercise. The content in which they use them will probably be far removed from the application of those words in Section 2. This is to be expected. Repeat the exercise asking that the sentences be related to business topics. Tell them if they are wrong and that they will learn entirely new meanings for these words in Section 2. Inform them that at the end of class you will again ask them to use these words in forming sentences related to business topics.

SUGGESTED ACTIVITIES

1. **Directed Reading.** As students read, have them define each of the words used in the Motivation and add the following: "merge," "unrestrained competition," "monopoly," "dividends," and "money trust." If students are able to define these terms, they should be able to comprehend the major concepts addressed in this section. As a summary, repeat the motivational exercise for *all* of the terms, including the three initially used as a starting point.

2. **History Study Skill.** Refer students to the activity *Getting Information from Newspapers* on textbook page 548. Ask students to provide specific details for those stories with headlines related to information in Sections 1 and 2. The publishers of your local newspaper may be willing to provide a class set of newspapers for free or at a reduced rate. This would allow all students to complete the activity simultaneously and for you to assist with any difficulties they may encounter.

3. **Time Line.** Have students begin constructing a time line of major events during the Gilded Age. They may use the presidential election years 1876-1892 as intervals on the time line, with a scale of 1 inch = 4 years. Have them briefly review Section 1 for events of importance, including the assassination of Garfield, the Pendleton Civil Service Act, and the McKinley Tariff, to be placed on the line. Ask them to go over Section 2 for additional events, such as the invention of the "trust" in 1882.

4. **Round Robin.** Use the Round Robin technique as introduced in Chapter 1. Call on a student volunteer to state one important fact from Section 2. The second student volunteer should repeat the fact and add a new one. The third student should repeat the second fact and add a new one. This activity should continue until all pertinent facts have been verbalized or until all students have had an opportunity to participate.

BUILDING AMERICAN CITIZENSHIP

During the Gilded Age, many of the nation's political leaders were businesspeople themselves. Do you think there are many wealthy business people among the political leaders of our nation today? (Answers will vary.) Should political leaders be allowed to make decisions about the businesses in which they are involved? (There is a danger that they show bias in favoring legislation to help that business.) What effect can the average citizen have on the relationship between business people and politicians? (Stay informed, vote for honest politicians, write letters and make phone calls to members of Congress about issues of concern.)

SECTION 2 REVIEW ANSWERS

1. **IDENTIFY: Samuel Dodd:** lawyer employed by John D. Rockefeller who created the business organization known as a trust; **J. Pierpont Morgan:** famous New York banker; **"money trust":** a small group of bankers and very wealthy business leaders who held great power over American Industry.

2. **DEFINE: pool:** an organization in which owners of business in an industry agreed on prices and amount of goods produced to avoid over-production and falling prices;

3. Many political leaders were business people themselves; politicians seeking office depended on campaign contributions from business leaders and corporations; political leaders had faith in the leadership and judgment of business leaders.

4. Monopolies, pools, and trusts were used to control competition and prices.

SECTION 3: Reformers Demand Business Regulation

OBJECTIVES

After completing this section, students will be able to:
- List the steps taken by state and federal governments to regulate business.
- Identify the laws passed by Congress to regulate business.
- Determine the causes and effects of the Pullman Strike.

MOTIVATION

Review the previous sections to be sure that students understand the concepts of monopoly and trusts. Also, ask them to explain the attitude of many political leaders towards business and the reasons for this attitude. Next, ask students to think about what circumstances would make political leaders change their minds about regulating businesses.

SUGGESTED ACTIVITIES

1. **Directed Reading.** As students read, have them answer the questions posed during the Motivation:
   A. What made the federal government start regulating business activities? (Farmers, workers, businessmen, and reformers demanded it.)
   B. How did they begin to regulate businesses? (Laws were passed.)
   C. What did the Pullman Strike prove about government efforts to control business? (Laws were used frequently to control workers rather than businesses.)
   Discuss the answer to each question. Have students quote exact passages from the text to prove that their answers are correct.

2. **Time Line.** Direct students to add important events

from Section 3 to their time line. These would include:

A. 1887—Interstate Commerce Act

B. 1890—Sherman Anti-Trust Act

C. 1894—Pullman Strike

3. **Cause and Effect**. Review the meaning of these terms with students. A "cause" is what makes something happen. An "effect" is a result. Have students label each of the following as a cause or effect of the Pullman Strike. These statements may be written on the chalkboard or on a transparency for the overhead projector.

A. The Pullman Company totally controlled the town in which its workers lived. (C)

B. State troopers were sent wherever there was danger of violence. (E)

C. Mail deliveries were stopped. (E)

D. George Pullman fired several of the workers' leaders. (C)

E. Men died in the fighting between strikers and soldiers. (E)

F. President Cleveland sent troops to break the strikers. (E)

G. George Pullman reduced salaries by almost 25 percent. (C)

H. Workers had to live in the company town to get a job at the Pullman factory. (C)

4. **Using Newspapers.** Duplicate Worksheet 63, *Urban Life.* You may wish to assign this activity for homework. This will allow students to work independently, applying the History Study Skill introduced in the previous section.

BUILDING AMERICAN CITIZENSHIP

Your textbook states that although the struggle against trusts began in the states, it became clear that it would have to be won by the federal government. Why do you think it is easier for the federal government to begin reforms and pass laws for American citizens than it is for state governments? (As is implied in Section 3, state governments often disagree among themselves about reforms and laws. Unlike the states, the federal government can pass laws that apply to American citizens all across the nation.)

SECTION 3 REVIEW ANSWERS

1. **IDENTIFY: Interstate Commerce Act:** law passed in 1887 requiring railroad fees to be "reasonable and just," forbidding rebates to big shippers, unfair long-haul/short-haul rates, and requiring publication of rate schedules; **Interstate Commerce Commission:** agency created to enforce the regulations under the Interstate Commerce Act to investigate complaints against the railroads and to order railroads to halt illegal practices; **Sherman Antitrust Act:** law passed in 1890 making it illegal to form trusts or to try to stop competition in any way; **Pullman strike:** 1894 strike by Pullman workers brought on by a 25 percent reduction in salaries; **American Railway Union;** labor union led by Eugene V. Debs, which supported the Pullman strike by shutting down all rail lines into and out of Chicago.

2. **DEFINE: rebates:** refunds of money.

3. They saw them as dangerous and dishonest people who threatened the survival of democracy.

4. President Cleveland said the strike was preventing mail from being delivered, which is a federal crime.

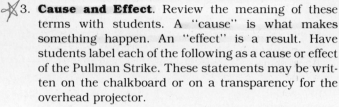

SECTION 4: Farmers Fight for a Better Life

OBJECTIVES

After completing this section, students will be able to:

• Describe the goals of the Populist Party.

• Explain the money problem that arose because of the gold standard.

• List the reasons for the Populists' failure to gain the support of the people.

MOTIVATION

Have students name the two major political parties that compete for political offices in America today. Tell them that the class is now going to start a new political party. Ask them what they think will be needed to make it successful? (A statement of goals, good leaders, a wide base of support) If they are unable to answer the question, tell them you will ask it again at the end of the class. If they offer ideas, tell them to see, as they read, whether the party started in the 1890's had what it needed to be successful.

SUGGESTED ACTIVITIES

1. **Directed Reading.** Have students scan the opening paragraph to find the name of the new political party. Write the two headings below on the chalkboard and ask students to write them in their notebooks. As they read, have them list the goals of the Populist Party under one of the two headings:

GOALS: FARMING ISSUES	OTHER ISSUES
Subtreasury plan	Graduated income tax
Silver dollars	Popular election of senators
Nationalization of transportation and communication	An eight-hour workday
	No more use of private police to break strikes

Discuss the entries under each heading to make sure that students understand the meaning of each. As a summary, return to the question posed during the Motivation and have students list what would be needed to make a new political party successful. Discuss which of these the Populists had (platform, leaders) and did not have (support).

2. **Time Line.** Have students add important events from Section 4 to their chapter time line. These would include:

A. 1890—Passage of the Sherman Silver Purchase Act

B. 1892—Formation of the Populist Party

C. 1892—Election of Cleveland

3. **Ideals in the Lives of Americans.** Point out that one of the most powerful speakers of the Populist Party was a woman. Ask students to name her. (Mary

Ellen Lease) Tell students that another famous woman was beginning her public life at about the same time that the Populist Party was formed. Have them read the selection of Carrie Chapman Catt on textbook page 545 and then answer the two questions at the end.

4. **Comprehension Check.** Use the following TRUE-FALSE questions to determine whether or not students understand what they have read.
   A. The Populist Party started a struggle between the silverites and the gold bugs. (T)
   B. The Populist Party won the support of workers and businessmen. (F)
   C. The "money problem" involved losses by bankers and businessmen as well as by farmers. (F)
   D. The Populists supported the nationalization of public transportation and communication. (T)
   E. The "subtreasury plan" called for the government to print paper dollars backed by silver (F)

BUILDING AMERICAN CITIZENSHIP

Review what is needed for a political party to become successful. Ask students if there are any reasons why a group of people might want to start a political party today? (Environmental issues, anti-nuclear movement) Which of the things required to start a political party would be the most difficult to acquire in today's society? Why? (Answers will vary.)

14

SECTION 4 REVIEW ANSWERS   P·542

1. **IDENTIFY: Populist Party:** political party organized by farmers in 1892 to demand broad reforms; **Greenback Labor Party:** political party that promised to print more paper money; **Sherman Silver Purchase Act:** 1890 law that required the government to buy silver each month; **James B. Weaver:** unsuccessful Populist candidate for President in 1892.
2. **DEFINE: nationalize:** the taking over by government of a privately owned industry, such as the railroads; **graduated income tax:** a federal tax according to income and earnings; **gold standard:** a monetary standard in which paper money is backed by and redeemable for gold.
3. To restore government to the "plain people"; to help farmers solve the problems of high production costs and low crop prices; to nationalize public transportation and communication; to institute a graduated income tax; to elect Senators by popular vote; an 8-hour workday; an end to the use of private armed police forces against strikers; and to get the government to issue silver dollars.
4. Farmers wanted paper money backed by silver as well as gold; owners of large businesses opposed both the greenback and silver-dollar plans.
5. Sherman Silver... ; Pop. Party, Cleveland

SECTION 5: Bryan Leads the Populist Movement

OBJECTIVES

After completing this section, students will be able to:
• Describe President Cleveland's actions to end the gold crisis.

• Explain the problems of the Populist Party in the election of 1896.
• Distinguish between the campaign styles of McKinley and Bryan in the election of 1896.

MOTIVATION

How do candidates for national offices win votes? Ask students this question and list their responses on the chalkboard. Ask them how well they think candidates would do in a national election if they did nothing but sit on their front porches and wait for the people to come to them? Tell them that that is exactly what McKinley did in 1896 and that they are going to find out just how well this worked.

SUGGESTED ACTIVITIES

1. **Directed Reading.** Have students answer the following questions as they read Section 5:
   A. What did Bryan mean when he referred to a "cross of gold"?
   B. How did Bryan try to win the support of the voters?
   C. How did McKinley try to win the support of the voters?
   D. Why did Bryan lose the election of 1896?
   Discuss the answers to these questions when students have finished the reading. As a summary, have students review the list of what a candidate must do to win a national election. Add anything they may have learned from Section 5 (get money, hire a good campaign manager, win the support of newspapers and other media).
2. **Time Line.** Have students add the important events of Section 5 to their chapter time line. These include:
   A. 1895—Repeal of the Sherman Silver Purchase Act
   B. 1896—Election of 1896
   C. 1896—End of the Populist Party
   Have students compare their time line to the one found in the textbook Chapter Opener. Have them describe the similarities and differences.
3. **Using Tables.** Duplicate Worksheet 64, *Presidential Elections, 1884-1896.* Have students study the table and answer the questions that follow.
   This election information may also be used to review the Chapter 11 History Study Skill, *Using Circle Graphs.* After students review this information, have them use the electoral vote results from one or more of the elections on the table to draw one or more circle graphs.
4. **Discussion.** Have students review the two paragraphs under the heading "McKinley Wins by a Landslide." Ask them to name those areas of the country that voted for Bryan and those that voted for McKinley. Geographically, who seemed to carry most of the nation? (Bryan) If this is true, how could McKinley have won by a landslide? (The areas carried by Bryan, though larger, had a lower population and therefore fewer electoral votes. The industrialized parts of the nation had a larger population and, therefore, more electoral votes.)

BUILDING AMERICAN CITIZENSHIP

Duplicate Worksheet 65, *Letters to Government Leaders.* Have students read the letters carefully and answer the questions that follow. In addition, ask students which candidates these letter writers probably would have supported in the election of 1896. Have them explain the reasons for their answers.

SECTION 5 REVIEW ANSWERS

1. **IDENTIFY: William Jennings Bryan:** unsuccessful Democratic candidate for President in 1896; **William McKinley:** Republican candidate elected President in 1896; **Mark Hanna:** brilliant campaign manager who helped get McKinley elected in 1896.
2. When President Cleveland borrowed gold from J. Pierpont Morgan to resupply the nation's treasury, Morgan and other bankers demanded a large profit. People felt that Cleveland was helping the rich get richer while many Americans went without jobs or money.
3. The graduated income tax, popular election of Senators, and subtreasury plans.

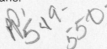

CHAPTER 23 REVIEW ANSWERS

REVIEWING KEY WORDS

1. e.   2. d.   3. a.   4. c.   5. b.

REMEMBERING IMPORTANT PEOPLE AND EVENTS

1. a.   2. c.   3. b.   4. b.   5. b.
6. c.   7. c.   8. c.   9. b.   10. d.
11. T   12. T   13. F   14. F   15. F

PLACING EVENTS IN TIME

1. B   2. A   3. B   4. A   5. B

LINKING GEOGRAPHY AND HISTORY

1. The East supported the gold standard because this was the center of business and industry. The gold standard kept the value of the dollar rising.
2. The Midwestern and Plains farmers supported the silver standard. So did silver miners in the Far West. They hoped to lower the value of the dollar and thus, the cost of goods.
3. The gold bugs in the East won most of the money battles because of their wealth and influence over the federal government.

THINKING ABOUT AMERICAN HISTORY

Answers will vary. However, students should include the following ideas from this chapter: The power of wealthy bankers and tycoons to control prices and competition through monopolies, pools, and trusts was becoming a threat to farmers and ordinary citizens. Farmers and workers were being crushed by high costs and low income and were therefore forced to take political action to defend themselves against big business. These actions eventually led to greater government regulation and an increasing role of government in business affairs.

APPLYING HISTORY STUDIES SKILLS

1. editorial page.   2. first section, or Section A.
3. index.   4. headline   5. lead sentence.

UNIT 7 REVIEW ANSWERS

VOCABULARY REVIEW

Answers will vary.

REVIEWING THE MAIN IDEAS

1. The search for gold and silver brought the miners, many of whom stayed after the ore veins gave out. Ranchers created the cattle kingdom. Farmers established homesteads and farms.
2. They lost their war against the settlers and were forced to move to reservations.
3. It had rich natural resources, wealthy people willing to invest in businesses, inventors who improved means of transportation, communication, and production of goods, public and government support for the growth of business, and a supply of cheap labor.
4. They were admired for their imaginative ideas, their abilities, their ambition, and their intelligence. They were feared because of their ruthless business practices and their power.
5. (a) Pressure from reformers to improve the lives of slum dwellers brought about some new government regulations requiring better plumbing and more fresh air in new city buildings. Fewer people in the slums died of disease as a result of new attention given to cleanliness. Churches set up schools and health clinics and loan associations for the poor in the slums. Settlement houses were opened to provide many services to the poor. They also brought political pressure on local governments for better garbage disposal, plumbing systems, and housing conditions in the slums. (b) Efforts of political reformers led to passage of the Pendleton Act in 1883, which was the first step toward ending the spoils system and the political corruption it entailed. (c) Efforts of business reformers brought about the first law to control big-business monopolies—the Interstate Commerce Act of 1887. The Sherman Antitrust Act was passed in 1890.
6. They joined the Grange, founded in the 1860's as a social organization to bring farm families closer together but later used as a political lobbying organization. They joined cooperatives and banded together to form the Populist Party in 1892.

APPLYING YOUR STUDY SKILLS

1. **Using a Time Line**
   a.   (1) First transcontinental railroad; invention of the telephone; first subway. (2) Custer's Last Stand; Battle of Wounded Knee. (3) 11 years.
   b.   Each Administration would equal one inch:

   1876 1880 1884 1888 1892 1896 1900

2. **Preparing an Outline**
   "Writers and Artists of the Late 1800's"

   I. Writers of realism
   A. Bret Harte
   B. Joel Chandler Harris
   C. Mark Twain
   D. William Dean Howells

   II. Writers of naturalism
   A. Frank Norris
   B. Stephen Crane
   C. Theodore Dreiser

   III. Painters of realism
   A. John Singer Sargent
   B. Winslow Homer
   C. Thomas Eakins
   D. James Whistler

3. **Using Maps**

   a. Sedalia, Abilene, Newton, Ellsworth, Dodge City, Cheyenne.

PROJECTS

Answers will vary.

BUILDING AMERICAN CITIZENSHIP

1. Individuals sometimes find it difficult to solve big problems on their own. A group or organizations can provide support. Also, people tend to listen to an organization more readily than an individual. Examples of groups with common interests: National Organization of Women (NOW); Common Cause, a citizens' lobby for good government; groups that oppose nuclear weapons; organizations that work for a clean environment; Vietnam veterans groups, and so on.

2. Examples include volunteering your time to help out at hospitals or visiting the sick or elderly or to help in other ways, donating whatever money you can to worthwhile causes, picking up litter left by others, donating used clothing and other items to charity organizations, and so on.

UNIT 8 (1890-1920)

America Expands Overseas

Introducing the Unit

Unit Eight covers the 30 year period from 1890 to 1920, a time of great flux and growth in America. During this time America turned to the international scene and began to gain power in world affairs. However, problems at home were not forgotten as reformers continued to search for ways of improving life for American citizens.

Chapter 24 traces the reform movement known as Progressivism from its Populist roots, through its numerous achievements, to its demise after the outbreak of World War I. The period from 1900 to about 1914 was especially noteworthy for its reform legislation in government at state and local levels. Then the Great War succeeded largely in diverting the attention of Americans away from reform. Nonetheless, two important amendments, Prohibition and Women's Suffrage, were passed by Congress in 1918.

Chapter 25 describes the transformation of America from an isolated nation to one heavily involved in world affairs. Seward's purchase of Alaska in 1867 signaled the beginning of American expansion. By the 1890's, Americans were caught up in the competition for trading rights in Asia and involved in a movement to annex Hawaii. In the 1860's as well, we had enforced the Monroe Doctrine and had intervened in Latin American affairs. The Spanish-American War in 1898 officially marked the end of America's century of isolation and initiated a period of expansionism. As a result of the war, America acquired possessions, some temporary others permanent. In the first decade and a half of the 20th century, America was involved in a rebellion in China, a war between Russia and Japan, and in some internal affairs in Mexico.

When war began in Europe in 1914, most Americans wanted to stay out of it. Chapter 26 describes our attempts at maintaining neutrality, the provocations by Germany that resulted in the failure of those attempts, and our subsequent involvement in the war. This chapter discusses the tremendous surge of activity on the home front and the terrible cost in American lives overseas. It also shows that by the end of the war, America had become a world leader, both politically and economically.

The Unit Opener in the textbook depicts many of the significant persons and events of the period. You may wish to use these illustrations to help introduce the unit. Beginning in the upper left-hand corner, a suffragist is shown, holding the nation's flag. Then proceeding in a clockwise direction are the Hawaiian Queen Liliuokalani, Kitty Hawk in North Carolina, Theodore Roosevelt, and a scene of World War I.

Another major feature in this and several other units in the textbook is a photo essay, *What Life Was Like.* It is designed to evoke the quality and flavor of daily life in different types of American communities at various times in the nation's history. In Unit Eight, the photo essay illustrates American life at the dawn of high technology.

Unit Themes and Ideas

Unit Eight is organized around three main themes—reform, expansionism, and war. The Progressives worked for reforms to end corruption in big business as well as in government, particularly on the state and local levels. Major reforms were pushed through in these and other areas even as the Progressive era was coming to an end in the second decade of the 20th century. Prohibition and women's suffrage were the final products of these years of reform.

America's expansion into Latin America, the Pacific Ocean, and Asia had strong underlying economic motivations—a shorter transportation route through the Panama Canal, coaling stations in Hawaii, and trade with China and Japan. The United States became an imperialist nation of sorts as it gained possessions in Latin America and the Pacific through war and annexations.

The failure of European nations to maintain a balance of power resulted in the outbreak of World War I. As a series of events seemed to be carrying the United States into that conflict, neutrality gave way to preparedness and then to war. The American mobilization effort was one of the most spectacular success stories in the nation's history. The same cannot be said of the efforts made to create a lasting peace. The defeat of the League of Nations ended one period in American history and began another as the United States returned to normalcy.

The themes and ideas of Unit Eight are organized into the three chapters below:

Chapter 24 - *America Begins an Age of Reform (1900 - 1920)*

Chapter 25 - *Americans Gain Power in World Affairs (1890 - 1914)*

Chapter 26 - *America Enters World War I (1914 - 1920)*

CHAPTER 24

America Begins an Age of Reform (1900-1920)

Chapter Objectives

After completing this chapter, students will be able to:
1. Identify reforms achieved by the Progressives.
2. Describe the contributions of Roosevelt, Taft, and Wilson to the reform movement.

3. Trace the movements for women's suffrage and prohibition.
4. Explain why the reform movement did not meet the needs of America's blacks and immigrants.

Chapter Chronology

Chapter 24 covers a period of intense concern with reform in many areas of American life. Two longtime reform goals—women's suffrage and prohibition, became law during this time. Several of the major events of the time are highlighted on the time line in the textbook Chapter Opener. The new century opened with the election of William McKinley as President. Assassinated in 1901, he was succeeded by his Vice President, Theodore Roosevelt. In the election of 1904, the voters chose Roosevelt to lead the nation for another four years. An important piece of legislation in the first decade of the 20th century was the Pure Food and Drug Act, passed in 1906. The Democrats returned to power in 1912 with the election, as president, of Woodrow Wilson. Prohibition became legal in 1919 with the ratification of the Eighteenth Amendment. In 1920, with the ratification of the Nineteenth Amendment, American women were given the right to vote.

Motivation

Lincoln Steffens and Upton Sinclair are two of the muckraking journalists about whom students will learn in Section 1. Read short, selected passages from the works of these muckrakers to the students or give them the excerpts below.

Adapted from *The Shame of the Cities* by Lincoln Steffens:

One of this city's judges had a criminal record. In a district where only 100 voters lived, 250 people voted. Voters included the names of dead dogs, children, and imaginary people. The same address, a four-story house, was given by 44 voters.

Adapted from *The Jungle* by Upton Sinclair

The factory owners had secret water lines, through which they stole billions of gallons of the city's water. A doctor discovered that the carcasses of diseased steers were sold in the city to unsuspecting buyers. Rats were a bother so the meat-packers put out poisoned bread for them. The rats would die and then rats, bread, and meat would be mixed together and made into sausage.

Discuss each selection with the class. Ask students what the problems were according to Steffens and Sinclair and what should have been done about them. Note their responses on the chalkboard and have students add to them as they study the chapter.

Geographical Setting

The Age of Reform encompassed the entire nation. Thus, Chapter 24 does not have a geographical focus, and there are no maps in this chapter. Still, it is important to reinforce students' knowledge of locational geography by having them locate such places, mentioned in the textbook, as Galveston, Chicago, Tuskegee, Wisconsin, Oregon, and Alaska.

History Study Skills

The History Study Skill in Chapter 24 is *Studying Photographs.* This activity is best used in conjunction with the photograph of coal miners in Section 2 and of the women's suffrage headquarters in Section 5.

Bibliography

Teacher References

Chambers, John W., *The Tyranny of Change: America in the Progressive Era.* St. Martin's Press, New York City, 1980.

Hofstadter, Richard, *The Age of Reform.* Knopf, New York City, 1955.

Student References

Fisher, Leonard, *The Newspapers: A Nineteenth Century America Book.* Holiday House, New York City, 1981. This book described the evolution of American newspapers from small weeklies to mass-produced, metropolitan dailies.

Patterson, Lillie, *Sure Hands, Strong Heart: The Life of Danial Hale Williams,* Abingdon Press, Nashville, Tenn., 1981. This is an excellent illustrated biography of Hale Williams, a black physician who was one of the first doctors to perform open heart surgery.

Audio-Visual Materials

The Progressive Era, Encyclopedia Britannica, black and white, 23 minutes. This film examines politics in the early 1900's and describes government practices that were the objects of reform.

Trust-Busting, Listening Library Inc., color. This sound filmstrip surveys the rise of trusts; legislation and judicial action against trusts; and individuals involved in trust-busting.

SECTION 1: The Progressives Work for Reforms

OBJECTIVES

After completing this section, students will be able to:
- List the goals of the Progressive movement.
- Describe the types of articles written by muckrakers.
- Name the methods used by Progressives to reform local and state governments.
- Explain how the Progressives gained control of the White House.

MOTIVATION

Use the short passages from the Motivation in the chapter introduction in this manual. Without naming the authors, ask students to identify the problems from each excerpt and to suggest solutions. Ask them also how they think the public would learn about the problems. Tell students you will read the passages again at the end of class, when you will require them to answer the above questions in detail and name the author of each passage.

SUGGESTED ACTIVITIES

1. **Directed Reading.** As students read, have them list the methods used by the various reformers to achieve

their goals. Ask them to define or explain each method. These include writing newspaper and magazine articles: working for "home rule," adopting the city commissioner and city manager system: and establishing such state-wide reforms as the direct primary, the initiative, the referendum, and the recall.

Summarize the lesson by returning to the Motivation. Reread each passage and ask students to identify the authors. Have them name the other "muckraker" mentioned in the chapter. Ask how the public learned about the problems and how they should have been dealt with.

2. **History Study Skills.** Have students complete the activity *Studying Photographs* on textbook page 575. Relate the material to the information in Section 1, by asking them what the "muckrakers" might have written about coal miners after visiting the mines or seeing this picture or one like it.

3. **Flash Cards.** The concepts introduced in this chapter might be difficult for slower students to grasp. To help reinforce the concepts, prepare two sets of flash cards. On one set write the terms: on the other, brief explanations of these concepts. Distribute the cards among the students at random. Have one student bring a card with a term on it to the front of the room. The student whose card had the matching explanation should then also come to the front of the room. This activity may be repeated as needed.

BUILDING AMERICAN CITIZENSHIP

Duplicate Worksheet 66, *Helping Improve Your Government*. This, too, will provide an opportunity for students to distinguish between several of the concepts introduced in Section 1. More importantly, it requires them to apply the concepts to given situations.

SECTION 1 REVIEW ANSWERS

1. **IDENTITY: Ida M. Tarbell:** journalist who wrote about secret deals and other methods used by Standard Oil to beat out its competitors; **Upton Sinclair:** author of *The Jungle*, a study of Chicago's meatpacking industry; **Lincoln Steffens:** muckraker who wrote about corrupt machines in city politics; **Robert LaFollette:** Progressive governor of Wisconsin who was responsible for reforms such as the direct primary, a state civil service, a conservation program, and a state income tax.

2. **DEFINE: Progressive movement:** reform movement of the early 1900's; so named because its members believed progress was possible; **muckrakers:** name given by Theodore Roosevelt to reporters who raked up the mud, or evils, of America's society so that the public would do something about them; **direct primary:** system in which political candidates are elected by the voters instead of by party leaders; **initiative:** a law allowing voters to introduce new ideas for legislation themselves; **referendum:** method allowing a law proposed by voters in petitions to be placed on a ballot for approval or rejection by voters; **recall:** a law giving voters the power to remove officeholders thought to be doing a poor job.

3. The goals of Progressivism included honest and democratic government, the regulation of big business, improvement in job conditions for workers, and better housing and medical care for the poor.

4. In a commissioner system, commissioners are elected to head each major department of government. In a manager system, elected commissioners chose a manager to conduct the city's business.

SECTION 2: Theodore Roosevelt Supports Reform

OBJECTIVES

After completing this section, students will be able to:
- State the reasons for Roosevelt's popularity among the American people.
- Describe Roosevelt's attitudes towards big business and unions.
- List the reforms undertaken during Roosevelt's administration.

MOTIVATION

Place the following terms on the chalkboard: reformer, "Rough Rider," "trust buster," champion of fairness, and conservationist. Ask students if they are familiar with any of these terms. Have them explain those they know. Tell students that all of the terms were used to describe the President they will read about today. Be sure to have students tell how each of these terms apply to Teddy Roosevelt after they have finished Section 2.

SUGGESTED ACTIVITIES

1. **Directed Reading.** As students read, have them complete the following outline: *Theodore Roosevelt's Presidency.*
   I. Reasons for his popularity
   II. Challenges to big business
   III. Increasing the power of the Presidency
   IV. Passage of major reform laws

   You may wish to assist low-ability students in developing their outlines by providing a specific number of subtopics or by providing partial statements for subtopics. Review important information that should be incorporated under each topic.

2. **Improving Your History Writing.** Have students review the Chapter 10 History Study Skill. Then, direct students to consider the statement below: Theodore Roosevelt once said he was "better suited" to the Presidency than anyone else. Ask the students, based on the information in Section 2, if they think that this is an honest statement. Have them write a paragraph stating their opinion and give evidence from their reading to support it.

3. **Comprehension Check.** Use the following matching exercise to determine whether students understand what they have read.

1. Hepburn Act	A. established Roosevelt's reputation as a military hero
2. Pure Food and Drug Act	B. ordered all companies to label their products honestly

3. Northern Securities Company

4. United Mine Workers Strike

5. Rough Riders

C. first labor dispute in which a President took an active role

D. increased the regulation of railroad companies

E. break-up of this monopoly established Roosevelt's reputation as a "trust buster"

ANSWERS: 1. D; 2. B; 3. E; 4. C; 5. A

4. **Studying Your History Vocabulary.** Review the "clues" for finding the meaning of terms as described in the Chapter 16 History Study Skill. Then, have students skim Section 2 to establish the meaning of the following terms: (A) welfare; (B) "bust;" (C) "square deal"; (D) leased.

BUILDING AMERICAN CITIZENSHIP

What characteristics did Roosevelt have that qualified him for the presidency of the United States? Section 2 stated that few Presidents before him possessed these same characteristics. Which past Presidents, do you think, had them? Which of our most recent Presidents, do you think, possessed these qualities? Give reasons for your selections.

SECTION 2 REVIEW ANSWERS

1. **IDENTIFY: Square Deal:** name given to Theodore Roosevelt's years in office, arising from the fair settlement of the coal strike of 1902; **Hepburn Act:** a 1906 law that gave the Interstate Commerce Commission greater control over the railroads by allowing inspection of a railroad company's accounts to determine the highest rates it could charge; **Pure Food and Drug Act:** 1906 law ordering all companies to label their products honestly; **Meat Inspection Act:** law requiring meat packers to keep their plants clean.

2. Applying the Sherman Antitrust Act, Roosevelt ordered the Justice Department to break up, or "bust," big monopolies, which led to suits by the federal government of 44 companies.

3. He called owners and union leaders to Washington and helped arrange a compromise.

SECTION 3: The Reform Movement Weakens

OBJECTIVES

After completing this section, students will be able to:
• Compare the personalities and achievements of Presidents Taft and Roosevelt.
• Describe the issues about which President Taft and Progressive reformers disagreed.
• Explain the reasons for Theodore Roosevelt's return to politics in 1910.

MOTIVATION

Use the following illustration. Think of an imaginary student whose older sister, now graduated, had attended the same school and had studied with most of the same teachers. This older sister had done just about *everything* right. Her grades were high, and she was involved in many afterschool activities. What might the teachers say to the imaginary student? (Why can't you be more like your older sister?)

Next, review the characteristics that made Roosevelt a good president, including his exceptional energy, his love of politics, his speaking ability. Ask students what problems any man elected to the presidency after Roosevelt might have. Tell them that they will be able to answer these questions after reading Section 3.

SUGGESTED ACTIVITIES

1. **Directed Reading.** As students read Section 3, have them answer the following questions:
   A. What were the major differences in personality between Taft and Roosevelt?
   B. Why did Taft become unpopular among Progressive reformers?
   C. In your opinion, what "mistakes" did Taft make?
   Discuss the answers to these questions. As a summary, ask students to state the positive actions taken by Taft to continue the reform movement.

2. **Research Activity.** Two prominent personalities are briefly described in this section, Gilbert Pinchot and Joseph Cannon. Ask students to prepare a written report on one of these individuals. Students should use library sources to investigate the public careers and private lives of these men so that they may better understand the conflicts that arose during Taft's administration.

3. **Time Line.** Have students study the time line in the textbook Chapter Opener. Ask them to try and select the events that occurred during Taft's administration. (There are none.) Using the previous activity, have them choose two important events from the section that they would include in the line. Ask them to state the reasons for their selection.

BUILDING AMERICAN CITIZENSHIP

As they did with Presidents Taft and Roosevelt, citizens often compare the performance of one public official with another. Can you think of any examples when this may have occurred in your community or state? What, in your opinion, is the purpose of such a comparison? (It often happens during political campaigns as voters try to make up their minds about whom to elect) Do you think such comparisons are fair to the individuals involved? Why? Why not?

p 560

10 ## SECTION 3 REVIEW ANSWERS

1. **IDENTIFY: Mann-Elkins Act:** law passed in 1910 increasing the power of the Interstate Commerce Commission enabling it to regulate telephone and telegraph companies as well as railroads; **Payne-Aldrich Tariff:** 1910 tariff that barely lowered rates but established a commission to study rate patterns; **Gilbert Pinchot:** chief of the United States Forest Service fired by President Taft for his constant criticism; **Joseph Cannon:**

powerful conservative Speaker of the House stripped of his power by Progressives, though supported by President Taft; **New Nationalism:** program introduced by Roosevelt in political speeches in 1910, calling for government regulation of industry and business and for programs to meet the needs of people at both the federal and state levels.

2. Taft brought 90 lawsuits against giant corporations and supported the passage of the Mann-Elkins Act.

3. Major disagreements involved tariff rates, returning land reserves for public sale, the firing of Gilbert Pinchot, and his support of conservatives in the 1910 Congressional elections.

4. Roosevelt was disappointed in Taft's conservative policies and returned to politics to support Progressive Republicans.

SECTION 4: Democrats Take Up the Fight for Reform

OBJECTIVES

After completing this section, students will be able to:
• State the reasons for the formation of the Progressive Party.
• Compare "New Nationalism" with "New Freedom."
• List and explain the major reforms introduced during President Wilson's first term of office.

MOTIVATION

Use pictures of Taft, Roosevelt, and Wilson (check the school library for these). Review the accomplishments of Roosevelt and Taft and the differences between them. Have students identify the year of the next Presidential election (1912) and tell them that Wilson was the third candidate in that election. Ask students to speculate on who would win it and why (at this point, they would probably say Roosevelt because of his popularity). Tell students that there will be a class discussion on the election, the winner, and his accomplishments as President after they have read Section 4.

SUGGESTED ACTIVITIES

1. **Directed Reading.** As students read, have them answer the following:
   A. What were the major goals of the Bull Moose Party?
   B. Who won the election of 1912? Why?
   C. What were the major accomplishments of the person elected in 1912?
   Review the answers to these questions when students have finished reading. In addition, you may wish to discuss the similarities and differences between Roosevelt and Wilson and between Wilson and Taft in terms of their personalities and political views. Be sure to compare Roosevelt's views of big business with those of Wilson.

2. **Writing Assignment.** To provide practice of the Chapter 23 History Study Skill, *Getting Information from Newspapers*, have students write a leading paragraph for each of the following headlines. Be sure

to tell them to include the 5W's and the H (Who, what, when, where, why, and how) as journalists would.
   A. "Roosevelt Walks Out; Taft Nominated"
   B. "Chicago Hosts Bull Moose Party"
   C. "New Freedom" Defeats "New Nationalism"
   D. "Big Business Unhappy With Presidential Policies"
   E. "Progressives Support New Tax Law"
   Below average students may be asked to select only two of these. You may wish to display the students' work in a bulletin board display.

3. **Landmarks of Liberty.** Have students read the selection on the Mount Rushmore National Memorial on textbook page 560. It is most appropriate for Section 4 since the reading provides an excellent point from which to review the accomplishments of Theodore Roosevelt. You might also ask students if they might have chosen other presidents for Mount Rushmore than those represented. They should be able to defend their selections.

4. **Acrostic.** Review the major accomplishments of Wilson's first administration by having students complete the following acrostic:

UnderWood Tariff	W - lowered import duties on 9,000 items
regulated competItion	I - Wilson's idea for making sure businesses competed fairly
CLayton Act	L - made it clear that labor unions were not to be prosecuted for holding back trade
Federal ReServe Act	S - created a centralized financial system for the U.S.
Federal Farm LOan Act	O - offered farmers loans at low interest rates
sixteeNth amendment	N - gave the federal government power to create an income tax

BUILDING AMERICAN CITIZENSHIP

In the election of 1912, voters seemed to make their choices along party lines. What does this mean? Do you think this happens in most Presidential elections? Give a reason for your answer.

SECTION 4 REVIEW ANSWERS

1. **IDENTIFY: "Bull Moose Party":** nickname given to the Progressive Party, formed in 1912; **New Freedom:** name given to Woodrow Wilson's reform program; **Underwood Tariff:** 1913 law lowering import duties on over 9,000 items; **Sixteenth Amendment:** amendment ratified in 1913 giving the federal government power to create an income tax; **Federal Reserve Act:** 1913 law that created the federal reserve system to centralize and stabilize the nation's financial system; **Federal Trade Commission:** created in 1914 to investigate corporations suspected of treating competitors unfairly; **Clayton Antitrust Act:** 1914 law that was stronger than the Sherman Antitrust Act, designed to regulate big business.

2. The party was formed because Roosevelt and his supporters refused to accept the renomination of Taft by the Republican Party.
3. Theodore Roosevelt believed big business was good for America but had to be regulated by government. Wilson favored small businesses because they gave more Americans chances to compete and prosper.
4. Wilson introduced tariff reform, an income tax, reform of the nation's banking system, and new measures such as the Federal Trade Commission to regulate big business.

SECTION 5: The Progressive Era Comes to an End

OBJECTIVES

After completing this section, students will be able to:
- Explain the arguments of the supporters and opponents of Prohibition.
- Explain the arguments of the supporters and opponents of women's suffrage.
- Describe the problems of blacks and immigrants during the late 19th and early 20th centuries.

MOTIVATION

Have students read the first paragraph of Section 5 to determine two movements in which Progressives were active and two movements which they largely ignored. List these on the blackboard. Then, divide students into four groups, and assign one of these movements to each group.

SUGGESTED ACTIVITIES

1. **Directed Reading.** Have students in each group read only that part of the section that deals with the movement to which they were assigned. When each group has finished, they are to discuss the following questions and prepare a brief report on their findings. Then, one member of each group should read the report to the class. Use Activity 2 as a summary.
   A. What were the major arguments offered by supporters and opponents of the movement?
   B. How successful was the movement in solving the problems of its people?
   C. Who were the leaders of the movement? (if any)
2. **Comprehension Check.** Place this exercise on the chalkboard or on a transparency for the overhead projector. If the statement is correct, have students place a check (✓) next to the statement. If it is incorrect, they should write nothing.
   A. America became "dry" with the ratification of the Eighteenth Amendment. (✓)
   B. The NAWSA worked for the vote, for better education, and for increased economic opportunities for women. (✓)
   C. Prior to 1900, most Americans opposed the women's suffrage movement. (✓)
   D. Booker T. Washington and William E.B. DuBois demanded an end to segregation and equal rights for all Americans. (No check)

E. Progressives tried to have laws passed to help immigrants get better housing and higher wages. (No check)
3. **Reading for the Main Idea.** Duplicate Worksheet 68, *Booker T. Washington.* The activity is designed to review the Chapter 5 History Study Skill while simultaneously providing additional information on one of America's best-known black leaders. As an extension activity you may wish to challenge above-average students to do research on the life of William E.B. DuBois and to create a similar activity using the details of his life.
4. **Picture Study.** Use the picture in Section 5 to assist students in reviewing the material on the women's suffrage movement. Ask the kinds of questions used in the History Study Skill Activity on textbook page 575 to help students interpret the photograph. For example: How many people are in the picture? What do they seem to be doing? How is this picture related to what you have read about the women's suffrage movement?
5. **Reading Photographs.** Duplicate Worksheet 67, *Sweatshops.* Have students study the photograph and answer the questions that follow. Relate the picture to the information in Section 5 by asking students to describe the attitudes of Progressives and other Americans toward immigrants.

BUILDING AMERICAN CITIZENSHIP

Identify the areas of the world from which immigrants have come in recent years. (Cuba, Haiti, Mexico, Southeast Asia) Review the arguments given by opponents of immigration in the 19th century. Ask students if some American citizens today still have the same concerns about immigrants. (Many do. They worry about jobs needed by Americans, the willingness of immigrants to work for low pay, and so on) Ask students to suggest a policy that our government might adopt to help solve immigration problems.

SECTION 5 REVIEW ANSWERS

1. **IDENTIFY: Prohibition:** forbidding the drinking of alcoholic beverages; **Eighteenth Amendment:** amendment ratified in 1919 making it illegal to manufacture, sell, or transport alcoholic beverages; **Carrie Chapman:** president of the National American Woman Suffrage Association who, in 1916, developed a plan for getting the vote for women; **Nineteenth Amendment:** amendment ratified in 1920 stating that citizens could not be denied the right to vote on account of sex; **Booker T. Washington:** former slave who founded Tuskegee Institute in 1881 to help train black workers for skilled jobs; **William E. B. Du Bois:** black leader who in 1905 established the "Niagara Movement," demanding an end to the separation of races; **National Association for the Advancement of Colored People (NAACP):** an organization created in 1909 by Du Bois and a group of white Progressives to demand equal rights for blacks.
2. People thought that politics should be left to men, that women should play the role of "wife" and "mother"; white Southerners feared that women voters might support equal rights for blacks; some feared that women

would support Prohibition; business owners feared that women would vote to improve working conditions and raise wages for workers.
3. Catt's plan was to work for passage of a national constitutional amendment and to work in each state to win the support of members of Congress.
4. Blacks worked to gain more skills and to make their needs known to all Americans. Booker T. Washington founded the Tuskegee Institute to train black workers, and William E. B. Du Bois worked for black equality by establishing the "Niagara Movement" and, with a group of white Progressives, the NAACP.

pp 576-577

21

CHAPTER 24 REVIEW ANSWERS

REVIEWING KEY WORDS

1. c.   2. a.   3. e.   4. d.   5. b.

REMEMBERING IMPORTANT PEOPLE AND EVENTS

1. c.   2. c.   3. a.   4. a.   5. b.
6. a.   7. d.   8. b.   9. c.   10. c.

REVIEWING THE FACTS

1. T   2. T   3. F   4. T   5. F

PLACING EVENTS IN TIME

1. E *4*   2. C *5*   3. D *2*   4. A *3*   5. B *1*

LINKING GEOGRAPHY AND HISTORY

In the East, state and city governments were run by political machines where reform candidates had little chance of winning. Only in the West did "bosses" have little control.

THINKING ABOUT AMERICAN HISTORY

1. lumber
2. Roosevelt set aside many forests as federal reserves.
3. air, water, and fuels such as coal and oil
4. the Environmental Protection Agency, which falls under the jurisdiction of the Department of the Interior

APPLYING HISTORY STUDIES SKILLS

1. They are first-hand accounts of events. They show scenes clearly and often capture the feelings of the people involved.
2. Answers will vary.
3. Answers will vary.

CHAPTER 25

Americans Gain Power in World Affairs (1890-1914)

Chapter Objectives

After completing this chapter, students will be able to:
1. Explain what motivated Americans to get involved in world affairs.
2. Identify causes, events, and results of the Spanish-American War.

3. Describe how Americans extended their power and influence in Asia.
4. List in order key events in the development and building of the Panama Canal.
5. Explain why America assumed the role of "guardian" of the Western Hemisphere.

Chapter Chronology

Chapter 25 discusses America's first forays into world affairs in the post-Civil War years and describes how our nation became a great power by the eve of World War I. The time line in the textbook Chapter Opener highlights some of the major international developments of the period. In 1895, rebellion against Spain broke out in Cuba. Three years later, in 1898, the United States declared war against Spain and the Spanish-American War began. In that same year, the United States annexed Hawaii. In 1899, America announced the Open Door policy in China. Shortly thereafter, in 1900, the Boxer Rebellion occurred in China. Events in the Caribbean led Roosevelt, in 1904, to issue the Roosevelt Corollary, a further extension of the Monroe Doctrine. In 1908, the United States entered into a Gentlemen's Agreement with Japan to halt Japanese immigration to America. Unrest in China continued, and 11 years after the Boxer Rebellion there, a political revolution took place in 1911. Back in the Western Hemisphere, 1914 saw the completion of the Panama Canal.

Motivation

Use a large wall map of the world to introduce students to the main theme of Chapter 25—expansion. Start with the time line in the textbook Chapter Opener. Have students read each event and then locate each place on the map. Have them keep in mind the "action" surrounding each event, such as Cuba rebels, war begins, and so on. Next, have students look at the photos in the chapter. Ask students to locate each place named and also to note the "action" involved. After this survey of place geography and events, students will be ready for the textbook Chapter Introduction.

Geographical Setting

Virtually all of the major events in Chapter 25 are related to geography. Far-flung trade routes required coaling stations and naval protection—hence, our interest in Samoa and Hawaii. Foreign influence in the Western Hemisphere threatened American security—hence, the purchase of Alaska; the continuing applications of the Monroe Doctrine to the Caribbean; and the fighting of the Spanish-American War. The desire to control a connecting link between the Atlantic and Pacific oceans prompted building of the Panama Canal.

The map *The Spanish-American War in the Caribbean, 1898* on textbook page 585 provides students with a good opportunity to pinpoint the area of that conflict in the Caribbean. The map *United States Possessions in 1900* on textbook page 587 shows American possessions worldwide and is particularly good for reinforcement of locational geography. The *Panama Canal Zone* map on textbook page 592 helps students visualize the effect of the canal. This is a good chapter for students to practice many of the skills they have learned so far.

133

History Study Skills

The History Study Skill introduced in Chapter 25 is *Locating Places on Maps.* Students will learn this skill in conjunction with the map *United States Possessions in 1900,* so the activity should be done after Section 2. You might prefer to use this activity as a summary of the chapter, thus providing reinforcement of most of the places mentioned in it.

Bibliography

Teacher References

Dobson, John, *America's Ascent: The United States Becomes a Great Power, 1880-1914.* Northern Illinois University Press, DeKalb, Ill., 1978.

Healy, David, *U.S. Expansionism.* University of Wisconsin Press, Madison, Wis., 1970.

Student References

Madison, Arnold, *American Global Diplomacy, 1800-1950.* Franklin Watts, New York City, 1977. The evolution of two dominant themes of American foreign policy—isolationism and imperialism—are traced in this survey.

Walsh, John E., *The Philippine Insurrection, 1899-1902.* Franklin Watts, New York City, 1973. This is an in-depth study of America's war with Filipino rebels, who wanted their independence following the Spanish-American War in 1898.

Audio-Visual Materials

The U.S. Becomes a World Power, McGraw Films, black and white, 25 minutes. This film analyzes events that led up to the Spanish-American War and also the results of that war.

The Age of Theodore Roosevelt, Guidance Associates, 3 filmstrips, 3 cassettes, library kit, teacher's guide. This program, which focuses on Roosevelt's life—his youth, young adult life, and his presidency—also contains much information on his foreign policy.

SECTION 1: America Enters World Affairs

OBJECTIVES

After completing this section, students will be able to:
* List the reasons for America's growing interest in world affairs.
* Explain how the United States acquired Alaska and Hawaii.
* Describe European challenges to the Monroe Doctrine in the late 19th century.

MOTIVATION

Use the Motivation suggested in the chapter introduction in this manual. This will provide students with a general overview of the chapter's contents. Then, have them read the Chapter Introduction on textbook page 579. Ask students to describe why the United States wanted Samoa and why the Samoans were willing to sign a treaty with America. Tell students that, after reading Section 1, they should be able to explain why the United

States became involved in world affairs. They should also be able to name seven areas of the world in which the United States became involved.

SUGGESTED ACTIVITIES

1. **Directed Reading.** As students read, have them answer the following questions:
   A. Why did the United States want to expand its power in the world?
   B. Name seven areas of the world in which the United States became involved between 1865 and 1900.
   Discuss the answers to these questions. As students list the seven areas in question, ask them to locate each one on an appropriate wall map or the map, *United States Possessions in 1900* on textbook page 587. These should include Alaska, Midway, Japan, China, Hawaii, Mexico, and Venezuela. Also, discuss why the United States became involved in those areas.

2. **Matching Exercise.** Use the following matching exercise to help students identify the individuals involved in America's expansion at this time. You may place it on the chalkboard or on a transparency for the overhead projector.

A. Alaska	1. Matthew Perry
B. China	2. Grover Cleveland
C. Japan	3. Sanford Dole
D. Hawaii	4. William Seward
E. Mexico	5. Andrew Johnson
F. Venezuela	6. Queen Liliuokalani
G. Midway	7. Emperor Maximilian

ANSWERS: (A) 4; (B) 4; (C) 1; (D) 6 and 3; (E) 4, 5, and 7; (F) 2; (G) 4

3. **Map Exercise.** Use the same map as in Activity 1 to help students answer the following questions. This activity is an extension of the skill exercise used in the section review. Have students apply their knowledge of cardinal and intermediate directions used to travel:
   A. From Japan to Hawaii (SE)
   B. From Hawaii to Midway (NW)
   C. From Venezuela to Washington, D.C. (N)
   D. From Alaska to Hawaii (SW)
   E. From Japan to China (E)

4. **Identification of Areas of Influence.** Use a chalkmap of the world or a transparency of an outline map of the world. Place a number on the location of each of the areas in which the United States became involved. Have students consult the above-mentioned map in their textbook to identify the areas. Then, have them close the book and repeat the exercise using the outline map. You may also make flashcards with the names of the seven areas and pass these out to students. Have them bring the appropriate flash card to the outline map and hold it on the number identifying the correct location.

BUILDING AMERICAN CITIZENSHIP

"Should the United States be allowed to acquire territory outside its own borders to increase its power in the world?" How would American citizens in the late 19th century have answered this question? How do you think today's American citizens would answer this question?

SECTION 1 REVIEW ANSWERS

1. **IDENTIFY: William Seward:** American Secretary of State who believed America should become a world power; responsible for the purchase of Alaska in 1867; **Queen Liliuokalani:** queen of Hawaii, overthrown by American settlers in 1893; **Sanford Dole:** American president of the Republic of Hawaii.
2. The purchase of Alaska was known as "Seward's folly."
3. America was looking for new foreign markets in which to sell its products; it wanted to find new sources of raw materials; it wanted to become a world leader.
4. Americans rebelled because when Queen Liliuokalani took power, she forced a new constitution taking away the power of Americans.

SECTION 2: America Fights a War with Spain

OBJECTIVES

After completing this section, students will be able to:
- Explain the causes of the Spanish-American War.
- Name and locate the important battles of the Spanish-American War.
- Identify the territories acquired by the United States as a result of the war.
- Describe the methods use by the United States to govern its overseas territories.

MOTIVATION

Discuss the concept of the war with emphasis on the question: Why do nations go to war? Ask students to consider what they have learned in Section 1. Then suggest reasons why the United States might go to war in the late 19th century. Have them read Section 2 to determine the correctness of their responses.

SUGGESTED ACTIVITIES

1. **Directed Reading.** As students read Section 2, have them complete an outline of the material, using the section title as their outline title. You may wish to provide the main topics, which are as follows:

   I. Causes of the War   III. Results of the War
   II. Events of the War

   When students have completed the assignment, have them write their topics and subtopics on the chalkboard. This will provide a good means of checking the information as well as outline style and form, including correct capitalization, punctuation, and indentation.
2. **Locating Places on Maps.** Use the History Study Skill activity on textbook page 597. This exercise allows students to practice the skill of locating lines of latitude and longitude. Students are to apply it to the information they acquired in Section 2. You may wish to provide additional practice by using the map from Section 1, Activies 1, 3, and 4. Select points in each of the seven areas. Then have students identify the lines of latitude and longitude.
3. **Improving Your History Writing.** Duplicate Worksheet 70, *The Spanish-American War.* Have

students review the Chapter 10 History Study Skill activity before beginning the assignment. You may wish to add a sixth topic sentence: "Today, the treaty ending the Spanish-American War was signed." The clue would be, "What did it say?"
4. **Cause and Effect.** Review the meaning of these terms. A "cause" is what makes something happen; an "effect" is a result. Have students identify each of the following as a CAUSE or EFFECT of the Spanish-American War.
   A. The Filipino Revolt of 1899 (E)
   B. Cuba gaining its independence (E)
   C. Newspaper stories about shocking events in Cuba (C)
   D. Sinking of the Battleship *Maine* (C)
   E. Death of thousands of Cubans in unsanitary camps (C)
   F. America gaining control of Puerto Rico (E)

   You may also wish to use these events to have students complete a sequencing activity. Have them place the events in the order in which they appeared in the section.

BUILDING AMERICAN CITIZENSHIP

Duplicate Worksheet 69, *Respecting the Rights of All Peoples.* The first part of the activity requires students to review material from Section 1 and to consider the effects of United States policy regarding Hawaii. The second part of the activity requires students to apply critical thinking skills to their knowledge of the Spanish-American War and its results.

SECTION 2 REVIEW ANSWERS

1. **IDENTIFY: José Marti:** leader of a Cuban rebellion against Spain in 1895; *Maine:* American battleship blown up in Havana harbor in 1898; **Commodore George Dewey:** leader of a successful American naval attack on Spain's Pacific fleet during the Spanish-American War; **Rough Riders:** a volunteer cavalry unit recruited by Theodore Roosevelt to fight in Cuba; **Emilio Aquinaldo:** leader of a Philippine rebellion against American occupation; **Platt Amendment:** amendment passed in 1901 giving the United States power to guard Cuban independence, to prevent Cuba from making treaties with foreign powers, and to set up naval bases in Cuba.
2. **DEFINE: imperialist nation:** a nation that rules over colonies or territories; **neutrality:** policy of not taking sides in a dispute; **protectorate:** a nation dependent on the protection of another nation.
3. America went to war against Spain in 1898 because the American people demanded it. Americans were angry about the sinking of the *Maine,* Spanish treatment of Cubans, and the destruction of American property in Cuba.
4. The Philippines, Guam, and Puerto Rico.

SECTION 3: America Becomes Involved in Asia

OBJECTIVES

After completing this section, students will be able to:
- Explain the "Open Door" Policy.

135

- Describe the "Boxer Rebellion."
- Describe American involvement with Japan during the first decade of the 20th century.
- Identify the reasons for the decline of American trade in Asia.

MOTIVATION

Review the locations of the Asian nations with which the United States had become involved and also the reasons for this involvement. Introduce the terms "Boxer Rebellion," "Chinese Revolution," "Open Door Policy," "Gentleman's Agreement," and "Russian-Japanese War." Tell students that they will learn how the above are related to the Asian nations with which the United States became involved.

SUGGESTED ACTIVITIES

1. **Directed Reading.** As students read, have them complete the following chart, using the five events identified in the Motivation as their entries for column 1:

EVENT   ASIAN NATION INVOLVED   DATE   DESCRIPTION

To check student responses, place the chart on the chalkboard and have students write in all entries. As a summary activity, have the students arrange the events in chronological order.

2. **Landmarks of Liberty.** Have students read the selection, *San Diego's Floating Museum* on textbook page 583 and answer the questions at the end. In addition, use the textbook map or chalkmap to have them identify the United States possessions in the Pacific that might have been regular stops of ships like the *Star of India* on voyages from San Diego to Asia. (Hawaii, Guam, and the Philippines)

3. **History Study Skills.** Have students state the location of San Diego using lines of latitude and longitude. Then distribute copies of Worksheet 71, *Major American Cities*. Ask students which other West coast cities probably served as major ports for trade between the United States and Asian countries. (San Francisco and Seattle) Then, have students review the study skill by answering the questions beneath the map.

4. **Comprehension Check.** To determine whether or not students understand what they have read, utilize the following TRUE-FALSE exercise. Have them correct FALSE statements to make them true.
   A. Admiral Alfred T. Mahan was responsible for the "Open Door" policy. (F)
   B. The Boxer Rebellion was a Japanese revolt against foreigners in their nation. (F)
   C. Theodore Roosevelt helped end the Russian-Japanese War. (T)
   D. Japanese immigration was halted by a Congressional law passed in 1918. (F)
   E. American trade in Asia declined because the risks and costs were too great. (T)

BUILDING AMERICAN CITIZENSHIP

Section 3 describes American involvement in the affairs of China and Japan. Do you think what the United States did was good for the citizens of China? Do you think what the United States did was good for the citizens of Japan? Explain your answers to these questions.

SECTION 3 REVIEW ANSWERS

1. **IDENTIFY: Alfred Thayer Mahan:** American naval officer and adviser who called for the United States to strengthen its naval power to protect American business interests abroad; **"Open Door" Policy:** policy proposed by American Secretary of State John Hay for equal trading rights for all nations in all areas of China, including the trading areas claimed by foreigners; **Boxer Rebellion:** an unsuccessful attempt in 1900 by Chinese secret societies to drive all foreigners out of China: **Gentlemen's Agreement:** a private agreement between President Roosevelt and Japan in which Japan agreed to voluntarily restrict the flow of Japanese workers into California to prevent passage of a law by Congress excluding Japanese immigration.

2. When President McKinley was assassinated in September 1901, Vice-President Roosevelt became President.

3. At first, the Chinese were forced to accept foreign control. Later, they began forming secret societies to drive the foreigners out.

4. The Japanese were dissatisfied with the 1905 treaty ending the Russian-Japanese War. They resented American business competition in Asia. Americans were upset about Japan's growing military and economic power and about the flood of Japanese immigrants into the United States from Japan.

SECTION 4: America Builds the Panama Canal

OBJECTIVES

After completing this section, students will be able to:
- Describe the political difficulties that had to be overcome before the Panama Canal was built.
- List the construction and health problems that had to be solved while building the Panama Canal.

MOTIVATION

Have students study the picture of the Panama Canal on textbook page 593. Ask them what they can learn about the Canal from the picture. Can they describe: What it looked like? Where it was built? When it was built? Why it was built? What problems were encountered in building it? Explain that Section 4 will answer the questions about the Canal which the picture cannot provide.

SUGGESTED ACTIVITIES

1. **Directed Reading.** Have students answer the following questions as they read Section 4.
   A. Why did the United States want to build a canal?
   B. How did the United States get the land that was needed to build a canal?
   C. What do you think was the biggest problem that the builders had to solve? Give a reason for your answer.

   Review the answers to the questions. Please note that question "C" requires students to give an opinion. Any of the problems may form a basis for their answer as long as a reason is given.

2. **History Study Skills.** Have students refer to the map, *The Panama Canal Zone* on textbook page 592 to locate Panama. Then have them refer to the map, *United States Possessions in 1900,* on textbook page 587 to state the location of the Canal using latitude and longitude.
3. **Research Activity.** There are three people, George W. Goethals, William Gorgas, and Walter Reed, without whom the Panama Canal could not have been built. Have students select one of the three and prepare a brief report concerning his contributions to the building of the canal.

   Average and above-average students might use library resources for this assignment. Below-average students might use the information in the textbook only to identify the contribution of each man.
4. **Studying Your History Vocabulary.** Have students apply the Chapter 16 History Study Skill to determine the meaning of the following words used in Section 4: isthmus, canal, locks, and elevation.

BUILDING AMERICAN CITIZENSHIP

American citizens criticized Theodore Roosevelt's interference in the affairs of Colombia to obtain the Canal Zone. Yet, the Panama Canal brought many benefits to the United States and other nations of the world. Do you think Roosevelt was right in his action toward Colombia? How else do you think the problem of acquiring land for a canal could have been solved?

SECTION 4 REVIEW ANSWERS

1. **IDENTIFY: George W. Goethals:** American army engineer who directed the construction of the Panama Canal; **Colonel William Gorgas:** army doctor in charge of public health in the Canal Zone who wiped out yellow fever and learned how to protect people against malaria.
2. **DEFINE: isthmus:** a narrow strip of land that separates two bodies of water.
3. To provide a waterway to connect the Atlantic and Pacific oceans.
4. Agreements had to be reached with Britain, the French company that owned building rights, and after Panamanian independence from Colombia, with the government of Panama.

SECTION 5: America Guards the Western Hemisphere

OBJECTIVES

After completing this section, students will be able to:
- Compare and contrast "Big Stick Diplomacy," "Dollar Diplomacy," and "Missionary Diplomacy."
- Describe the conflicts between Mexico and the United States.
- Explain the benefits and problems associated with the United States becoming a world power.

MOTIVATION

Have students recall the important features of the Monroe Doctrine. If necessary, refer them to Chapter 11,

Section 5. Ask students which nations challenged the Monroe Doctrine in the later 1800's. Have them skim the end of Section 1 to refresh their memory. Tell them that Theodore Roosevelt added to the doctrine while he was President, and that they will find out about this addition in Section 5.

SUGGESTED ACTIVITIES

1. **Directed Reading.** As students read the section, have them complete the following table. One sample is provided below.

PRESIDENT	METHODS	NATION(S) INVOLVED	OUTCOME
T. Roosevelt	"Big Stick Diplomacy"	Dominican Republic	Took temporary control of finances; later withdrew

   Place the column headings on the chalkboard and have students complete their entries. As a summary, discuss the differences and similarities among the types of diplomacy favored by the Presidents.
2. **History Study Skills.** Apply the History Study Skill for Chapter 25 by providing students with a list of points of latitude and longitude for each of the areas included on their table. Using the map *United States Possessions in 1900* on textbook page 587, have them locate and identify those areas. Include the following: Dominican Republic, Haiti, Nicaragua, Cuba, and Veracruz, Mexico.
3. **Chronology.** Review the Chapter 19 History Study Skill. Then have students place the following events in chronological order:
   A. President Wilson sent the American Navy to seize Veracruz.
   B. President Taft sent Marines to Nicaragua.
   C. President Wilson sent Marines to Haiti.
   D. The Roosevelt Corollary was first used in the Dominican Republic.
   E. Pancho Villa led a raid into New Mexico.
   ANSWERS: D - B - A - C - E

BUILDING AMERICAN CITIZENSHIP

You have just finished reading about America's expanded role as a world power. During this period, the United States interfered in the affairs of many nations. Should our nation have done this? Was it lawful? Why did American citizens allow this interference to continue? (National pride in the nation's accomplishments) How could the interference have been stopped? (Elect candidates who promised not to do it.)

SECTION 5 REVIEW ANSWERS

1. **IDENTIFY: Roosevelt Corollary:** added meaning given the Monroe Doctrine by President Roosevelt stating that the United States has the duty to act as an "international police power" in the Western Hemisphere; **Dollar Diplomacy:** President Taft's policy of investing money in Latin American nations to bring progress to those nations and drive out European influence; **Victoriano Huerta:** leader of Mexico forced from power as a result of political and military pressure from the United

States and the ABC Powers; **Pancho Villa:** Mexican rebel who led a raid into the United States in 1917 in an effort to cause trouble between the two nations; **General Pershing:** leader of the United States troops sent to Mexico to find Villa.

2. **DEFINE: diplomacy:** the management of relations between nations.
3. Roosevelt's two main goals were to keep control of the Panama Canal and enforce the Monroe Doctrine in the Western Hemisphere.
4. To stop a German ship from delivering arms to Huerta.

CHAPTER 25 REVIEW ANSWERS

REVIEWING KEY WORDS

| 1. e. | 2. d. | 3. c. | 4. a. | 5. b. |

REMEMBERING IMPORTANT PEOPLE AND EVENTS

| 1. a. | 2. c. | 3. e. | 4. d. | 5. b. |
| 6. b. | 7. e. | 8. d. | 9. c. | 10. a. |

REVIEWING THE FACTS

| 1. C | 2. P | 3. P | 4. P | 5. C |

PLACING EVENTS IN TIME

| 1. A | 2. D | 3. C | 4. B | 5. E |

LINKING GEOGRAPHY AND HISTORY

1. Panama is located on an isthmus, a narrow strip of land that separates the Atlantic and Pacific oceans. Roosevelt chose Panama because it provided a short route for the canal.
2. Spain had to transport troops and materials a much greater distance.

THINKING ABOUT AMERICAN HISTORY

1. It brought new markets for their products and new sources of raw materials.
2. Answers will vary.

APPLYING HISTORY STUDIES SKILLS

1. 20°N, 170°E.	2. 15°N, 145°E.
3. 15°S, 165°W.	4. 18°N, 67°W.
5. 20°N, 160°W.	

CHAPTER 26

America Enters World War I (1914-1920)

Chapter Objectives

After completing this chapter, students will be able to:
1. Explain how war broke out in Europe.
2. Describe the efforts of the United States to avoid war.
3. Identify ways in which the war changed the lives of Americans.
4. Evaluate the impact of America's participation on the outcome of the war.
5. Describe Wilson's efforts to create a lasting peace.

Chapter Chronology

Chapter 26 covers the events leading to the outbreak of World War I, the war itself, America's growing involvement and final participation in it, and its end and aftermath. The time line in the textbook Chapter Opener traces major events of these years. Austrian Archduke Franz Ferdinand was assassinated in 1914. This event precipitated World War I, which started a few weeks later. One year later, in 1915, the British luxury liner the *Lusitania* was sunk by the Germans. In 1916, Wilson was reelected President. In 1917, Wilson asked Congress to declare war on Germany, and the nation entered into World War I. Americans were drafted and went overseas to fight. The armistice declared by the Allies and the Germans late in 1918 ended the war, and soon thereafter, Wilson announced his Fourteen Points program. In the next year, Congress rejected Wilson's proposal for a League of Nations.

Motivation

Ask students to read the Chapter Introduction on textbook page 601 on the assassination of Archduke Franz Ferdinand. Have them think back on assassinations that have occurred in American history:

Lincoln 1865	Kennedy 1963
Garfield 1881	King 1968
McKinley 1901	

Ask students what happened after each of these assassinations. Were there riots, rebellions? Ask students if they think the assassination of Archduke Franz Ferdinand was really a *cause* of World War I or an excuse taken by countries that had been ready to go to war for some time before.

Geographical Setting

Chapter 26 deals primarily with events in Europe and the United States during World War I. The major geographical focus is on the European nations that went to war. The map *Europe in World War I, 1914-1918* illustrates the opposing sides in World War I and their specific military activities. This is a good place to review military map skills developed in Chapter 18 with maps of the Civil War. The map *Europe After World War I* illustrates some of the dramatic changes that resulted from the conflict. This is a good place to review the skill of comparing historical maps, introduced in Chapter 7.

History Study Skills

The History Study Skill introduced in Chapter 26 is *Recognizing Propaganda*. The propaganda used, which dates from the World War I period, was designed to influence Americans to join the war. The best place to use this activity is in conjunction with Section 2. This is where students will read about the pressure put on Americans to go to war on the side of the Allies.

Bibliography

Teacher References

Graham, Otis L., *The Great Campaigns: Reform and War in America, 1900-1928.* Kreiger, Melbourne, Fla., 1971.

Hardach, Gerd. *The First World War, 1914-1918.* University of California Press, Berkeley, Calif., 1977.

Link, Arthur, *Woodrow Wilson: Revolution, War, and Peace.* Harper, New York City, 1979.

Student References

Dupuy, Trevor, *Stalemate in the Trenches, November 1914-March, 1918.* Franklin Watts, New York City, 1967. This military history describes the horrors of trench warfare in World War I and includes detailed descriptions of such major battles of the Western front as Verdun.

This Fabulous Century, Vol. II, 1910-1920, Time-Life Books, New York City, 1970. America at war is well illustrated in this volume. Information on the home front and the battlegrounds is included.

Audio-Visual Materials

U.S. Neutrality, Films Inc., black and white, 14 minutes. This film shows most of the major events that led to the entry of the United States into World War I.

World War I, Educational Enrichment Materials, 1 sound filmstrip. This filmstrip is chronologically organized, from prewar politics through postwar peace initiatives.

SECTION 1: Europe Goes to War

OBJECTIVES

After completing this section, students will be able to:
- Identify the reasons why World War I began.
- Name and locate the European nations that became involved in World War I.
- Describe the reactions of the American government and citizens to the outbreak of World War I.
- Explain how the opposing armies became involved in trench warfare.

MOTIVATION

Use the Motivation suggested in the introduction to Chapter 26 in this manual. Have students speculate about the assassination of Archduke Franz Ferdinand as a cause of war. Tell them that they will be able to answer the question with a greater degree of certainty when they have finished reading Section 1.

SUGGESTED ACTIVITIES

1. **Directed Reading.** As students read, have them write a sentence or two telling how each of the following contributed to the outbreak of World War I.
   A. The System of Alliances
   B. Nationalism
   C. Imperialism
   D. Assassination of Archduke Franz Ferdinand
   Review the sentences students wrote to determine their understanding of the above. As a summary, return to the question posed during the Motivation. Have students speculate about what might have happened without any one of these elements. For example, suppose there had been no system of alliances.

2. **Map Study.** A knowledge of the geography of Europe is essential if students are to understand World War I. Therefore, have students study the map *Europe in World War I, 1914-1918* on textbook page 604 to identify the nations of the Triple Alliance, the nations of the Triple Entente, and the nations that remained neutral. Help the class in locating these nations in the following ways:
   A. Cut out silhouettes of the nations and place them, in isolation, on the overhead projector for students to identify.
   B. Use a blank chalkmap and point to specific nations so that students can name them.
   C. Use a transparency of an outline map of Europe on which students may write the names of the countries.
   D. Provide students with a blank outline map of Europe on which to label each nation and create a key.
   One or all of these activities can be utilized to reinforce geographical relationships.

3. **Interpreting Maps.** Duplicate Worksheet 72, *Neutrality and World War I.* The exercise will require students to apply the knowledge gained in the previous activity. Students should NOT be allowed to use their textbook or any other references to assist them.

4. **Discussion.** Two topics that were not incorporated in the directed reading could form the basis for a class discussion.
   A. How did the American government and American citizens react to the war? Was there any difference between the government's attitude and that of the citizens?
   B. Why did the fighting in World War I become "trench warfare"? How did attitudes toward "trench warfare" lead to America being affected by the war?

BUILDING AMERICAN CITIZENSHIP

Recall the definition of the term "compromise." Why do you think the nations of Europe were unable, or unwilling, to solve their differences through compromises? Do you think the citizens of those nations were able to influence the decisions made by their leaders? Explain your answer.

p. 605

1b

SECTION 1 REVIEW ANSWERS

1. **IDENTIFY: Triple Entente:** alliance of Russia, France, and Great Britain; **Triple Alliance:** alliance of Austria-Hungary, Germany, and Italy; **Gavrilo Princip:** Serbian nationalist who assassinated Archduke Francis Ferdinand and his wife Sophie; **Central Powers:** Germany, the Ottoman Empire, and Austria-Hungary; **Allies:** Great Britain, France, Russia, and the United States; **Schlieffen Plan:** German strategy for quick conquest of France so that its armies would be free to attack Russia.

2. **DEFINE: balance of power:** groups of European nations tied together by treaties to defend each other in case of attack; **ultimatum:** demands that must be met to avoid war; **mobilize:** to prepare for war; **neutral:** not taking sides in a war; **trench warfare:** in World War I, 600 miles

of parallel ditches from which the Allied and German armies attacked each other; **contraband:** war materials carried by neutral ships to warring nations, forbidden by international law.

3. The Serbian plea for Russian help brought Russia into the war, which in turn brought Germany, thus activating the balance of power and bringing in other nations bound by treaties to defend each other.

4. It was difficult for the United States to remain neutral because 32 million Americans were foreign-born or were children of immigrants.

5. *Dove & olive branch*

SECTION 2: America Tries to Stay Out of the War

OBJECTIVES

After completing this section, students will be able to:
- List developments that helped move America closer to the Allies during 1914 and 1915.
- Explain how America began preparing for war.
- Identify the events that led to the American declaration of war against Germany.

MOTIVATION

When the war began, what was the government's official position regarding United States involvement? (Neutrality) However, the United States did eventually go to war. Why? What events between 1914 and 1917 led to American involvement? Ask students to read the headings in boldface type to get ideas. (List these on the board.) Have students read the section and then add to the list when they are finished.

SUGGESTED ACTIVITIES

1. **Directed Reading.** Use the following questions to guide students' reading of Section 2:
   A. Why were Americans so concerned about German submarine attacks?
   B. Why did some American leaders oppose the preparedness movement?
   C. What steps were taken by President Wilson to try to avoid war?
   Review the answers to these questions with students. In addition, return to the partial list of events recorded during the motivation. Add others the students read about, discussing each event. Use Activity 2 below as a summary.

2. **Putting Events in Chronological Order.** Review and apply the Chapter 19 History Study Skill by having students arrange the following events in chronological order:
   A. The Zimmerman Note is published.
   B. Germany issues the "Sussex Pledge."
   C. The Lusitania is sunk.
   D. Congress declares war on Germany.
   E. Woodrow Wilson is reelected.
   ANSWERS: C - B - E - A - D

3. **History Study Skills.** Have students complete the activity for this chapter's History Study Skill, *Recognizing Propaganda*, on textbook page 622. This exercise may stimulate interest in World War I pro-

paganda posters. Encourage students to use library sources to find other examples, which may be copied or drawn for display in the classroom. You may also wish to suggest to students that they draw their own posters. Have other class members attempt to identify the themes of the posters, the nations they support, and their messages.

4. **Improving Your History Writing.** Have students review the Chapter 10 History Study Skill. Then ask them to write a paragraph answering the following question: Why did the United States declare war on Germany?

BUILDING AMERICAN CITIZENSHIP

The American debate about Germany's submarine warfare in 1915 presented a serious problem: Which is more important—the right of American citizens to travel without restriction, or the government's responsibility to save lives by restricting the freedom of citizens to travel? How would you solve this problem?

SECTION 2 REVIEW ANSWERS

1. **IDENTIFY:** *Lusitania:* British passenger ship sunk by German U-Boats, killing 128 Americans; **"Sussex pledge":** a German promise in 1916 not to sink another ship without warning; **Charles Evans Hughes:** Supreme Court Justice who was the unsuccessful Republican candidate in the presidential election of 1916; **Colonel Edward House:** close friend of President Wilson who was sent on an unsuccessful peace mission to Europe in 1916; **Zimmerman note:** secret German message to Mexico from Germany proposing an alliance between the two nations.

2. It started with a preparedness movement in the United States and ended with approval by Congress of an increase in military spending.

3. In response to Germany's renewal of surprise attacks on Allied and neutral ships.

4. Disclosure of the Zimmerman note to Mexico and the sinking of three American ships by German submarines.

SECTION 3: The War Changes the American Nation

OBJECTIVES

After completing this section, students will be able to:
- List the changes in the American nation that resulted from our entry into the war.
- Describe the efforts taken to mobilize the nation.
- Explain how the war affected the lives of women, blacks, and Mexican Americans.
- Describe the action taken by supporters and opponents of the war.

MOTIVATION

Write the following on the chalkboard: LIBERTY, CABBAGE and SALISBURY STEAK. Ask students if they know what these things are and how they are related to World War I. (They will probably say "Food that the soldiers were given to eat.") Tell them that they should be able to identify the connection between the foods and World War I by the end of the lesson. (Anti-German propagandists changed the names of sauerkraut and hamburger to the above.)

SUGGESTED ACTIVITIES

1. **Directed Reading.** Below are four scrambled sentences which, if properly written and organized in sequence, will provide an overview of the lesson. Place them on the chalkboard or on a transparency for the overhead projector. Have students read Section 3, unscramble the sentences, and place them in sequential order. (Clue: The first word of each sentence is capitalized)

   A. women opportunities blacks Mexican new war Americans The opened for end (The war opened new opportunities for women, blacks, and Mexican-Americans.)

   B. men, weapons, Mobilizing supplies to and to send food ships Europe involved organizing America (Mobilizing America involved organizing men, ships, weapons, food, and supplies to send to Europe.)

   C. propaganda anything German The on Public found Information in Waged America a against campaign Committee (The Committee on Public Information waged a propaganda campaign against anything German found in America.)

   D. war Wilson the against President not Americans protested who tolerate did (President Wilson did not tolerate Americans who protested against the war.)

   As a summary, see if students can connect one of the sentences to the foods mentioned in the Motivation. If they still cannot identify the relationship between the foods and World War I, provide an explanation.

2. **Acrostic.** Use the following puzzle to check students' understanding of the factual information in Section 3.

   CLUES:

   Bernard BaruCh   C - appointed to head the War Industries Board

   Herbert Hoover   H - appointed to head the food Administration Board

   EspionAge Act   A - law that forbade anti-war writing through the U.S. Mail

   SeditioN Act   N - law that made a crime of any disloyal act

   propaGandist   G - an opinion maker

   George CrEel   E - appointed to head the Committee on Public Information

3. **Separating Facts from Opinions.** Review the Chapter 12 History Study Skill with students. Then have them decide whether each of the following is a FACT or an OPINION.

   A. Perhaps the most successful war mobilization program was the Food Administration Board (O)

   B. Farm production rose from 7 million tons in 1914 to 19 million tons in 1919. (F)

   C. American men claimed that women slowed down factory production. (O)

   D. The Supreme Court rules that the government could limit free speech during a national crisis. (F)

E. President Wilson created an agency to encourage public support for the war. (F)

BUILDING AMERICAN CITIZENSHIP

Duplicate Worksheet 73, *Propaganda and Loyalty in Time of War.* This activity requires students to think critically about four situations involving freedom of speech during a national crisis. You may wish to discuss the first situation orally, to give students an opportunity to articulate their opinions before writing them down.

SECTION 3 REVIEW ANSWERS

1. **IDENTIFY: War Industries Board:** advisory board created by Wilson in July 1917 to direct the nation's economic shift from peacetime to wartime production; **Bernard Baruch:** business genius appointed head of the War Industries Board in 1918; **Food Administration Board:** agency headed by Herbert Hoover to provide food for the Allies and expand American farm production; **Committee on Public Information:** an agency created by Wilson to encourage public support of the war; **George Creel:** head of the Committee on Public Information.

2. **DEFINE: propagandist:** opinion maker.

3. Millions of men had to be drafted and trained as soldiers; factories had to be converted to make war materials.

4. Heavy artillery was not delivered in time for the war; factories produced few tanks; the navy had to buy Dutch ships or use captured German ships; the railway systems were unable to carry all the needed supplies to army camps and naval bases.

SECTION 4: America Turns the Tide of Battle

OBJECTIVES

After completing this section, students will be able to:
- Describe the American fighting forces, including their numbers, their training, and their problems.
- Identify the problems the Allies faced on European battlefields in 1917.
- Explain how the American army and navy helped to win the war.
- Graph the human costs of war.

MOTIVATION

Place the following figures on the chalkboard and have students study them. Ask how the figures might be related to World War I. If students are unable to establish the relationship, tell them that you will discuss the figures again after they have read the section. If a viable answer is given, ask why they think the figures for some nations are so high and those for others lower. This can also be discussed again when students have finished reading.

Germany 1.8 million	France 1.38 million
Austria-Hungary 1.2 million	England 947,000
Russia 1.7 million	United States 104,000

SUGGESTED ACTIVITIES

1. **Directed Reading.** As students read, have them answer the following questions:
   A. What problem was the United States having in preparing men for war?
   B. Based on what you have just read, could the Allies have won the war without the help of the Americans? Explain your answer.
   C. How did the American army and navy contribute to the defeat of the Central Power Nations?

   Review the answers to these questions. Then return to the Motivation. Discuss the reason for the deaths of so many people. Be sure to emphasize that not all of those killed were soldiers but that many European civilians died as well. Summarize by having students state why American casualties were so much lower. (The United States entered the war late, fighting in the last year).

2. **Constructing a Graph.** Have students review the Chapter 17 History Study Skill, *Using Bar Graphs.* Then, have them construct a bar graph using the figures from the Motivation. Students should place the names of the countries on the vertical axis and the number of deaths, in 1/4 million intervals, on the horizontal axis.

   Next, have students review the Chapter 11 History Study Skill, *Using Circle Graphs.* Ask them to use the military service figures for the United States to construct a circle graph. These include: 24 million men registered for the draft, 4.8 million drafted, 2 million who served in combat, and 104,000 casualties.

3. **Research Activity.** The human cost of the war was terribly high. This was partly due to powerful weapons and war machines that were used on a massive scale for the first time. Have students select one of the following on which to prepare a report. The assignment should emphasize the development of the weapon and its use during World War I: gas, grenades, airplanes, tanks, land mines, and submarines.

4. **Audiovisual Activity.** Use the sound filmstrip, *World War I* from Audio-Visual Materials in the chapter introduction in this manual. It will help students visualize the destruction caused by World War I, and the role of the United States in it, and will enhance their understanding of its global nature and its high human and material costs. If this filmstrip is unavailable, check your library or instructional materials center for a suitable alternative.

BUILDING AMERICAN CITIZENSHIP

During World War I, some 300,000 citizens evaded the draft. During the Vietnam War, the same situation arose again. What can the government do about this problem? (Answers will vary.)

SECTION 4 REVIEW ANSWERS

1. **IDENTIFY: Selective Service Act:** law requiring all men between the ages of 20 and 30 years to register for military service; **William S. Sims:** American admiral who helped the British mine the North Sea and who persuad-

ed the Allies to use the convoy system; **Second Battle of the Marne:** Germany's last great drive on Paris, which took place in July 1918 and lasted for three days.

2. **DEFINE: conscientious objectors:** men who were granted special status because they opposed the war on moral or religious grounds; **convoy system:** system in which several navy ships accompanied a group of merchant ships crossing the ocean; **armistice:** a break in the fighting.

3. Initially, the Germans were successful and drove back both the British and the French. By June 1918 the Germans had reached the Marne River, 37 miles from Paris.

4. American troops played important roles in the Second Battle of the Marne and at St. Mihiel and in the Meuse-Argonne campaign.

SECTION 5: America Refuses to Join the League

OBJECTIVES

After completing this section, students will be able to:
- Compare Wilson's plans for a peace treaty with the plans of the Allied leaders.
- Identify specific parts of the Treaty of Versailles.
- Explain the arguments of American supporters and opponents of the Treaty of Versailles and the League of Nations.

MOTIVATION

Remind students that they have studied several wars this year. Ask them to name some. (Revolutionary War, War of 1812, Mexican War, Civil War, Spanish-American War) Then ask the following questions: What do the warring nations usually do soon after the fighting ends? (Sign a treaty) What matters are discussed and included in a treaty? (the assignment of territory and money, usually to the victors, arrangements concerning prisoners and so on) Which nations would you expect to be included in reaching such an agreement after World War I? (United States, France, Russia, Britain, Germany, Austria-Hungary, Italy) Tell students that in Section 5, the World War I treaty, what it said, and how Americans reacted to it, will be examined and discussed.

SUGGESTED ACTIVITIES

1. **Directed Reading.** As students read, have them complete the following paragraph. This may be written on the chalkboard or on a transparency for the overhead projector.

   President ___(WILSON)___ wrote a plan for peace called the ___(FOURTEEN POINTS)___. The last part called for a creation of a ___(LEAGUE OF NATIONS)___. The peace ___(CONFERENCE)___ was held in ___(PARIS)___ where other leading ___(ALLIED)___ nations formed plans to punish ___(GERMANY)___. The Treaty of ___(VERSAILLES)___ punished ___(GERMANY)___ by making it pay ___(REPARA-TIONS)___, taking away its ___(COLONIES)___ and forcing it to accept ___(RESPONSIBILITY)___ for the war. In the United States, the ___(REPUBLICANS)___ in Congress ___(OPPOSED)___ the treaty. Although President Wilson ___(TOURED)___ the United States to gain support for the treaty, it was ___(DEFEATED)___ by the ___(SENATE)___.

You may wish to provide a word bank of answers for low-ability students.

2. **Comparing Historical Maps.** Review the Chapter 7 History Study Skill. Have students apply this skill to the two maps in this chapter. Then have them answer the following questions:
   A. Compare Germany before and after World War I. What changes do you see? (Lost land to Poland in the East and to France in the West)
   B. Look at the map of Europe after World War I. What new nation was created to replace Serbia and Montenegro? (Yugoslavia)
   C. What nations gave up land to Greece? (Bulgaria and Turkey)
   D. What nations were created from land that had belonged to Russia? (Poland, Finland, Estonia, Latvia, Lithuania)
   E. Did Great Britain gain any land in Europe as a result of the war? (No)
   F. Did Italy gain any land as a result of the war? (Yes—a small part of the Austro-Hungarian Empire)

3. **The Treaty of Versailles.** Duplicate Worksheet 74 of this title. This activity provides specific details concerning the punishment of Germany, that were not included in the textbook. To do this activity, students will have to apply critical thinking skills to the various points included in the Treaty of Versailles.

4. **Ideas in the Lives of Americans.** Have students read the selection on Oliver Wendell Holmes, on textbook page 610. Ask students what was happening to the Treaty of Versailles when Justice Holmes ruled on the case involving free speech in 1919. (Congress rejected the Treaty of Versailles.) In addition, ask students when he was appointed to the Supreme Court (1902); when he retired (1932); and how old he was at retirement (91). These questions may be answered from information in the selection. Finally, discuss the answers to the two questions at the end of the reading.

BUILDING AMERICAN CITIZENSHIP

Do you think the citizens of France and Great Britain agreed with the decision of their leaders to punish Germany? Think about the specific punishments handed to Germany. How do you think the German nation and its citizens were affected by these punishments?

SECTION 5 REVIEW ANSWERS

1. **IDENTIFY: Fourteen Points:** President Wilson's outline of a policy for world peace presented in a speech in January 1918; **League of Nations:** an international organization to guarantee independence to both large and small states, called for as Wilson's fourteenth point in his speech; **Treaty of Versailles:** agreement ending World War I; **Henry Cabot Lodge:** Republican Senator who led the fight to change the Treaty of Versailles.

2. **DEFINE: reparations:** payments to make up for the costs of war.

3. The European Allies wanted to divide up the Central Powers' land and colonies and make Germany pay heavy reparations. Wilson called for the independence of Europe's overseas colonies and less severe punishment of Germany.

4. The Republicans were angry because Wilson invited no Republicans to take part in the peace conference. Also, they objected to the League of Nations because it would have the right to call on American troops to protect the independence of a member nation. Others felt that the United States should avoid permanent promises to other nations. Progressives felt Americans should concentrate on their own problems, not international problems.

CHAPTER 26 REVIEW ANSWERS

REVIEWING KEY WORDS

1. b.	2. b.	3. a.	4. b.	5. a.

REMEMBERING IMPORTANT PEOPLE AND EVENTS

1. c.	2. b.	3. a.	4. e.	5. d.
6. d.	7. e.	8. b.	9. c.	10. a.

REVIEWING THE FACTS

1. T	2. F	3. F	4. T	5. T

PLACING EVENTS IN TIME

1. C	2. A	3. B	4. E	5. D

LINKING GEOGRAPHY AND HISTORY

1. They were located in Central Europe and had to fight enemy nations both to the east and to the west. Their armies, therefore, had to be divided to fight in two directions at the same time.

2. The North Sea was the route taken by U-boats to travel from Germany to the Atlantic Ocean.

THINKING ABOUT AMERICAN HISTORY

1. An armistice stops the fighting, but it may be a temporary truce. A treaty stops the fighting permanently and arranges for a peace settlement.

2. Answers may vary, but in general, students should point to the difficulties experienced by the Allies in 1917, i.e., the defeat of the French along the Aisne River, the increase in U-boat sinkings of Allied ships, and Russia's withdrawal from the war. The information in Section 4 suggests the possibility of an Allied defeat.

APPLYING HISTORY STUDIES SKILLS

1. To persuade citizens to do things and to make sacrifices during wartime that would not be expected during peacetime.

2. Information presented to influence public opinion.

3. Television and radio commercials, newspaper ads, posters, etc.

UNIT 8 REVIEW ANSWERS

VOCABULARY REVIEW

Answers will vary.

REVIEWING THE MAIN IDEAS

1. Roosevelt ordered the prosecution of big businesses that had established monopolies, took an active part in settling the Pennsylvania coal miners strike, fought for passage of the Hepburn Act and the Pure Food and Drug Act, and supported conservation. Taft ordered prosecution of huge corporations, signed the Mann-Elkins Act, and campaigned for mine-safety legislation and an 8-hour workday for federal employees. Wilson supported reduced tariffs and an income tax. He reformed the nation's banking system, created the Federal Trade Commission, and signed into law the Clayton Anti-Trust Act.

2. They paid little attention to the lack of civil rights for blacks and the terrible conditions under which immigrants had to work.

3. The industrial growth of the United States led to a search for new markets and new sources of raw materials. The United States wanted to protect its business interests, and so it took a more active role in world affairs. Strong national pride also caused Americans to seek world leadership.

4. The United States purchased Alaska, annexed Hawaii, and as a result of fighting in the Spanish-American War, gained control of the Philippines, Guam, and Puerto Rico. It also expanded its world leadership through its "Open Door" Policy in China. In addition, President Roosevelt helped end the Russian-Japanese War and used his influence to improve relations between Japan and the United States. The United States also gained influence through the building of the Panama Canal and the Monroe Doctrine.

5. The causes of World War I were the European alliance treaties (balance of power system), a growing spirit of nationalism in Europe, increased competition among the Great Powers, and the assassination of Austria-Hungary's Archduke Francis Ferdinand and his wife Sophie.

6. Numerous surprise U-boat attacks on Allied and neutral American ships and consequent loss of American lives, the sinking of the *Lusitania*, the Zimmerman note to Mexico, and public support for the Allies led President Wilson to ask Congress to declare war on April 7, 1917.

APPLYING YOUR STUDY SKILLS

1. **Using a Time Line**
   a. (1) 31 years

   (2) American fighting in World War I lasted longer —over a year; the Spanish-American War lasted about 8 months.
   (3) The Sixteenth Amendment—income tax—was ratified in 1913. (The Eighteenth Amendment—Prohibition—was ratified in 1919.)

2. **Making a Chart**

Date	Territory Acquired	Methods Acquired
1867	Alaska	Treaty - Bought
1898	Philippines	War
1898	Hawaii	Annexation
1898	Guam	War
1898	Puerto Rico	War
1903	Panama Canal	Treaty

3. **Using Maps**
   a. (1) Wilson   (2) McKinley   (3) Roosevelt
   (4) Roosevelt   (5) Taft   (6) Wilson

4. **Using your Textbook**
   a. (1) Germany; Austria-Hungary; Russia; Bulgaria; Ottoman Empire
   (2) Russia had become the Union of Soviet Socialist Republics as a result of a Communist revolution in 1917.
   (3) During the war it was part of Austria-Hungary; after the war it was located in Austria.
   (4) Finland; Estonia; Latvia; Lithuania; Poland; Czechoslovakia; Austria; Hungary; Yugoslavia

PROJECTS

Answers will vary.

BUILDING AMERICAN CITIZENSHIP

1. a. Answers will vary. b. Answers will vary.
2. The United States is the leader of the free world. It protests unfair actions taken by other nations, such as the Soviet Union's invasion of Afghanistan. It has played an active role in trying to reach peaceful solutions in troubled areas of the world, such as the Middle East. It has also played an active role in trying to help solve the world's economic problems. The United States is a leading member of such alliances as NATO and SEATO and is an active member of the United Nations, and so on.

America Has Troubled Times

Introducing the Unit

Unit Nine surveys the events, both at home and abroad, of the years between 1920 and 1945, the period spanning the end of World War I to the end of World War II. This period falls into three relatively distinct parts. The first, 1920 to 1929, treated in Chapter 27 and known as the "Roaring Twenties", ends with the Wall Street crash in October 1929. This was a decade of Republican Presidents. By and large, it was also a decade of economic prosperity, "boom times," for Americans as well as a period which saw great social change, as many citizens throughout the nation were able to partake of the "good life." The decade had its dark side, however, as large numbers of Americans did not reap the benefits of the generally booming postwar period.

The crash that ended the 1920's signaled the beginning of the Great Depression, the worst business depression in the nation's history. Chapter 28 covers this period, the decade of the 1930's, up to the eve of our involvement in World War II. The Great Depression affected all Americans. In 1932 alone, people suffered through a banking crisis, a dust bowl, and a Bonus Army march. By 1933, 13 million workers were unemployed. Under the new Democratic President Franklin D. Roosevelt, inaugurated in 1933, the federal government instituted massive public assistance programs. Roosevelt's New Deal reforms seemed to be popular with the people, who returned Roosevelt to the White House in 1936. As life gradually was beginning to improve in the United States, serious rumblings of war resounded through Europe and Asia.

Chapter 29 covers the rise in Germany, Italy, and Japan, of dictators whose unbridled military aggression resulted in the outbreak of World War II. In the 1930's, Japan invaded China, Italy invaded Ethiopia, and Germany annexed Austria and Czechoslovakia and invaded Poland. By September 1939, Europe was once again at war. The United States, while proclaiming its neutrality, aided Europeans defending themselves against the Germans and Italians. In Asia the United States was trying to stem the rising tide of Japanese imperialism. The Japanese attack on Pearl Harbor plunged America into war both in the Pacific and Europe for the next four years. Victory in Europe came in April 1945. The use of atomic weapons in Japan in August 1945 ended the war in the Pacific and ushered in a new era, the Atomic Age.

The Unit Opener in the textbook depicts many of the significant persons and events of this period. You may wish to use these illustrations to help introduce the unit. President and Mrs. Roosevelt dominate the left and center of the page. Beginning in the upper left-hand corner in a clockwise direction are a Nazi swastika, the atomic bomb, the Japanese flag, the U.S. Marines at Iwo Jima, a flapper, Louis Armstrong, a dustbowl farm, and the symbol of the NRA, an agency of the New Deal.

Unit Themes and Ideas

Unit Nine is organized around three major themes: prosperity, depression, and war. Prosperity in the 1920's was evident in many ways. Many industries, especially the automobile industry and related businesses, flourished. People learned to buy on the installment plan and also began to spend more money on clothes and entertainment, including sports events and movies. Unfortunately, the "good life" did not seem to extend to several groups of Americans, blacks and farmers. Poverty and racism were twin specters during this time, signaling serious domestic problems to come.

With the crash of the stock market the prosperity bubble burst. President Hoover did little to stem the deepening crisis. He was defeated in 1932 by Roosevelt, who tried many innovative remedies to bring back prosperity. Controversial from the start, his programs did get the country out of the worst part of the depression. His New Deal included something for business and labor. It also saw the beginnings of deficit spending and social security. However, it took a war to finally end the Great Depression.

World War II, plunged the World into global conflict for the second time in the 20th century. The United States, though neutral for the first two years of the war, lent support and supplies to the British. American neutrality was abruptly ended in 1941 with the Japanese attack on Pearl Harbor. The United States fought in Europe and Asia concurrently, while again achieving remarkable economic production at home. A relatively clear-cut postwar peace plan was the result of Allied conferences throughout the war. The use of atomic weapons and the creation of a world peace-keeping organization were two important legacies of this period.

The themes and ideas of Unit Nine are organized into the three chapters below:

Chapter 27 - *Boom Times Change to Hard Times (1920 - 1929)*
Chapter 28 - *The New Deal Tries to End the Depression (1929 - 1941)*
Chapter 29 - *Rise of Dictators Leads to World War II (1920 -1945)*

CHAPTER 27

Boom Times Change to Hard Times (1920-1929)
Chapter Objectives

After completing this chapter, students will be able to:
1. Identify signs of economic prosperity in the 1920's.
2. Describe how many Americans spent their leisure time.

3. Explain why the government supported big business.
4. Identify economic and social problems evident in the 1920's.
5. List the major causes of the stock market crash of 1929.

Chapter Chronology

Chapter 27 covers the years from 1920 to 1929, a period of booming industrial production and soaring profits that ended abruptly with the collapse of the stock market and the most serious financial crisis in the nation's history. Several important persons and events of the time are highlighted on the time line in the textbook Chapter Opener. The decade opened with the election of the Republican Warren Harding as President. Following Harding's death in 1921, Calvin Coolidge became President. In 1921, also, the Veteran's Bureau was formed. Coolidge was elected President in 1924. Three years later Charles Lindbergh flew across the Atlantic Ocean. In the same year, 1927, the first sound motion picture was made. Herbert Hoover was elected President in 1928, just one year before the crash of the stock market.

Motivation

Have students read the title of Chapter 27 and explain what they think the terms "Boom Times" and "Hard Times" mean. Next ask them to turn to the History Study Skill activity on textbook page 647. Have students work through the skill exercises and questions. When they have completed their work, ask them which years included the "Boom Time" and when the "Hard Times" started.

Geographical Setting

Chapter 27, which deals largely with nationwide political, economic, and social events, does not have a geographical focus. However, ask students to locate, on a map or globe, various American cities and states mentioned in the text. Have them trace Lindbergh's flight route across the Atlantic.

History Study Skills

The History Study Skill in Chapter 27 is *Using a Line Graph*, an extension of the skill introduced in Chapter 13. The information used for this activity is stock prices from 1920 through 1929. This activity may be used to introduce the chapter or in conjunction with Section 5 of the text.

Bibliography

Teacher References

Leuchtenburg, William E., *The Perils of Prosperity*. University of Chicago Press, Chicago, Ill., 1958.

Tentler, Leslie W., *Wage-Earning Women: Industrial Work and Family Life in the United States, 1900-1930*. Oxford, New York City, 1979.

Student References

Yates, Elizabeth, *My Diary—My World*. Westminster Press, Philadelphia, Pa., 1981. These entries from the diaries of Elizabeth Yates, an award-winning writer, date from her teenage years in 1917 to 1925, when, as an upper-class schoolgirl, she lived during a period of great social change in America.

Collins, David R., *Charles Lindbergh: Hero Pilot*. Garrard, Champaign, Ill., 1978. This is a well-illustrated and interesting biography of the first man to fly solo across the Atlantic Ocean.

Audio-Visual Materials

The Reckless Years: 1919-1929, Guidance Associates, 2 filmstrips, 2 cassettes, library kit, teacher's guide. The filmstrips illustrate the social, political, and economic changes that took place during the decade after World War I.

The 1920's, Listening Library, Inc., 6 sound filmstrips with a teacher's guide. This program uses the art styles of the 1920's to illustrate the decade's major themes.

SECTION 1: Prosperity Comes to Postwar America

OBJECTIVES

After completing this section, students will be able to:
- Identify the reason for naming the decade following World War I the "Roaring Twenties."
- Describe the nation's economic problems immediately following World War I.
- Explain how the automobile helped America achieve prosperity in the 1920's.

MOTIVATION

Use the Motivation suggested in the chapter introduction in the manual. Have students complete the History Study Skill activity, and discuss with them which years were the "Boom Times" and when the "Hard Times" began. Tell students that, by the end of this section, they will be able to explain what factors led to the "Boom Times."

SUGGESTED ACTIVITIES

1. **Directed Reading.** As students read Section 1, have them answer the following questions:
   A. Why did the economy get off to a shaky start after World War I?
   B. How did the automobile contribute to the rapid growth of the economy during the 1920's?
   C. What effect did "installment buying" have on the nation's economy?
   Review the answers to the guide questions. As a summary, ask students to identify all of the factors that led to "Boom Times" during the 1920's.
2. **Research Activity.** Section 1 informs students that 108 manufacturers produced 23 million cars in the 1920's. Students also learn that Henry Ford did not invent the auto, although he was responsible for the growth of the industry. Have students use library sources to research the history of the automobile. Ask them to discover who invented it, to name some manufacturers other than Ford, and to draw pictures of different models. Student illustrations of different

models of automobiles may be used to create a bulletin board display.

3. **Studying Your History Vocabulary.** Review the Chapter 16 History Study Skill. Then, have students apply the skill to define each of these terms by using information found in Section 1: a) skyrocketed; b) inflation; c) assembly line; d) conveyor belt; and e) installment plan.

4. **Class Discussion.** The automobile helped lead America to "Boom Times" partly because it stimulated other related industries. Have students review these industries. Then, discuss this concept of interdependence by applying it to another machine, such as the computer or the airplane. Have students speculate on what other industries might grow as a result of its popularity and why.

BUILDING AMERICAN CITIZENSHIP

Manufacturers encouraged people to "Buy! Spend!" and to "Enjoy the good life!" during the 1920's. Is this a good attitude to promote among the citizens of a nation? Is it fair to all citizens of the nation? Explain your answer. (This should bring students to the realization that not all citizens enjoyed the prosperity equally. The poor were not able to buy, spend, and enjoy the good life.)

SECTION 1 REVIEW ANSWERS

1. **IDENTIFY: Henry Ford:** king of the auto industry, whose use of the assembly line enabled him to offer Americans the first inexpensive car, the Model T.

2. **DEFINE: assembly line:** factory system in which each worker is assigned to one task in making a product as it moves along a conveyor belt; **installment plan:** a payment plan in which customers make a small cash payment and pay the remainder in weekly or monthly payments.

3. It was a time when the nation was busy and booming—the economy was growing, sports were exciting, "hot jazz" was popular, and Americans were enjoying life and were proud that their young and strong country was growing richer and more powerful every day.

4. All industries related to the auto industry—steel, lead, nickel, glass, gasoline, oil, service stations, and road building.

SECTION 2: Americans Enjoy the Good Life

OBJECTIVES

After completing this section, students will be able to:
- List the types of entertainment that became popular during the 1920's.
- Describe the fun-seeking lifestyle of the young.
- Explain the reasons for the failure of Prohibition.

MOTIVATION

Write the following list of 1920's expressions on the chalkboard:

"Bootlegging"   "Talkie"   "Jazz"
"Speak easies"   "Dreammaker"   "Sultan of Swat"
"Flappers"

Ask students if they have ever heard of any of these terms. Have them try to determine to what area of 1920's life each might apply.

SUGGESTED ACTIVITIES

1. **Directed Reading.** As students read, have them jot down the meaning of each of the expressions discussed during the Motivation and to which type of 1920's entertainment each was related. For example, the "Sultan of Swat" was the nickname given to Babe Ruth, the nation's greatest baseball hero during the 1920's. Review the information, then use the following activity as a summary.

2. **Matching Activity.** This exercise may be written on the chalkboard or on a transparency for the overhead projector. Directions: Match the left-hand column with the type of entertainment to which it is related in the right-hand column.

   1. *Amos 'n Andy*   A. nightclubs
   2. *The Jazz Singer*   B. baseball
   3. "Sultan of Swat"   C. vacations
   4. Yosemite National Park D. movies
   5. Dixieland Jazz   E. radio

   ANSWERS: E - D - B - C - A

3. **Improving Your Writing.** Review the Chapter 10 History Study Skill. Then have students apply it by writing a paragraph in answer to the question below: What are some of the similarities and some of the differences between forms of entertainment enjoyed in the 1920's and forms of entertainment enjoyed today?

4. **Putting Events in Chronological Order.** Review the Chapter 19 History Study Skill. Then have students apply it by arranging the following events in chronological order:

   A. The first commercial radio broadcast was made.
   B. The St. Valentine's Day Massacre occurred.
   C. Jack Dempsey became the "Heavyweight Champion of the World."
   D. Prohibiton was repealed.
   E. The first film with sound was produced.

   ANSWERS: A - D - E - B - C

BUILDING AMERICAN CITIZENSHIP

Many citizens rejected Prohibition because they felt it was an "attempt to control their private behavior." Are there any laws in your community or state that attempt to control private behavior? (motorcycle safety helmets, seat belts in the car, no smoking in public areas) Do you think it proper for the United States government to pass these types of laws? Explain your answer.

SECTION 2 REVIEW ANSWERS

1. **IDENTIFY: Al Jolson:** star of the first motion picture with sound, *The Jazz Singer;* **George Herman "Babe" Ruth:** America's greatest baseball hero of the 1920's; **Jack Dempsey:** boxing champion from 1921 to 1926; **Prohibition:** the outlawing of the sale, manufacture, or transport of liquor by the Eighteenth Amendment; **Al Capone:** famous Chicago gangster involved in "bootlegging" liquor in the 1920's.

2. The radio, movies, jazz, sports such as baseball and boxing, and taking vacations.

3. "Flappers" were young women who cut their hair short and wore short, loose clothing; they wore makeup and openly flirted with men.
4. Americans rejected the law as an attempt to control their private behavior; there weren't enough agents to enforce the law.

SECTION 3: The Government Supports Big Business

OBJECTIVES

After completing this section, students will be able to:
- List the methods used by Presidents Harding and Coolidge to promote business interests.
- Describe the scandals that occurred during Harding's Presidency.
- Explain the reasons for the election of Herbert Hoover in 1928.

MOTIVATION

Have students recall the 20th-century Presidents that they have discussed so far and ask them to briefly describe each one. (McKinley, Roosevelt, Taft, and Wilson) Tell students that three Presidents served during the 1920's and that by the end of this lesson, they will be able to name and describe them. If available, display photographs.

SUGGESTED ACTIVITIES

1. **Directed Reading.** As students read Section 2 have them write the name of each President and the year he became President. Ask them also to write several adjectives describing each man.

   Warren Harding —1920—handsome, hard working, friendly
   Calvin Coolidge —1923—honest, quiet, deeply religious
   Herbert Hoover —1929—quiet, reserved, serious

   Display pictures of the three Presidents. Have students identify the pictures on the basis of the adjectives they have written. Discuss student descriptions of the Presidents. To summarize, compare these individuals to those who served during the first decades of the 20th century.
2. **Identification.** Place the following statements on the chalkboard or on a transparency for the overhead projector. Have students read them and identify the President to whom they apply.
   A. He defeated Alfred Smith in the election of 1928. (Hoover)
   B. He released Eugene V. Debs from prison. (Harding)
   C. He worked only a few hours a day. (Coolidge)
   D. He opposed insurance for veterans and aid to farmers. (Coolidge)
   E. He was concerned about his friends being involved in scandals. (Harding)
   F. He served as Secretary of Commerce before his election to the Presidency. (Hoover)
3. **Comprehension Check.** To determine students' understanding of what they read, have them complete the following TRUE-FALSE exercise. If the response is

"FALSE," students should be able to rewrite the statement to make it TRUE.
   A. All of the men elected to the Presidency during the 1920's were Republicans. (T)
   B. Both Harding and Coolidge allowed government agencies to promote business rather than regulate it. (T)
   C. President Coolidge appointed reformers to head important government agencies. (F)
   D. During the 1920's, the Supreme Court continued to support labor reform and laws passed by Congress to improve working conditions. (F—Court ruled against unions and laws to improve working conditions.)
   E. Many citizens did not vote for Alfred Smith because he supported big business. (F—He was against Prohibition, and he was a Catholic.)

BUILDING AMERICAN CITIZENSHIP

Should the religion of a political candidate make any difference to the voters? Would the religion of a candidate make any difference to you? Why or why not?

SECTION 3 REVIEW ANSWERS

1. **IDENTIFY: Warren Harding:** Republican candidate elected President in 1920; **Teapot Dome scandal:** scandal resulting from Secretary of the Interior Albert Fall's release of the navy's oil reserves to private companies in exchange for $400,000; **Calvin Coolidge:** succeeded as President after the death of Warren Harding in 1923; **Andrew Mellon:** Secretary of the Treasury under Presidents Harding and Coolidge; **Herbert Hoover:** Republican candidate elected President in 1928.
2. **DEFINE: "yellow dog" contracts:** contracts giving companies the right to fire any worker who joined a union.
3. Harding approved the highest tariff in the nation's history, reduced the income tax rates, and fought against anything that raised government expenses. Coolidge appointed people to regulatory commissions that supported business, cut taxes, and opposed increases in government spending.
4. Both candidates held many of the same political beliefs. However, some people did not like Smith's views on Prohibition, his ties to New York politicians, or the fact that he was a Catholic. Americans believed that a vote for Hoover would mean "four more years of prosperity."

SECTION 4: Problems Arise in the Good Life

OBJECTIVES

After completing this section, students will be able to:
- Identify the groups of Americans who did not share in the prosperity of the 1920's.
- Explain the reasons why some Americans did not share in the prosperity of the 1920's.
- Identify the problems of black Americans and immigrants during the 1920's.
- Describe the writings of the "lost generation."

MOTIVATION

Have students read the first paragraph in Section 4 to name those groups of Americans who did not share in the prosperity of the 1920's. (Farmers, many factory workers, blacks, radicals, and immigrants) Ask students which people did share in the prosperity if these groups were left out. (The wealthy) Ask students why so many people were not able to share in the good life. Tell them they should be able to discuss this when they have finished reading Section 4.

SUGGESTED ACTIVITIES

1. **Directed Reading.** As students read, have them complete an outline using the following title and topics:

   HARD TIMES DURING THE 1920'S
   I. Farm families
   II. Workers
   III. Black families
   IV. Immigrants

   As they select information for subtopics, remind students to place emphasis on the reasons why these groups did not share in the prosperity of the period. Review the subtopics selected by the students. Discuss the "lost generation" with the class as well. Did those poets and writers write about these groups of people? Explain. Use the following activity as a summary.

2. **Comprehension Check.** Have the students copy the following sentences from the chalkboard or a transparency and supply the missing information.
   A. Farmers lost money because ___(PRICES)___ fell and ___(COSTS)___ rose.
   B. Workers in the ___(COAL-MINING)___ and ___(TEXTILE)___ industries suffered hard times because of low ___(WAGES)___ and high ___(PRICES)___.
   C. The ___(KU KLUX KLAN)___ reappeared in the 1920's with hate campaigns against various groups, including ___(BLACKS)___, Jews, Catholics, and ___(IMMIGRANTS)___.
   D. The ___(SACCO AND VANZETTI)___ Case involved the execution of two radical immigrants who had been convicted of ___(MURDER)___.
   E. In 1924, the ___(NATIONAL ORIGINS ACT)___ set limits on the number of immigrants allowed into the country each year.
   F. The "lost generation" disapproved of the ___(MATERIALISM)___ of Americans.

3. **Using a Line Graph.** Duplicate Worksheet 75, *Immigration.* This activity provides practice in applying the History Study Skill introduced in the Motivation in Section 1. You may wish to familiarize students with the graph before they begin, by having them answer the following questions:
   A. What is the title of the graph? (*Immigration to the United States, 1860's-1930's)*
   B. What information is given on the vertical axis? (Millions of immigrants)
   C. What information is given on the horizontal axis? (Decades from the 1860's to the 1930's)

4. **Using Bar Graphs.** Review the Chapter 17 History Study Skill *Using Bar Graphs.* Then duplicate Worksheet 76, *Farm Production and Prices.* Before students complete the exercises for the two graphs, familiarize them with the contents by asking questions similar to those suggested for the previous activity.

BUILDING AMERICAN CITIZENSHIP

What were the major economic problems faced in the 1920's by citizens who were not wealthy? (Low wages and high prices) Given what you have learned in Section 3, can you tell why the government did not help citizens solve their problems? (Government supported business) How do you think the situation in the 1920's compares with life in the 1980's—are the problems similar? Is the attitude of the government similar? Explain your answer.

SECTION 4 REVIEW ANSWERS

1. **IDENFITY: Ku Klux Klan:** organization that reappeared in the 1920's to terrorize such minority groups in America, as blacks, Jews, Catholics, and immigrants; **Sacco and Vanzetti case:** famous murder trial in which two Italian immigrants who belonged to a radical political group were convicted and executed; **Harlem Renaissance:** period in the 1920's and 1930's when blacks made many cultural contributions.
2. **DEFINE: quota:** proportional share, or limit.
3. They were caused by prejudice and white resentment of blacks who were migrating in increasing numbers to Northern cities and competing for jobs and housing.
4. The "lost generation" was a group of writers and artists who left America to work in Europe because they believed America was losing many of its ideals and values.

SECTION 5: The Crash of 1929 Ends Prosperity

OBJECTIVES

After completing this section, students will be able to:
* Explain how the stock market works.
* Identify reasons for people's belief in continued prosperity.
* Describe the Great Crash and how it affected businesses in America.

MOTIVATION

Use the time line on the textbook Chapter Opener page to review the major events discussed in the previous sections. Have students identify the one event that has not yet been discussed. (1929—Stock market crash) Discuss the stock market. What is it? What city is its center of activity? How does it work? What is meant when we say the stock market "crashed"? These questions are answered in Section 5.

SUGGESTED ACTIVITIES

1. **Directed Reading.** Have students use the guide questions below as they read Section 5. They should not attempt to write answers to the questions, but

should be prepared to discuss them when they finish reading.

A. How does the stock market work?

B. Why did it "crash" in 1929?

C. What were the effects of the crash?

Discuss each question thoroughly, then summarize by using the following activity.

2. **Comprehension Check.** Have students answer TRUE or FALSE to each of the following. If the statement is FALSE, students should be able to give the reason(s).

A. Stock bought on margin must be paid for immediately. (F—Margin means "bought on credit.")

B. People believed that stock prices would continue to rise. (T)

C. The stock market crash occurred on October 24, 1929. (F—October 29, 1929)

D. Many investors in the stock market lost all of their money. (T)

E. Business people who wish to buy new equipment or expand their operations may sell stock or shares of ownership in their companies in order to raise money. (T)

3. **Predicting Outcomes.** Conduct a class discussion based on what students learned in this chapter. What effect, do students think, did the loss of fortunes of wealthy business people have on the average American citizen? (Factories closed. People were out of work and unable to pay their bills or buy new goods. As a result, more factories were forced to close, and more people lost their jobs. Without jobs and incomes, many citizens lost their homes and their savings and became destitute.)

4. **Ideals in the Lives of Americans.** Have students read the selection on Frances Perkins on textbook page 640. In addition to discussing the two questions at the end of the reading, ask students how Frances Perkins served her country during the "Boom Times" and the "Hard Times" of the 1920's.

BUILDING AMERICAN CITIZENSHIP

Duplicate Worksheet 77, *Rights and Responsibilities.* You may wish students to complete the activity, first from a "Twenties" perspective, and then from a current point of view. Their answers could then be compared to note differences and similarities, resulting from changes in attitudes in the last six decades.

SECTION 5 REVIEW ANSWERS

1. **IDENTIFY: Great Depression:** the worst economic hard times in American history, suffered during the 1930's; **Great Crash:** the sudden and drastic drop in stock market prices on October 29, 1929; **Black Thursday:** the name given to October 24, 1929, when stock prices plunged.

2. **DEFINE: stock:** shares of ownership in a corporation; **margin:** buying stock with borrowed money; **broker:** stock dealer.

3. They believed political and business leaders who told them that prosperity would continue; many people didn't understand how the economy worked; people wanted to believe that the economy was strong.

4. Many people had bought stock on margin, expecting the stock prices to continue to rise. When the prices fell, they had no money to pay for the stock. The rush of frightened investors to sell their stock at any price drove prices even lower.

P. 648-49

CHAPTER 27 REVIEW ANSWERS   32

REVIEWING KEY WORDS

1. e.	2. b.	3. c.	4. a.	5. d.

REMEMBERING IMPORTANT PEOPLE AND EVENTS

1. c.	2. b.	3. a.	4. d.	5. e.
6. c.	7. b.	8. b.	9. a.	10. c.

REVIEWING THE FACTS

1. F	2. T	3. T	4. T	5. T

PLACING EVENTS IN TIME

1. b.	2. e.	3. c.	4. a.	5. d.

LINKING GEOGRAPHY AND HISTORY

Answers will vary but should include the point that white workers felt they had to compete with newly arrived black workers for jobs and housing.

THINKING ABOUT AMERICAN HISTORY

1. Answers will vary.

2. Answers will vary but could include the following points: (a) having laws to regulate the purchase of stocks on credit; (b) demanding that politicians and business leaders be accurate and responsible in their statements regarding the state of the nation's economy; (c) educating citizens so that they have a better understanding of economic matters.

APPLYING HISTORY STUDIES SKILLS

1. 1929.   2. 1924.   3. 1931.

4. About $3,700 million.   6 + 7 billion

CHAPTER 28

The New Deal Tries to End the Depression (1929-1941)

Chapter Objectives

After completing this chapter, students will be able to:

1. Describe how the Great Depression developed after the stock market crashed in 1929.

2. Identify the major programs of the New Deal.

3. Evaluate the success of New Deal programs.

4. Explain how the New Deal changed American society.

5. Describe the strengths and weaknesses of Roosevelt's Presidency.

Chapter Chronology

Chapter 28 describes the aftermath of the stock market crash in 1929 and the nation's efforts to recover its economic stability under the leadership of President

Roosevelt. Several of the major events of this period can be found on the time line in the textbook Chapter Opener. The Great Depression began in 1929 with the collapse of the stock market. In 1932, Franklin D. Roosevelt was elected President. By the following year, the New Deal was underway. One of its most ambitious projects, the TVA, was created in 1933. Many important new laws were passed, including the Social Security Act in 1935. In that year, as well, John L. Lewis created the CIO. Roosevelt was reelected in 1936. A major social reform was effected in 1938 when child labor ended. In the same year, the Agricultural Adjustment Act, helping farmers, was passed. In the election of 1940, Roosevelt was elected President for an unprecedented third term.

Motivation

Several days before starting Chapter 28, ask students to talk with adults in the family or in the community who lived through the Great Depression. Have students write down a few of the recollections of these people. In class, have students read the textbook Chapter Introduction and then add to it the information they gathered in the homework assignment. Categorize the students' information under such headings as *Effects of the Depression on Families* or *Kinds of Work Done During the Depression.* Use this information for reference as students work through the chapter.

Geographical Setting

Chapter 28 does not have a specific geographical focus, and there are no maps in this chapter. However, review with the class the location and geographical characteristics of the Great Plains. Have students locate, on a map of the United States, the area electrified by the TVA projects.

History Study Skills

The History Study Skill introduced in Chapter 28 is *Finding Out About Your Local History.* The emphasis is on the local history of the students' community during the Depression. Specific attention is given to the WPA, the Works Progress Administration, an agency that had programs in communities throughout the United States. This activity could be done in conjunction with Section 3 of the text or as a long-range project.

Bibliography

Teacher References

Terkel, Studs, *Hard Times: An Oral History of the Great Depression.* Pantheon, New York City, 1970.

Conklin, Paul, *The New Deal.* Harlan-Davidson, Arlington Heights, Ill, 1975.

Student References

Burch, Robert, *Ida Early Comes Over the Mountain.* Viking, New York City, 1980. This novel focuses on the struggles of a family in rural Georgia to survive during the Great Depression.

Katz, William L., *An Album of the Great Depression.* Franklin Watts, New York City, 1978. Both the pictures and the text of this book poignantly illustrate how the Great Depression affected the lives of ordinary Americans.

Audio-Visual Materials

Life in the Thirties, McGraw Films, 1965, black and white, 52 minutes. This film focuses on the critical early years of the Great Depression and the leadership of Roosevelt.

Presidents of the United States: Part VI, Hoover and Roosevelt, 2 sound filmstrips, National Geographic, 1980. These filmstrips survey the personal lives and administrations of the two men who served as President during the Great Depression.

SECTION 1: The Great Depression Deepens

OBJECTIVES

After completing this section, students will be able to:
- Describe the effects of the Great Depression on people's lives.
- Explain how the area once known as the "breadbasket of the world" became known as the "dust bowl."
- Identify reasons why President Hoover was blamed for the Depression.

MOTIVATION

If possible, use the Motivation suggested in the chapter introduction in this manual. If students have been unable to gather information from their parents or members of the community, place the following headlines on the chalkboard:

A. Farmers Block Food Shipments to Cities
B. Dairymen Dump Milk—Prices Too Low
C. Coal Miners Attack Company Stores Demanding Food
D. Veterans Army Removed From Washington by Force

Have students study the headlines carefully. Ask them to explain why these violent incidents may have occurred in the years following the stock market crash. Tell them the headlines are based on information in Section 1 and that each will be discussed when they have finished reading.

SUGGESTED ACTIVITIES

1. **Directed Reading.** As students read Section 1, ask them to list all of the problems faced by farmers and workers during the Great Depression. Review the list with students. Have students use it as a homework assignment, asking their parents and neighbors which of the problems, if any, they experienced during the Depression. As a summary, discuss the facts related to each of the headlines used as part of the Motivation.

2. **Using a Line Graph.** This section gives unemployment figures for 1930, 1931, and 1933. List the following statistics on the board. Then, have students review the Chapter 27 History Study Skill and create a line graph using these figures.

Millions of People Unemployed

1929—1.5	1933—12.8	1937—7.7
1930—4.3	1934—11.3	1938—10.3
1931—8.0	1935—10.6	1939—9.4
1932—12.1	1936—9.0	1940—8.1

Below-average students may need assistance in determining the intervals for placing the information on both the vertical and horizontal axes. For example, each year on the horizontal axis might be 1/4 inch or 1 cm. Each "million" on the vertical axis might be 1/2 inch or 2 cm.

3. **Separating Facts from Opinions.** Review the Chapter 12 History Study Skill. Then have students decide whether each of the following statements is a "fact" or an "opinion." Require students to give reasons for their selections.

4. **Reading for the Main Idea.** Review the Chapter 5 History Study Skill. Then, have students state, in their own words, the main idea of Section 1. It might be something like this: "During the Great Depression, many people lost their jobs and their savings, and were forced to struggle just to survive."

BUILDING AMERICAN CITIZENSHIP

During the early years of the Depression, the government did little to help American citizens in their struggle to survive. Why do you think that this was so? In today's society, what help is available to citizens who have lost their jobs and must struggle to survive? (Unemployment insurance, food stamps)

SECTION 1 REVIEW ANSWERS

1. **IDENTIFY: "Hoovervilles":** shantytowns consisting of sheds built by people who had lost their jobs and their homes; **"Bonus Army":** 11,000 veterans who marched to Washington to demand their bonuses for fighting in World War I.

2. **DEFINE: bread lines:** lines of unemployed people waiting for free food.

3. People lost their jobs, homes, and farms; they used up their savings, and many had to accept charity; banks failed.

4. The Great Plains was hit by a long-lasting drought, and dust storms blew away the topsoil.

SECTION 2: President Roosevelt Starts the New Deal

OBJECTIVES

After students have completed this section, they will be able to:
- Describe the background and experiences that qualified FDR for the Presidency.
- List the "alphabet soup" agencies and the purpose for which each was created.
- Describe the criticisms against some of the New Deal agencies.

MOTIVATION

List the following on the chalkboard: FERA, CCC, FDIC, PWA, CWA, NRA, AAA, TVA. Try not to use any references as you do this. Students' initial reaction will be one of amazement. Next, tell them that these initials stand for "alphabet soup" agencies created by the

government during the 1930's. Ask students why they were called that. Ask if they have any idea why they may have been created. Tell them that after reading Section 1 they will be able to identify each agency and the reason for its creation.

SUGGESTED ACTIVITIES

1. **Directed Reading.** Duplicate Worksheet 78, *New Deal Programs.* As students read Section 1, have them complete the table. Be sure to inform them before they begin that the last three entries cannot be completed.

   As a summary, review the information on the chart. Then, have students put it away. Go back to the list of "alphabet soup" agencies on the chalkboard. Ask students to give the full name of each agency and to state its purpose.

2. **Putting Events in Chronological Order.** Discuss Roosevelt's life and the experiences that qualified him for the Presidency. Review the Chapter 19 History Study Skill. Then have students place the following events from his life in chronological order:
   A. Stricken with polio
   B. Ran unsuccessfully as a candidate for Vice President of the United States
   C. Elected President of the United States
   D. Elected Governor of New York
   E. Served as Assistant Secretary of the Navy
   ANSWERS: E - B - A - D - C

3. **Recognizing Primary and Secondary Sources.** Review the Chapter 15 History Study Skill. Then have students apply the skill by determining whether each of the following is a primary or secondary source. Have students give reasons for their choices.
   A. The original hand-written copy of FDR's inaugural address (P)
   B. A tape of one of FDR's "Fireside Chats" (P)
   C. An interview with a 70-year-old CCC veteran recalling his experiences during the Depression (S)
   D. A "Blue Eagle" (P)
   E. A newspaper article criticizing the "alphabet soup" agencies (S)

4. **Flash Cards.** Make two sets of flash cards, using two different colors of tagboard. On one set, place the names of the "alphabet soup" agencies. On the second set, place a brief description of each agency's purpose. Distribute these among students. Have students come to the front of the room to match the appropriate cards. This exercise may be repeated as needed. The cards may then be placed on the bulletin board or taped to the chalkboard for a subsequent matching exercise in Section 3.

BUILDING AMERICAN CITIZENSHIP

What method did FDR use to inform American citizens of actions taken by the government to solve Depression problems? (Fireside Chats) Why do Presidents usually announce major government decisions to the people? (To get their support) How do Presidents today make such announcements? (Make a speech on television or call a televised press conference)

SECTION 2 REVIEW ANSWERS

1. **IDENTIFY: FDIC:** (Federal Deposit Insurance Corporation) federal agency that originally provided insurance for all savings accounts up to $5,000; **Hundred Days:** Roosevelt's first 100 days in office, during which time many new government agencies were created to help the needy and aid economic recovery; **FERA:** (Federal Emergency Relief Administration) federal agency to aid the unemployed and provide federal money to state and local relief agencies; **CCC:** (Civilian Conservation Corps) federal agency that gave jobs to young men between the ages of 18 and 25; **NRA:** (National Recovery Administration) federal agency created to regulate industry; **AAA:** (Agricultural Adjustment Administration) federal agency created to regulate agriculture; **TVA:** (Tennessee Valley Authority) federal agency created to build dams and power plants in the Tennessee River Valley.

2. **DEFINE: bank holiday:** the closing of all banks for examination by government officials, called for by President Roosevelt the day after he took office.

3. He announced a "bank holiday" for examination of banks by government officials and allowed only those in good financial condition to reopen; he created the FDIC.

4. To inspire and restore people's confidence in America and to explain what actions the government was taking to bring about economic recovery.

SECTION 3: New Deal Reforms Continue

OBJECTIVES

After completing this section, students will be able to:

- Identify the opponents of New Deal programs and explain the reasons for their opposition.
- List the programs started during the "Second New Deal" and state their purposes.
- Describe the progress made by workers and unions during the "Second New Deal."

MOTIVATION

Review the "alphabet soup" agencies discussed in Section 2. Have students refer to Worksheet 78, if necessary. Then, have them name the three programs not discussed in Section 2. (WPA, Social Security Act, NLRB) Ask students which of the programs is still in effect (Social Security) and to identify its purpose. Also, ask what problems would be dealt with by the NLRB.

SUGGESTED ACTIVITIES

1. **Directed Readings.** As students read Section 3, have them complete Worksheet 78, stating the purpose and results of the final three programs. As a summary, add three new flash cards to the set created for the activities in Section 2. Again, distribute the set of flash cards among students.

   Have them match all 11 programs with their purposes. Then, have students orally state the results of each program, without the use of the chart.

2. **Matching Exercise.** Discuss the criticisms of New Deal programs as stated by FDR's opponents. To check students' understanding of the attacks, place the following exercise on the chalkboard or on a transparency for the overhead projector. Have students match the statement with the person responsible for it.

A. Dr. Francis Townsend	(B, E) Claimed that New Deal programs were socialistic and an attack on private property.
B. Al Smith	
C. Father Charles E. Coughlin	
D. Huey P. Long	(C) Proposed heavy taxation of the rich and a guaranteed income for everyone.
E. John W. Davis	
	(A) Proposed a retirement fund for senior citizens.
	(D) Proposed that the government provide every family with a home, $2,000 a year, and a free college education for the children.

3. **Improving Your Writing.** Review the Chapter 10 History Study Skill. Have students apply the skill by writing a paragraph in answer to the following question: "What progress was made by workers and unions during the 'Second New Deal'?"

4. **History Study Skills.** Refer students to the activity *Finding Out About Your Local History* on textbook page 665. You may wish to assign this as a long-range project. However, have students read it through in class first, so that you can make any necessary modifications and answer any questions.

BUILDING AMERICAN CITIZENSHIP

The "alphabet soup" agencies and the Social Security Act involved the government in the lives of American citizens more than ever before in our nation's history. What were the advantages of this involvement? (Provided help to people who needed it.) Were there any disadvantages of this increased involvement by the government? (Everything had to be done according to the regulations of the agencies.) How much is our government involved in the lives of citizens today? Do you think it is too much or not enough? Explain your answer.

SECTION 3 REVIEW ANSWERS

1. **IDENTIFY: Father Charles Coughlin:** the "radio priest" from Detroit who had a weekly radio program, during which he attacked the New Deal; **Dr. Francis Townsend:** critic of FDR who proposed that citizens over 60 be given a pension of $200 a month; **Senator Huey P. Long:** enemy of FDR who proposed a "share our wealth" plan for the nation; **WPA:** (Works Progress Administration) federal agency that set aside $5 billion for "useful projects," giving jobs to over 5 million Americans; **Social Security Act:** law passed in 1935 to create (1) pensions for workers on retirement at age 65, (2) unemployment insurance to help workers who lost their jobs, and (3) aid to dependent mothers and children and the handicapped.

2. **DEFINE: sitdown strike:** strike in which workers sat down by their machines and refused to move.

3. WPA and Social Security.

4. The Wagner Act created the National Labor Relations Board, which protected workers' rights to organize and protection against unfair labor practices by employers. John L. Lewis created the CIO, giving unskilled as well as skilled workers the opportunity to join unions.

SECTION 4: The New Deal Runs Into Problems

OBJECTIVES

After completing this section, students will be able to:
- List the groups of voters that supported FDR in the 1936 election.
- Explain how FDR's court-packing plan and the "Roosevelt depression" affected New Deal programs.
- Describe the lasting effects of the New Deal on American society.

MOTIVATION

Use the time line at the beginning of Chapter 28. Ask students when FDR was elected for the second time. (1936) Have students look at the programs started during each of his first two administrations. Ask them if he was able to accomplish more to end the Depression during his first term or his second term. Have them support their answer with evidence from the time line. Also, ask if they feel the time line provides enough factual evidence to answer the question fully. Tell students that they will be asked the same question after reading Section 4 to see if their opinions have changed.

SUGGESTED ACTIVITIES

1. **Directed Reading.** As students read Section 4, have them answer the following questions:
   A. Why was FDR able to win the election of 1936 so easily? (Candidate of economic recovery, stirred pride in the people, won support from labor, liberals, and blacks)
   B. What new problems did FDR face during his second term in office? (Opposition to his proposed reorganization of the Supreme Court; a recession; new conservative Congress elected in 1938)
   C. How did the New Deal increase the power of the Presidency? (President suggested legislative reforms to Congress; new agencies and programs were headed by presidential appointees)
   Review the answers to these questions with students. Summarize by returning to the question posed during the Motivation. Discuss it again. Have students give evidence to support their answers.

2. **Ideals in the Lives of Americans.** Ask students to read the selection on Mary McLeod Bethune on textbook page 662. Have them discuss the two questions at the end of the reading. In addition, ask why Mrs. Bethune's appointment to a government position during FDR's administration was important. (She was black and a woman. FDR sought the support of both of these groups during the 1936 campaign. Her appointment may have helped him win support.) You may also wish to have students compare the careers of Mary McLeod Bethune and Frances Perkins (see textbook page 640).

3. **Finding Out About Your Local History.** Duplicate Worksheet 79, *A Small Town in the 1930's.* This exercise reinforces the History Study Skill for Chapter 28 and also requires students to use and familiarize themselves with library sources. Encourage students to complete the brief report suggested as a part of this exercise by suggesting topics of local interest.

4. **Round Robin.** Use the method as introduced in Chapter 1. Ask a student volunteer to state an important fact from Section 4 or any of the other sections in Chapter 28. Have a second student volunteer repeat that fact and add another. Have a third student volunteer repeat the fact stated by the second, and state another. Continue this activity as time and resources allow.

BUILDING AMERICAN CITIZENSHIP

Your textbook states that the New Deal established the idea that it was the federal government's duty to provide for the people's welfare. Is this idea still popular? What do you think of it? Would you recommend any changes in the government's current policy to improve the lives of American citizens?

SECTION 4 REVIEW ANSWERS

1. **IDENTIFY: Court-packing plan:** FDR's plan to add more justices to the Supreme Court, which would allow him to appoint people who supported the New Deal; **Fair Labor Standards Act:** law passed in 1938 that ended child labor and set minimum wages and maximum hours for workers.
2. Organized labor, people who considered themselves progressives or liberals, and black Americans.
3. Many people disapproved of his Court-packing plan; many also blamed him for the 1937 recession.
4. Increased power of the Presidency; increased size of the federal government; increased role of certain groups, such as organized labor and farmers, in political decision making; some political gains for minorities; establishment of the idea that it is the government's job to provide for the welfare of the people.

CHAPTER 28 REVIEW ANSWERS
REVIEWING KEY WORDS

1. c.   2. e.   3. a.   4. b.   5. d.

REMEMBERING IMPORTANT PEOPLE AND EVENTS

1. a.   2. d.   3. d.   4. c.   5. b.
6. c.   7. e.   8. a.   9. d.   10. b.

REVIEWING THE FACTS

1. T   2. T   3. F   4. T   5. T

PLACING EVENTS IN TIME

1. E   2. D   3. A   4. C   5. B

LINKING GEOGRAPHY AND HISTORY

Shortage of some farm products which led to higher prices; many farmers lost their land and moved to the cities, competing for jobs that were already scarce.

THINKING ABOUT AMERICAN HISTORY

1. **Advantages:** greater federal aid to citizens and to state and local governments; more jobs for the unemployed; protection of workers' rights; insurance for saving accounts; a more stable banking system, and so on. **Disadvantages:** more rules and regulations; cost of federal spending.
2. Answers will vary.

APPLYING HISTORY STUDIES SKILLS

1. No.   2. Yes.   3. Yes.   4. No.
5. Yes.   6. Yes.   7. Yes.   8. No.

CHAPTER 29

Rise of Dictators Leads to World War II (1920's-1945)

Chapter Objectives

After completing this chapter, students will be able to:
1. Explain how the military aggression of German, Italian, and Japanese dictators caused war.
2. Describe how the United States became involved in World War II.
3. Identify important events during World War II.
4. Describe the impact of World War II on Americans at home.

Chapter Chronology

Chapter 29 surveys the background, causes, major events, and conclusion of World War II. Many of the most significant events of the period are highlighted on the time line in the textbook Chapter Opener. Italy became a dictatorship in 1922 when Benito Mussolini took power. In 1931, Japan seized Manchuria. Two years later, in 1933, Adolf Hitler gained power in Germany. In 1935, Italy invaded Ethiopia. Meanwhile, in Asia, Japan attacked China in 1937. In 1941, Japan attacked Pearl Harbor, bringing the United States into World War II. Western Europe was liberated by the Allies in 1944, and the war came to an end in 1945.

Motivation

Have students turn to the time line on the textbook Chapter Opener page, carefully note each event, and locate each place mentioned on a map or globe. Next, have them identify the countries they think were aggressors (Japan and Italy) as well as the individuals who gained power (Mussolini and Hitler). Ask them to name people or events that they may have heard of before (Hitler and Pearl Harbor). Then have students read the textbook Chapter Introduction and discuss the summary questions with them.

Geographical Setting

Chapter 29 has a strong geographical focus. Students will learn about areas of Europe, Africa, and Asia that may be unfamiliar to them. The map *Axis Expansion in Europe Before September 1939*, on textbook page 671, allows students to identify the countries discussed in Section 1. The map, *Japanese Expansion in Asia Before World War II*, on textbook page 672, illustrates Japanese imperialism and the sites of important battles of the Pacific. The maps *World War II in Europe, 1939-1945*, on textbook page 676, and *The United States in World War II in the Pacific*, on textbook page 679, both illustrate the influence of geography on the war. For example, the United States adopted a strategy, known as "island hopping," in the Pacific, in order to reduce the time spent driving back the Japanese.

History Study Skills

The History Study Skill in Chapter 29 is *Using Organizational Charts*. The information illustrated is the organization of the major bodies of the United Nations. This activity is best used at the end of the chapter, where the United Nations is discussed.

Bibliography

Teacher References

Iriye, Akira, *Power and Culture: The Japanese-American War, 1941-1945*. Harvard University Press, Cambridge, Mass., 1981.

Morison, Samuel Eliot, *The Two-Ocean War*. Little, Brown, Boston, Mass., 1963.

Student References

Lidz, Richard, *Many Kinds of Courage*. G.P. Putnam's Sons, New York City, 1980. A collection of oral history accounts of people who survived World War II; this book recreates the chaos and anguish of the period.

Maxer, Harry, *The Last Mission*. Delacorte, New York City, 1979. In this exciting novel, the teenage hero lies about his age to enlist as a bomber crewman in World War II and then finds that war is not as glamorous as he had thought.

Audio-Visual Materials

World War II, Educational Enrichment Materials, 5 color sound filmstrips. This well-documented program vividly illustrates the key events before, during and after World War II.

American People in World War II, McGraw Films, color, 25 min., 1973. This film, about life on the home front in World War II, describes how the United States mobilized its people and other resources during this time.

SECTION 1: Dictators Threaten World Peace

OBJECTIVES

After completing this section, students will be able to:
• Identify the dictators of Germany, Italy, and Japan.

- Tell how World War II began.
- Describe the methods used by the United States to support the fight against the Axis Powers.
- Explain the Soviet Union's involvement in World War II.

MOTIVATION

Use the strategy suggested in the chapter introduction in this manual. Emphasize the countries involved in World War II as depicted on the time line: Italy, Japan, Manchuria, Germany, Ethiopia, and China. Have students locate these nations on the map in their textbook. Then, use a blank chalkmap or a transparency of an outline map to have them identify each nation. Tell them that in Section 1 they will learn how each of these nations was involved in events that led to World War II.

SUGGESTED ACTIVITIES

1. **Directed Reading.** As students read, have them complete the following table:

NATIONS THAT THREATENED WORLD PEACE

Nation	Leader	Promises to the People	Countries Invaded
Germany			
Italy			
Japan			

Draw the table on the chalkboard and have students complete all entries. As a summary, discuss what the title was that was given to the leaders of these nations, and what their governments had in common.

2. **Discussion.** Conduct a class discussion on the following question: How did World War II begin? Be sure to make comparisons with the start of World War I. What were the similarities (alliances, imperialism) and the differences (the event responsible for the start of the fighting, the different nations involved)? Also, discuss the involvement of the Soviet Union and how it changed between 1939 and June 1941.

3. **Putting Events in Chronological Order.** Review the Chapter 19 History Study Skill. Then have students place the following events from Section 1 in correct chronological order.
   A. Germany attacked the Soviet Union.
   B. Germany invaded Poland.
   C. Japan attacked China.
   D. Japan took control of Manchuria.
   E. The Nazis gained control of Germany.
   F. Mussolini attacked Ethiopia.
   G. The Fascists took control of the Italian government.
   H. The United States began sending aid to the Allies.
   ANSWERS: G - D - E - F - C - B - H - A

   Use the exercise to review the important facts in the section. For example: G - Who were the Fascists? How did they gain control of the Italian government? When?

4. **Matching Exercise.** Place the following activity on the chalkboard or on a transparency for the overhead projector. It will determine whether or not students

know the leaders of the major nations involved in World War II.

(D)___Benito Mussolini	A. Soviet Union
(A)___Josef Stalin	B. Germany
(F)___Emperor Hirohito	C. United States
(B)___Adolf Hitler	D. Italy
(E)___Winston Churchill	E. Great Britain
(C)___Franklin Roosevelt	F. Japan

Once again, review which of these were Axis nations and which were Allied nations or supported the Allied nations.

BUILDING AMERICAN CITIZENSHIP

How can dictators persuade the citizens of their nation to support their rise to power? Once in power, how do dictators control the citizens of their nation? Do you know of any dictators in the world today? How do you think their methods of staying in power compare with those of Hitler and Mussolini?

SECTION 1 REVIEW ANSWERS

1. **IDENTIFY: Benito Mussolini:** founder and organizer of the Fascist Party in Italy in 1922; **Fascists:** members of the Fascist Party in Italy; **Adolf Hitler:** head of the Nazi Party and dictator of Germany; **Nazi Party:** political party that took control of Germany in 1933; **Axis Powers:** Germany, Italy, and Japan; **Hirohito:** emperor of Japan: **Josef Stalin:** dictator of the Soviet Union; **Winston Churchill:** Prime Minister of Great Britain during World War II; **Lend-Lease Act:** law passed in 1941 permitting the President to lend or sell war materials to the Allies; **Allies:** Great Britain, France, the Soviet Union, and the United States.

2. **DEFINE: dictatorship:** a government in which the leader or leaders hold complete authority over the people they rule; **concentration camps:** prison camps.

3. World War II began with Germany's attack on Poland on September 1, 1939. Two days later, Great Britain and France declared war on Germany.

4. It passed the Lend-Lease Act to lend or sell war materials to the Allies; it placed an embargo on scrap metal, oil, and other raw materials to Japan.

SECTION 2: America Enters World War II

OBJECTIVES

After completing this section, students will be able to:
- Describe the Japanese attack on Pearl Harbor.
- Identify major naval battles fought in the Pacific Ocean.
- Explain how Allied forces halted the advances of Axis forces in Europe and North Africa.

MOTIVATION

On the board, list the major battles that students will be reading about: El Alamein, Coral Sea, Pearl Harbor, Stalingrad, and Midway. Have them use the maps *World War II in Europe* and *The United States in World War II in the Pacific* to identify the location of each of these battles. If any students are familiar with these battles, allow them to contribute what details they know. Ask if the maps give information about who won the battles or when.

SUGGESTED ACTIVITIES

1. **Directed Reading.** As students read, have them answer the following questions:
   A. Why were the Japanese able to do so much damage to the American navy at Pearl Harbor? (Surprise attack, ships lined up in dock)
   B. How were the Japanese advances on territories in the Pacific Ocean stopped? (Battle of the Coral Sea, Battle of Midway)
   C. How were German advances in the North Atlantic, Europe, and North Africa stopped? (North Atlantic —sonar and "depth charges"; Europe—Battle of Stalingrad; North Africa—El Alamein)
   Review the answers to the questions and discuss the details of each battle. As a summary, have students arrange the names of the battles listed on the board for the Motivation in chronological order.
2. **Research Activity.** The names of important Axis and Allied military leaders are mentioned in Section 2. They include: General Douglas MacArthur, Admiral Yamamoto, General Erwin Rommel, General Dwight D. Eisenhower, General Bernard Montgomery, and Rear Admiral Isaac Kidd. Assign students to use library sources to write reports on the lives of these individuals. Below-average students may be directed to identify them by using information from the textbook.
3. **Reviewing Map Skills.** Review the Chapter 25 History Study Skill. Duplicate Worksheet 80, *Latitude, Longitude, and Location* and ask students to complete it. If a class set of world atlases is available, you may wish to have students consult them to locate the points of longitude and latitude for the other battles described in Section 2.
4. **Landmarks of Liberty.** Have students read the selection *The U.S.S. Arizona Memorial at Pearl Harbor* on textbook page 675. Ask students to recall important details about the U.S.S. *Arizona* from the text: How many lives were lost on the battleship? How many other battleships were sunk? What was the total loss of life at Pearl Harbor that day? Discuss the answers to the two questions at the end of the reading selection.

BUILDING AMERICAN CITIZENSHIP

The Japanese attack on Pearl Harbor was a surprise. Do you think a nation has an obligation to warn another nation that it is going to attack? What would be the advantages and disadvantages of giving such advance warning?

SECTION 2 REVIEW ANSWERS

1. **IDENTIFY: Pearl Harbor:** naval base where the United States Pacific Fleet was stationed, attacked by Japan on December 7, 1941; **General Douglas MacArthur:** general appointed by President Roosevelt to head the Allied forces in the South Pacific; **Battle of the Coral Sea:** 1942 naval battle off the coast of Australia in which American forces so badly damaged the Japanese fleet that Japan canceled its plans to invade Australia; **Erwin Rommel:** German general, called the "Desert Fox," who commanded German and Italian troops in North Africa; **General Dwight D. Eisenhower:** joint commander of the Allied troops in North Africa; **General Bernard Montgomery:** joint commander of the Allied troops in North Africa.
2. **DEFINE: convoys:** groups of merchant ships accompanied by warships for protection.
3. The day after the Japanese attack on Pearl Harbor on December 7, 1941, the United States declared war on Japan. Britain quickly did the same, and then Germany and Italy joined Japan in declaring war on the United States.

SECTION 3: The Allies Take the Offensive

OBJECTIVES

After completing this section, students will be able to:
- Name and locate the Allied victories in Europe and the Pacific from 1942 to 1945.
- Explain the important decisions made at the Yalta and Potsdam Conferences.
- Describe how the Allies forced the Japanese to surrender.

MOTIVATION

The students have read about the first four years of the war thus far. Discuss one year at a time. Ask who was winning the war in 1939, and have students give evidence to support their answer. Repeat the process for 1940, 1941, and 1942. Students should name the important battles fought each year as part of their reply. Ask why it took three more years to win the war if the Axis advance had been halted by 1942. Discuss responses before reading Section 3.

SUGGESTED ACTIVITIES

1. **Directed Reading.** Ask students to draw two columns on a sheet of paper. As they read, have them list, in the first column, the major battles fought in the Pacific and, in the second column, those fought in Europe. As a summary, review the entries made by students and have them discuss the important details of each battle.
2. **Class Discussion.** Discuss the issue of the atomic bomb with the students. Why was the bomb dropped? Why didn't Japan surrender when it was issued an ultimatum? Where was the first bomb dropped? What were the effects? Why was a second bomb dropped? Where? What were the effects?
3. **Comparison.** Have students compare the Yalta Conference with the Potsdam Conference. Discuss the dates, the leaders who were there, the issues discussed, the decisions made, and so on. Conclude the discussion by having students decide whether each of the following refers to the Potsdam Conference or to the Yalta Conference.
   A. Attended by FDR, Churchill, and Stalin (Y)

B. Made decision to try Nazi leaders for their crimes (P)

C. Agreed to divide Germany into four occupied zones. (Y)

D. Promised to work for an international organization to promote world peace (Y)

E. Agreed to demand the immediate surrender of Japan (P)

F. Agreed to bring about free elections in Europe after the war (Y)

4. **Organizing Facts.** Duplicate Worksheet 81, *Which War?* This worksheet requires students to apply their knowledge of both World Wars to complete a categorization activity. You may wish to work with students to complete the first three or four statements in order to be sure they are following the directions accurately.

BUILDING AMERICAN CITIZENSHIP

The last paragraph of Section 3 describes the cost of World War II in lives and property loss. However, it does not mention the personal costs or sacrifices that had to be made by the citizens of warring nations. How do you think the lives of civilian citizens in the Axis nations were affected? In the Allied nations?

SECTION 3 REVIEW ANSWERS

1. **IDENTIFY: Guadalcanal:** island in the Solomon Islands where Americans began their offensive against Japan in August 1942. **D-Day;** the day of the Allied invasion of Europe—June 6, 1944; **Battle of the Bulge:** unsuccessful German counterattack in Belgium in December 1944; **Yalta Conference:** meeting of Roosevelt, Churchill, and Stalin at Yalta in the Soviet Union in January 1945; **Clement Atlee:** Prime Minister of Britain who replaced Churchill in 1945.

2. **DEFINE: holocaust:** the destruction of the Jewish people in Nazi concentration camps; **ultimatum:** a last chance for immediate surrender.

3. The dropping of the second atomic bomb, this time on Nagasaki in Japan on August 9, 1945.

4. American, British, and Canadian troops from the west and Russian troops from the east invaded Germany and met at the Elbe River in April 1945, bringing final defeat to the Germans.

5. G, S, D

SECTION 4: The War Brings Worldwide Changes

OBJECTIVES

After completing this section, students will be able to:
• Explain why the United Nations was created and describe its organization.
• Describe changes that occurred in America as a result of our involvement in World War II.

MOTIVATION

Every war in which the United States participated brought about changes. Have students recall the major changes brought about by the American Revolution (freedom from Great Britain); the Civil War (freedom for black Americans, a reunited nation); the Spanish-American War (new lands overseas); and World War I. Ask students what major changes they think came about in the lives of Americans after World War II. Write suggested answers on the chalkboard. Tell students they will be able to add or to remove items from this list after they have read Section 4.

SUGGESTED ACTIVITIES

1. **Directed Reading.** Have students skim the headings to note areas in which life changed as a result of World War II. Use these, with students, to create the major topics for an outline.

War Brings About Change
   I. United Nations Created
   II. American Industry Boomed
   III. Black Americans Gained Opportunities
   IV. Women Took on New Roles
   V. Some Americans Faced Troubles
   VI. War Affected All Americans

When the major topics have been selected, have students read the chapter carefully to list two or three subtopics for each major topic. Then, have selected students write the completed outline on the chalkboard. Finally, check this information against the list developed during the Motivation.

2. **Using Organizational Charts.** Have students complete the History Study Skill activity on textbook page 688. After students answer the questions that are part of the activity, ask them to state the purpose of an organizational chart. (To show relationships between the various parts of an organization.) Ask what information the chart does *not* contain? (A description of the various tasks of the UN agencies.) Depending upon the level of the students, you may wish to have them attempt to create an organizational chart of your school, including such parts as those of the principal, the vice-principal(s), the department heads, the teachers, the librarian, the cafeteria staff, the counseling staff, the custodial staff, the students, the student council, and so on.

3. **History Study Skills.** Duplicate Worksheet 82, *The Normandy Campaign.* The purpose of this activity is to have students apply the History Study Skill they have just learned. In order to determine their degree of success in working independently, you may wish to assign this activity for homework.

4. **Comprehension Check.** In order to determine whether students have understood the material in Section 4, have them complete the following TRUE-FALSE exercise. This can be written on the chalkboard or on a transparency for the overhead projector. If a statement is FALSE, have students rewrite it to make it TRUE.

A. Industry "boomed" during World War II because labor unions did not strike and advanced technology led to production increases. (T)

B. America's armed forces became integrated during World War II. (F)

C. By 1945, women made up one-third of the labor force of the United States. (T)

D. All Japanese Americans living in the United States during World War II were placed in internment (relocation) camps until 1945. (F)

E. Over 1,000,000 Americans were killed in World War II. (F)

BUILDING AMERICAN CITIZENSHIP

Duplicate Worksheet 83, *Japanese Americans and World War II*. The first three questions in this activity add to students' knowledge of Japanese-American problems during the war and require them to apply the Chapter 5 History Study Skill, *Reading for the Main Idea*. Questions 4 and 5 focus on the problem of citizens whose rights are suspended during a time of war, and require students to think critically about them.

SECTION 4 REVIEW ANSWERS

1. **IDENTIFY: United Nations:** an international organization dedicated to freedom and cooperation among peoples everywhere; **Colonel Benjamin O. Davis:** highest ranking black officer in the Army Air Force; **Dr. Charles Drew:** inventor of a new way to store and use plasma, the fluid part of blood.
2. **DEFINE: rationing:** making available limited amounts of scarce goods.
3. To create a world organization dedicated to world peace and justice.
4. Black Americans worked in industry and served in the armed forces. Many women worked in factories and in businesses, and some served in the armed forces.

CHAPTER 29 REVIEW ANSWERS

REVIEWING KEY WORDS

1. a.   2. c.   3. e.   4. b.   5. d.

REMEMBERING IMPORTANT PEOPLE

1. c.   2. b.   3. a.   4. e.   5. d.

REVIEWING THE FACTS

1. G   2. I   3. G   4. J   5. G
6. F   7. T   8. T   9. T   10. T

PLACING EVENTS IN TIME

1. A   2. B   3. C   4. E   5. D

LINKING GEOGRAPHY AND HISTORY

1. Supplying all areas with needed materials simultaneously; dividing the armed forces so that there were enough military personnel in all combat areas.
2. Australia and New Zealand's proximity to the battle zone in the South Pacific made them vulnerable to Japanese aggression. They were fighting to protect themselves from possible invasion.

THINKING ABOUT AMERICAN HISTORY

1. Both groups were placed in camps and thus lost their homes and businesses and had their lives ruined. The big difference was that Japanese Americans were not killed.
2. The United States had highly developed technology, rich natural resources, and an industrial system—which had grown rapidly during the war—untouched by bombs or invaders.

APPLYING HISTORY STUDIES SKILLS

1. It shows the relationship between the parts of the organization, the importance of each part, and what part has control over another.
2. General Assembly.
3. Five.
4. It hears disputes between countries.
5. Economic and Social Council.

UNIT 9 REVIEW ANSWERS

VOCABULARY REVIEW

Answers will vary.

REVIEWING THE MAIN IDEAS

1. Wages rose, and people had more money to spend; more goods and services were available at lower prices.
2. Farm families; miners and mill workers; blacks who migrated to Northern cities; immigrants.
3. People had been investing heavily in the stock market. They believed prices would continue to rise, and they could sell their stock to make a profit. Many had bought on margin, or borrowed money, and when prices started to fall, frightened investors rushed to sell their stock to recover their losses. Panic selling drove prices down even more.
4. By providing jobs for the unemployed, creating a system of pensions for workers who retire at 65, insuring savings accounts, raising farm prices, protecting workers' rights to form unions, and so on.
5. The rise of dictatorships in Italy, Germany, and Japan, and the ambition of these nations for wealth and power. Hitler's attack on Poland started the war in 1939.
6. Initially, the United States provided the Allies with supplies through direct sale and lend-lease. After the bombing of Pearl Harbor, it declared war on all of the Axis Powers.

APPLYING YOUR STUDY SKILLS

1. **Using a Time Line**
   a. (1) 11 years
      (2) Social Security Act
      (3) 2 years
2. **Using a Map**
   a. (1) Spain, Portugal, Ireland, Sweden, and Turkey
3. **Using a Chart**
   a. (1) T (2) F (3) T (4) F (5) T (6) T
4. **Using Your Textbook**
   a. (1) 13 years   (2) 4 times
      (3) Twenty-second Amendment

PROJECTS

Answers will vary.

BUILDING AMERICAN CITIZENSHIP

1. Answers will vary.
2. Answers will vary but may include the following:
   a. To make their nations rich and powerful.
   b. Freedom of speech, press, religion, assembly, trial by jury, and so on.
   c. Answers will vary.

UNIT 10 (1945-1980's)
America Is Challenged Anew

Introducing the Unit

Unit Ten surveys the period from 1945 to the 1980's, a turbulent time marked by progress, violence, determination, and hope. There were many contradictions—sweeping social reforms and yet periods of great unrest at home; continuing efforts to find peaceful, equitable solutions to world problems and yet heavy American involvement in two wars in Asia. Our citizens, in the time-honored American tradition, disagreed and argued about many issues and problems. On one subject, however, their response was unanimous—pride in America's spectacular achievements in space.

Chapter 30 describes how Americans, with World War II behind them, picked up their lives and adjusted to a peacetime society. Under President Truman, their standard of living rose, and, on the whole, they enjoyed a period of growing prosperity. On the world scene, the United States, already a major power before World War II, emerged in the postwar period even stronger. America, now the leader of the world's free nations, was committed to a policy of containing communism abroad and eliminating it at home.

Chapter 31 deals with the 1950's, a period when the American economy was at an all-time high under a popular President, Dwight Eisenhower. However, not all Americans could share equally in the nation's good times. During this decade, black Americans began to work harder than ever to achieve their civil rights. Meanwhile, the Cold War between the United States and the Soviet Union continued.

The period of the 1960's, covered in Chapter 32, was marked by violence, social upheaval, and war in Southeast Asia. It was also the period in which, under President Johnson, the Great Society program, the broadest program of social and economic change since the New Deal, was launched.

In the 1970's and 1980's, the United States continued its role as the leader of the free world. The Cold War continued though relations with Communist China improved dramatically. The nation remained well ahead in the space race. Major domestic concerns included civil rights, women's rights, and the environment.

The Unit Opener in the textbook depicts many of the significant persons and events of the period. You may wish to use these illustrations to help introduce the unit to the students. In the center is the first U.S. space shuttle. In the lower left-hand corner is a representation of the first space walk. Continuing in a clockwise direction, are President John F. Kennedy and Martin Luther King, a suburban housing development, two scientists, military helicopters of the type used in Korea and Vietnam, and a computer analyst.

Unit Themes and Ideas

Several major themes dominate Unit Ten. One is America's role in the maintenance of the balance of power between the "Communist World" and the "Free World." The conflict inherent in the opposing values and attitudes of communist dictatorships and democratic governments continues to be a crucial problem in our foreign relations.

Another important theme is the ongoing struggle to ensure equal rights for all Americans. In the 1960's, 1970's, and 1980's, blacks were vigorously joined in their struggle for civil rights by American Indians and women. Although great progress has been made, much work still remains to be done.

A third major theme of this unit is the ongoing search for economic stability and prosperity for all. In the world's richest nation, there is poverty. Economic security has continued to be threatened by periodic inflation, recession and unemployment. These are problems that have eluded easy solutions. These three issues—political, social, and economic—set against the background of ever more sophisticated technological development in both civilian and military spheres, promise to continue into the next century, where they will challenge the imagination, resourcefulness, and stamina of today's young people.

The themes and ideas of Unit 10 are organized into the four chapters below:

Chapter 30 - *The Postwar Years Bring New Problems (1945 - 1953)*

Chapter 31 - *Eisenhower Leads a Prosperous Nation (1953 - 1960)*

Chapter 32 - *Americans Face Conflict and Change (1960's - 1970's)*

Chapter 33 - *Americans Look Ahead with Hope (1970's - 1980's)*

CHAPTER 30

The Postwar Years Bring New Problems (1945-1953)

Chapter Objectives

After completing this chapter, students will be able to:

1. Describe how America changed after World War II.
2. Explain what Truman hoped to accomplish with his Fair Deal.
3. Identify accomplishments of the Truman Presidency.
4. Define the concept of "iron curtain."
5. Explain why Americans were concerned about the threat of communism at home and abroad.
6. Describe American participation in the Korean War.

Chapter Chronology

Chapter 30 covers the period from the end of World War II through the conclusion of the Truman Presidency. This was a time of tremendous adjustment and change on the home front as well as in world affairs. Several important persons and events of the period are highlighted on the time line in the textbook Chapter Opener. Early in 1945, shortly before the end of the war, Franklin D. Roosevelt died and Harry S. Truman became President. In 1947, the Marshall Plan was announced. In the same year, the Taft-Hartley Act, limiting the power of unions, was passed. Truman won the Presidential election in 1948. The Berlin Airlift began in 1949, the same year in which the North Atlantic Treaty Organization was formed. In the following year, war broke out in Korea. The Twenty-second Amendment, limiting American presidents to two four-year terms in office was ratified in 1951.

Motivation

Have students think back to the period immediately following World War I. Ask them what changes occurred in the country at that time. Jot their responses on the board. Once you have a short list, have students look at the section titles and headings in this chapter. Ask students for any evidence that the 1950's may have been similar to the 1920's. Use this activity for reference as students work through the chapter.

Geographical Setting

Two international geographical settings are emphasized in this chapter. The first, dealing with the cold war in Europe, Asia, and Africa illustrates the extent of communist aggression after World War II. The second emphasis is on Korea where the Korean War began in 1950. Students should locate the 38th parallel and the Yalu River on the map, *The Korean War, 1950-1953.*

History Study Skills

The History Study Skill introduced in Chapter 30 is *Reading Political Cartoons.* The cartoon used to develop this skill deals with the Cold War, and Stalin's establishment of "puppet" countries in Eastern Europe. This activity is best used in conjunction with Section 3.

Bibliography

Teacher References

Goldman, Eric, *The Crucial Decade—And After, 1945-1960.* Random House, New York City, 1960.

Graebner, Norman, *Cold War.* D. C. Heath, Boston, Mass., 1976.

Student References

Devaney, John, *Douglas MacArthur: Something of a Hero.* G. P. Putnam's Sons, New York City, 1979. This is a fine biography of Douglas MacArthur, a great World War II general.

Irving, Clifford, *Spy: The Story of Modern Espionage.* Macmillan, New York City, 1969. This well-illustrated book, which focuses primarily on the Soviet spy network and its evolution during the Cold War, also discusses British and American intelligence organizations.

Audio-Visual Materials

Harry S. Truman: Man of Decision, Guidance Associates, 3 filmstrips, 3 cassettes, library kit, teacher's guide.

This program surveys Truman's presidency, with emphasis on Cold War events and the Fair Deal.

McCarthyism: Era of Fear, Educational Enrichment Materials, 2 filmstrips, 2 cassettes, 1 spirit master, teacher's guide.

This program traces the rise and fall of Joseph McCarthy, the Wisconsin senator who created a climate of fear with his charges of Communist infiltration of the American government.

SECTION 1: America Returns to Peacetime Living

OBJECTIVES

After completing this section, students will be able to:

- Describe major changes in America's economy immediately following World War II.
- List new products that improved Americans' standard of living.
- Identify areas of American life in which black Americans were able to make progress in their struggle for equality.

MOTIVATION

Use a display of pictures of the following: a pair of nylons, a toaster, any items made of plastic, a television set (other items mentioned in Section 1 may be substituted). Have students identify the items. Take an informal survey to determine how many of the students have each item in their homes. Ask if anyone recalls a time when they did not have such items in their homes. Tell students that in Section 1 they will be reading about how these items were developed.

SUGGESTED ACTIVITIES

1. **Directed Reading.** Have students copy the following sentences from the chalkboard. As they read, have them fill in each blank with the correct answer. You may wish to provide a word bank for below-average students.

A. After World War II, several __(UNIONS)__ went on strike to demand higher __(WAGES)__. President __(TRUMAN)__ ended strikes by __(RAILROAD)__ workers and __(MINERS)__ because they threatened the nation's __(WELFARE)__.

B. New __(PRODUCTS)__ and materials became available to __(CONSUMERS)__ after the war. These included __(NYLON)__, __(PLASTICS)__, __(TOASTERS)__ and __(MIXERS)__. __(TELEVISION)__ became a popular form of family entertainment.

161

C. Two organizations that worked to get equal __(RIGHTS)__ for black people were the __(NAACP)__ and __(CORE)__. __(JACKIE ROBINSON)__ became the first black American to play on a major league baseball team.

As you review the answers for each sentence, discuss related information. For example, with "A," ask what the result was of the constant demand for higher wages. (Higher prices and inflation)

2. **Reading for the Main Idea.** Review the Chapter 5 History Study Skill. Then, have students apply it by stating the main idea of Section 1 in their own words. Their statement should contain the following information: Many changes occurred in America after World War II. These included an improved standard of living; an increased variety of consumer goods; and some progress in the struggle of black Americans to gain equal rights.

3. **Separating Facts from Opinions.** Review the Chapter 12 History Study Skill. Then, have students apply it by determining whether each of the statements below is a "fact" or an "opinion."
   A. Critics charged that President Truman had no right to end strikes. (O)
   B. When demand is greater than supply, prices rise. (F)
   C. Most people were willing to pay higher prices for goods after World War II. (O)
   D. One of the biggest changes in family life was brought about by television (O)
   E. In 1951, color television was introduced. (F)
   F. Many white people supported the idea of equality for black Americans. (O)

BUILDING AMERICAN CITIZENSHIP

In 1946, President Truman acted to end strikes by miners and railroad workers because he said these strikes threatened the nation's welfare. What do you think he meant by that? Do unions have a right to strike? Do you think Presidents should have the right to end any strike? (Answers will vary.)

SECTION 1 REVIEW ANSWERS

1. **IDENTIFY: NAACP:** National Association for the Advancement of Colored People; organization that worked to gain equality for black Americans under the law; **CORE:** Congress for Racial Equality; organization that used peaceful public demonstrations and protests to gain equal rights for blacks; **Jackie Robinson:** first black American to play on a major-league baseball team.
2. **DEFINE: inflation:** rapid increase in prices for goods and services; **standard of living:** quality of life; **segregation:** separation of races.
3. Factories turned from producing war materials to producing consumer goods; greater consumer demand; inflation; higher wages.
4. Getting better jobs and higher salaries; entering professions such as law and medicine; right to play on major-league baseball teams.

SECTION 2: President Truman Starts the Fair Deal

OBJECTIVES

After completing this section, students will be able to:
• Identify actions taken by President Truman to secure equal rights for black Americans.
• Describe the relationship between President Truman and Congress.
• Explain the results of the election of 1948.

MOTIVATION

Write the following headlines on the chalkboard:
"Twenty-Second Amendment Approved"
"Taft-Hartley Act Passed Over President's Veto"
"Hoover Commission Submits Report"
"Truman Upsets Dewey"
"Segregation Ended In Armed Forces"
Have students study each headline carefully. Tell students that each event occurred during the administration of one President. Ask them to identify the President.

SUGGESTED ACTIVITIES

1. **Directed Reading.** As students read, have them copy each of the above headlines. Require them to write a "lead" sentence for a proposed article based on each headline, including what it refers to and when it happened. When the assignment is complete, have student volunteers read their lead sentences. Discuss each event fully. Summarize by having students place the headlines in chronological order.
2. **Putting Events in Chronological Order.** Review the Chapter 19 History Study Skill. Then, have students arrange the following events in Truman's life in chronological order. This activity may be placed on the chalkboard or on a transparency for the overhead projector.
   A. Elected County Judge in Kansas City
   B. Served as a lieutenant in the army in World War I
   C. Became President of the United States
   D. Elected Senator from Missouri
   E. Failed in the clothing business
   ANSWERS: B - E - A - D - C
   Compare Truman's life story with that of other Presidents with whom students are familiar. These might include Theodore Roosevelt, Woodrow Wilson, and FDR.
3. **Acrostic.** Use the following puzzle to review the major events of Truman's administration. This activity may be written on the chalkboard or on a transparency for the overhead projector.

TaFt-Hartley Act	F - 1947 law limiting the power of labor unions
Twenty-second Amendment	A - limited a President to two four-year terms in office
Central Intelligence Agency	I - created to keep the President informed about matters concerning the nation's security
HooveR Commission	R - appointed to reorganize the Executive Branch of the federal government

Thomas E. Dewey	D - unsuccessful Republican candidate in the election of 1948
DixiEcrats	E - conservative Southern Democrats who opposed Truman in the election of 1948
Housing Act	A - provided low-cost housing for poor people
"whistLe-stop"	L - Truman's 1948 campaign to speak directly to the voters

4. **Ideals in the Lives of Americans.** Ask students to read the selection on Felisa Rincón de Gautier, on textbook page 701. Have them discuss the questions at the end of the reading. Also, have students tell what events were occurring in the United States at the time of Gautier's election. Ask if they think Gautier would have had the same political opportunities in New York if she had chosen to remain in the United States.

BUILDING AMERICAN CITIZENSHIP

This section emphasizes the role of Congress in making laws for the nation. Why did Truman complain about a "do-nothing Congress?" (They didn't cooperate with him.) What is the role of Congress—to support programs suggested by the President or to represent the views of the citizens that elect them? Explain your answer.

SECTION 2 REVIEW ANSWERS

1. **IDENTIFY: Fair Deal:** the name President Truman gave to his programs to provide greater equality and fair treatment to all Americans; **Taft-Hartley Act:** law passed in 1947 limiting the power of labor unions by banning the "closed shop" and giving the President the right to call for a "cooling off" period during a strike; **Hoover Commission:** commission appointed by Truman and headed by former President Hoover to suggest ways to improve the operation of the Executive Branch of the federal government; **CIA:** Central Intelligence Agency; agency charged with keeping the President informed on security matters; **Twenty-second Amendment:** amendment limiting a President to two four-year terms in office; **Dixiecrats:** members of the States' Rights Party, also called the Dixiecrat Party, made up of conservative Southern Democrats who opposed Truman's civil rights programs.

2. Truman formed a President's Committee on Civil Rights to study problems of black citizens, ended segregation in all the armed forces, and asked Congress to pass several laws providing job opportunities, education, and housing for blacks and needy Americans.

3. Public-opinion polls showed that he was less popular than his Republican opponent Thomas Dewey, and the Democratic Party was divided into three groups.

SECTION 3: America Leads the Free Nations

OBJECTIVES

After completing this section, students will be able to:
• List the European nations that became "satellites" of the Soviet Union.

• Identify specific areas in which the United States became involved in the struggle to contain communism.
• Describe the programs and organizations established to help various nations ward off communism.
• Describe the activities of Senator McCarthy.

MOTIVATION

Use the History Study Skill, *Reading Political Cartoons* on page 711. Have students study the cartoon, complete the brief reading, and answer the questions. Ask them how the nations got to be "puppets." Ask if they think the United States was able to do anything about Soviet control of these nations? Explain that Section 3 will provide details about the struggle against communism in Europe and elsewhere after World War II.

SUGGESTED ACTIVITIES

1. **Directed Reading.** As students read, have them answer the following guide questions:
   A. How did the Soviet Union get control of the nations of Eastern Europe? (Soviet troops occupied them during World War II and stayed after the war.)
   B. Which nations were helped by the United States in their struggle to contain communism? (Turkey, Greece, Yugoslavia, and West Germany)
   C. What programs and organizations were established to help stop the spread of communism? (Truman Doctrine, Marshall Plan, Point Four Program, and NATO)
   D. How did Senator McCarthy influence the struggle against communism? (He tried to uncover Communists and disloyal Americans, but wrongly accused many innocent people in the process.)

   Discuss the answers to the four questions. Have students identify each of the four programs named in answer to question "C." Use the following activity as a summary.

2. **Selecting Details.** Have students copy the following statements and use the information in Section 3 to provide the correct answer. This activity may be placed on the chalkboard or on a transparency for the overhead projector.
   A. Three "captive" nations controlled by the Soviet Union in Eastern Europe were __(POLAND)__, __(HUNGARY)__, __(CZECHOSLOVAKIA)__. (Others may be named.)
   B. The __(TRUMAN DOCTRINE)__ provided funds to help free nations block the growth of communism.
   C. __(GERMANY)__ was split into two parts after World War II, one free and one "captive."
   D. The __(MARSHALL PLAN)__ provided money to help European nations rebuild after the war.
   E. Non-Communist countries in Asia, Africa, and Latin America were aided by the __(POINT FOUR PROGRAM)__.
   F. The organization known as __(NATO)__ was established in 1949 to provide for the defense of all member nations in Europe and North America.
   G. The __(WARSAW PACT)__ was a military alliance between the Soviet Union and the Eastern European satellites.

163

3. **Map Interpretation.** Ask students to study the map, *The Cold War in Europe, Asia, and Africa, 1968* on textbook page 704. Then, have them use the map legend to answer the following:
   A. Which European nations remained neutral?
   B. Which Communist nations were not controlled by the Soviet Union?
   C. How many nations were considered members of the Soviet bloc?
4. **Studying Your History Vocabulary.** Have students review the Chapter 16 History Study Skill. Then, ask them to apply the skill by giving the meanings of the following terms found in Section 3: "Cold War," "satellites," "iron curtain," containment, airlift, and censure.

BUILDING AMERICAN CITIZENSHIP

Duplicate Worksheet 84, *Herblock's McCarthy*. This activity is designed to provide students with an opportunity to practice the History Study Skill introduced in the Motivation. It will also give them an opportunity to think critically about the violation of the rights of many innocent American citizens by Senator McCarthy during his campaign to uncover Communists in the United States.

SECTION 3 REVIEW ANSWERS

1. **IDENTIFY: Cold War:** conflict fought without war between the United States and the Soviet Union following World War II; **Satellite nation:** nation of Eastern Europe whose leaders take orders from the Soviet Union; **iron curtain:** symbol for the division of Europe between the free nations of the West and the captive nations of Eastern Europe dominated by the Soviet Union; **Truman Doctrine:** Truman's policy of helping free nations block the growth of communism; **Josef Broz Tito:** Communist leader of Yugoslavia; **Berlin Airlift:** operation of flying in American supplies to Berlin as a response to the Soviet blockade of the city in 1948; **Marshall Plan:** a European recovery plan created by Secretary of State George Marshall to help European nations rebuild farms, factories, and cities after World War II; **Point Four Program:** Truman's foreign-policy program to provide aid to non-Communist countries in Asia, Africa, and Latin American; **NATO:** North Atlantic Treaty Organization; organization formed by the Unites States and the free nations of Europe and Canada for the joint defense of its members; **Warsaw Pact:** military alliance between the Soviet Union and its East European satellites in response to NATO; **Senator Joseph McCarthy:** Senator who led a campaign to uncover Communists and disloyal Americans in the United States.

2. **DEFINE: policy of containment:** same as the Truman Doctrine—giving aid to free nations to help them "contain" the growth of communism.
3. Poland, Czechoslovakia, Hungary, Rumania, Bulgaria, Yugoslavia, and Albania.
4. Primarily through the Truman Doctrine and the Point Four Program.

164

SECTION 4: America Fights in Korea

OBJECTIVES

After completing this section, students will be able to:
• Describe the causes, events, and results of the Korean War.
• Explain why President Truman fired General MacArthur.

MOTIVATION

Review the concept of "Cold War." Ask students what would happen if suddenly it became a "hot war." (Nations would begin fighting.) Ask where they would expect such a "hot war" to begin. (The probable responses would be "Europe.") Tell the students that the war actually became "hot" in Asia. Have them look at the map of *The Korean War* on textbook page 708 to determine the actual location of the war. Also, use an outline map or chalkmap of the world and ask them to locate Korea and to name the countries or bodies of water North, South, East, and West of it.

SUGGESTED ACTIVITIES

1. **Directed Reading.** As students read, have them complete the following outline, using the title *The Korean War.*
   I. Causes
   II. Events
   III. Results
   Have students review the subtopics. Review them by having students write the completed outlines on the chalkboard. Summarize by discussing the outcome of the war—what was gained and what was lost?
2. **Using Map Skills.** Duplicate Worksheet 85, *The Korean War.* In this activity, students are required to apply skills they have learned in earlier chapters. This activity should also increase their understanding of the major events of the Korean War.
3. **Putting Events in Chronological Order.** Review the Chapter 19 History Study Skill. Then, have students apply it by placing the following events from Section 4 in chronological order.
   A. MacArthur was removed from command of American troops in Korea.
   B. Truman appealed to the United Nations to stop the Korean War.
   C. North Korea invaded South Korea.
   D. American forces staged a surprise landing at Inchon.
   E. Chinese communist troops began helping North Korea.
   ANSWERS: C - B - D - E - A

BUILDING AMERICAN CITIZENSHIP

Discuss President Truman's dismissal of General MacArthur. Do government officials have the right to criticize government policies in public? Why did President Truman fire MacArthur? Do you think MacArthur should have followed the President's orders even though he disagreed with them? What constitutional principle was involved in their disagreement?

SECTION 4 REVIEW ANSWERS

1. **IDENTIFY: 38th parallel:** dividing line between North Korea and South Korea; **General Douglas MacArthur:** commander of the UN troops in Korea; **General Matthew Ridgeway:** general appointed by Truman to replace MacArthur after MacArthur's dismissal in April 1951; **Ted Williams:** baseball star who left the Boston Red Sox to fight as an air force pilot in the Korean War; **Cornelius Charlton:** black American who won the Congressional Medal of Honor during the Korean War.
2. The Korean War began when the North Korean Army crossed the 38th parallel in a surprise attack on South Korea in June 1950.
3. It ended in a stalemate. Korea remained divided at the 38th parallel.

CHAPTER 30 REVIEW ANSWERS

REVIEWING KEY WORDS

1. b.   2. d.   3. e.   4. c.   5. a.

REMEMBERING IMPORTANT PEOPLE AND EVENTS

1. a.   2. a.   3. b.   4. b.   5. b.
6. a.   7. b.   8. a.   9. a.   10. b.

REVIEWING THE FACTS

1. F   2. F   3. F   4. T   5. F

PLACING EVENTS IN TIME

1. D   2. E   3. B   4. C   5. A

LINKING GEOGRAPHY AND HISTORY

1. The Soviet Union would gain control of the Black Sea and also have had an outlet to the Mediterranean Sea.
2. The stronger force might attack and overtake the weaker force.

THINKING ABOUT AMERICAN HISTORY

1. Truman worried that if the United States did not put up a fight in Korea, the Communists would feel that they could get away with attacking other countries.
2. Answers will vary.

APPLYING HISTORY STUDIES SKILLS

1. To give an opinion on political events.
2. Six European nations.
3. Answers will vary.

CHAPTER 31

Eisenhower Leads a Prosperous Nation (1953-1960)

Chapter Objectives

After completing this chapter, students will be able to:
1. Describe how life improved for Americans in the 1950's.
2. Identify significant changes in American society after the war.
3. Trace the Civil Rights movement from 1954 to 1960.
4. Explain the concept of the Cold War.

Chapter Chronology

Chapter 31 surveys the years 1953 through 1960, the time of Eisenhower's Presidency. Several of the important persons and events of the period are highlighted on the time line in the textbook Chapter Opener. Dwight D. Eisenhower was elected President in 1952. One year later, in 1953, the Korean War ended. In 1954, in a landmark decision, the Supreme Court ruled against segregated schools. The following year, in 1955, Civil Rights leaders initiated the Montgomery bus boycott. Eisenhower was reelected President in 1956. In 1957, the Soviet Union launched Sputnik. One year later, the first American satellite was launched. In 1958, also, Fidel Castro took control of Cuba. The 49th and 50th states, Alaska and Hawaii, were added to the Union in 1959.

Motivation

Ask students to recall the three main themes of Chapter 30 (return to peacetime; social reforms of Fair Deal; and Cold War). Have them skim Chapter 31, looking at section titles and illustrations. Ask students which themes are carried into Chapter 31 and how they develop. This activity will provide a flow between Chapters 30 and 31 and demonstrate the continuation of historical themes in the post-World War II period.

Geographical Setting

The Eisenhower years were marked by Cold War confrontation in Europe, Asia, and Latin America. Students should use a map or globe to locate important places mentioned in the chapter, including East Germany, West Germany, Poland, Hungary, Cuba, China, Taiwan, and South Vietnam. Important sites in the growing American Civil Rights movement include Montgomery, Alabama and Little Rock, Arkansas.

History Study Skills

The History Study Skill introduced in Chapter 31 is *Using Picture Graphs.* The information graphed illustrates the increasing affluence of Americans during the 1950's and 1960's. This activity is best used in conjunction with Section 1.

Bibliography

Teacher References
Grantham, Jr., Dewey W., *The United States Since 1945.* McGraw-Hill, New York City, 1975.
Hughes, Emmet J., *The Ordeal of Power: A Political Memoir of the Eisenhower Years.* Atheneum, New York City, 1975.
Student References
Webb, Sheyann, *Selma, Lord, Selma: Girlhood Memories of Civil Rights Days.* University of Alabama Press, Montgomery, Alabama, 1980. An elementary school student during the Selma civil rights demonstra-

tions, the author here presents her personal recollections of those demonstrations in a highly readable manner.

Wilson, Beth P., *Giants for Justice: Bethune, Randolph and King.* Harcourt, New York City, 1978. This well illustrated book provides a good introduction to the lives of three important black Americans and the civil rights movement in general.

Audio-Visual Materials

Dwight D. Eisenhower: Soldier and Statesman, Guidance Associates, 2 filmstrips and cassettes, library kit, teacher's guide. This program uses extensive first person interviews with Eisenhower to trace his youth, army career, and presidency.

The 1950's, Listening Library, Inc., 6 filmstrips and cassettes. These filmstrips provide an extensive survey of postwar America as it wrestled with technological change, social change, and the Cold War.

SECTION 1: America Enjoys an Era of Prosperity

OBJECTIVES

After completing this section, students will be able to:
• Explain how automation led to increased productivity.
• Describe the changes in American life brought about by modern technology and increased productivity.

MOTIVATION

Refer students to the History Study Skill, *Using Picture Graphs* on textbook page 727 to introduce Section 1. Have them read the information and answer the questions about the picture graphs. Ask students why there was such an increase in the number of automobiles and television sets during this period. Ask if they think there was an increase in the production of other goods too. Ask what must happen to consumption if production increases. Ask what brought about the increase in production and the increase in consumption during the period?

SUGGESTED ACTIVITIES

1. **Directed Reading.** As students read Section 1, have them answer the following guide questions:
   A. How did automation help to increase productivity? (Computers used to operate machines on large scale; this speeded up production.)
   B. What factors led to an increase in consumption of goods? (Mass marketing, mass media, mass culture, growth of big business, unions protecting the needs of workers)
   C. Why did more people begin moving to the suburbs? (It was a sign of the good life to be able to afford the housing and transportation required for living there.)
   Discuss the answers to these questions carefully. Return to the final question posed in the motivation and have students identify all factors that led to increased productivity and consumption. Use the following activity to summarize.

2. **Cause and Effect.** Review the meaning of the terms "cause" and "effect." A "cause" is what makes something happen. An "effect" is a result. Have students determine whether each of the following was a "cause" or "effect" of prosperity in the 1950's.
   A. People watching and taking part in organized sports (E)
   B. Unions working to improve wages and working conditions (C)
   C. Use of the computer (C)
   D. Movement to the suburbs (E)
   E. Use of mass marketing techniques (C)

3. **Making a Line Graph.** Duplicate Worksheet 86, *Shifts from Small Towns.* You may wish to have students review the Chapter 27 History Study Skill before completing the activity. When students have finished drawing the line graph, ask specific questions to help them interpret it. For example: Which year shows the greatest difference between the numbers of people living in the suburbs and those living in the rural areas? (1930) Which year shows the smallest difference? (1960) What does the graph tell you about the choices Americans were making about where they lived? (An increasing number were choosing to live in the suburbs.)

4. **Ideals in the Lives of Americans.** Have students read the selection on Jonas Salk on textbook page 719. Discuss the two questions that follow the reading. Be sure to explain to students that this period of history was marked not only by increases in productivity and consumption, but also by major medical breakthroughs, such as the anti-polio vaccine.

BUILDING AMERICAN CITIZENSHIP

Which group of citizens in the United States would be classified as neither rich nor poor? (Middle Class) Why do you think the American middle class is important? (Largest group of citizens, great voting power, source of most tax income to government, group that advertisers appeal to and are most likely to reach and profit from) (Opinions will vary.)

SECTION 1 REVIEW ANSWERS

1. **IDENTIFY: Howard Aiken:** computer scientist at Harvard University whose work in 1939 led to the development of the first modern computer; **AFL-CIO:** giant labor union formed when the CIO and the A.F. of L. merged in 1955; **Levittown:** an example of the new suburbs of the 1950's, located near New York City.

2. **DEFINE: automation:** using machines to operate other machines; **computer:** an electronic machine that can be programmed to solve complicated problems much more quickly and accurately than the human brain; **mass consumption:** demand for the same goods and services by millions of people; **mass marketing:** selling of products and services through nationwide advertising; **mass media:** means of communication, such as radio, television, newspapers, and magazines, used for mass marketing; **mass culture:** similarity of life styles shared by millions of people; **suburb:** a smaller community near a large city.

3. The computer.

4. Americans enjoyed greater prosperity and more leisure time. There was a great demand for goods and services, resulting in mass consumption, mass marketing, and the development of a mass culture.

SECTION 2: Black Americans Work for Civil Rights

OBJECTIVES

After completing this section, students will be able to:
- List the methods used by black Americans during the 1950's to gain equal rights.
- Describe specific victories of the Civil Rights movement in Montgomery, Alabama and Little Rock, Arkansas.
- Discuss the migration of black citizens to big cities outside the South.

MOTIVATION

Review the history of the struggle for equal rights that began during Reconstruction. How much progress was made between 1865 and 1950? (Very little) Which 20th century President had so far been the greatest supporter of equal rights? (Truman) How successful were his efforts? (Not very—Congress opposed his proposals.) If a President was unable to gain equal rights for all Americans, who else would be able to do it? How could civil rights be gained for all citizens?

SUGGESTED ACTIVITIES

1. **Directed Reading.** As students read, have them complete the following table.

CIVIL RIGHTS MOVEMENT

METHODS USED TO GAIN RIGHTS	EXAMPLE	DEGREE OF SUCCESS
1. (Taking cases to court)	(Brown vs. Board of Ed. of Topeka)	(Ended segregation of public schools)
2. (Bus boycott)	(Montgomery, Ala.)	(Ended segregation of buses)
3. (Establishing groups)	(SCLC)	(Organized peaceful protests to win civil rights)
4. (Sit-ins)	(Took seats at lunch counters and refused to move)	(Ended segregation of public eating places)
5. (Attending school)	(Little Rock, Ark.)	(Black students allowed to attend school)

Review the answers with students by having them place the entries for each column on the chalkboard. For low-ability students, you may wish to provide the entry for one column in each case. This will assist them in providing accurate information in the other columns.

2. **Discussion.** Discuss the migration of black citizens to the big cities of the North and West. Why did they move? In which decade did the greatest migration oc-

cur? What problems did the newcomers experience in the big cities? How did segregation in the North differ from segregation in the South? How did the National Urban League help the people who migrated?

3. **Using Picture Graphs.** Duplicate Worksheet 87, *American Farms (1940-1960)*. The activity enables students to apply the History Study Skill introduced in the Motivation for Section 1. Have students carefully read and study the worksheet. Then ask them how black migration from the South might have affected the number of farms. (Movement of blacks from the South would help account for the decreasing number of farms.)

4. **Comprehension Check.** To determine students' grasp of the information in Section 2, have them complete the following matching activity. This may be placed on the chalkboard or on a overhead projector.

A. *Brown v. Board of Education of Topeka*
B. Montgomery Bus Boycott
C. SCLC
D. Civil Rights Commission
E. National Urban League

(D) Reported that most black citizens in the South were denied the right to vote
(B) Ended segregation of transportation facilities in one Southern city
(E) Helped black newcomers in Western and Northern cities
(C) Organized peaceful protests to win civil rights for blacks
(A) Ended segregation of public schools

BUILDING AMERICAN CITIZENSHIP

Duplicate Worksheet 88, *Local Governments*. This activity will allow students to practice the Chapter 28 History Study Skill and will familiarize them with the various types of local government. Have them answer the following questions:
A. Which type of local government was involved in the Supreme Court case to end segregation of public schools? (School Districts)
B. Which type of government had to deal with problems resulting from black migration? (Cities)

SECTION 2 REVIEW ANSWERS

1. **IDENTIFY: NAACP:** organization that work for the civil rights of black Americans; **Brown v. Board of Education of Topeka:** 1954 Supreme Court case that ended segregation in public schools; **Earl Warren:** Chief Justice of the Supreme Court who presided in the *Brown v. Board of Education* case; **Rosa Parks:** black citizen arrested in Montgomery, Alabama, for refusing to move to the section reserved for blacks on a bus: **Martin Luther King, Jr.:** black civil rights leader who urged followers to use peaceful means to end segregation; **National Urban League:** organization created to help black newcomers find jobs and places to live in cities in the North and West.

2. **DEFINE: boycott:** to refuse to use; "**sit-ins**": nonviolent protests in which blacks took seats in restaurants and refused to move when they were denied service.

23. They turned to the courts; they held marches and demonstrations and used peaceful protests, such as boycotts and sit-ins; they worked through such organizations as the NAACP.

24. In the South, segregation was a matter of law; for example, black people could not attend white schools. In the North, people were separated by economic and social factors; because blacks and whites lived in different neighborhoods, they went to different schools.

5. Brown, Boycott, Little Rock

SECTION 3: The Cold War Continues

OBJECTIVES

After completing this section, students will be able to:
* Explain the methods used by the United States and Soviet Union in their attempts to prevent war.
* Describe efforts to contain communism in Asia.
* Identify specific events that led to an increase of Soviet power and influence during the 1950's and 1960's.

MOTIVATION

Have students recall earlier events of the Cold War. List these on the board, and state important facts about each. These might include the communization of Poland, Hungary, Czechoslovakia, and several other countries of Eastern Europe; division of Germany; the formation of the Truman Doctrine, NATO, and the Warsaw Pact; and so on. Ask students to look at the title of Section 3 and to write in their notebooks what they would "expect" to happen during a "continuation" of the Cold War. These ideas should not be shared with the class at this point. First, have students read Section 1 to complete the Directed Reading activity.

SUGGESTED ACTIVITIES

1. **Directed Reading.** As students read, ask them to answer the following questions:
   A. What steps were taken by the United States and the Soviet Union to prevent war? (Arms race, meeting between leaders of the two nations)
   B. In which areas of the world did the United States try to contain communism, and how? (Asia—formation of SEATO; South Vietnam—sending American advisors; China—support for Nationalists on Taiwan; Middle East—Eisenhower Doctrine)
   C. In which areas of the world did the Soviet Union try to strengthen its power and influence, and how? (East Germany, Hungary—putting down revolts; Cuba—sent military and economic aid; space—putting the first satellite into orbit)
   D. How did the actual events of the Cold War compare to what you *expected* to happen? (Answers will vary.)
   Review the answers to the first three questions. Then summarize the lesson by having individual students read their expectations—as written during the Motivation—and their answers to question "D."

2. **Studying Your History Vocabulary.** Review the Chapter 16 History Study Skill. Then have students apply it by skimming the contents of Section 3 in order to find the meanings of the following terms: arms race, guided missiles, peaceful coexistence, orbit, summit meeting.

3. **Acrostic.** Check students' knowledge of individuals and ideas involved in the events described in Section 3 by having them complete the following acrostic:

	CLUES:
Ho Chi Minh	C - leader of Communists in North Vietnam
ExplOrer I	O - first American satellite sent into orbit
Joseph StaLin	L - leader of the Soviet Union before Nikita Khrushchev
FiDel Castro	D - established close ties between his Cuban government and that of the Soviet Union
EisenhoWer Doctrine	W - promised American aid to Middle Eastern countries threatened by Communists
SEATO	A - regional alliance of Asian nations for defensive purposes
John FosteR Dulles	R - American Secretary of State during the administration of President Eisenhower

4. **Comprehension Check.** To determine whether or not students can distinguish between the roles of the superpowers during the Cold War, have them tell whether each of the following statements refer to the United states (US) or the Soviet Union (SU).
   A. First to develop the H-bomb (US)
   B. Introduced the concept of peaceful coexistence (SU)
   C. First to orbit a satellite in outer space (SU)
   D. Sent military advisors to South Vietnam (US)
   E. Sent an army to crush a rebellion in Hungary (SU)
   F. Sent an army to protect the government in Lebanon (US)
   G. Captured a spy plane taking photographs of military bases (SU)

BUILDING AMERICAN CITIZENSHIP

Recall the concept of compromise.
1. What things are necessary if two sides are to settle a dispute through compromise? (Willingness on each side to give something up; trust)
2. What were some of the differences that the two superpowers needed to settle by compromise? (Arms race, reuniting Germany)
3. Why did their efforts to settle differences frequently fail? (They did not trust each other.)

SECTION 3 REVIEW ANSWERS

1. **IDENTIFY: John Foster Dulles:** Secretary of State in the Eisenhower administration; **Nikita Khrushchev:** leader of the Soviet Union; **Sputnik I:** first Soviet satellite sent

into space, on October 4, 1957; **Explorer I:** first American satellite sent into space, on January 31, 1958; **SEATO:** Southeast Asia Treaty Organization; an alliance of nations formed to stop the spread of communism in Southeast Asia; **Ho Chi Minh:** Communist leader of North Vietnam; **Eisenhower Doctrine:** foreign policy announced by Eisenhower in 1957 promising American aid to Middle Eastern countries threatened by a Communist takeover; **Fidel Castro:** Cuban revolutionary who set up a Communist government in Cuba in 1959.

2. **DEFINE: free world:** nations with democratic ways of life; **H-bomb:** hydrogen bomb, developed by the United States in 1952; **missiles:** rockets carrying nuclear explosives; **summit meeting:** a conference attended by heads of governments.
3. The development of the H-bomb by both the United States and the Soviet Union.
4. By forming friendship treaties with America's allies; meeting with the new Soviet leader Nikita Khrushchev in 1955; forming the Southeast Asia Treaty Organization (SEATO); sending military advisers to South Vietnam; supporting the Chinese anti-Communist government of Chiang Kai-shek; establishing the Eisenhower Doctrine.

32

CHAPTER 31 REVIEW ANSWERS

REVIEWING KEY WORDS

1. d.   2. c.   3. a.   4. b.   5. e.

REMEMBERING IMPORTANT PEOPLE

1. b.   2. d.   3. c.   4. a.   5. e.

REVIEWING THE FACTS

1. T   2. T   3. T   4. F   5. F

PLACING EVENTS IN TIME

1. d.   2. c.   3. e.   4. b.   5. a.

LINKING GEOGRAPHY AND HISTORY

Because Cuba is only 90 miles from the United States, and the Soviet Union was setting up military bases there.

THINKING ABOUT AMERICAN HISTORY

1. To overthrow their Soviet-controlled Communist governments and become free nations again.
2. High wages made possible by higher productivity brought a high standard of living for most Americans. They had more leisure time, and they could afford to buy new homes and things they had once only dreamed of owning.

APPLYING HISTORY STUDIES SKILLS

1. circle; bar; line; picture
2. symbols or pictures
3. about 61 million
4. about 45 million
5. 5 complete sets and a 6th that is nearly complete
6. more

CHAPTER 32
Americans Face Conflict and Change (1960's-1970's)

Chapter Objectives

After completing this chapter, students will be able to:
1. Assess Kennedy's impact on the nation during his presidency.
2. Describe progress made in the civil rights movement.
3. Identify successes and failures of Johnson's presidency.
4. Explain how the Vietnam War divided Americans.

Chapter Chronology

Chapter 32 surveys a time of great turbulence and change both at home and abroad. It was a period of social upheaval and war and, at the same time, of major reforms and social progress. Several of the important persons and events of the time are highlighted on the time line in the textbook Chapter Opener. The decade opened with the election of John F. Kennedy in 1960. Two years into his administration, in 1962, the Cuban Missile Crisis occurred. After Kennedy was assassinated in 1963, Lyndon B. Johnson became President. He was elected President in 1964 and in the same year, the Civil Rights Act was passed. By 1967, anti-Vietnam War protests were on the increase. In 1968, Richard Nixon was elected President. In that same year, Martin Luther King, Jr. was killed. Five years later, in 1973, Americans withdrew from the Vietnam War.

Motivation

Have students turn to the textbook Chapter Introduction and read about the Kennedy-Nixon debate. When they have completed the final paragraph about the social conflicts and changes, have them look at the heads in Sections 1 and 2. Ask them to describe and list "social conflicts and changes" that are indicated there. Save this list for reference as students work through the chapter.

Geographical Setting

Chapter 32 focuses on important international geographical settings. These include Cuba, a continuing source of problems for the United States, and Vietnam, site of the longest continuous war in American history. The maps in this chapter illustrate the setting of the war in Southeast Asia. A third geographical focus is the divided city of Berlin in Germany. Have students also look at a map of the United States, to review the locations of important places associated with the civil rights movement.

History Study Skills

The History Study Skill introduced in Chapter 32 is *Using Flow Charts.* The information shown is presidential succession as defined by the Twenty-Sixth Amendment. This activity is best used in conjunction with Section 2.

Bibliography

Teacher References

Sundquist, James L., *Politics and Policy: The Eisenhower, Kennedy, and Johnson Years.* Brookings, Washington, D.C., 1969.

White, Theodore H., *The Making of the President, 1968.* Atheneum, New York City, 1969.

Student References

Fincher, E. B., *The Vietnam War.* Franklin Watts, New York City, 1980. This well-illustrated book, which includes a history of Vietnam and the invasion of Cambodia, examines the impact of the war on American servicemen and Americans at home.

Clark, Ann Nolan, *To Stand Against the Wind.* Viking, New York City, 1978. This novel about a Vietnamese boy who emigrates to the United States, describes the many difficult decisions he has to make while adapting to American society.

Audio-Visual Materials

The 1960's, A Decade of Hope, Guidance Associates, 2 filmstrips, 2 cassettes, Library Kit, and teacher's guide. This program surveys many of the social changes that occurred in the United States in the 1960's.

America in 1968: People and Culture, BFA, 19½ minutes, color. This film illustrates many of the events of the 1960's, some resulting in the reexamination of our values as a nation.

SECTION 1: President Kennedy Leads the Nation

OBJECTIVES

After completing this section, students will be able to:
- List important events in the life of John F. Kennedy.
- Describe domestic issues and foreign policy problems faced by President Kennedy.
- Explain how relations between the United States and the Soviet Union began to improve during Kennedy's administration.

MOTIVATION

Write the following slogans on the blackboard: Square Deal (TR); New Deal (FDR); New Freedom (Wilson); Fair Deal (Truman). Have students recall the individuals who used these slogans to describe their programs and why they did so. Then, write New Frontier on the chalkboard. Ask students if they can identify the President who introduced this program. Ask why he may have chosen this name. Tell the class that these questions will be answered in Section 1.

SUGGESTED ACTIVITIES

1. **Directed Reading.** Have students draw two columns on a sheet of paper, as indicated below. As they read, they should select details from the reading to be entered in the appropriate column. Samples are provided.

NEW FRONTIER

CHALLENGES WITHIN THE NATION	CHALLENGES WITH OTHER NATIONS
Poverty	Space race
Disease	Cuban Missile Crisis

Have students review their entries for columns 1 and 2 and discuss important details associated with each. As a summary, return to the two questions posed during the motivation and have students answer them.

2. **Putting Events in Chronological Order.** Review the Chapter 19 History Study Skill. Then have students apply it by chronologically arranging the following events in President Kennedy's life:
A. Wrote *Profiles in Courage*
B. Elected Senator from Massachusetts
C. Served as a naval officer in the Pacific
D. Lived in Europe and met many political leaders
E. Elected to the House of Representatives from Massachusetts
F. Elected President
G. Graduated from Harvard University
   ANSWERS: G - D - C - E - B - A - F

3. **Comprehension Check.** Determine student understanding of the important events described in Section 1 by having them answer TRUE or FALSE to each of the following statements. If a statement is FALSE, have students rewrite it to make it TRUE.
A. The United States was the first nation to send a person into space. (F - Soviet Union)
B. Anti-Castro Cubans invaded Cuba but were defeated by Castro's soldiers. (T)
C. A naval blockade of Cuba led to the building of missile bases there. (F - led to their being removed)
D. The United States and its allies forced the Communists to leave East Berlin. (F - the Communists stayed and built the Berlin Wall.)
E. Relations between the United States and the Soviet Union gradually worsened during Kennedy's administration. (F-relations improved after the missile crisis.)
F. Peace Corps volunteers taught people of developing nations new skills and gave them the ability to help themselves. (T)

BUILDING AMERICAN CITIZENSHIP

A good citizen takes pride in a President's ability to earn the respect of other nations. Do you think American citizens were proud of President Kennedy's handling of foreign affairs? Give evidence from Section 1 to support your answer.

SECTION 1 REVIEW ANSWERS

1. **IDENTIFY: John Glenn:** first American to orbit the earth, in February 1962; **Berlin Wall:** wall built by the Communists to separate East Berlin from West Berlin; **Alliance for Progress:** President Kennedy's program to help developing nations in Latin America, established in 1961; **Peace Corps:** program established by President Kennedy in 1961 in which volunteer Americans lived and worked in developing nations and taught the people new skills and knowledge to help them help themselves.

2. **DEFINE: "hot line":** direct telephone line between the heads of government of the United States and the Soviet Union, to be used in a time of crisis to prevent war.
3. Kennedy invoked an image of Americans' past ability to overcome obstacles on the frontier. His "new frontier" called for overcoming the problems of poverty, disease, and social injustice.
4. The space race, Cuban missile crisis, Bay of Pigs invasion, Berlin Wall.

SECTION 2: The Civil Rights Movement Makes Progress

OBJECTIVES

After completing this section, students will be able to:
- Identify events that led to increased equality for black Americans during Kennedy's administration.
- Describe the assassination of President Kennedy.

MOTIVATION

Use the excerpts from Martin Luther King's "I Have A Dream" speech, one of the Sources of Freedom on textbook page 736. Select volunteers to read the excerpts and to interpret Dr. King's words. Ask students what methods black Americans had used in the 1950's to try to gain equal rights. (sit-ins, boycotts, court cases) Tell them when they finish reading Section 2, they will be able to identify new methods used in the early 1960's.

SUGGESTED ACTIVITIES

1. **Directed Reading.** As students read Section 2, have them write a sentence telling how each of the following led to increased civil rights for black citizens.
   A. Twenty-third Amendment (Washington, D.C. citizens given the right to vote)
   B. Twenty-fourth Amendment (outlawed poll taxes)
   C. Freedom Riders (led to desegregation of public transportation)
   D. James Meredith (helped desegregate colleges)
   E. Demonstrations in Birmingham, Alabama (television coverage won sympathies of many Americans)
   F. March on Washington (caused many citizens to strengthen their support of the civil rights movement)

   Discuss the sentences students have written. As a summary, return to the challenge presented in the Motivation. Have students identify *new* methods used by those working for the civil rights movement. (Freedom riders, March on Washington)
2. **Class Discussion.** Focusing on the details provided in Section 2, have students discuss the assassination of President Kennedy. When did the assassination occur? Why was Kennedy there? Who was the assassin? What happened to him? Why did he shoot the President? Who became the President after Kennedy's death?
3. **History Study Skills.** Ask students to complete the activity *Using Flow Charts* on textbook page 747.

Have them answer the questions at the end as well as the ones below:
A. Which amendment to the Constitution established the succession depicted in the flow chart? (Twenty-seventh)
B. Suppose the Speaker of the House is unable to become President. Who is next in line? (President Pro Tempore)
C. Who are the other members of the cabinet that might become President if the Secretary of State is unable to serve? (Secretary of Defense, Secretary of the Treasury, Secretary of the Interior, Attorney General)
4. **Round Robin.** Use this review and summary technique as introduced in Chapter 1. Select a student volunteer to give one important fact from Section 2. Then select a second volunteer to repeat that fact and give a new one. Select a third volunteer to repeat the fact stated by the previous student and give a new one. Repeat as often as time and resources allow.

BUILDING AMERICAN CITIZENSHIP

Duplicate Worksheet 89, *Non-Violent Protest.* This activity emphasizes the strengths and weaknesses of non-violent protest. Ask students to think of various types of violent protests. After discussing their strengths and weaknesses, have students compare them with the strengths and weaknesses of non-violent protests. Ask students to express an opinion about the forms of protest they think are effective.

SECTION 2 REVIEW ANSWERS

1. **IDENTIFY: Twenty-third Amendment:** amendment giving residents of Washington, D.C., the right to vote in presidential elections; **Twenty-fourth Amendment:** amendment passed in 1962 outlawing payment of a poll tax before allowing a citizen to vote; **Freedom Riders:** groups of young people, both black and white, who traveled through the South on buses protesting segregation laws; **James Meredith:** first black student to enroll at the University of Mississippi, in 1962; **March on Washington:** 1963 demonstration of more than 200,000 people to influence Congress to pass new laws against segregation; **Lee Harvey Oswald:** assassin who killed President John F. Kennedy.
2. Millions of people saw televised news programs showing police violence against the demonstrators, and their sympathies went to the non-violent protestors.
3. To influence Congress to pass new laws against segregation.

SECTION 3: President Johnson Plans the Great Society

OBJECTIVES

After completing this section, students will be able to:
- Identify programs started and laws passed, during Johnson's administration, to help the needy and benefit the Civil Rights movement.
- Explain why some black Americans participated in the riots during the 1960's.

- Identify black Americans who were able to take advantage of new opportunities opened by the Civil Rights movement and Great Society programs.

MOTIVATION

There are some periods of American history in which the actions, and in some cases, the ideas of certain individuals seem to shape the course of events. Have students name some of the people who left their mark on history in the early 1960's. (John F. Kennedy, Martin Luther King, Jr., James Meredith, and Lee Harvey Oswald) Ask students how each of these people "made" history during the early 1960's. Tell them that today they will study the individuals whose actions influenced history during the rest of the decade.

SUGGESTED ACTIVITIES

1. **Directed Reading.** Relate this to the Motivation by having students copy the names of individuals who "made" history during the 1960's and write a sentence or two about each one. These individuals include: Lyndon Johnson, Robert C. Weaver, Martin Luther King, Jr., Edward Brooke, Shirley Chisholm, and Thurgood Marshall. Have students read the sentences they have written. Then summarize the lesson by having students complete the following activity.

2. **Comprehension Check.** Have students complete the matching exercise below to determine whether or not they understand the roles played by the individuals listed in the previous activity.

1. Edward Brooke	A. first black woman to serve in Congress
2. Robert C. Weaver	B. first black justice of the Supreme Court
3. Shirley Chisholm	C. first black citizen elected to the Senate since Reconstruction
4. Martin Luther King, Jr.	D. black civil rights leader famous for highly effective nonviolent protests
5. Lyndon Johnson	E. first black official to serve as a cabinet member
6. Thurgood Marshall	F. challenged Americans to build a "Great Society"

ANSWERS: C - E - A - D - F - B

1. **Categorization.** Many of the laws passed and programs started during Johnson's administration benefitted the Civil Rights movement or aided the needy. Have students categorize each of the following as a Civil Rights (CR) program or a "Great Society" (GS) program or law for the poor and needy.
   A. Economic Opportunity Act (GS)
   B. VISTA (GS)
   C. 1964 Civil Rights Act (CR)
   D. Project Head Start (GS)
   E. Medicare (GS)
   F. Elementary and Secondary Education Act (GS)
   G. Twenty-fourth Amendment (CR)
   H. Voting Rights Act (CR)
   I. Neighborhood Youth Corps (GS)
   J. Upward Bound (GS)

Have students explain the purpose of each law or program. You may also wish to have students practice the Chapter 19 History Study Skill, *How to Put Events in Chronological Order* by rearranging the list in the order of occurrence.

4. **Reading a Flow Chart.** Duplicate Worksheet 90, *How a Bill Becomes a Law.* This activity will allow students to practice the History Study Skill introduced in Section 2. Before having students answer the questions, be sure to read through each block of the chart with them to clarify vocabulary and to answer questions.

BUILDING AMERICAN CITIZENSHIP

How did the Civil Rights Act of 1964 and the Voting Rights Act of 1965 benefit *all* American citizens? (Civil Rights Act—No one could be denied a job because of race or religion; Voting Rights Act—led to an increase in the number of black voters and, therefore, resulted in more representative government in the states and the entire nation.)

SECTION 3 REVIEW ANSWERS

1. **IDENTIFY: Civil Rights Act of 1964:** law forbidding segregation or discrimination in all public places and making discrimination in business and education illegal; **War on Poverty:** President Johnson's program of new laws to help poor people; **Barry Goldwater:** unsuccessful Republican candidate for President in 1964; **"Great Society:"** Johnson's term for his programs for social and economic reforms to give equal opportunities to all Americans; **Medicare:** health-care program for people over 65; **Robert C. Weaver:** first black official to serve as a Cabinet member; **Voting Rights Act of 1965:** a law that gave the federal government the right to supervise the registration of black voters; **Thurgood Marshall:** first black Justice of the Supreme Court, appointed in 1967.

2. The Office of Economic Opportunity set up job-training and educational programs; the Job Corps for adults and the Neighborhood Youth Corps for teenagers taught work skills; project Head Start taught skills to preschool children; Upward Bound prepared high-school students for college; VISTA was a program of volunteers working in inner-city neighborhoods to help the needy.

3. The march was to call attention to the fact that many blacks in the South still could not vote or take part in government.

SECTION 4: The Vietnam War Divides Americans

OBJECTIVES

After completing this section, students will be able to:
- List the actions taken by President Johnson to support the South Vietnamese.
- Explain the strategy of the North Vietnamese.
- Describe the differences between "hawks" and "doves."
- Identify the steps taken by President Nixon to end American involvement in the Vietnam War.

MOTIVATION

Ask students to name all the wars in the 20th century in which the United States was involved. (World War I, World War II, Korean War, and Vietnam War) Ask if the United States lost or supported the losing side in any of these wars? (Vietnam) Tell students that the Vietnam War was the only war not won by the United States. Ask if they know the reasons. Tell students that this question will be discussed when they have read Section 4.

SUGGESTED ACTIVITIES

1. **Directed Reading.** As students read, have them answer the following questions about the Vietnam War:
   A. What caused the civil war in Vietnam?
   B. How did America become more involved in the war during Johnson's administration?
   C. What methods were used by United States forces to try to defeat the Viet Cong?
   D. Why did some Americans begin opposing the war in Vietnam?
   E. How did America's involvement in the war end?
      Discuss the answers to these questions with students. As a summary, repeat the questions posed during the motivation: Why did the United States fail to win the Vietnam War?
2. **Map Interpretation Exercise.** Use the map, *The Vietnam War, 1961-1973* on textbook page 744. Have students answer the following questions based on the information depicted on the map.
   A. Vietnam is located on the continent of __(ASIA)__.
   B. The capital of North Vietnam was __(HANOI)__; the capital of South Vietnam was __(SAIGON)__.
   C. The capitals of North and South Vietnam were about __(700)__ miles apart.
   D. The body of water that borders North Vietnam in the east is the __(GULF OF TONKIN)__.
   E. The countries located west of South Vietnam were __(CAMBODIA)__ and __(LAOS)__.
   F. The Ho Chi Minh Trail extended from North Vietnam, through __(LAOS)__ and into South Vietnam.
3. **Ideals in the Lives of Americans.** Have students read the selection on S. I. Hayakawa, on textbook page 741 and answer the two questions that follow. Ask students what important events occurred in 1968, when Hayakawa's life changed. (Election of Nixon; assassinations of Dr. King and of Robert Kennedy; growing opposition to the Vietnam War)
4. **Organizing Facts.** Duplicate Worksheet 91, *Kennedy and Johnson.* This activity requires students to apply the skill of categorization. It also serves as an excellent review of the major events in Chapter 32. As you check the answers with students, have them recall important details related to each event.

BUILDING AMERICAN CITIZENSHIP

During every major war, there have been some citizens who protest America's involvement. Why do you think that the antiwar movement became so strong during the Vietnam War? (For the first time Americans had same-day television coverage of our soldiers being killed; Americans felt too much money was being spent on the

war instead of on social programs here; unlike the situation during earlier wars, no laws were passed making antiwar protests illegal) Did the protests of American citizens have any influence on continued American involvement in the war? (Yes—Nixon promised to end the war. He was elected and worked to end it.)

SECTION 4 REVIEW ANSWERS

1. **IDENTIFY: Viet Cong:** Communist rebels of South Vietnam; **Gulf of Tonkin Resolution:** Congressional resolution giving President Johnson the power to take all necessary measures to repell Communist attacks on American forces in South Vietman; **Robert Kennedy:** brother of President John Kennedy, who challenged Johnson for the Presidency in 1968 but was assassinated during the campaign in June 1968; **Hubert Humphrey:** unsuccessful Democratic candidate for President in 1968; **Henry Kissinger:** President Nixon's foreign-policy adviser and chief American negotiator in the peace talks with North Vietnam.
2. **DEFINE: "doves":** Americans who opposed the Vietnam War; **"hawks":** Americans who supported the Vietnam War.
3. President Johnson ordered the bombing of North Vietnam, sent more troops and supplies to South Vietnam, and ordered American planes to attack Communist supply lines.
4. The Nixon plan was to provide for the training of the South Vietnamese army to defend itself while gradually reducing the number of American troops.

CHAPTER 32 REVIEW ANSWERS
REVIEWING KEY WORDS

1. b.	2. b.	3. a.	4. a.	5. b.

REMEMBERING IMPORTANT PEOPLE

1. a.	2. d.	3. b.	4. e.	5. c.

REVIEWING THE FACTS

1. b.	2. e.	3. c.	4. d.	5. a.
6. T	7. F	8. F	9. T	10. T

PLACING EVENTS IN TIME

1. E	2. D	3. A	4. C	5. B

LINKING GEOGRAPHY AND HISTORY

1. Because most of the segregation laws and customs that discriminated against blacks were in Southern states.
2. If South Vietnam became Communist, the neighboring nations of Laos, Cambodia, and Thailand were also in danger of falling under Communist control.

THINKING ABOUT AMERICAN HISTORY

1. The civil rights movement was more successful because it had far greater public support as well as powerful political support from Presidents Kennedy and Johnson.
2. As the war dragged on, a military victory over the Communists appeared doubtful, and the costs of the war in dollars and in lives lost kept increasing. People came to believe that the goals of the Great Socie-

ty and the civil rights movement could not be achieved while the United States was wasting precious resources in Vietnam. By 1968 only 30 percent of Americans backed the war.

APPLYING HISTORY STUDIES SKILLS

1. Answers will vary.
2. Twenty-fifth Amendment.
3. President Pro Tempore of the Senate.

CHAPTER 33

Americans Look Ahead with Hope (1970's-1980's)

Chapter Objectives

After completing this chapter, students will be able to:
1. Identify challenges confronted by Nixon during his presidency.
2. Describe Carter's major problems as President.
3. Explain why Reagan believed that the United States needed to be strengthened.
4. Identify future goals of Americans.

Chapter Chronology

Chapter 33 surveys the decades of the 1970's and 1980's. Several important persons and events of this period are highlighted on the time line in the textbook Chapter Opener. The decade opened with the formation of the Environmental Protection Agency in 1970. In 1972, Richard Nixon was reelected President. In the same year he also visited China. After Nixon resigned as the nation's Chief Executive in 1974, Gerald Ford became President. He was followed by James E. Carter, who was elected President in 1976. Two years later, the Panama Canal Treaty was signed. In 1979, Americans in Iran were seized as hostages. In the following year, Ronald Reagan was elected President.

Motivation

Write "Nixon-Ford-Carter-Reagan" on the board. Ask students what they know about each President or what they associate with each name. List students' responses under each name. Keep the list for reference as students read the chapter.

Geographical Setting

Chapter 33 includes discussion of several countries, including Iran and Afghanistan, with which students may be unfamiliar. Iran is mentioned in connection with the revolution that occurred there and Afghanistan in connection with the Russian invasion and occupation of that country. Students may be able to find maps and other information on these countries in newspapers and magazines. Students should also review the geographical location and importance of the Panama Canal, China, the Middle East, and the USSR. Within the United States, the changes in population are illustrated in the map, *United States Population Changes, 1970-1980*.

History Study Skills

The History Study Skill introduced in Chapter 33 is *Using a Population Map*. The information on the map illustrates population shifts to the Sun Belt. This activity is best used in conjunction with Section 4.

Bibliography

Teacher References
Sirica, John J., *To Set the Record Straight: The Break-in, the Tapes, the Conspirators, the Pardon.* Norton, New York City, 1979.
Shoup, Laurence H., *The Carter Presidency and Beyond.* Ramparts Press, Palo Alto, Calif., 1980.
Student References
Radding, Charles, *The Modern Presidency.* Franklin Watts, New York City, 1979. In this excellent and well-illustrated account of the role of the Chief Executive in modern American government, important aspects of the presidency are analyzed.
Hoobler, Dorothy and Thomas, *An Album of the Seventies*, Franklin Watts, New York City, 1981. This is a well-illustrated album that includes such events as the Kent State crisis, Watergate, and the Iranian Hostage crisis.

Audio-Visual Materials

American Decades: The 1970s, United Learning, 1981, 6 sound filmstrips, teacher's guide. This lively and informative program includes such titles as Popular Culture; US Politics; People and Issues; the US and the World; Science in the 70s; Women; and Newsmakers.

The World to Come: Exploring the Future, Educational Enrichment Materials, 6 sound filmstrips, teacher's guide. In this program, a study of the probable and the possible, the focus is on food, energy, transportation, medicine, architecture, and recreation.

SECTION 1: The Nixon Years Are a Time of Challenge

OBJECTIVES

After completing this section, students will be able to:
- Describe steps taken during Nixon's administration to improve relations with the People's Republic of China and with the Soviet Union.
- Explain why President Nixon resigned.
- Tell how President Ford tried to restore confidence in the American government.

MOTIVATION

Use the Motivation suggested in the chapter introduction in this manual. Before writing the names on the board, ask students if they can identify individuals who have served as President since 1968. Then, list events associated with each President. Retain a copy of this list or have students keep a copy in their notebooks for reference.

SUGGESTED ACTIVITIES

1. **Directed Reading.** Have students start an outline of the administrations of Presidents Nixon, Ford, Carter, and Reagan. Students may use the title of the chapter as the title of the outline, or they may create their own. The major topics should be the names of the four Presidents. The sub-topics should include important events that occurred while each served as Chief Executive. Suggested entries follow:

   I. Nixon Administration
   - A. First landing on the moon
   - B. Laws passed to protect the environment
   - C. Nixon visited China and the Soviet Union
   - D. Watergate Affair occurred
   - E. Vice-President Agnew resigned
   - F. Nixon resigned

   II. Ford Administration
   - A. Appointed Rockefeller to serve as vice-president
   - B. Dealt with problems of oil shortages

   Review students' entries by having them write the outline on the chalkboard. Summarize by discussing the important facts related to each subtopic.

2. **Ideals in the Lives of Americans.** Have students read the selection on Rachel Carson on textbook page 754. Then discuss the answers to the two guide questions at the end. Ask students what steps were taken during Nixon's administration to avoid the "silent spring" that Rachel Carson feared.

3. **Class Discussion.** The topic for the discussion is the resignation of Richard Nixon as President. Ask students what 1972 event eventually led to Nixon's resignation in 1974. How did the break-in at the Watergate involve the President? How did Congress get involved in the investigation? What charges were brought against the President? Who became President after Nixon's resignation?

4. **Creating a Puzzle.** Have students use the people, laws, events and so on, listed under Identify in the Section 1 Review in the textbook. Require students to create an acrostic, crossword, or word search puzzle from these entries. Set a minimum number of items to be included in the puzzle and specify that clues must be given. You may ask students to trade puzzles and work them out, or collect puzzles from one class to distribute to another.

BUILDING AMERICAN CITIZENSHIP

President Nixon both helped and hurt the citizens of the United States. Can you tell how his trips to China and the Soviet Union helped American citizens? (They reduced the threat of Cold War conflicts with these nations.) Can you tell how the Watergate Affair hurt the citizens of the United States? (Many lost confidence in the government.)

SECTION 1 REVIEW ANSWERS

1. **IDENTIFY: NASA:** National Aeronautics and Space Administration; federal agency responsible for space exploration; **Clean Air Act:** 1970 law requiring auto makers to produce cars that caused less air pollution; **Water Quality Improvement Act:** 1970 law creating regulations for industries to reduce water pollution; **EPA:** Environmental Protection Agency; federal agency created to enforce laws to control pollution; **Leonid Brezhnev:** leader of the Soviet Union during the 1970's; **George McGovern:** unsuccessful Democratic candidate for President in 1972; **Twenty-sixth Amendment:** amendment ratified in 1971 lowering the voting age to 18 years; **Gerald Ford:** Vice-President who became President when Richard Nixon resigned in August 1974; **Energy Policy and Conservation Act:** 1975 law that provided for a national reserve of petroleum in case of emergency.

2. Americans celebrated the first "Earth Day" on April 22, 1970; Congress passed the Clean Air Act and the Water Quality Improvement Act and set up the Environmental Protection Agency (EPA) to enforce laws controlling pollution.

3. Nixon visited both the People's Republic of China and the Soviet Union in 1972, encouraging trade and cooperation with both countries.

4. President Nixon resigned when it appeared that he would be impeached for failing to uphold the law in the Watergate affair.

SECTION 2: President Carter Faces Serious Problems

OBJECTIVES

After completing this section, students will be able to:
- List the problems faced by President Carter within the United States and in dealing with other nations.
- Describe President Carter's most important achievement.
- Explain why President Carter lost the election of 1980.

MOTIVATION

Use a wall map of the world or one that can be projected on the overhead. Have students locate Israel, Egypt, Afghanistan, Iran, and Panama. Ask students what they know about each of these nations. (They should recall the building of the Panama Canal.) Tell students that President Carter had to deal with them all and that, by the end of this lesson, they should be able to determine how successful he was with each.

SUGGESTED ACTIVITIES

1. **Directed Reading.** Use the theme developed in the Motivation. As students read, have them explain the problems that President Carter faced at home and with each of the nations mentioned above.
   - A. In the United States—inflation, unemployment, energy crisis
   - B. Israel and Egypt—brought the two countries together to work out a treaty ending the fighting between them
   - C. Panama—signed a treaty providing for the return of the canal in 1999
   - D. Iran—its new government held 52 American hostages for over a year
   - E. Afghanistan—to protest this country's invasion by the Soviet Union, called for a boycott of the 1980 Olympics held in Moscow.

Discuss the facts associated with each of the nations.

As a summary, have students determine the nations with which President Carter had the greatest success and the nations with which he had the least success. Also, ask which nations and their situations helped influence the outcome of the 1980 election.

2. **Outline.** Continue the outline started in Section 1. The major topic would be III—President Carter. The subtopics could include any or all of the events described in the previous activity. Have students compare Carter and Nixon. Who seemed to have greater success in dealing with other nations? Who seemed to have greater success dealing with problems within the United States?

3. **Categorization.** Introduce the term *domestic* and explain that it refers to things that happen in America. Ask students what the opposite of "domestic" would be. (foreign) Have students characterize the following events from the administrations of Nixon, Ford, and Carter as "domestic" or "foreign."
   A. Controlling pollution (D)
   B. Ending the Cold War (F)
   C. Watergate Affair (D)
   D. Shortage of oil (D)
   E. Inflation (D)
   F. Unemployment (D)
   G. Control of Panama Canal (F)
   H. Middle East Peace (F)
   I. "Hostage Crisis" (F)
   J. 1980 Olympic boycott (F)

BUILDING AMERICAN CITIZENSHIP

Presidents Nixon and Carter spent a great deal of time dealing with foreign affairs. In general, do you think Presidents should devote more time to domestic issues, more to foreign affairs, or equal time to both? Give reasons for your answers.

SECTION 2 REVIEW ANSWERS

1. **IDENTIFY: Energy Security Act:** 1980 law providing federal funds to develop synthetic gas and oil; **Camp David Peace Agreement:** peace agreement worked out with the help of President Carter and signed by Israel and Egypt at Camp David, Maryland, in September 1978.

2. President Carter established the Department of Energy, urged Americans to stop all wasteful use of energy, proclaimed "Sun Day," and urged businesses and universities to discover ways to use solar energy.

3. Arab opposition to the Egypt-Israeli peace treaty; Americans taken as hostages in Iran; Soviet invasion of Afghanistan.

SECTION 3: Reagan Seeks To Strengthen America

OBJECTIVES

After completing this section, students will be able to:
• List the major points of Reagan's "Economic Recovery" plan and its expected results.

• Identify the nations supported by Reagan in their struggle against communism.
• Explain the major purpose of the 1982 Cancún Conference.

MOTIVATION

Write the following on the chalkboard:

President	Governor	Republican
Film Actor	Rancher	Sportscaster

Ask students to determine whom the above titles describe. If they are able to identify Ronald Reagan, ask which would refer to his present life (President, Republican, Rancher) and which to his careers before becoming President (Actor, Republican, Governor, Rancher, Sportscaster). Explain to students that Section 3 describes Reagan's problems and achievements as President.

SUGGESTED ACTIVITIES

1. **Directed Reading.** Continue the theme developed in Activity 3 in Section 2. Have students write two columns on their papers as indicated below and place the events described in the proper column:

DOMESTIC ISSUES	FOREIGN AFFAIRS
"Economic Recovery" plan	Military aid sent to El Salvador
Assassination attempt	Marines sent to Lebanon
Air traffic-controllers strike	Cancún Conference

Place the chart on the chalkboard and have students list the events in the appropriate columns. As a summary, have students add a final topic in their outline of the chapter and select and add subtopics from the reading.

2. **Comprehension Check.** Have students answer TRUE or FALSE to each of the following statements. This activity may be placed on the chalkboard or on a transparency for the overhead projector. Students should be able to give reasons for their answers.
   A. Ronald Reagan was the oldest person ever elected President. (T)
   B. One of President Reagan's major goals was to cut the size of the federal government's budget. (T)
   C. The purpose of President Reagan's "Economic Recovery" Plan was to increase the government's control of big business. (F)
   D. The air traffic-controller's strike closed the nation's airports (F)
   E. President Reagan sent American troops to El Salvador and Lebanon. (F)
   F. The President and Congress agreed to increase military spending. (F)

3. **Organizing Facts.** Duplicate Worksheet 92, *Recent Presidents.* This activity will provide an excellent summary of Sections 1, 2, and 3. You may wish to have students characterize the events as dealing with domestic issues or with foreign policy.

4. **Improving Your History Writing.** Review the Chapter 10 History Study Skill. Then, ask students to write a paragraph answering the following questions: Why do the developing nations of the world look to the United States for leadership and help? What is your

opinion of the efforts of the United States to help these nations?

BUILDING AMERICAN CITIZENSHIP

Duplicate Worksheet 93, *Our Presidents As Leaders*. You may wish to introduce the activity by having students answer the questions as they apply to the President now in office. Then, have students complete the activity. As a follow-up, conduct a class discussion during which students may talk about the responses they received.

SECTION 3 REVIEW ANSWERS

1. Reduction in federal spending; cut in individual income taxes; ending many government regulations of business and industry; tightening the nation's money supply.
2. Afghanistan, Poland, and El Salvador.
3. To discuss how the developed nations could help developing nations strengthen their economies.

SECTION 4: Americans Strive for Progress

OBJECTIVES

After completing this section, students will be able to:
- List the areas in which women have made gains in their efforts to gain equal rights.
- Identify America's minority groups and the gains they have made in recent years.
- Describe the changes and shifts in America's population in recent years.
- Tell how advances in science and technology have improved life for American citizens.

MOTIVATION

Use the History Study Skill *Using a Population Map* on textbook page 768. Have students look at the map, before they read the explanation, and ask if they can figure out what the numbers mean. Ask them to tell you which part of the country seems to have the highest numbers, and which the lowest numbers. Then have them read the explanation and answer the questions. Explain to students that the shift in population is only one of the changes that has occurred in America in recent years. By the time they finish reading this final section, they should be able to identify several others.

SUGGESTED ACTIVITIES

1. **Directed Reading.** As students read Section 4, have them answer the following question: "What changes have occurred in American society in recent years?" Among the items they might list are the following?
   A. New opportunities for women
   B. Gains made by minority groups
   C. The growth and movement of America's population
   D. Use of computers in businesses, factories, homes
   E. Improved buying power for most Americans

F. Increased leisure time
Discuss the items listed by students, and summarize the lesson by using the following activity.

2. **Summary Activity.** This activity is similar to the one found in the Section 4 Review. Ask students whether there has been an increase or decrease recently in each of the following areas.
   A. The number of women holding elected offices in government (I)
   B. The number of minority students who have graduated from college (I)
   C. The age at which people retire (I)
   D. The number of people moving into large urban areas (D)
   E. The number of computers used in business and industry (I)

3. **Population Maps.** Duplicate Worksheet 94, *Centers of Population*. This activity allows students to practice reading population maps, as introduced in the Motivation. You may wish to assign this exercise for homework, permitting students to apply the skill in an independent setting.

BUILDING AMERICAN CITIZENSHIP

The main idea of Section 4 is that the citizens of America have been meeting the challenges of the time. Once again, have students identify these challenges. (Refer to list compiled in the *Directed Reading* activity) Which of these problems are likely to continue to challenge Americans in the immediate future? (Struggle for equal rights, productivity of American factories, unemployment, inflation) Can you think of any new problems that are currently challenging American citizens? (Answers will vary.)

SECTION 4 REVIEW ANSWERS

1. IDENTIFY: **Sandra Day O'Connor:** the first woman appointed to the Supreme Court, in 1981; **NOW:** National Organization for Women, formed in 1966 to work for equal rights for women: **ERA:** Equal Rights Amendment; amendment granting women "equality of rights under the law"; **Gross National Product:** GNP; total output of goods and services in the United States.
2. They are still working for passage of an Equal Rights Amendment.
3. Black Americans, Hispanic Americans, Asian Americans, and American Indians made progress in getting key jobs in business and industry; more blacks were elected to Congress; more children of minority groups attended college.
4. Computers have changed work patterns in factories and offices and teaching and learning patterns in schools. They are being used in homes to entertain, store and process information, and help solve problems.

CHAPTER 33 REVIEW ANSWERS
REVIEWING KEY WORDS

1. c.   2. e.   3. b.   4. d.   5. a.

REMEMBERING IMPORTANT PEOPLE

1. a.   2. c.   3. d.   4. b.   5. c.

REVIEWING THE FACTS

1. F   2. F   3. T   4. T   5. T
6. c.   7. b.   8. b.   9. a.   10. b.

PLACING EVENTS IN TIME

1. C   2. A   3. D   4. E   5. B

LINKING GEOGRAPHY AND HISTORY

1. To try to stop the spread of communism in Central America.
2. Answers will vary.

THINKING ABOUT AMERICAN HISTORY

1. Answers will vary.
2. Answers will vary.

APPLYING HISTORY STUDIES SKILLS

1. Mountain.
2. About the same.
3. Mountain, Alaska, Hawaii.
4. Answers will vary.
5. Northeast and Central states.

UNIT 10 REVIEW ANSWERS

VOCABULARY REVIEW

Answers will vary.

REVIEWING THE MAIN IDEAS

1. It was clear that South Korea needed help when it was invaded by Communist North Korea in June 1950. If the United States failed to provide military aid, President Truman feared that the Communists would take that as a signal of weakness and perhaps then attack other nations. He therefore decided to send American troops to South Korea.
2. Business boom; higher productivity made possible through automation and the use of computer technology; increased profits and higher salaries; increased spending by workers leading to mass consumption and mass production; use of mass marketing and mass media to increase consumer demand, leading to greater prosperity.
3. They used court cases, got political candidates elected to office, boycotts, sit-ins, freedom rides, marches, peaceful demonstrations, violence and rioting.
4. At first, Americans supported President Johnson when he stepped up America's military involvement. Later the nation became divided into "hawks" and "doves." As the costs in American lives and money grew and still

there was no victory, more and more people opposed the war. Finally, President Nixon ended American involvement in the war in 1973.
5. Race riots, violence, and crime in cities, equal rights for minorities, the Watergate affair, the oil crisis, the hostage crisis in Iran, decreased productivity, unemployment, recession, nuclear arms race.
6. Eisenhower met Khrushchev in Geneva, Switzerland, in 1955; Kennedy met with Khrushchev in Vienna in 1961 and also set up a "hot-line" between Washington, D.C., and Moscow; Nixon visited the People's Republic of China and the Soviet Union in 1972. All Presidents have worked on treaties for arms control.

APPLYING YOUR STUDY SKILLS

1. **Using a Time Line**
   a. (1) America's involvement in the Vietnam War ended.
   (2) 12 years.
   (3) 1954.

2. **Separating Facts from Opinions**
   (1) O.   (2) F.   (3) O.   (4) O.   (5) F.

3. **Arranging Events Chronologically**
   (6) (Truman)   (3) (Eisenhower)   (1) (Kennedy)
   (2) (Johnson)   (5) (Carter)   (4) (Reagan)

4. **Making an Outline**

   CIVIL RIGHTS

   I. Truman
      A. Desegregation of the armed forces
      B. Desegregation of major-league baseball

   II. Eisenhower
      A. Desegregation of public schools
      B. Desegregation of buses in Alabama
      C. SCLC formed by Martin Luther King, Jr.
      D. Civil Rights Commission appointed
      E. National Urban League formed

   III. Kennedy
      A. Desegregation of colleges
      B. Freedom Riders
      C. March on Washington

   IV. Johnson
      A. Civil Rights Act of 1964
      B. Voting Rights Act of 1965

PROJECTS

Answers will vary.

BUILDING AMERICAN CITIZENSHIP

1. Answers will vary.
2. Answers will vary.

Locating Information In A Book

In Chapter 1 the History Study Skill helped you learn to locate information in your textbook. This may be used to find information in many kinds of books. Knowing how to use a table of contents, for example, will help you save time in studying and doing homework. Review the History Study Skill in Chapter 1, and then answer the question below.

USING THE TABLE OF CONTENTS, GLOSSARY, AND INDEX

Below are questions about where to find information in a book. Read each question carefully and then decide if the information is best found by using the Table of Contents, the Glossary, or Index.

1. Where would you find a page reference for Christopher Columbus?_____

2. Where would you find the page number of the beginning of Unit 1? _____

3. Where would you find the meaning of the word "colony"? _____

4. Where would you most easily find a reference to the Aztec Indian? _____

5. Where would you find the title of Chapter 2?_____

6. Where would you find a definition of "pueblo"? _____

7. Where would you find the page number for the first page of the Glossary? _____

8. Where would you find a list of the maps in the book?_____

_____

LOCATING INFORMATION ABOUT THE CHAPTERS OF YOUR TEXT

9. What are the section titles in Chapter 1?_____

_____

_____

_____

_____

10. In which section would you expect to find information about climate conditions in the different

geographical regions of the United States? Look over the subtitles under the section head to help

you decide. _____

_____

_____

_____

_____

Making a Table Culture and Environment

In Chapter 1 you read about different groups of Indians and where they lived. Each group had its own ways of living, or *culture*. And each group lived in a specific *environment*, or region. Many times, the ways Indians lived, or their culture, was influenced by where they lived, or their environment. Use your textbook to complete the table below. It will help you understand the relationship between culture and environment better. The first answer will help you complete the table.

INDIAN GROUPS	CULTURE	ENVIRONMENT
Shoshone	nomads; gathered wild plants and nuts; hunted small animals.	Great Basin; high, rocky, barren land (not good for farming)
Maya	town dwellers; built great pyramids; had a written language and mathematics; grew corn and other crops.	
Zuñi and Hopi	town dwellers; built adobe pueblos; grew corn and other crops on irrigated land.	
Apache	nomads; gathered wild plants and nuts; hunted animals; grew some crops.	
Iroquois	lived in towns; grew corn and other crops; gathered wild plants and nuts, hunted forest animals.	
Aztecs	city dwellers; built huge pyramids; grew corn and other crops; won a large empire by military conquest.	
Navajo	lived in small settlements; hunted animals; grew some corn and other crops; raised sheep after they were introduced by the Spanish.	

Name _____Class_____Date_____

Using Time Lines Explorers, 1499-1609

In Chapter 2 you learned form the History Study Skill that time lines can help you see clearly the order in which events happened. This information will help you know when events happened during the period when European explorers came to the Americas. Below is a time line which shows the dates of European explorers' voyages to the Americas. Study the time line carefully and then answer the questions below.

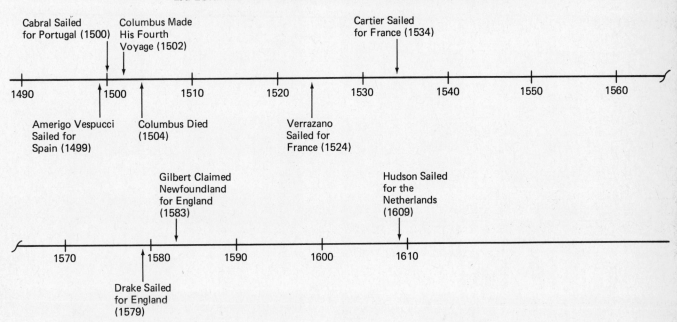

EXPLORERS AND THE COUNTRIES THEY SAILED FOR, 1499-1609

1. Between 1499 and 1610 how many different European countries does the time line show sent explorers to the Americas? _____

2. Name these countries._____

_____

3. Which European country began exploring the Americas in 1524? _____

4. In what year did Drake set sail to explore the Americas? _____

5. What was the last European nation to begin the exploration of the Americas? _____

_____

6. In what year did Portuguese exploration in the Americas begin? _____

7. Name the two explorers shown on the time line who explored America for France. _____

_____

8. Name the two explorers shown on the time line who explored America for England._____

_____

9. How many years did Columbus live after his fourth voyage? _____

10. How many years in total are shown on the time line? _____

Worksheet 3, Chapter 2

Crossword Puzzle European Exploration

Use your text to complete the crossword puzzle below. You can find all the information you will need to complete the puzzle in Chapter 2.

ACROSS
1. The name of the people who attacked the Vikings in America.
5. Another name for the Vikings.
7. Complete control of a market.
9. Sailed around the Cape of Good Hope.
10. The weather during the first part of Columbus's voyage was _____ .
11. A sturdy ship built by the Portuguese.
12. People who tried to win the Holy Land from the Muslims.

DOWN
1. The name of Columbus's flagship.
2. Norse settlement was found here in 1966.
3. Sailors used this to find latitude.
4. The Prince who started a school for sailors.
6. Portugal traded with this African kingdom.
8. An instrument that indicates all directions accurately.

Chronological Order The Spanish in America

The Spanish explored and established settlements in America during a period of almost 300 years. Chapter 3 covers a long part of that period. Below are eight events that are described in this chapter. In the table below, add to the dates of the events in the order in which they occurred. Then give the name or names of the leaders or other persons who took part in the event listed. Sometimes the same leader took part in more than one event.

1532   Spanish soldiers attack the Inca Empire
1609   The town of Santa Fe in New Mexico is started
1774   An overland trail to California is made
1521   The Aztecs surrender
1565   The Spanish land on the east coast of Florida
1523   The Spanish plan a new city to replace Tenochtitlan
1769   Spanish missionaries establish San Diego
1542   Spaniards sail along the Pacific Coast of California

DATE	EVENT	LEADER
1521		
1523		
1532		
1542		
1565		
1609		
1769		
1774		

Now answer these questions about the table above:

1. How many of these events happened in the 1500's? _____

2. How many of these events happened in the 1600's? _____

3. How many of these events happened in the 1700's? _____

4. How many years passed between the first event and the last event? _____

5. What three states in the present-day United States are mentioned in the table above? _____

_____

The Parts of a Map Spanish Conquests

As you learned in the History Study Skill for Chapter 3, knowing the different parts of a map helps you understand the information shown on the map. Also, when you know these parts of a map, you will be able to make a map yourself.

The title of a map tells you exactly what it is about. The key, or legend, helps you understand the symbols and colors on a map. Below is an outline map of parts of North and South America. Follow the instructions below to complete the outline map on this page. Use the maps and other information in your text to complete the map.

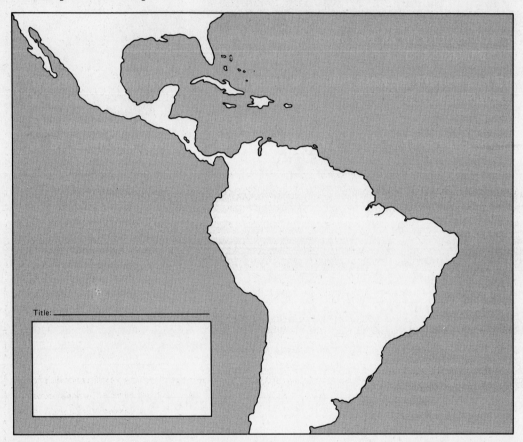

Title: _____

1. Color in the location of the Aztec empire and the Inca empire. Be sure to use two different colors. If you don't have crayons or colored pencils cover the areas with different patterns of dots, dashes, or wavy lines. Label the two empires.

2. Show the routes Cortés took to defeat the Aztecs and the route Pizarro took to defeat the Incas.

3. Label each of the following on the map:
   Hispaniola   Cuba   Panama
   Florida   Pacific Ocean   Atlantic Ocean
   Caribbean Sea   Puerto Rico

4. Show the Andes Mountains.

5. Use the box in the lower right-hand corner of the map to make your key or legend. Remember, you will need to explain your colors or shading and the map symbols you use.

6. Give your map a title that describes the information you have placed on it.

©Macmillan Publishing Co.

Name _____ Class_____ Date_____

Studying History Maps French Explorers

In Chapter 4 in the History Study Skill you learned about reading History Maps. The map below shows the routes followed by early French explorers in America. Study the map on this page. Then use the skills you learned in the chapter to answer the questions below.

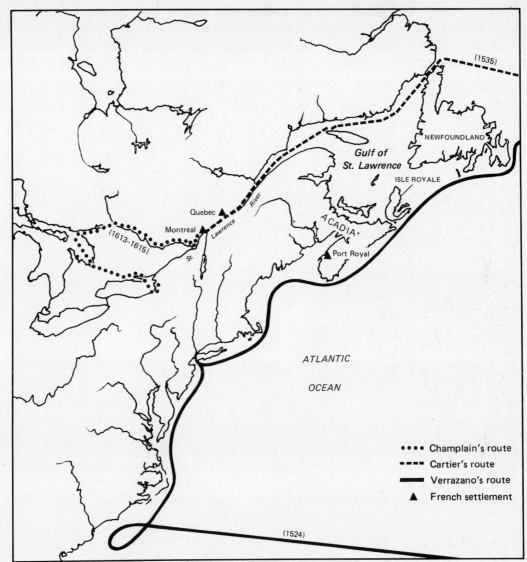

1. Which of the three explorers did not sail into the Gulf of St. Lawrence? _____

2. Which of the three explorers went farthest west? _____

3. Which of the three explorers was the first to enter the St. Lawrence River?_____

4. List the three French explorers in the correct order in which they arrived in America.

    First: _____   Second: _____

                Third: _____

5. Give the three French settlements shown on the map. _____

_____

Worksheet 7, Chapter 4

Making Comparisons Spain and France

In Chapter 3 you learned how Spain explored and colonized in North America. In this chapter you studied about French exploration and colonization. Complete the table below that compares what the Spanish and French did in the New World. You may use your textbook to help you.

	SPAIN	FRANCE
1. What areas were explored? By what names are the North American countries they explored known today?		
2. What were these explorers looking for?		
3. How did people from each country treat the Indians?		
4. Did their settlements grow quickly or slowly? Why?		
5. What things did the colonists send back home?		
6. Which countries tried to colonize the same land claimed by this nation?		

The Main Idea Jamestown and Plymouth

In Chapter 5 the History Study Skill helped you learn how to find the main idea in a paragraph. Read each of the paragraphs below and then read the sentences following them. Select the sentence in each group that best states the main idea of the paragraph.

1. Jamestown was built on low, swampy marshland. It was located on a small peninsula that jutted out into the James River. In the summer months, mosquitoes spread disease. The damp climate caused the food supplies to spoil quickly. The tents that many settlers lived in began to rot.

    a. Jamestown was an unsuccessful settlement.

    b. Jamestown's location was poorly chosen.

    c. The winter months were the worst time of year at Jamestown.

2. During the first few months, the colonists at Jamestown suffered from disease, hunger, and Indian attacks. Most of the supplies they brought from England were used up searching for gold. They failed to build strong shelters or a fort and did not clear land or plant gardens. There was no strong leader at the settlement.

    a. More buildings and supplies were needed to save Jamestown.

    b. The Indians could have helped the colonists solve their problems.

    c. The new colony at Jamestown got off to a poor start.

3. At Plymouth, the Pilgrims found a good harbor and a hill on which to locate a fort. There were many cornfields left by the Indians and many running streams. The land was full of game and the waters were full of fish.

    a. The place the Pilgrims chose for their settlement had many advantages.

    b. The Pilgrims avoided many of the hardships of the colonists at Jamestown.

    c. Colonists at Plymouth were most concerned about building homes.

4. The Pilgrims at Plymouth built houses and planned gardens. They also built a community storehouse. But because it was winter, the Pilgrims could not grow food. Before long, the supply of food brought from England was gone. Over half of the Pilgrims died during the first four months.

    a. The Pilgrims were saved by the strong, warm houses they built.

    b. The Plymouth colonists solved the problem of shelter but not their food problems.

    c. What Plymouth needed was a strong leader.

© Macmillan Publishing Co.

★Building American Citizenship

The Mayflower Compact

The Pilgrims were very concerned about setting up rules of government for the colony they were planning. Before landing at Plymouth, they drew up a compact, or agreement. Below is an easy-to-read version of the Mayflower Compact. Read it, and then answer the questions that follow.

In the name of God, Amen. We whose names are signed below are the loyal subjects of King James. We have undertaken for the glory of God, and the advancement of our Christian faith, and the honor of our king and country, a voyage to plant the first colony north of Virginia. We do solemnly and mutually combine ourselves together into a political body. We do this to keep order and to preserve and advance our goals. This document allows us to make and carry out just and equal laws from time to time as are necessary for the good of the colony. We all promise to obey these laws.

1. What three reasons do the Pilgrims give for their voyage to start a new colony?

_____

_____

_____

_____

2. What two reasons are given for combining together into a political body? _____

_____

_____

_____

3. What does the Mayflower Compact allow the colonists to do? _____

_____

_____

_____

4. What are the responsibilities of the Pilgrims to the Compact? _____

_____

_____

_____

5. What ideas in the Mayflower Compact are part of our democratic beliefs today? _____

_____

_____

_____

Organizing Facts English Colonies

In Chapter 5 you have read how England succeeded in setting up colonies along the East Coast of North America. These colonies were divided into three groups: the New England Colonies, the Middle Colonies, and the Southern Colonies. Below are twenty statements about English colonies in North America. In front of each statement write **NE** if it applies to one of the New England Colonies, **M** if it applies to one of the Middle Colonies, **S** if it applies to one of the Southern Colonies.

_____ 1. The first successful English colony was started here in 1607.

_____ 2. The "Mayflower" landed here in 1619.

_____ 3. The Dutch bought land here for $24 in tools and other items.

_____ 4. This colony split into two colonies in 1744.

_____ 5. The first log cabins were built here.

_____ 6. The Puritans controlled this colony.

_____ 7. Peter Stuyvesant was a colonial governor here.

_____ 8. This colony was started as a haven for debtors.

_____ 9. Roger Williams established his own colony here.

_____ 10. The Quakers established a colony here.

_____ 11. This colony was started by Catholics.

_____ 12. Four British warships captured this colony from the Dutch without firing a shot.

_____ 13. The first Africans arrived here in 1619.

_____ 14. The *Frame of Government* was a plan of government here.

_____ 15. The charter here separated church and government.

_____ 16. Anne Hutchinson was forced out of this colony.

_____ 17. A large German population settled here.

_____ 18. Rice and indigo were grown in this colony.

_____ 19. The plan of government here was called the *Fundamental Orders*.

_____ 20. The largest of all the English colonies in North America was here.

Tables Life in the English Colonies

In many ways the people in the thirteen English colonies had much in common. However, the colonists had very different ways of life, depending on where they lived. Use information from Chapter 6 in the textbook to fill in the table below. You may use the same answer in more than one box.

	NEW ENGLAND COLONIES	MIDDLE COLONIES	SOUTHERN COLONIES
1. What was produced in each region?			
2. What kind of work was done by young people?			
3. What kind of work was done by women?			
4. Name two important cities in each region and tell why they were important.			
5. Name the main religious groups in the region.			
6. Describe education in the region.			

© Macmillan Publishing Co.

Maps of Trade Routes Spanish Trade

In Chapter 6 you have read about the triangular trade route between Great Britain, Africa, and the British colonies in North America. Spain also had a well-developed system of trade with its colonies in the New World. Use the skills you learned in the History Study Skill of Chapter 6 to answer the questions that follow the map below.

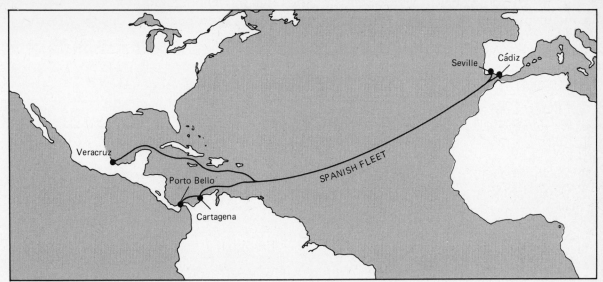

1. What things did Spain send to its colonies in the New World? _____
   _____
   _____

2. What were two important cities in Spain that took part in trade with the Americas?
   _____

3. What three leading colonial cities traded with Spain?_____

4. What things were sent from the colonies to Spain? _____
   _____

5. Write a three-sentence paragraph comparing trade between Britain and its colonies with the trade
   between Spain and its colonies. _____
   _____
   _____
   _____
   _____
   _____
   _____

★Building American Citizenship

Colonial Government

During the years described in Chapter 6, many Americans became more involved in government, and their political rights were expanded. The table below contains words from Chapter 6 as well as some new words which you will soon learn. Complete the table by defining and giving the purpose of the person and institution in British and Colonial political life that are listed in the table. Then answer the questions that follow.

BRITISH POLITICAL LIFE

INSTITUTION	DEFINITION AND PURPOSE
Monarch	
Parliament	
House of Commons	
House of Lords	

COLONIAL POLITICAL LIFE

INSTITUTION	DEFINITION AND PURPOSE
Proprietor	
Colonial Governor	
House of Burgesses	
Colonial Assemblies	
Governor's Council	

1. What part of the British Parliament did the House of Burgesses resemble most? _____

2. What were the duties of colonial assemblies? _____

3. What part of the British Parliament did the governor's councils resemble most?_____

4. What were the duties of the colonial governor's councils? _____

5. Who was allowed to vote in colonial America?_____

©Macmillan Publishing Co.

Name _____ Class _____ Date _____

Comparing Maps Colonies in 1650 and 1700

In the History Study Skill in Chapter 7 you learned how to compare two historical maps to see how colonial America changed. The maps in the Study Skill of Chapter 7 showed that France lost its American colonies to the British. Below are two maps of the East Coast of America. One map is of 1650 and the other is of 1700. Study the maps, and then answer the questions that follow.

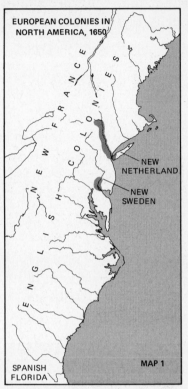
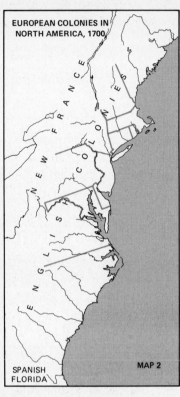

1. What European countries with American colonies are shown in Map 1? _____

   _____

2. What year does Map 1 represent? _____

3. What European country or countries are shown with colonies in Map 2? _____

   _____

4. What year does Map 2 represent? _____

Now review Chapter 5 and answer the following questions:

5. What British colony replaced New Netherland? _____

6. What British colony replaced New Sweden? _____

7. In what year did the Dutch take control of New Sweden? _____

8. Explain how England took control of New Netherland. _____

   _____

   _____

   _____

© Macmillan Publishing Co.

Name _____ Class _____ Date _____

Cause and Effect The American Revolution

In Chapter 7 you read about the events leading up to the American Revolution. Some of the events *caused* other events to happen. These other events are called *effects.* For example, French and British disputes over the same land *caused* the French and Indian War. The large *debt* the British had at the end of the French and Indian War was an *effect* of the war. Below are statements about events that were causes. These are followed by three possible effects of the events. Identify the correct cause and effect relationship by choosing the effect that relates to the cause above it.

CAUSE

1. In 1764, Parliament passed the Sugar Act and sent customs collectors to make sure that the tax was paid.

EFFECT:

   a. Colonial merchants and shippers were angered by the searches made by customs collectors.
   b. Colonists were relieved that the new tax was actually lower than the old tax.
   c. Most Americans knew that higher taxes would help protect them from Indians.

CAUSE:

2. The Stamp Act of 1765 was passed by Parliament.

EFFECT:

   a. Americans protested by drawing up petitions and boycotting British goods.
   b. Colonists did not protest because the Stamp Act was better than the Sugar Act.
   c. Colonists protested by printing their own stamps.

CAUSE:

3. In 1773 a Tea Act was passed by Parliament.

EFFECT:

   a. Colonists were happy that tea prices were lowered.
   b. Tea was thrown overboard in Boston harbor by angry Americans.
   c. British soldiers fired on the angry mob of colonists, killing 5 men.

CAUSE:

4. One of the Intolerable Acts closed the port of Boston.

EFFECT:

   a. Colonists armed themselves and attacked British troops.
   b. Thomas Paine wrote a famous essay called *Common Sense.*
   c. The First Continental Congress met in Philadelphia.

CAUSE:

5. Groups of militia called minutemen organized throughout Massachusetts.

EFFECT:

   a. The minutemen carried out daring raids against British troops.
   b. Britain opened the port of Boston.
   c. British troops marching toward Concord fired on colonists at Lexington.

© Macmillan Publishing Co.

Name _____ Class_____ Date_____

★**Building American Citizenship**

Methods of Protest

In Chapter 7 you read how the colonists struggled with Great Britain for many years before war actually broke out. During this time the colonists used many different methods of protests to show that they were unhappy with what they considered to be unjust British laws, taxes, and actions. Below is a table that lists some colonial methods of protest. Complete the table and answer the questions that follow.

Method of Protest		**Give an example of when colonists used it**
Petition	to make formal, usually written requests that laws or conditions be changed	
Boycott	to join together with others to refuse to buy or sell certain goods when the tax on them is considered unjust	
Destruction of Property	to destroy goods or buildings belonging to people considered responsible for unjust laws or taxes	

1. Which of these methods of protest do you feel were lawful? _____

_____

2. Which of these methods of protest do you feel were illegal? _____

_____

3. Give one example you have seen or read about in recent times that illustrates each of these

   methods of protest.

   petition _____

   _____

   boycott_____

   _____

   speeches _____

   _____

   destruction of property _____

   _____

© Macmillan Publishing Co.

195

Worksheet 17, Chapter 7

★ **Building American Citizenship**

Declaration of Independence

Understanding the Declaration of Independence is essential for good American citizenship. The Declaration is important to all the people of the world who value freedom. It is worth careful study. Turn to the Declaration in your textbook. Notice that after a short introduction which tells why the Declaration of Independence was written, there is a statement of principle about human rights and government. This is followed by specific complaints against the government of King George III. Then there is a summary of how Americans tried to work with the British to end this unfair treatment. The claim of freedom and independence for the United States of America ends the document. Answer the questions below as you read the document.

AMERICANS BELIEVED CERTAIN TRUTHS TO BE SELF-EVIDENT

1. List three truths named in the Declaration of Independence that Americans believed to be self-

    evident. _____

    _____

    _____

    _____

AMERICANS BELIEVED THE KING HAD "INJURED" THE COLONISTS

2. List three "injuries" that the King had done to the colonists._____

    _____

    _____

3. Do you think these "injuries" were serious enough for the colonists to have rebelled?

    Explain your answer._____

    _____

    _____

AMERICANS TRY TO END UNFAIR TREATMENT

4. What step did Americans take to try to end unfair treatment by the British? _____

    _____

    _____

AMERICANS DECLARED THEIR INDEPENDENCE

5. Copy below the phrase or phrases used to formally declare America's independence.

    _____

    _____

    _____

    _____

    _____

© Macmillan Publishing Co.

Making a Time Line The American Revolution

Using time lines is a skill that you have known about since Chapter 2. Each of the chapters of your textbook begins with a time line. Now make your own time line in the space provided below. Look at each item, decide if it is a British victory or an American victory, and then place it to the left or right of the time line under the correct heading. Be sure to check in your textbook to find the date of each event. Include the month, if it is available, and the year of each event in your time line.

Events to Be Shown on Time Line

- Battle of New York
- Battle at Yorktown
- Battle of Bunker and Breed's Hills
- Winter at Valley Forge
- Battle of Trenton

- Battle of Moore's Creek Bridge
- Battle at Saratoga
- Battle of Fort Ticonderoga
- Battle of King's Mountain
- Battle of Quebec

TIME LINE

British Victories   **American Victories**

1775

1776

1777

1778

1779

1780

1781

Worksheet 19, Chapter 9

The Main Idea The Swamp Fox

Read each paragraph below and choose the answer that best gives the main idea of that paragraph.

1. Francis Marion was a captain in the South Carolina militia. He commanded 60 volunteers who were sworn to fight the British in the American Revolution. Their job was to repair the forts that protected Charleston harbor. The militia wanted to fight, not build forts, and so many of the volunteers deserted. But Francis Marion helped to see that the work continued on the forts. When the British fleet arrived at Charleston in June of 1776, it could not destroy the well-made forts. The British sailed away and Charleston was saved.

   a. A soldier must be prepared to do many things other than fight.

   b. Francis Marion was a very colorful leader who ruled his men with an iron hand.

   c. Men who deserted Marion's group were Loyalists who sided with the British.

2. Two years later, the British returned and captured Charleston. Many people in South Carolina joined the British Army. Francis Marion decided to fight on against the British even though his group of soldiers was small. He decided to use "hit-and-run" tactics. Soon his group was the only Patriot force in the state. Marion and his men began by burning British boats along the Santee River. Next, they rescued some American prisoners being taken to Charleston.

   a. The British capture of South Carolina eliminated all Patriot forces in the state.

   b. A small group of Patriots was successful against the British in South Carolina.

   c. Francis Marion became famous in the North because of his victory at Charleston.

3. Marion and his men continued to raid small British and Loyalist camps. They captured guns, ammunition, and food. More volunteers joined Marion's forces. The British tried to catch Marion, but he was too smart. He hid among the pine woods and dark swamps of South Carolina. Soon people began to call him the "Swamp Fox." Finally, the British stopped chasing Marion. They knew he was too sly to catch.

   a. Marion and his men were not successful against British troops.

   b. The "Swamp Fox" was a nickname given to Marion because he was smart and hard to catch.

   c. British and Loyalist troops forced Marion to live in a swamp where he could not attack them.

4. In 1781 Marion joined with Colonel Harry Lee. They built a tall tower and dragged it outside Fort Watson, a British-held fort. From the tower, sharpshooters could shoot at the soldiers inside the fort. The British quickly surrendered. It was the first American victory against a major British strongpoint in three years. Six months later, the war was over and Americans had their independence. All during the war, Francis Marion had kept Patriot hopes alive in South Carolina.

   a. British troops were tired of the long war and surrendered to Marion.

   b. Marion and his men ended the war at the Battle of Fort Watson.

   c. The "Swamp Fox" never gave up hope and fought on until the Americans won the war.

©Macmillan Publishing Co.

Tables The Articles of Confederation

There were many tasks facing the new government under the Articles of Confederation. Review the discussion of the Confederation government in Chapter 9, and then describe in the table below how the government under the Articles of Confederation showed strength or weakness in performing the governing tasks listed at the left.

TASK	STRENGTHS OF THE GOVERNMENT UNDER THE ARTICLES OF OF CONFEDERATION	WEAKNESS OF THE GOVERNMENT UNDER THE ARTICLES OF OF CONFEDERATION
Raising Money through Taxes		
Printing Money		
Repaying Foreign Loans		
Dealing with Foreign Governments		
Organizing the Northwest Territory		

1. Write a paragraph explaining what you think was the greatest success of the government under the Articles of Confederation. _____

   _____

   _____

   _____

2. Write a paragraph explaining what you think was the greatest failure of the government under the Articles of Confederation._____

   _____

   _____

   _____

©Macmillan Publishing Co.

Studying Illustrations Shays' Rebellion

In Chapter 9 you learned how to get information from the study of illustrations. Use those skills to study the illustration below and answer the questions that follow.

Daniel Shays, followed by the poor farmers and debtors that joined his rebellion, brings his protest to the state supreme court in Springfield, Massachusetts, in 1786.

1. What does the caption of this illustration tell you? Ask yourself the questions Who? What? Where? When? How? _____

   _____

   _____

2. Which person in the illustration do you think is Daniel Shays? Explain your answer. _____

   _____

   _____

3. What person in the illustration do you think is the state official Daniel Shays and his followers are bringing their protest to? Explain your answer. _____

   _____

4. What clues in the illustration suggest that the meeting involves some sort of problem? _____

   _____

   _____

5. What conditions was Daniel Shays protesting? _____

   _____

©Macmillan Publishing Co.

The Constitution Branches of Government

Use the copy of the Constitution in your textbook to complete the fill-in-the blank exercise below.

PREAMBLE

The people of the United States established the Constitution for the United States of America to form

a more perfect union, _____

_____

ARTICLE 1. THE LEGISLATIVE BRANCH

Section 1. All legislative powers are given to _____, which has two parts, a

_____, and a _____.

Section 2. The House of Representatives is chosen every_____years.

Section 3. The Senate is made up of_____ Senators from each State. Senators

serve for_____ years. The _____ is President of the Senate, but

he or she does not vote unless there is a _____.

Section 7. All bills for _____ shall start in the House of Representatives. Once a

bill passes both the House and Senate, it must be signed by the _____ before it

becomes law.

Section 8. Congress has the power to: (Select three powers that you think are important.)

_____

_____

_____

ARTICLE 2. THE EXECUTIVE BRANCH

Section 1. The executive power is given to _____ whose term of office is

_____.

Section 2. The President's powers include: (Select three powers you consider important.)

_____

_____

_____

ARTICLE 3. THE JUDICIAL BRANCH

Section 1. The judicial power is given to _____ and _____.

Section 2. The Supreme Court does not listen to all cases but only certain kinds of cases.

These include: (Select three kinds of cases that are tried in federal courts.)

_____

Organizing Facts Which Branch?

The three branches of government share powers. The President, governors, or mayors have executive power. Congress, state legislatures, or city councils have legislative power. The Supreme Court and other federal, state, and local courts have judicial power. Look at each of the powers listed below. In front of the number, mark each of the powers of the federal government as **E** Executive, **L** Legislative, or **J** Judicial. Use the copy of the Constitution in your text for reference.

_____ **1.** coin money

_____ **2.** make treaties

_____ **3.** decide controversies between states

_____ **4.** declare war

_____ **5.** raise armies

_____ **6.** levy taxes

_____ **7.** appoint ambassadors

_____ **8.** establish post offices

_____ **9.** grant pardons

_____ **10.** make rules for government

_____ **11.** borrow money

_____ **12.** appoint Supreme Court Justices

_____ **13.** call out the militia

_____ **14.** make laws

_____ **15.** see that laws are executed

_____ **16.** interpret laws

_____ **17.** approve treaties

_____ **18.** regulate commerce

_____ **19.** command the army

_____ **20.** collect taxes

★**Building American Citizenship**

The Bill of Rights

You read in Chapter 10 that one of the first things the new American government did in 1789 was to add the Bill of Rights of the Constitution. You will find the Bill of Rights in your textbook. Read the situations below and decide which basic rights of Alvin Goldman, an American citizen, were violated.

Situation	Right Violated
1. Mr. Goldman was prevented by the authorities from speaking on the subject of his religion.	
2. Mr. Goldman was reading a book when local police officers broke down his door and began searching for stolen property. They did not say a word to Mr. Goldman about why they were there.	
3. Mr. Goldman was put in jail for failing to pay a parking fine. Bail was set at $10,000.	
4. Mr. Goldman was found guilty for failing to pay his parking fine. The judge ordered Mr. Goldman to turn in his driver's license and not to drive again for five years.	
5. Five years later, after Mr. Goldman was put in jail, he was tried again in court for the same crime and was fined $500.	
6. Mr. Goldman was told by the head of local National Guard that five soldiers were going to spend the next month in his home.	
7. Mr. Goldman owned a newspaper and was told that he could not print a newspaper because the governor did not like Mr. Goldman's ideas.	
8. Mr. Goldman was not told why when he was arrested for speeding and put in jail for over a week before the trial date was set. He was told that he could not have a lawyer to help him at the trial.	

Worksheet 25, Chapter 10

Improving Your Writing   The Barbary Pirates

In Chapter 10 you worked on an exercise to improve your history writing. One of the most important parts of good writing is to present facts and details that explain or support the main idea or topic. Below are five main idea, or topic, sentences that deal with an American ship captured by the Barbary pirates. Pretend you were on that ship and make up the details to complete each paragraph. Some clues about what to write are given at the left.

(What were your feelings about the trip?)

1. When I was 13 years old, my family sailed from Baltimore to visit friends in England. _____
_____
_____
_____

(What were your feelings? How did your parents react? What did your captain do?)

2. One day, about three weeks after we left port, a pirate ship suddenly appeared, and sailed swiftly toward us. _____
_____
_____
_____

(What were your feelings? What did other people feel? What did the pirate do?)

3. A cruel looking pirate captain came on board ship. _____
_____
_____
_____

(What were your feelings? What had the pirates done on your ship?)

4. At last, the pirates decided to leave our ship. _____
_____
_____
_____

(What were your feelings?)

5. We watched the pirate ship sail away._____
_____
_____
_____
_____

Name _____ Class_____ Date_____

Election Maps The Election of 1800

In Chapter 10 you read about the important differences between the Federalists and the Republicans. Below is a map of the United States in 1800, showing how each state voted in the election that year. Study the map carefully and answer the questions that follow.

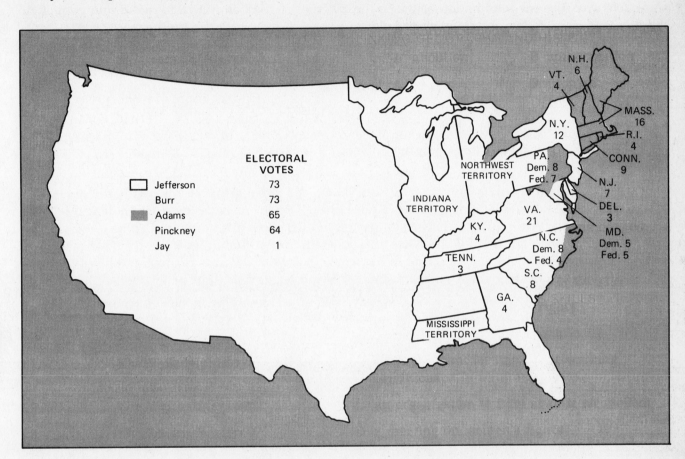

1. Place each of the 16 states under one of the headings below:

STATES THAT VOTED FOR ADAMS
(electoral vote)

1.   5.
2.   6.
3.   7.
4.

STATES THAT VOTED FOR JEFFERSON
(electoral vote)

1.   4.
2.   5.
3.   6.

STATES THAT SPLIT THEIR VOTES

1.
2.
3.

2. How many electoral votes did each candidate receive?_____

_____

_____

© Macmillan Publishing Co.

205

Worksheet 27, Chapter 10

Name _____ Class _____ Date _____

Circle Graphs The Elections of 1812 and 1816

In Chapter 11 you learned how to interpret and then how to make circle graphs that showed results from elections. Making circle graphs is not hard at all once you learn a few simple rules. Circle graphs are good to include in history reports and projects because they *show* information in an easily understandable way. Use the information below on the Election of 1812 and 1816 to make your own circle graphs. Be sure to follow the steps given below.

ELECTION OF 1812

Candidates	Electoral Vote	Percentage
James Madison	128	59%
DeWitt Clinton	89	41%

Step 1 Determine how many sections your circle graph will have. It should have as many sections as there are candidates. In this election, there were two candidates so make sure to make a graph with two parts.

Step 2 Look at the percentages in the table above. On the circle graph below divide the circle into four equal parts in light pencil that can be erased. Divide one of the quarters in half and divide each of the two halves in half again (into eighths). Now take a quarter, plus one half of a quarter (one eighth), plus a bit less than one third of still another half of a quarter. Added together they make a section that is very close to 41%. Now draw permanent lines that mark off the area of the circle that represents 41% and erase your light pencil lines.

Step 3 Label each of the parts of the circle graph. Each part should be labeled with the candidate's name and number of votes.

ELECTION OF 1812

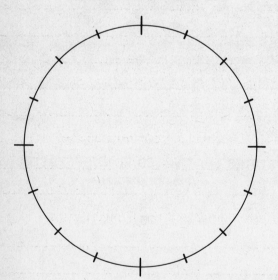

ELECTION OF 1816

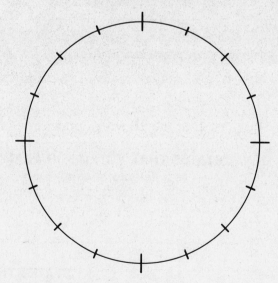

Now see if you can make a circle graph for the Election of 1816. Use the blank above.

ELECTION OF 1816

Candidates	Electoral Vote	Percentage
James Monroe	183	84%
Rufus King	34	16%

Divide the circle into four quarters first. Then further divide and combine the segments until they show percentages that are close to the percentages in the table above.

★ Building American Citizenship

The Star-Spangled Banner

The "Star-Spangled Banner" is the national anthem of the United States. You read in Chapter 11 how it was written by Francis Scott Key in 1814 during the British invasion of the United States. Key wrote the words as a poem. Within a few days of the battle, however, the words had been set to music. The song was an immediate success and was soon recognized by the Army and Navy as our country's anthem. In 1931, Congress officially adopted the "Star-Spangled Banner" as our national anthem.

Below is the first verse of "The Star Spangled Banner." Read it carefully and answer the questions that follow.

THE STAR-SPANGLED BANNER

Oh! say! can you see, by the dawn's early light,
What so proudly we hailed at the twilight's last gleaming?
Whose broad stripes and bright stars through the perilous fight,
O'er the ramparts we watched were so gallantly streaming?
And the rockets' red glare, the bombs bursting in air,
Gave proof through the night that our flag was still there.
Oh, say, does that Star-Spangled Banner yet wave
O'er the land of the free and the home of the brave?

1. Look up in a dictionary and write down the meaning of the following words:

   twilight _____

   perilous _____

   ramparts_____

   star-spangled (Look up "Spangled" first.) _____

2. What is the star-spangled banner? _____

   _____

3. What questions does Francis Scott Key ask? (Restate the question in your own words.)

   _____

   _____

4. Write down the words of "The Star Spangled Banner" that described the United States.

   _____

   _____

5. About what time of day do you think Francis Scott Key wrote his verse? Explain your answer. ____

   _____

   _____

Putting Events In Order   1800 to 1824

A great many events happened in the United States in the years between 1800 and 1824. There were three different Presidents, a major war, and important additions to the country's territory. Below are 18 important events from Chapter 11. After each event put the name of the President who was in office at the time it happened. Also, put the correct year after each event.

	President	Year
1. Lewis and Clark began their exploration.	_____	_____
2. The "Star-Spangled Banner" was written.	_____	_____
3. The Embargo Act was passed by Congress.	_____	_____
4. A protective tariff was passed.	_____	_____
5. Congress impeached John Pickering.	_____	_____
6. The United States acquired Florida.	_____	_____
7. The Non-Intercourse Act was passed.	_____	_____
8. *Marbury v. Madison* set up judicial review.	_____	_____
9. British troops burned Washington, D.C.	_____	_____
10. Congress declared war on Britain.	_____	_____
11. The Navy sailed against the Barbary pirates.	_____	_____
12. The Rush-Bagot Agreement was signed.	_____	_____
13. The Judiciary Act was repealed.	_____	_____
14. The *Leopard* assaulted the *Chesapeake*.	_____	_____
15. Jackson defeated British at New Orleans.	_____	_____
16. Perry's fleet defeated the British.	_____	_____
17. The Monroe Doctrine was issued.	_____	_____
18. The Louisiana Territory was purchased.	_____	_____

Fact or Opinion? Pioneers Move Westward

In Chapter 12 you learned how to separate fact from opinion. You have read several paragraphs about Abraham Lincoln. Some of the paragraphs were facts that are supported by actual evidence. Other paragraphs were opinions. They might, in fact, be true, but there is no solid evidence to support what is said. Below are passages from your textbook. Decide if each passage is fact or opinion. Then explain why you think that way.

1. "Pioneers had started to move to the western side of the Appalachian Mountains even before the Revolutionary War. However, the British tried to stop this westward movement. They were afraid the settlers would cause trouble with the Indians who lived there and harm the fur trade."

   Fact or opinion? _____ Explain your answer. _____
   _____
   _____

2. "A new period in water transportation began in 1825. In that year, the *Seneca Chief*, a freight barge, was pulled from Buffalo at the eastern end of Lake Erie to Albany on the Hudson River. The barge traveled 363 miles (580.8 kilometers) on the brand-new Erie Canal."

   Fact or opinion? _____ Explain your answer. _____
   _____
   _____

3. "Most American pioneers moved westward because they hoped life there would be better. It was becoming harder to be successful and to get ahead in the East. Many Americans felt that in the West they would have the chance to improve their lives. Others were looking for adventure or trying to escape crowded city life."

   Fact or opinion? _____ Explain your answer. _____
   _____
   _____

4. "Soon, other mills were built in New England. One reason factories were built in this section of the country was that New England had many swift-running rivers. They supplied the power needed to turn the water wheels that ran the machines in the factories. By this time a number of New Englanders had made money from trade and were willing to spend it building factories."

   Fact or opinion? _____ Explain your answer. _____
   _____
   _____

5. "John Quincy Adams had been a brilliant Secretary of State. However, he was not a good President. He was hardworking, but it was difficult to get him to change his mind. Moreover, he did not know how to get support for his programs in Congress."

   Fact or opinion? _____ Explain your answer. _____
   _____
   _____
   _____

★**Building American Citizenship**

Americans Compromise

You learned in Chapter 9 that compromises were very important at the Constitutional Convention in 1787. In Chapter 12, you read about another compromise—the Missouri Compromise of 1820. Below are some questions that will help increase your understanding of why compromises are such an important part of citizenship.

1. What was the problem about Missouri's becoming a state?_____
_____
_____
_____

2. How did the Missouri Compromise of 1820 give something to both sides?_____
_____
_____
_____

3. Much of the land in the West was sold by the government for $2.00 an acre. But many settlers had "squatted" on the land without buying it. To evict these settlers would cause anger among Americans. Give one possible compromise that would satisfy both the government and the "squatters."_____
_____
_____
_____

4. Suppose your school's student government decides to hold a dance. Some people want a 50's dance but others want a dress-up dance. What are some possible compromises?
_____
_____
_____
_____

5. Why do you think compromises are so important in American life? _____
_____
_____
_____
_____
_____
_____
_____

© Macmillan Publishing Co.

Worksheet 32, Chapter 12

Giving Examples Causes of Sectionalism

In Chapter 12 you read about the problems that created strong sectional feelings in the United States. Give examples showing how each of the following helped cause sectionalism. Use your textbook to help you.

Slavery _____
_____
_____
_____

The factory system in Northeast _____
_____
_____
_____

Cotton as the South's number-one cash crop _____
_____
_____
_____

East-West transportation routes _____
_____
_____
_____

Tariffs _____
_____
_____
_____

Summarize what you consider to be the most important cause of sectionalism in 1828. Be sure to write the main idea in the topic sentence and then support it with statements of the facts.

_____
_____
_____
_____
_____
_____

Worksheet 33, Chapter 12

Name _____ Class_____ Date_____

Reviewing Map Skills Indian Relocation, 1830-1842

Here is a map that shows the relocation of the Indians who lived in the Southeast to the Indian Territory west of the Mississippi. Study the map and then answer the questions that follow it.

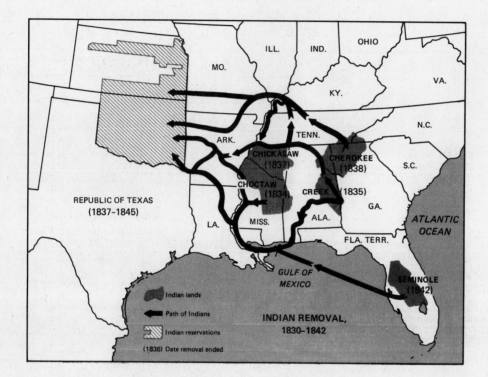

1. In one sentence tell what this map shows. _____

_____

2. What does this symbol stand for? _____

3. How many American Indian tribes are shown on the map?_____

   Name them. _____

_____

4. What does this symbol stand for? _____

_____

5. Name the four different Indian tribes who lived in Alabama before their removal. _____

_____

6. Which tribe ended up settling in the southernmost part of the Indian Territory? _____

_____

7. Which Indian tribe was removed first? _____

   Which tribe was removed last? _____

8. In what direction did all of the Indian tribes move? _____

©Macmillan Publishing Co.

Worksheet 34, Chapter 13

Line Graphs Farm Size and Land Prices

In the History Study Skill for Chapter 13 you learned how to use a line graph to show changes in numbers over a period of years. The table below shows the minimum purchase, or the smallest amount of land a person could buy from the government. The line graph shows the "Average Price per Acre" that people had to pay to buy land from the government. Use the skills learned in Chapter 13 to study the graph below. Then study the table and answer the questions that follow.

AVERAGE PRICE PER ACRE OF GOVERNMENT LAND

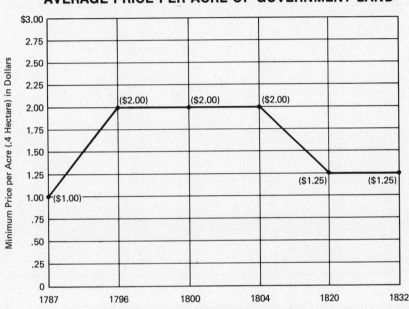

MINIMUM FARM SIZE, 1787-1832

Year	Acres/Hectares
1787	640 acres/26 hectares
1796	640 acres/26 hectares
1800	320 acres/13 hectares
1804	160 acres/6.5 hectares
1820	90 acres/4.6 hectares
1832	40 acres/1.6 hectares

1. What was the smallest amount of land a settler could purchase from the government in 1787? _____ in 1804? _____ in 1832? _____

2. What was the price per acre a settler paid for government land in 1787? _____ in 1800? _____ in 1820? _____

3. Generally, did the minimum number of acres a person could buy from the government increase or decrease between 1787 and 1832? _____

4. Generally, did the price per acre of land purchased from the government increase or decrease between 1796 and 1832? _____

5. If you had purchased the minimum number of acres in 1820, about how much would you have paid? _____

Worksheet 35, Chapter 13

★Building American Citizenship

Planning a Political Campaign, 1840

In the Presidential election of 1840, the winner had to get at least 148 electoral votes out of a total of 294 to win. The table below shows the number of electoral votes each state had. Use this information to answer the questions that follow.

ELECTORAL VOTES OF THE STATES IN 1840

Slave States		Free States	
Delaware	3	New Hampshire	6
Maryland	8	Massachusetts	12
Virginia	17	Rhode Island	4
North Carolina	11	Connecticut	6
South Carolina	9	New York	36
Georgia	10	New Jersey	26
Kentucky	12	Vermont	6
Tennessee	13	Ohio	23
Louisiana	6	Indiana	12
Mississippi	6	Illinois	9
Alabama	9	Maine	9
Missouri	7	Michigan	5
Arkansas	3	Pennsylvania	26
	114		**180**

1. Which state has the most electoral votes? _____

2. Is it a slave state or a free state?_____

3. Of the slave states, which one has the most electoral votes?_____

4. How many free states have more electoral votes than the slave state with the most electoral votes? _____

5. Of the free states, which one has the fewest electoral votes? _____

6. Could a candidate win the election without getting some electoral votes from the slave states?
_____

7. Could a candidate win without getting some electoral votes from the free states? _____

8. Was it more important for Van Buren and Harrison to campaign in free states or slave states?
_____ Why? _____
_____

9. If you were trying to help one of the candidates get elected, in what four states would you campaign the most? _____

10. In advising a candidate and in helping a candidate with speeches, would you tell the candidate to pay more attention to the needs of the slave states or the free states? _____
_____

★**Building American Citizenship**

A Nation of Immigrants

Below are several paragraphs about the immigrants who contributed so much to American life. After reading the information, choose the sentence that best states the main idea of the paragraph.

1. Immigrants who wanted to come to the United States had to come over on one of the many ships sailing from Europe. Conditions on these ships for poor passengers were harsh. It took at least six weeks to cross from Great Britain to New York in the 1840's. Sometimes the trip took three months! People were crowded together in cramped spaces. Food and water often were bad tasting or spoiled. Thousands of would-be immigrants died every year just trying to reach America.

   a. Very few immigrants made it to America because they died trying to get here.

   b. Immigrants suffered many hardships before they arrived in America.

   c. It was probably better to stay in Europe than to risk the dangers of crossing the Atlantic Ocean.

2. Irish immigrants left Ireland in the 1840's because of famine. There was not enough food to feed the people. Most of the Irish who landed here were too poor to buy land so they stayed in cities along the Atlantic coast. The Irish worked hard and started schools to help their children become good Americans. Much of the Irish heritage became a part of American culture. Irish music and writing were popular. Some Irish became political leaders. Many Americans today trace their ancestry back to Ireland.

   a. Irish immigrants were more successful than other immigrants.

   b. The United States welcomed Irish immigrants in the 1840's.

   c. Irish immigrants contributed to building the United States and added much to American culture.

3. Almost 2 million Germans came to the United States between 1820 and 1860. German immigrants included farmers, craftspeople, politicians, and shopkeepers. Germans settled throughout the country. They settled in large numbers in the Great Lakes region. German farmers taught Americans about new and better ways to farm. Germans insisted that their children get a good education in order to become good citizens. Today many Americans trace their ancestry back to Germany.

   a. Germans were a very important immigrant group coming to America from 1820 to 1860.

   b. German immigrants did not have a difficult time coming to the United States.

   c. More immigrants came from Germany than from all other countries put together.

Circle Graphs Immigration, 1820-1860

Between 1820 and 1860, over 2 million people came to the United States from Europe. Most of these immigrants came from Ireland, Great Britain, and Germany. In Chapter 11, you learned how to study information on circle graphs. Use the skills you learned to study the graphs below, and then answer the questions that follow.

1821–1830

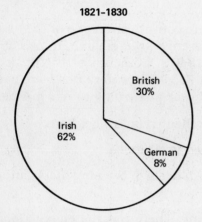

British 30%
Irish 62%
German 8%

1831–1840

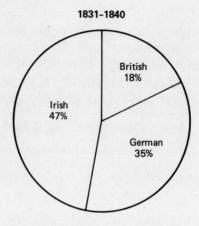

British 18%
Irish 47%
German 35%

1841–1850

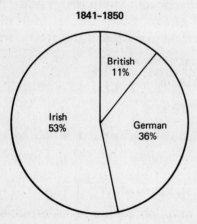

British 11%
Irish 53%
German 36%

1851–1860

British 20%
Irish 40%
German 40%

1. What overall time period is shown on these graphs? _____

2. What was the largest group of immigrants during each of the decades shown?

   1821-30 _____   1841-50 _____

   1831-40 _____   1851-60 _____

3. Look at British immigration between 1821 and 1850. Does their part of the graph increase or

   decrease during each of these three decades? _____

4. Look at German immigration between 1821 and 1860. Does their part of the graph increase or

   decrease during each of these four decades?_____

5. Look at Irish immigration between 1821 and 1860. Does their part of the graph increase or

   decrease during each of these four decades?_____

Details in Maps Roads in 1840

In the History Study Skill in Chapter 14 you learned how to study the details in maps. The map below shows the important roads in the United States in 1840. It also shows states, territories, cities, the nation's capital, rivers, mountains, and bodies of water. Study the map carefully and then answer the questions that follow.

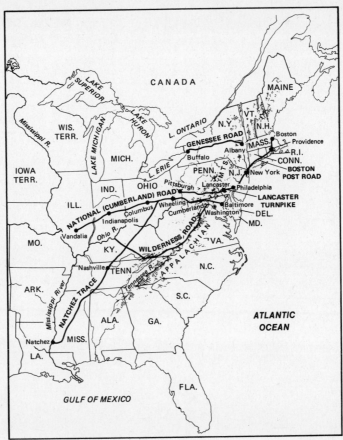

1. What is the main purpose of the map? _____

2. What five major roads are shown on the map? _____,

   _____, _____, _____,

   _____

3. Which of these roads go through the Appalachian Mountains? _____

   _____

4. Do most of these roads generally run east to west or north to south? _____

5. At what city in the East does the Cumberland Road start? _____

6. At what city in the West does the Cumberland Road end? _____

7. Which road goes all the way to the Mississippi River? _____

8. Name the states that you would pass through if you traveled on the National Road from Maryland

   to Illinois. _____

   _____

★Building American Citizenship

Reformers Work to Improve American Life

An important part of being a good citizen is trying to help improve the lives of other people. Use the information from the text and from classwork to complete the table below. If you are not able to fill in all of the boxes, ask your teacher or the librarian to help you.

REFORMERS	PROBLEMS TO SOLVE	METHODS REFORMERS USED
Dorothea Dix		
Thomas Gallaudet		
Horace Mann		
Frederick Douglass		
William Lloyd Garrison		
Elijah Lovejoy		
Lucretia Mott		

Primary Sources Slaves Tell Their Story

William Wells Brown was a slave who ran away to the North. He wrote about his experience as a slave and the feelings he had about slavery. Brown's writing is a primary source. After you have read the paragraphs below, answer the questions that follow.

My mother was a field hand, and one morning was ten or fifteen minutes behind the others in getting into the field. As soon as she reached the spot where they were at work, the overseer began whipping her. Though the field was some distance from the house, I could hear every crack of the whip, and every groan and cry of my poor mother. I remained at the door, not daring to venture any farther. The cold chills ran over me, and I wept aloud.

Solomon Northrup was a free man who was kidnapped and sold into slavery. Years later, when he was freed, he wrote about his life as a slave.

The hands are required to be in the cotton field as soon as it is light in the morning. With the exception of ten or fifteen minutes given them at noon to swallow their allowance of cold bacon, they are not permitted to be idle a moment until it is too dark to see . . . . They do not dare to stop even at dinner time, nor return to the quarters, however late it be, until the order to halt is given by the driver. The day's work over in the field, the baskets are carried to the gin-house, where the cotton is weighed. No matter how tired and weary he may be—no matter how much he longs for sleep and rest—a slave never approaches the gin-house with his basket of cotton without fear. If it falls short in weight—if he has not performed the full task appointed him, he knows that he must suffer.

1. Make a list of all of the things that happened to slaves that did not happen to free people that are

   mentioned in the accounts above. _____

   _____

   _____

   _____

   _____

2. Why do you think the slaveowners treated these slaves the way they did? _____

   _____

   _____

   _____

3. Why are these accounts of slavery believable? _____

   _____

   _____

   _____

4. Is Solomon Northrup's story a primary source? _____

   Explain. _____

   _____

   _____

Crossword Puzzle Reform in America

Use your text to complete the crossword puzzle below.

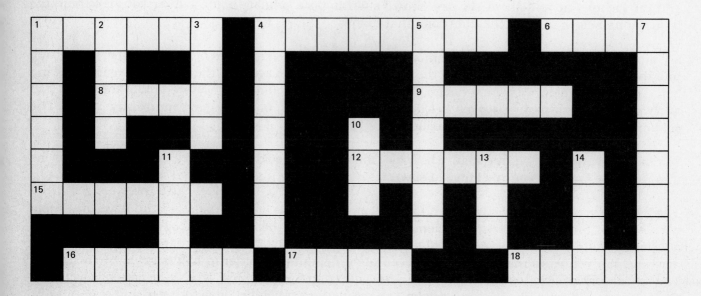

ACROSS

1. to improve, or change for the better.
4. He published the *Liberator.*
6. Abolitionist speaker Theodore_____.
8. The "North_____" was published by Frederick Douglass.
9. A famous religious community in Iowa.
12. The _____ community made silverware.
15. Mr. Gallaudet's first name.
16. He left his Alabama plantation and joined the abolitionists.
17. A women's-rights advocate, she helped found the American Anti-Slavery Society.
18. The Declaration of Sentiments was read at Seneca _____, New York.

DOWN

1. Mr. Owen's first name.
2. A form of protest in which a person eats no food.
3. "Dear Father, Drink no_____."
4. Two sisters who fought against slavery and for women's rights.
5. They "danced" away their sins.
7. Abolitionist Frederick _____.
10. Elijah Lovejoy was killed by a _____.
11. Education reformer Horace _____.
13. She worked with the mentally ill.
14. Southern leaders demanded that Garrison be put in _____.

©Macmillan Publishing Co.

221

★**Building American Citizenship**

Setting up a Government

In 1836 Texas won its independence from Mexico, but it did not become part of the United States until 1845. In the meantime, Texans had set up their own government. Pretend you were living in Texas in 1836. Look at the problems below and decide what kind of a government you would set up to solve these problems.

PROBLEM 1 Texans had been governed by Santa Anna, a dictator, when they were part of Mexico. The United States, a country that Texas wants to join, is a democracy. Which kind of government would you, as a Texan, choose? Explain why.

_____

_____

_____

_____

_____

_____

PROBLEM 2 Texas was led in its fight for independence by a strong leader, Sam Houston. Do you want one person to lead the new Texas government, or do you want to limit the powers of its leader? Explain your answer.

_____

_____

_____

_____

_____

PROBLEM 3 Who should make the laws for the people of Texas? Should there be a group of lawmakers, or should all the people make their own laws? Explain your answer.

_____

_____

_____

_____

_____

_____

© Macmillan Publishing Co.

Map Keys Westward Expansion

In Chapter 16 you have read how the United States gained new Western lands. In fact, by 1853 all of what is now the United States (except Alaska and Hawaii) was included within today's boundaries. In Chapter 16 you read how territory was gained after the war with Mexico, how territory was added by a treaty with Great Britain, how territory was bought from Mexico, and how Texas was added by annexation. On the map below, show each of these territories that were added to the United States.

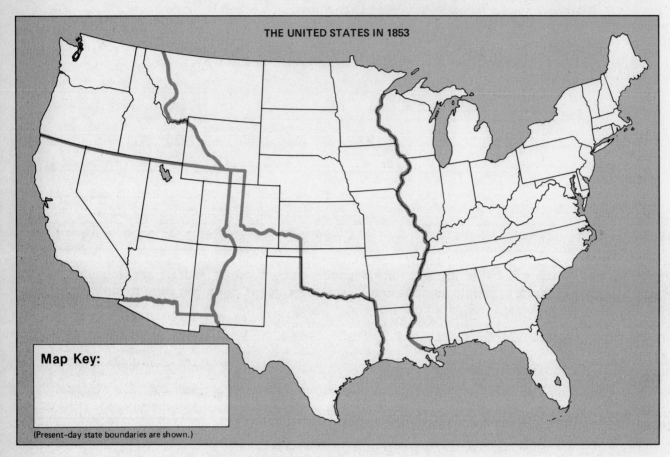

THE UNITED STATES IN 1853

Map Key:

(Present-day state boundaries are shown.)

1. Write in the names of the states east of the Mississippi.

2. Color the thirteen states that were part of the Louisiana Purchase YELLOW.

3. Color the state of Texas GREEN.

4. Color the territory gained from the Mexican War RED.

5. Color the Oregon Territory PURPLE.

6. Color the Gadsden Purchase BROWN.

7. Make a key for your map showing what each color means.

© Macmillan Publishing Co.

History Words Using Vocabulary Clues

In the History Study Skill for Chapter 16 you learned several ways to find the meanings of new history words in your textbook. You can figure out the meaning of some words by using vocabulary clues such as "or" and "that is." These vocabulary clues let you know that the definition of the history word follows the clue. Find the history words in the column at the left in your textbook. Page numbers are given for each word. Then copy the meaning of the word and any vocabulary clues from your textbook in the space provided. Underline the vocabulary clues.

History Words	Vocabulary Clues and Definitions
1. illegally (p. 370)	
2. reforms (p. 370)	
3. cavalry (p. 371)	
4. siesta (p. 372)	
5. annex (p. 373)	
6. missionaries (p. 375)	
7. expansion (p. 379)	
8. ceded (p. 382)	
9. vigilantes (p. 384)	
10. polygamy (p. 386)	

© Macmillan Publishing Co.

★ Building American Citizenship

Compromise Fails in the 1850's

One of the important ideals of democracy is that citizens should try to settle disputes in peaceful and orderly ways. In Chapter 17 you have read that Americans living in the 1850's tried to settle their differences by compromise. A compromise is the settlement of a dispute in which each side gives up part of what it wants and each side gets part of what it wants. Read over Chapter 17 in your textbook and answer the following questions.

1. The North and South tried to settle their differences in the Compromise of 1850. Congress passed five laws that made up the Compromise of 1850. Two laws clearly favored the North and the anti-slavery forces. What were these laws? _____

_____

2. Only one of the laws of the Compromise of 1850 clearly favored the South and the pro-slavery forces. What was this law? _____

_____

3. Two of the laws of the Compromise of 1850 dealt with "popular sovereignty." Define "popular sovereignty." _____

_____

_____

4. Why were people in the North *and* the South unhappy with the laws dealing with popular sovereignty?_____

_____

5. Why do you think the Compromise of 1850 failed to solve sectional differences? _____

_____

_____

6. In 1854, Americans tried another compromise, the Kansas-Nebraska Act. Look at the map in your textbook. According to the Missouri Compromise of 1820, would Kansas and Nebraska have been slave states or free states? _____

_____

7. What did Northerners and anti-slavery forces gain from the Kansas Nebraska Act?_____

_____

_____

_____

8. What did Southerners and pro-slavery forces gain from the Kansas-Nebraska Act? _____

_____

_____

© Macmillan Publishing Co.

Bar Graphs The Election of 1860

You learned how to get information from bar graphs in the History Study Skill for Chapter 17. Study the two bar graphs below, and then answer the questions that follow.

ELECTORAL VOTE IN THE ELECTION OF 1860

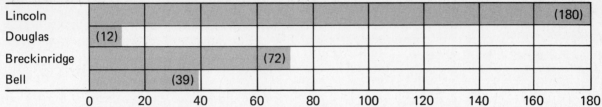

Candidate									
Lincoln									(180)
Douglas	(12)								
Breckinridge				(72)					
Bell		(39)							

0   20   40   60   80   100   120   140   160   180

POPULAR VOTE IN THE ELECTION OF 1860
(in millions)

Candidate									
Lincoln							(1,865,593)		
Douglas						(1,382,713)			
Breckinridge			(848,356)						
Bell		(592,906)							

0   .2   .4   .6   .8   one   1.2   1.4   1.6   1.8   two
                          million   million

1. According to the Constitution, the person with a majority of the electoral votes wins the election. Who won the election of 1860? _____

2. How many electoral votes did the winner have? _____

3. How many popular votes did the winner have? _____

4. Which candidate received the second highest number of popular votes? _____

5. How many electoral votes did that candidate get? _____

6. Which candidate received the second highest number of electoral votes? _____

7. How many popular votes did that candidate get? _____

8. Did the winner of the election of 1860 receive a *majority* of the electoral votes? _____

9. Did the winner of the election of 1860 receive a *majority* of the popular votes? _____

10. How do you explain Douglas's large popular vote and small electoral vote? _____

_____

Cause and Effect The 1850's

Events in history don't just happen. There were *causes* for all the events you have read about in Chapter 17. Actually, most events may have more than one cause. Besides causes, events also have *effects.* That is, something happens as a result of another event. Below are 9 groups of statements. In each group, there is one cause, one effect, and one event that is neither a cause or effect. Read each group of items and mark **C** for the *causes,* **E** for the *effects,* and **N** for those events that are neither.

1. _____ Representative Preston Brooks attacked Senator Sumner.

   _____ Senator Sumner spoke out against South Carolina.

   _____ John Brown attacked Harpers Ferry.

2. _____ Kansas and Nebraska entered the Union as slave states.

   _____ The Compromise of 1850 was passed.

   _____ California and New Mexico asked to be free states.

3. _____ Northerners were angered by the Fugitive Slave Law.

   _____ Kansas joined the Union as a slave state.

   _____ The Compromise of 1850 was passed.

4. _____ *Uncle Tom's Cabin* was written.

   _____ The Kansas-Nebraska Act was passed.

   _____ The Missouri Compromise was dead.

5. _____ Popular sovereignty was accepted.

   _____ A troubled territory was called "bleeding Kansas."

   _____ Calhoun put forth his "Platform of the South."

6. _____ The Supreme Court ruled that slavery was protected by the Constitution.

   _____ A Constitutional amendment was passed in 1860.

   _____ Dred Scott lost his case before the Supreme Court.

7. _____ Lincoln and Douglas debated.

   _____ Lincoln won the election for Senator from Illinois.

   _____ Lincoln became famous across the country.

8. _____ Slaves were freed in Virginia.

   _____ John Brown raided the town of Harpers Ferry.

   _____ Fear of slave uprisings spread throughout the South.

9. _____ Lincoln was elected President in 1860.

   _____ South Carolina seceded from the Union.

   _____ The Compromise of 1850 was passed.

Military Maps The Battle of Antietam

In Chapter 18 you learned how to use military maps to understand major campaigns and battles. Below is a military map of the important battle of Antietam, fought near Sharpsburg, Maryland, on September 17, 1862. With this battle the Confederate army's invasion of the North was stopped. Soon after this victory President Lincoln issued his Emancipation Proclamation. Study the map carefully, and then fill in the blanks to complete the story below.

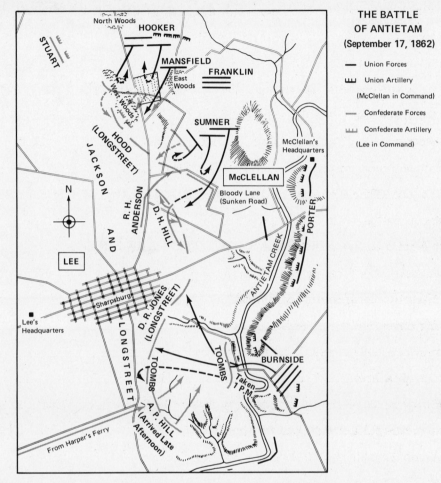

On the morning of September 17, the two Union generals, _____ and _____ , on the northernmost part of the battlefield attacked the Confederate army. The Union attack was stopped by Confederate General _____ . At midday, Confederate General D.H. Hill was attacked by Union General _____ north of Sharpsburg. Again, the Confederates held the line. Strangely one Union general, _____ , and his troops did not join in the morning and midday battle even though he was close by. In the afternoon, General Burnside attacked Confederate General _____ south of Sharpsburg. He was just about to break through the Confederate lines when the Confederate General _____ , who arrived late in the afternoon, came to the rescue. At the end of the day on September 17, 1862, the battle ended.

Name _____ Class _____ Date _____

The Emancipation Proclamation

The Emancipation Proclamation is a historic document that led to the end of slavery in the United States. Read the parts of the Proclamation given below and then answer the questions that follow.

THAT ON THE FIRST DAY OF JANUARY, 1863, ALL PERSONS HELD AS SLAVES WITHIN ANY STATE THAT IS CURRENTLY IN REBELLION AGAINST THE UNION, SHALL BE THEN AND FOREVERMORE FREE.

1. According to this part of the Emancipation Proclamation, only certain slaves were freed.

   Which slaves were freed? _____

   Which slaves were not freed? _____

MILITARY FORCES OF THE UNION WILL RECOGNIZE AND MAINTAIN THE FREEDOM OF SUCH PERSONS AND WILL DO NO ACTS TO HARM THOSE PEOPLE FREED. I ASK ALL PEOPLE SO DECLARED TO BE FREE TO ABSTAIN FROM ALL VIOLENCE, UNLESS IN SELF-DEFENSE. I ASK THEM TO WORK FAITHFULLY FOR WAGES ONCE THEY ARE FREED.

2. Who does Lincoln say will protect the freed slaves? _____

   _____

3. What two things does Lincoln ask of the freed slaves? _____

   _____

I FURTHER DECLARE THAT FREED SLAVES WILL BE ALLOWED TO JOIN THE ARMED SER-VICES OF THE UNITED STATES, TO DEFEND THE FORTS, BATTLE STATIONS, AND VESSELS OF ALL SORTS.

4. In your own words, explain what Lincoln's words mean. _____

   _____

5. The Emancipation Proclamation was a good *first step* in ending slavery in the United States. What

   other things had to be done before all slavery was ended? _____

   _____

   _____

Primary Sources Letters from a Soldier

During the long years of the Civil War, soldiers did not spend all of the time in battle. The two letters below were written by Samuel McClelland, a Union soldier. Read each letter, and then answer the questions that follow.

January 6, 1862, Camp Woods, Kentucky

Dear Cousin Flora,

I am very well at present with the exception of a cold in my chest for over a week. We had to go out on picket duty last Friday, and it rained on us all the time we were out. This gave me a fresh case of cold. I can scarcely speak today. We had a very pleasant Christmas and New Year, but I could have had more fun at home where I would have my liberty. Our camp's sick list has been increasing very fast of late due to measles. There is a rumor that Confederate General Buckner is moving this way, but I don't believe it. We are about to move on Bowling Green, and I expect in a few days that the Stars and Stripes will float triumphantly on the hills overlooking that city. Our flag has never been dishonored nor shall it be, so long as there are good men left with us. So goodbye.

From Sam

1. What seems to be the main concern Sam expresses in this letter? _____

2. Where does Sam show signs of home sickness? _____

_____

3. Does Sam seem to be a patriotic soldier? Explain. _____

_____

December 1, 1864, Nashville, Tennessee

Dear Cousin Marg,

When I wrote you last, I was in Atlanta, but I am in Nashville now. I was sick shortly after the battle of Jonesboro, so I missed being discharged with many of my comrades after we took Atlanta. We are having quite exciting times here at present. Their Rebel General Hood has taken it into his head to attack Nashville, and is fool enough to think that he can force the state of Tennessee into their Confederacy again. General Thomas is in command here. Our lines had not yet been formed, however, when the Rebs attacked in force. They charged our works four different times and with four columns of men, but they were only charging on to destruction. They did not succeed in a single instance, losing between 5,000 and 6,000 men.

Your Cousin,
S. A. McClelland

4. Which parts of the letter make you think that Sam is confident of victory? _____

_____

5. What do these letters tell you about the life of an ordinary soldier in the Union Army during the

Civil War? _____

_____

_____

Worksheet 51, Chapter 18

Chronological Order Reconstruction

In Chapter 19, you learned that the former Confederate states were "reconstructed." That meant that each state had to satisfy certain conditions before it could be readmitted to the Union. Occupation by federal troops of states readmitted to the Union continued for a time. When federal troops were withdrawn, Reconstruction Republicans lost control of state governments. The map below shows two things: (1) the date when each state was readmitted to the Union and (2) the date when the Reconstruction Republican governments lost control of state governments. Use the information on the map and what you learned in the History Study Skill in Chapter 19 on chronological order to answer the questions below.

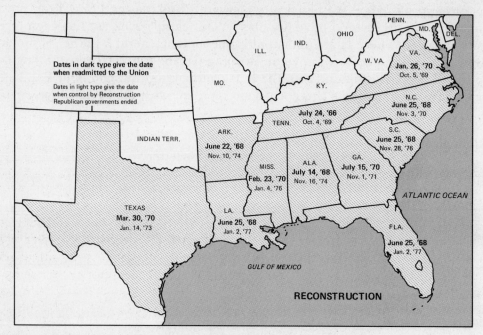

1. List the states in the order they were readmitted to the Union.

   1st _____   7th _____

   2nd _____   8th _____

   3rd _____   9th _____

   4th _____   10th _____

   5th _____   11th _____

   6th _____

2. List the states in the order in which Reconstruction Republican control of the reconstructed state governments ended.

   1st _____   7th _____

   2nd _____   8th _____

   3rd _____   9th _____

   4th _____   10th _____

   5th _____   11th _____

   6th _____

The Main Idea Andrew Carnegie

In Chapter 21 you read how Andrew Carnegie built the largest steel company in the world. Below are some statements adopted from Carnegie's autobiography. Read each one, and then answer the questions that follow.

1. When Andrew Carnegie was still a young boy, he got his first job in a local textile mill. The job paid $1.20 a week. As Carnegie wrote many years later, "I have made millions since, but none of these gave me so much happiness as my first week's earnings. I was now a helper of the family, a bread-winner."

   Explain why Carnegie was so proud of his first job. _____

   _____

   _____

2. When Carnegie was 21, he purchased 10 shares of stock. Several months later, the first dividend check for $10 arrived in the mail. Carnegie wrote, "I shall remember that check for as long as I live. It gave me [my first income] that I had not worked for with the sweat of my brow. 'Eureka,' I cried, 'Here's the goose that lays the golden eggs'."

   Explain what Carnegie means in this passage. _____

   _____

   _____

3. Carnegie once read a saying that he liked very much. He had this saying placed in his own library. It read:

   > He that cannot reason is a fool
   > He that will not is a bigot
   > He that dare not is a slave

   Explain why you think Carnegie liked this saying so much. _____

   _____

   _____

4. While still a young man, Carnegie had become rich in several different businesses. Then he decided to put all of his time and energy into the iron and steel industry. He wrote, "Put all your eggs in one basket, and then watch that basket."

   Explain what he meant. _____

   _____

   _____

5. When Carnegie was 33, he wrote, "Man must have an idol—the amassing of wealth is one of the worst [kinds] of idolatry."

   Explain how Carnegie, later in his life, showed how he felt about this "idol." _____

   _____

   _____

© Macmillan Publishing Co.

Name _____ Class _____ Date _____

★Building American Citizenship

To Strike or Not to Strike

You read in Chapter 21 that American workers struggled to get ahead during the Industrial Revolution. Many workers went on *strike*, in order to try to improve their wages, hours, and working conditions. Today, American workers often use strikes as a way to win benefits from their employers. Strikes, however, often seriously disrupt the life of the community. What do you think are the duties and responsibilities of workers who want to strike?

ALLOWED TO STRIKE ▲————————▲————————▲————————▲————————▲ NOT ALLOWED TO STRIKE

NOT SURE

Look at the line above. There are several jobs listed below. Place each of the jobs above the line according to how you feel about the right of this worker to strike. Those who you think have a right to strike should go at the left. Those who you think should not be allowed to strike should go at the right. Put those about whom you are not sure in the middle.

DOCTOR   POLICE OFFICER   TEACHER

FIREFIGHTER   CARPENTER   AUTO WORKER

Explain why you placed each person where you did on the line.

DOCTOR _____

_____

FIRE FIGHTER _____

_____

POLICE _____

_____

CARPENTER _____

_____

TEACHER _____

_____

AUTO WORKER _____

_____

© Macmillan Publishing Co.

238 _____

Studying Statistics Immigration

In Chapter 22 you read about Americans who had immigrated here from Europe. The bar graphs below give you more information about the number of immigrants who lived in America in 1890 and in 1910. Study the bar graphs carefully. Then use the skills you learned in the History Study Skill in Chapter 22 on statistics to answer the questions below.

FOREIGN-BORN POPULATION OF THE UNITED STATES, 1890 AND 1910

FOREIGN-BORN POPULATION OF THE UNITED STATES, 1890 AND 1910

Place of Birth

England, Scotland, and Wales
- (1,251,000) 1890
- (1,221,000) 1910

Ireland
- (1,871,000) 1890
- (1,352,000) 1910

Germany
- (2,784,000) 1890
- (2,311,000) 1910

Eastern Europe
- (635,000) 1890
- (3,702,000) 1910

Southern Europe
- (206,000) 1890
- (1,525,000) 1910

(in millions) 0   0.5   1.0   1.5   2.0   2.5   3.0   3.5   4.0

1. What two years does each of the bar graphs compare? _____

_____

2. In 1890 more non-native born people living in the United States had been born in _____than anywhere else.

3. In 1910 more non-native born people living in the United States had been born in _____ than anywhere else.

4. Between 1890 and 1910 did the foreign-born population from England, Scotland, Wales, Ireland, and Germany increase or decrease? _____

5. Between 1890 and 1910 was there an increase or decrease in the foreign-born population from Southern Europe? _____ from Eastern Europe? _____

★**Building American Citizenship**

The Tweed Ring

In Chapter 22 you read about a corrupt "big city boss" named William "Boss" Tweed. Below is some more information about Boss Tweed. Read each paragraph and then choose the sentence that best tells the main idea of the paragraph.

1. William Tweed loved his family. He did not drink or smoke. He was a good husband and a loving father. Tweed gave money to the poor, to hospitals, to schools and churches. He once wrote, "I dare any politician in New York to point out one instance where I've broken my word."

   a. William Tweed was not a corrupt, crooked politician.

   b. William Tweed had many good personal qualities.

   c. William Tweed never broke his word.

2. Tweed ran for Congress in 1852 and won. Yet, he was not happy during his two years in the House of Representatives. He did not achieve much in Washington, D.C. Tweed never took part in congressional debates, and he made only one speech during his term. That speech was in favor of the Kansas-Nebraska Act. When he returned to New York, he was broke and unpopular. He was considered a failure at age thirty-one.

   a. Tweed's years in Washington as a Congress member were not successful.

   b. If Tweed had worked harder in Congress, he would have been more powerful.

   c. Tweed became a "boss" in Congress.

3. Tweed began his rise to power in New York in 1857 as a member of the Board of Supervisors. The Board was a powerful group that had control over taxes, city planning, and the courts. Soon Tweed was on his way to becoming rich and corrupt. Tweed once said that he and the other supervisors passed bills only if they received a bribe. Tweed once paid $5 each for 300 old benches and then sold them to the city of New York for $169,800. Tweed and his friends on the Board of Supervisors became very rich.

   a. Tweed was the only corrupt politician in New York.

   b. Tweed worked with other supervisors to gain power in New York City.

   c. Tweed made $169,800 during his term in office.

4. Boss Tweed was a very generous man. He could afford to be. The money he gave to the poor was money that he had stolen from the city government. During the winter of 1870, he gave $50,000 to people in his neighborhood for food and coal. The people loved Tweed for his gifts. When Tweed asked them to vote for him or his friends, the people were glad to repay Tweed for his kindness. This is how Tweed was able to keep power for such a long time.

   a. William Tweed helped a lot of people with his charity, and in return they voted to support him.

   b. William Tweed paid people $5 to vote for him.

   c. William Tweed fixed the ballot boxes so that none of his opponents could win.

5. Why should citizens refuse to vote for a politician like Tweed? _____

   _____

   _____

   _____

Using Newspapers Urban Life

In Chapter 23 you have read about urban life in America at the end of the nineteenth century. Newspapers were the principal way of getting information to people at the time. Newspapers are still a very important source of news today. From newspapers you can learn about important events, political developments, sports, and much more. Get a recent copy of a local newspaper and use it to help you with this activity.

One of the first things you notice about the newspaper is that it is divided into *sections*. A *section* contains articles on the same basic subject. A newspaper's sections are listed in an *index* on the first or second page. Find the *index* in your newspaper and identify the different sections listed there. *Section A* usually contains the important national and world news. *Section B* often has the important state and local news. Is this how your newspaper is organized? Other parts of the newspaper are the sports section, classified section, and the entertainment section. What other sections are listed in the index of your newspaper?

_____

_____

_____

The first thing to do when reading a newspaper is to skim the *headlines*. Headlines are printed in large, dark letters that summarize the main idea of the leading articles. A headline in the 1880's about corruption in a city government might have been:

BUILDERS CHEAT CITY GOVERNMENT

This headline gives the reader an idea what the article is about so that the reader can decide whether to read the article. Notice that the headline used few words.

Read the headlines below and then explain what you think the story is about:

TRAGIC FIRE IN TENEMENT _____

ELECTION FRAUD EXPOSED _____

Each section of the newspaper is written with a specific audience in mind. The *classified section* lists items for sale and job openings. The *business section* is for people interested in business.

Now, let's see how well you can use the newspaper to find the answers to the questions below.

1. What is the date of the newspaper? _____

2. In what section is local news located? _____

3. Find a classified ad for a house for sale and copy it. _____

_____

_____

4. Write down one of the headlines in the national news section. _____

_____

5. Find and write down the score of a local sports event. _____

_____

Worksheet 63, Chapter 23

Tables Presidential Elections, 1884 to 1896

The table below shows the results of four of the presidential elections discussed in Unit Seven. Study the table carefully, and then answer the questions that follow.

ELECTION	CANDIDATE	PARTY	POPULAR VOTE	ELECTORAL VOTE
1884	Cleveland Blaine	Democratic Republican	4,911,017 4,848,334	219 182
1888	Cleveland Harrison	Democratic Republican	5,540,050 5,444,337	168 233
1892	Cleveland Harrison	Democratic Republican	5,554,414 5,190,802	277 145
1896	Bryan McKinley	Democratic Republican	6,467,946 7,035,638	176 271

1. In the table above, how many elections were won by the Republicans? _____

2. How many elections were won by the Democrats?_____

3. Which person won two elections? _____

4. In which election was the popular vote the closest? _____

5. Who received the most popular votes in the election of 1888? _____

6. Who received the most electoral votes in the election of 1888? _____

7. Who was chosen President in the election of 1888? _____

8. How many elections were decided by fewer than 400,000 votes?_____

9. When voters switch back and forth from party to party in elections, what does this tell you about

   what the voter thinks of the parties? _____

   _____

   _____

10. In 1896 almost 3,000,000 more people voted than in 1892. How would you explain this

    increase?_____

    _____

    _____

    _____

    _____

© Macmillan Publishing Co.

★ **Building American Citizenship**

Letters to Government Leaders

In Chapter 23 you learned that many Americans did not share in the nation's prosperity. One action that these Americans might have taken was to write letters to try to influence their local, state, or national representatives in government to help them. Below are examples of letters that people of the 1920's might have written to government leaders. Study these letters carefully, and then answer the questions that follow.

LETTER A

I am writing to strongly request that you help the poor farmers of our state. Prices are very low, and we cannot earn enough money to pay our bills. I think you should pass a law that sets prices for our crops so that we can make a profit. Also, it would be a good idea if the government bought some of our products to give to poor people.

> Sincerely yours,
> An Unhappy Farmer

LETTER B

I am writing for all of our members who want you to do something about unequal pay for women. We do the same kinds of jobs as men, yet we are paid only half as much as men are. There should be a law to prevent this kind of unfair treatment.

> Sincerely,
> President of
> the OAWW

LETTER C

I am writing to request that you hire black workers for the new fire department that is being set up. Many people in this community are black, and it would be unfair to have an all-white fire department. There are many well-qualified black persons in our community who want to be firefighters. Please consider them for the new jobs.

> Sincerely,
> A Concerned Citizen

LETTER D

I have voted for you in the last three elections. However, if you try to put a state prison near our town, I will never vote for you again. And I will get all my friends to vote against you, too.

> Sincerely,
> A Concerned Voter

1. Which letter was probably written to a member of Congress? _____

   Explain your answer. _____

2. Which letter was probably written to a member of the state legislature?_____

   Explain your answer. _____

3. Which letter was probably written to a member of the local government? _____

   Explain your answer. _____

4. Which letter was written by a member of an organization for women? _____

   Explain your answer. _____

5. Which letter tries to influence the political leader with a threat? _____

   What is the threat? _____

★Building American Citizenship

Helping Improve Your Government

The initiative, referendum, and recall were three reforms the Progressives used to improve government.

Initiative — is a way in which groups of voters can have new laws introduced in their law-making bodies.

Referendum — is a way in which voters can approve or reject a bill in a special election after it has been passed by the legislators.

Recall — is a way in which voters can sign a petition to remove an elected official from office.

Several situations are described below. Study each one carefully and then decide which of the three reforms you would use to solve the problem—initiative, referendum, or recall.

1. The town council passed a law last year requiring that all bicycles have tags. These tags cost $20 but you and your friends think the cost is too high. You have written to members of the council, but none of them will introduce a bill to lower the cost of tags. What should you do? Explain why.

_____

_____

_____

2. The president of the student council at your school is a nice person, a good student, and a hard worker. Recently, however, the president has been absent from all student council meetings because of an after-school job. The student council does not get much done because it has no real leadership. What would you do? Explain why.

_____

_____

_____

3. The three members of your county council passed a bill raising their salaries from $5,000 to $25,000 a year. You and your friends do not like the bill and you feel that these legislators are not doing their jobs properly. What should you and your friends do? Explain why.

_____

_____

4. A judge in your community no longer punishes people convicted of parking violations. The judge thinks the law is too harsh and he will not punish anyone who breaks the law. You were once in an accident caused by a double-parked car and you disagree with the judge. What should you do? Explain why.

_____

_____

_____

© Macmillan Publishing Co.

Name _____ Class_____ Date_____

Reading Photographs Sweatshops

In the History Study Skill in Chapter 24 you learned how photographs can help you understand the past. Photographers like Jacob Riis took pictures to show what life was like for immigrants and other poor people in American cities. The photograph below shows an immigrant family at work at home. They are making cigars. Study the photograph carefully and answer the questions that follow.

Library of Congress

1. How many people do you see in the photograph? _____

2. What members of the family do you see in the picture? _____
_____

3. Why do you think they are working at home rather than in a factory?_____
_____
_____

4. How would you describe the working conditions for this American family? _____
_____
_____

5. Why do you think the children are at home instead of at school? _____
_____
_____

Worksheet 67, Chapter 24

The Main Idea Booker T. Washington

In Chapter 24 you have read about Booker T. Washington. Washington, a former slave, devoted his life to helping black Americans. Below are several selections about this great man. Read each selection and then choose the sentence that best describes the main idea.

1. In 1872 Booker T. Washington began studying at Hampton Institute, a college for black Americans in Virginia. Students at Hampton were taught that hard work was the best way to achieve success in life. Hard work, they were told, helped you earn more money and made you honest, intelligent, and reliable. By the time Washington was graduated, he was convinced that black Americans could be successful if they worked hard and learned useful skills.

   a. Booker T. Washington entered Hampton because he believed in hard work.

   b. At Hampton, Washington became convinced that hard work was the best way to meet the needs of most black Americans.

   c. Washington was successful because he attended Hampton Institute.

2. Washington helped to start a college in Tuskegee in 1881. When he started, there were no buildings or books for a college. Moreover, many white people did not like the idea of a college for black students. Washington quickly organized the students into teams, and they began to build their own college. Meanwhile, he talked with members of the white community and told them how good it would be to have a college for black Americans. He told them that black students would obey the laws and cooperate with white authorities in keeping the peace. His actions were successful. Washington was able to calm the white community while his students finished building Tuskegee Institute.

   a. Washington had to overcome many problems in order to get Tuskegee built.

   b. Whites and blacks worked together to build Tuskegee.

   c. Tuskegee suffered because there were no funds for buildings.

3. Washington did not demand equal rights for black people. He pushed forward a program of training black Americans to become farmers, mechanics, teachers, and servants. He urged blacks to "cast down your bucket where you are," and do the best they could with conditions as they were. Washington was upset by the large numbers of black Southerners who were moving to Northern cities. He wanted Southern blacks to develop habits and skills that would encourage white Southerners to accept them as equals.

   a. Washington worked hard to gain equal rights for all Americans.

   b. Washington urged black Southerners to migrate to Northern cities.

   c. Washington encouraged Southern blacks to stay where they were and learn a trade and good work skills.

★Building American Citizenship

Respecting the Rights of All Peoples

In Chapter 25 you have read how America gained control over many islands in the Caribbean and the Pacific. There were people living on these islands, and the United States tried to do what it believed was best for these people. Review the information in your text and then answer the following questions.

HAWAII

1. In 1893 United States Marines helped overthrow the Queen of Hawaii. Why do you think many Americans felt it was wrong for the United States to annex Hawaii at that time? _____

   _____

   _____

   _____

2. What is the status of Hawaii today? _____

   _____

3. Do you think that the United States did what was best for the people of Hawaii? Explain your

   answer. _____

   _____

   _____

   _____

PUERTO RICO

4. Congress declared war on Spain in 1898. In the treaty with Spain that ended the war, the United States was given the island of Puerto Rico. Why did Congress keep control of Puerto Rico after the

   war? _____

   _____

   _____

5. What is the status of the Puerto Rico today?_____

   _____

6. Do you think the United States did what was best for the people of Puerto Rico? Explain your

   answer. _____

   _____

   _____

   _____

Improving Your Writing The Spanish-American War

Throughout the year you have worked on exercises to improve your history writing. In good writing it is very important to write clear, factual statements that support the topic sentence of each paragraph. Below are five topic sentences that a newspaper reporter in Cuba might have written telling about the Spanish-American War. Pretend you are that newspaper reporter and that you are writing the story. Complete each paragraph with at least two sentences of your own. Some clues about what to write are given at the left.

(Did you see it?

Who caused it?

Was anyone hurt?

What might happen

next?)

1. Today, our battleship *Maine* exploded and sank in Havana harbor.
_____
_____
_____
_____

(What do you think will

happen in Cuba now?

What do you want to

happen?)

2. We just learned that 17,000 American troops have left Florida to invade Cuba. _____
_____
_____
_____

(Describe the battle

action. Did you see the

Rough Riders?)

3. Last week, I went along with American troops as they captured San Juan Hill._____
_____
_____
_____

(Describe what happened.

What did the American

fleet do?)

4. Yesterday, the Spanish fleet tried to sneak out of Santiago harbor.
_____
_____
_____

(Was this surrender

important for the war

in Cuba? Do you think

the war will end soon?)

5. Today, the Spanish army at Santiago surrendered. _____
_____
_____
_____

© Macmillan Publishing Co.

248 _____

Name _____ Class_____ Date_____

● Maps Locating Major American Cities

In the History Study Skill in Chapter 25 you learned to measure distances on a map. In this exercise you will practice locating places on a map. Use the indicators of latitude at the left and right side of the map and the longitude marking at the top and bottom of the map to answer the questions below.

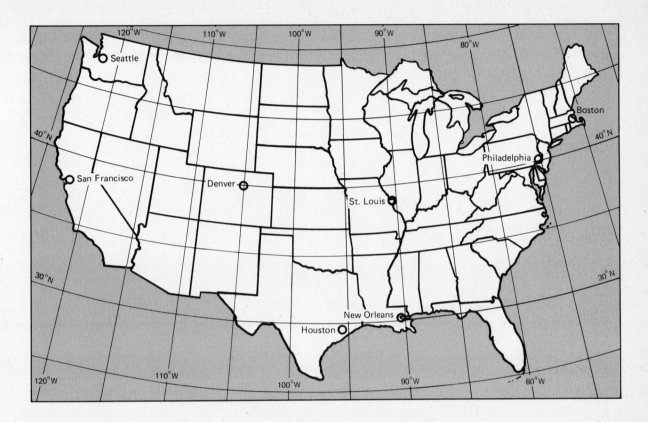

1. Which parallel of latitude goes through both Houston and New Orleans? _____

   (Reminder: Be sure to indicate North (N) or South (S) latitude.)

2. Which parallel of latitude goes through both Denver and Philadelphia? _____

3. Which meridian of longitude goes through both St. Louis and New Orleans? _____

   (Reminder: Be sure to indicate East (E) or West (W) longitude.)

4. What city is located near 40°N, 105°W? _____

5. What is the latitude and longitude for each of the following cities?

   a. Houston _____   c. San Francisco_____

   b. Philadelphia_____   d. Seattle _____

        e. Boston _____

Name _____ Class _____ Date _____

★ Building American Citizenship

Neutrality in World War I

In Chapter 26 you read about how war broke out in Europe. Some countries (the Central Powers) belonged to an alliance called the Triple Entente. Other countries (the Allies) belonged to the Triple Alliance. Some nations did not join either alliance—they were neutral. In America, at first, most citizens wanted their country to remain neutral. But the feelings of citizens gradually changed, and America came into World War I on the side of the Allies, who were members of the Triple Alliance. The map below shows the three groups of countries in Europe. Study the map carefully, and then answer the questions that follow.

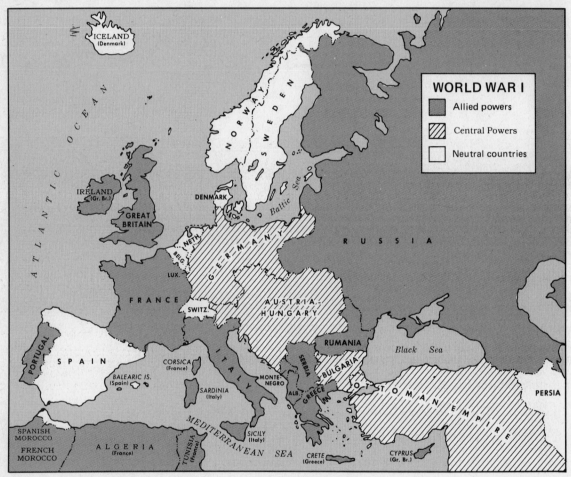

1. Name the countries that belonged to the Central Powers. _____
_____

2. Name the countries that belonged to the Allied Powers. _____
_____

3. As an American citizen in 1914, would you have wanted the United States to remain neutral?
Explain your answer. _____
_____
_____

© Macmillan Publishing Co.

★Building American Citizenship

Propaganda and Loyalty in Wartime

In Chapter 26 you read about some Americans who did not support the nation's war effort in World War I. These people often tried to convince others, with propaganda, that they too should not support the nation's war effort. The Supreme Court has ruled that the government had the right to limit free speech during a national crisis. How much free speech Americans should have during a time of national crisis is an important question. Below are several imaginary cases involving freedom of speech in a national crisis. You be the judge and decide what should be done in each case. Keep in mind the provisions of the Constitution and the Bill of Rights.

1. Sally Malinski is a newspaper editor. She has been writing editorials asking people to protest against the war by not paying taxes and by refusing to make guns and weapons. Government lawyers want her to be put in jail. What do you think should be done? Explain your answer.

_____

_____

_____

2. Steve Becker works on the docks loading supplies to go to Europe to help the British. His grandparents came from Germany, and Steve does not want American weapons to be used to kill German soldiers. He begins passing out leaflets urging all German-American dockworkers to go on strike and refuse to load supplies. Government lawyers want to put Steve in jail. What do you think should be done with Steve? Explain your answer.

_____

_____

_____

3. Helen Chen is a librarian in a small town. The mayor and town council decide that all pro-German books should be taken from the library because Germany is an enemy country. Helen Chen refuses to do this and she writes letters defending her actions to the local newspaper. The mayor demands that she resign because she is unpatriotic, but she refuses. The mayor files a lawsuit to fire Helen. What do you think should be done? Explain your answer.

_____

_____

_____

4. You have been invited to speak at an assembly in a local high school. Students want to hear your opinion on how much freedom of speech a person should have during a time of war. What would you say to them?

_____

_____

_____

_____

© Macmillan Publishing Co.

Worksheet 73, Chapter 26

Documents The Treaty of Versailles

Woodrow Wilson went to Paris after World War I to help write a peace treaty that would prevent future wars. Most of the Treaty of Versailles was written by Great Britain, France, Italy, and the United States. Germany was *not* permitted to attend.

1. The Treaty of Versailles forced Germany to take all the blame for causing World War I. The treaty says, . . . "Germany accepts the responsibility of Germany and her allies for causing all the loss and damage [in World War I]." Why do you think the German people were unhappy with this part of the treaty?

    _____

    _____

2. From what you have read in Chapter 26, do you think that Germany alone was to blame for the war? Explain your answer.

    _____

    _____

3. Germany lost thirteen percent of its land. Parts of Germany were given to Belgium, Denmark, Poland, and Czechoslovakia. Do you think it was fair to Germany to take away this territory? Explain your answer.

    _____

    _____

4. Germany was not allowed to have a standing army. Germany was forced to destroy most of its navy and had to turn over most of its air force to the Allies. Why do you think these terms were put in the Treaty?

    _____

    _____

5. How do you think the Germans felt about being disarmed after World War I?

    _____

    _____

6. The Allies insisted that Germany pay for all damages done in World War I. Germany was forced to pay the Allies many billions of dollars as well as to turn over property and resources. Germany had to give up 400 million tons of coal and 1 million tons of new ships. How did the payment for damages affect the German people?

    _____

    _____

7. Historians have written that the Treaty of Versailles was an important cause of World War II. Do you agree with them? Explain your answer.

    _____

    _____

Line Graphs Immigration

In Chapter 27 you have read how Congress passed new immigration laws that limited the number of immigrants allowed into the United States. The line graph below illustrates immigration patterns in the decades after the Civil War. Study it carefully. Use the skills you learned in the History Study Skill for Chapter 27 to answer the questions that follow.

IMMIGRATION TO THE UNITED STATES, 1860's to 1930's

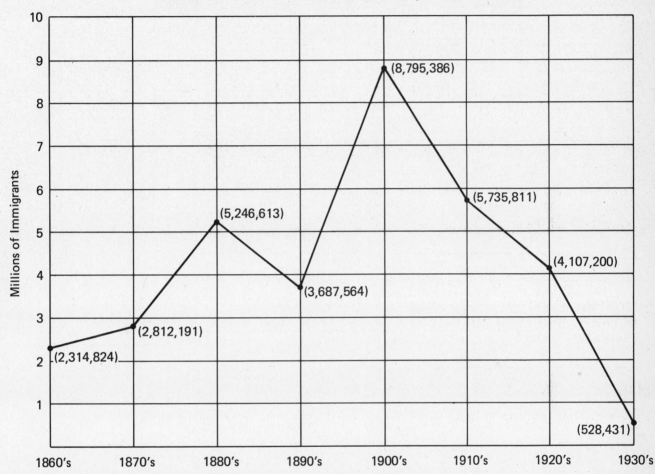

1. About how many immigrants entered the United States in the 1920's? _____

2. Which decade had the greatest number of immigrants? _____

3. Which decade had the smallest number of immigrants? _____

4. As a general trend, did immigration increase or decrease in the decade before 1900?_____

_____

5. Did immigration increase or decrease after 1900? _____

_____

Worksheet 75, Chapter 27

Bar Graphs Farm Production and Prices

During the year you have learned how to use bar graphs. Comparing information in bar graphs is another skill. Below are two bar graphs. One shows farm production and the other shows the value of crops. Study each graph carefully and then answer the questions that follow.

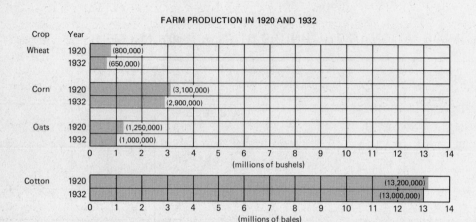

FARM PRODUCTION IN 1920 AND 1932

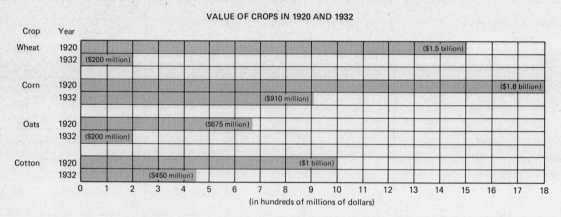

VALUE OF CROPS IN 1920 AND 1932

1. Was farm production in 1932 greater, about the same, or much less than it had been in 1920?

_____

2. Was the value of crops in 1932 greater, about the same, or much less than it had been in

   1920? _____

3. Which crop fell in value the most between 1920 and 1932? _____

4. Was production of this crop in 1932 greater, about the same, or much less than it had been in

   1920? _____

5. Why do you think production of crops remained high even though prices fell between 1920 and

   1932? _____

   _____

   _____

   _____

★Building American Citizenship

Rights and Responsibilities

In Chapter 27 you have read how Americans enjoyed prosperity in the 1920's. Americans in those years felt that things had never been so good. Still, there were many problems in American society. Many people refused to obey the laws against drinking alcoholic beverages. Congress limited immigration into the United States, and there were racial tensions. It seemed almost that some Americans did not want to accept the *responsibilities* that went along with their many rights and privileges.

Below is a table that lists some of the rights and privileges that Americans enjoy. List some of the responsibilities that go along with each right.

RIGHTS AND PRIVILEGES	RESPONSIBILITIES
Freedom of Speech	
Freedom of Press	
Freedom of Religion	
The Right to Assemble in Groups	
The Right to Bear Arms	
The Right to Vote	
Equal Opportunity for Jobs	
The Right to Own Property	

Worksheet 77, Chapter 27

Tables New Deal Programs

In Chapter 28 you have read about the many new programs started by government to help people during the Great Depression. All of these programs were part of the New Deal. Some of these programs are still in effect. Use the information in the chapter to complete the table below on the New Deal.

PROGRAM	YEAR	WHAT THE PROGRAM DID
Federal Deposit Insurance Corporation (FDIC)	1933	Provided insurance for all savings accounts up to $5,000.
Federal Emergency Relief Administration (FERA)		
Civilian Conservation Corps. (CCC)		
Civil Works Administration (CWA)		
Public Works Administration (PWA)		
National Recovery Act (NRA)		
Agricultural Adjustment Act (AAA)		
Tennessee Valley Authority (TVA)		
Works Progress Administration (WPA)		
Social Security Act		
National Labor Relations Board (NLRB)		

© Macmillan Publishing Co.

Name _____ Class _____ Date _____

Local History A Small Town in the 1930's

In the History Study Skill in Chapter 28 you learned several ways to find out about life in your community during the 1930's. You learned about how interviews with older persons and how materials in the library can help you find out about the New Deal in the 1930's and how it changed American life. Libraries are an especially good source of information on local history. The materials in your local library can help you to learn more about the impact of the Great Depression on your own community.

USING THE CARD CATALOG

Imagine that you live in the small town of Crisfield, Maryland. Suppose you want to find information about how the Great Depression of the 1930's affected your community. One of the first things you should do is search through your library's Card Catalog. Understanding the Card Catalog can make finding the books you need easy. Below are three cards from a Card Catalog. They are found under the subject category, MARYLAND HISTORY. You could search under other subject categories that you think might have the information you need. Study each card carefully and then answer the questions that follow.

A. MARYLAND HISTORY

975.2 Radoff, Morris
       The old line state: a history of Maryland, by Morris Radoff. Annapolis: Hall of Records,
       © 1971   312 pages

B. MARYLAND HISTORY

975.22W Wilson, Woodrow T.
         History of Crisfield, by Woodrow Wilson. Baltimore: Gateway Press,
         © 1973   277 pages

C. MARYLAND HISTORY

973.916T Terkel, Louis
          An oral history of the Great Depression, by Louis Terkel. New York: Pantheon.
          © 1970   418 pages

1. Which of these three books would be a good source on the Great Depression throughout the United States? Explain your answer. _____

2. Which of these books would tell about conditions in the state of Maryland? _____

3. Do you think Book A will contain information on the effects of the Great Depression on Crisfield, Maryland? Explain your answers. _____

4. Which parts of the book would you use to locate information on the effects of the Great Depression on people in Crisfield, Maryland? _____

© Macmillan Publishing Co.

257

Worksheet 79, Chapter 28

Maps Latitude, Longitude, and Location

Study the map below, and then answer the questions that follow it.

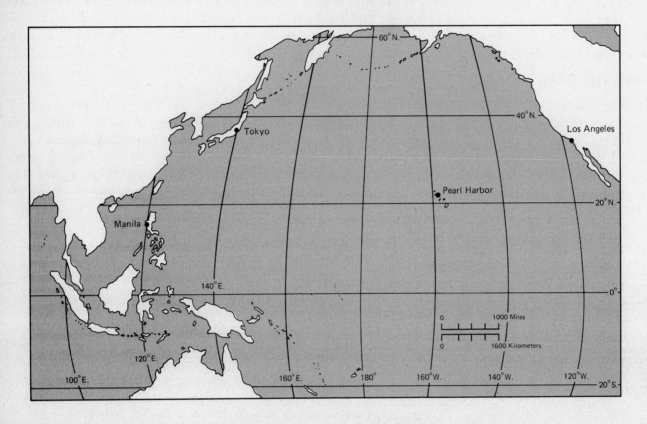

1. Give the correct latitude and longitude for the following cities:

   a. Los Angeles, California _____   **b.** Pearl Harbor, Hawaii _____

   c. Tokyo, Japan _____   **d.** Manila, Philippines _____

2. How far is it between each of the two places given below? Use the map scale at the lower right of

   the map.

   a. Los Angeles and Pearl Harbor _____

   b. Pearl Harbor and Tokyo _____

   c. Tokyo and Manila _____

Categorizing Which War?

The United States has fought in two wars that were called "World Wars"—World War I from 1917 to 1918 and World War II from 1941 to 1945. Below are statements about these wars. If the statement is true for World War I *only*, put a **WWI** in front of it. If the statement is true for World War II only, put a **WWII** in front of it. If the statement is true of *both* wars, write **WWI** and **WWII** in front of it. If the statement is true of **neither** war, put an **N** in front of the statement.

_____ 1. The United States fought on the side of Britain and France.

_____ 2. An atomic bomb was dropped on Hiroshima.

_____ 3. The United States fought against Germany.

_____ 4. The British assassinated the German ruler.

_____ 5. "Blackjack" Pershing led American troops in battle.

_____ 6. The United States invaded Canada.

_____ 7. President Wilson attended the peace conference.

_____ 8. Black Americans fought bravely.

_____ 9. The United States tried to remain neutral.

_____ 10. Teddy Roosevelt led a famous charge.

_____ 11. The Zimmerman Note angered Americans.

_____ 12. Japanese Americans were put in relocation camps.

_____ 13. Americans mobilized their resources and made sacrifices at home.

_____ 14. Submarine warfare was used.

_____ 15. The League of Nations was created.

_____ 16. America fought on the side of Russia.

_____ 17. Trench warfare and poison gas were used.

_____ 18. The United Nations was created.

_____ 19. The United Nations fought against Japan.

_____ 20. Sweden and Switzerland fought on the side of Britain and France.

Organizational Charts Normandy Campaign

In Chapter 29 you learned how charts can help you understand an organization like the United Nations. Charts can also help you understand how a business is organized or how a labor union works. The chart below shows how Allied armies that invaded France in World War II were organized. This Allied invasion was called the Normandy Campaign. Troops from the United States, Britain, Canada, and France all fought together to defeat the Germans. Even though these countries had joined together to fight, there were times when only one person or one group had to make important decisions. The chart below shows the persons and groups that made all the important decisions about the Normandy Campaign. Study the chart carefully and answer the following questions.

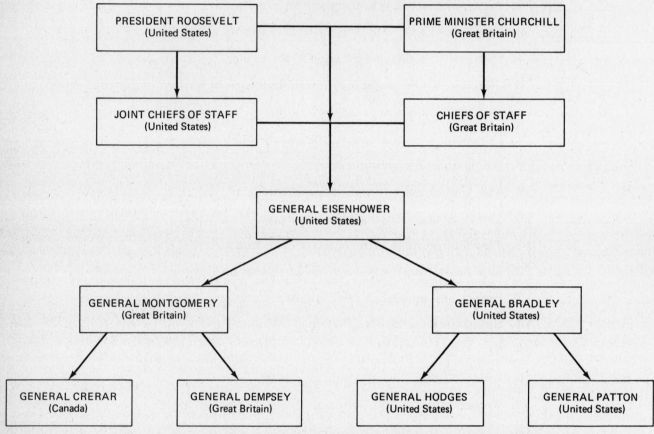

1. Who are the highest-ranking persons on this chart, and what country do they represent? _____

    _____

2. Who is the Supreme Commander of all Allied military forces, and what country does this person

    represent? _____

3. What two groups does General Eisenhower have to get approval from before he can put his plans

    into action? _____

    _____

4. What two generals received their orders directly from General Eisenhower? _____

    _____

5. General Crerar was Canadian. What other generals were his equal? _____

    _____

★ Building American Citizenship

Japanese Americans and World War II

Below are several paragraphs about the treatment of Japanese Americans in World War II. Read each paragraph, and then select the sentence that tells the main idea of the paragraph.

1. When Japan bombed Pearl Harbor on December 7, 1941, thousands of Japanese immigrants were living in California, Oregon, and Washington. Even though many of them had lived there for 10 or 15 years, the United States had a law that prevented them from becoming citizens. However, children of Japanese immigrants were American citizens if they had been born in the United States. Japanese Americans were very unhappy when Japan declared war on the United States.

   a. When World War II started, many Japanese Americans were living in the United States.

   b. All Japanese Americans in California were children of Japanese immigrants.

   c. Japanese immigrants and their families were forced to return to Japan when war broke out.

2. In 1942 President Roosevelt signed an order that greatly upset Japanese Americans. The order allowed General John DeWitt to force them to leave their homes and move to relocation camps. General DeWitt felt that Japanese Americans were enemies of the United States. He ordered all Japanese Americans to move into army shelters located in western desert land, Alabama, and Arkansas. Here, the General thought they could do no harm during the war.

   a. Roosevelt ordered Japanese Americans and German Americans to be relocated.

   b. General DeWitt moved the Japanese Americans because he thought they would support Japan against the United States in World War II.

   c. Only disloyal Japanese Americans were forced to leave their homes.

3. Relocation of Japanese American families happened so quickly that many had no time to sell their homes and property. Families were only allowed to pack one or two suitcases. Everything else had to be left behind. When the war finally was over, most Japanese Americans found that they could not reclaim their homes and property. They had lost everything.

   a. The relocation of Japanese Americans was done to protect them from harm.

   b. Japanese Americans were treated unfairly during the relocation process.

   c. After the war, Japanese Americans were allowed to return to their homes and claim their personal property.

4. Why do you think that President Roosevelt decided to move Japanese Americans to relocation camps? _____

   _____

   _____

   _____

5. Do you think some other group might be treated like this again if the United States is involved in another war? Explain your answer. _____

   _____

   _____

★ Building American Citizenship

Political Cartoons

In Chapter 30 you read about Senator Joseph McCarthy of Wisconsin, who started a campaign to un-cover Communists and disloyal Americans in the United States. Below is a political cartoon that appeared in many newspapers in 1954. Study the cartoon carefully, and then answer the questions that follow.

"I Have Here In My Hand ——"

...from Herblock's *Here And How* (Simon & Schuster, 1955)

1. Who is the person represented in the cartoon? _____

2. What is the person holding in his hand?_____
   _____

3. Look at the microphone at the bottom right of the cartoon. What is the person in the cartoon doing
   with the "doctored photo" and "faked letter"? _____
   _____
   _____

4. How would you describe the person's looks? (Happy, sad, something else?)_____
   _____
   _____

5. What do you think is the meaning of this cartoon? _____
   _____
   _____

Name _____ Class_____ Date_____

Maps The Korean War

In Chapter 30 you read about Americans' fighting in the Korean War. Below is a map of Korea showing places where major battles were fought. Study the map carefully, and then answer the questions below.

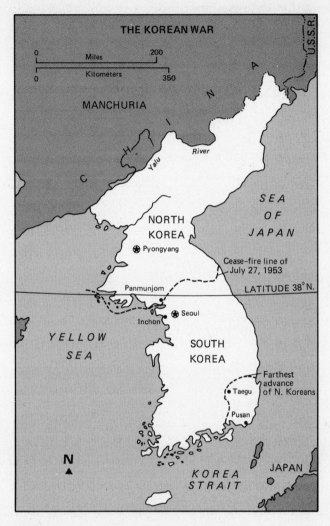

1. What body of water is located to the east of South Korea? _____ to the south? _____ to the west? _____

2. What river that flows into the Yellow Sea is part of the northern border of North Korea?

_____

3. In which part of South Korea is Seoul, the capital city, located? _____

4. Inchon, the town where General MacArthur's forces landed, is located on what body of water?

_____

5. Which parallel of latitude was the original border between North and South Korea? _____

_____

Worksheet 85, Chapter 30

Name _____Class_____Date_____

Line Graphs Shifts from Small Towns

In Chapter 31 you read about Americans who moved from cities to the suburbs. At the same time, other Americans were still moving from rural areas to cities. Below are the percentages of Americans who lived in suburbs or rural areas and small towns from 1930 to 1960. Use the figures given below to make line graphs showing this information.

	SUBURBS	RURAL AREAS AND SMALL TOWNS
1930	18%	50%
1940	20%	49%
1950	24%	44%
1960	31%	37%

Directions: Use a blue or black pen to draw a line on the graph showing the percent of Americans living in suburbs, and label that line. Use a pencil to draw a line on the graph showing the percent of people who lived in rural areas and small towns, and label that line.

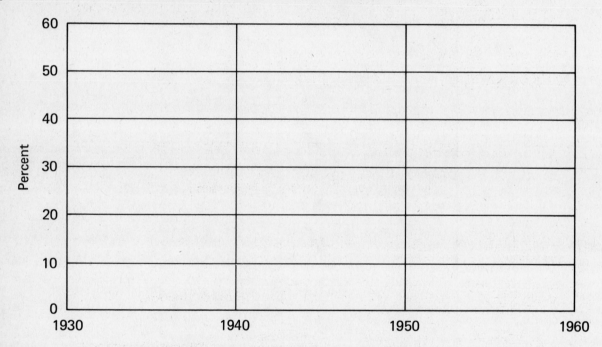

In your textbook you studied about the increase in the population of the suburbs during the 1950's. Study the graph you have drawn. How would you describe the changes in the population of rural areas and small towns during the period from 1930 to 1960?

_____

_____

_____

_____

_____

264 _____

© Macmillan Publishing Co.

Picture Graphs American Farms, 1940 to 1960

In the History Study Skill in Chapter 32 you learned how to read picture graphs. Picture graphs help you see the differences between numbers. Below are two picture graphs. Study them carefully, and then answer the questions that follow.

NUMBER OF FARMS IN THE UNITED STATES

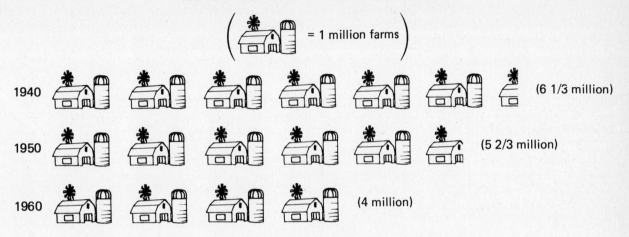

AVERAGE SIZE OF FARMS IN THE UNITED STATES

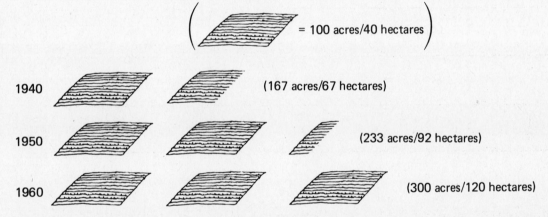

1. According to the picture graph, did the number of farms increase or decrease between 1940 and

   1960? _____

2. How many fewer farms were there in 1960 than in 1940? _____

3. According to the picture graph, did the size of farms increase or decrease between 1940 and 1960?

   _____

4. How much bigger was the average farm in 1960 than in 1940? _____

5. Do you think the number of farmers who worked the farms increased or decreased between 1940

   and 1960? Explain your answer._____

   _____

   _____

Worksheet 87, Chapter 31

★**Building American Citizenship**

Local Government

In Chapter 31 you have read about some of the conflicts in American society during the 1950's. One of the most important jobs of government is to resolve conflicts. Some of the conflicts of the 1950's were settled by the federal government. Others were solved by state and local governments.

There are many different kinds of "local governments." For some people, the city government is their local government. In most rural areas, the county government is the people's local government. The table below give the numbers of different kinds of local governments from 1942 to 1967. Study the information carefully, and then answer the questions that follow.

TOTAL NUMBERS OF DIFFERENT KINDS OF LOCAL GOVERNMENTS, 1942-1972

Local Governments	1942	1952	1957	1962	1967	1972
Cities	16,200	16,778	17,183	17,997	18,048	18,517
Counties	3,050	3,049	3,047	3,048	3,049	3,044
Townships	18,919	17,202	17,198	17,144	17,105	16,991
School Districts	108,579	67,846	50,446	34,678	21,782	15,781
Other Special Districts	8,299	12,319	14,405	18,233	21,264	23,885
TOTAL	155,067	116,694	102,279	91,185	81,248	78,218

1. How many different kinds of local governments are shown in the table? _____

2. Name the different kinds of local governments shown in the table. _____
_____

3. How many different years does the chart include?_____

4. What was the total number of local government units in 1942? _____

   in 1967?_____

5. Was there an increase or a decrease in the total number of local government units between 1942

   and 1967? _____

6. What two kinds of local governments showed large increases between 1942 and 1967? _____
_____

7. What kind of local government stayed almost the same between 1942 and 1967? _____

8. What two kinds of local governments showed large decreases between 1942 and 1967? _____
_____

9. What kinds of local governments do you have in your community? _____
_____

10. According to the table, was there more or less local government in 1967 than in 1942?
    _____ Why do you think this was so? _____
_____
_____
_____

©Macmillan Publishing Co.

Name _____ Class _____ Date _____

Non-Violent Protests

In Chapters 31 and 32 of your textbook you learned how the civil rights movement used many forms of non-violent protests to win equal rights for black Americans.

Three different methods of non-violent protest—sit-ins, freedom riders, and boycotts—are the subject of this activity. Use the information in your textbook to answer the questions below.

1. Define "sit-in." _____

   _____

   _____

2. Give an example of a "sit-in." _____

   _____

   _____

3. What do you think are the strengths or weaknesses of sit-ins as a form of non-violent protest?

   _____

   _____

4. Define "freedom riders." _____

   _____

   _____

5. Give an example of protests made by freedom riders. _____

   _____

   _____

6. What do you think are the strengths or weaknesses of the freedom riders' activities as a form of

   non-violent protest?_____

   _____

   _____

7. Define a "boycott." _____

   _____

   _____

8. Give an example of the use of a boycott. _____

   _____

   _____

9. What do you think are the strengths or weaknesses of a boycott as a form of non-violent protest?

   _____

   _____

   _____

Worksheet 89, Chapter 32

Name _____ Class _____ Date _____

Flow Charts How a Bill Becomes a Law

You have read in Chapter 32 about important civil rights laws that were passed in the 1960's by Congress. Law-making is sometimes a long and difficult process. It was not easy getting civil rights laws passed. The flow chart below shows how one of the civil rights bills became a law. Study the chart carefully, and then answer the questions that follow. Remember, some bills start in the House of Representatives, while others begin in the Senate. The bill below started in the House of Representatives.

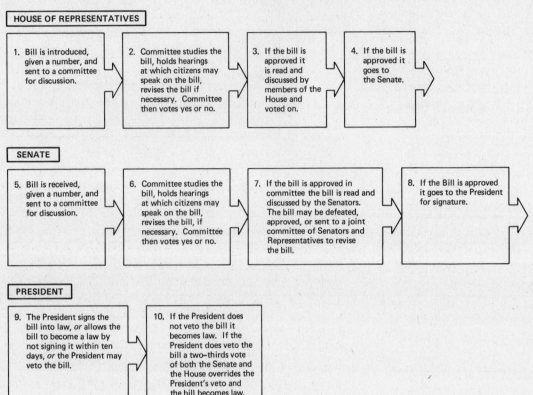

HOUSE OF REPRESENTATIVES

1. Bill is introduced, given a number, and sent to a committee for discussion.

2. Committee studies the bill, holds hearings at which citizens may speak on the bill, revises the bill if necessary. Committee then votes yes or no.

3. If the bill is approved it is read and discussed by members of the House and voted on.

4. If the bill is approved it goes to the Senate.

SENATE

5. Bill is received, given a number, and sent to a committee for discussion.

6. Committee studies the bill, holds hearings at which citizens may speak on the bill, revises the bill, if necessary. Committee then votes yes or no.

7. If the bill is approved in committee the bill is read and discussed by the Senators. The bill may be defeated, approved, or sent to a joint committee of Senators and Representatives to revise the bill.

8. If the Bill is approved it goes to the President for signature.

PRESIDENT

9. The President signs the bill into law, *or* allows the bill to become a law by not signing it within ten days, *or* the President may veto the bill.

10. If the President does not veto the bill it becomes law. If the President does veto the bill a two-thirds vote of both the Senate and the House overrides the President's veto and the bill becomes law.

BILL: Segregation in jobs, schools, and housing is unlawful in the United States.

1. If citizens wanted to speak in favor of the proposed bill, at what step or steps in the process would they be able to do it? _____

_____

2. If the Senate and House disagree on the wording of the bill, what can they do? _____

_____

_____

3. Are the steps in the law-making process similar in both the House and the Senate? Explain your answer. _____

_____

4. If the President had vetoed the civil rights bill, what could Congress have done to get the bill passed? _____

_____

Organizing Facts Kennedy and Johnson

In Chapter 32 you have read about the two Presidents, Kennedy and Johnson, who served between 1961 and 1969. These years were a period of great change and conflict at home and abroad. Below is a list of events that occurred while Kennedy and Johnson were President. Decide if the event occurred during Kennedy's or Johnson's terms in office. Then list each event on the table below.

Glenn and Carpenter Travel in Space
Job Corps Started
Riots Break Out in Watts
16,000 American Military Advisers Sent to Vietnam
United States Blockades Cuba
Voting Rights Act Is Passed
Dr. King Is Assassinated
Great Society Started
Peace Corps Is Started
Brooke Becomes a Senator
The March on Washington Occurs
Civil Rights Act Is Passed

Soviets Place Missiles in Cuba
Tonkin Gulf Resolution Is Passed
Hawks and Doves Disagree
Dr. King Wins Nobel Prize
President Visits the Berlin Wall
Goldwater Is Defeated
Freedom Riders Protest Segregation
New Frontier Is Started
Weaver Heads HUD
Meredith Attends University of Mississippi
Oswald Assassinates President Kennedy
Medicare Law Is Passed

KENNEDY	JOHNSON

Organizing Facts Recent Presidents

In Chapter 33 you have read about many important events that happened during the 1970's and 1980's. Many of these events happened because Presidents helped cause them to happen. Other events that happened were not caused by Presidents. Below are some of these events. Put each event under the name of the person who was President at that time. If the President caused, or helped cause the event, put a **C** after the event.

Department of Energy Was Created
Watergate Break-in Occurred
Iranians Seized American Hostages
President Was Wounded by an
Assassin
Skylab 1 Was Put in Orbit
Air Traffic Controllers Went on Strike

Americans Celebrated the Bicentennial
Environmental Protection Agency Was Created
Marines Were Sent to Lebanon
Panama Canal Treaty Was Signed
Energy Policy and Conservation Act Was Passed
Treaty Between Egypt and Israel Was Signed
Joint American-Soviet Space Project Took Place

PRESIDENT NIXON

PRESIDENT FORD

PRESIDENT CARTER

PRESIDENT REAGAN

© Macmillan Publishing Co.

★Building American Citizenship

Our Presidents as Leaders

In Chapter 33 and throughout the book you have read about American Presidents. Some Presidents were good leaders, others were less successful. Many of the adults in your family, school, and neighborhood have lived under the Presidencies of Nixon, Ford, Carter, and Reagan. These adults probably have opinions about how good these Presidents were as leaders. Use the questions below to interview adults in your family, school, or community. Record your findings on the table below. Be sure to include opinions about all four Presidents in your table.

Question 1. Do you remember actions that President Nixon, Ford, Carter, or Reagan took that you thought showed good leadership? Would you please explain what you liked about the President's actions?

Question 2. Do you remember some actions that President Nixon, Ford, Carter, or Reagan took that you thought showed poor leadership? Would you please explain what you disliked about these actions?

President	Actions that Showed Good Leadership	Actions that Showed Poor Leadership
NIXON		
FORD		
CARTER		
REAGAN		

Worksheet 93, Chapter 33

Population Maps Center of Population

In the History Study Skill in Chapter 33 you learned to read a population map. That map illustrated the movement of Americans into the Sun Belt states of the South and Southwest. The map below is another kind of population map. It shows where the "center" of our country's population was located in every decade since 1790. The population "center" means that the population in all directions away from the center is equally dense. Find the "center" in 1800. You will see that it was located between Baltimore and Washington. By 1810 the center was about 50 miles farther west, in Virginia. The movement of the center had many causes, but one of the most important was that more and more Americans moved west as the year went by. Study the map below, and then answer the questions that follow.

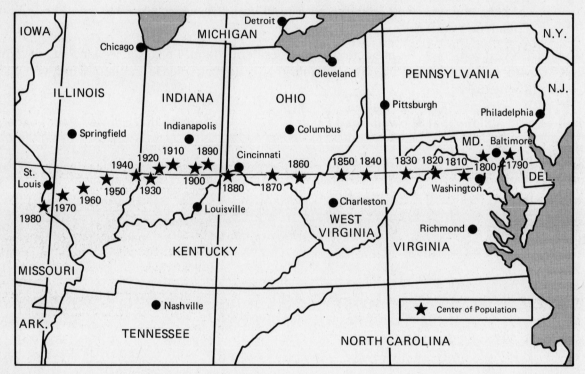

1. What would be the best title for this map?

   a. Population Map of the United States

   b. America's Population Center Moves West

   c. How Our Country's Population Has Grown

2. According to the map's legend, the ★ stands for

   a. the place where most Americans lived

   b. population centers along America's first railroad

   c. an imaginary point in all directions from which the United States population is equally dense

3. Between 1910 and 1960 the United States population moved mostly toward the

   a. south and west

   b. north and west

   c. south and east

Chapter 1 Test

REVIEWING KEY WORDS

Write the letter of the answer that correctly defines each word.

1. _____ confederation   **A** a group's way of life

2. _____ archaeologists   **B** traditions handed down from the past

3. _____ glaciers   **C** the loose union of Iroquois Indians

4. _____ heritage   **D** huge masses of ice and snow

5. _____ culture   **E** scientists who study physical remains

CHECKING UP ON THE FACTS

Write the letter of the answer that correctly completes each statement or correctly answers each question below.

6. _____ The first people who came to North America were
   A farmers.   **C** gatherers.
   B nomads.   **D** fishermen.

7. _____ All of the following are true of the first people who came to America *except*
   A they knew how to use fire.   **C** they knew how to farm.
   B they lived in caves.   **D** they made tools from stones.

8. _____ Evidence of the first Americans has been found in
   A Folsom, New Mexico.   **C** Koster, Illinois.
   B Ross County, Ohio.   **D** all of these.

9. _____ Each natural region of North America is different from other natural regions because of
   A the shape of the land.   **C** the soil, rainfall, and weather.
   B the plants and vegetables.   **D** all of these.

10. _____ The highest place in North America is
   A the Cascade Range.   **C** Mount Mitchell.
   B Mount McKinley.   **D** the White Mountains.

11. _____ The river which flows through the middle of the North American continent is the
   A Mississippi.   **C** Missouri.
   B Colorado.   **D** Ohio.

12. _____ The Continental Divide can be found in which region of North America?
   A Rocky Mountains   **C** Appalachian Mountains
   B Pacific   **D** Canadian Shield

13. _____ The early Indian people of Mexico were the
   A Creek.   **C** Iroquois.
   B Aztecs.   **D** Chippewa.

© Macmillan Publishing Co.

14. _____ From which group did the tribes come that were united by the Iroquois League?
   A Plains   C Eastern Woodlands
   B Mexican   D Eskimos

15. _____ Which of the following is an example of the Indian heritage?
   A oranges   C cabbage
   B spinach   D corn

WHERE DID IT HAPPEN?

Write the letter of the natural region in which each of the following places is located.

16. _____ Great Basin   A Intermountain Plateau

17. _____ Great Plains   B Central Lowlands

18. _____ Blue Ridge Mountains   C Appalachian Mountains

19. _____ Hudson Bay   D Rocky Mountains

20. _____ Continental Divide   E Canadian Shield

WHEN DID IT HAPPEN?

Write the letter of the event that happened first in each of the following pairs of events.

21. _____ A Discovery of artifacts in Loucheaux, Alaska
           B Discovery of artifacts in Folsom, New Mexico

22. _____ A Hunters reached South America
           B Hunters crossed the land bridge from Asia

23. _____ A Indians of Mexico began to farm
           B Farmers of the Southwest dug irrigation canals

24. _____ A Maya culture develops
           B Incas build an empire in Peru

25. _____ A Iroquois League is organized
           B Aztecs build an empire in Mexico

Chapter 2 Test

REVIEWING KEY WORDS

Write the letter of the answer that correctly defines each word.

1. _____ colony   **A** a sturdy ship that used the lateen sail

2. _____ monopoly   **B** an instrument that indicates directions

3. _____ compass   **C** total control of trade or business

4. _____ astrolabe   **D** territory controlled and settled by people from another country

5. _____ caravel   **E** instrument used to find North and South by measuring the location of the stars

CHECKING UP ON THE FACTS

Write the letter of the answer that correctly completes each statement.

6. _____ Columbus received the money and ships for his voyages from
   A Prince Henry.   **B** King John II.   **C** Ferdinand and Isabella.

7. _____ The Pacific Ocean was discovered by
   A Marco Polo.   **B** Vasco de Balboa.   **C** Ponce de Leon.

8. _____ The explorer whose three year expedition proved that the world was round was
   A Ferdinand Magellan.   **B** Vasco da Gama.   **C** Bartholomeu Diaz.

9. _____ The Viking explorer who sailed to several places along the North American coast was
   A Bjarni Herjolfsson.   **B** Leif Ericsson   **C** Thorfin Karlsveni.

10. _____ A Spanish colony started in the Caribbean was
   A Cuba.   **B** Brazil.   **C** the Philippines.

Read each statement carefully. If it is TRUE, write the letter A. If it is FALSE write the letter B.

11. _____ The Crusades led to the growth of trade with Asia.

12. _____ Christopher Columbus made only one voyage to the New World.

13. _____ English explorers found a Northwest Passage to Asia.

14. _____ In general, Indians were treated cruelly by the Spaniards.

15. _____ The English and French firmly controlled the Caribbean.

WHERE DID IT HAPPEN?

Write the letter of the answer that correctly completes each sentence.

   A The Holy Land   **B** San Salvador   **C** Cape of Good Hope
     D The "Indies"   **E** Puerto Rico

16. _____ Columbus named the islands he founded ___?___ because he thought they were off the coast of Asia.

17. _____ Columbus called the island on which he first landed ___?___.

18. _____ The Crusades were wars fought to gain control of___?___.

19. _____ Indians on the island of ___?___ rebelled against Spanish rule.

20. _____ The Portuguese were the first to sail around the ___?___ at the southern tip of Africa.

WHEN DID IT HAPPEN

Write the letter of the year in which each event happened.

21. _____ Marco Polo and his father began their trip to China.   A 1498

22. _____ Da Gama discovers a new trade route to Asia.   B 1271

23. _____ Magellan's crew completes the voyage around the world.   C 1522

24. _____ Columbus discovers America.   D 1001

25. _____ Viking sailors sail along the coast of North America.   E 1492

Chapter 3 Test

REVIEWING KEY WORDS

Write the letter of the answer that correctly defines the following words.

1. _____ hacienda   **A** to persuade someone to change from one religion to another

2. _____ pueblo   **B** unsettled lands along the edges of a country's territory

3. _____ convert   **C** a town in New Spain

4. _____ mestizo   **D** a person who is part Spanish and part Indian

5. _____ borderland   **E** a large Spanish estate

CHECKING UP ON THE FACTS

Read each statement carefully. If it is TRUE, write the letter A. If it is FALSE, write the letter B.

6. _____ Under Spanish rule, the Indian population of New Spain increased.

7. _____ Spain's empire in America was divided into two parts so that it would be easier to govern.

8. _____ Both Russia and Spain claimed land in California.

9. _____ Spain ruled its empire in America for over 300 years.

10. _____ The policy of mercantilism led to wealth and power for both colonies and parent countries.

11. _____ From its earliest days, California had a mixture of many different peoples.

12. _____ The criollos held the highest social and economic positions in New Spain.

13. _____ Estéban was a former slave who met his death while searching for gold north of Mexico.

14. _____ The Spaniards introduced the Indians to new animals, a new language, a new religion, and new methods of farming.

15. _____ A viceroy was appointed to govern the colonies of New Spain in the name of the King of Spain.

WHEN DID IT HAPPEN?

Write the letter of the year in which each event happened.

16. _____ The Spaniards built a fort at St. Augustine, Florida.   **A** 1718

17. _____ The French established New Orleans.   **B** 1769

18. _____ Cortés conquered the Aztecs.   **C** 1532

19. _____ Pizarro conquered the Incas.   **D** 1521

20. _____ The Spaniards settled at San Diego.   **E** 1565

© Macmillan Publishing Co.

WHERE DID IT HAPPEN?

Write the letter of the answer that correctly completes each statement.

21. _____ The first of the borderlands to be settled by people from New Spain was
    A Texas.   C Arizona.
    B Florida.   D California.

22. _____ The oldest city in the United States is
    A Mexico City.   C Albuquerque.
    B San Diego.   D St. Augustine.

23. _____ Hernando de Soto was the first Spaniard to explore
    A the Mississippi River.   C the Rio Grande.
    B Florida.   D California.

24. _____ The areas in the Americas colonized by Spain, Portugal, and France were called
    A New Spain.   C South America.
    B Latin America.   D Central America.

25. _____ The capital of the Aztec Empire was
    A Moctezuma.   C Lima.
    B Tenochtitlán.   D Cajamarea.

Chapter 4 Test

REVIEWING KEY WORDS

Write the letter of the answer that correctly completes each sentence below.

A missionaries   B coureurs de bois   C habitants

D portage   E seigneurs

1. _____ The ___?___, or woods runners, were French fur trappers who became friendly with the Indians.

2. _____ Carrying canoes overland between two bodies of water is called ___?___.

3. _____ People who wanted to spread the Christian religion among the Indians were called ___?___.

4. _____ The government of France gave grants of land to ___?___, who were French nobles.

5. _____ ___?___ often ran away because they did not like farming land that was not their own.

CHECKING UP ON THE FACTS

Write the letter of the name of the person who is described in each of the following sentences.

6. _____ He was the "father of Louisiana."   A Champlain

7. _____ He was the first French explorer to discover Canada.   B Cartier

8. _____ He was the missionary who helped explore the Mississippi River.   C LaSalle

9. _____ He was the "father of New France."   D Marquette

10. _____ He was the first European to travel down the Mississippi to the Gulf of Mexico.   E de Bienville

Read each statement carefully. If it is TRUE, write the letter A. If it is FALSE, write the letter B.

11. _____ People who chose to settle in New France were granted freedom of religion.

12. _____ The French fur traders treated the Indians very differently from the way the Spanish treated the Indians.

13. _____ Britain and France fought four wars over the control of land in North America.

14. _____ The coureurs de bois looked for the Northwest Passage while they searched the wilderness areas for furs.

15. _____ In North America, French ways of living are most alive today in the state of Illinois.

WHEN DID IT HAPPEN?

Write the letter of the year in which each of these events took place.

16. _____ The French lost their empire in North America.   A 1682

17. _____ New Orleans was founded.   B 1718

18. _____ LaSalle claimed Louisiana for France.   C 1535

19. _____ Champlain founded Quebec.   D 1763

20. _____ Cartier discovered the St. Lawrence River.   E 1608

WHERE DID IT HAPPEN?

Write the letter of the answer that correctly completes each statement or correctly answers each question below.

21. _____ The city that became the center of the French empire in North America was
   A Montreal.   **B** Quebec.   **C** St. Louis.

22. _____ The river explored by Joliet was the
   A St. Lawrence.   **B** Mississippi.   **C** Ohio.

23. _____ All the land through which the Mississippi River and its tributaries flow was called
   A Illinois.   **B** Canada.   **C** Louisiana.

24. _____ Which of the following was *not* a point of conflict between France and England?
   A Montreal   **B** Ohio Valley   **C** Great Plains

25. _____ The Mississippi River flows into the
   A St. Lawrence River.   **B** Gulf of Mexico.   **C** Great Lakes.

© Macmillan Publishing Co.

Chapter 5 Test

REVIEWING KEY WORDS

Write the letter of the answer that correctly defines each word.

1. _____ charter

    A a fleet of warships

2. _____ armada

    B a person who agreed to work for a certain number of years in exchange for passage to America

3. _____ proprietor

    C a person who received a charter from the king granting land in America to start a new colony

4. _____ patroon

    D Dutch landowner in New Netherland

5. _____ indentured servant

    E document granting a person or group land and rights to govern colonists who settled there

CHECKING UP ON THE FACTS

Write the letter of the name of the colony started by each person.

6. _____ James Oglethorp   **A** Maryland

7. _____ William Penn   **B** Pennsylvania

8. _____ Roger Williams   **C** Rhode Island

9. _____ Lord Baltimore   **D** Georgia

10. _____ John Smith   **E** Virginia

Write the letter of the name of the colony that is described in each of the following sentences.

11. _____ The people who settled here mysteriously disappeared.   **A** Jamestown

12. _____ The first Africans arrived here in 1619.   **B** Maryland

13. _____ Indians taught the colonists here to hunt, clear fields, and plant crops.   **C** Roanoke

14. _____ Settlers were given land here for each member of the family and for each indentured servant.   **D** Pennsylvania

15. _____ The Frame of Government established a representative assembly and freedom of religion.   **E** Plymouth

WHEN DID IT HAPPEN?

List the following events in the order they happened by placing the letter of each event in the correct order.

16. _____ (first event)   **A** The first settlers arrived in Jamestown.

17. _____ (second event)   **B** The Carolinas were started.

18. _____ (third event)   **C** The Pilgrims landed at Plymouth Bay.

19. _____ (fourth event)   **D** England defeated the Spanish Armada.

20. _____ (fifth event)   **E** The English captured New Netherland.

WHERE DID IT HAPPEN?

Write the letter of an important town located in each of the colonies.

21. _____ Georgia   **A** Philadelphia

22. _____ Pennsylvania   **B** New York City

23. _____ Massachusetts   **C** Savannah

24. _____ Virginia   **D** Jamestown

25. _____ New York   **E** Boston

Chapter 6 Test
REVIEWING KEY WORDS

Write the letter of the word that is defined in each of the following descriptions.

1. _____ An economy in which families grow or produce just what they need for themselves:
   A triangular trade   **B** subsistance economy   **C** commercial farming economy

2. _____ A person learning a skill, trade, or craft:
   A apprentice   **B** artisan   **C** pagan

3. _____ A thinly settled area beyond which the wilderness lay:
   A royal colony   **B** assembly   **C** frontier

4. _____ The buying and selling of goods:
   A commerce   **B** economy   **C** staple

5. _____ A king or a queen:
   A monarch   **B** proprietor   **C** parliament

6. _____ A colony under the direct control of the king:
   A proprietary colony   **B** royal colony   **C** self-governing colony

7. _____ A crop grown for sale:
   A economy   **B** staple   **C** cash crop

8. _____ One of many Protestant religious groups:
   A denomination   **B** toleration   **C** apprentice

9. _____ An unmarried woman in the colonies:
   A spinster   **B** apprentice   **C** a craftsworker

10. _____ A crop grown to sell after harvest:
    A artisan   **B** staple   **C** economy

CHECKING UP ON THE FACTS

Read each statement carefully. If it is TRUE, write the letter A. If it is FALSE, write the letter B.

11. _____ In colonial America, a child's education consisted mainly of watching adults and listening to what they said.

12. _____ Many people living in the New England colonies made their living in jobs that had to do with shipping and trade.

13. _____ Most people who moved to the frontier were searching for gold.

14. _____ The Indians were unable to stop the westward movement of the colonists.

15. _____ Cato was a freed slave who became a self-educated scientist and mathematician.

WHEN DID IT HAPPEN?

Write the letter of the years during which each of the following happened.

       A in the 1600's   **B** in the 1700's

16. _____ The indigo plant was introduced into South Carolina.

17. _____ Colonists began calling for separation of church and state.

18. _____ New Englanders set up a system of education.

19. _____ Most of the American colonies were controlled by the British monarch.

20. _____ The first representative assembly was created.

WHERE DID IT HAPPEN?

Read each statement or phrase carefully.
If it refers to the NEW ENGLAND COLONIES, write A in the answer blank.
If it refers to the MIDDLE COLONIES, write B in the answer blank.
If it refers to the SOUTHERN COLONIES, write C in the answer blank.
If it refers to the FRONTIER, write D in the answer blank.

21. _____ The edge of the Appalachian Mountains, from Virginia to Georgia

22. _____ The colonies where most of the African slaves were taken in America

23. _____ The colonies where the church was the center of community social life

24. _____ The "break basket" of the colonies

25. _____ The colonies where the chief crop was tobacco

© Macmillan Publishing Co.

Chapter 7 Test

REVIEWING KEY WORDS

Write the letter of the answer that correctly defines each word.

1. _____ boycott   **A** a representative

2. _____ repeal   **B** doing away with a law

3. _____ delegate   **C** refusing to buy or sell goods

4. _____ monopoly   **D** a group of citizens trained to fight in emergencies

5. _____ militia   **E** sole control over the buying and selling of a product

CHECKING UP ON THE FACTS

Write the letter of the answer that correctly completes each of the following statements.

6. _____ Benjamin Franklin's 1754 suggestion for a colonial government with representatives from each colony was known as the
A Proclamation of 1763.   C Treaty of Paris.
B· Albany Plan of Union.   D Declaration of Rights.

7. _____ The French and Indian War began in
A Boston.   C the Ohio Valley.
B Lexington.   D Quebec.

8. _____ The event that took place in 1770 in which Crispus Attucks was killed was the
A Boston Massacre.   C Battle of Lexington.
B Boston Tea Party.   D Battle of Concord.

9. _____ The colonists used all of the following means of protest against Britain *except*
A boycotts.   C repealing laws.
B protest meetings.   D petitions.

10. _____ The law that placed customs duties on paint, lead, tea, paper, and wine coming to America was part of the
A Quartering Act.   C Townshend Acts.
B Intolerable Acts.   D Quebec Act.

11. _____ All of the following were leaders in the colonial protest against British actions *except*
A Patrick Henry.   C Samuel Adams.
B Thomas Hutchinson.   D John Dickinson.

12. _____ Groups of people in each colony who communicated news of important happenings in the colonies were called the
A Committees of Correspondence.   C Continental Congress.
B writs of assistance.   D Stamp Act Congress.

13. _____ Thomas Paine's book urging the colonists to seek independence from Great Britain was called
A *The Albany Plan.*   C The Declaration of Rights and Grievances.
B *Common Sense.*
   D The Olive Branch Petition.

14. _____ The first battle of the American Revolution took place in
   A Lexington.   C Boston.
   B Concord.   D Charleston.

15. _____ The Second Continental Congress did all of the following *except*
   A declared war against Spain.   C approved raising an army.
   B appointed a military commander.   D approved an "Olive Branch Petition"
                                            to the king.

WHEN DID IT HAPPEN?

List the following events in the order they happened by placing the letter of each event in the correct order.

16. _____ (first event)   A The Boston Tea Party

17. _____ (second event)   B The Treaty of Paris marking the end of the French and Indian
                                  War

18. _____ (third event)   C The repeal of the Stamp Act

19. _____ (fourth event)   D The Battles of Lexington and Concord

20. _____ (fifth event)   E The Boston Massacre

WHERE DID IT HAPPEN?

Read each statement carefully. If it is TRUE, write the letter A. If it is FALSE, write the letter B.

21. _____ To end trouble with the Indians, the British government stopped further settlement of land in the Ohio Valley in 1763.

22. _____ The Intolerable Acts were meant to punish the people of Boston for the Boston Tea Party.

23. _____ The first battles of the American Revolution took place in two villages located east of Philadelphia.

24. _____ The French and Indian War doubled the size of the British empire in North America.

25. _____ The First Continental Congress met in Boston.

Chapter 8 Test

REVIEWING KEY WORDS

Write the letter of the answer that correctly defines each word.

1. _____ soldiers hired to fight in an army

2. _____ privately owned ships that attack enemy ships in time of war

3. _____ to set people free

4. _____ to take possession of another person's property

5. _____ an introduction that tells the purpose of a document

A privateers

B emancipate

C preamble

D mercenaries

E confiscate

CHECKING UP ON THE FACTS

Write the letter of the name of the person who is described in each of the following sentences.

A Thomas Jefferson   B John Paul Jones   C General Cornwallis
D General von Steuben   E John Burgoyne

6. _____ The British commander who was defeated at the battle of Saratoga.

7. _____ The author of the Declaration of Independence.

8. _____ The commander of the *Bonhomme Richard* who won a famous naval battle against the British warship *Serapis*.

9. _____ The German officer who helped train American troops at Valley Forge.

10. _____ The commander of the British troops who surrendered at Yorktown.

Write the letter of the sentence that correctly answers each question below.

11. _____ Which of these was *not* an idea stated in the Declaration of Independence?
A All people were born with the same basic rights.
B People's rights come from God.
C Governments were made by people.
D Parliament was responsible for all of the wrongs against the colonies.

12. _____ Which of the following was an advantage held by the American army at the beginning of the war?
A A well-equipped, highly trained army
B A large navy
C Soldiers who believed in their cause
D Mercenaries willing to fight for money

13. _____ Which of these battles was won by the British?
A Yorktown   C Trenton
B New York   D Saratoga

14. _____ Which one of the following people was *not* a British commander?
A Burgoyne   C Greene
B Howe   D Clinton

15. _____ How did American women support the Revolution?
A They organized boycotts.   C They took charge of family
B They collected money for   businesses.
the army.   D All of these

History of the American Nation

WHEN DID IT HAPPEN?

Write the letter of the year in which each event took place.

16. _____	The battle at Saratoga	**A**	1775
17. _____	The Battle of Bunker Hill	**B**	1776
18. _____	The Battle of Yorktown	**C**	1777
19. _____	The signing of the Declaration of Independence	**D**	1781
20. _____	The signing of the Treaty of Paris	**E**	1783

WHERE DID IT HAPPEN?

To tell where each of the following battles took place, write A for the NORTH, B for the SOUTH, C for the WEST, or D for the MIDDLE STATES.

21. _____ Vincennes

22. _____ Bunker Hill

23. _____ Charleston

24. _____ Trenton

25. _____ King's Mountain

Chapter 9 Test
REVIEWING KEY WORDS

Write the letter of the word that is defined in each of the following descriptions.

1. _____ a form of government in which power is divided between the national and state governments

   A convention

2. _____ an agreement in which each side gives up something it wants and each side gets something it wants

   B quorum

3. _____ a meeting of delegates

   C compromise

4. _____ the number of delegates that must be present at a meeting in order to conduct business

   D federalism

5. _____ powers that are shared by the national and state governments

   E concurrent powers

CHECKING UP ON THE FACTS

Write the letter of the answer that correctly completes each statement below.

6. _____ One of the greatest weaknesses of the Articles of Confederation was that it
   A could borrow and coin money.
   B. could make laws for the states to obey.
   C had no strong executive.
   D could build and equip a navy.

7. _____ During the period from 1783 to 1787, the new United States had trouble with
   A a breakdown of law and order in the states.
   B merchants, farmers, and manufacturers finding markets for their goods.
   C foreign countries that would not cooperate.
   D all of these.

8. _____ All of these were accomplished by the national government under the Articles of Confederation *except*
   A establishing a policy for settling the Northwest Territory.
   B raising an army to stop Shays' Rebellion.
   C working out a peace treaty with Great Britain.
   D guaranteeing civil liberties to those who settled in the Northwest Territory.

9. _____ The only state that did not send delegates to the Constitutional Convention was
   A Rhode Island.   **B** Georgia.   **C** Virginia.   **D** New York.

10. _____ The leader who influenced the work of the Constitutional Convention more than any other delegate was
   A James Madison.   **C** Benjamin Franklin.
   B George Washington.   **D** Thomas Jefferson.

11. _____ People who did not approve the Constitution because they preferred strong state governments were called
   A executives.   **C** Anti-Federalists.
   B Federalists.   **D** Senators.

© Macmillan Publishing Co.

History of the American Nation

12. _____ The number of states needed to approve the Constitution before it became effective was

    A 7.   **B** 9.   **C** 11.   **D** 13.

13. _____ The Preamble to the Constitution

    A lists the reasons the Constitution was written.
    B divides power between the national government and state governments.
    C describes the functions of the three branches of government.
    D tells how to amend the Constitution.

14. _____ The lower house of the legislature, in which the number of representatives depends upon the population of each state, is the

    A Senate.   **C** Supreme Court.
    B House of Representatives.   **D** State Department.

15. _____ The first Ten Amendments to the Constitution are called the

    A Northwest Ordinance.   **C** Articles of Confederation.
    B *Federalist Papers.*   **D** Bill of Rights.

WHEN DID IT HAPPEN?

List the following events in the order they happened by placing the letter of each event in the correct order.

16. _____ (first event)   **A** ratification of the Constitution

17. _____ (second event)   **B** passage of the Northwest Ordinance

18. _____ (third event)   **C** ratification of the Articles of Confederation

19. _____ (fourth event)   **D** approval of the Bill of Rights

20. _____ (fifth event)   **E** end of the War of Independence

WHERE DID IT HAPPEN?

Write the letter of the answer that correctly completes each of the following sentences.

    A Pennsylvania   **B** Massachusetts   **C** Connecticut
        D the Northwest Territory   **E** New Hampshire

21. _____ An ordinance was written in 1787 that outlined the way in which parts of __?__ could become states.

22. _____ __?__ became the ninth state to appove the Constitution, thereby completing the ratification process.

23. _____ Delegates from the state of __?__ proposed a compromise that created a two-house legislature for the new government.

24. _____ The Constitutional Convention was held in the state of __?__.

25. _____ Shays' Rebellion, in the state of __?__, helped to prove that the national government under the Articles of Confederation was weak.

© Macmillan Publishing Co.

Chapter 10 Test

REVIEWING KEY WORDS

For each two groups of words below, write the letter of the correct definition for each word.

1. _____ Cabinet

2. _____ appeal

3. _____ census

4. _____ tariff

5. _____ revenue

A income

B a count of the population

C a tax on imports

D heads of executive departments who advise the President

E a request that a case be heard by a higher court

6. _____ precedents

7. _____ executive privilege

8. _____ caucuses

9. _____ sedition

10. _____ deport

A secret meetings of political parties

B a President's right to keep certain documents secret

C unwritten laws or customs used as examples for future action

D to force to leave the country

E to act or speak against a government in order to cause unrest or rebellion

CHECKING UP ON THE FACTS

Write the letter of the answer that correctly completes each statement or correctly answers each question below.

11. _____ All of these executive departments were created by President Washington *except*
A the Department of the Treasury.
B the Department of State.
C the Department of War.
D the Department of Transportation.

12. _____ Which of the following laws were passed while John Adams was President?
A the Judiciary Act
B the Landing Bill
C the Alien Acts
D the Neutrality Act

13. _____ The Virginia and Kentucky Resolutions first raised the issue of
A loose construction v. strict construction.
B states' rights v. national sovereignty.
C farmers' and workers' interests v. the interests of the wealthy.
D the Federalists v. the Republicans.

14. _____ Jay's Treaty, ratified by the Senate in 1795, was made with
A Spain.
B Great Britain.
C France.
D French West Indies.

15. _____ In the election of 1800, there was a tie vote for President between Aaron Burr and
A Thomas Jefferson.
B John Adams.
C Alexander Hamilton.
D Thomas Pinckney.

WHEN DID IT HAPPEN?

Write the letter of the year in which each event took place.

16. _____ John Adams was elected President.   A 1791

17. _____ Thomas Jefferson was elected President.   B 1794

18. _____ The Alien Acts were passed.   C 1796

19. _____ The Bill of Rights was added to the Constitution. D 1798

20. _____ The Whiskey Rebellion occurred.   E 1800

WHERE DID IT HAPPEN?

Write the letter of the answer that correctly completes each sentence below.

A New Orleans   **B** Washington, D.C.   **C** Philadelphia   **D** New York City

21. _____ The first capital of the United States was located in ___?___.

22. _____ According to the 1790 census, ___?___ was America's largest city.

23. _____ American use of the port at ___?___ was controlled by Spain.

24. _____ The first national bank of the United States was located in the city of ___?___.

25. _____ John Adams was the first President to live in the capital city of ___?___.

© Macmillan Publishing Co.

Chapter 11 Test

REVIEWING KEY WORDS

Write the letter of the answer that correctly defines each term.

1. _____ judicial review

A to bring charges of wrongdoing against a federal official

2. _____ protective tariff

B a government order to stop trade

3. _____ embargo

C the power of the Supreme Court to declare a law unconstitutional

4. _____ interstate commerce

D a tax on imports that results in higher prices for goods from other nations

5. _____ impeach

E trade between the states

CHECKING UP ON THE FACTS

Write the letter of the answer that correctly completes each sentence or correctly answers each question below.

6. _____ The Supreme Court case which established the precedent of judicial review was
   A *Marbury v. Madison.*
   B *McCulloch v. Maryland.*
   C *Gibbons v. Ogden.*

7. _____ Which of the following was *not* a cause of the War of 1812?
   A abuse of American rights at sea
   B Tecumseh's attacks on Western settlers
   C the burning of the nation's capital

8. _____ Which battle of the War of 1812 was fought after the peace treaty was signed?
   A Thames
   B Baltimore
   C New Orleans

9. _____ Who was President when the Louisiana Territory was purchased?
   A Jefferson
   B Madison
   C Monroe

10. _____ Florida was purchased from which European nation?
    A France
    B Spain
    C Russia

11. _____ The statement that warned European nations to stay out of the political affairs of the Western Hemisphere was
    A the Treaty of Ghent.
    B the Monroe Doctrine.
    C the Rush-Bagot Agreement.

12. _____ The Shoshone Indian who served as a guide on the Lewis and Clark Expedition was
    A Sacajawea.
    B Tecumseh.
    C Sequoya.

13. _____ Which of the following Americans was a military leader during the war with the Barbary states?
A Francis Scott Key
B Andrew Jackson
C Stephen Decatur

14. _____ The "Era of Good Feeling" took place during the Presidency of
A Thomas Jefferson.
B James Madison.
C James Monroe.

15. _____ The "Star-Spangled Banner" was written by
A William Henry Harrison.
B Francis Scott Key.
C John Quincy Adams.

WHEN DID IT HAPPEN?

List the following events in the order they happened by placing the letter of each event in the correct order.

16. _____ (first event)   **A** The purchase of Florida

17. _____ (second event)   **B** "Mr. Madison's War"

18. _____ (third event)   **C** The Monroe Doctrine

19. _____ (fourth event)   **D** The Louisiana Purchase

20. _____ (fifth event)   **E** The *Chesapeake-Leopard* affair

WHERE DID IT HAPPEN?

Write the letter of the answer that correctly completes each sentence below.

A Baltimore   **B** New Orleans   **C** St. Louis

D Derna   **E** Tippecanoe

21. _____ Lewis and Clark left the city of ___?___ and traveled up the Missouri River to begin their exploration of the Louisiana Territory.

22. _____ An American officer led an army of Americans, Greeks, and Arabs in the capture of the Tripolitan city of ___?___.

23. _____ The "Star-Spangled Banner," was a poem written at the battle at Fort McHenry, near the city of ___?___.

24. _____ Andrew Jackson led an American army at the Battle of ___?___, America's greatest victory of the War of 1812.

25. _____ Tecumseh's village was destroyed at the Battle of ___?___

© Macmillan Publishing Co.

Chapter 12 Test

REVIEWING KEY WORDS

Write the letter of the answer that correctly completes each statement.

A factory system   **B** mass production   **C** protective tariff
         D interchangeable parts   **E** division of labor

1. _____ Producing large amounts of goods in a short time is called ___?___.

2. _____ The system of using workers and machines in special buildings to produce large amounts of goods in a short time is called ___?___.

3. _____ Dividing up work so that each worker has only one or two jobs to perform is called ___?___.

4. _____ Pieces of goods made exactly alike are called ___?___.

5. _____ Business owners and manufacturers asked the government to help them by passing a ___?___ to raise the price of imported goods.

CHECKING UP ON THE FACTS

Write the letter of the sentence that correctly describes each of the following people.

6. _____ Eli Whitney   **A** He worked out the Missouri Compromise.

7. _____ Robert Fulton   **B** He built the steamboat *Clermont*.

8. _____ Samuel Slater   **C** He invented the cotton gin and the system of mass production.

9. _____ Nat Turner   **D** He led an unsuccessful slave rebellion in Virginia in 1831.

10. _____ Henry Clay   **E** He set up the first American factory in 1791.

Write the letter of the answer that correctly completes each statement or answers each question below.

11. _____ All of the following improved transportation in the early 1800's *except*
     A the Erie Canal.   **B** the *Clermont*.
     C The National Road.   **D** the airplane.

12. _____ Factories were built in the Northeast because
     A New England had many swift-moving rivers to supply power.
     B people there were willing to invest money to build factories.
     C many people there needed jobs.
     D all of these.

13. _____ Which of the following statements is *true*?
     A Most white Southerners owned no slaves
     B Most plantations were very large
     C Most black people were happy to be slaves
     D Most slaveowners were willing to end slavery

14. _____ Which of the following was *not* a method used by slaves to resist unfair treatment?

    A running away   **C** doing little work

    B going on a walkout   **D** joining a rebellion

15. _____ John Quincy Adams won the election of 1824 because he

    A received the greatest number of popular votes.

    B won the most electoral votes.

    C received a majority vote in the House of Representatives.

    D none of these.

WHEN DID IT HAPPEN?

For each pair of events, write the letter of the event that occurred first.

16. _____   **A** The Missouri Compromise

             B The Tariff of Abominations

17. _____   **A** the end of the slave trade

             B the invention of the cotton gin

18. _____   **A** the election of Andrew Jackson

             B the election of John Quincy Adams

19. _____   **A** the opening of the Wilderness Road

             B the opening of the National Road

20. _____   **A** the opening of the Erie Canal

             B the first trip of the *Clermont*

WHERE DID IT HAPPEN?

For each statement below, choose the letter of the correct answer.

    A the Northeast   **B** the West   **C** the South

21. _____ This section favored the National Republican Party.

22. _____ For a time, the issue of slavery was settled for this section with the Missouri Compromise.

23. _____ This section opposed a protective tariff.

24. _____ In this section cotton was "king."

25. _____ People moved to this section for a chance to own more land.

Chapter 13 Test
REVIEWING KEY WORDS

Write the letter of the correct definition for each of the following words.

1. _____ specie
2. _____ bank notes
3. _____ speculator
4. _____ nullification
5. _____ charter

A a contract to operate

B a state's refusal to enforce a federal law

C a person who invests money hoping to make a quick profit

D gold or silver

E paper money

CHECKING UP ON THE FACTS

Read each statement carefully. If it is TRUE, write the letter A. If it is FALSE, write the letter B.

6. _____ The Seminoles were the only Indians who resisted Jackson's Indian removal policy.

7. _____ Senator Robert Hayne supported the doctrine of states' rights.

8. _____ Jackson's policy of "rotation in office" hired experts to fill government jobs.

9. _____ Martin Van Buren was blamed for the business depression of 1837.

10. _____ By the time Andrew Jackson was elected President, all adult white males had the right to vote.

DO YOU KNOW YOUR PRESIDENTS?

Read each phrase below. If it refers to *President Jackson*, write the Letter A in the answer blank; if it refers to *Martin Van Buren*, write the letter B in the answer blank; if it refers to *William Henry Harrison*, write the letter C in the answer blank.

11. _____ the "Little Magician"

12. _____ "Tippecanoe and Tyler, too!"

13. _____ "Our Union, it must be preserved!"

14. _____ The "log cabin and cider" campaign

15. _____ "Old Hickory"

WHEN DID IT HAPPEN?

Write the letter of the year in which each of these events occurred.

16. _____ President Jackson was elected to a second term as President
A 1828   B 1832   C 1836

17. _____ The Indian Removal Act was passed by Congress.
A 1828   B 1830   C 1832

18. _____ President Jackson destroyed the Second Bank of the United States.
A 1830   B 1832   C 1834

© Macmillan Publishing Co.

History of the American Nation

19. _____ The Whigs conducted the "log cabin and cider" campaign.
  A 1832   **B** 1836   **C** 1840

20. _____ A sharp downturn in business took place
  A 1830   **B** 1837   **C** 1840

WHERE DID IT HAPPEN?

Write the letter of the state in which each of the following events took place.

  A New York   **B** Tennessee   **C** South Carolina
        D Oklahoma   **E** Illinois

21. _____ Andrew Jackson was elected as this state's first Senator.

22. _____ The Sauk and Fox tribes fought to keep their lands in this state.

23. _____ This state passed a Nullification Act that nearly involved the nation in a war over the tariff question.

24. _____ The Indian Territory, to which the five Southeastern tribes were removed, is located in this state.

25. _____ This state was where President Martin Van Buren was born.

Chapter 14 Test

REVIEWING KEY WORDS

Write the letter of the answer that correctly completes each sentence below.

A metropolis   **B** prejudice   **C** Lyceum
       D clipper ship   **E** packet line

1. _____ People who traveled by sea preferred to take their trips on a ___?___ because these ships ran on a regular schedule.

2. _____ During the 1800's Americans showed their ___?___ against foreigners by voting against immigrants who ran for public office.

3. _____ During the 1800's Americans who wished to hear the latest information on science, politics, or religion, often attended lectures at the ___?___.

4. _____ The ___?___ was a beautiful ocean-going vessel that used many sails to increase its speed.

5. _____ A big city like New York or Philadelphia is called a ___?___ because it serves as a center of business, education, culture, and politics.

CHECKING UP ON THE FACTS

Write the letter of the answer that correctly completes each statement below.

6. _____ All of the following are examples of literature in the 1800's *except*
   A *Rip Van Winkle.*
   B *The Pathfinder.*
   C "Raftsmen Playing Cards."
   D *The Yemmassee.*

7. _____ The *Tom Thumb*, a steam-powered locomotive, was built by
   A Richard Hoe.
   B Peter Cooper.
   C Cyrus McCormick.
   D John Griffith.

8. _____ All of these means of transportation were improved in the early 1800's *except*
   A the stagecoach.
   B the steam-powered locomotive.
   C steamships.
   D automobiles.

9. _____ The telegraph was invented by
   A Samuel F. B. Morse.
   B John Deere.
   C Samuel Colt.

10. _____ All of the following were major problems faced by cities *except*
   A poor housing.
   B few amusements.
   C poor sanitation.
   D crime.

Write the letter of the answer that gives the correct field of art in which each of the following people worked.

11. _____ Stephen Foster   **A** poetry

12. _____ Thomas Cole   **B** history

13. _____ George Bancroft   **C** literature

14. _____ Henry Wadsworth Longfellow   **D** music

15. _____ Washington Irving   **E** painting

WHEN DID IT HAPPEN?

List the following events in the order they happened by placing the letter of each event in the correct order.

16. _____ (first event)   **A** first clipper ship was designed

17. _____ (second event)   **B** invention of the telegraph

18. _____ (third event)   **C** invention of the steel plow

19. _____ (fourth event)   **D** George Bancroft's history of the United States was completed.

20. _____ (fifth event)   **E** American trade with China began.

WHERE DID IT HAPPEN?

Write the letter of the city in which each of the events below took place.

21. _____ This city had the first paid police force in the United States.   **A** Lowell, Massachusetts

22. _____ The *Tom Thumb* challenged a horse-drawn coach here.   **B** Boston, Massachusetts

23. _____ This city was where most of the immigrants arrived.   **C** Concord, Massachusetts

24. _____ Many mills where workers were on the job 12 to 13 hours were built here.   **D** Baltimore, Maryland

25. _____ Many New England writers lived in this village.   **E** New York City, New York

Chapter 15 Test

REVIEWING KEY WORDS

Write the letter of the correct word that is defined in each of the following descriptions.

1. _____ the right to vote	**A** suffrage	**B** temperance
2. _____ places where teachers were trained	**A** normal schools	**B** religious revivals
3. _____ the freeing of slaves	**A** abolition	**B** emancipation
4. _____ to improve or correct society's social problems	**A** reform	**B** utopian

CHECKING UP ON THE FACTS

For each of the two groups of words below write the letter of the correct answer for each of the following.

5. _____ Horace Mann	**A** She helped the mentally ill.
6. _____ Dorothea Dix	**B** He improved the lives of the handicapped.
7. _____ Lucretia Mott	**C** He improved education.
8. _____ William Lloyd Garrison	**D** He worked for the abolition of slavery.
9. _____ Thomas Gallaudet	**E** She worked for women's rights.
10. _____ The American Temperance Union	**A** an experiment in cooperative living
11. _____ The Philadelphia system	**B** an experiment for improving working conditions
12. _____ The Waltham system	**C** an organization to fight against alcoholism
13. _____ The Amana Society	**D** a meeting on women's rights
14. _____ The Seneca Falls Convention	**E** a plan for improving prison conditions

WHEN DID IT HAPPEN?

Write the letter of the answer that tells in which decade each of the following events took place.

15. _____ The Shakers came to America.
    A in the 1760's   **B** in the 1770's   **C** in the 1780's

16. _____ Brook Farm was established.
    A in the 1840's   **B** in the 1850's   **C** in the 1860's

17. _____ The first issue of *The Liberator* was published.
    A in the 1820's   **B** in the 1830's   **C** in the 1840's

18. _____ The American Anti-Slavery Society was formed.
    A in the 1820's   **B** in the 1830's   **C** in the 1840's

19. _____ Elijah Lovejoy was killed.
    A in the 1820's   **B** in the 1830's   **C** in the 1840's

20. _____ The Seneca Falls Convention was held.
    A in the 1820's   **B** in the 1830's   **C** in the 1840's

History of the American Nation

WHERE DID IT HAPPEN?

Write the letter of the answer that correctly completes each of the following sentences below.

A Indiana	**B** Vermont	**C** Illinois
D Massachusetts	**E** New York	

21. _____ The first normal school was established in ___?___.

22. _____ The utopian community of New Harmony was started in ___?___.

23. _____ John Noyes started the Oneida Community in Putney, ___?___.

24. _____ The Seneca Falls Convention met in the state of ___?___.

25. _____ Elijah Lovejoy was murdered in Alton, ___?___.

Chapter 16 Test

REVIEWING KEY WORDS

Write the letter of the answer that correctly defines each word.

1. _____ annex
A groups formed by citizens to help keep order and enforce the laws

2. _____ expansionists
B to add territory

3. _____ vigilantes
C Americans who supported the westward growth of the United States

CHECKING UP ON THE FACTS

Write the letter of the state or area that is described by each of the phrases below.

A Texas   B Oregon   C Mexican Cession
D California   E Utah

4. _____ "Fifty-four forty or fight!"

5. _____ The Mormon settled here.

6. _____ The Lone Star Republic

7. _____ The Bear Flag Republic

8. _____ The Treaty of Guadalupe Hidalgo

9. _____ The Forty-Niners arrived here

10. _____ "Remember the Alamo!"

Write the letter of the state or area in which each of these persons became famous.

A Texas   B Oregon   C Mexican Cession
D California   E Utah

11. _____ Brigham Young

12. _____ John Sutter

13. _____ Sam Houston

14. _____ Zachary Taylor

15. _____ Jason Lee

WHEN DID IT HAPPEN?

List the following events in the order they happened by placing the letter of each event in the correct order.

16. _____ (first event)
A settlement of the Oregon boundary dispute with Britain

17. _____ (second event)
B Gadsden Purchase

18. _____ (third event)
C declaration of independence by Texas

19. _____ (fourth event)
D Treaty of Guadalupe Hidalgo

20. _____ (fifth event)
E gold discovered in California

History of the American Nation

WHERE DID IT HAPPEN?

Write the letter of the place where each of these events happened.

21. _____ The Mormons established a desert community.

22. _____ Gold was discovered on the American River.

23. _____ Mountain men and missionaries blazed the first trails.

24. _____ The Austin family began an American colony.

25. _____ The United States paid $15 million for the Mexican Cession

A Oregon

B the territories known as California and New Mexico before the Mexican War

C California

D Texas

E Utah

First Semester Test

I. VOCABULARY REVIEW

Write the letter of the word that correctly completes each sentence below.

A colonies	D declaration	G representative	J veto
B constitution	E embargo	H revolution	
C culture	F nullify	I tariff	

1. _____ A ___?___ is a tax on goods brought into a country.

2. _____ When Andrew Jackson was President, he opposed South Carolina's attempt to reject, or ___?___ a law.

3. _____ The President has a right to ___?___ laws that are passed by Congress.

4. _____ The English established 13 ___?___ on the East Coast of North America.

5. _____ Thomas Jefferson wrote a ___?___ stating the reasons why the American colonies wanted their freedom from England.

6. _____ A ___?___ is a written plan of government.

7. _____ An ___?___ forbids ships to enter or leave a country's ports.

8. _____ The way of life of a group or society is called its ___?___.

9. _____ A ___?___ is a person elected to act for a large group of citizens.

10. _____ The overthrow of a government, often as a result of fighting, is called a ___?___.

II. REVIEWING THE FACTS

Write the letter of the answer that correctly completes each statement or correctly answers each question.

11. _____ Scientists believe the first people came to America from
   A Africa.
   B Asia.
   C Europe.
   D Australia.

12. _____ All of the following were Spanish explorers of the Americas *except*
   A Christopher Columbus.
   B Ponce de León.
   C Francisco Coronado.
   D Jacques Cartier.

13. _____ The first English colony in America was
   A Plymouth, Massachusetts.
   B Jamestown, Virginia.
   C Quebec.
   D Philadelphia, Pennsylvania.

14. _____ In which part of your book would you find the unit titles, chapter, and section titles?
   A Index
   B Glossary
   C Table of Contents
   D Title Page

15. _____ Tobacco and rice plantations were found in the ___?___ Colonies.
   A New England
   B Middle
   C Southern
   D Western

16. _____ As a result of the French and Indian War, which one of the following nations lost land in North America?
   A France
   B England
   C Spain
   D Russia

17. _____ Which of the following events helped to cause the American Revolution?
  A The Boston Massacre.   C The Boston Tea Party.
  B The tax laws passed by Parliament.   D All of the above.

18. _____ The Declaration of Independence was signed in the year
  A 1763.   C 1783.
  B 1776.   D 1812.

19. _____ The Constitution provided that
  A slavery was no longer allowed in the United States.
  B each state could print its own money.
  C the Executive, Legislative, and Judicial branches of government were created.
  D states could declare a law unconstitutional.

20. _____ The Bill of Rights guarantees
  A freedom of speech.   C freedom of the press.
  B freedom of religion.   D all of these.

21. _____ The United States doubled its size with the purchase of
  A Louisiana.   C Florida.
  B Canada.   D Oregon.

22. _____ All of the following happened during the War of 1812 except
  A the burning of Washington, D.C.
  B the Lewis and Clark Expedition.
  C the writing of the Star-Spangled Banner.
  D the Battle of Lake Erie.

23. _____ The man who was President during the War of 1812 was
  A James Madison.   C Andrew Jackson.
  B James Monroe.   D John Q. Adams.

24. _____ The Monroe Doctrine stated that European nations
  A could not start new colonies in the Americas.
  B could not interfere with governments of independent countries.
  C could keep the colonies they already had in the Americas.
  D all of these.

25. _____ Which one of the following events happened first?
  A Louisiana Purchase   C Monroe Doctrine
  B War of 1812   D Ratification of the Constitution

26. _____ The first person from the West to be elected President was
  A George Washington.   C Andrew Jackson.
  B Thomas Jefferson.   D James Monroe.

27. _____ The Battle of the Alamo was called the "Cradle of Texas Liberty" because
  A the battle fought there ended Texas' war with Mexico.
  B a small number of men fought to the death there with great bravery.
  C a Mexican Army was completely destroyed there and the leader captured.
  D none of these.

©Macmillan Publishing Co.

First Semester Test

28. _____ The territory which completed the boundaries of all the states in the continental United States was
    A Texas.   C the Gadsden Purchase.
    B Oregon.   D the Louisiana Purchase.

29. _____ The "Forty-Niners" moved to California in order to search for
    A buffalo.   C land.
    B gold.   D jobs.

30. _____ Andrew Jackson was responsible for all of the following *except*
    A granting the Supreme Court the power to declare laws unconstitutional.
    B preserving the Union during the Nullification crisis.
    C forcing the Indians to move west from their homelands.
    D fighting the Bank of the United States.

Read each sentence carefully. If the sentence is TRUE, write the letter A. If the sentence is FALSE, write the letter B.

31. _____ In mercantilism, colonies existed to increase the wealth and power of the parent countries.

32. _____ Only the French, English, and Spanish established colonies in the Americas.

33. _____ The lives of people living in the Northern, Middle, and Southern colonies were very similar.

34. _____ The Articles of Confederation provided a weak central government for the United States after the American Revolution.

35. _____ Tobacco became the most important crop grown in the South by the mid-1800's.

36. _____ John Paul Jones became a naval hero in the War of 1812.

37. _____ The Constitution can be changed by adding new parts, or amendments.

38. _____ During the early 1800's, reformers worked to abolish slavery, increase opportunities for women, and help many groups of Americans.

39. _____ The first successful American locomotive was put to use during the War of 1812.

40. _____ Samuel Morse invented the telegraph in 1844.

III. REVIEWING AMERICAN HISTORY

In your own words, answer each of the following questions.

1. Why did Europeans wish to come to the Americas during the 1400's and 1500's?

_____

_____

_____

_____

2. How did people's lives develop differently in the Northern, Middle, and Southern Colonies?

_____

_____

_____

_____

3. What actions were taken by the citizens of the United States to develop a strong government for the nation after the American Revolution?

_____

_____

_____

_____

4. What methods did the United States use to gain territory between 1783 and 1853?

_____

_____

_____

_____

5. How did reformers work to improve American life during the early 1800's?

_____

_____

_____

_____

©Macmillan Publishing Co.

Chapter 17 Test

REVIEWING KEY WORDS

Write the letter of the answer that correctly defines each term.

1. _____ underground railroad

    A all the jobs people do to make a living

2. _____ economic activities

    B the idea of letting people in each territory vote to decide on whether to allow slavery in their territory

3. _____ proviso

    C escape routes from the South to free states in the North

4. _____ secede

    D to leave the Union

5. _____ popular sovereignty

    E a special condition added to a bill or a treaty

CHECKING UP ON THE FACTS

Write the letter of the answer that correctly completes each statement or correctly answers each question below.

6. _____ Which of the following did *not* increase the differences between the North and South?
   A the Compromise of 1850   C the Dred Scott case
   B *Uncle Tom's Cabin*   D the raid on Harpers Ferry

7. _____ The North and South differed in all of the following *except*
   A economic activities.   C language.
   B slavery.   D secession.

8. _____ Which of the following is *true* about slavery?
   A Slaves were generally happy.
   B Only a small number of Southerners owned slaves.
   C Most slaves escaped from their owners.
   D Slave labor was not an important part of Southern life.

9. _____ Which political party was formed in the mid-1850's to oppose slavery?
   A the Whig Party   C the Republican Party
   B the Free-Soil Party   D the Constitutional Union Party

10. _____ Which of the following was *not* part of the Compromise of 1850?
   A The slave trade was ended in the District of Columbia.
   B The federal government would help catch runaway slaves.
   C California became a free state.
   D The Missouri Compromise was repealed.

11. _____ The Crittenden Compromise would have
   A guaranteed slavery where it already existed.
   B banned slavery in the territories acquired from Mexico.
   C granted popular sovereignty to all western territories.
   D none of these.

12. _____ Which of the following supported slavery?
   A Harriet Beecher Stowe   C Daniel Webster
   B John C. Calhoun   D John Mason

© Macmillan Publishing Co.

13. _____ A slave who went to court to fight for freedom—and lost—was
   A Harriet Tubman.   C Solomon Northrup
   B Dred Scott.   D George Fitzhugh.

14. _____ Abraham Lincoln's opponent in the 1858 Illinois debates on slavery was
   A Daniel Webster.   C John C. Breckinridge.
   B Stephen A. Douglas.   D John Bell.

15. _____ The person responsible for the 1859 attack on Harpers Ferry arsenal was
   A John Brown.   C John Mason.
   B John Bell.   D Dred Scott.

WHEN DID IT HAPPEN?

Write the letter of the year in which each of these events took place.

16. _____ Abraham Lincoln is elected.   A 1852

17. _____ The Dred Scott case is decided.   B 1854

18. _____ *Uncle Tom's Cabin* is published.   C 1857

19. _____ The Kansas-Nebraska Act is passed.   D 1860

20. _____ Confederate States of America is formed. E 1861

WHERE DID IT HAPPEN?

Write the letter of the state or territory that is described in each of the sentences below.

21. _____ This state became free as a result of the Compromise of 1850.   A Virginia

22. _____ This territory became a battleground between pro-slavery and
   anti-slavery forces as a result of an 1854 law.   B Kansas

23. _____ Harpers Ferry, where John Brown led a raid in 1859, was in this
   state.   C Alabama

24. _____ In this state the Confederate States of America was formed.   D Illinois

25. _____ This was the home state of Abraham Lincoln.   E California

Chapter 18 Test

REVIEWING KEY WORDS

Write the letter of the term that is correctly defined by each of the following descriptions.

A habeas corpus   **B** total war   **C** unconditional surrender
D bounty system   **E** emancipation

1. _____ Involving all of a nation's resources in fighting

2. _____ Giving freedom to slaves

3. _____ The right to appear in court before being put in jail

4. _____ Being forced to give up everything

5. _____ Offering money to army volunteers

CHECKING UP ON THE FACTS

Write the letter of the answer that correctly completes each statement or correctly answers each question below.

6. _____ The Confederate Constitution provided for all of the following *except*
   A citizens' right to own slaves.
   B a national draft law.
   C limits on federal spending.
   D strong states' rights.

7. _____ The President of the Confederacy was
   A Robert E. Lee.
   B Joseph Johnston.
   C Jefferson Davis.
   D George McClellan.

8. _____ The "border states" of Missouri, Kentucky, Delaware, and Maryland
   A seceded but did not join the Confederacy.
   B chose to stay in the Union.
   C abolished slavery and stayed in the Union.
   D none of the above.

9. _____ Which of the following was *not* part of the Union plan to win the war?
   A capture the Confederate capital
   B control the Mississippi River
   C stop Confederate trade with other nations
   D hold out until the Confederate army asked for peace

10. _____ Which of the following was an advantage of the South at the start of the war?
    A a large population
    B a well-organized railway system
    C a strong military tradition
    D industrial power

Write the letter of the name of the person who is described in each sentence below.

11. _____ She aided wounded soldiers on the battlefield.

A Dorothea Dix

12. _____ He commanded the Union troops in their march from Atlanta to Savannah, Georgia.

B Clara Barton

13. _____ He was the commander of the Confederate Army.

C William Sherman

14. _____ He was the Democratic presidential candidate in the election of 1864.

D Robert E. Lee

15. _____ She was Superintendent of Nurses for the federal government.

E George McClellan

WHEN DID IT HAPPEN?

List the following events in the order they happened by placing the letter of each event in the correct order.

16. _____ (first event)   **A** re-election of Abraham Lincoln

17. _____ (second event)   **B** Confederate surrender at Appomattox

18. _____ (third event)   **C** Emancipation Proclamation

19. _____ (fourth event)   **D** First Battle of Bull Run

20. _____ (fifth event)   **E** Battle of Gettysburg

WHERE DID IT HAPPEN?

Write the letter of the places where each of these events took place.

21. _____ This city became the capital of the Confederacy.

A Fort Sumter, South Carolina

22. _____ The first battle of the Civil War was fought here.

B Richmond, Virginia

23. _____ This battle gave Union troops control of the Mississippi

C Vicksburg, Mississippi

24. _____ At this battlefield Lincoln gave his most famous speech.

D Hampton Roads, Virginia

25. _____ A naval battle was fought between the *Monitor* and the *Virginia* here.

E Gettysburg, Pennsylvania

Chapter 19 Test

REVIEWING KEY WORDS

Write the letter of the answer that correctly completes each sentence.

A sharecroppers	**B** carpetbaggers	**C** scalawags
D impeached	**E** Black Codes	

1. _____ White Southerners who joined the Republican Party and supported Reconstruction were called ___?___ by former Confederates.

2. _____ One reason President Andrew Johnson was ___?___ by the House of Representatives was that he failed to uphold the Reconstruction Act.

3. _____ Northern Republicans who gained control of state governments in the South during Reconstruction were called ___?___.

4. _____ Farmers who pay for the rent of their land by giving part of their crops to the land-owners are called ___?___.

5. _____ Laws passed by Southern state governments to limit the rights and opportunities of former slaves were called ___?___.

CHECKING UP ON THE FACTS

Write the letter of the sentence that correctly describes each person.

6. _____ Thaddeus Stevens

7. _____ Edwin Stanton

8. _____ Ulysses S. Grant

9. _____ Blanche K. Bruce

10. _____ Rutherford B. Hayes

A He was chosen President as a result of the Compromise of 1877.

B He was one of the first black Americans elected to the Senate.

C This Secretary of War was fired by President Johnson.

D He was the leader of the Radical Republicans in Congress.

E This military hero was elected President in 1868.

Write the letter of the answer that correctly completes each sentence or correctly answers each question below.

11. _____ The final plans for Reconstruction of the Southern states were written by
   A President Lincoln.
   B President Johnson.
   C Congress.

12. _____ The Amnesty Act of 1872
   A required the President to get Congress's approval before firing a federal official.
   B set up military governments in the Southern states.
   C pardoned most former Confederate soldiers and officials.

13. _____ Which of the following was created to help former slaves?
   A Black Codes
   B Freedmen's Bureau
   C Ku Klux Klan

14. _____ Which amendment to the Constitution granted black Americans the right to vote?
   A the Thirteenth Amendment
   B the Fourteenth Amendment
   C the Fifteenth Amendment

15. _____ Which of the following was *not* part of the Compromise of 1877?
   A Only Northerners would be named to Hayes's Cabinet.
   B Southerners were to receive a share of patronage in federal jobs.
   C The Southern states were to receive funds for internal improvements.

WHEN DID IT HAPPEN?

Write the letter of the event that took place in each of the following years.

16. _____ 1865   **A** The Civil Rights Act was passed.

17. _____ 1866   **B** The Fifteenth Amendment was passed.

18. _____ 1868   **C** President Johnson was impeached.

19. _____ 1869   **D** The Hayes-Tilden election was disputed.

20. _____ 1876   **E** The Ku Klux Klan was founded.

WHERE DID IT HAPPEN?

Read each statement carefully. If it refers to the NORTH, write the letter A. If it refers to the SOUTH, write the letter B.

21. _____ It was the home of Radical Republicans.

22. _____ State governments there adopted Black Codes during Reconstruction.

23. _____ Many of its citizens were disenfranchised after the Civil War.

24. _____ Many people there felt the goals of black citizens had been achieved by 1876.

25. _____ Democrats there were determined to get rid of the Republicans.

Chapter 20 Test

REVIEWING KEY WORDS

Write the letter of the term that is defined in each of the following statements.

1. _____ Communities that grew because of the mines located nearby
   A boom towns   B cowtowns   C ghost towns

2. _____ A person who received a grant of land in the Great Plains
   A tycoon   B vaquero   C homesteader

3. _____ Planting crops that keep the soil moist as long as possible
   A dry farming   B wet farming   C bonanza farms

4. _____ Land that was set aside especially for Indians
   A lode   B open range   C reservation

5. _____ Special government aid, such as grants of land or money
   A nomads   B subsidies   C sinew

CHECKING UP ON THE FACTS

Read each statement carefully. If it is TRUE, write the letter A. If it is FALSE, write the letter B.

6. _____ The transcontinental railroads were built mostly by immigrants and Civil War veterans.

7. _____ Life in the small towns of the West was often difficult and violent.

8. _____ Settlers moved to the Great Plains to mine, ranch, and start farms.

9. _____ The problems of farmers on the Great Plains included bad weather, insect plagues, and lack of water and building materials.

10. _____ The Dawes Act allowed Indians to keep their ways of living and customs on Indian reservations.

Write the letter of the answer that correctly completes each of the following sentences.

11. _____ Barbed wire was invented by
    A Oliver Dalrymple.   B Joseph Glidden.   C Fred Wenner.

12. _____ The railway tycoon who became known as the "empire builder" was
    A James J. Hill.   B Leland Stanford. C Cornelius Vanderbilt.

13. _____ Joseph McCoy's cattle trail that went through the grasslands from Texas to Kansas was called the
    A Western Trail.   B Pecos.   C Chisholm Trail.

14. _____ The law that granted 160 acres of land to any citizen or to any person who intended to become a citizen was
    A the Dawes Act.   B the Homestead Act. C the Oklahoma Settlement Act.

15. _____ The long war between the Indians and settlers ended at the Battle of
    A Sand Creek.   B the Little Bighorn. C Wounded Knee.

WHEN DID IT HAPPEN?

Write the letter of the years in which each of the following events took place.

16. _____ The transcontinental railroad was completed.   **A** the 1860's

17. _____ Barbed wire was invented.   **B** the 1870's

18. _____ The frontier came to an end.   **C** the 1880's

19. _____ Wars with the Indians ended.   **D** the 1890's

20. _____ The Chisholm Trail was opened.

WHERE DID IT HAPPEN?

Write the letter of the answer that correctly completes each of the following sentences.

    A Promontory Point, Utah   **B** Virginia City, Nevada   **C** Abilene, Kansas
        D Oklahoma Territory   **E** the Bighorn River in Montana Territory

21. _____ One of the few battles won by the Indians took place at ___?___.

22. _____ The last "frontier" opened to settlement was in ___?___.

23. _____ ___?___ was a bustling mining community in the 1870's that became a ghost town in the 1880's.

24. _____ The cattle trail from Texas ended at a railroad station in ___?___, where cattle were loaded onto railroad cars.

25. _____ The transcontinental railroad was completed at ___?___.

© Macmillan Publishing Co.

Chapter 21 Test

REVIEWING KEY WORDS

Write the letter of the term that is defined in each of the following statements.

1. _____ The government's "hands-off" policy that supported business and industry
   A laissez-faire   B patent systems   C capital

2. _____ Large stores that offered many different kinds of goods for sale, such as clothing, furniture, and food
   A chain stores   B specialty shops   C department stores

3. _____ Business people who bring together all the elements needed for the growth of an industry
   A artisans   B stockholders   C entrepreneurs

4. _____ Total control over an industry
   A trust   B monopoly   C union

5. _____ Employers' system of breaking strikes by closing down factories so that striking workers have no jobs
   A merger   B lockout   C competition

CHECKING UP ON THE FACTS

Write the letter of the answer that correctly completes each sentence below.

6. _____ The telephone was invented by
   A Thomas Edison.   C. Alexander Graham Bell.
   B Cyrus Field.   D Frank Sprague.

7. _____ In the late 1800's transportation for city workers was provided by
   A subways.   C elevated railways.
   B trolleys.   D all of these.

8. _____ The first chain store in America was
   A The A & P.   C Sears Roebuck and Company.
   B Wanamaker's.   D R. H. Macy's.

9. _____ Aaron Montgomery Ward started a
   A department store.   C specialty shop.
   B chain store.   D mail-order house.

10. _____ America had all of the following advantages that helped the growth of business and industry *except*
    A government policies favoring business.   C people willing to invest in new business.
    B new inventions.   D a small labor supply.

11. _____ The entrepreneur of the meat-packing industry was
    A Andrew Carnegie.   C John D. Rockefeller.
    B Gustavus Swift.   D Cornelius Vanderbilt

12. _____ The first trust company formed in the United States was
    A Standard Oil.   C United States Steel.
    B National Biscuit.   D New York Central Railroad.

13. _____ The Bessemer process improved the method for producing
   A steel.   C petroleum.
   B electricity.   D biscuits.

14. _____ The union blamed for the Haymarket Affair was the
   A National Labor Union.   C Knights of Labor.
   B American Federation of Labor.   D National Trade Union.

15. _____ The major concerns of the working people during the last part of the 1800's were
   A low wages.   C lack of jobs.
   B job safety.   D all of the above.

WHEN DID IT HAPPEN?

List the following events in the order they happened by placing the letter of each event in the correct

answer blank below.

16. _____ (first event)   A The telephone was invented.

17. _____ (second event)   B The Knights of Labor was formed.

18. _____ (third event)   C The first trust company was established.

19. _____ (fourth event)   D Laying the first transatlantic cable was begun.

20. _____ (fifth event)   E The nation's first subway was opened.

WHERE DID IT HAPPEN?

Write the letter of the place where each of these events happened.

21. _____ Thomas Edison set up his laboratory here.   A Boston, Massachusetts

22. _____ The meat-packing industry was started here.   B Chicago, Illinois

23. _____ The first subway was built here.   C Menlo Park, New Jersey

24. _____ The steel industry was established here.   D Philadelphia, Pennsylvania

25. _____ Wanamaker's was a major department store   E Pittsburgh, Pennsylvania

   here.

© Macmillan Publishing Co.

318 _____

History of the American Nation

Chapter 22 Test

REVIEWING KEY WORDS

Write the letter of the answer that correctly completes each of the following statements.

1. _____ Rundown sections of cities are called
   A slums. **B** tenements. **C** cooperatives.

2. _____ Writers who wrote about the struggles of people against an unjust society and their own human weaknesses are called
   A romantics. **B** realists. **C** naturalists.

3. _____ A person trained to deal with the affairs of a city government is a
   A city boss. **B** commissioner. **C** city manager.

4. _____ People who design buildings are
   A immigrants. **B** architects. **C** reformers.

5. _____ Places set up in city neighborhoods to provide services and aid to the poor were
   A skyscrapers. **B** settlement houses. **C** environments.

REVIEWING THE FACTS

Read each statement carefully. If it is TRUE, write the letter A. If it is FALSE, write the letter B.

6. _____ Before 1896 most immigrants came to America from Northern and Western Europe.

7. _____ During the last half of the 1800's, farmers felt left out and looked down upon by others in American society.

8. _____ The Grange was only a social organization.

9. _____ Reformers were more successful in gaining political control of cities than in helping people in the slums.

10. _____ Realism was a major force in art and literature in the late 1800's.

Write the letter of the answer that correctly completes each of the following statements.

11. _____ The most famous local-color writer was
    A Theodore Dreiser. **C** Mark Twain.
    B Winslow Homer. **D** Henry James.

12. _____ Farmers' problems during the last half of the 1800's were caused by
    A insects. **C** bad weather.
    B low prices for crops. **D** all of these.

13. _____ The corrupt politicians who ruled New York City were known as
    A White City. **C** the Grange.
    B the Populists. **D** the Tweed Ring.

14. _____ The painter who became famous for realistic portraits of people was
    A Winslow Homer. **C** Mark Twain.
    B John Singer Sargent. **D** Jacob Riss.

15. _____ The first skyscraper was designed by
    A William Le Baron Jenney. **C** Oliver Kelley.
    B Jacob Riis. **D** Louis Sullivan.

WHEN DID IT HAPPEN?

Write the letter of the years in which each event happened.

A in the 1860's   **B** in the 1870's   **C** in the 1880's   **D** in the 1890's

16. _____ Immigrants began coming to America from southern and eastern Europe.

17. _____ The Statue of Liberty was presented to the United States from France.

18. _____ The Grange was founded.

19. _____ A worldwide depression in farm prices began.

20. _____ The Tweed Ring lost its control of New York City.

WHERE DID IT HAPPEN?

Write the letter of the place where each of these events happened.

21. _____ The first skyscraper was built here.   **A** New York

22. _____ An official immigration center was established here.   **B** San Francisco

23. _____ First permanent lodge of the Grange was established here.   **C** White City

24. _____ A small model city was built here.   **D** Chicago

25. _____ Chinese immigrants created a "Chinatown" here.   **E** Ellis Island

Chapter 23 Test

REVIEWING KEY WORDS

Read each of the following sentences. If the underlined term is used correctly, write the letter A. If it is not used correctly, write the letter B.

1. _____ A monopoly is an organization that owns all of the stock in many companies.

2. _____ People who receive Civil Service jobs must pass a test to show that they are able to do this work.

3. _____ The gold standard required that all paper money printed in the U.S. must be backed by gold.

4. _____ The nationalized company is taken away from its owners and placed under government control.

5. _____ A graduated income tax taxes everyone equally, no matter how much income they earn.

CHECKING UP ON THE FACTS

Write the letter of the statement that correctly describes each President.

6. _____ Rutherford B. Hayes   **A** The only President elected to two non-consecutive terms.

7. _____ James Garfield   **B** He was assassinated by a young office seeker.

8. _____ Chester A. Arthur   **C** The Pendleton Act to reform Civil Service was passed when he was President.

9. _____ Grover Cleveland   **D** He conducted a "front porch" campaign in the election of 1896.

10. _____ William McKinley   **E** His election ended Reconstruction.

Write the letter of the answer that correctly completes each sentence or correctly answers each question below.

11. _____ Which of the following was organized by Samuel Dodd?
    A the first trust   C the Civil Service system
    B the Populist Party   D the Silverites

12. _____ The "cross of gold" election campaign was conducted by:
    A James G. Blaine.   C William Jennings Bryan.
    B J. Pierpont Morgan.   D none of the above.

13. _____ The law which made it illegal to interfere with competition or to form organizations to control several companies was
    A the Pendleton Civil Service Act.   C the Interstate Commerce Act.
    B the Sherman Anti-Trust Act.   D the Sherman Silver Purchase Act.

14. _____ The major goal of the Populist Party was
  A the "Subtreasury Plan."
  B the adoption of a "silver standard."
  C helping farmers solve problems.
  D the popular election of Senators.

15. _____ President Cleveland attempted to solve the nation's gold crisis by
  A raising the tariff.
  B repealing the Sherman Anti-Trust Act.
  C adopting a silver standard.
  D borrowing gold from powerful bankers.

WHERE DID IT HAPPEN?

Write the letter of the answer that correctly completes each of the sentences below.

  A New York City   **B** Omaha, Nebraska   **C** Chicago, Illinois
      D St. Louis, Missouri   **E** Canton, Ohio

16. _____ The city where the Pullman Strike occurred was ___?___.

17. _____ ___?___ was the city where the first official convention of a new national party, the Populist Party, was held.

18. _____ ___?___ was the city where the Populist Party was first formed.

19. _____ In the election of 1896, the Republican candidate conducted a "front porch" campaign from the city of ___?___.

20. _____ The corrupt Tammany Hall machine controlled politics in ___?___.

WHEN DID IT HAPPEN?

Write the letter of the year in which each event took place.

21. _____ The Pullman Strike began.   **A** 1880

22. _____ The Populist Party was formed.   **B** 1881

23. _____ President Garfield was assassinated.   **C** 1883

24. _____ The first trust was set up.   **D** 1892

25. _____ The Pendleton Act was passed.   **E** 1894

Chapter 24 Test

REVIEWING KEY WORDS

Write the letter of the answer that correctly defines each of the following words.

1. _____ suffragists
2. _____ recall
3. _____ Prohibition
4. _____ muckrakers
5. _____ referendum

A to forbid the sale or use of alcoholic beverages

B the power to remove officials from office who do a poor job

C people who supported the right of women to vote

D reporters who wrote about the need to reform American society

E allows voters to place a proposed law on a ballot to be voted on

CHECKING UP ON THE FACTS

Write the letter of the name of the President who is described in each of the following sentences.

A Theodore Roosevelt   B William Taft   C Woodrow Wilson

6. _____ He was the candidate of the Bull Moose Party.

7. _____ He favored the passage of the income-tax amendment.

8. _____ He helped settle the coal miners' strike of 1902.

9. _____ He supported the Payne-Aldrich tariff.

10. _____ He helped reform the banking system and created the Federal Trade Commission.

Read each statement carefully. If it is TRUE, write the letter A. If it is FALSE, write the letter B.

11. _____ Woodrow Wilson was the first President to set aside land for a National Park system.

12. _____ The NAACP was founded by William E. B. DuBois.

13. _____ The Eighteenth Amendment granted women the right to vote.

14. _____ The Federal Reserve System established a commission to investigate monopoly trusts.

15. _____ The Sixteenth Amendment gave the federal government the power to create an income tax.

WHERE DID IT HAPPEN?

Write the letter of the state in which each of these events took place.

16. _____ Oregon
17. _____ Texas
18. _____ Virginia
19. _____ Wisconsin
20. _____ Illinois

A birthplace of the Bull Moose Party

B the first state that used the recall to remove officials from office

C the state in which the city manager system was first used

D the state that started the direct primary system

E the state in which the city commission form of government was first used

© Macmillan Publishing Co.

WHEN DID IT HAPPEN?

List the following events in the order they happened by placing the letter of each event in the correct order.

21. _____   A The income tax amendment was ratified.

22. _____   B Women gained the right to vote.

23. _____   C Theodore Roosevelt was elected President.

24. _____   D The NAACP was formed.

25. _____   E Woodrow Wilson was elected President.

Chapter 25 Test

REVIEWING KEY WORDS

Write the letter of the answer that correctly defines each word.

1. _____ imperialism
2. _____ neutrality
3. _____ protectorate
4. _____ isthmus
5. _____ diplomacy

A A policy of not taking sides in a dispute

B The way nations handle their relations with other nations

C A nation's desire to take over other lands.

D A narrow strip of land connecting two larger bodies of land

E A territory that is ruled by a more powerful nation

CHECKING UP ON THE FACTS

Write the letter of the answer that correctly completes each statement or correctly answers each question below.

6. _____ The Secretary of State responsible for the purchase of Alaska was
   A Walter Reed.   **B** William Seward.   **C** Daniel Webster.

7. _____ The first President of the Republic of Hawaii was
   A Liliuokalani.   **B** Sanford Dole.   **C** Victoriano Huerta.

8. _____ Which of the following was *not* a cause of the Spanish-American War?
   A Newspaper stories about events in Cuba
   B The sinking of the *Maine*
   C "Big Stick" diplomacy

9. _____ General "Blackjack" Pershing commanded black American troops in
   A Cuba.   **B** Mexico.   **C** both Cuba and Mexico.

10. _____ Which nation rebelled against American rule after the Spanish-American War?
    A The Philippines.   **B** Puerto Rico.   **C** Cuba.

11. _____ Equal trading rights for all nations in China were guaranteed by the
    A "Open Door" Policy.   **B** Platt Amendment.   **C** "Gentlemen's Agreement."

12. _____ The Russian-Japanese War was ended with the help of President
    A Roosevelt.   **B** Taft.   **C** Wilson.

13. _____ The nation of Panama was originally part of
    A Mexico.   **B** Nicaragua.   **C** Colombia.

14. _____ The engineer who directed the building of the Panama Canal was
    A George Goethals.   **B** William Gorgas.   **C** Walter Reed.

15. _____ Relations with other nations that were based on fair and honest dealings was called
    A "Big Stick Diplomacy.   **B** missionary diplomacy.   **C** imperialism.

WHERE DID IT HAPPEN?

Write the letter of the answer that correctly completes each of the sentences below.

  A Mexico   **B** Alaska   **C** Cuba   **D** China   **E** Hawaii

16. _____ ___?___ was annexed by the United States after it had been a Republic for seven years.

17. _____ The purchase of ___?___ was known as "Seward's Folly."

18. _____ The French challenged the Monroe Doctrine by sending troops to ___?___.

19. _____ The "Boxer Rebellion" was an attempt to drive all foreigners out of ___?___.

20. _____ ___?___ became an independent nation as a result of Spanish-American War.

WHEN DID IT HAPPEN?

Write the letter of the year in which each event took place.

21. _____ The Panama Canal was completed.   **A** 1867

22. _____ The Spanish-American War was fought.   **B** 1893

23. _____ Alaska was purchased from Russia.   **C** 1898

24. _____ The Roosevelt Corollary was established.   **D** 1905

25. _____ Americans in Hawaii overthrew the queen.   **E** 1914

Chapter 26 Test
REVIEWING KEY WORDS

Write the letter of the answer that correctly completes each statement.

A reparations   **B** mobilization   **C** an ultimatum
D contraband   **E** a balance of power

1. _____ European nations signed treaties to try to keep ___?___ in Europe by agreeing to defend each other in case of attack.

2. _____ ___?___ means preparing for war by ordering up troops and supplies of weapons.

3 _____ Neutral ships were forbidden to carry ___?___, or supplies of weapons to warring nations.

4. _____ A list of demands that must be met in order to avoid a conflict is called ___?___.

5. _____ ___?___ are payments that a defeated nation is required to make to pay for the cost of a war.

CHECKING UP ON THE FACTS

Write the letter of the answer that correctly completes each statement or correctly answers each question below.

6. _____ The causes of World War I include all of the following *except*
A nationalism.   **C** demilitarization.
B imperialism.   **D** treaties of friendship.

7. _____ Archduke Francis Ferdinand was assassinated in
A Russia.   **C** Germany.
B Serbia.   **D** France.

8. _____ Germany's plan for winning World War I was outlined in the
A Triple Entente.   **C** Schlieffen Plan.
B Sussex Pledge.   **D** none of these.

9. _____ Which of the following best describes U-boat warfare?
A U-boats had to use surprise attacks.
B U-boats warned enemy ships before attacking.
C U-boats were swift and heavily armed.
D U-boats respected the rights of neutral ships.

10. _____ Which of the following actions were taken by President Wilson to keep America out of war?
A Sent a representative to Europe to propose a peace conference to end the war.
B Ended all diplomatic relations with Germany.
C Warned Germany to end its submarine attacks.
D All of the above.

11. _____ Which one of the following statements is true?
A Black soldiers served in integrated units of the armed forces.
B More women worked in factories than ever before.
C Mexican Americans were subject to the draft.
D "Freedom of speech" was supported by an important Supreme Court decision.

History of the American Nation

12. _____ The job of the War Industries Board was to
  A mobilize ships, weapons, soldiers, and equipment to be sent to Europe.
  B organize food shipments to the Allied nations.
  C draft soldiers to fight in the war.
  D arrest anti-war protestors who violated the law.

13. _____ The Committee on Public Information was headed by
  A George Creel.   C. Edward House.
  B Bernard Baruch.   D Henry Cabot Lodge.

14. _____ American soldiers fought in which of the following battles?
  A The Second Battle of the Marne.   C The Meuse-Argonne campaign.
  B The Battle of St. Mihiel.   D All of the above.

15. _____ "Peace without victory" was the idea of
  A George Clemenceau.   C Woodrow Wilson.
  B David Lloyd George.   D Vittorio Orlando.

WHERE DID IT HAPPEN?

Write the letter of the nation that is described in each sentence.

A Germany   B Austria-Hungary   C Mexico
          D Russia   E Belgium

16. _____ Fighting on the Eastern Front ended when this nation withdrew from the war.

17. _____ Germany invaded this neutral nation in order to attack France.

18. _____ This nation was the first nation to declare war.

19. _____ This nation was forced to accept responsibility for starting World War I.

20. _____ The Zimmermann Note outlined a secret plan to have this nation declare war on the United States.

WHEN DID IT HAPPEN?

Write the letter of the year in which each event happened.

A 1914   B 1915   C 1917   D 1918   E 1919

21. _____ The armistice that ended World War I was signed.

22. _____ Congress rejected the League of Nations.

23. _____ The *Lusitania* was sunk.

24. _____ World War I began.

25. _____ The United States entered the war.

Chapter 27 Test
REVIEWING KEY WORDS

Write the letter of the answer that correctly defines each word.

1. _____ broker

   A agreements that companies used to fire workers who joined unions

2. _____ business

   B using a small downpayment to buy something

3. _____ quota

   C a person who sells stocks

4. _____ installment plan

   D a limit set on the number of immigrants to America

5. _____ "yellow dog" contracts

   E any commercial or industrial activity

CHECKING UP ON THE FACTS

Write the letter of the answer that correctly completes each sentence or answers each question below.

6. _____ The industry that led the way to the "boom times" of the 1920's was
   A construction.   **C** mining.
   B automobile.   **D** steel.

7. _____ The first "talking" motion picture was called
   A "The Jazz Singer."   **C** "Amos 'n' Andy."
   B "The Sultan of Swat." **D** "The A & P Gypsies."

8. _____ The gangster who "bootlegged," or sold illegal whiskey, during the 1920's was
   A Al Jolson.   **C** Al Capone.
   B Walter Johnson.   **D** Rudolph Valentino.

9. _____ All of these events took place during the 1920's *except*
   A The Sacco and Vanzetti case.
   B The Dempsey-Tunney fight.
   C The first jet plane crossed the Atlantic.
   D Young women, or flappers, became more independent.

10. _____ In the 1920's jazz became a popular form of
    A writing.   **C** sports.
    B music.   **D** painting.

11. _____ The President who died in office during the 1920's was
    A Woodrow Wilson.   **C** Calvin Coolidge.
    B Warren G. Harding.   **D** Herbert Hoover.

12. _____ The President who was known for his honesty, religious faith, and quiet life-style was
    A Woodrow Wilson.   **C** Calvin Coolidge.
    B Warren G. Harding.   **D** Herbert Hoover.

13. _____ Which of the following groups benefited the most from the booming American economy of the 1920's?
    A farmers   **C** immigrants
    B black Americans   **D** bankers

14. _____ All of these persons were members of the "lost generation" *except*
    A Sinclair Lewis.   **C** Edna St. Vincent Millay.
    B Ernest Hemingway.   **D** Andrew Mellon.

15. _____ People believed in the "boom economy" for all of these reasons *except*
    A Political and business leaders told Americans it would continue.
    B They did not understand how the nation's economy worked.
    C They believed that a sharp increase in immigration would result.
    D They wanted to believe in it.

WHERE DID IT HAPPEN?

Write the letter of the name of the place that correctly completes each sentence.

    A New Orleans   **B** Chicago   **C** St. Louis
           D New York   **E** Teapot Dome

16. _____ A government scandal involved oil reserves at ___?___, Wyoming.

17. _____ One of the world's largest stock exchanges is in the city of ___?___.

18. _____ The St. Valentine's Day Massacre took place in ___?___.

19. _____ Race riots between white and black citizens broke out in ___?___, Missouri.

20. _____ Jazz was a combination of blues and Dixieland music that began in the city of ___?___.

WHEN DID IT HAPPEN?

Write the letter of the year in which each event took place.

    A 1923   **B** 1924   **C** 1927   **D** 1928   **E** 1929

21. _____ President Harding died in office.

22. _____ Lindbergh flew across the Atlantic.

23. _____ The Stock Market crashed.

24. _____ Herbert Hoover was elected President.

25. _____ Calvin Coolidge was elected President.

© Macmillan Publishing Co.

Chapter 28 Test

REVIEWING KEY WORDS

Write the letter of the answer that correctly defines each word.

1. _____ Depression   **A** veterans who were seeking added pay for fighting in World War I

2. _____ charity   **B** aid to poor and needy people

3. _____ "Dust Bowl"   **C** workers refuse to work but stayed by their machines

4. _____ "Bonus Army"   **D** a sharp business downturn and hard times

5. _____ Sitdown strike   **E** the Great Plains area in the early 1930's

CHECKING UP ON THE FACTS

Read each statement carefully. If it is TRUE, write the letter A. If it is FALSE, write the letter B.

6. _____ Many banks were forced to close during the Depression because borrowers were unable to repay their loans.

7. _____ President Hoover did nothing to help the nation recover from the Depression.

8. _____ During FDR's two terms, the federal government regulated business and industry more than it ever had before.

9. _____ During his second term of office, FDR began more programs to help America recover from the Depression than during his first term.

10. _____ FDR was able to end the Depression.

Write the letter of the answer that correctly completes each sentence.

11. _____ The law which created a system of old-age pensions for American workers was
    A The Wagner Act.   **C** the Banking Act.
    B The Social Security Act.   **D** The Fair Labor Standards Act.

12. _____ Before becoming President, FDR served in all of these offices *except*
    A Vice-President.   **C** State Senator.
    B Governor.   **D** Assistant Secretary of the Navy.

13. _____ The government agency that created jobs for over 5 million Americans was the
    A FERA.   **C** PWA.
    B CCC.   **D** WPA.

14. _____ The "radio priest" who attacked the New Deal and FDR's recovery program was
    A Huey Long.   **C** John Davis.
    B Francis Townsend.   **D** Charles Coughlin.

15. _____ The Congress of Industrial Organizations (CIO) was created by
    A Harry Hopkins.   **C** John L. Lewis.
    B Al Smith.   **D** Mary McLeod Bethune.

WHERE DID IT HAPPEN?

Write the letter of the state in which each of these events took place.

        A Louisiana   **B** Tennessee   **C** Wisconsin
                D Michigan   **E** New York

16. _____ Dairy farmers dumped their milk rather than sell it at low prices.

17. _____ The TVA built dams and electric power plants here.

18. _____ FDR served as governor of this state.

19. _____ Huey Long was governor of this state.

20. _____ The sit-down strike was first used in this state.

WHEN DID IT HAPPEN?

Write the letter of the year in which each event took place.

      A 1932   **B** 1933   **C** 1935   **D** 1936   **E** 1937

21. _____ FDR was first elected President.

22. _____ The TVA was established.

23. _____ The Social Security Act was passed.

24. _____ FDR's court-packing plan failed.

25. _____ FDR was elected to a second term.

Chapter 29 Test

REVIEWING KEY WORDS

Write the letter of the word that is defined by each of the following descriptions.

A sonar	**B** dictator	**C** rationing
D ultimatum	**E** concentration camps	

1. _____ Limiting the amount of goods or food that people may buy.

2. _____ Places where Jews and enemies of the Germans were sent during World War II.

3. _____ Electronic device used to find submarines.

4. _____ A final demand that an enemy nation surrender.

5. _____ A leader who holds complete power over the people.

CHECKING UP ON THE FACTS

Write the letter of the answer that correctly completes each statement.

6. _____ The Axis nations in World War II included
   A Germany.   C. Japan.
   B Italy.   D all of these.

7. _____ All of these statements about the Axis nation dictatorships are true *except*
   A One person or a small group had all the power.
   B The people had only those rights the government allowed them to have.
   C The people were free to criticize the leader's decisions.
   D The government wanted to add more territory to the nation.

8. _____ All of these lands were conquered by the Nazi armies *except*
   A Soviet Union.   C Poland.
   B Czechoslovakia.   D France.

9. _____ The leader of Great Britain during most of World War II was
   A Clement Atlee.   C Winston Churchill.
   B Bernard Montgomery.   D Dwight Eisenhower.

10. _____ The Japanese followed up their victory at Pearl Harbor by capturing
   A Australia.   C Manchuria.
   B Alaska.   D the Philippines.

11. _____ The Japanese navy was stopped for the first time at the Battle of
   A Midway.   C Iwo Jima.
   B Coral Sea.   D Leyte Gulf.

12. _____ The Axis threat in North Africa was stopped at the Battle of
   A Stalingrad.   C El Alamein.
   B Yalta.   D Cairo.

13. _____ *Operation Overlord* was the code name for the Allied invasion of
   A Sicily.   C Italy.
   B France.   D Germany.

14. _____ The conference at which Allied leaders agreed to bring Nazi war criminals to trial was
   A Nuremberg.   C Potsdam.
   B San Francisco.   D Normandy.

15. _____ During World War II, more American women than ever before were
   A working in factories.   C members of the League of Nations.
   B soldiers in battle.   D emigrants to Europe.

WHERE DID IT HAPPEN?

Write the letter of the nation that is described in each of the statements below.

   A Poland   B Japan   C Ethiopia
            D the Soviet Union   E Austria

16. _____ World War II began with the German invasion of ___?___.

17. _____ ___?___ signed a treaty with the Germans which Hitler broke by invading that nation a year later.

18. _____ The first atomic bomb was dropped on ___?___.

19. _____ In 1938 Hitler annexed ___?___ because he claimed most of the people there were Germans.

20. _____ In 1935 Italy conquered the African nation of ___?___.

WHEN DID IT HAPPEN?

Write the letter of the event that happened first in each of these groups of three events.

21. _____ The enemy attack on: A Poland   B China   C Soviet Union

22. _____ The surrender of: A Italy   B Germany   C Japan

23. _____ The bombing of: A Hiroshima   B Nagasaki   C Pearl Harbor

24. _____ The Allied invasion of: A Italy   B France   C North Africa

25. _____ The Battle of: A Coral Sea   B Midway   C Leyte Gulf

Chapter 30 Test

REVIEWING KEY WORDS

Write the letter of the answer that correctly defines each word.

1. _____ satellites

2. _____ inflation

3. _____ standard of living

4. _____ Cold War

5. _____ Iron Curtain

A a conflict without fighting or using weapons

B nations controlled by the Soviet Union

C symbol of Europe's division into free and Soviet-controlled nations

D quality of people's lives

E a rapid increase in the prices of goods and services

CHECKING UP ON THE FACTS

Write the letter of the answer that correctly completes each sentence below.

6. _____ After World War II a major feature of America's economy was
A strikes by unions for higher wages.
B continuing inflation.
C a higher standard of living.
D all of the above.

7. _____ One of the biggest changes in family life after World War II was brought about by
A television.   C radio.
B plastic.   D nylon.

8. _____ The organization which worked for equal rights by bringing lawsuits into court was
A NAACP.   C NATO.
B CORE.   D none of these.

9. _____ The first black person to become a major league baseball player was:
A Branch Rickey.   C Jackie Robinson.
B Cornelius Charlton. D Ted Williams.

10. _____ The 1947 law passed to limit the power of labor unions was the
A Legislative Reorganization Act.   C Housing Act.
B Taft-Hartley Act.   D Twenty-second Amendment.

11. _____ The policy of containing communism became known as the
A NATO.   C Warsaw Pact.
B Point Four Program. D Truman Doctrine.

12. _____ The leader of Senate investigations of disloyal Americans was
A Branch Rickey.   C Cornelius Charlton.
B Joseph McCarthy.   D Matthew Ridgeway.

13. _____ The commander of the UN troops at the start of the Korean War was
A Matthew Ridgeway.   C Dwight Eisenhower.
B Douglas MacArthur.   D Thomas Dewey.

14. _____ All of the following are true of the Korean War *except*
          A Communist North Korea invaded South Korea.
          B The UN sent troops to aid South Koreans.
          C North and South Korea became one nation when the war ended.
          D Nearly 34,000 Americans died in the war.

15. _____ President Truman's program providing equal rights for all Americans was called the
          A New Deal.   **C** New Frontier.
          B Square Deal.   **D** Fair Deal.

WHERE DID IT HAPPEN?

Write the letter of the answer that correctly completes each statement.

A Greece   **B** Canada   **C** Germany   **D** Turkey   **E** Yugoslavia

16. _____ The Soviet Union backed rebels who tried to gain control of ____?____.

17. _____ and ____?____.

18. _____ The United States helped Josef Tito, the leader of ____?____, keep that country independent of the Soviet Union.

19. _____ The divided country of ____?____ became a symbol of the Cold War.

20. _____ The United States and ____?____ were two North American nations that belonged to NATO.

WHEN DID IT HAPPEN?

Write the letter of the year in which each of these events happened.

        A 1947   **B** 1948   **C** 1949   **D** 1950   **E** 1951

21. _____ Color television was introduced.

22. _____ The first black player was on a major league baseball team.

23. _____ Harry S. Truman was elected President.

24. _____ NATO was formed.

25. _____ The Korean War began.

©Macmillan Publishing Co.

Chapter 31 Test

REVIEWING KEY WORDS

Write the letter of the term that is correctly defined in each of these descriptions.

1. _____ Millions of Americans buying the goods that factories produced

2. _____ Life styles in all parts of the nation becoming similar

3. _____ Smaller communities surrounding large cities

4. _____ A non-violent protest in which people refuse to leave their seats

5. _____ A gathering of leaders of the superpowers

A Mass culture

B Mass consumption

C Suburbs

D Summit meeting

E Sit-in

CHECKING UP ON THE FACTS

Write the letter of the answer that correctly completes each statement or correctly answers each question below.

6. _____ Progress in technology and increased productivity led to
   A increased consumption.
   B more leisure time.
   C people moving to the suburbs.
   D all of these.

7. _____ Most Americans were members of a class of income earners called the
   A middle class.
   B upper class.
   C lower class.
   D none of these.

8. _____ The most popular leisure-time activity of the 1950's was
   A taking part in organized sports.
   B working with computers.
   C going shopping for consumer goods.
   D watching television.

9. _____ The NAACP worked to end segregation mainly by
   A holding marches.
   B bringing lawsuits in the courts.
   C staging peaceful protests.
   D starting riots.

10. _____ A black Southerner who refused to move from a seat on an Alabama bus was
   A Martin Luther King, Jr.
   B Rosa Parks.
   C Earl Warren.
   D Jesse Jackson.

11. _____ President Eisenhower's actions involving civil rights included
   A enforcing federal laws.
   B speaking out for civil rights.
   C speaking out against civil rights.
   D none of the above.

12. _____ The Soviet Union gained power and influence in all of these nations *except*
   A Hungary.
   B Cuba.
   C East Germany.
   D Portugal.

13. _____ The person who became the new leader of the Soviet Union during the 1950's was
   A Fidel Castro.
   B Ho Chi Minh.
   C Nikita Khrushchev.
   D Chiang Kai-shek.

14. _____ The United States followed a policy of containment in all of these areas *except*
    A South Vietnam.   C Asia.
    B Middle East.   D Canada.

15. _____ The 1960 summit meeting was cancelled because of
    A the development of the H-bomb.
    B the launching of Sputnik.
    C the Soviet capture of an American spy plane.
    D the Communist takeover of Cuba.

WHERE DID IT HAPPEN?

Write the letter of the answer that correctly completes each of the sentences below.

    A Little Rock, Arkansas   B Levittown, N.Y.   C Taiwan
        D Topeka, Kansas   E Montgomery, Alabama

16. _____ A bus boycott led to an end to segregation on public transportation in the city of ___?___.

17. _____ ___?___ is an example of a new suburb of the 1950's.

18. _____ A Supreme Court case involving the Board of Education of ___?___ ruled that segregation in public schools must be ended.

19. _____ The Nationalist Chinese fled to the island of ___?___ in 1949.

20. _____ Federal troops were sent to ___?___ to enforce the law and to allow students to attend Central High School.

WHEN DID IT HAPPEN?

Write the letter of the year in which each of these events happened.

21. _____ The A.F. of L. merged with C.I.O.   A 1955

22. _____ The summit meeting collapsed.   B 1957

23. _____ Federal troops were sent to Arkansas to enforce school desegregation.   C 1958

24. _____ A Communist government was established in Cuba.   D 1959

25. _____ The first American satellite was sent into space.   E 1960

Chapter 32 Test

REVIEWING KEY WORDS

Write the letter of the word that is correctly defined in each of the following descriptions.

1. _____ Surprise attack tactics used by the Viet Cong in the Vietnam War

   A "hit and run"   **B** "search and destroy"

2. _____ Americans who opposed the Vietnam War

   A hawks   **B** doves

3. _____ Nixon's plan to end America's involvement in Southeast Asia

   A demobilization   **B** Vietnamization

4. _____ Term used to describe the Presidency of John Kennedy

   A New Frontier   **B** Great Society

5. _____ A Soviet space explorer

   A cosmonaut   **B** astronaut

CHECKING UP ON THE FACTS

Write the letter of the answer that correctly completes each statement.

6. _____ As President, John F. Kennedy called on Americans to solve the problems of
   A poverty.   **C** social injustice.
   B disease.   **D** all of the above.

7. _____ During Kennedy's Presidency, the United States and the Soviet Union competed in all of these *except*
   A space.   **C** Germany.
   B Cuba.   **D** Canada.

8. _____ The program established by Kennedy to send Americans to help people of developing nations learn new skills and knowledge was called
   A VISTA.   **C** The Alliance For Progress.
   B the Peace Corps.   **D** Upward Bound.

9. _____ A form of protest used to end segregation on buses and other transportation facilities was
   A freedom rides.   **C** boycotts.
   B sit-ins.   **D** riots.

10. _____ James Meredith helped to achieve the desegregation of
   A colleges.   **C** restaurants.
   B buses.   **D** courts.

11. _____ President John F. Kennedy was assassinated by
   A Robert C. Weaver.   **C** Lee Harvey Oswald.
   B Earl Warren.   **D** James Earl Ray.

12. _____ The law passed by Congress to end discrimination in business and education was the
   A Voting Rights Act of 1965.   **C** Economic Opportunities Act.
   B Civil Rights Act of 1964.   **D** Elementary and Secondary Education Act.

13. _____ The unsuccessful Republican candidate for the Presidency in 1964 was
   A Richard Nixon.   **C** Hubert Humphrey.
   B Lyndon Johnson.   **D** Barry Goldwater.

14. _____ President Johnson increased American involvement in the Vietnam War by
   A sending more American troops to Vietnam.
   B sending more American planes to Vietnam.
   C sending more supplies to Vietnam.
   D signing a treaty with Mexico.

15. _____ The main objection to the Vietnam War was the
   A high cost of weapons.
   B terrible loss of American lives.
   C slowdown in civil rights reform.
   D danger to our Allies.

WHERE DID IT HAPPEN?

Write the letter of the city that is described by each of these events.

16. _____ The assassination of John F. Kennedy took place here.

A Los Angeles, California

17. _____ The assassination of Martin L. King, Jr. took place here.

B Birmingham, Alabama

18. _____ The Twenty-third Amendment gave citizens there the right to vote.

C Washington, D.C.

19. _____ Peaceful demonstrations here led to many arrests and the jailing of Dr. King.

D Dallas, Texas

20. _____ Riots occurred in the black neighborhood here known as "Watts."

E Memphis, Tennessee

WHEN DID IT HAPPEN?

Write the letter of the event that happened first in each of the following pairs of events.

21. _____ A The assassination of Martin L. King, Jr.   B The assassination of John F. Kennedy

22. _____ A The "Great Society"   B The "New Frontier"

23. _____ A The Gulf of Tonkin Resolution   B Nationwide protests against the Vietnam War

24. _____ A The end of the Vietnam War   B The election of Richard Nixon

25. _____ A The Voting Rights Act was passed   B The Civil Rights Act was passed

©Macmillan Publishing Co.

Chapter 33 Test

CHECKING UP ON THE FACTS

Write the letter of the name of the person who is described in each statement.

1. _____ The first woman appointed to the Supreme Court.   **A** Neil Armstrong

2. _____ The first person to walk on the moon.   **B** Betty Friedan

3. _____ The first President to resign from office.   **C** Gerald Ford

4. _____ The first person to serve as Vice-President and then as President without being elected.   **D** Sandra O'Connor

5. _____ The founder of the National Organization for Women.   **E** Richard Nixon

Choose the letter of the answer that correctly completes each sentence.

6. _____ The agency that organized America's first space flight to the moon with humans was
    A NASA.   **C** GNP.
    B NOW.   **D** NATO.

7. _____ While he was President, Richard Nixon improved American relations with
    A Communist China   **C** both A and B.
    B Soviet Union.   **D** neither A nor B.

8. _____ Nixon resigned the office of President because
    A he favored Congress's investigation of Watergate.
    B he knew he no longer had enough Congressional support to stay in office
    C the Vice-President had been accused of taking bribes.
    D his foreign policy had failed.

9. _____ The person chosen as the Vice-President after Nixon's resignation was
    A Spiro Agnew.   **C.** George Bush.
    B Hubert Humphrey.   **D** Nelson Rockefeller.

10. _____ All of the following were problems within the United States that were faced by President Carter *except*
    A inflation.   **C** hostage crisis.
    B energy crisis.   **D** unemployment.

11. _____ President Carter's greatest foreign policy achievement was
    A negotiating a treaty with Panama.
    B ending the fighting between Israel and Egypt.
    C boycotting the 1980 Olympics.
    D ending the Cold War.

12. _____ One goal of Ronald Reagan's "Economic Recovery" plan was to
    A increase the rate of unemployment.
    B help the economy to grow by encouraging business activity.
    C help the developed nations of the world.
    D none of the above.

13. _____ President Reagan was responsible for
   A ending the air traffic-controllers strike.
   B solving the nation's energy problems.
   C paying the debts of developing nations.
   D shifting the population of the United States.

14. _____ The largest minority group in the United States today is
   A Hispanic Americans.   **C** Black Americans.
   B American Indians.   **D** Handicapped Americans.

15. _____ All of the following statements are true *except*
   A Unemployment has been a serious problem in recent years.
   B More Americans are moving to urban areas than ever before.
   C The buying power of Americans nearly doubled during the 1970's and 1980's.
   D The computer has not been used to help produce goods and services.

WHERE DID IT HAPPEN?

Write the letter of the answer that correctly completes each of the sentences below.

   A Communist China   **B** Afghanistan   **C** Iran
              D Egypt   **E** Mexico

16. _____ President Reagan played a leading role at a conference in ___?___ at which problems of developing nations were discussed.

17. _____ President Carter helped negotiate a treaty between Israel and ___?___.

18. _____ A boycott of the 1980 Olympics was designed to protest the Soviet Union's invasion of ___?___.

19. _____ The government of ___?___ held 52 Americans hostage for 444 days.

20. _____ President Nixon's visit to ___?___ helped ease the tensions of the Cold War.

WHEN DID IT HAPPEN?

List the following events in the order they happened by placing the letter of each event in the correct order.

21. _____ (first event)   **A** Nixon resigned as President.

22. _____ (second event)   **B** Humans first walked on the moon.

23. _____ (third event)   **C** Jimmy Carter was elected President.

24. _____ (fourth event)   **D** President Reagan sent American troops to Lebanon.

25. _____ (fifth event)   **E** The first American President visited the Soviet Union.

Second Semester Test

I. VOCABULARY REVIEW

Write the letter of the word that correctly completes each sentence below.

A abolitionists   D computer   G détente   J strike
B astronaut   E depression   H immigrants
C Cold War   F dictatorship   I neutrality

1. _____ One method used by union workers to gain their demands is to ___?___.

2. _____ ___?___ were people who worked to end slavery in the United States.

3. _____ ___?___ was a policy of improving relations between the United States and the Soviet Union.

4. _____ A person who is trained for American space flights is an ___?___.

5. _____ ___?___ are people who move to a new country where they were not born.

6. _____ A nation's policy of not taking part in a conflict or war is called ___?___.

7. _____ A ___?___ is a machine that is able to process information very rapidly and direct the work of other machines.

8. _____ The ___?___ began after World War II, when the United States and the Soviet Union became rivals for world leadership.

9. _____ In a ___?___ many businesses are forced to close and many workers lose their jobs.

10. _____ A nation ruled by one person, or one political party, where the people have few rights is called a ___?___.

II. REVIEWING FACTS

Write the letter of the answer that correctly completes each statement or correctly answers each question.

11. _____ Which of the following helped cause the Civil War?
    A slavery
    B disputes over tariffs
    C disagreements over the right of a state to secede
    D all of these.

12. _____ The President of the Confederate States of America during the Civil War was
    A Jefferson Davis.   C Robert E. Lee.
    B Abraham Lincoln.   D Andrew Jackson.

13. _____ Which of the following events happened last?
    A General Lee's Surrender at Appomattox.
    B Assassination of Abraham Lincoln.
    C Impeachment of Andrew Johnson.
    D The Emancipation Proclamation.

14. _____ After the Civil War, gold and cheap land attracted settlers to the
    A reconstructed Southern states.   C Oregon Territory.
    B Great Plains.   D Southwest.

© Macmillan Publishing Co.

15. _____ Which of the following contributed to America's development as an industrial nation?
A plentiful natural resources
B new inventions
C both A and B
D neither A nor B

16. _____ The inventor best known for his invention of electric light was
A Alexander Graham Bell.
B Cyrus W. Field.
C Thomas A. Edison.
D Henry Ford.

17. _____ Which of the following methods was not used to increase companies' control of an entire business?
A monopolies
B unions
C trusts
D corporations

18. _____ The goals of the Progressive movement included helping
A women get the right to vote.
B aliens return to their homelands.
C big business influence government policies.
D prevent passage of an income tax law.

19. _____ As a result of the Spanish-American War, the United States acquired all of the following _except_
A Puerto Rico.
B Alaska.
C Guam.
D Philippines.

20. _____ The Panama Canal opened in the year
A 1904.
B 1912.
C 1914.
D 1917.

21. _____ The United States became involved in World War I because
A Allied propaganda forced Americans to abandon neutrality.
B Germany tried to get Brazil to fight against the United States.
C Germany's submarines sank many American ships.
D An Austrian prince and his wife were assassinated.

22. _____ The Treaty of Versailles, which ended World War I,
A blamed Germany for starting the war.
B established the League of Nations.
C was never approved by the United States.
D all of these.

23. _____ Which of the following is true of the 1920's?
A Most Americans shared in America's growing prosperity.
B The government increased its control of big business.
C President Harding was assassinated.
D Prohibition was repealed.

24. _____ All of the following nations established dictatorships before World War II _except_
A Russia.
B Germany.
C Italy.
D France.

25. _____ The President of the United States during World War II was
A Woodrow Wilson.
B Herbert Hoover.
C Franklin Roosevelt.
D Dwight Eisenhower.

©Macmillan Publishing Co.

Second Semester Test

26. _____ An important result of World War II was
   A the creation of the United Nations.
   B the increased power of France and England.
   C the end of the Communist government in Russia.
   D the annexation of more territory by Germany.

27. _____ Which of the following was intended to unite Western European nations against the danger of a Communist attack?
   A Truman Doctrine   C Warsaw Pact
   B NATO   D Marshall Plan

28. _____ All of the following were conflicts in the Cold War *except*
   A the Cuban Missile Crisis.   C the Vietnam War.
   B the Korean War.   D the energy crisis.

29. _____ Who was the first President in American history to resign from office?
   A Spiro Agnew   C Gerald Ford
   B Richard Nixon   D Jimmy Carter

30. _____ All of the following non-violent methods were used to gain civil rights for black Americans *except*
   A court cases.   C riots.
   B boycotts.   D sit-ins.

Read each sentence carefully. If the sentence is TRUE, write the letter A. If the sentence is FALSE, write the letter B.

31. _____ Before the Civil War, most white Southerners owned slaves.

32. _____ Many immigrants came to America to start a new life and find freedom to worship and to work as they wished.

33. _____ Miners, ranchers, and farmers helped settle the Great Plains.

34. _____ The Pendleton Civil Service Act of 1883 changed the method of selecting people for government jobs.

35. _____ The Nineteenth Amendment granted women the right to vote.

36. _____ The Great Depression began with the Stock Market Crash of 1929.

37. _____ Many of the programs established during the New Deal, including the Social Security system, still operate today.

38. _____ The first atomic bomb was dropped on Nuremberg, Germany in 1945.

39. _____ Both John F. Kennedy and Martin Luther King, Jr., were assassinated during the 1960's.

40. _____ The United States helped South Vietnam establish an independent nation after defeating North Vietnam in 1973.

III. REVIEWING AMERICAN HISTORY

In your own words, answer each of the following questions.

1. Why was the North able to defeat the South in the Civil War?

_____

_____

_____

_____

2. What problems were created by the growth of American cities during the late 1800's?

_____

_____

_____

_____

3. How did the United States gain territories outside its continental boundaries?

_____

_____

_____

_____

4. What were the major events that led to World War II?

_____

_____

_____

_____

5. How has the United States contributed to the world's knowledge of space and space flight?

_____

_____

_____

_____

ANSWER KEY FOR WORKSHEETS

Worksheet 1, Chapter 1   **1.** Index; **2.** Table of Contents; **3.** Glossary; **4.** Index; **5.** Table of Contents; **6.** Glossary; **7.** Table of Contents; **8.** At the end of the Table of Contents; **9. 1.** People Move into North America, **2.** America Has Many Regions, **3.** Indians Develop Many Different Cultures; **10. 2.** America Has Many Regions

Worksheet 2, Chapter 1

Mayans Yucatan Peninsula; hot jungle with rainy season (good for farming)

Zuñi and Hopi High desert; some rainfall (good for farming with irrigation)

Apache Great Basin; high, rocky, barren land (not good for farming)

Iroquois Eastern Woodlands, hot summers; high rainfall (good for farming)

Aztecs Valley of Mexico; high moderate climate; well watered by runoff from mountains (good for farming)

Navajo High Desert; some rainfall (good for sheep raising)

Worksheet 3, Chapter 2   **1.** 5; **2.** Spain, England, Portugal, France, the Netherlands; **3.** France; **4.** 1579; **5.** the Netherlands; **6.** 1500; **7.** Verrazano and Cartier; **8.** Drake and Gilbert; **9.** 2 years; **10.** 120 years

Worksheet 4, Chapter 2

```
 1                    2            3      4
 S K R A E L I N G S  N  G  S      A      H
 A                    E            S      E
 5               6
 N O R S E       S    W            T      N
 T             O      F            R      R
 A             N    7 M  O N O P O L Y
 M             G    8 C  U            L
 A             H    C U  L
 R             O    O 9  D  I  A  S   B
 I            10    M     E
 A             C A L M    P
 I             I       N
 A          11 C A R A V E L
              S       N
            12 C R U S A D E R S
```

Worksheet 5, Chapter 3   Events should be organized in chronological order. Leaders of the events given are: 1521, Cortés; 1523, Cortés; 1532, Pizarro; 1542, Cabrillo; 1565, Menéndez de Avilés; 1609, Oñate; 1769, Portolá and Serra; 1774, Anza: **1.** 5; **2.** 1; **3.** 2; **4.** 253; **5.** California, Florida, and New Mexico

Worksheet 6, Chapter 3   Student maps can be checked against the map in Chapter 6 of the textbook to verify answers.

Worksheet 7, Chapter 4   **1.** Verrazano; **2.** Champlain; **3.** Cartier; **4.** 1st, Verrazano; 2nd, Cartier; 3rd, Champlain; **5.** Port Royal, Quebec, Montreal

Worksheet 8, Chapter 4   **Spain 1.** Florida, the Mississippi valley, and the Southwestern United States/United States, Mexico, Central American nations; **2.** Gold and silver; **3.** Answers will vary, but Indians generally were treated poorly. **4.** Quickly; many settlers came from Spain. **5.** Silver, gold, agricultural products; **6.** France and England

France 1. The St. Lawrence valley and the Mississippi valley/United States and Canada; **2.** Furs; **3.** Answers will vary, but Indians generally were treated fairly well. **4.** Slowly; only a few settlers were allowed to come from France. **5.** Furs; **6.** England

Worksheet 9, Chapter 5   **1.** b, **2.** c, **3.** a, **4.** b

Worksheet 10, Chapter 5   **1.** "the glory of God, the advancement of our Christian faith, and the honor of our king and country," **2.** "to keep order and to preserve and advance our goals," **3.** "to make and carry out just and equal laws from time to time as are necessary for the good of the colony" **4.** They all promise to obey the laws. **5.** Answers will vary.

Worksheet 11, Chapter 5   **1.** S, **2.** NE, **3.** M, **4.** S, **5.** M, **6.** NE, **7.** M. **8.** S, **9.** NE, **10.** M, **11.** S, **12.** M, **13.** S, **14.** M, **15.** M, **16.** NE, **17.** M, **18.** S, **19.** NE, **20.** S

Worksheet 12, Chapter 6

New England 1. Fish, timber, rum; **2.** Fishing, farming; **3.** Farming, household management; **4.** Answers will vary; **5.** Puritans; **6.** Elementary education for most children; colleges to train ministers

Middle Colonies 1. Grain, iron, furs; **2.** Farming; **3.** Farming, household management; **4.** Answers will vary; **5.** Church of England, Presbyterians, Quakers, Dutch Reformed; **6.** Some elementary education, colleges to train ministers

Southern Colonies 1. Tobacco, rice, indigo; **2.** Farming; **3.** Farming, household management; **4.** Answers will vary. **5.** Church of England; **6.** Not very much elementary education; one college in Virginia

Worksheet 13, Chapter 6   **1.** Manufactured goods; **2.** Seville and Cádiz; **3.** Veracruz, Porto Bello, and Cartagena; **4.** Silver, gold, and agricultural products like sugar, tobacco, and cocoa; **5.** Answers will vary.

Worksheet 14, Chapter 6   Monarch—Head of state; Parliament—Legislative body; House of Commons—Lower legislative house; House of Lords—Upper legislative house; Proprietor—Owner of the land of the colony by grant from the king; Colonial Governor—Head of state usually appointed by the king; House of Burgesses—Lower legislative house in Virginia; Colonial Assemblies—Lower house in many colonies that voted on taxes and oversaw the government; Governor's Council—Governor's advisory body; **1.** House of Commons; **2.** To vote on tax assessments; to oversee the government; **3.** The House of Lords; **4.** To advise the governor; **5.** Property owners who were members of the established church

Worksheet 15, Chapter 7   **1.** England, the Netherlands, Sweden, France, and Spain. **2.** 1650; **3.** England, France, and Spain; **4.** 1700; **5.** New York; **6.** Delaware, part of Pennsylvania; **7.** 1655; **8.** Answers will vary.

Worksheet 16, Chapter 7   **1.** a, **2.** a, **3.** b, **4.** c, **5.** c,

Worksheet 17, Chapter 7
Petition—Petitions from the colonial assemblies to the king and Parliament to end unjust taxation

boycott on tea and other British goods that
...o be taxed unjustly
...roperty—The Boston Tea Party **1, 2,** and **3.**
...ill vary.

Worksheet 18, Chapter 8   **1.** That all people are created
equal, are endowed by their Creator with certain unalienable
rights, that among these are life, liberty, and the pursuit of hap-
piness; **2.** Answers will vary. **3.** Most students will consider that
the injuries were serious enough. **4.** They petitioned for redress;
they appealed to the British people; **5.** From "We therefore, the
Representatives of the United States of America..., to "...and
that all political connection between them and the State of
Great Britain, is and ought to be totally dissolved"

Worksheet 19, Chapter 8
British Victories   June 1775, Battle of Bunker and Breed's Hill;
Dec. 1775-May 1776, Battle of Quebec; Aug.-Sept. 1776, Battle of
New York.
American Victories   May 1775, Battle of Fort Ticonderoga; Feb.
1776, Battle of Moore's Creek Bridge; Dec. 1776-Jan. 1777, Battle
of Trenton; Oct. 1777, Battle of Saratoga; 1777-1778, Winter at
Valley Forge; Oct. 1780, Battle of King's Mountain; Oct. 1781,
Battle of Yorktown

Worksheet 20, Chapter 8   **1.** a, **2.** b, **3.** b, **4.** c

Worksheet 21, Chapter 9   Answers will vary.

Worksheet 22, Chapter 9   **1.** Daniel Shays and the poor
farmers and debtors who joined him bring their protest to the
state supreme court in Springfield, Mass., in 1786. **2.** Daniel
Shays is the man at the right with one foot on the step. **3.** The
man standing at Daniel Shays left is the state official.
4. Answers will vary. **5.** Heavy taxes, the jailing of debtors, and
laws that favored rich creditors.

Worksheet 23, Chapter 9   **Preamble** Establish justice,
insure domestic tranquility, provide for the common defense,
promote the general welfare, and secure the blessings of liberty
to ourselves and our posterity.
Article 1. Section 1. Congress; House of Representatives,
Senate; **Section 2.** 2; **Section 3.** 2; 6; Vice President; tie; **Section
7.** Raising revenue; President; **Section 8.** Answers will vary. **Article 2. Section 1.** President; 4; **Section 2.** Answers will vary. **Article 3. Section 1.** A Supreme Court; inferior courts established by
Congress; **Section 2.** Answers will vary.

Worksheet 24, Chapter 9   **1.** L, **2.** E, **3.** J, **4.** L, **5.** L, **6.** L, **7.** E,
8. L, **9.** E, **10.** L, **11.** L, **12.** E, **13.** L, **14.** L, **15.** E, **16.** J, **17.** L, **18.** L,
19. E, **20.** E

Worksheet 25, Chapter 10   **1.** 1st Amendment, freedom of
speech; **2.** 4th Amendment, freedom from unreasonable search
and seizure; **3.** 7th Amendment, excessive bail shall not be required; **4.** 7th Amendment, no cruel or unusual punishments;
5. 5th Amendment, Double jeopardy; **6.** 3rd Amendment, no
soldiers will be quartered in private homes in time of peace;
7. 1st Amendment, freedom of the press; **8.** 6th Amendment, the
right to a speedy trial, to be informed of the nature and cause of
the accusation, and to have the assistance of a lawyer.

Worksheet 26, Chapter 10   Answers will vary.

Worksheet 27, Chapter 10   **1. Adams** Mass., N.H., Vt.,
R.I., Conn., N.J., Del. **Jefferson** N.Y., Va., Ky., Tenn., S.C., Ga.
Split Pa., Md., N.C. **2.** Jefferson, 73; Burr, 73; Adams, 65;
Pinckney, 64; Jay, 1

Worksheet 28, Chapter 11

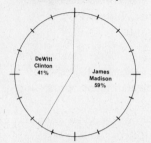 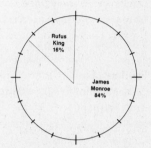

Worksheet 29, Chapter 11   **1. twilight**   soft, hazy light
reflected from the sun after sunset; **perilous**   full of peril;
hazardous; dangerous; **ramparts**   embankments built for
defense; **2.** The American flag; **3.** Answers will vary. **4.** "O'er the
land of the free and the home of the brave" **5.** Dawn. Explanations will vary.

Worksheet 30, Chapter 11   **1.** Jefferson, 1804; **2.** Madison,
1814; **3.** Jefferson, 1807; **4.** Monroe, 1816; **5.** Jefferson, 1804; **6.**
Monroe, 1819; **7.** Madison, 1809; **8.** Jefferson, 1803; **9.** Madison,
1814; **10.** Madison, 1812; **11.** Jefferson, 1804; **12.** Monroe, 1818;
13. Jefferson, 1801; **14.** Jefferson, 1807; **15.** Madison, 1814; **16.**
Madison, 1813; **17.** Monroe, 1823; **18.** Jefferson, 1803

Worksheet 31, Chapter 12 **1.** Fact, **2.** Fact, **3.** Fact, **4.** Fact,
5. Opinion. Explanations will vary.

Worksheet 32, Chapter 12   **1.** Should Missouri be admit-
ted as a slave state or as a free state? **2.** Missouri entered the
Union as a slave state; Maine as a free state. **3, 4,** and **5.**
Answers will vary.

Worksheet 33, Chapter 12   Answers will vary.

Worksheet 34, Chapter 13   **1.** Answers will vary. **2.** Indian
lands; **3.** 5; Cherokee, Creek, Seminole, Chickasaw, Chocktaw; **4.**
The path of the Indians' journey to the West; **5.** Chocktaw,
Chickasaw, Cherokee, Creek; **6.** Chocktaw; **7.** Chocktaw;
Seminole; **8.** West

Worksheet 35, Chapter 11   **1.** 640 acres, 160 acres, 40
acres; **2.** $2.00, $1.25; **3.** Decreased; **4.** Decreased; **5.** $50.

Worksheet 36, Chapter 13   **1.** New York; **2.** Free state; **3.**
Virginia; **4.** 4; **5.** Rhode Island; **6.** Yes; **7.** No; **8.** Free states. The
election could not be won without some votes from the free
states. **9.** Answers will vary. **10.** Free states

Worksheet 37, Chapter 14   **1.** b, **2.** c, **3.** a

Worksheet 38, Chapter 14   **1.** 1821-1860; **2.** 1821-1830,
Irish; 1831-1840, Irish; 1841-1850, Irish; 1851-1860, Irish and Germans; **3.** Decreases; **4.** Increases; **5.** Decreases.

Worksheet 39, Chapter 14   **1.** To show roads in 1840; **2.**
Wilderness Road, National (Cumberland) Road, Upper Road,
Natchez Trace, Fall Line Road; **3.** National (Cumberland) Road

and Wilderness Road; **4.** East to West; **5.** Baltimore; **6.** Vandalia; **7.** Natchez Trace; **8.** Md., Va., Ohio, Ind., Ill.

Worksheet 40, Chapter 15
Dix   Prison conditions/Speeches and influencing leaders;
Gallaudet   Care of the Deaf/Founded school for deaf people;
Mann   Education/Developed public school system in Mass.;
Douglass   Slavery/Speeches, published a newspaper;
Garrison   Slavery/Speeches, published a newspaper;
Lovejoy   Slavery/Published a newspaper;
Mott   Women's Rights/Speeches, Demonstrations

Worksheet 41, Chapter 15   **1.** Whipping, forced labor; **2.** Answers will vary. **3.** Because they are accounts by people who were slaves. **4.** Yes. Answers will vary.

Worksheet 42, Chapter 15

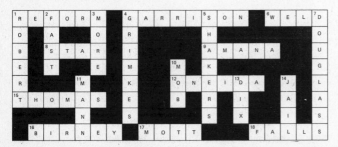

Worksheet 43, Chapter 16   Answers will vary.

Worksheet 44, Chapter 16   Student maps can be checked against the map in Chapter 16 of the textbook to verify answers.

Worksheet 45, Chapter 16   **1.** "<u>that is</u>, against the law"; **2.** "<u>or</u> things they wanted changed"; **3.** "<u>or</u> soldiers on horseback"; **4.** "<u>or</u> map"; **5.** "<u>or</u> add"; **6.** "These men and women set out to teach Christianity to non-Christian people."; **7.** "<u>or</u> growth"; **8.** "<u>or</u> gave up"; **9.** "To be vigilant means to be watchful and alert." **10.** "In polygamy a man may have more than one wife at a time."

Worksheet 46, Chapter 17   **1.** California was to be admitted as a free state and the slave trade was to end in the District of Columbia. **2.** The Fugitive Slave Law; **3.** The plan by which the people of each state or territory would decide by majority vote whether or not to ban slavery. **4.** Answers will vary. **5.** Answers will vary. **6.** Kansas and Nebraska would have been free. **7.** Some Northern politicians hoped for a more rapid settlement of the West that would bring advantages to their area. **8.** Kansas and Nebraska were opened to slavery.

Worksheet 47, Chapter 17   **1.** Lincoln; **2.** 180; **3.** 1,865,593; **4.** Douglas; **5.** 12; **6.** Breckinridge; **7.** 848,356; **8.** Yes; **9.** No; **10.** Douglas came in second in several states where Lincoln won by a narrow margin.

Worksheet 48, Chapter 17   **1.** E, C, N; **2.** N, C, E; **3.** E, N, C; **4.** N, C, E; **5.** C, E, N; **6.** E, N, C; **7.** C, N, E; **8.** N, C, E; **9.** C, E, N

Worksheet 49, Chapter 18   Hooker and Mansfield; Hood; Sumner; Franklin; D. R. Jones; A. P. Hill

Worksheet 50, Chapter 18   **1.** Slaves within any state in rebellion; Slaves in the border states that did not secede; **2.** The military forces of the Union; **3.** That they abstain from violence and that they work faithfully for wages once they are free; **4.** Lincoln made it Union policy to recruit former slaves to serve in the Union army. **5.** The Confederacy had to be defeated to make good the promise of the Emancipation Proclamation. Also, the 13th Amendment that ended slavery in 1865 had to be ratified.

Worksheet 51, Chapter 18   **1.** Sickness; **2.** When he talks about Christmas and New Year's Day; **3.** Yes. He talks about the Union flag never being dishonored. **4.** When he talks about General Hood attacking Nashville. **5.** Answers will vary.

Worksheet 52, Chapter 19   **1.** 1st, Tenn.; 2nd, Ark.; 3rd through 6th can be either La., Fla., S.C., or N.C.; 7th, Ala.; 8th, Va.; 9th, Miss.; 10th, Tex.; 11th, Ga.; **2.** 1st, Tenn.; 2nd, Va.; 3rd, N.C.; 4th, Ga.; 5th, Tex.; 6th, Ark.; 7th, Ala. 8th, Miss.; 9th, S.C.; 10th and 11th can be either La. or Fla.

Worksheet 53, Chapter 19   **1.** Answers will vary. **2.** Citizenship, **3.** Answers will vary.

Worksheet 54, Chapter 19   **1.** Increased; **2.** A big change. There were almost twice as many voters in 1876 than in 1860. **3.** 1876, 8.4 million; **4.** 1864, 4.0 million; **5.** Answers will vary, but students might mention the great increase in population caused by immigration and the large number of freed slaves who were able to vote.

Worksheet 55, Chapter 20

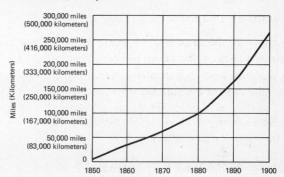

Worksheet 56, Chapter 20   Answers will vary.

Worksheet 57, Chapter 20   **1.** E, **2.** B, **3.** A, **4.** C, **5.** D

Worksheet 58, Chapter 21   **1.** 8; **2.** 1820, 1900; **3.** 1900, 1820; **4.** 1880; **5.** 1860, the Civil War

Worksheet 59, Chapter 21   Answers will vary.

Worksheet 60, Chapter 21   Answers will vary.

Worksheet 61, Chapter 22   **1.** 1890 and 1910; **2.** Germany; **3.** Eastern Europe; **4.** Decreased; **5.** Increase, Increase

Worksheet 62, Chapter 22   **1.** b, **2.** a, **3.** b, **4.** a, **5.** Answers will vary.

Worksheet 63, Chapter 23   Answers will vary.

Worksheet 64, Chapter 23   **1.** 2, **2.** 2, **3.** Cleveland, **4.** 1884, **5.** Cleveland, **6.** Harrison, **7.** Harrison, **8.** 3, **9.** That voters are not too happy with either party. **10.** Answers will vary, but perhaps Bryan's candidacy was important.

Worksheet 65, Chapter 23   **1.** A, Farm prices are a national concern. **2.** D, Prisons are usually built by the state. **3.** C,

Local governments hire firefighters. **4.** B, It is clear that the writer represents a women's group. **5.** D, Not to vote for the leader again.

Worksheet 66, Chapter 24   Answers will vary.

Worksheet 67, Chapter 24   **1.** 4; **2.** A mother, a father, and two children; **3.** Answers will vary, but the job can be done easily at home on a small scale. **4.** Answers will vary, but conditions do not seem pleasant. **5.** Answers will vary, but it seems evident that the parents need the money their children earn.

Worksheet 68, Chapter 24   **1.** b, **2.** a, **3.** c

Worksheet 69, Chapter 25   **1.** Answers will vary. **2.** Hawaii is a state. **3.** Answers will vary. **4.** Puerto Rico was considered necessary for the defense of the Panama Canal. **5.** Puerto Rico is a Commonwealth, and the people of Puerto Rico are citizens of the United States. **6.** Answers will vary.

Worksheet 70, Chapter 25   Answers will vary.

Worksheet 71, Chapter 25   **1.** 30°N; **2.** 40°N; **3.** 90°W; **4.** Denver; **5. a.** 30°N, 95° W; **b.** 40°N, 75°W; **c.** 37°N, 123°W; **d.** 48°N, 122°W; **e.** 43°N, 71°W

Worksheet 72, Chapter 26   **1.** Germany, Austria-Hungary, Bulgaria, and the Ottoman Empire; **2.** Great Britain, France, Russia, Italy, Portugal, Serbia, Montenegro, Greece, and Rumania; **3.** Answers will vary.

Worksheet 73, Chapter 26   Answers will vary.

Worksheet 74, Chapter 26   Answers will vary.

Worksheet 75, Chapter 27   **1.** 5,000,000; **2.** 1900's; **3.** 1860's; **4.** Increased; **5.** Decreased

Worksheet 76, Chapter 27   **1.** About the same, **2.** Much less, **3.** Wheat, **4.** About the same, **5.** Answers will vary.

Worksheet 77, Chapter 27   Answers will vary.

Worksheet 78, Chapter 28
FERA 1933, Gave federal money to the states as direct relief.
CCC 1933, Gave jobs in conservation to young people.
CWA 1933, Created jobs for the unemployed.
PWA 1933, Set up public works projects to create jobs for the unemployed and stimulate the economy.
NRA 1933, Set up codes of cooperation for industries; gave labor the right to bargain collectively.
AAA 1933, Limited farm production to cut down on surpluses and raise prices; helped farmers get mortgages at low interest rates.
TVA 1933, Set up public authority to develop the resources of the Tennessee Valley.
WPA 1935, Set up large-scale national public works programs.
Social Security Act 1935, Gave unemployment compensation and set up a system of old-age pensions.
NLRB 1935, Helped settle labor differences.

Worksheet 79, Chapter 28   **1.** Book C; answers will vary. **2.** Book A; **3.** Answers will vary. **4.** The Index and the Table of Contents.

Worksheet 80, Chapter 29   **1. a.** 38°N, 118°W; **b.** 21°N, 158°W; **c.** 35°N, 140°E; **d.** 15°N, 120°E; **2. a.** About 2,700 miles; **b.** About 3,600 miles; **c.** About 2,200 miles

Worksheet 81, Chapter 29   **1.** WWI & WWII, **2.** WWII, **3.** WWI & WWII, **4.** N, **5.** WWI, **6.** N, **7.** WWI, **8.** WWI & WWII, **9.** WWI & WWII, **10.** N, **11.** WWI, **12.** WWII, **13.** WWI & WWII, **14.** WWI & WWII, **15.** WWI, **16.** WWI & WWII, **17.** WWI, **18.** WWII, **19.** WWII, **20.** N

Worksheet 82, Chapter 29   **1.** Roosevelt and Churchill; United States and Britain; **2.** Eisenhower; United States; **3.** The American Joint Chiefs of Staff and the British Chiefs of Staff; **4.** Montgomery and Bradley; **5.** Generals Dempsey, Hodges, and Patton

Worksheet 83, Chapter 29   **1.** a, **2.** b, **3.** b, **4.** Answers will vary. **5.** Answers will vary.

Worksheet 84, Chapter 30   **1.** Senator Joseph McCarthy, **2.** A doctored photo and a faked letter—falsified evidence. **3.** Answers will vary. **4.** Answers will vary. **5.** Answers will vary.

Worksheet 85, Chapter 30   **1.** Sea of Japan, Korea Strait, Yellow Sea; **2.** The Yalu River; **3.** West Central; **4.** The Yellow Sea; **5.** The 38th Parallel

Worksheet 86, Chapter 31   Answers will vary.

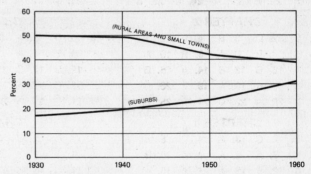

Worksheet 87, Chapter 31   **1.** The number decreased. **2.** 2.3 million; **3.** It increased. **4.** 130 acres, or 92 hectares; **5.** The number of farmers decreased dramatically because of the increased mechanization of farm work.

Worksheet 88, Chapter 31   **1.** 5; **2.** Cities, Counties, Townships, School Districts, Other Special Districts; **3.** 6 years; **4.** 155,067, 81,248; **5.** Decrease; **6.** Cities and Other Special Districts; **7.** Counties; **8.** Townships and School Districts; **9.** Answers will vary. **10.** Less. Answers will vary.

Worksheet 89, Chapter 32   **1.** A sit-in is a peaceful protest in which black Americans occupied seats, or held sit-ins, at segregated lunch counters, restaurants, or other public facilities. **2.** Answers will vary. **3.** Answers will vary. **4.** Freedom riders were peaceful protesters who traveled to places where segregation was practiced to make large-scale public protests such as marches and demonstrations. **5.** Answers will vary. **6.** Answers will vary. **7.** A boycott is the joining together into groups to refuse to buy or use certain goods or to deal with certain people or businesses, as a protest. **8.** Answers will vary. **9.** Answers will vary.

Worksheet 90, Chapter 32   **1.** Steps 2 and 6, when the House and Senate hold hearings on the bill. **2.** Send the bill to a joint committee of Senators and Representatives to revise the bill. (Step 7); **3.** Yes. Explanations may vary. **4.** Congress could have tried to pass the bill by overriding the President's veto with a two-thirds vote in both the House and Senate.

Worksheet 91, Chapter 32   **Kennedy** Glenn and Carpenter travel in space, Brooke becomes a Senator, New Frontier is started, United States blockades Cuba, Peace Corps is started, Soviets place missiles in Cuba, Freedom riders protest segregation, the March on Washington occurs, Meridith attends University of Mississippi, Oswald assassinates President Kennedy, President visits Berlin wall.
Johnson Job Corps started, Dr. King wins Nobel Prize, Voting Rights Act is passed, Dr. King is assassinated, Riots break out in Watts, Great Society is started, Weaver heads HUD, Civil Rights Act is passed, Goldwater is defeated, 16,000 American military advisers sent to Vietnam, Tonkin Gulf Resolution is passed, Hawks and Doves disagree, Medicare Law is passed

Worksheet 92, Chapter 33   **Nixon** Watergate break-in occurred, Skylab 1 was put in orbit, Environmental Protection Agency was created **(C)**, Joint American-Soviet space project took place **(C)**
Ford America celebrated Bicentennial, Energy Policy and Conservation Act was passed
Carter Department of Energy was created **(C)**, Panama Canal Treaty was signed **(C)**, Treaty between Israel and Egypt was signed **(C)**, Iranians seized American hostages
Reagan President was wounded by an assassin, Air traffic controllers went on strike, Marines were sent to Lebanon **(C)**.

Worksheet 93, Chapter 33   Answers will vary.
Worksheet 94, Chapter 33   1. b, 2. c, 3. a

ANSWER KEY FOR TESTS

CHAPTER 1
1. C	2. E	3. D	4. B	5. A
6. B	7. C	8. D	9. D	10. B
11. A	12. A	13. B	14. C	15. D
16. A	17. B	18. C	19. E	20. D
21. B	22. B	23. A	24. A	25. B

CHAPTER 2
1. D	2. C	3. B	4. E	5. A
6. C	7. B	8. A	9. B	10. A
11. A	12. B	13. B	14. A	15. B
16. D	17. B	18. A	19. E	20. C
21. B	22. A	23. C	24. E	25. D

CHAPTER 3
1. E	2. C	3. A	4. D	5. B
6. B	7. A	8. A	9. A	10. B
11. A	12. B	13. A	14. C	15. A
16. E	17. A	18. D	19. C	20. B
21. B	22. D	23. A	24. B	25. B

CHAPTER 4
1. B	2. D	3. A	4. E	5. C
6. E	7. B	8. D	9. A	10. C
11. B	12. A	13. A	14. C	15. B
16. D	17. B	18. A	19. E	20. C
21. B	22. B	23. C	24. A	25. **B**

CHAPTER 5
1. E	2. A	3. C	4. D	5. B
6. D	7. B	8. C	9. A	10. E
11. C	12. A	13. E	14. B	15. D
16. D	17. A	18. C	19. E	20. B
21. C	22. A	23. E	24. D	25. B

CHAPTER 6
1. B	2. A	3. C	4. A	5. A
6. B	7. C	8. A	9. A	10. B
11. A	12. A	13. B	14. A	15. B
16. B	17. B	18. A	19. B	20. A
21. D	22. C	23. A	24. B	25. C

CHAPTER 7
1. C	2. B	3. A	4. E	5. D
6. B	7. C	8. A	9. C	10. C
11. B	12. A	13. B	14. A	15. A
16. B	17. C	18. E	19. A	20. D
21. A	22. A	23. B	24. A	25. B

CHAPTER 8
1. D	2. A	3. B	4. E	5. C
6. E	7. A	8. B	9. D	10. C
11. D	12. C	13. A	14. C	15. D
16. C	17. A	18. D	19. B	20. E
21. C	22. A	23. B	24. D	25. B

CHAPTER 9
1. D	2. C	3. A	4. B	5. E
6. C	7. D	8. B	9. A	10. A
11. C	12. B	13. A	14. B	15. D
16. E	17. C	18. B	19. A	20. D
21. D	22. E	23. C	24. A	25. B

CHAPTER 10
1. D	2. E	3. B	4. C	5. A
6. C	7. B	8. A	9. E	10. C
11. D	12. C	13. B	14. B	15. A
16. E	17. C	18. D	19. A	20. B
21. D	22. C	23. A	24. C	25. B

CHAPTER 11
1. C	2. D	3. B	4. E	5. A
6. A	7. C	8. C	9. A	10. B
11. B	12. A	13. C	14. C	15. B
16. D	17. E	18. B	19. A	20. C
21. C	22. D	23. A	24. B	25. E

CHAPTER 12
1. B	2. A	3. E	4. D	5. C
6. C	7. B	8. E	9. D	10. A
11. D	12. D	13. A	14. B	15. C
16. A	17. B	18. B	19. A	20. B
21. A	22. B	23. C	24. C	25. B

CHAPTER 13
1. D	2. E	3. C	4. B	5. A
6. B	7. A	8. B	9. A	10. A
11. B	12. C	13. A	14. C	15. A
16. B	17. B	18. B	19. C	20. B
21. B	22. E	23. C	24. D	25. A

CHAPTER 14
1. E	2. B	3. C	4. D	5. A
6. C	7. B	8. D	9. A	10. B
11. D	12. E	13. B	14. A	15. C
16. E	17. D	18. B	19. A	20. C
21. B	22. D	23. E	24. A	25. C

CHAPTER 15
1. A	2. A	3. B	4. A	5. C
6. A	7. E	8. D	9. B	10. C
11. E	12. B	13. A	14. D	15. B
16. A	17. B	18. B	19. B	20. C
21. D	22. A	23. B	24. E	25. C

CHAPTER 16
1. B	2. C	3. A	4. B	5. E
6. A	7. D	8. C	9. D	10. A
11. E	12. D	13. A	14. C	15. D
16. C	17. A	18. D	19. E	20. B
21. E	22. C	23. A	24. D	25. B

FIRST SEMESTER TEST

I. VOCABULARY REVIEW
1. I	2. F	3. J	4. A	5. D
6. B	7. E	8. C	9. G	10. H

II. REVIEWING THE FACTS
11. B	12. D	13. B	14. C	15. C
16. A	17. B	18. B	19. C	20. D
21. A	22. B	23. A	24. D	25. D
26. C	27. B	28. C	29. B	30. A

31. A 32. B 33. A 34. A 35. B
36. B 37. A 38. A 39. B 40. A

III. REVIEWING AMERICAN HISTORY

1. At first, they hoped to find a shorter route to the riches of the East. Later, they developed colonies to contribute to the wealth and power of their own countries.
2. Geography played an important role. New England's rocky soil caused many people to turn to the sea for a living. Fertile valleys in the Middle Colonies turned it into a region of farms, and people then developed a variety of occupations. The fertile land in the Southern Colonies led to the growth of plantations.
3. They wrote a Constitution, elected a President, established a system of courts, and proved during the War of 1812 that the United States was capable of meeting challenges from other nations.
4. War, treaty, purchase.
5. Some worked to abolish slavery, others to increase opportunities for women and to help various other groups of Americans who needed their help.

CHAPTER 17

1. C 2. A 3. E 4. D 5. B
6. A 7. C 8. B 9. C 10. D
11. A 12. B 13. B 14. B 15. A
16. D 17. C 18. A 19. B 20. E
21. E 22. B 23. A 24. C 25. D

CHAPTER 18

1. B 2. E 3. A 4. C 5. D
6. B 7. C 8. B 9. D 10. C
11. B 12. C 13. D 14. E 15. A
16. D 17. C 18. E 19. A 20. B
21. B 22. A 23. C 24. E 25. D

CHAPTER 19

1. C 2. D 3. B 4. A 5. E
6. D 7. C 8. E 9. B 10. A
11. C 12. C 13. B 14. C 15. A
16. E 17. A 18. C 19. B 20. D
21. A 22. B 23. B 24. A 25. B

CHAPTER 20

1. A 2. C 3. A 4. C 5. B
6. A 7. A 8. A 9. A 10. B
11. B 12. A 13. C 14. B 15. C
16. A 17. B 18. D 19. D 20. A
21. E 22. D 23. D 24. C 25. A

CHAPTER 21

1. A 2. C 3. C 4. B 5. B
6. C 7. D 8. A 9. D 10. D
11. B 12. A 13. A 14. C 15. D
16. D 17. B 18. A 19. C 20. E
21. C 22. B 23. A 24. E 25. D

CHAPTER 22

1. A 2. C 3. C 4. B 5. B
6. A 7. A 8. B 9. B 10. A
11. C 12. D 13. D 14. B 15. A
16. D 17. C 18. A 19. D 20. B
21. D 22. E 23. A 24. C 25. B

CHAPTER 23

1. B 2. A 3. A 4. A 5. B
6. E 7. B 8. C 9. A 10. D
11. A 12. C 13. B 14. C 15. D
16. C 17. B 18. D 19. E 20. A
21. E 22. D 23. B 24. A 25. C

CHAPTER 24

1. C 2. B 3. A 4. D 5. E
6. A 7. C 8. A 9. B 10. C
11. B 12. A 13. B 14. B 15. A
16. B 17. E 18. C 19. D 20. A
21. C 22. D 23. E 24. A 25. B

CHAPTER 25

1. C 2. A 3. E 4. D 5. B
6. B 7. B 8. C 9. C 10. A
11. A 12. A 13. C 14. A 15. B
16. E 17. B 18. A 19. D 20. C
21. E 22. C 23. A 24. D 25. B

CHAPTER 26

1. E 2. B 3. D 4. C 5. A
6. C 7. B 8. C 9. A 10. D
11. B 12. A 13. A 14. D 15. C
16. D 17. E 18. B 19. A 20. C
21. D 22. E 23. B 24. A 25. C

CHAPTER 27

1. C 2. E 3. D 4. B 5. A
6. B 7. A 8. C 9. C 10. B
11. B 12. C 13. D 14. D 15. C
16. E 17. D 18. B 19. C 20. A
21. A 22. C 23. E 24. D 25. B

CHAPTER 28

1. D 2. B 3. E 4. A 5. C
6. A 7. B 8. A 9. B 10. B
11. B 12. A 13. D 14. D 15. C
16. C 17. B 18. E 19. A 20. D
21. A 22. B 23. C 24. E 25. D

CHAPTER 29

1. C 2. E 3. A 4. D 5. B
6. D 7. C 8. A 9. C 10. D
11. B 12. C 13. B 14. C 15. A
16. A 17. D 18. B 19. E 20. C
21. B 22. A 23. C 24. C 25. A

CHAPTER 30

1. B 2. E 3. D 4. A 5. C
6. D 7. A 8. A 9. C 10. B
11. D 12. B 13. B 14. C 15. D
16. A 17. D 18. E 19. C 20. B
21. E 22. A 23. B 24. C 25. D

CHAPTER 31

1. B 2. A 3. C 4. E 5. D
6. D 7. A 8. D 9. B 10. B
11. A 12. D 13. C 14. D 15. C
16. E 17. B 18. D 19. C 20. A
21. A 22. E 23. B 24. D 25. C

CHAPTER 32

1. A 2. B 3. B 4. A 5. A
6. D 7. D 8. B 9. C 10. A
11. C 12. B 13. D 14. D 15. B
16. D 17. E 18. C 19. B 20. A
21. B 22. B 23. A 24. B 25. B

CHAPTER 33

1. D 2. A 3. E 4. C 5. B
6. A 7. C 8. B 9. D 10. C
11. B 12. B 13. A 14. C 15. C
16. E 17. B 18. B 19. C 20. A
21. A 22. E 23. B 24. C 25. D

SECOND SEMESTER TEST

I. VOCABULARY REVIEW

1. J 2. A 3. G 4. B 5. H
6. I 7. D 8. C 9. E 10. F

II. REVIEWING FACTS

11. D 12. A 13. C 14. B 15. C
16. C 17. B 18. A 19. B 20. C
21. C 22. D 23. A 24. D 25. C
26. A 27. B 28. D 29. B 30. C
31. B 32. A 33. A 34. A 35. A
36. A 37. A 38. B 39. A 40. B

III. REVIEWING AMERICAN HISTORY

1. The North was able to defeat the South because it had a larger population, more railroads and factories, a larger army, etc.
2. Problems in the cities included overcrowding, tenements and slums, crime, and corruption among government officials.
3. The United States purchased Alaska in 1867; annexed Hawaii in 1898; took possession of the Philippines, Guam, and Puerto Rico after the Spanish-American War; and purchased the Panama Canal Zone in 1903.
4. World War II began as a result of the rise of dictatorships in Europe, the conquest of other nations by these dictators, and finally the German invasion of Poland in 1939. The United States went to war after the bombing of Pearl Harbor, in December 1941.
5. The United States began to launch space satellites shortly after Russia's Sputnik I in 1957. In the 1960's, America's first manned space flights were sent into space. In 1969, the first American landed on the moon. In the 1970's United States astronauts pioneered in space shuttles.